Strategic Investment

Strategic Investment
Real Options and Games

Han T. J. Smit
Lenos Trigeorgis

Princeton University Press

Princeton and Oxford

Published by Princeton University Press,

41 William Street, Princeton, New Jersey 08540

In the United Kingdom: Princeton University Press,

3 Market Place, Woodstock, Oxfordshire OX20 1SY

Library of Congress Cataloging-in-Publication Data

Smit, Han T. J., 1967–

   Strategic investment : real options and games / Han T.J. Smit and Lenos Trigeorgis.

      p.   cm.

   Includes bibliographical references and index.

   ISBN: 0-691-01039-0

   1. Options (Finance)   2. Investments.   3. Game theory.   I. Trigeorgis, Lenos.

   II. Title.

   HG6042.S63   2004

   332.64'53'015193—dc22   2003066385

British Library Cataloging-in-Publication Data

is available

This book has been composed in Univers and Sabon.

Printed on acid-free paper. ∞

pup.princeton.edu

Printed in the United States of America

10 9   8   7   6   5

ISBN-13: 978-0-691-01039-7 (cloth)

Contents

Part III: Applications and Implications

Figures

Tables

Boxes

Acknowledgments

We are indebted to Carliss Baldwin,
Karel Cool, Marco Dias, Avinash
Dixit, W. Carl Kester, Scott P. Mason,
and Stewart C. Myers for useful
comments on earlier work that
provided the basis for this book.

Introduction:
Strategic Investment as
Real Options and Games

*I used to think I was indecisive — but now
I'm not so sure.*
— Anonymous

I.1. About This Book

In this book we present a new perspective on strategic investment, drawing on and synthesizing new valuation methods from finance, such as real options, and basic concepts from industrial organization and game theory. This book on new approaches to strategic valuation aims at both a *professional* and an *academic* audience. We synthesize cutting-edge ideas on strategic valuation, which are communicated in accessible language and illustrated with examples and applications. Our approach will be helpful to professional managers and students of strategy in developing a conceptual framework and choosing the tools for strategic investment decisions. Such an applied orientation provides critical insight into both the opportunities and the potential pitfalls of strategy implementation.

The gap between finance and corporate strategy remains embarrassingly large, as academics and practitioners alike have recognized for some time now. The most important managerial decisions — in terms of both the size of expenditures and their impact on the future of the firm — are strategic decisions, yet they are the least well understood and often are made without the discipline of rigorous analysis. For such strategic decisions, the traditional discounted-cash-flow (DCF) approach is often short-sighted. Strategic thinking and capital budgeting should be combined explicitly when firms make capital investments to gain strategic advantage. Traditional methods of appraising projects do well when valuing bonds, deciding on maintenance or replacement, or determining other passive investments in a stable environment where a stream of cash flows can be well specified. These methods, however, have serious shortcomings in valuing investments when management has the ability to control future cash flows and revise future decisions, particularly when current investment may interact with future investments (growth options), may

Special thanks to Mikhael Shor of Vanderbilt University for identifying some of the quotations appearing in the chapter headings in this book.

confer future strategic advantages, or may affect (and be affected by) actions and reactions of other parties external to the firm (such as competitors and suppliers).

In this book we synthesize the newest developments in corporate finance and related fields, in particular real options and game theory, to help bridge the gap between traditional corporate finance and strategic planning. We use practical examples and references from company experiences to demonstrate the relevance of this approach. The book discusses strategic valuation examples from various industries, such as R & D investment in high-tech industries, joint research ventures, product introductions in consumer electronics, infrastructure and public investment (e.g., airport expansion), and examples from oil exploration investment. Our treatment of "strategic investment" goes far beyond use of standard real-options analysis; we extend the potential of real options by combining it with principles from industrial organization and game theory to capture the competitive dimensions and endogenous interactions of strategic decisions between the firm and its competitors.

We believe that now is the right time to bring these new ideas on strategic valuation to a broader audience. Strategy has been a stagnant field (in terms of concrete quantitative valuation tools) for some time, and the gap between finance and strategy has been apparent. The relatively new fields of game theory and real options have now gained academic credibility and recognition. In 1994 the Central Bank of Sweden awarded the Nobel Prize in economic science to John Nash, John C. Harsanyi, and Reinhard Selten for their contributions to game theory. Box I.1 reveals what's behind the Nash Prize. In 1997 the Nobel Prize was awarded to Myron Scholes and Robert Merton for developing options pricing. In the last several years, all the major consulting firms have attempted to apply these ideas in their practice.

We hope that our book appeals to academics in finance and strategy as well as to high-ranking professionals and a general audience. We are pleased to bring material developed in our work and the work of others to a broader audience and integrate it with other fascinating concepts and approaches from strategy, corporate finance, and related fields. Every attempt was made to make the book accessible to a wide audience, yet at the same time it should be challenging, engaging, and, though not mathematical, compelling to an intellectually rigorous reader.

I.2. Real Options and Games: Linking Corporate Finance and Strategy

In an increasingly uncertain and dynamic global marketplace, strategic adaptability has become essential if firms are to take advantage of favor-

Box I.1 Behind the Nobel Prize Awards

Often the winner of a Nobel Prize is an obscure academic, noticed by few in his community until he is thrust into the spotlight. But when photographs of John Nash appeared in the press last week, a common reaction in and around Princeton, New Jersey, was a shock of recognition: "Oh, my gosh, it's him!" Nash, who shared the Economics Prize with John Harsanyi of the Haas School of Business at the University of California, Berkeley, and Reinhard Selten of the University of Bonn, is a familiar eccentric in the university town — a quiet, detached man who frequently spends his time riding the local "Dinky" train on its short hop between Princeton and Princeton Junction, reading newspapers discarded by other passengers. Some knew him as the author of the enormously complicated mathematical equations that appeared on classroom blackboards from time to time — the product of a splendid but troubled mind working out his thoughts when no one was around.

The work that earned Nash his prize was largely completed by 1950 when, at age 22, he submitted the Princeton Ph.D. thesis that has been described as the rock on which the mathematics of game theory is based. Game theory tries to explain economic behavior by analyzing the strategies "players" in the marketplace use to maximize their winnings. Nash, drawing on the dynamics of such games as poker and chess, introduced the distinction between cooperative games, in which players form binding agreements, and noncooperative ones, in which they don't. His "Nash Equilibrium" has been used by generations of corporate and military strategists to help decide when to hold 'em and when to fold 'em.

Source: Excerpts from "Bittersweet Honors," *Time*, October 24, 1994. © 1994 Time Inc., reprinted by permission.

able future investment opportunities, respond appropriately to threatening competitive moves, and limit losses from adverse market developments. The conceptual approach to strategic decision-making developed in this book considers a firm's growth opportunities as a package of corporate real options that is actively managed by the firm and that may influence and be affected by competitive actions. In this way, strategic considerations of importance to practicing managers can be brought into the analysis in a rigorous fashion that is consistent with the tenets of both industrial organization and modern finance theory.

A combination of real-options analysis and game theory, such as the one presented in this book, can help answer many strategic questions that are important for corporate success. Thinking in terms of options, games, and adaptive strategies may help managers address strategic questions, such as these: What is the value of growth opportunities in our business? When is it appropriate to speed up investment in order to capture a larger market share or preempt entry by competitors? When is it better to maintain a "wait and see" approach to benefit from resolution of market uncertainty? When should the firm proceed in stages? Should the firm compete in R & D, or take an accommodating stance via a joint research venture? Is another form of strategic alliance more appropriate?

In an ever-changing technological and competitive landscape, precisely these strategic decisions determine the firm's competitive success and market value — and sometimes its very survival. Yet managers often have to make these decisions using intuition and experience alone, with little guidance from structured, quantitative analysis.

We provide quantitative guidance by integrating two complementary fields: strategy and finance. In strategic management theory, the resource-based view and core-competence arguments explain why firms should invest in resources or competencies to acquire a distinctive advantage in pursuing market opportunities in a dynamic environment. Valuation techniques from finance help quantify those resources that enable the firm to adjust and redeploy assets, develop and exploit synergies, and generate new opportunities (e.g., time-to-market and first- or second-mover advantages).

Investment decisions that have a major *strategic* impact on the firm's future path have been more difficult to analyze than standard discounted cash flow (DCF) techniques would suggest. Rapid technological changes and intensified competition necessitate an analysis of the project's strategic growth potential that is more dynamic than just a forecast of expected cash flows. Thinking of future investment opportunities in terms of "real options" has provided powerful new insights and has already enabled substantial progress in modern corporate decisions on allocation of resources.

Real-options theory utilizes the insights and techniques derived from financial option pricing to quantify the thus far elusive elements of strategic adaptability to capitalize on better-than-expected developments (e.g., expand into new growth markets) or retreat to limit losses from market setbacks. Real options stresses the importance of wait-and-see flexibility, suggesting that managers should wait until major uncertainties are resolved and the project is more clearly beneficial, requiring a positive premium over the zero-NPV (net present value) threshold. During postponement, new information can be revealed that might affect the future desirability of the project; if future prospects turn sober, the firm has implicit insurance cushioning it against downside losses by choosing not to proceed with (subsequent stages of) the project.

Since it recognizes that investments tend to be sequentially related over time, real-options analysis is particularly suitable to valuing strategy instead of isolated projects. In this framework, strategic projects are not considered as stand-alone investments, but rather as links in a chain of interrelated investment decisions, the earlier of which set the path for the ones to follow.

Real-options analysis also gives new insight into the effect of uncertainty on an investment opportunity's value, insight that runs counter to traditional thinking. If management is asymmetrically positioned to capitalize on upside opportunities but can cut losses on the downside, more uncertainty can actually be beneficial when it comes to option value. Gains can be made in highly uncertain or volatile markets by staging the investment because of the exceptional upside potential and limited downside losses, since management can default on planned investments or simply not proceed to the next stage.

Of course, it may not always be advisable to follow a flexible wait-and-see strategy from a competitive perspective. When a competitor's investment decisions are contingent upon others' moves, a more rigorous *game-theoretic* treatment becomes necessary. The optimal investment timing under uncertainty and competition often involves a trade-off between wait-and-see flexibility and the "strategic value" of early commitment. Early commitment generates value when it can influence how competing firms assess their options in the market in a way favorable for the incumbent. Consider a pioneer firm that makes an aggressive, large-scale investment in a new geographical market. The firm's competitors may view this entry as a threat, inducing them to enter the market later on a reduced scale to avoid a battle over market share. By reducing the likelihood of competitive intrusion, the project can produce higher profits for the pioneer. Such aspects of competition and flexibility are essential in strategic analysis, but they are not properly captured in the standard tools for evaluating projects.

Appropriate competitive strategies can henceforth be analyzed using a combination of option valuation and game-theoretic principles. To bring the flexibility and competitive aspects together in a holistic framework, we adopt an expanded (or strategic) NPV criterion. This expanded NPV criterion can capture the strategic commitment value of competitive interactions, as well as the value of managerial flexibility to alter planned investment decisions within the firm's overall strategy. Strategic commitment can have significant value. For example, by making an early strategic R & D investment, a firm may develop more cost-efficient or higher-quality products or processes that can result in a sustainable cost or other competitive advantage and a higher market share down the road. A firm anticipating competitive entry may commit to excess production capacity early on to preempt competitors. The "strategic value" of early investment can sometimes be negative. This may be the case when the realized value of the strategic investment is vulnerable to the firm's ability to appropriate for itself the resulting benefits. Competitors can often benefit from the commercial results created by another firm's R & D, while competition or rivalry later in the commercialization stage can erode the value of strategic investments for the pioneer. Besides the proprietary or shared nature of the investment, the competitor's expected reaction to counter or reinforce the pioneer's strategic investment action can also affect the value and desirability of the strategic investment.

The options and games approach in this book provides a novel framework that enables valuing various competitive strategies in different circumstances under uncertainty. The valuation explicitly allows capturing important strategic aspects and views the option chain of investments within a broader competitive environment. Proper strategy valuation and design, in this view, requires careful consideration of the capabilities for growth created by strategic investments, of the effect of competitive moves and the type of competitive reactions, of the value of commitment and deterrent strategies, as well as of the development of successful commercial investment opportunities. Box I.2 shows that even Bill Gates could benefit from game theory.

I.3. An Overview of the Book

The book is organized in three parts. Part I (chaps. 1–4), "Approaches to Strategic Investment," provides an overview and develops step by step the conceptual frameworks and principles useful for strategic investment analysis. It reviews modern approaches to strategic management and introduces new valuation principles for strategic investment. The rationale for this part of the book can be seen by referring to figure I.1 (discussed in more detail in chapter 1), which brings out the connection between corporate strategic planning and the market value of the firm. Chapter 1 provides a motivation by linking strategy to the market value of investment opportunities (via the expanded NPV criterion), taking a first step toward closing the gap between traditional corporate finance and strategic planning. Discounted cash flow (DCF), real-options theory, game theory, and strategic planning are brought together in a comprehensive framework capable of incorporating management's flexibility to respond to market opportunities and competitive moves or threats in an uncertain and evolving environment. We view an expanded or strategic NPV as the sum of standard NPV plus flexibility value and strategic value. We discuss the value drivers of standard NPV, as well as of flexibility and strategic value. In the subsequent chapters we review the basic concepts and foundations of these three building blocks: strategic manage-

Box I.2 Reciprocity: Bill Gates Could Gain a Lot from a Little Game Theory

It's too bad that Bill Gates, chairman and founder of Microsoft Corp., decided to drop out of college and become a billionaire. He might have learned from game theory that in the long run the best competitive strategy is to be nice, or at the very least to do unto others as they do unto you. If others are nice and play fair, do likewise. And if not, treat them accordingly: reciprocity, as the social scientists say, and tit-for-tat, as the game theorists put it. What you don't do is grind them into dust on the assumption that the best competition is no competition. Game theory says that is not a good strategy for long-term survival. With no competition, why innovate?

John von Neumann, who made fundamental contributions to computer science and quantum theory, called game theory a mathematical analysis for modeling competition and cooperation in living things, from simple organisms to human beings. Game theory has become useful in helping scientists determine how entities cooperate and compete and which strategies are most successful.

Source: Excerpts from "Bill Gates Could Gain a Lot from a Little Game Theory," by Bernard Cole, *EE Times,* June 19, 2000. Reprinted by permission.

ment and portfolio planning, corporate real options, and economics of strategy (industrial organization game theory).

Chapter 2, "Strategic Management: Competitive Advantage and Value Creation," reviews various strategic paradigms that analyze the underlying sources of value creation for the firm, focusing on industry and competitive analysis, firms' internal resources and dynamic capabilities, and portfolio planning of growth options. Industry analysis, competitive forces, and portfolio approaches each approach the problem from an external perspective. Internal approaches, such as the resource-based view or the dynamic capabilities framework, approach this issue of the sources of value creation from within the firm. Value creation is seen as resting on distinctive resources and capabilities, as well as on the ability to adapt to a changing environment.

Chapter 3, "Corporate Real Options," reviews the basic concepts and valuation principles of real options within a framework that views investment opportunities as collections of corporate options on real assets. Examples include valuing a license or patent giving a firm an option to invest in commercial production of a new product, valuing R & D and other growth opportunities as multistage growth options, and analyzing a mine concession with options to shut down and reopen. Chapter 4,

FIGURE I.1 IMPACT OF CORPORATE STRATEGIC PLANNING ON THE
MARKET VALUE OF THE FIRM

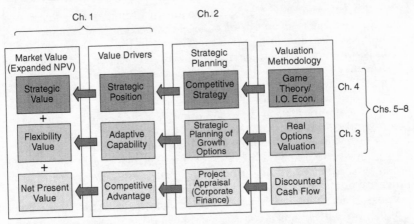

The broader strategy framework recognizes three levels of planning that have an effect on the market value (expanded NPV) of investment opportunities. First (bottom row), project appraisal from corporate finance aims at determining the effect on the net present value of the projected cash flows resulting from establishing a competitive advantage. Second, strategic planning of growth opportunities aims at capturing the flexibility value resulting from the firm's adaptive capabilities through real-options valuation. Third, competitive strategy aims at capturing the strategic value from establishing, enhancing, or defending a strategic position vis-à-vis competitors based on game theory analysis and industrial organization economics.

"Games and Strategic Decisions," provides an overview of basic principles of game theory and industrial organization/strategy that are essential for our understanding of strategic decisions. Strategic investment decisions are often made in a context where decision makers must take into account the deliberate (re)actions of other players and firms. Practical examples from consumer electronics, such as the development of CD technology, and from other industries illustrate the potential use of combined options concepts and game theory principles in developing a better understanding of competitive behavior under uncertainty in oligopolistic markets.

Part II (chaps. 5–7), "Competitive Strategy and Games," brings out in more detail the interaction and integration of the real-options approach with game theory and industrial organization concepts to capture the competitive aspects of investment strategy. Again, competitive investment strategy is based on the strategic or expanded NPV criterion that incorporates not only the direct cash-flow value (NPV) and the flexibility or option value, but also the strategic commitment value from competitive interaction.

Chapter 5, "Simple Strategic Investment Games," provides a simplified overview of many of the ideas that follow. The reader can take part in a thought experiment involving a series of strategic investment problems of increasing complexity. Questions addressed include the following: What is the impact of exogenous competitive entry (substitute products) on a firm holding a license giving it an option to invest in commercial production of a new product? What if an early strategic investment can preempt competitive entry altogether? What is the impact on the firm's first-stage R & D strategy of exogenous competition in production (in a later stage) that can influence asymmetrically the production decisions and profits of competing firms? Can the optimal R & D strategy differ depending on whether it generates proprietary or shared benefits? Does it differ according to the type of industry? What happens in innovation races where the first mover can achieve an advantage that may preempt its competitor and "win all"? What if both competitors invest early (overinvest), hurting both? What are the benefits of cooperating via a joint research venture (while preserving the right to compete in commercialization and sales)? The reader is guided through such stylized problems supported by practical examples of the strategies of leading companies.

Chapter 6, "Flexibility and Commitment," focuses on the trade-off between the value of timing flexibility and early strategic commitment, revisiting previous ideas in a more rigorous framework that accounts for proper modeling of different competitive equilibrium games. The focus here is on second-stage competition in product markets. This analysis provides guidelines for the circumstances in which strategic investment may be advantageous or disadvantageous. The key factors influencing the optimal competitive strategy are (1) whether the firm's strategic investment makes the firm "tough" or "vulnerable" (related to whether the resulting strategic benefits are exclusive or shared with competition); and (2) how the competitor is expected to respond when it is hurt or benefits from the pioneer's investment. According to the anticipated reaction of competitors, we distinguish various exercise games and determine appropriate investment strategies in different settings, such as investments in R & D and goodwill (advertising).

Chapter 7, "Value Dynamics in Competitive R & D Strategies," extends the preceeding analysis to a broader range of issues in the case of strategic R & D investments. The chapter discusses extensions accounting for an uncertain outcome of the R & D effort and considers the benefit of cooperation in a joint research venture.

Part III (chaps. 8–10), "Applications and Implications," discusses various applications, continuous-time analytic models, and the implications of the approach presented here. Chapter 8 provides case applications illustrating the powerful potential of a combined options and games approach. In general, real options and competitive games have complex structures. Thus, it is difficult to provide credible analysis without using realistic examples. An in-depth analysis of typical situations is important in validating the framework described in the first two parts of the book. We first discuss examples of actual situations facing competing firms in a particular industry (consumer electronics), to show the real-life flavor of typical problems. Subsequently we discuss an acquisition strategy known as "buy and build," in which an investor initially undertakes a "platform" acquisition in an industry and then leverages core competencies onto follow-on acquisitions in a broadened geographical base. Important questions for a successful acquisition strategy are these: How valuable are the growth opportunities created by the acquisition? When is it appropriate to grow organically or through strategic acquisitions? Finally, the chapter discusses in depth the case of an infrastructure investment for expansion of a European airport. Airports in Europe face a changing competitive environment. We analyze the flexibility and strategic characteristics of infrastructure investments that generate other investment opportunities, and in so doing change the strategic position of the enterprise.

In chapter 9, "Continuous-Time Analytic Models and Applications," we review various analytic models in continuous time that have made a significant contribution to the literature and provide interesting applications. We also extend our own framework (discussed in chapters 6 and 7) in continuous time. The chapter reviews related literature in terms of continuous-time analytic models and discusses more applications. It also supplements the rest of the book, which follows a discrete-time analysis for expositional simplicity and accessibility to a broader audience.

The last chapter, "Overview and Implications," pulls things together. It reviews the strategic framework integrating options and competitive games, and recaps the main conclusions and implications (including empirically testable hypotheses). The chapter ends with suggestions for implementation and ideas for future work.

Part I

Approaches to
Strategic Investment

Chapter 1

Corporate Finance and Strategic Planning: A Linkage

Life can be understood backward,
but . . . it must be lived forward.
— Søren Kierkegaard (1813–1855)

1.1. Introduction

This chapter takes a first step toward closing the gap between traditional corporate finance theory and strategic planning. To put issues in a broad perspective, figure 1.1 summarizes three approaches to strategic planning and their impact on the market value of the firm. This conceptual framework aligns the design of an investment strategy with the value of the firm. Consider the various sources of economic or market value a firm can create. As shown in the left-hand column, the market value of a firm is not completely captured by the expected cash flow generated by the tangible assets that are currently in place (measured by NPV). Stock market prices partly reflect a firm's strategic growth potential. This value derives from investment opportunities that the firm may undertake in the future under the right circumstances, and is sensitive to competitive moves. The strategic option value of a firm can be vulnerable not just to the actions of incumbents, but also to the unanticipated entry of new rivals with entirely new technologies that can modify the competitive landscape in which the firm operates.

Investment appraisal methods should capture the components of flexibility and strategic value, as they may contribute significantly to the firm's market value in an uncertain competitive environment. The flexibility and strategic considerations of importance to practicing managers can now be brought into a rigorous analysis in a fashion consistent with the tenets of modern finance and the maximization of shareholder value. The right-hand column in figure 1.1 shows the valuation approach based on insights from real options and game theory, which captures additional flexibility and strategic value not measured by cash flow benefits per se. This approach considers growth opportunities to be a package of corporate real options that is actively managed by the firm and may be affected by competitors actions and by new technologies. If a firm's investment decisions are contingent upon and sensitive to competitors' moves, a *game-theoretic*

FIGURE 1.1 IMPACT OF CORPORATE STRATEGIC PLANNING ON THE MARKET VALUE OF THE FIRM

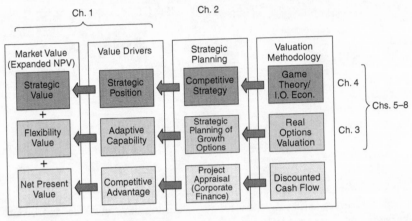

The broader strategy framework recognizes three levels of planning that have an effect on the market value (expanded NPV) of investment opportunities. First (bottom row), project appraisal from corporate finance aims at determining the effect on the net present value of the projected cash flows resulting from establishing a competitive advantage. Second, strategic planning of growth opportunities aims at capturing the flexibility value resulting from the firm's adaptive capabilities through real-options valuation. Third, competitive strategy aims at capturing the strategic value from establishing, enhancing, or defending a strategic position vis-à-vis competitors based on game theory analysis and industrial organization economics.

treatment can be helpful. Competitive strategies should be analyzed using a combination of option valuation and game-theoretic industrial organization principles, as the two may interact.

To link corporate strategy with the value creation of the firm, one should identify the investment opportunity's value drivers. These value drivers provide an interface between the quantitative project valuation methodology and the qualitative strategic thinking process, focusing on the sources of value creation in strategic planning. The second column in figure 1.1 suggests that to understand total strategic value creation, one must examine, not only the traditional value drivers that focus on *why* a particular investment is more valuable for a company than for its competitors, but also the important value drivers for capitalizing on the firm's future growth opportunities, and *how* strategic moves can appropriate the benefits of those growth opportunities, as well as limiting risk if unfavorable developments occur.

This broader framework provides deeper insights for competitive strategic planning. As the strategies of firms in a dynamic, high-tech environment confirm, adaptability is essential in capitalizing on future investment opportunities and in responding appropriately to competitive moves. Adapting to, or creating, changes in the industry or in technology is crucial for success in dynamic industries.

The rest of this chapter is organized as suggested by the columns of figure 1.1. Starting from the left with shareholders' (market) value, and the components of this value observed from stock prices in financial markets, we reason back to the origins of this value in the real (product) markets and to corporate strategy. The market value components are discussed in section 1.2. Section 1.3 reviews the relevant valuation approaches, and the need for an expanded NPV criterion. Games are used to capture important competitive aspects of the strategy in a competitive environment. The value drivers of NPV, flexibility value, and strategic value, are discussed in section 1.4, relating the qualitative nature of competitive advantage and corporate strategy with quantifiable value creation measures for the firm. Section 1.5 discusses the options and games approach to capturing value creation in corporate strategy.

1.2. The Market Value of Growth Opportunities

In a dynamic environment, strategic adaptability is essential in capitalizing on favorable future investment opportunities or responding appropriately to competitive moves. A firm's growth opportunities and its strategic position in the industry are eventually reflected in stock market prices. Of course, not all stocks generate the same earnings stream or have the same growth potential. Growth stocks (e.g., in biotech, pharmaceuticals, or information technology) typically yield high price-earnings and market-to-book ratios. In fact, it is precisely the intangible and strategic value of their growth opportunities that determines most of the market value of high-tech firms in a continuously changing environment. As box 1.1 suggests, a proper analysis of this strategic growth option value is more difficult than price-earnings ratios or other multiples might imply. An underlying theory that can explain this market valuation is now available if we consider the strategic option characteristics of a firm's growth opportunities. There is indeed a clear appreciation in the market for a firm's bundle of corporate real options (present value of growth opportunities, or PVGO).[1]

Table 1.1 shows that industries with higher volatility and (market, firm-specific, or total) risk (and as we will see, more option value) — such as information technology, pharmaceuticals, and consumer electronics — tend to have more valuable growth opportunities and a higher proportion of

---

[1]See for instance Smit (1999b) for an empirical study on the prevalance of PVGO in share value.

TABLE 1.1

Industry (average) Volatility (Market and Firm-Specific Uncertainty) and Proportion of PVGO to Price for a Number of Representative Industries, as of June 30, 1998

Industry	Uncertainty			Average PVGO/P	
	Total = (σ_T^2)	Firm + (σ_S^2)	Market (σ_M^2)	Market Model	$r + 6\%$
Pharmaceuticals	14	12	2	92	83
Information technology	23	20	3	84	83
Consumer electronics	26	21	5	83	70
Food	6	5	1	81	72
Banking	6	4	2	81	55
Transportation	9	7	2	62	38
Electric power	4	3	1	60	48
Chemicals	6	4	2	46	47

Note: Numbers are percentages. Averages per industry are equally weighted (to avoid excessive influence of large firms), based on monthly returns over the period 1988–98. Total risk (volatility), σ_T^2, is estimated as the variance of monthly returns; market (or systematic) risk, $\sigma_{M,i,t}^2$, is estimated from $\sigma_{M,i,t}^2 = \beta_{i,t}^2 \sigma_{m,t}^2$, where $\sigma_{m,t}^2$ is the volatility of the S&P 500 market index at time t, and $\beta_{i,t}$ is the beta or sensitivity of monthly returns of firm i to monthly market returns of the S&P 500 index estimated over a period of 10 years. The present value of growth opportunities (PVGO) for firm i is estimated by subtracting the discounted value (with the discount rate estimated from the market model or the risk-free rate (r) plus a 6% risk premium) of its perpetual stream of earnings (under a no-growth policy) from its market price.

PVGO to price on average (above 80%) than other industries — such as transportation, chemicals, and electric power (below 60%). The former industries involve more unexpected technological changes and competitive moves; as the firm's (or the industry's) dynamic path unfolds, management must be better prepared to learn, adapt, and revise future investment decisions. The market appropriately rewards with higher market valuations those firms better able to cope with change, capitalizing on the upside potential while mitigating downside risk.

Growth firms (e.g., leading firms in information technology, pharmaceuticals, and consumer electronics) tend to have a higher option value component (PVGO) than income stocks, for two reasons. First, they tend to operate in more volatile industries (characterized by more frequent technological innovations and a more intensely competitive environment),

Box 1.1 REAL OPTIONS, GROWTH OPPORTUNITIES, AND MARKET VALUATION

Companies have all kinds of options: to raise production, to buy rivals, to move into related fields. Studying a company's portfolio of options provides insight into its growth prospects and thus its market value.

"It's an important way of thinking about businesses and their potential," says Michael J. Mauboussin, a strategist at Credit Suisse First Boston (CSFB). "The thought process itself is very valuable."

Real-options analysis is a big step beyond static valuation measures such as price-earnings and price-to-book ratios. Comparing two companies on the basis of their P/E ratios is valid only if they have the same expected earnings growth. They hardly ever do. Real-options analysis zeroes in on what really matters: the earnings growth itself. It values companies by studying the opportunities they have for growth and whether they can cash in on them. Management's skill becomes a major focus. Take America Online Inc., whose P/E is stratospheric. AOI stock would be only about 4% of what it is today if the market expected it to maintain profits at the current level forever.

CSFB cable-TV analyst Laura Martin recently used real-options analysis to conclude that cable stocks are undervalued. Real-options analysis can also conclude that companies are overvalued. Coming up with a target price for a company by evaluating its real options is harder than lining up companies by their P/E's five-year sales growth. It means understanding the companies, their industries, and managers' ability to take advantage of the options open to them. Then again, who said stock picking was supposed to be easy?

Source: excerpts from Coy 1999b.

with the higher underlying volatility being translated into higher (simple) option value. Second, they tend to have a greater proportion of compound (multistage or growth) options as opposed to simple (cash-generating) options, which amplifies their option value (being options on options). This higher (growth) option value, in turn, is translated into higher market valuations, which may appear excessive from the perspective of standard DCF valuation methods.

Figure 1.2 shows competitive strategies and relative market (price) performance over a two-year period in various high-tech industries. Panel A shows Microsoft's strategic moves and superior market performance in comparison to Netscape and other computer software rivals; panel B shows superior market performance by Intel and Sun Microsystems in

FIGURE 1.2 COMPETITIVE STRATEGIES AND RELATIVE MARKET (PRICE) PERFORMANCE OF FIRMS IN THREE HIGH-TECH INDUSTRIES OVER A TWO-YEAR PERIOD.

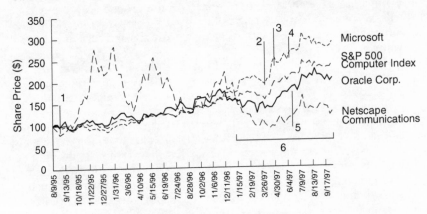

Panel A. Microsoft's strategic moves and superior market performance over rivals

Notes:
1. In August 1995 Netscape goes public in providing software for the Internet (all firms indexed at 100 on August 9, 1995).
2. In March 1997 Microsoft allies with rival Hewlett-Packard to push its Windows NT program into corporate servers.
3. In April 1997 Microsoft agrees to buy WebTV, a start-up company that delivers Internet information directly to television sets.
4. In May 1997 Microsoft announces an all-out attack into the lucrative heavy-duty corporate computing market.
5. In May 1997 Oracle buys into Navio Communications, established by Netscape to develop Internet software for consumer electronics.
6. Netscape and Microsoft make further strategic moves to gain an advantage in their continuing battle over who will be the Internet standard bearer. Through its superior strategic moves Microsoft gains a clear advantage over Netscape, whose relative position is eroding.

comparison to IBM, Hewlett-Packard, and other computer hardware rivals; panel C shows Texas Instruments and Philips' performance relative to Sony, Time Warner, Matsushita, and other rivals in consumer electronics. We later provide specific examples of intelligent strategic decisions made by some of these leading companies.

1.3. From NPV to an Expanded (Strategic) NPV Criterion

In corporate finance, value creation for the firm's shareholders is the accepted criterion for making investment decisions or selecting business alternatives. A standard assumption is that financial markets are efficient

FIGURE 1.2 *continued*

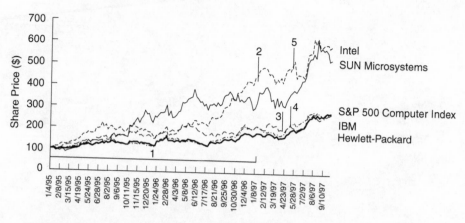

Panel B. Intel's and Sun Microsystems' superior market performance over rivals

Notes:

1. Intel is established as the product standard in the microprocessor market with its Pentium chip.

2. In January 1997 Intel moves aggressively in networking products (and in April announces further investment), forcing competitors to reduce their prices (Novell announces 18% cut in its workforce in May).

3. In April 1997, Hewlett-Packard agrees to buy Verifone, leading maker of credit card authorization devices, for its potential to dominate the emerging electronic commerce business.

4. In May 1997 Microsoft announces an all-out attack into the lucrative heavy-duty corporate computing market, at the expense of IBM, Sun Micosystems, and Oracle. IBM responds aggressively, claiming this to be Microsoft's "Vietnam."

5. In May 1997 Intel announces its next-generation microprocessor, the Pentium II. A week later, Digital sues Intel charging remarkable similarities with its Alpha chip.

and that the prices of all traded securities adjust rapidly to reflect relevant new information. When unanticipated information about a firm's investment opportunities or profits comes out in the financial markets, investors bid prices up or down until the expected return equals the return on investments with comparable risk. Under the assumption of a perfectly competitive financial market, all investors will apply the same risk-adjusted required return to discount the expected cash flows in valuing a particular asset.[2] Standard valuation methodologies, such as NPV, aim at selecting investments that, to create value for existing shareholders, yield an expected return in excess of the return required in financial markets from assets of comparable risk.

---

[2]This is a capital market with essentially no barriers to entry, minimal trading costs, and costless access to all relevant information.

FIGURE 1.2 *continued*

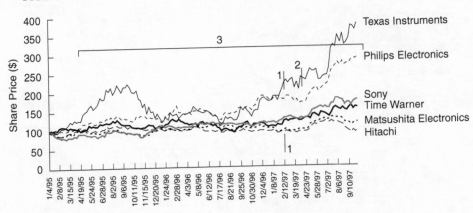

Panel C. Texas Instruments' and Philips' superior market performance over rivals

Notes:
1. In February 1997 Texas Instruments, Hitachi and Mitsubishi announce they will jointly develop a 1 gb DRAM.
2. In April 1997 Texas Instruments gambles on Digital TV with its light-processing technology (turning heads in technology circles although currently losing money), as part of a new higher-risk, higher-margin strategy.
3. Philips and Sony's strategy to commercialize the digital video disc faces competitive pressures by Toshiba and Time Warner. In 1995 the alliance of Philips and Sony (which developed the Multi-Media CD) agrees with the alliance of Toshiba and Matsushita (which developed the Super-Density Disk) to set a common industry standard for the new-generation high-density CD (the digital video disc). There follows ongoing fight between these manufacturers in dividing the market pie to maximize the value of their investment in the product standard.

Consider an investment opportunity in competitive real (product) markets characterized by costless entry and exit and homogeneous products. Early investment in such a project can produce only a temporary excess return. Competitors will eventually enter the industry and catch up. In the long run, equilibrium rates of return in competitive industries should be driven down to required returns. Most real markets, however, have significant entry barriers and are less competitive. In such imperfect real markets, it is possible for a firm to consistently earn excess returns that exceed the risk-adjusted return or the opportunity cost of capital. Firms can only earn excess returns because of some competitive advantage, such as achieving lower costs (e.g., as a result of absolute cost advantage or economies of scale) or earning a premium in product prices (e.g., as a result of product differentiation or monopoly power; see Porter 1980 and Shapiro 1991). Firms may also achieve higher returns because of more creative management, adaptive strategic planning, or organizational capabilities that enable it to better adapt to changes in the environment and to competitive moves.

In a DCF valuation, the project's expected cash flows, $E(CF_t)$ over a prespecified life (T) are discounted at a risk-adjusted discount rate k (derived from the prices of a twin traded security in the same risk class, typically from the Captial Asset Pricing Model, or CAPM) to arrive at the project's value V_0, that is,

$$V_0 = \sum_{t=1}^{T} \frac{E(CF_t)}{(1 + k)^t}. \tag{1.1}$$

The *net* present value (NPV) is the above gross present value of discounted cash flows, V_0, minus the present value of the necessary investment cost outlay, I_0. If positive, it represents the value creation for the shareholders undertaking this project.

With a standard NPV analysis, it is not practical to capture the full value of an investment strategy that involves real options. The NPV method implicitly assumes precommitment to future plans and defines an investment decision as a "now or never" proposition; it does not properly take into account the value of a wait-and-see strategy to make decisions as the value of the project evolves and uncertainty is revealed. Consider, for example, capacity expansion in the steel industry (see Dixit and Pindyck 1994, 8). If steel prices fall and the project turns out to be a bad investment, it may not be possible to recover the investment cost by selling the plant to another steel company (i.e., the investment may be irreversible).[3] Such an irreversible decision should be made with caution, and flexibility in the timing of the investment becomes important. Managers should not invest immediately in such a project if they expect to earn just the opportunity cost of capital. In fact, timing flexibility in an uncertain environment gives management an incentive to wait until the project is more clearly successful, requiring a premium over the zero-NPV cutoff value, equal to the option value of deferment. This option value is analogous to an insurance premium because waiting may avoid the mistake of investing prematurely.

In fact, the opportunity to invest in a project is analogous to having a call option. Figure 1.3 illustrates this analogy. A call option gives its holder the right, by paying a specified cost within a given period, to exercise the option and acquire the underlying asset. If there are no opportunity costs of waiting or dividend-like benefits to holding the asset, the holder will postpone the decision to exercise until the expiration date (t). In the real-option case, the underlying asset is the present value of the cash flows

---

[3]Investments in marketing and goodwill are typically irreversible, and many capacity decisions may be partly irreversible.

FIGURE 1.3 ANALOGY OF A CALL OPTION WITH THE FLEXIBILITY TO WAIT

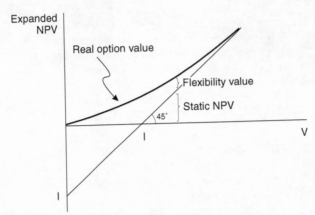

Project	Variable	Call Option
Present value of expected cash flows	V	Stock price
Present value of investment outlays	I	Exercise price
Length of deferral time	T	Time to maturity
Time value of money	r	Risk-free rate
Volatility of project's returns	σ^2	Variance of stock returns

Expanded NPV = Static NPV + Flexibility Value

from the completed and operating project, V_t, while the exercise price is the necessary investment outlay (at time t), I_t. The ability to defer a project with an uncertain value, V_t, creates valuable managerial flexibility. If, during the later stage, market demand develops favorably and $V_t > I_t$, the firm can make the investment and obtain the project's net present value at that time, $NPV_t = V_t - I_t$. If, however, the project value turns out to be lower than originally expected ($V_t < I_t$), management can decide not to make the investment and its value is truncated at zero. In this case, the firm only loses what it has spent to obtain the option. The curve in figure 1.3 illustrates the current value of the option characterized by this truncated payoff. The value represented by this curve can be divided in two components, the static NPV of cash inflows and the timing flexibility component of value. The latter captures the premium over the zero-NPV threshold, representing the option value of deferment. This premium is generally lower if other options (besides the expected cash flows) may be generated from the project.

Investment decisions should thus be based on an expanded NPV criterion that incorporates, along with the direct NPV of expected cash flows from an immediate investment, the flexibility value of the combined options embedded in the project. That is,

Expanded NPV = passive NPV + flexibility (or option) value.   (1.2)

An important next step in bridging the gap between traditional corporate finance theory and strategic planning is combining this real-options approach with game theory, taking into account competitive counteractions. For instance, the commercialization decision of Digital's Alpha chip was in fact greatly influenced by Intel's decisions regarding its Pentium processor; similarly, Philips' and Sony's strategy to commercialize the digital video disc was affected by competitive decisions by Toshiba and Time Warner, and vice versa. These decisions are better seen as *strategic games* against both *nature* and *competition*. Management's investment decisions are made with the explicit recognition that they may influence competitive reaction, which in turn impacts the value of the firm's investment opportunity.

The strategic value of early commitment in influencing competitive behavior must therefore be offset by the flexibility or option value of waiting. In the expanded or strategic NPV framework, investment has two main effects on a firm's value compared to a wait-and-see strategy: (1) *A flexibility or option-value effect*. This reflects management's ability to wait to invest under uncertain conditions. Early investment, although enhancing the commitment value of future growth opportunities, sacrifices flexibility value compared to a wait-and-see strategy. (2) *A strategic commitment effect*. Early investment can signal a credible commitment that can influence competitors' investment decisions. In part II of this book we illustrate how to quantify these value components when determining the expanded NPV for various (R & D) investment strategies. Box 1.2 provides a simple numerical example of an option game.

In the broader context incorporating both flexibility and strategic considerations of competitive interaction, in addition to the value of cash flows from passively committing to future plans, expanded NPV (reflecting total market value) becomes

Expanded (strategic) NPV = (passive) NPV + flexibility (option)
value + strategic (game-theoretic) value.   (1.3)

This formula combines the three components of value presented in figure 1.1.

1.4. Value Drivers of NPV, Flexibility Value, and Strategic Value

Where do positive expanded NPV's come from? Positive NPV investments are supposed to yield an excess return above the opportunity cost of capital. To understand the value creation of a project's positive expanded NPV, one must first examine the various value drivers to explain *why* a particular project is more valuable for one company than for its competitors.

How firms achieve and sustain competitive advantage and earn a return in excess of the opportunity cost of capital is a fundamental question in the field of strategic management. This literature is complementary for the design and valuation of an investment strategy.

A key step in building a framework that relates corporate finance with strategic planning is to understand the foundations on which can be built the distinctive and difficult-to-imitate competitive advantages that determine NPV, flexibility value, and strategic value. The externally based view of the firm emphasizes imperfections, strategic behavior, and market power, which may create an opportunity to generate returns that exceed the opportunity cost of capital. The resource-based view focuses internally on the exploitation of firm-specific assets and capabilities. These are discussed in detail in chapter 2. These views and sources of competitive advantage provide an interface between the quantitative project valuation employing corporate finance tools and the qualitative process of strategic planning.

1.4.1. VALUE DRIVERS OF NPV

Value creation has two underlying sources. First, it depends on the general attractiveness of the industry in which the company operates. Second, it depends on the establishment of a competitive advantage over rivals. One strand of literature generally sees value creation as deriving from economic rents in industries characterized by strategic behavior and market power. The excess returns over the opportunity cost of capital underlying positive NPV projects cannot be sustained without market imperfections.

In a competitive market characterized by costless entry and exit and homogeneous products, early investment can produce only temporary excess profits. Eventually, competitors catch up and enter the industry. In the long run, the increased supply lowers prices such that equilibrium rates of return are driven down to their required returns. Then excess profits and NPVs (determined from the present value of the expected excess profits) are expected to be driven down to zero. Therefore, the "average" firm operating in a highly competitive market will be unable to consistently undertake positive NPV projects.

In a competitive environment, excess profits can exist if the firm can generate a competitive advantage. According to Shapiro (1991, chap. 10), entry barriers and a distinct advantage over existing competitors (e.g., economies of scale and scope, absolute cost advantages, or product differentiation) are the real source of excess profits. Such value drivers may result in a cost advantage, for example, absolute cost advantage, economies of scale or economies of scope. Differentiation can be achieved by creating

Box 1.2 Innovation Race: Example of an Option Game

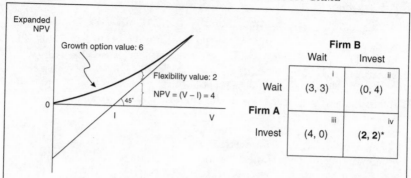

Consider an investment opportunity shared by two firms. Suppose that the total market value (NPV pie) from immediate investment (whether by a single firm or shared equally among the two firms) is $4 billion. The additional value of the flexibility to "wait and see" under demand uncertainty (without adverse competitive interaction) is $2 billion. This results in a total (shared) growth option value (option pie or expanded NPV) of $6 billion if the two firms could fully appropriate the flexibility value of waiting. The above is summarized in the option value diagram on the left-hand side. The right-hand side two-by-two table presents the payoffs (firm A, firm B) in four investment-timing scenarios: (i) when both firms decide to wait, they equally share the value of the investment option ($\frac{1}{2} \times 6$), resulting in a (3, 3) payoff; (ii)/(iii) when one firm (A or B) invests first while the other waits, it preempts its competitor and captures the full NPV value (4) for itself, resulting in a payoff of (4, 0) or (0, 4), respectively; and (iv) when both firms invest immediately (simultaneously), they share equally the total NPV ($\frac{1}{2} \times 4$), resulting in a (2, 2) value payoff for each firm.

The above value-payoff structure results in a Nash equilibrium outcome of Invest-Invest (2, 2). Firm A's payoff from immediate investment (lower row) exceeds its payoff from a wait-and-see strategy (upper row), regardless of which strategy firm B chooses (4 > 3 in left "wait" column, 2 > 0 in right "invest" column); that is, firm A has a dominant strategy to invest, regardless of the timing decision of its competitor. Firm B also has a dominant strategy to invest regardless of firm A's decision, resulting in a Nash equilibrium (*) outcome in the lower right cell, from which neither firm can improve by making a unilateral move; here, both firms receive their second-worst payoff of (2, 2), an example of the well-known *prisoners' dilemma* (In the classic prisoners' dilemma, two prisoners accused of a crime would be worse off if they both confess (2, 2) than if they do not (3, 3), but

continued . . .

Box 1.2 continued

the fear of the other prisoner confessing (0, 4) puts pressure for both to do so even though not confessing would have been preferable for both). Here, both firms would be better off to coordinate and fully appropriate the option value of waiting (3, 3).

The Nash equilibrium depends of course on the payoff in the four investment-timing scenarios. If the flexibility value would be equal or higher than the full NPV if the firm invests first, a *second* Nash equilibrium might arise in the game (Wait, Wait), for example, if this strategy payoff of waiting passes from (3, 3) to (4, 4) or (5, 5) due to a higher specific uncertainty. In short, depending on the parameters, the options strategy (Wait, Wait) can be a Nash equilibrium, but the required option premium (flexibility value) is much higher than it would be in the real-options approach alone.

---

brand identification and customer loyalty. This is supported by trademark laws, copyrights and patents, and advertising coupled with promotional and R & D activities. The most important project value drivers that lead to differentiation are the following.

Developing and introducing innovative products. Innovation in product development helps firms to differentiate themselves from competitors, particularly if patents can successfully protect new products. For instance, in the pharmaceutical industry firms have earned high returns by developing unique products. In consumer electronics, companies like Philips and Sony did so by introducing the new CD technology. The uncertainty of innovative product introductions is both technological and commercial in nature. The success of a new technology or product introduction depends critically on the value added for customers. Therefore, these innovative products are often accompanied with a real-time marketing program during development.

Reputation buildup. Companies develop track records through large advertising expenditures and marketing skills (for instance, Coca-Cola, Philip Morris, etc.). Company reputation for quality and integrity permits charging a premium price. Reputation becomes a valuable intangible asset and is sometimes referred to as brand-name capital. New competitors are forced to invest heavily in advertising and marketing to overcome existing loyalties. The large advertising outlays necessary can themselves create an entry barrier.

Project value drivers stemming from cost advantages include the following.

Absolute cost advantages over competition. Examples include

• A proprietary product technology. Often, patents or corporate secrecy can restrict competitors' access to a more efficient production technique, and thus allow the firm to produce more cheaply or at a higher quality than its competitors. Process efficiencies may result from the implementation and use of mechanization in product development, generating cost savings due to a more efficient use of materials, labor costs, or design. Cost advantages are rarely permanent. Even with patent protection and licenses, expected economic rents or excess returns can diminish in the long term as competitors catch up and invent similar or better products to satisfy the same consumer needs.

• Control of important inputs or efficient production facilities. This can result when there are locational advantages of specific raw materials, when the firm may exercise bargaining power with suppliers and establish cooperation relationships, or when other unique characteristics can be exploited. A pioneer firm can gain control over an important production factor's more efficient sources of supply, and may therefore be able to earn more than its (potential) competitors. However, a firm can expect to earn excess profits only if it can avoid paying the full value for a certain production factor.[4]

• Early-mover preemption advantages. Pioneer firms often appropriate favorable locations early on. For example, McDonalds has acquired at relatively low cost many of the best fast food restaurant locations.

• Learning and experience curve effects. In some businesses, unit costs can decline as the firm gains more experience. These effects are related to cumulative volume. Learning effects result as the firm accumulates experience and know-how, internalizes its procedures, and increases the level of coordination and organization of its activities. Learning and experience curves are particularly significant if labor is performing intricate tasks or complex assembly operations. For example, in the shipbuilding and airplane-manufacturing industries, unit cost declines up to 70% as cumulative production increases. The market leader accumulates experience the fastest and thus gains a cost advantage. As costs continue to decline, it becomes more difficult for imitators to catch up. Texas Instruments, Sony,

---

[4]For instance, the Boeing 757 is a much more efficient plane than older ones. However, an airline company that operates a 757 does not have to expect excess profits in a particular line. Boeing may be overcharging for the greater efficiency provided. An airline company can only expect economic rents from this source if it operates the Boeing 757 more efficiently than its competitors (see Brealey and Myers, 2003, Chapter 11).

Black and Decker, and aircraft-manufacturing corporations, for example, have developed strategies based on building cumulative volume through aggressive investments in capacity and pricing policies that anticipate future cost declines.

• Managerial organization advantages. Such advantages can be obtained by decreasing agency costs through efficient management compensation systems or by reducing transaction costs along the organization's vertical chain.

Economies of scale. With economies of scale, the unit cost of a product declines as the absolute production volume per period increases. Scale economies can be available in many areas of a business, for example, in production, R & D, and marketing. Economies of scale are an important factor determining the structure of a market. The higher the break-even demand necessary, the larger the need to develop economies of scale, and the more concentrated the sector tends to be. On the other hand, if the minimum efficient scale is small relative to the level of demand, a fragmented market can be exploited by several firms. Significant economies of scale in production can deter entry because they force new competitors to invest heavily in capacity, while risking an aggressive response from established firms. The competitors' alternative is to enter at small scale and accept a cost disadvantage compared to incumbent firms. When economies of scale are present, firms direct their strategy to building volume. For example, Philips' strategy for some of its business units in consumer electronics has been directed towards building large production volume.

Economies of scope. With economies of scope, cost advantages can result from producing and selling multiple products related by a common technology, production facilities, or network. R & D spillovers are sources for achieving economies of scope, as the findings in one area can be applied to another. For instance, modular design, which prevails in electronics and in car and airplane manufacturing, allows firms to make product variations using standard modular parts.

The externally oriented view of the firm deals with issues of limited or imperfect competition that may result from exclusionary behavior, for example, due to entry barriers or a threat of increasing entry costs. Market imperfections make it possible to create a strategic position that enables the firm to earn more than the opportunity cost of capital. Strategic decisions concerning the choice between cost- and differentiation-based advantages, or between a broad and focused market scope, shape the firm's strategic position. However, fundamental to imperfections and strategic position are the resources of the firm. To establish a strategic position based on a cost advantage, for instance, a firm must possess resources such as scale-efficient plants, superior process technology, ownership of low-cost sources of raw materials, or access to low-wage labor. Similarly, a position based on a differentiation advantage can be built based on brand reputation, proprietary technology, or an extensive sales and service network.

Another view, also discussed at length in chapter 2, emphasizes that building competitive advantage and capturing and sustaining entrepreneurial rents stem from the utilization of firm-specific resources. In this "resource-based" view of the firm, the source of excess profits cannot be found in the external environment; rather, it lies in the exploitation of unique internal resources and capabilities that confer competitive advantage over and above the real costs of these resources. The resource-based view of the firm emphasizes that the use of resources and capabilities that are specific for the organization are the real source for value creation. Mechanisms that "isolate" the specific resources from competitors make it hard to imitate the firm's position and help sustain its competitive advantage. For instance, patents can "isolate" or protect the knowledge position of the firm from its competitors, while early-mover advantages may protect its production position under economies of scale.

To be a source of competitive advantage, external opportunities to exploit the firm's unique resource position must exist. Excess profits that derive from market power may find their source in the unique resources of the firm. For instance, barriers to entry, based on economies of scale, advantages in patents or experience, or brand reputation, are often resources that the incumbent already possesses but which an entrant can acquire only gradually and at a cost. Figure 1.4 portrays various resources of the firm that may lead to competitive advantage and profitability. These resources are inputs into the production process and support the competitive position of the firm.

In a context where valuable growth opportunities derive from control over scarce intangible resources, such as knowledge assets, accumulation of such intangible assets and management of their valuable growth opportunities are fundamental strategic issues. The notion that competitive advantage requires the exploitation of firm-specific capabilities, as well as investing and building new ones, is fundamental for the resource-based view (Wernerfelt 1984). A new strand of literature in strategic management theory, referred to as "dynamic capabilities," offers additional insights into how firms can renew competences to respond flexibly and capitalize on a changing environment (Teece, Pisano, and Shuen 1997). In the corporate finance and real-options literature, investing in intangible assets can generate valuable growth opportunities. This method introduces uncertainty into the valuation equation and is therefore particularly appropriate for analyzing investment in an uncertain and changing environment.

FIGURE 1.4 RESOURCES AS A BASIS FOR PROFITABILITY

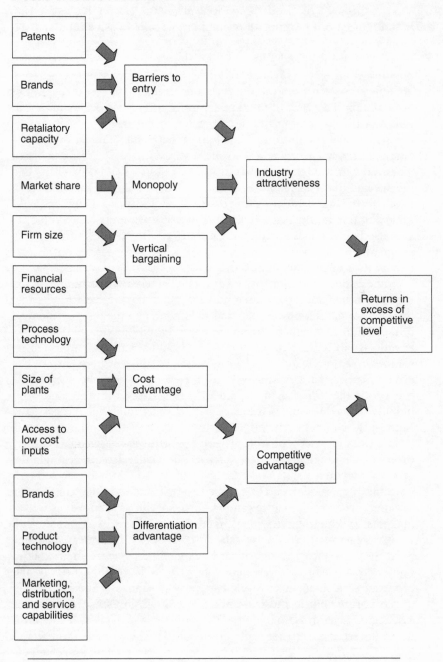

Source: Based on Grant 1991.

1.4.2. Drivers of Flexibility or Growth Option Value

It is well accepted that the intangible value of investments that make up part of the firm's resources does not derive so much from direct cash inflows, as from the options to invest in future growth. Indeed, strategic plans often encompass investments that, if measured by cash flows alone, appear to have a negative net present value (NPV), when in fact they may generate a strategic position to invest in valuable follow-on opportunities. An early investment in research and development, for instance, may seem unattractive if its direct measurable cash flows are considered in isolation. Such a strategic R & D investment should not be seen as a one-time investment at the outset; proper analysis requires explicit consideration of its follow-on commercial options (i.e., to commercialize the end product of the R & D program) and related applications. Of course, it is well understood that firms use strategic investments to enhance their position, and appreciate the value of flexibility to react to an uncertain environment. The option perspective suggests that, as information over the success of R & D is revealed, management has flexibility to proceed to the next stage, terminate, or otherwise alter its future investment plans. An R & D investment, a pilot project, or entry into a new geographical market have an add-on strategic value because they may create future investment opportunities. Viewing strategic investments, such as R & D, through an options perspective can offer several interesting, and sometimes unconventional, insights. As an equivalent to a call option, the value of the growth options of a firm is influenced by uncertainty, time to maturity, and interest rates.

Project uncertainty or risk measures the variability, or dispersion, of future values of the underlying asset and can exert substantial influence on the value of real growth options. On one hand, high systematic risk results in a high required return by the capital market and a low market value of the project from immediate investment. On the other hand, high (total) risk has a positive influence on the value of a real option. When business is good, extreme values are more likely, making options more valuable. If two R & D projects, for example, have the same expected payoffs and the same costs, but uncertainty over the value of the projects' commercialization differs (with different ranges of possible outcomes), a perceptive R & D manager would choose the riskier one (Kolbe, Morris, and Teisberg 1991) because it would have a higher payoff if the R & D turns out successful. This insight, which may be surprising at first glance, hinges on the fact that if the R & D phase fails, the enormous follow-on investment expenditure for production and commercialization need not be made. In other words, if research fails, then only the relatively small R & D investment is lost and the two projects give the same payoff of zero. On the other hand, more can be gained from the riskier project because of its better chance of exceptionally high returns in the commercial stage. The option to invest in the commercialization of a project involves an asymmetry. As a result, the growth option value today of the high-risk project will be larger. Downside losses are limited when management decides to default on planned investment installments, while at the same time the full upside potential of the project is preserved.

The *length of time* that project outlays can be deferred makes a real growth option more valuable. A strategic investment, such as a pilot plant or R & D project, often provides an interval before investing in the follow-on project during which the decision maker can safely wait to examine the course of future events. More time to option maturity increases option value since it gives management a wider choice with respect to timing. Consider, for example, a new product introduction. Management may invest first in a pilot project to test the market before it invests large irreversible outlays in commercial exploitation. If competitive pressure is low, management may postpone projects in new markets and decide to invest large irreversible outlays only when the project appears to be clearly profitable. The dispersion of the underlying commercial value is likely to increase as the length of time increases, while at the same time the present value of the investment cost is lower. Sometimes it may be preferable to continue with the wait-and-see strategy, even though this may require ongoing expenses in market research or further product development.

The level of *interest rates* also may influence the value of a real growth option. For any given project, higher interest rates generally translate into higher required return and a lower market value on immediate investment. But high interest rates also influence the value of a real option if management believes that large investment outlays of the follow-on investment may be postponed. When interest rates increase, this tends to decrease the present value of the follow-on investment outlay. A strategy that encompasses low immediate investments and large growth opportunities will have a higher value as interest rates increase.

Kester (1984) and Trigeorgis (1988) propose a real-options classification scheme that is motivated by similarities and differences with financial options. Figure 1.5 illustrates a version of this real-options classification that distinguishes between simple and compound options, and proprietary and shared options. To appreciate this, let us distinguish the basic problems managers may face. The first strategic question concerns the value characteristics of the project: Does this business alternative realize its value primarily through direct measurable cash inflows, or does it have a strategic value? Commercial one-stage projects that derive their value from expected cash flows would be classified as simple options. Other projects do not derive their value primarily from cash inflows, but from strategic value. For instance, a pilot project that might create a new market, R & D, or exploration investments in natural resources may derive their value from future multistage commercial opportunities and are classified as compound options.

The second question that is important to the evaluation process considers the firm's ability to fully appropriate the value of the option for itself. Some investment opportunities provide an exclusive right of when to invest. These options, which are unaffected by competitive initiatives, are classified as proprietary options. A concession to develop natural resources, a patent for developing a product that has no close substitutes, the unique know-how of a technological process, or market conditions that competitors are unable to duplicate for at least some time are just a few examples of such proprietary real options. If, however, competition can influence the timing and value of investment, then the investment opportunity is shared. Shared real options are opportunities that are jointly held by a number of competing firms, or even by an entire industry, and can be exercised by any one of the collective owners.

Figure 1.5 provides some examples of the preceeding option-based classification scheme.

FIGURE 1.5 A CLASSIFICATION FOR REAL GROWTH OPTIONS

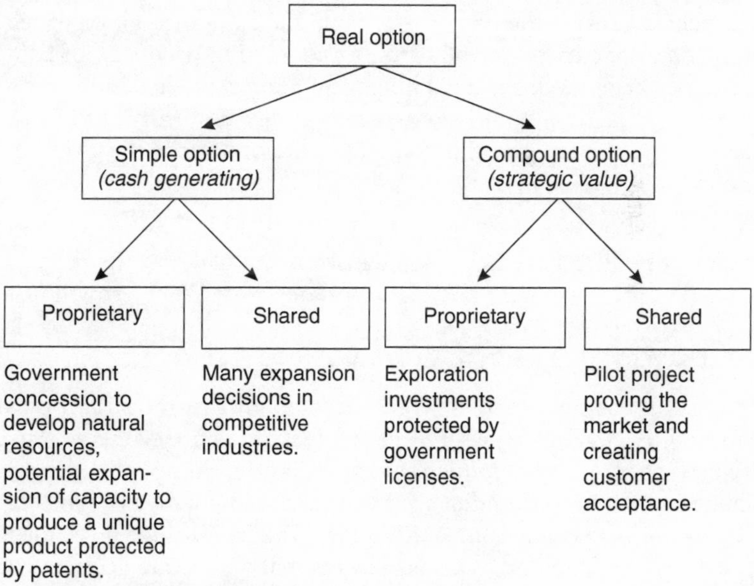

Proprietary	Shared	Proprietary	Shared
Government concession to develop natural resources, potential expansion of capacity to produce a unique product protected by patents.	Many expansion decisions in competitive industries.	Exploration investments protected by government licenses.	Pilot project proving the market and creating customer acceptance.

Source: Based on Trigeorgis 1988.

1. A production license that gives the right for a specified period to invest in production facilities and produce proven reserves can be classified as a *simple proprietary* option.

2. An exploration license that allows an oil company to invest in exploration wells can be viewed as a *compound proprietary* option. The investment in test and appraisal wells in a petroleum development program, while typically yielding a low return, actually creates an option to invest in subsequent production facilities.

3. Many expansion decisions in competitive industries can be seen as *simple shared* options. Examples of such options include the opportunity to introduce a new product impacted by introduction of close substitutes or to penetrate a new market without barriers to competitive entry. For instance, the introduction of the multimedia compact disk developed by Sony (and Philips) in 1995 faced exogenous competitive erosion from companies like Toshiba, Time Warner, and Matsushita (with the Super-Density Disk). Similarly, Texas Instruments' entry into the digital TV with its digital light-processing technology for high-quality big-screen television, developed over a decade for over $500 million, faced anticipated competitive erosion with substitute products by Sony, Fujitsu, and Sharp.

4. Investment in R & D for the production of a new product with close substitutes can be classified as a *compound shared* option. Research success may lead to commercialization, and potentially follow-on generations of the product (a compound option), all of which may be impacted by introduction of competing products. In consumer electronics, firms like Philips and Sony competed (and cooperated) in the development of technologically innovative products, such as video and CD technology. The development of the CD technology resulted in various new product introductions.

Box 1.3 shows the development of the shared growth options of Amazon.com vis-à-viz competitor Barnes & Noble, and the difficulties observed in financial markets to appropriately value such growth firms.

1.4.3. DRIVERS OF STRATEGIC VALUE AND STRATEGIC MOVES

Game theory, also referred to as strategic conflict in the strategic management literature, analyzes the nature of competitive interaction between rival firms. The main focus of game theory is to reveal under which circumstances a firm can influence the behavior and actions of rival firms and thus the market environment. Such moves may include investment in capacity, R & D, and advertising. Players make strategic decisions with an explicit recognition that their actions affect each other, and each individual player takes this into account. It is the interaction between firms that makes strategic decisions different from other types of decisions.

Game theory can help structure complex competitive situations and formalize various types of competitive business behavior. The relevance of game theory for strategic management as a tool to analyze strategic decisions depends on the strategic context and in particular on the positions of the rivals. Game theory is most applicable when management can readily ascertain the strategic alternatives in an environment with few rivals that are not too dissimilar.

A game represents a strategic context in which decisions of firms are interdependent. This can be a zero-sum game, or a game for the division of a given economic pie, as well as cooperation or mutual benefit decisions that enhance total value. In the first case, the gain of one firm is the other firm's loss. For instance, in electronics and pharmaceuticals firms enter into patent races to improve their competitive position and their ability to capture the growth opportunities in the industry. Patents and proprietary use of information can prevent the creation of valuable opportunities for competition. Whereas opportunities of common interest or cooperation may increase the total value (positive-sum games), threats of conflict or competition may reduce the total economic pie (negative-sum games). The benefits of firms simultaneously pursuing competition and cooperation, or "co-opetition," are described by Brandenburger and Nalebuff (1995, 1996).

Consider, for instance, the battle over a technology standard in the video recorder market. In the late seventies, the introduction of three types of video recorders resulted in intense rivalry. Philips launched the V2000 system to compete with Sony's Betamax and JVC's VHS system. The war of attrition in video systems resulted in a destruction of value for Philips and Sony. By contrast, in the subsequent development of the CD technology, Philips recognized that the CD player would be a success only if other firms produced compatible or standard CDs and CD players. Philips and Sony's joint agreement on the CD player turned out to be a success, resulting in a range of subsequent growth opportunities.

A strategic move alters a rival's belief or action in a way that is favorable to the pioneer firm and can enhance its value. With a strategic move, such as an early irreversible investment, a threat of a price war or lawsuit, a promise to cooperate, or an announcement of a pathbreaking discovery, a firm may influence the investment behavior of a rival. To be effective, such strategic moves require irreversible or costly commitments. The moves in question will have no effect or credibility if they can be costlessly undone. Contrary to option theory, game theory shows that it is not always preferable to keep options open. A distinguishing feature is that a strategic move may purposefully limit the options of the firm.

Box 1.3 Observed Firm Behavior: Amazon.com vs. Barnes & Noble

The book retail market via the Internet is an example of oligopolistic competition. Amazon.com is by far the pioneer Internet book retailer. Amazon introduced its services on the Internet in 1995. In May 1997 Amazon went public, with a stock price of $18, which rose to over $100 in the summer of 1999. By the spring of 2000, it became (finally) clear to investors that the new economy could not meet the high expectations embedded in their stock prices, and Amazon's stock price made a free fall. The figure at the end of this box shows Amazon's stock price behavior, as well as its Internet competitor BN.com and the traditional Barnes & Noble bookstores until March 2001 (adjusted for stock splits).

The creation of value for Amazon.com results from its strategic position to provide a selection of online products and services (books, music CDs, software). Will Amazon.com be able to preempt growth in this industry and sustain its position as leader in the online book market? Successful strategies attract imitators, and growth opportunities in these markets are likely to be shared with competitors down the road. In May 1997 the leading bookstore chain in the United States, Barnes & Noble, launched an online book service, Barnes & Noble.com (BN.com). The services of BN.com are nearly identical to those of Amazon.com, and its web site closely resembles Amazon's. Barnes & Noble entered the online business with heavy upfront advertising expenditures, and it initiated a high-profile lawsuit against Amazon.com. It also discounted the books it sells online 30% below its bookstore prices.

The growth period for e-commerce that lasted until the spring of 2000 is characterized by the increasing value for firms operating in the new economy. The stock price behavior of Amazon.com relative to the traditional Barnes & Noble confirms the high expectation of the Internet firms. However, earnings per share and the value of assets in place were much lower for Internet book retailers such as Amazon.com than for traditional book retailers such as Barnes & Noble. The stock price derived more from its embedded growth options. These firms were competitively priced using relative pricing (multiples); however, their stocks turned out to be overpriced compared to their future growth prospects. The high volatility exhibited by Amazon.com is partly explained by the implicit leverage of its embedded growth options. The prospective nature of growth opportunities (amplified by leverage) makes these stocks highly sensitive to the prospects of the overall economy or to factors that are idiosyncratic to the firm. Amazon.com stock price declined heavily with the rest of the new economy in 2000 as losses increased and the U.S.

continued . . .

Box 1.3 continued

economy slowed down. The same happened to BN.com, while the traditional Barnes & Noble remained more stable.

After the adjustment of the growth expectations in financial markets, e-commerce is still a rapidly evolving industry, and the playing field is changing. Thousands of companies are developing capabilities in this area. One may wonder whether Amazon.com will be able to sustain its position as leading Internet book provider. Depending on the development of this market via the Internet, there probably is room for more than one competitor. Amazon.com was still about eight times larger than BN.com. The gross turnover of Amazon.com was $148 million in 1997 and increased to $1,640 million in 1999. However, this growth was accompanied by increasing losses from $31 million in 1997 to $720 million in 1999. BN.com turnover was $62 million in 1998 and $203 million in 1999 with a loss of $17 million and $21 million respectively. Increased competition may trigger a war of attrition, and firms may have to fight to gain a position in this growth market.

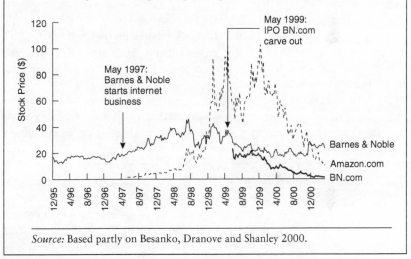

Source: Based partly on Besanko, Dranove and Shanley 2000.

Commitment to a certain action has strategic value that can sometimes be turned into an advantage. If rivals know you do not have the freedom to capitulate, you may prevent a war.

The order of the play or of strategic moves determines the interactions of the decisions. To seize the advantage in a game, one can take initiative by being the first mover, or alternatively use a response rule. Opponents who fail to cooperate may be threatened, or promises can be made in order to alter their investment strategy. In effect, a response rule can also change the

order of the play. Dixit and Nalebuff (1991) distinguish between unconditional strategic moves and conditional moves (see figure 1.6 for a classification of strategic moves). An unconditional move is a response rule in
which the firm moves first and the action is predetermined. For instance,
preemptive development of a technology protected by patents is an unconditional strategic move. With a conditional move, a firm potentially limits
or conditions its own actions by specifying a rule for how to react under
different circumstances, for instance, a threat to respond with a price war
if a rival should lower its prices. Both strategic moves are described below.

Unconditional investment moves. Precommitment to invest may provide
an opportunity to advantageously influence competitive behavior. Investment commitment can be viewed as an unconditional move with a credible
intent to alter the rival's response. Consider a pioneer firm that moves first
with an early large-scale investment in a new geographic market. Competitors may view this strategic investment as a threat to their future profit
base in this market, and may choose to stay out altogether or enter later at
a reduced scale to avoid a battle over market share. By reducing the
likelihood of competitive intrusion, this strategic investment can lead to
higher long-term profits for the pioneer firm. This type of investment
entails "commitment value" for the pioneer by virtue of influencing the
investment decisions of competitors (e.g., see Dixit 1979, 1980).

Although early commitment kills the option value to invest later, it can
make the firm better off strategically. The inability to retreat from the market alters the beliefs about the intensity of potential competition and future
profitability in the market. As noted, for a credible commitment, a competitive move must be costly or impossible to reverse. An important aspect
of credibility in strategic moves is the irreversible nature of investment. Investment projects are often irreversible or "sunk," that is, once the investment is made, the project cannot be undone and the expenditures cannot
be recovered. This inflexibility signals commitment to pursue the chosen
strategy to the very end. If a competitor is forced to react in a favorable way
for the firm, then this inflexibility can have significant commitment value.

Conditional investment moves. Alternatively, a firm can adopt a conditional response rule to influence competitive behavior. With a conditional response rule, the firm moves second, following the rule. Firms can
use threats or promises to influence a rival's strategy.

A *threat* is a response rule by which a firm threatens to punish rivals if
they take actions that work against its interest. When Microsoft announced
its entry into mainframes in 1997, incumbents such as IBM threatened a
battle over market share. Both sides may suffer if a threat is carried out.

Figure 1.6 A Classification of Strategic Moves

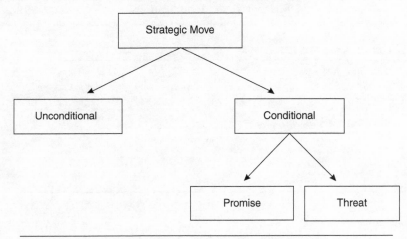

Source: Based on Dixit and Nalebuff 1991.

A *promise* is a response rule by which a firm rewards others if they take actions that work in its interest. For instance, in the development of CD technology, Philips recognized that its player would be a success only if other firms produced CDs and CD players. Philips and Sony exchanged licenses to acquire a product standard for the CD player and promised to coordinate in future product developments.

Since anyone can make threats or promises, they are not always credible. Response rules have no effect if they can be undone without cost. Establishing credibility means that you cannot readily reverse your move, and that you keep your promises and execute your threats. Several authors have emphasized that reputation may establish credibility (e.g., Ghemawat 1991; Dixit and Nalebuff 1991). Confrontation between rivals is properly seen as a repeated game, and firms establish a reputation by being consistent in their actions over time. Procter and Gamble has built a reputation for responding aggressively through its hard-fought battles in disposable diapers, household detergents, and toothpaste. This reputation may deter competitors that want to enter the market with similar products.

An alternative approach is via contracts. Firms may agree to cooperate with standardization agreements. Philips made cooperative standardization contracts with Sony in CD technology, and later with Time Warner in the development of the DVD, over the design of a single common standard. These contracts helped establish the credibility of the promise that both firms would cooperate in technology and produce the same standard, avoiding a war of attrition with different technologies.

Table 1.2
Value Determinants, Strategies, and Real Options

Value Driver	Strategy
Differentiation with unique, innovative products	*Aim:* The value creation is based on achieving proprietary knowledge, coupled with a marketing program for customer acceptance. *Important in:* Industries involving innovative or unique products, e.g., pharmaceutical industry, information technology, and electronics.
Leverage of reputation	*Aim:* Strategy aimed at creating a leading position in quality or service, differentiating the product from competitors. *Important in:* Industries with large brand-name capital, e.g., soft drinks or cigarette industry. The platform company should be a respected company to beome a successful foothold for future growth opportunities.
Cost advantage based on economies of scope	*Aim:* Expansion is aimed at gaining cost advantages associated with producing and selling multiple products related by a common technology, product facilities or network. *Important in:* Industries where a cost advantage exists when the same investment can support multiple profitable activities at different locations.
Building up of scale	*Aim:* The key toward competitive advantage here is building size in a fragmented market. The strategy is aimed at market leadership with an investment and pricing policy that fully exploits economies of scale in the firm's functions. *Important in:* Fragmented industries with large fixed investments in R & D or production, banking, automobiles, oil.
Absolute cost advantage	*Aim:* Expansion is aimed at achieving the lowest delivered cost position in the industry, especially if cost reduction can be made proprietary to the firm. *Important in:* Industries where proprietary knowledge, a learning cost effect, efficient supply, or favorable locations result in a cost advantage, e.g., natural resource industries.

Option Game Interactions	
Portfolio of Options	Strategic Moves
The strategy encompasses a portfolio mix of compound options, e.g., R & D followed by prototyping pilot projects in new markets. High technical uncertainty over success of R & D, due to implicit leverage, coupled with high commercial uncertainty and strategic uncertainty over product acceptance. Adaptive capabilities enhance the value of flexibility.	Commitment effect of first-mover advantages due to, e.g., patents, buyer switching costs, and network externalities. When the product has a network externality, an early mover that made more sales than its competitors in early periods develops a larger installed base. However, increased technological intensity coupled with shorter life cycles makes preventing early imitation increasingly difficult. In many cases the costs of imitation have become lower than the cost of innovation.
Strategic/ goodwill investments in advertising and marketing generate future expansion options. Low technological and commercial uncertainty.	Commitment effect may depend on position of the firm and competitive reaction. Reputation and buyer choice under uncertainty may also be isolating mechanisms for the early mover. If buyers have imperfect information regarding product quality, they may hold on to the first brand that performs satisfactorily. Threat of reciprocating reactions: advertising may result in more advertising and price competition may make everybody worse off.
Options that allow switching between different technologies or products and leverage of competences onto a broad geographical or financial base. For instance, R & D generating compound options resulting from critical technologies that cut across businesses. Various simple, commercial options over a broad product line.	An advantaged strategic position results from resources that can be used in several products. As a result, a given resource position will often have consequences for several products, each yielding part of the resulting return.
Infrastructure investments that generate options to expand more quickly than competitors. This resource position enables the firm to preempt expansion opportunities in the market.	Value of early commitment is present when the minimum efficient scale is large relative to the market size and a limited number of firms can fit in the market without creating overcapacity. Capacity games often involve contrarian reactions. Late movers would be reluctant to pay for the resource since they would be faced with higher cost or might face the threat of price competition due to excess capacity.
Early exercise of options may generate a cost advantage or experience curve effects. For instance, acquisition of favorable locations or exploration investments in the petroleum industry to acquire favorable areas at low cost.	Early commitment of capital (exercise of real option) to acquire a cost advantage or experience effect. Capitalizing on expansion opportunities in case of experience effects depends on the ability of the firm to keep experience effects proprietary. When experience effects are proprietary, later resource producers will face an uphill battle with earlier producers who have lower costs. Later acquirers would thus face less valuable expansion opportunities.

1.5. Value Creation in Strategic Planning

Value creation suggests that the investment strategy should be focused explicitly on the relevant value drivers. Table 1.2 provides a summary of the value drivers, resources, and real options that can help build a strategic position. The two columns on the left show that a value-creating strategy depends on opportunities or market imperfections in the external environment. For instance, in one market a market-leader strategy may be successful because economies of scale are present, while in another market an innovative strategy may be successful if differentiation and technological innovation are critical to success. Each strategy encompasses a set of specific operational decisions in addition to investment decisions in resources. The cost-leader strategy, for example, would accompany a low product-price policy to enable a firm to quickly expand its market share, the construction of facilities of efficient scale, and investment in cost-reducing production (Shapiro 1991, chap. 10).

The resource position of the firm is essential not only for supporting competitive advantage underlying the net present value component, but also for creating valuable growth options (table 1.2, third column), and helping win the competitive game to appropriate these opportunities via strategic moves (fourth column). For example, if a firm wants to build a learning cost advantage, it must enlarge cumulative production volume more rapidly than its competitors. When it executes first the experience curve strategy, later resource producers will be in a disadvantaged position in exercising their expansion options. Such entry should be assessed on the basis of its ability to create proprietary future opportunities and to rapidly expand production. The strategic aspects of early commitment are critical in the valuation of growth options, particularly if the learning effects can be made proprietary to the firm. Competitors may view such investment as an erosion of their potential profit base in the market and stay out or enter later at reduced scale.

Firms scan the environment for resources that fit well with the assets they have in place and for which they are likely to face only a few competitors. Proper strategy design requires careful consideration of strategic investments that will build competitive advantage and successful commercial projects. Multistage (compound) options have strategic value in that they create or enhance the value of subsequent commercial options. The benefits of later commercialization that may be made possible by a strategic investment must be properly captured by determining the value of the overall strategy. Each project in a strategic investment program can be viewed as a necessary link in creating future commercial opportunities, and should therefore be analyzed with option valuation techniques. Compound options, such as R & D, pilot projects in a new market, or an up-front goodwill investment, create a resource barrier and a competitive advantage that builds a defense against potential entrants. Patents, proprietary technologies, reputation, and brand-name capital are resources that enhance the value of commercialization options. In general, the more proprietary the strategic benefits of the growth option, the more the option enlarges competitive advantage when investing in a subsequent simple option, and the more valuable the strategy will be.

In designing and valuing a strategic investment program, we must be careful to recognize competitive interactions. When the benefits of the pioneer's growth options are proprietary, later entrants would expect lower value for their expansion opportunities. But when the benefits are shared, the effect is to reduce the costs for later entrants, as in the case of an unpatented innovation for which no sustainable first-mover advantage exists. This is the case with many production systems and procedures. Innovative investments are critically dependent on the ability of the innovative firm to appropriate the resulting benefits. When these benefits are proprietary, a technological lead enables the firm to capitalize on valuable follow-on options later. It also enables the firm to retain better people in a more stimulating setting so that the organization can cultivate more advanced ideas than its followers. But when the results are shared or can be easily replicated by followers, imitation may be easier than the original invention.

1.6. Conclusions

The valuation tools from corporate finance need to be integrated with the ideas and principles from the fields of strategic management and industrial organization to develop strategic investment tools that can better capture the full value creation observed in financial markets. This chapter takes a first step toward bridging the gap between traditional corporate finance and strategic planning. The focal point here is the value creation of the firm in financial markets. Total value is made up of a static NPV component that derives from assets that are already in place, and a dynamic component consisting of flexibility and strategic value. For many stocks, a significant proportion of firm value is generated by the expectation of future opportunities and exploitation of future competencies. Strategic decisions must be made and adjusted throughout the process of creating business value. The embedded growth option value depends on the capability of management to identify and flexibly exploit available options. Flexibility in decision making is necessary for successfully responding to technological and competitive challenges. Project value drivers can be viewed as an interface between the quantitative project valuation obtained via corporate finance evaluation tools and the qualitative process of strategic planning.

The investment decision should thus be based on an *expanded* or *strategic* NPV criterion that incorporates not only the direct NPV of measurable cash flows but also the flexibility and the strategic commitment value components. The dynamic risk characteristics of growth opportunities may be more difficult to capture than the standard valuation methodology (NPV) would have us believe. The growth option component reflects the value of possible future investment (or divestment) opportunities and differs, by nature, from standard DCF value. The entrepreneurial side of strategy — how opportunities are created and protected — is largely ignored by standard analysis. We need to build a more dynamic view of the business enterprise and develop an acceptable descriptive theory of strategic planning that can assist practitioners in the development of long-run competitive advantage and strategic adaptability. The combined options and games perspective proposed herein is particularly relevant for innovative oligopolistic industries (e.g., pharmaceuticals or consumer electronics) facing high innovation costs in multiple stages in a technologically uncertain and competitive setting.

Suggested Readings

Myers, S. C. "Finance Theory and Financial Strategy." *Midland Corporate Finance Journal* 5, no. 1 (1987): 6–13.

Kester, W. C. "Today's Options for Tomorrow's Growth." *Harvard Business Review* 62 (1984): 153–60.

Shapiro, A. C. "Corporate Strategy and the Capital Budgeting Decision." *Midland Corporate Finance Journal* 3, no. 1 (1985): 22–36.

Smit, J.T.J., and L. A. Ankum. "A Real Options and Game-Theoretic Approach to Corporate Investment Strategy under Competition." *Financial Management* 22 (1993): 241–50.

Strategic Management: Competitive Advantage and Value Creation

*Instead of breaking that bridge, we
should, if possible, provide another, that
he may retire the sooner out of Europe.*
— Aristides, referring to a proposal to
destroy Xerxes' bridge of ships over
the Hellespont

2.1. Introduction

The development of the strategy debate from strategic corporate planning to strategic management theory follows the evolution of the business environment.[1] Box insert 2.1 reviews this strategy evolution since
the 1960s. In the past decade, the strategic management field has seen the
development of two main views. One view is that flexibility is valuable.
As the competitive environment of most firms changes quite frequently,
flexibility in investments should allow firms to optimize their investments
and value creation. The other view is that commitment is valuable because it can influence the strategic actions of competitors. This creates the
opportunity to realize better payoffs (and shareholder value).

Both views are supported by theoretical arguments and a large body of
research. The flexibility view partly draws on the resource-based view of
the firm and core-competence arguments: a firm should invest in resources and competencies that give it a distinctive chance to pursue a set
of market opportunities. During the nineties, this was the dominant paradigm in the strategy field. Today, it still is one of the main views and has
seen a further development in what some call the "knowledge-based
view" of the firm. The commitment view is firmly anchored in industrial
organization and game theory, which during the nineties were increasingly
adopted in the strategy field.

Since both views have a theoretical justification, a key question is
under what circumstances each can inform strategic decisions. In this
chapter we review some of the important developments in strategic management theory, and consider how they relate to real options and games.
First, we review the different traditional strategic management paradigms,

[1]This chapter describes basic concepts of strategic management and relates them to real-
options thinking. For a treatment of many of these strategy concepts in greater depth, see
also the textbooks of Grant, *Contemporary Strategy Analysis* (1995), and Besanko, Dranove, and Shanley, *Economics of Strategy* (2000).

distinguishing those with an external view from those with an internal view of the firm. External approaches share the position that value creation derives from external market forces and strategic competitive behavior. Internal views posit that competitive advantages depend on unique or firm-specific resources and capabilities that enable the firm to create or exploit advantaged opportunities. Subsequently, we discuss an integrated real-options and games approach that recognizes the link between internal resources and market opportunities, enabling a quantitative strategic analysis under conditions of uncertainty and change. This approach recognizes the value of the ability to flexibly exploit resources and capabilities when opportunities present themselves in a competitive environment.

We also examine the sources of competitive advantage when the industry evolves. Competitive advantage may be temporary because industries and competition within industries continuously change. Firms make tremendous efforts to *sustain* competitive advantage and protect their future growth options from duplication efforts by competitors. Whether or not competitive advantage can be sustained depends on mechanisms put in place to isolate the firm's resource position from competitors. Richard Rumelt refers to the firm's protections as *isolating mechanisms*. Sustaining competitive advantage in an uncertain and changing environment means that firms must actively and continually create and appropriate future growth options. The timing of exercising corporate real options is an isolating mechanism that properly considers the trade-off between preempting advantages, late-mover advantages, and the ability of the firm to appropriate for itself the resulting benefits of its growth options.

Next we discuss and extend strategic planning approaches to help manage corporate opportunities as a portfolio of options in an uncertain and rapidly changing environment. In the last decade we witnessed a revival of conglomerate diversification and acquisitions. But while the synergy in the 1960s conglomerate wave was financial in nature, the new diversification strategy focused on synergies that created value by establishing or augmenting core businesses with related resources and capabilities. Adaptive resources and capabilities that enable the firm to adjust and redeploy assets, exploit cross-time synergies, and generate new opportunities, have become important extensions of the Boston Consulting Group's traditional growth-share matrix for portfolio planning.

The rest of this chapter is organized as follows: Section 2.2 reviews the internal and external views of value creation of the firm. In section 2.3 we discuss competitive advantage that underlies value creation and consider how it can be sustained. Section 2.4 discusses portfolio planning approaches and extensions under uncertainty focused on spillover effects of growth options.

Box 2.1 The Evolution of Strategy

The word *strategy* derives from the Greek *strategos*, translated "to lead an army." Indeed many concepts of strategy and game theory go back to military antecedents and principles already used by Alexander the Great and Julius Caesar. In modern times, corporate strategy is still a force shaping the success or failure of many companies in various industries.

In the last decades, the debate on strategy in the strategic management literature is as dynamic as the evolution of the business environment itself. The 1960s and early 1970s were characterized by the rise of conglomerates and were focused on the management of growth. New financial management techniques, strategic planning systems, and organizational developments such as the multidivisional structure and strategic business units were developed to help manage multibusiness corporations. Planning and diversification also played an important role in corporate business. The work of Igor Ansoff in the 1960s became a dominant business paradigm. Significant interest arose in portfolio-planning techniques such as the Boston Consulting Group growth-share matrix and balanced portfolio management of business units. In a stable period of growth for diversified firms, portfolio-planning also became popular in combination with the experience or learning curve.

By the mid-1970s, the increased macroeconomic uncertainty after the first oil shock and the failure to realize synergies with diversification strategies changed the business environment. This conglomeration trend reversed itself during the mid-1970s and 1980s. Conglomerates divested unattractive business units and were forced to focus their attention more on competitiveness and strategic flexibility. Changing markets and economic turbulence made conglomerates inefficient, and many of them showed poor stock market performance. In moving "back to the core business," many firms divested unrelated and inefficient business units that had not created value, often through leveraged buyouts. The interest shifted away from diversification and portfolio planning toward competitiveness and industry analysis. In the 1980s Michael Porter's industry and competitive analysis became the leading paradigm. Porter introduced industrial organization economics in strategic management to analyze the determinants of firm profitability. The early structure-conduct-performance paradigm provided a basis for Porter's "five forces" framework.

During the late 1980s and early 1990s, corporate restructuring and business engineering became important ideas for corporate survival, reviving the internal view of the firm that originated from the early 1960s. In the 1990s, C. K. Prahalad and Gary Hamel presented

continued . . .

Box 2.1 *continued*

their "core competences" framework, which in a way popularized the resource-based view of strategy developed earlier by Wernerfelt and others. However, the mid-1990s saw a revival of diversification and acquisitions. But while the synergy in the 1960s conglomerates was financial in nature, the new diversification strategy focused on synergies that created value by establishing or augmenting core businesses with related resources and capabilities.

See also Grant 1995 for a more complete overview of the development of strategic management theory.

2.2. Views of Value Creation of the Firm

Various paradigms in strategic management approach the underlying sources of value creation by the firm from different perspectives (for further discussion see Teece, Pisano, and Shuen 1997). Table 2.1 summarizes the different frameworks for strategy and competitive advantage discussed in this chapter. These approaches indicate that competitive advantage is a function of the firm's resources and capabilities, the opportunities they create in a dynamic environment, and the firm's adaptive capability to respond to market changes.

In the strategic management literature we distinguish approaches with an external orientation from those with an internal focus. The former share an approach to competitive advantage and value creation from an external perspective. The external environment of the firm is shaped by competitors, suppliers, and customers. External approaches generally take an industrial organization perspective and view value creation as arising from economic profits in industries with market structure imperfections, from synergies from product market combinations, or from strategic behavior. The sources of competitive advantage reside at the level of industry or groups within an industry.

The industry and competitive analysis or "five forces" framework developed by Michael Porter (1980) views strategy in terms of industry structure, entry deterrence, and strategic positioning. Porter emphasizes the actions a firm can take to create a defensive position against competitive forces. He proposes an "extended rivalry" framework in which the competitive position is affected by suppliers of substitute products, the possibility of new firms entering the market, and the bargaining power of suppliers and buyers.

Another external approach in the strategic management literature, that of strategic conflict based on game theory developed by Carl Shapiro

TABLE 2.1
External and Internal Views of the Firm and Approaches to Strategy

Paradigm	Representative Authors	Unit of Analysis	Focal Concern
External			
Industry and competitive analysis	Porter (1980)	Industry (firms/ products)	Structural conditions and competitor positioning
Strategic conflict/ game theory	Ghemawat (1986) Shapiro (1989) Brandenburger and Nalebuff (1995)	Firms/ products	Strategic interactions
Internal			
Resource-based view	Rumelt (1984) Chandler (1966) Wernerfelt (1984) Teece (1980,1982)	Internal capabilities/ resources	Asset accumulation
Dynamic capabilities	Prahalad and Hamel (1990) Hayes and Wheelwright (1984) Dierickx and Cool (1989) Teece, Pisano, and Shuen (1997)	Processes/ positions/ paths	Asset accumulation, replicability
Linkage of Internal and External			
Real options and games	McGahan (1993b) Smit and Ankum (1993) Kulatilaka and Perotti (1998) Bowman and Hurry (1993) McGrath (1997)	Above under uncertainty	Adjusting decisions in a dynamic and competitive environment

(1989), explicitly analyzes strategic behavior and sees value creation as a function of how one plays the game in its competitive environment. Insights from game theory are used to help management understand strategic interaction rivalry between players and determine the optimal competitive strategy.

A different perspective is presented by the second category of approaches. Here, competitive advantage arises from within the firm. These ideas, first described in *The Theory of the Growth of the Firm* by Edith Penrose (1959), later became more well known as the "resource-based theory" in articles by Birger Wernerfelt (1984) and others (e.g., Rumelt

1984; Teece 1984). The resource-based approach sees firms as profitable not because they engage in strategic investments, but because they have achieved significantly lower costs, or offer higher quality or product performance. Excess profits stem from imperfect factor markets for nontradable or intangible assets like distinctive competences, know-how, and capabilities. A more recent development is based on corporate capabilities to adapt and focuses on value creation for firms operating in environments of rapid technological change. This theory of "dynamic capabilities," proposed by Teece, Pisano, and Shuen (1997), views competitive advantage and capabilities to adapt in a changing environment as resting on distinctive processes, shaped by the firm's asset position and the evolutionary paths it has adopted or inherited.

In the rest of this section we discuss first the various external views of the firm. We start with the industry and competitive analysis framework of Porter in section 2.1, and then discuss the strategic conflict approach based on ideas from game theory in section 2.2. Subsequently, we turn to the internal views. The resource-based perspective focusing on strategies for exploiting firm-specific assets is presented in section 2.3, while the dynamic capabilities framework is discussed in section 2.4.

2.2.1. INDUSTRY AND COMPETITIVE ANALYSIS

The industry and competitive analysis framework of Michael Porter (1980), the leading strategy paradigm in the 1980s, has its roots in industrial organization. The foundation of Porter's framework for business strategy is the structure-conduct-performance paradigm, based on a survey performed by Scherer. This paradigm asserts that conditions of supply and demand in an industry determine its structure. The competitive conditions that result from this industry structure influence the behavior of companies and in turn dictate the performance of the industry. The profitability of an industry, of course, depends on a variety of factors, for example, how valuable a product or service offered by the firm is, the level of competition and rivalry within the industry, and the relative bargaining power of the different parties along the value chain, from suppliers to manufacturers and distributors. Porter's framework emphasizes that management must understand how industry structure drives competition and affects the profitability and attractiveness of being in a particular market, identifying developments that may be translated into opportunities and events that may threaten the firm's current or intended position in the industry. The key success factors are constantly changing and as such are continuously being challenged by competitors in the industry.

Porter's industry and competitive analysis helps managers focus on the most significant forces in their specific industry. Porter separates the rele-

FIGURE 2.1 PORTER'S "FIVE FORCES" INDUSTRY AND COMPETITIVE ANALYSIS

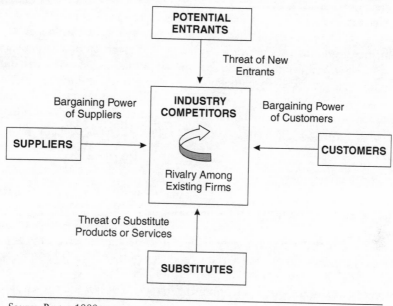

Source: Porter 1980.

vant economic factors of competition into five categories, what is known as the "five forces" analysis. This "extended rivalry" is summarized in figure 2.1. Direct competition comes from rival companies from within the same industry. The intensity of rivalry and competition within the industry is affected by the competitive pressure or threat of substitute products, the possibility of new firms entering the market, and the bargaining power of suppliers and buyers. Assessing the impact of these factors can help management act to enhance the firm's market position or create defensible positions against competitive forces.[2]

Internal Rivalry

The centerpiece of Porter's industry and competitive analysis is internal rivalry, which involves strategic moves of firms to gain market share within an industry. The intensity of rivalry between established competitors in

[2]In analyzing strategic priorities, managers should look for opportunities in industries with weak competitive forces—few rivals, no close substitutes, high barriers to entry, suppliers and buyers with weak bargaining power, etc.

the industry, and therefore their profitability, is affected by the other four factors. Rivalry may involve price competition but may also be driven by other dimensions. In price competition, a reduction in the price-cost margin erodes profitability. The extent to which industry profitability is reduced by aggressive price competition depends upon the industry's concentration, the degree of product differentiation, the diversity of competitors, excess capacity, and exit barriers. In some situations, aggressive price competition can give way to competition in advertising or innovation. Increases in fixed and variable costs (e.g., due to innovation or quality improvement) can be passed on from the manufacturer to the customer if the improvement in the product or service quality justifies a higher price.

Threat of Substitutes

The possibility that customers may switch to a substitute product limits pricing and profitability. New substitutes, involving novel technologies, may pose large threats to existing products. The extent to which a company's products or services may be replaced by substitute products depends on several factors, such as the tendency of buyers to substitute, the level of value added by the company's products or services in the clients' perception, and the price-performance characteristics of the substitutes.

Threat of Potential Entrants

If some firms in the industry earn excess profits on their new investments, these positive-NPV opportunities may also attract new entrants. Unless profitability is protected by entry barriers, capacity expansion by new entrants reduces the market share of incumbents, increasing internal rivalry and lowering price-cost margins until the return on these projects diminishes to the opportunity cost of capital. The threat posed by entrants is sufficient to force incumbent firms to limit their prices. How easy or difficult it is for a potential entrant to penetrate an incumbent's market depends on several factors. These include specificity and cost of the capital assets required to compete in the industry; access to basic resources or distribution channels; the presence of legal and regulatory barriers; the possibility of retaliation by established firms; the need to establish brand identity; and cost advantages, such as economies of scale, scope, and learning cost effects.

Incumbents in an industry naturally try to use entry barriers to avoid intensification of rivalry and erosion of profits. These barriers may be structural but may also be the result of strategic behavior. Structural entry barriers occur when established firms possess cost, marketing, location, or distributional advantages over potential entrants. When incumbents take deliberate actions to deter the entrance of new competitors, barriers are said to be *strategic*. When credible, these actions can change the entrants' expectations about the level of competitive rivalry they will face if they enter the market. Such actions include manipulating prices before entrance (limit pricing) or after entrance (predatory pricing), expanding capacity, obtaining patents (even for small variants of a product), advertising aggressively to create brand loyalty, and so on. Strategic barriers are more likely to succeed if an established firm enjoys a monopolistic position, allowing it to raise prices after the original move is made.

Bargaining Power of Customers and Suppliers

Both suppliers and customers can extract value from manufacturers, depending on how the latter set prices when buying inputs from suppliers or selling their products to customers. If price setting with suppliers and customers involves extensive and complex negotiations, the company's bargaining power with these parties may be affected. The company's ability to be a price setter (rather than a price taker) with suppliers and customers generally depends on the concentration of customers and suppliers in the sector; costs of switching if customers decide to buy from competitors or suppliers sell to others; the ability of customers to integrate backwards, and of suppliers to integrate forward; the price elasticity of the market; and the company's long-term relationships with its customers and suppliers.

Porter posits in *The Competitive Advantage of Nations* (1990) that competitive advantage in particular industries is strongly concentrated in specific locations. Criticism against the "five forces" framework and the structure-conduct-performance paradigm focused on its failure to take explicit endogenous competitive behavior into account (Grant 1995) and its inability to (explicitly) handle uncertainty. The five-forces framework is limited in helping management decide when to compete and when not to compete, in detailing the interaction of sequential moves, and in accounting for the impact of promises and threats. Game theory is better suited to address such issues.

2.2.2. Strategic Conflict and Game Theory

In 1944 John von Neumann and Oskar Morgenstern published their *Theory of Games and Economic Behavior* with Princeton University Press. During the last three decades game theory has reshaped microeconomic analysis and greatly expanded the depth of competitive analysis in business strategy. Game theory reveals how a firm can make strategic moves in order to influence the strategic position of competing firms or the intensity of industry rivalry. The approach is relevant for analyzing investments in oligopolistic market environments, as well as for negotiations, bargaining, or bidding situations, in which firms base their actions and strategies on what they think other players will do. Game theory has been used in economics to formalize and quantify intuitive arguments about various types of firm behavior, for instance R & D competition, patent races, capacity investment, or signaling.

Since the 1980s there has also been a growing interest in game theory applications in strategic management theory, although the strategic management literature has relied more on the intuitive appeal of game theory concepts rather than on its mathematical formality. *The Strategy of Conflict* by Thomas Schelling (1980) opened the way for our understanding of strategic conflict situations. Alan Shapiro's "The Theory of Business Strategy" (1989) applied strategic conflict to better understand business strategy. It showed how a firm can leverage competitive advantage to improve its strategic position or influence the behavior and actions of rival firms and thus the market environment. There are many situations in which firms can make use of strategic moves to gain competitive advantages that may influence their future competitive position and expected profitability. Such moves may sometimes involve signaling. Credible strategic moves demand that commitments are costly to reverse. Recent treatments discuss the role of commitment and reputation (e.g., Ghemawat and del Sol 1998).

Game theory can also be used to help analyze which factors affect the trade-off between cooperation and conflict. For instance, when does advertising result in more advertising by competitors, and when is it likely to gain market share? This trade-off is important in price competition. Lowering prices in a bid to gain market share often prompts competitors to match the cuts to regain lost share. This simply restores the status quo, but at lower prices, leaving everyone worse off. Brandenburger and Nalebuff (1995, 1996) recommend "co-opetitive" strategies involving cooperation when it comes to creating the industry pie and competition when dividing it up.

The strategic conflict approach to game theory is particularly relevant in stable environments when the strategic alternatives can be easily ascertained and when competitors are not too dissimilar, as in the case of Unilever and Procter and Gamble, Coca-Cola and Pepsi, or Boeing and Airbus. Excess profits in such a view are eventually the result of how managers "play the game," for example, by competing in zero-sum games or collaborating in positive-sum games.

In many cases, game theory is used to formalize observed firm behavior. A general criticism is that by trying to rationalize known behavior in a stylized way, standard game theory models often fail to produce testable predictions. When there are significant cost-, price-, or information-based asymmetries in a competitive game situation between firms, the insights from the analysis are likely to be self-evident (Sutton 1992; Teece, Pisano, and Shuen 1997). In industries with a changing technological and market environment, competitors can be dissimilar in many ways. Further, the strategic conflict approach does not fully recognize that, besides strategic moves, competition also involves the protection and accumulation of unique resources and capabilities as well as the cultivation and optimal exercise of strategic options.[3]

When combined with real-options theory, however, new and less obvious variables, such as volatility and correlation, may help explain more subtle differences in investment behavior. For example, a firm with relatively higher firm-specific uncertainty or exercise cost may prefer to wait. This insight may shed a different light on the sources of first- or second-mover advantages. Our extended view of game theory combined with real-options valuation better accounts for these important aspects, particularly in an uncertain and changing environment. In such a changing environment the strategic position of the firm depends on the creation of new opportunities, which are by their prospective nature very sensitive to competitive interactions.

2.2.3. Internal, Resource-Based View of the Firm

We now turn to internal approaches that view the source of value creation as residing within the firm. In addition to the competitive forces and how the firm "plays the game" in the external environment, competitive advantage and interfirm profit differences can be attributed to the internal resources of the firm itself. Internally focused approaches share the view that corporate strengths and weaknesses are true sources of enduring competitive advantage through increased efficiency and effectiveness. There are several strands of the internal view literature that focus on leveraging the internal resources and capabilities to the advantage of the firm. Understanding the firm's strategic position requires an assessment of the current or required internal resources and capabilities to meet the external market conditions and turn them into favorable forces that enable the firm to perform better than its competitors.

The main strand of the internal approaches is the resource-based view (Penrose 1959; Wernerfelt 1984; Rumelt 1984; Teece 1984). The resource-based theory of strategy emphasizes that each firm is characterized by its own collection of resources and capabilities. Exploitation of scarce firm-specific resources and capabilities is the fundamental determinant of value

---

[3]See Teece, Pisano, and Shuen 1997 and section 2.2.4 for a discussion of dynamic capabilities.

creation by the firm. It is the leveraging and scarcity of firm-specific resources and capabilities that enable the firm to generate a profit stream in excess of the opportunity cost of capital.

Resources are firm-specific assets, the basic inputs in the production process. The firm's resources at a given time include those tangible and intangible assets that add to the strengths and weaknesses of the firm (Wernerfelt 1984), for instance its brand name, in-house knowledge of technology, trade contracts, and so on. Capability is the capacity for a set of resources to perform a given task or activity. Any productive activity requires the cooperation and integration of several resources. Those activities that the firm is able to perform better than its competitors are particularly important. Prahalad and Hamel (1990) use the term *core competencies* to describe the firm's central capabilities.[4] They encompass the collective learning in the organization, such as how to coordinate diverse production skills or integrate multiple streams of technology. Examples of core capabilities include NEC's integration of computer and telecommunications technology, Philips' optical-media expertise, and Canon's know-how in optics and precision mechanics. Distinctive or core competences center attention on competitive advantage.

In order to create value, the bundle of the firm's resources should have several important features (Barney 1986; Grant 1995): (1) The resources should be distinctive, scarce, and relevant to establish competitive advantage; (2) they should be durable and hard to imitate so the competitive advantage is sustainable; (3) the firm should be able to appropriate the excess profits that result from the resources. When the firm has no such resources, it has little competitive advantage, and so will make an average return on capital.

Resources Should Be a Source of Competitive Advantage

Excess profits derive from utilizing resources and competences that are scarce. However, such scarce and distinctive resources are only valuable when they are relevant. The important question for value creation to ask is, What opportunities exist for economizing use of these resources? A firm's resources are most valuable when they are explicitly linked to market opportunities. So what is needed in defining a company's strategy is to identify growth opportunities in markets and activities in which its distinctive capabilities are relevant, and then put together the other resources needed to capitalize on these growth opportunities.

Clearly, the value of intangible resources, such as patents, critically depends on the generation of future valuable "growth options" for the firm.

---

[4]The literature oftentimes uses the terms *capabilities* and *competences* interchangeably.

In addition, a firm's tangible resources, such as plant, machinery, or human capital, may have embedded options to expand to increase productivity and efficiency. There may also be options to "switch use" when the resources, for instance of an acquired company, can be more profitably employed elsewhere. Once management knows which of the resources and core capabilities are most important, it should use the option-leverage to enhance its competitive advantage. To leverage the option potential of its unique resources and capabilities, the firm must be properly organized. Complementary resources, such as appropriate reporting structures, management control systems and compensation policies, should be well coordinated with other resources and capabilities to fully realize the potential of the firm's available growth options.

The Advantage Should Be Sustainable

An important step in understanding the nature of sustainable competitive advantage is to distinguish between those resources which are truly idiosyncratic to the firm and those which can be readily acquired in the marketplace. Creating value requires that the firm possess unique resources and capabilities that make it impossible for competitors to duplicate its strategy. If its strategy yields excess profits, others will be induced to acquire the same resources, and the resulting competition will erode profit margins. Those resources or capabilities that can be bought readily in the marketplace or are shared by several competing firms, are unlikely to be a source of sustainable competitive advantage (Barney 1986).[5]

Microsoft's dominant position has been based on its distinctive capability in programming its operating system, which allowed it to also stay in the lead in other software products, such as Word and Excel. Coca-Cola's competitive advantage is based on its Coke brand name, not its drink technology. The distinctive capability for McDonalds is its ability to supply hamburgers of the same quality from several thousands of outlets around the world. When McDonalds wants to apply its distinctive capability in a new geographical market, it can go out and buy the other resources it needs. Although others may be able to buy similar resources, the true sources of the company's competitive advantage — quality and identity — are much harder to imitate.

To sustain competitive advantage, the resource strategy should be difficult, if not impossible, to imitate. Distinctive resources should be imperfectly

---

[5]Even if a firm has distinctive resources, it may not necessarily generate lasting excess profits. To be an enduring form of competitive advantage, resources should be durable. Technological resources, for instance, often lose their relevance even before their patents expire. Other resources, such as reputation, may sustain the passage of time.

mobile. It is the heterogeneity and imperfect transferability of resources that precludes imitation. Some intangible assets are difficult to transfer among firms not only because of transaction and transfer costs, but also because the assets themselves may contain tacit knowledge. Trade secrets and certain specialized production facilities and engineering experiences are such examples.

If a firm cannot buy a distinctive resource or capability, it must build it gradually. However, to build a unique position often takes a history of systematic investment. History matters. As firms evolve over time, they accumulate unique skills, assets, and resources. The strategic position of the firm is therefore path dependent; that is, it depends on the particular path the firm has followed, and the unique experience, relationships, and reputation it has built over time are embedded in the firm's resources and capabilities. As a result, firms are heterogeneous, and their exploitation of their firm-specific resources and capabilities may enable them to generate a profit stream in excess of the opportunity cost of capital. Firms such as Intel, Nokia, and Microsoft have built a strong market position based on their intangible technical resources. Coca-Cola Corporation, on the other hand, has built a strong market position based on its brand name. In section 2.3 we discuss the isolating mechanisms a firm may use to sustain its competitive advantage.

The Value of the Resource Should Be Appropriable

Is the firm able to appropriate for itself the profit stream resulting from its resources? Again, if resources are traded in a competitive and efficient market, any potential profit stream would be fully reflected in market prices. To generate excess profits, the firm needs to acquire the resources without paying the full premium that reflects the future potential profit stream.

Acquisitions may be a way to trade a bundle of firm resources, even though in some cases these resources may otherwise be unmarketable. Often there is a low degree of transparency regarding the resources of a firm, which should be partly eliminated through careful due diligence. Even without information asymmetries, the buyer value of the target can be different because buyers are heterogeneous and may perceive different synergies. The organizational capabilities and the bundle of corporate real options, like uncertainty itself, will likely be different for each buyer. As a result, the value of a target may be different for each buyer, depending on the firm's other resources and its past strategies.[6]

[6] A resource-based acquisition strategy is *related supplementary* when the resources of the target are related to the resources of the bidding firm. Acquisitions can also be *related complementary* when resources combine effectively and can be used in several products. As a result, a given resource position barrier will often have consequences for several products.

When there are several similar buyers, competition will likely bid up the price of the target. In this perspective, a buyer's chance of exploiting market imperfections and getting a cheap target are greatest if it has a distinctive resource position with relatively little competition.[7] But with a more unique position, the firm may face relatively fewer targets. In theory, it is best, of course, to be a sole buyer with a lot of identical targets (Wernerfelt 1984).

2.2.4. DYNAMIC CAPABILITIES

The notion that competitive advantage requires the exploitation of firm-specific capabilities and constantly developing new ones is central to the resource-based view.[8] A recent strand of literature in strategic management, referred to as "Dynamic Capabilities," offers additional insights as to how firms can renew competencies to respond flexibly and capitalize on opportunities in a changing environment (Teece, Pisano, and Shuen 1997). The dynamic capabilities approach explicitly focuses on competitive advantage in an environment with rapid changes.[9]

Two aspects of competitive advantage and value creation are the main focus in the dynamic capabilities approach. The first aspect is dynamic, focusing on the capacity of firms to renew their competencies and adapt flexibly to a changing business environment. The second aspect focuses on capabilities, emphasizing the key role of strategic management in appropriately adapting and reconfiguring skills, resources, and competencies to match the requirements of a changing environment. The dynamic capabilities framework emphasizes not only how organizations first develop firm-specific capabilities, but also how they renew their competencies to respond to shifts in the business environment.

In this view, firms follow a trajectory of competence development. An investment strategy can be seen as a series of long-term, partly irreversible commitments to certain domains of competence, which in our view is similar to a chain of options. Of course, a competence-building strategy is path- or history-dependent. The chosen path not only determines which investment alternatives are open to the firm today, but also constrains the firm's choices in the future. Excess profits tend to flow not just from the asset base

---

[7]Too often, prospective buyers perform their valuation using certain simple criteria based on average or benchmark companies, such as earnings multiples or payback. However, buyer value is idiosyncratic. Estimating the true buyer value of the set of resources that a specific buyer can take advantage of requires a more sophisticated option valuation.

[8]This section is based on the article by Teece, Pisano, and Shuen (1997).

[9]The foundations of this framework can be found in Schumpeter 1934; Penrose 1959; Williamson 1975, 1985; Barney 1986; Nelson and Winter 1982; Teece 1988; and Teece et al. 1994.

of the firm and the degree of its inimitatibility; they also derive from the firm's ability to reconfigure and transform itself.

Building a competitive advantage in an environment in which time-to-market is critical, the rate of technological change is rapid, and the nature of future competition and markets is uncertain requires that the firm's capabilities be dynamic and adaptable. Teece, Pisano, and Shuen (1997) focus on three main factors that shape a firm's dynamic capabilities and its ability to create value in a changing environment: *processes, positions,* and *paths.*

A firm's competencies and dynamic capabilities are embedded in the firm's organizational processes. The content of these processes and the opportunities for the firm to develop competitive advantage are formed by the assets of the firm and by the evolutionary path it is following. This evolutionary path is often rather narrow. A firm's future path, what the firm can do and where it can go, is bounded by its current positions and the path it has followed to get there. Firm behavior and performance are hard to imitate when competitors are equally constrained.

Managerial and Organizational Processes

Dynamic capabilities emphasize the role of learning and reconfiguration.[10] Learning is a process by which repetition and experimentation allow tasks to be performed more efficiently, but it also supports identification of new opportunities. Obviously, there is value in the ability to reconfigure the firm's asset and resource base in response to a changing environment.

The capacity of a firm to reconfigure and transform is itself a learned organizational skill, one that requires continuous observation of markets and technologies for various types of options and the implementation of an adaptive strategy. Implementing the necessary adjustments depends on the firm's ability to monitor markets and competitors, and to complete reconfiguration and transformation ahead of its competition.

Positions

The strategic position of a firm is partly determined by its specific asset base, for example its specialized plant and equipment, knowledge assets and complementary assets to them, as well as its relational assets and reputation. To produce and deliver new products and services, technological innovations require the use of certain complementary assets, such as financial and organizational assets. The reputation of the organization af-

---

[10]Organizational processes have three roles: integration, learning, and reconfiguration.

fects the responses of customers, suppliers, and competitors, and as such it is an intangible asset that enables it to achieve its goals in the marketplace. Of course this product market position affects the position of the firm in its external environment. However, the market position in a period of technological change is often fragile, so continually identifying growth options is essential for sustaining competitive advantage.

Paths and Path Dependencies

"History matters" in this view. The available future paths for the firm depend on its current position and the past decisions that helped it to create a competitive advantage. Path dependencies emphasize the fact that investments are to some extent costly to reverse and affect the value of future investment alternatives. Therefore, investments tend to have longer-term implications. A firm's previous investments and its built-in competencies (its "history") also shape its probable future opportunities and constrain the number of its investment alternatives.

Path dependencies are particularly important when there are increasing returns to adoption. Technologies and products tend to become more attractive in the presence of network externalities, complementary assets, supporting infrastructure, learning effects, or scale economies in production and distribution.

Innovation in an industry depends on the technological opportunities that happen along the future paths. Technological opportunities are not exogenous to the industry. Hence, investment by firms may generate new firm-specific or proprietary technological opportunities along the way. Both the variety of technological choices and the cost of these alternatives depend on decisions made in the past. Investment occurs when the path ahead is attractive. However, these technology options are uncertain, and trailblazing breakthroughs in related areas may block the route ahead for specific R & D applications. The size and variety of the set of technological opportunities that are similar to the prior research activities on this path are likely to impact a firm's growth options value.

2.2.5. OPTIONS AND GAMES: A LINKAGE APPROACH

As noted, a firm's future growth opportunities that potentially can result from its unique resource position should eventually be reflected in the firm's market value. Tangible resources, such as financial resources and physical assets, are easiest to identify and value. But an increasingly important though elusive component of value derives from intangible assets, resources and capabilities to adapt and generate options to undertake operations in the future under the right circumstances.

Intangible assets are often fuzzy in nature, and their value is hard to quantify. This is especially true for intangible technological resources. A classic example is the failure of Xerox Corporation to fully exploit the opportunities in its personal computer technology. Options and games can provide an explicit valuation of strategy under uncertainty. It can help determine which unique internal or intangible resources have value and economic relevance in generating valuable opportunities in a competitive environment.

The important contribution of the options and games framework in strategic management is that it can enable a quantification of qualitative strategic thinking. It offers a dynamic strategy valuation that encompasses NPV analysis as a special case and incorporates the tree approaches of real-options and game theory when they are relevant. NPV analysis can capture the value of an expected scenario of strategic plans and resulting cash flows that derive from the firm's tangible assets and resources. Real options represent a more appropriate valuation procedure when the firm's bundle of distinctive resources generates future opportunities and when the plan is likely to unfold differently than expected. When competitors can affect each other's behavior, an expanded strategic analysis that also draws on principles of game theory is called for.

Although the various strategic management frameworks discussed herein take a different perspective, we think that both the resource-based view and the competitive analysis approach could benefit from a closer linkage with the options and games approach.[11] A purely external view on competitive strategy is first based on the identification of structural industry attractiveness and subsequently on the acquisition of the requisite assets. Such a pure external view does not provide a strong foundation for the formulation of a dynamic long-term strategy in volatile markets where technologies are evolving rapidly or customer preferences and identity change.

When the external environment is in a state of flux, the adaptive resources of the firm and the corporate growth options these resources can generate in a competitive environment should form a better basis for strategy formulation. In line with the resource-based view, strategic growth options should be exercised with reference to the competences and capabilities that the firm has relative to its competitors. Analyzing the firm's unique resources and capabilities helps identify those options that are more likely to be available to the company than to its competitors.

---

[11]Although the real-options literature dates from the mid-1980s, it only became important for strategic management theory in the 1990s. McGrath (1997) uses real-options logic for initiating and amplifying the impact of technology investments, while Bettis and Hitt (1995) and Bowman and Hurry (1993) suggest real-options theory as an alternative valuation lens for technology and other strategic investments under uncertainty.

Options and games analysis can help frame complex investment problems under uncertainty, recognizing that the firm's (internal) resources and (external) strategic position to capture new market opportunities are strongly interrelated. This framework can help identify the appropriate market opportunities in which the firm's resources have the potential to earn the highest excess profits and design a preemptive strategy to sustain this competitive advantage.

From an options perspective, multistage investment problems are seen as links in a chain of interrelated projects, accumulating resources over time and generating new opportunities in an uncertain environment. Isolating mechanisms for future growth options, such as early preemptive investment, patents, or a unique asset-accumulation path, can be used to avoid duplication efforts by competitors, and help the firm to appropriate future opportunities and sustain and strengthen its competitive advantage.

Firms who use their adaptable internal resources and capabilities to exploit external opportunities along favorable paths, while limiting investment and losses along unfavorable paths, are more likely to exploit competitive advantages. In the rest of this book we propose a dynamic view of the business enterprise that disciplines the acceptable descriptive theory of strategic management via a more rigorous analytical process to help managers create and sustain long-run competitive advantage and adaptive flexibility.

2.3. COMPETITIVE ADVANTAGE AND INDUSTRY EVOLUTION

Where do positive expanded NPVs come from? To understand the value creation behind an investment's positive expanded NPV, one must first examine the various strategies that explain *why* certain investments are valuable. Value creation, or the ability to generate an excess return above the opportunity cost of capital, has two underlying sources. First, it depends on the general attractiveness of the industry in which the firm operates. Second, it depends on the establishment of a competitive advantage over its rivals. In this sense the profitability of a firm consists of two components, depending on the average added value of the industry and the value created relative to its competitors.[12]

Strategies that pursue competitive advantage can generate excess profitability in an industry. However, excess returns may be temporary. Pervasive competitive forces may erode returns. The threat of competitive

[12]This does not mean that firms having competitive advantage always show an excess profitability over the industry. Under uncertainty, performance may be partly the result of luck, and sometimes bad luck results from unfavorable events that are out of the hands of the management of the enterprise.

entry, imitation by competitors, or price rivalry can drive a firm's rate of return down to its cost of capital. When the advantage can persist over a longer period and resists competitors' attempts to imitate, it is said to be sustainable. If firms were identical, their strategies could be readily replicated by rivals and competitive forces would erode their competitive advantage.

Industry profitability may also be temporary, as industries and competition within industries continuously evolve. New competitors and new strategies emerge, which can transform products, processes, distribution channels, even the industry structure itself. To maintain an enduring competitive advantage in such a changing environment requires firms to adjust effectively to the changing environment. Those firms that are better able to adjust prosper and grow, while those that are more passive or pursue inappropriate strategies may not survive.

In this section we use typical patterns of industry evolution to explore implications for achieving and sustaining competitive advantage. The life cycle model is used as a simplified characterization of the principal stages in an industry's development.[13] The well-known S-shaped curve in the life cycle is used to characterize changes in industry growth over time along the stages. According to the life cycle, demand is initially low after a product is introduced. Subsequently, the product enters a growth phase. As demand becomes increasingly driven by replacement sales rather than by new adopters, and as competitors settle in, the product reaches a maturity stage. Demand for the product finally declines, as superior substitute products eventually come in.

The evolution of growth in demand and production and the creation and diffusion of resultant knowledge are such that each stage is associated with particular structural features that determine competitive advantage and rivalry. Since the relevant distinctive resources and the appropriate strategy vary over the life cycle stages, firms need to factor in industry evolution and make necessary strategic adjustments in response to this changing environment.

2.3.1. COMPETITIVE ADVANTAGE IN THE EARLY AND GROWTH STAGES

In the *early stage* of the life cycle, the product produced by a pioneering firm may not be well known by potential customers, although product technologies advance rapidly. Competition is based primarily on alternative technologies or design configurations with rival technologies competing to become the dominant standard. This competitive process involves

---

[13]See Grant 1995 for a thorough discussion of competitive advantage and the life cycle model.

the selection of the more successful technologies or designs until eventually a dominant technology or design emerges.

During the *growth stage* there is a transition from technological heterogeneity to increased standardization in product technology. As market penetration accelerates and product prices fall, the ability to adopt large-scale manufacturing in order to achieve cost reduction is enhanced. As the industry advances, established standards that form around the dominant design are more difficult to replace. Learning effects associated with continuing product development and increasing volumes can take hold, while network effects can arise whenever externalities exist among users.

In the introduction and growth stages various isolating mechanisms can be used to exploit preempting advantages.[14] Investment timing in particular affects the exercise of corporate real options as well as competitive behavior. It thus involves a trade-off between two main effects: *a strategic commitment effect* and *a flexibility effect*. While early preemptive investment enhances the commitment value of future growth opportunities, it sacrifices flexibility value as compared to a wait-and-see strategy during the later uncertain stages of industry evolution. When early-mover advantages are present, early commitment can be an important isolating mechanism during the growth stage. While early-mover advantages can help sustain a competitive strategy, late-mover advantages may erode this early-mover sustainability. Wait-and-see flexibility can be an important late-mover advantage in this case.

Early-Mover Preemption Advantages

In the design of a strategy based on a resource barrier the firm aims to create a situation in which its own resource position directly or indirectly makes it more difficult for others to catch up with (Wernerfelt 1984). The early exercise of real options can be an important isolating mechanism. Once expansion options are exercised, for example, the leading position of the early mover may be hard to match by competitors.[15] A strong resource position of an early mover can affect the acquisition cost (exercise price) and profit stream (underlying value) of firms with a weaker position. Firms should gather those resources to create a resource barrier that

[14]Competitive advantage reflects the firm's ability to perform better than its competitors in later stages. Firms can use isolating mechanisms to avoid imitation of their capabilities by competitors. Similar to mechanisms to protect the profitability of an industry, like high entry barriers or other structural conditions to soften price competition, a firm can act to protect its competitive advantage vis-à-vis its competitors in a specific sector.

[15]Competitors have to make a timely diagnosis of the company's competitive advantage if they are to try to imitate it. This task becomes more difficult if the company relies on multiple sources of competitive advantage, creating casual ambiguity.

others would find difficult to replicate in areas where no one currently has an advantage. They must also attract new resources that combine well with those they already have. Wernerfelt (1984) discusses several situations where preemption may strengthen a resource position and increase the firm's ability to invest in future expansion options.

Technological leads. In the introduction stage, R & D investments can be seen as a first link in a chain of expansion options at later stages. A technological lead allows the firm to preempt commercialization expansion options, in particular when the firm is able to establish a dominant technology or design. Again, the value of future growth options depends on the proprietary nature of these options. If followers can imitate the pioneer's ideas, the technological lead might soon disappear. Patent and legal protection are examples of isolating mechanisms that can prevent competitors from imitating. The pioneer can strengthen entry barriers if it can keep growing technological capabilities to protect its position. This should be feasible if it reinvests a significant part of its returns to support R & D.

A firm can also make other strategic moves to undermine competitors' incentives for imitation. A deterrence strategy may involve threatening signals to persuade rivals that by imitation they will invite a reciprocating response. As noted, these moves have an effect only if they are credible, and establishing credibility requires costly commitment. This can be done, for example, via reputation. Confrontation among rivals is usually a repeated game, and firms establish a reputation by being consistent in their actions over time. Intel, for instance, has built a reputation for aggressively suing firms that develop technologies resembling its chip technology.

Network externalities. Early-mover advantages in exercising real options are also present in situations where the network of users increases. These so-called network externalities are present in industries such as software or consumer electronics. When the product has a network externality, an early mover that makes more sales than its competitors in early periods can develop a larger installed base. This installed base can be viewed as an infrastructure investment that generates a set of expansion options.

Customer loyalty, buyer switching costs, and reputation. A pioneer may preempt competition and capture a significant share of the market by setting the product standard early on. Companies with the best products may not always win a battle for the product standard. Luck may cause "lock-in" on inferior technologies and in some cases may generate switching costs for consumers. Such switching costs can arise when buyers develop brand-specific know-how that is not useful in competitive products and can be an important isolating mechanism for an early mover in combination with network externalities. In such a case, it will be easier for the pioneer to exercise expansion options than it is for followers who have to replace an existing standard or face buyer-switching costs.

Reputation and buyer choice under uncertainty may also be important isolating mechanisms during the introduction and growth stages. When buyers have imperfect information on product quality, they may hold on to the first brand that performs satisfactorily, or they may follow a brand name.

Production experience. When heterogeneity turns into standardization in the growth stage, experience curve effects may arise whereby costs decline as cumulative production increases. Capitalizing on expansion opportunities based on such resource position depends on the ability of the firm to keep experience effects proprietary. When experience effects are proprietary, later resource producers will face an uphill battle with earlier producers who have lower costs, and thus will face less valuable expansion opportunities. However, when experience efficiencies are shared with competitors, they will also reduce the costs of the later entrants, as is the case with many production systems and procedures.

Production capacity. From a resource-based perspective, a product entry barrier based on economies of scale can translate into a resource position barrier since it lowers expected revenues for prospective acquirers. In particular, when the minimum efficient scale is large relative to the market size, the market can only accommodate a limited number of firms without creating overcapacity. This resource position enables the firm to preempt expansion opportunities in the market. Early movers are in an increasingly improving position to exercise their expansion options along the option chain due to the idiosyncratic nature of their costs or underlying asset value. Late movers would be reluctant to exercise their options since they would be faced with higher costs or might face the threat of price competition due to excess capacity.

Erosion of Sustainability and Late-Mover Advantages

Most isolating mechanisms are based on early-mover advantages. However, occasionally there may also be disadvantages from moving early. Early-mover disadvantages are therefore advantages of the late mover (or late-mover advantages). Late-mover advantages erode fist-mover sustainability. Lieberman and Montgomery (1988) show that late movers may benefit from (1) the ability to free-ride on early-mover investments; (2) flexibility and the resolution of technological and market uncertainty; and (3) switching benefits.

Free-rider effects of shared growth options. In cases that the benefits of the strategic option are shared, later movers may free-ride on the pioneering firm's early investment. The strategic compound options that present themselves in the introduction stage, such as R & D, some types of infrastructure investments, buyer education, and so on may generate benefits that are shared with followers. Innovators may enjoy monopoly profits during a short period before later movers exercise their entry options. The increased technological intensity coupled with shorter life-cycles, however, makes preventing early imitation increasingly difficult. In most cases imitation is less expensive than innovation. If the up-front strategic investment is high, as in R & D, there is an increased incentive in many cases not to pioneer but to follow a coordinated R & D strategy with rivals, for example, via joint research ventures.

Resolution of technological and market uncertainty. The option value to wait is important when uncertainty is high and there is a benefit from waiting to exercise investments as uncertainty is resolved. Sometimes early movers may fail to establish a sustainable competitive advantage if they bet on the wrong technology. The timing of investment depends critically on the type of uncertainty. When there is substantial uncertainty about the future product standard, for example, early entry may potentially be attractive when the firm can influence the way uncertainty is resolved or if it provides the firm with better information than its competitors.

Switching benefits in changing markets. While substantial switching costs may favor an early mover, in regimes of rapid technological change, costs of switching must be traded off against the benefits of switching to a new product. New products employing different standards often appear in market environments that experience technological change, and incumbents can be readily challenged by superior products and services that yield switching benefits. The degree to which switching costs and network externalities may cause "lock-in" of the early-mover technology depends on such factors as the speed of technological change and the broader competitive environment.

2.3.2. COMPETITIVE ADVANTAGE IN MATURE BUSINESSES

During the *maturity stage* of the life cycle, saturation of demand is reached as new demand gives way to replacement demand. In this stage, the technological knowledge among producers has grown and has been diffused. A typical development when the industry reaches maturity is for competition to shift from non-price to price competition and for its intensity to increase. Competition in technological innovation and brand reputation gives way to price competition, driven by the increasing cost efficiency of manufacturers, excess capacity, and growing international competition.

The maturity stage may witness exit of weaker companies and consolidation of the industry around a few big players that can more efficiently utilize economies of scale or scope. When the industry enters into a decline stage, price competition may intensify into destructive price wars, depending upon the height of exit barriers and the strength of international competition.

Companies enjoying competitive advantage in mature industries tend to have higher profitability than the industry average. Competitive advantage is usually seen to depend on a preferential cost position or a differentiation position of the firm relative to its competitors. There are two principal implications for competitive advantage when the industry reaches maturity: first, the strategic positions and competitive advantage of firms become more entrenched; second, the nature of competitive advantage usually shifts from differentiation-based factors to cost-based factors.

According to Michael Porter, value creation and competitive advantage can derive from two broad generic strategies: either a cost advantage that allows a firm to produce at lower cost than competitors, or a differentiation advantage that allows the firm to earn a premium in prices. A cost leadership is appropriate when the price elasticity of demand is high and the value from customers' perspective is based on a low price. Differentiation is an important competitive advantage when the firm can create distinctive capabilities and core competences that allow it to charge a price premium due to the differentiated characteristics of its product or service.

Cost Leadership Strategy

A cost leadership strategy is based on offering products similar to the firm's competitors but at lower cost. This strategy exploits opportunities that can lower costs, if they are not currently exploited by others. For instance, a firm can exploit economies of scale or learning economies by operating in large quantities while keeping the quality similar to its competitors. When there are shared growth options in the market, strategies that are aimed at a larger share or more experience can generate a momentum that later entrants or smaller firms find difficult to contest. A cost leadership position is more likely to be attractive when demand's sensitivity to price is highly elastic, when the product is more commodity-like, and when customer services are hard to differentiate.

Differentiation Strategy

Competitive advantage based on differentiation creates a higher consumer surplus and allows the firm to set a premium price. A differentiation strategy involves not only the product or service itself, but the whole relationship between the suppliers, firm, and customers. This strategy is likely to be effective in a context where the company offers a product or service that is perceived to be more valuable to customers than the ones offered by its competitors due to distinctive physical features, better performance reliability, brand status, quicker customer response, faster delivery of products, or other features. Competitive advantage based on differentiation can be relatively more attractive when price elasticity of demand is low, sources of cost advantage are already exploited by competitors, and the nature of products or services allows for enhancing the perceived value to customers.

A generic cost leadership or differentiation strategy can be attractive when a major market segment has an overriding preference either for the price attribute or the quality features of the product or service, when market conditions remain stable over time, and when it is difficult for competitors to meet these clients' needs. However, in dynamic markets these conditions might change, and strategic flexibility to adapt becomes an important source of competitive advantage.

2.3.3. Creative Destruction and Adaptation as Source of Advantage

Firms that pay attention only to harvesting their existing resources face the danger of becoming obsolete when the overall environment changes. Depending on the dynamism and volatility of the industry, core competencies that served the firm well in the past may become rigidities when skills and managerial systems are no longer productive. Sooner or later discontinuities will arise, and entire new technologies may destroy prevailing sources of competitive advantage and create new ones. The value of a firm's resources can be vulnerable not just to the actions of incumbents, but also to entirely new technologies that can modify the very competitive landscape the firm operates under. New research shows that industry evolution can be affected by technological developments. Carliss Y. Baldwin and Kim B. Clark in *Design Rules: The Power of Modularity* (2000) propose a technological theory of modularity and design evolution that can inform economic theories of industry evolution (see box 2.2).

Schumpeter (1942) observed that markets have an evolutionary process of "creative destruction." In periods of relative stability, firms develop superior products, technologies, or organizational capabilities that allow them to earn excess profits. These periods are occasionally disrupted or ended by discontinuities or shocks. New entrants can exploit such technological discontinuities, and these late movers can become early movers in the new technology. In this sense, technological discontinuities open up options for new technologies.

Schumpeter's process of creative destruction helps explain why isolating mechanisms are not everlasting. Sustainable competitive advantages

Box 2.2 Modularity, Real Options, and Computer Industry Evolution

Carliss Y. Baldwin and Kim B. Clark in their book *Design Rules,* volume 1, *The Power of Modularity,* propose a technological theory of modularity and design evolution that can inform economic theories of industry evolution. Using the computer industry as a case, they show the effect that modularity can have on the structure of an industry. Based on data on the market values of substantially all the public corporations in the computer industry from 1950 to 1996, broken down into 16 subsectors, they tell a story of industry evolution that runs counter to conventional wisdom. The dominant theories of industry evolution describe a process of preemptive investment by large, well-capitalized firms, leading to stable market structures and high levels of concentration over long periods of time. The figure shows that there was indeed a period in which the computer industry was highly concentrated, with IBM playing the role of dominant firm. (IBM's market value is the "mountain range" that forms the backdrop of the chart.) But in the 1980s, the computer industry "got away" from IBM. In 1969, 71% of the market value of the computer industry was tied up in IBM stock; by 1996, no firm accounted for more than 15% of the total value of the industry.

THE MARKET VALUE OF THE COMPUTER INDUSTRY
By sector, 1950–1996 (in constant 1996 US dollars)

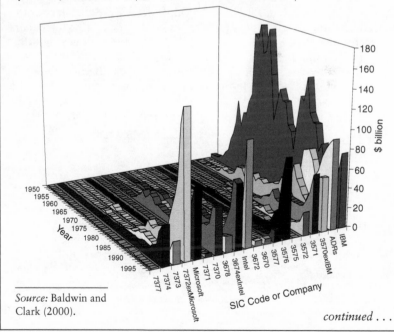

Source: Baldwin and Clark (2000).

continued . . .

Box 2.2 continued

By 1996, the computer industry consisted of a large *modular cluster* of over 1,000 firms, no one of which was very large relative to the whole. The total market value of the industry, which increased dramatically through the 1980s and 1990s, was dispersed across the 16 subindustries. Finally, the connections among products in the subindustries are quite complicated. Most computer firms did not design and make whole computer systems. Instead, they designed or made *modules* that were parts of larger systems.

In *Design Rules,* Baldwin and Clark argue that a fundamental *modularity* in computer designs caused the industry to evolve from its initial concentrated structure to a highly dispersed structure. Modularity allows design tasks to be divided among groups that can work independently, and do not have to be parts of the same firm. Compatibility among modules is ensured by "design rules," which govern the architecture and interfaces of the system. The design rules must be adhered to by all, and hence can be a source of economic power to the firms that control them. The theory of modular design and design evolution is based on two main ideas: (*a*) modularity creates options; and (*b*) modular designs evolve as the options are pursued and exercised.

Modularity Creates Options

When the design of an artifact is "modularized," the elements of the design are split up and assigned to modules according to a formal architecture or plan. Some of the modules are "hidden," meaning that design decisions in those modules do not affect decisions in other modules; some of the modules are "visible," meaning that they embody "design rules" that hidden-module designers must obey if the modules are to work together. In general, modularizations serve three purposes, any of which may justify an investment in modularity:

- Modularity makes complexity manageable.

- Modularity enables parallel work.

- Modularity is tolerant of uncertainty.

In this context, "tolerant of uncertainty" means that particular elements of a modular design may be changed *after the fact* and *in unforeseen ways* as long as the design rules are obeyed. Thus, modular designs offer alternatives that nonmodular ("interdependent") designs do not provide. Specifically, in the hidden modules, designers may replace early, inferior solutions with later, superior solutions. Such alternatives can be modeled as "real options." *The real options*

continued . . .

Box 2.2 continued

in a modular design are valuable. Baldwin and Clark categorize the major options implicit in a modular design, and explain how each type can be valued in accordance with modern finance theory. The key drivers of the "net option value" of a particular module are (1) the "technical potential" of the module (operating like volatility in financial option theory); (2) the cost of mounting independent design experiments; and (3) the "visibility" of the module in question. The option value of a system of modules in turn can be approximated by adding up the net option values inherent in each module and subtracting the cost of creating the modular architecture. A positive value in this calculation justifies investment in a new modular architecture.

Modular Designs Evolve as the Options Are Pursued and Exercised

Modular designs create value in the form of valuable real options. But how will that value be realized? The value of a modular system will be realized over time via *modular design evolution* (MDE). The promise implicit in a modular design is that parts of the system — the modules — can be modified after the fact at low cost. Foresighted actors seeking financial rewards will thus be motivated to pursue these options, and they will exercise the ones that are "in the money" at some future point in time (the actual date may be uncertain). Exercising an "in the money" option in this case means introducing a new, superior version of a particular module and reaping the economic rewards. The rewards may take the form of higher product revenue, or lower process cost, or both. The valuable options in a modular design thus motivate economic actors to pursue innovation, and the exercise of the options constitutes innovation. It follows that a modular design defines a set of evolutionary paths or trajectories. There will be at least one trajectory per hidden module, and there may be more if the full potential of the actions called "modular operators" is realized. As the history of a modular design unfolds, if the promise of the options is realized, we will "see" design evolution. The economically motivated actors in the system will pursue and then exercise design options on the basis of their inherent economic value. Their innovations will cause the individual hidden module designs to change over time in ways that create economic value. Architectures and interfaces will sometimes change, too, but less frequently.

This is how innovation works in the microcosm of a modular system. Most changes will not be big sweeping disruptions of the whole, although those are not ruled out. Most changes instead will involve replacing one small modular element with another correspondingly

continued . . .

Box 2.2 *continued*

small element that will do the same job in the system, only better. The overall picture is one of ordered, *but not wholly predictable,* progress toward higher economic value over time.

Source: Baldwin and Clark 2000.

may become obsolete and replaced by new ones. In many markets, periods of stability and maturity have become shorter, and some markets are characterized by a series of short cycles of creative destruction and frequent discontinuities. A passive strategy that focuses on the sustainability of a given competitive advantage in highly competitive markets will not likely be successful for long.

Whether the competitive advantage of a firm can be sustainable depends on the life cycle, the dynamism of the industry and market structure, and its own adaptive capabilities. The route to long-term success in competitive markets is for firms to proactively anticipate changes and to constantly adapt their strategy, flexibly exercising their options and creating new ones as the environment changes and new opportunities (or threats) arise. In intensively competitive environments, long-term success cannot be achieved by seeking only to sustain a given long-term advantage. Rather, achieving a sequential advantage across time is essential to place the firm on a leadership position.

An active adaptive strategy in a changing environment requires three key ingredients: timely information, proactive thinking, and adaptive capability. Proactive thinking involves anticipating changes in the basis of competitive advantage over time, as the industry moves through the life cycle, or as customer requirements and patterns of competition change.

Despite the best proactive thinking, unanticipated changes can lead to new threats or opportunities if the firm is able to adapt. Flexible strategies allow the firm to capitalize on better-than-expected developments or retreat to limit losses from market setbacks. Flexibility, or the ability to adapt to a changing environment while keeping one's options open, can be critically important for the survival and success of the firm. Strategic investments cannot be looked at as stand-alone opportunities, but as links that set the path for opportunities to follow. Whether these follow-on investment options will be exercised is uncertain at the time of the initial investment. In oligopolistic environments, a firm may use such strategic investments to shape industry developments, rather than passively wait for external forces to disrupt its currently preferential internal resources and capabilities. Box 2.3 projects a new vision of strategy in the changing competitive landscape ahead.

Box 2.3 Strategy in a Changing Competitive Landscape

Many of the concepts used in strategy were developed during the late 1970s and 1980s when underlying competitive conditions evolved within a well-understood model. Japan's manufacturing success with its emphasis on operating efficiency challenged some of the traditional assumptions — but it is only in the last decade that a new competitive landscape has emerged and the rules of engagement have changed. While the canvas available to today's strategists is large and new, companies will need to understand global forces, react quickly, and innovate when defining their business models.

The Emerging Competitive Landscape

The decade of the 1990s has witnessed significant and discontinuous change in the competitive environment. There is now an accelerating global trend to deregulate and privatize. Large and key industries like telecom, power, water, healthcare, and financial services are being deregulated. Countries as diverse as India, Russia, Brazil and China are at various stages of privatizing their public sectors. Technological convergence — such as that between chemical and electronic companies; computing, communications, components, and consumer electronics; food and pharmaceuticals; and cosmetics and pharmaceuticals — is disrupting traditional industry structures. Whether it is Eastman Kodak, the US photographic giant, Sony, the global electronics group, International Business Machines, Unilever, the Anglo-Dutch consumer giant, Revlon, the US cosmetics group, or Ford, managers must come to terms with the nature of transformation that technological convergence and digitalization will have on their industries. Further, the impact of the spread of the world wide web and the internet is just beginning to be felt. Ecological sensitivities and the emergence of non-governmental organizations such as the green movement are also new dimensions of the competitive landscape. Are these discontinuities changing the very nature of the industry structure — the relationships between consumers, competitors, collaborators, and investors? Are they challenging the established competitive positions of incumbents and allowing new types of competitors and new bases for competition to emerge (e.g., Barnes and Noble, and Amazon.com, both internet-based book retailers)? We can identify a long list of discontinuities and examples to illustrate each one of them. However, that is not our purpose here. We need to acknowledge the signals (weak as they may be) of the emergence of a new competitive landscape where the rules of engagement may not be the same as they were during the decade of the 80s. Strategists have to make the transition from asking

continued . . .

Box 2.3 continued

the question: "How do I position my company and gain advantage in a known game (a known industry structure)?" Increasingly the relevant question is: "How do I divine the contours of an evolving and changing industry structure and, therefore, the rules of engagement in a new and evolving game?" Industries represent such a diversity of new, emerging and evolving games. The rules of engagement are written as companies and managers experiment and adjust their approaches to competition.

Strategy in a Discontinuous Competitive Landscape

Strategists must start with a new mindset. Traditional strategic planning processes emphasised resource allocation — which plants, what locations, what products and sometimes what businesses — within an implicit business model. Disruptive changes challenge the business models. Four transformations will influence the business models and the work of strategists in the decades ahead: The strategic space available to companies will expand. Consider for example, the highly regulated power industry. All utilities once looked alike and their scope of operations were constrained by public utility commissions and government regulators. Due to deregulation, utilities can now determine their own strategic space. Today utilities have a choice regarding the level of vertical integration — "do I need to be in power generation? Do I need to be in power transmission?" Companies can unbundle assets and can also segment their businesses. "Should we focus more on industrial or domestic consumers?" They can decide their geographical scope. "Should I become global, regional, national or just remain local?" And finally, they can change their business portfolio. "Should I invest in water, telecoms, gas lines, services?" The forces of change — deregulation, the emergence of large developing countries such as India, China and Brazil as major business opportunities — provide a new playing field. Simultaneously, forces of digitalization, the emergence of the Internet and the convergence of technologies, provide untold new opportunities for strategists. The canvas available to the strategist is large and new. One can paint the picture one wants.

Speed is also an element in how fast a company learns new technologies and integrates them with the old. As all traditional companies are confronted with disruptive changes, the capacity to learn and act fast is increasingly a major source of competitive advantage. Innovation is the new source of competitive advantage. Innovation was always a source of competitive advantage. However, the concept of

continued . . .

Box 2.3 continued

innovation was tied to product and process innovations. In many large companies, the innovation process is still called the "product creation process." Reducing cycle time, increasing modularity, tracking sales from new products introduced during the last two years as a percentage of total sales, and global product launches were the hallmarks of an innovative company. Increasingly the focus of innovation has to shift towards innovation in business models. For example, how does an auction-based pricing market (e.g., airlines, hotels) in an industry with excess capacity change the business model? How do you think about resources available to the company for product development when customers become co-developers of the product or service? The 400,000–500,000 people, who beta tested Microsoft 2000, represent a development investment of $500 million (at a modest Dollars 1000 per person testing) outside the investment made by the company. Should we have an expanded notion of resource availability? What impact does mass customization or, more importantly, personalization of products and services have on the total logistics chain? Business innovations are crucial in a competitive landscape subject to disruptive changes.

Strategy in the Next Millennium

Given the dramatic changes taking place in the competitive landscape, I believe that both the concept of strategy and the process of strategy making will change. Older approaches will not suffice. Managers will have to start with two clear premises.

Firstly, that they can influence the competitive environment. Strategy is not about positioning the company in a given industry space but increasingly one of influencing, shaping and creating it. What managers do matters in how industries evolve. This is not just about the reactions of large, well-endowed companies like Citicorp, Merrill Lynch, Hilton Hotels, IBM or General Motors. Smaller companies can also have an impact on industry evolution. For example, E*Trade, Ebay, Price.com, and Amazon.com (all relatively new commercial enterprises created as a result of the internet), have significantly influenced the dynamics of well-established and traditional industries.

Secondly, it is not possible to influence the evolving industry environment, if one does not start with a point of view about how the world can be, not how to improve what is available but how radically to alter it. Imagining a new competitive space and acting to influence the migration towards that future is critical. Strategy is, therefore, not

continued . . .

Box 2.3 continued

an extrapolation of the current situation but an exercise in "imagining and then folding the future in." This process needs a different starting point. This is about providing a strategic direction — a point of view — and identifying, at best, the major milestones on the way. There is no attempt to be precise on product plans, or budgets. Knowing the broad contours of the future is not as difficult as people normally assume. For example, we know with great uncertainty, the demographic composition of every country. We can recognize the trends — the desire for mobility, access to information, the spread of the web and increasing dependence of all countries on global trade. The problem is not information about the future but insights about how these trends will transform industries and what new opportunities will emerge. While a broad strategic direction (or strategic intent and strategic architecture) is critical to the process, it is equally important to recognize that dramatic changes in the environment suggest managers must act and be tactical about navigating their way around new obstacles and unforeseen circumstances.

Tactical changes are difficult if there is no over arching point of view. The need constantly to adjust resource configuration as competitive conditions change is becoming recognized. A critical part of being strategic is the ability quickly to adjust and adapt within a given strategic direction. This may be described as "inventing new games within a sand box," the sand box being the broad strategic direction.

Finally, creating the future is a task that involves more than the traditional stand-alone company. Managers have to make alliances and collaborate with suppliers, partners, and often competitors to develop new standards (DVD digital versatile disc technology, for example), infrastructure (like broadband), or new operating systems (like Java). Alliances and networks are an integral part of the total process. This requirement is so well understood that it is hardly worth elaborating here. Resources available to the company are dramatically enhanced through alliances and networks.

Source: Excerpts from Prahalad 1999.

2.4. Portfolio Planning of Growth Opportunities

At the strategic level, firms must manage a portfolio of projects, structure business units or divisions, and determine the proper balance between cash-generating activities and the future growth of the firm. Portfolio planning, a framework for selecting strategies and allocating resources within a diversified portfolio, became popular along with the learning curve and product life cycle.[16] Active management of the firm's portfolio of investment options presupposes that we consider not only current synergies among projects, but also their sequential interdependencies with future investment opportunities. A firm's strategy for managing its portfolio of current and future options cannot be based on timing growth alone; it is proper management of *profitable* growth that results in value creation. An important question is, When and to what extent should we invest in projects with short-term profitability versus projects with long-term growth potential or strategic significance? Portfolio approaches have therefore two dimensions, a short-term profitability metric and a growth potential metric, both of which are prerequisites for the long-term success of the firm.

In this section we first discuss the traditional (static) portfolio planning approaches. The well-known Boston Consulting Group (BCG) growth-share matrix, which maps businesses according to profitability (or market share) and overall market growth, is the framework most used in portfolio planning for business units and acquisitions. This model, often used in conjunction with the learning curve and life cycle, was well suited for portfolio planning of diversified firms in a stable period of growth, such as the conglomerate era of the 1970s. In the revival of the 1990s diversification and acquisitions focused more on synergies that created value by establishing or augmenting core businesses with related resources and capabilities. However, the static perspective of the BCG growth-matrix planning approach is not always suitable for analyzing platform investments or follow-on opportunities under uncertainty.

With the increased dynamism and volatility of today's business there is a need for portfolio planning that satisfies the renewed awareness of uncertainty and builds in a degree of flexibility in investment decision making. Timothy Luehrman (1998) proposed a qualitative portfolio framework for the exercise timing of real options. This framework trades off a measure of immediate profitability against a measure of cumulative volatility (proxying for option value). Options should be managed toward exercise as they mature and as their cumulative volatility declines.

Our real-options growth (ROG) matrix goes a step further and embeds a dynamic real-options-based *valuation* in the planning and management of a portfolio of opportunities in an uncertain and competitive environment. As such, the real-options growth matrix combines the best features of traditional portfolio planning and modern valuation analysis,

---

[16]The concept of diversification is as old as the financial markets. There is significant evidence, going back to the thirteenth century, that investors were investing significant proportions of their wealth in foreign assets. During the eighteenth century the Dutch invested heavily in British and French securities. Like shareholders, conglomerate corporations have long been diversifying in international businesses.

such as real options and games. For value creation, we must consider both the value added by the cash flows of the firm's existing investments (or assets in place) and a proper measure of overall growth option value.[17] This new framework may help answer important questions such as the following: How does a firm play the game in a rapidly changing environment? How can a firm adjust its resource position to preserve and enhance its competitive advantage when the environment changes rapidly? The adaptive capabilities that enable the firm to adjust and redeploy assets, develop and exploit synergies, and generate new opportunities (e.g., time-to-market and first- or second-mover advantages) are valuable extensions of standard portfolio planning. We discuss the BCG matrix next.

2.4.1. Boston Consulting Group (BCG) Matrix

The proper balance between commercialization of profitable investments and the development of future opportunities plays a prominent role in strategic planning. One of the first portfolio planning approaches based on the idea of trading off current profitability vs. future growth was the growth-share matrix for portfolio planning developed by Boston Consulting Group in the 1970s. In the BCG matrix, each business is mapped on a two-dimensional grid. One dimension represents the business's profitability, and the other industry attractiveness or growth. Figure 2.2 depicts the BCG matrix. The vertical axis shows the relative profitability of a business unit or project, measured by return on assets (ROA) or market share.[18] The horizontal axis depicts the unit's future growth prospects, typically measured by the unit's projected real market growth.

---

[17]Our ROG framework recognizes that the present value of future growth opportunities is a more general measure for *growth option value,* reflecting volatility, adaptability, and competitive responsiveness. The value of assets in place and the value of future growth opportunities are incorporated in the stock prices of traded companies. Thus, both components of value can be extracted from financial market data. In addition, our framework can accommodate game theory analysis, which may be necessary when competitors affect investment opportunities.

[18]The belief that market share is vital for competitive positioning and profitability underlies this popular planning technique. Marketing applications of the BCG matrix use market share instead of ROA as a measure of present profitability, to capture market dominance. Typically the market share is related to the firm's largest competitor. It is likely that market share and profitability are strongly related. However, the BCG matrix does not explicitly capture this relation nor the value of exploration for potential profitable investment opportunities. A high market share in the pharmaceutical industry, for instance, can be the result of successful innovation. High market share and profits for a number of years resulted from successful and defensible R & D efforts. The successful strategy is no longer to price and market so as to win market share, but to launch an intensive R & D effort and use patent protection (see Oster 1999).

FIGURE 2.2 THE BOSTON CONSULTING GROUP'S (BCG) GROWTH-PROFITABILITY MATRIX

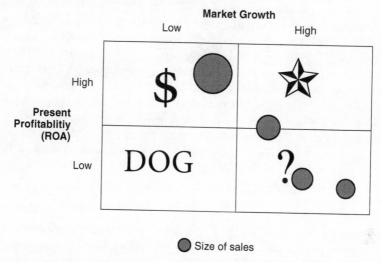

The BCG growth vs. profitability matrix categorizes projects (or product-market combinations) into four quadrants according to their potential for future growth and current profitability. Rising stars are projects in growth markets with relative high profitability. Question marks represent projects with high growth prospects, but with lower profitability. A cash cow is a project in a stable market environment with high present profitability. A dog is a project in a stable or declining market with low present profitability. Portfolio management recommends that firms use the profits earned by cash cows to fund development of rising stars and question marks.

The size of the circles indicates the value (or sales) of a unit or project. There are four quadrants. "Question marks" are defined as opportunities with low profitability but high growth prospects. Proper cultivation and active management may turn these "question marks" into "stars," or projects with high growth and profitability. Often this requires a sequence of additional investments, for instance in technological development or advertising campaigns. A rising "star" is a business unit with increasing profitability, a high growth rate, and increasing sales and size, as presented by the larger circles. "Cash cows" ($) are business units in stable or declining markets with relatively solid profitability. Low-profit business units in slow-growth markets are "dogs," and are generally to be avoided or divested. Management may use this matrix for the active management of their portfolio of business units in a relatively stable environment. Such a portfolio management approach recommends that firms use the profits earned by "cash cows" to generate/explore "question marks" and for further development of "rising stars." That is, one should balance commercialization and development.

With the BCG matrix, management can project a portfolio of business units into the future, developing a trajectory that starts with "question marks" with the intention to develop them into "rising stars" and finally turn them into "cash cows." This trajectory will depend in large part on the product life cycle. As noted, for most products, demand is initially low when the product is first introduced. The product subsequently enters a growth phase. As demand becomes increasingly driven by replacement sales rather than by first-time purchases, the product reaches its maturity stage. Demand for the product will then decline as superior substitute products emerge.

2.4.2. Exercise Timing of Options: The Tomato Garden Analogy

Option theory can add significant insight to this strategy framework.[19] Option analysis allows for switching along various strategic paths, which makes it possible to determine the value of a flexible strategy. Additional investment only becomes necessary if demand continues to develop favorably. This does not treat the trajectory and pattern of related outlays as a static scenario, but instead permits adjustments depending on market developments.

Timothy Luehrman (1998) proposed a gardening metaphor for classifying and managing growth options (see box insert 2.4). The development of growth options in a changing business environment is seen analogous to the ripening of tomatoes in a garden, and managing a portfolio of strategic options is like gardening tomatoes in an unpredictable climate. Growth options, like tomatoes, grow differently. Some tomatoes are ripe and perfectly ready to be picked; others would benefit from more time on the vine; some are not yet edible. Cultivation can improve the crop. An experienced gardener knows when to cultivate the crop, and when to pick tomatoes before squirrels or other competitors take their share.

With this gardening metaphor, Luehrman suggested using an "option space" for thinking about active management of portfolios of options, by analogy with the tomato garden. Corporate strategy is viewed as exercising the various options should the investment follow a path that makes an option worth exercising. The option space suggested by Luehrman, illustrated in figure 2.3, has two dimensions. Along the horizontal axis is

---

[19]This section is based in part on Luehrman 1998.

BOX 2.4 A GARDENING METAPHOR: OPTIONS AS TOMATOES

Managing a portfolio of strategic options is like growing a garden of tomatoes in an unpredictable climate. Walk into the garden on a given day in August, and you will find that some tomatoes are ripe and perfect. Any gardener would know to pick and eat those immediately. Other tomatoes are rotten; no gardener would ever bother to pick them. These cases at the extremes — now and never — are easy decisions for the gardener to make.

In between are tomatoes with varying prospects. Some are edible and could be picked now but would benefit from more time on the vine. The experienced gardener picks them early only if squirrels or other competitors are likely to get them. Other tomatoes are not yet edible, and there's no point in picking them now, even if the squirrels do get them. However, they are sufficiently far along, and there is enough time left in the season, that many will ripen unharmed and eventually be picked. Still others look less promising and may not ripen before the season ends. But with more sun or water, fewer weeds, or just good luck, even some of these tomatoes may make it. Finally, there are small green tomatoes and late blossoms that have little likelihood of growing and ripening before the season ends. There is no value in picking them, and they might just as well be left on the vine.

Most experienced gardeners are able to classify the tomatoes in their gardens at any given time. Beyond that, however, good gardeners also understand how the garden changes over time. Early in the season, none of the fruit falls into the "now" or "never" categories. By the last day, all of it falls into one or the other because time has run out. The interesting question is: What can the gardener do during the season, while things are changing week to week?

A purely passive gardener visits the garden on the last day of the season, picks the ripe tomatoes, and goes home. The weekend gardener visits frequently and picks ripe fruit before it rots or the squirrels get it. Active gardeners do much more. Not only do they watch the garden but, based on what they see, they also cultivate it: watering, fertilizing, and weeding, trying to get more of those in-between tomatoes to grow and ripen before time runs out. Of course, the weather is always a question, and not all the tomatoes will make it. Still, we would expect the active gardener to enjoy a higher yield in most years than the passive gardener.

In option terminology, active gardeners are doing more than merely making exercise decisions (pick or do not pick). They are monitoring the options and looking for ways to influence the underlying

continued . . .

---

the value of the project divided by the present value of the investment cost, or the value-to-cost ratio, which can be viewed as a proxy for current profitability. Along the vertical axis is the cumulative volatility metric, which represents the potential for changes in the value of the project (before the investment decision is made). This metric, which combines the project's volatility and the life of the growth option, is intended as a proxy for option value.

Luehrman then distinguishes six regions in the option space. Along the very top of the option space (region 1 and region 6), investment is a "now or never" decision, once time has run out or uncertainty has been resolved. Here, the option problem collapses back to a standard NPV application. The options located on the right-hand side of the option space are more promising. These options have high prospects but (like early tomatoes) may not yet be mature; some of them are in-the-money while others are still out-of-the-money, as indicated by the curve in the diagram. Options in region 3, labeled *Probably later*, are similar to green tomatoes: they are not edible now but could be picked later. In this region fall options that have valuable prospects, but immediate exercise of these out-of-the-money options may result in value destruction. Options in region 2, *Maybe now,* on the other hand, can be exercised immediately, though they should still be timed carefully. These tomatoes are edible now but could benefit from more time on the vine. An experienced gardener will pick them early if there is a threat of erosion, for example, if squirrels are likely to get them. Projects in region 1, *Invest now*, are like ripe tomatoes. The options are in-the-money and have run out of time. Options in the left half of the space, on the other hand, are less promis-

FIGURE 2.3 EXERCISING OPTIONS IN OPTION-VALUE SPACE

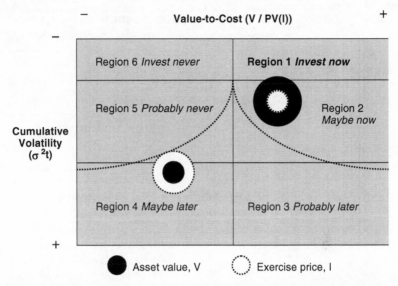

The option space is defined by two metrics: the value-to-cost metric, defined as the value of the underlying asset divided by the present value of expenditures or the value of the underlying asset divided by the present value of the exercise price, $V/PV(I)$. The second metric is the cumulative volatility defined as the variance per period of asset returns cumulated over the time to option expiration, $\sigma^2 t$.

Source: Luehrman 1998.

ing. Here we find the *Maybe later* and *Probably never* regions. In region 5, *Probably never* projects have dim prospects. These are like the late blossoms and small green tomatoes that are unlikely to ripen before the season ends. Projects in the lower region 4 have better prospects because there is still time for change.

The locations of these options are determined by their value-to-cost and volatility characteristics. The value of the underlying asset is indicated by the filled (solid) circle, while the exercise price or investment cost is depicted by the dashed (empty) circle. Options that are in-the-money have the dashed circle inside the solid one. Whether or not an investment is undertaken depends on uncertain future conditions. In "option space," as in nature, there are basic laws of time and motion. As time passes, investment opportunities tend to move upwards and to the left in option space: upwards because cumulative volatility declines as uncertainty is resolved over time, and to the left because the options need to be nurtured for further favorable development and in-the-money exercise.

As soon as an option starts down a particular path, it is exposed to uncertainty about industry developments, competitive moves etc. Management thus requires flexible responsiveness to these developments. As the path of a project develops over time, options move upwards and reach maturity at the top of the option space (regions 1 or 6), at which point the investment decision must be made or the option will expire. A strategy can be depicted in option space as a sequence of options, with each project or business unit in a strategic investment program seen as a link in generating another option, or as part of a bundle of projects that extends over the long term.

2.4.3. REAL-OPTIONS GROWTH (ROG) MATRIX

We now discuss the real-options growth (ROG) matrix as a tool that combines and extends the best features of the BCG matrix and the options space described above in addressing the classic trade-off between short-tem profitability and long-term growth potential. For value creation, we must consider both the value of the firm's existing investments (or assets in place) and its future growth option value. As a better proxy for the latter, we use the present value of future growth opportunities (PVGO) that combines both volatility and adaptability. Volatility may involve not just project demand, but also technological change, competitive moves, and so forth. PVGO can be normalized by being expressed as percentage of the firm's share price and can often be extracted from financial market data.

Consider the ROG matrix shown in figure 2.4 and how growth opportunities may evolve. The matrix proposes that growth opportunities be represented along two dimensions of value. The horizontal axis measures the direct NPV component of value, capturing present profitability from immediate investment (exercise). The vertical axis measures the relative value of the firm's growth options (PVGO). At any stage of an asset's development, total value can be viewed as the sum of the present value of the cash flows from existing assets plus a component capturing the potential of new growth opportunities.

The extension proposed via the ROG matrix is to embed such a dynamic real-options-based *valuation* (current value plus growth option value) within portfolio management analysis. That is, we recast our expanded (or strategic) NPV criterion, which captures the total value of management's flexibility to alter planned investment decisions as future market conditions change, within an active portfolio management context, as follows:

FIGURE 2.4 THE REAL-OPTIONS GROWTH (ROG) MATRIX

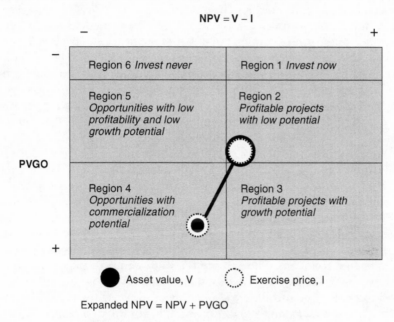

Asset value, V   Exercise price, I

Expanded NPV = NPV + PVGO

Total value creation (expanded NPV) consists of the net present value (NPV) plus the value of the growth opportunities (PVGO). The ROG matrix is defined by these two metrics. The first is the net present value, NPV $= V - I$. In case of an acquisition it is the value of assets in place minus the price of the target. The second metric is the present value of the growth opportunities, PVGO, of the project or acquisition.

Expanded (strategic) NPV = direct NPV + PVGO.   (2.1)

In this way the ROG matrix distinguishes between value components that can be traced back to financial markets, since both the current operating value and the value of future growth opportunities (PVGO) are reflected in the stock prices of traded companies. It is a key advantage of the ROG matrix that it can distinguish between value components that can be traced back to financial markets.

Coordinates: Estimating Assets in Place and Growth Option Value

PVGO can be estimated directly or indirectly from the financial markets. With the direct method, we can use option valuation methods to value the firm's set of strategic options. Such direct estimation of the value of the growth option component using option valuation methods requires identifying the individual strategic options for the firm and their interactions,

and estimating their parameters. The second method avoids these estimation and valuation complexities by using the consensus market assessment
of the firm's bundle of strategic options. This indirect method "backs out"
the value of the growth option bundle from the firm's equity value by de-
ducting from the observed market equity value the value of the static or
nongrowth component associated with continued current operations estimated from standard DCF techniques. This residual value reflects the
value of the bundle of growth options and is depicted along the vertical
axis of our ROG matrix. The horizontal coordinate measures the value of
assets in place minus the amount invested (the direct NPV).

We can relate the PVGO/stock price ratio to a number of empirically
observable variables related to option characteristics, such as firm-specific
volatility, market uncertainty, skewness of returns, and a proxy for the
exploration-exploitation mix of the bundle of growth options (measured
by R & D/sales).[20] The value share of growth options may further change
over time, due to changes in interest rates, moneyness of the options, maturity, and the volatility of the firm over time. Typical data from a variety
of industries seems to support the option value nature of the PVGO component (Smit 1999a). Volatile firms in rapidly evolving, uncertain and
high-technology industries, such as pharmaceuticals, computers, and consumer electronics, exhibit a higher proportion of growth option value embedded in their stock price. Effective portfolio strategies in volatile or
fast-developing industries must be flexible enough to enable the firm to
adjust effectively to an uncertain and changing competitive and technological environment. Indeed, the strategies of leading firms in such industries involve acquisitions that are undertaken in part or primarily for their
potential strategic growth option value, e.g., to enable the firm to acquire
options on evolving technologies in the industry. Even though the cash
flow benefits of such strategic investments may be elusive, dispersed, or
contingent on follow-on investments, they are clearly reflected in the equity values and acquisition premiums paid for high-tech firms.

Identifying Opportunities in the ROG Matrix

In the real-options growth matrix of figure 2.4, opportunities (projects,
business units, or firms) may fall in different regions in option-value
space based on their current profitability (NPV) versus relative growth
option potential (PVGO/price). The bottom left of the option-value space

---

[20]That is, $PVGO_{i,t}/P_{i,t} = f\left(R \& D_{i,t}/Sales_{i,t}, \sigma^2_{S,i,t}, \beta^2_{i,t}\sigma^2_{m,i,t}, sk_{i,t}, \alpha_{jt}\right) + \epsilon_i$;
The intercept α_j is the fixed effect that separates time series effects. The idiosyncratic com-
ponent is captured by the residuals of the regressions, ϵ_i. In such a regression we can also
control for financial leverage, firm size, etc.

(region 4) comprises opportunities that are currently unprofitable but have high growth potential and may be commercialized later. These "strategic" investments or acquisitions may generate other investment opportunities, and as such often represent "options on options." This region contains opportunities that are similar to the "question marks" in the BCG matrix and have typical compound (growth) option characteristics — they are at an innovation stage and have not yet proven themselves in the marketplace. At this stage, management focuses on the innovative activity and on defining what the customers want.

The economic value of such an opportunity or business unit (represented by the small solid circle in figure 2.4) derives primarily from its future potential, since current assets have a negative NPV, probably due to high investment outlays. Development of such opportunities involves a process analogous to developing or exercising a chain of options. The first project in line typically faces higher uncertainty, and must be exercised before proceeding to the next stage of the sequential investment chain. R & D expenditures or strategic acquisitions of high-tech research ventures in volatile industries typically appear to generate a low return when considered in isolation, but may have considerable strategic option value due to such follow-on opportunities. These strategic projects can no longer be looked at as independent investments, but rather as links in a chain of interrelated projects, the earlier of which are prerequisites for the ones to follow.

The lower-right region in figure 2.4 (region 3) comprises projects that are currently in-the-money (NPV > 0) but may be even more valuable if commercialized later. These might be projects or businesses that are valuable in and of themselves but which may derive additional value from technologies or applications currently under development. A pilot venture, a first-generation technology, a new drug with multiple extensions, or a strategic acquisition in a new geographical area may not only generate cash flows but may also bring additional strategic value to the firm by generating further investment opportunities. Often it pays to develop projects that are in this stage of business evolution. It is, however, important to preempt implementations of similar ideas by competitors to ensure that the firm enjoys proprietary benefits (e.g., if the product becomes the market standard in its class).

In the top-right region of the option-value space in figure 2.4 (region 2), growth option value declines as the option expires or as the remaining cumulative uncertainty decreases. This region hosts businesses with low uncertainty and growth option potential, held mostly for cash generation rather than for strategic growth option value. The projects here have positive NPVs, and standard DCF techniques are adequate to evaluate and develop such stable businesses.

In the top-left region (region 6), businesses with both low commercial and low growth option value should be abandoned or divested. An essential feature of the options approach to portfolio management lies in the recognition that investment opportunities along the development trajectory are discretionary. R & D, a start-up venture, or an exploration investment in natural resources may lead to a trajectory of commercialization, harvesting of patents, technological advantage, or valuable resources, but implies no obligation to invest further in case of failure. Favorable trajectory developments eventually end up in the top-right region (region 1), while unfavorable trajectories end up in the top-left region (region 6), as a consequence of uncertainty and a natural selection process. Many projects can end up in this "divest" region — even before investing large amounts in capacity — if conditions turn out to be unfavorable.

Balancing the Mix between Operational and Strategic Opportunities in the Options Portfolio

Management of the firm's "bundle of opportunities" requires a balance between exploiting current cash-generating advantages and generating new options.[21] The starting point for the portfolio management of options and the strategic analysis of project interactions is the proper definition of investment categories. The first strategic question management must address concerns the value characteristics of the project: Does this business opportunity realize its value primarily through direct measurable cash inflows, or does it have strategic growth option value? Most companies classify investment opportunities into two broad categories, operating and strategic investments. Projects that generate limited synergistic or follow-on effects are simple options or basic operating projects. These projects typically have a positive NPV, but generate limited growth opportunities. By contrast, strategic investment opportunities do not derive their value primarily from direct cash inflows, but from strategic follow-on investment opportunities. As shown in figure 2.4, a compound option with a typical low NPV in region 4 can generate a simple option in region 2 (the two are connected with a solid line). Examples of compound options include a pilot project that might create a new market or an exploration investment in natural resources that may derive value from future multistage commercial opportunities. Such opportunities or strategies have different time and growth-option profiles in option-value space.

The overall value of the portfolio of options depends on the mix of operational and strategic projects and their correlations and interactions. It

[21]This section relies on Kasanen 1993; and Trigeorgis and Kasanen 1991.

is important to recognize that different stages in the option chain may have distinctly different risk characteristics. The first stage explores and creates options that can be exploited in later stages, and is inherently more risky. There is also a distinction between uncertainties that can be resolved through further investment and those that cannot. Simple options typically face *market uncertainty* over operating cash flows that results primarily from uncertainties in demand or the prices of factors of production. These uncertainties are largely exogenous to the firm. Exploratory compound options, such as R & D, involve additional firm-specific uncertainties (that may or may not be reduced by further investment). These include technical, strategic, and organizational uncertainties.

Kasanen (1993) and Trigeorgis and Kasanen (1991) propose a framework that helps balance the optimal exploration-exploitation mix among strategic and operational investment opportunities in the options portfolio. One of the important characteristics of an investment category is its ability to generate other growth options. Different spillover effects can distinguish investments.

Intertemporal (compound option) effects. If successful, growth options generate new investment opportunities that become profitable commercial projects. Such growth options include R & D, advertising, visionary development of new technology investments, and positioning and pilot projects.

Interproject (operational) interaction effects. When implemented, these projects create interproject interactions and may generate further investment opportunities. Learning curve and constant improvement effects are some practical examples. For instance, cost efficiency and routines may lead to innovations in production or product design. The key here is to harness and build upon the experiences obtained at the operating level.

The expanded NPV of a business unit is thus determined by the composition of its portfolio of investment opportunities, taking into account the interproject and intertemporal synergies. Operational projects have a higher NPV, but the exploration capacity and growth option potential of operating projects is naturally much lower.

The intertemporal and interproject relationships or synergies between the various investment opportunities can be represented via a growth (or spawning) matrix as in figure 2.5 (Kasanen 1993). This matrix helps determine the optimal investment based on the trade-off between the value of growth opportunities (PVGO) from strategic investments, and the value generated by direct operating cash flows (NPV) from operating projects. It provides a way of assessing the proper mix between strategic

FIGURE 2.5 THE GROWTH MATRIX

TO

	Strategic Growth Options (Exploration)	Operational Investments (Exploitation)
Strategic Growth Options (Exploration)	Generates many new strategic options	Generates many new operational investments
Operational Investments (Exploitation)	Generates a limited feedback effect on exploitation opportunities	Generates a feedback effect on new strategic opportunities

FROM

Expanded NPV = NPV + PVGO

The growth matrix considers the generation of future growth opportunities by different categories of projects. Real investment opportunities can be divided into two broad categories: strategic and operational (normal) projects. The growth matrix defines the cross-time relationship for each investment category and its future investment opportunities. The vertical metric measures the current investments in strategic or operating projects. The second metric is future operational and strategic projects that are generated by these investments. The spawning structure defines the investment interactions among the categories with the objective of determining an optimal mix to maximize value.

Source: Kasanen 1993.

projects that pave the way for future growth and projects that exploit or commercialize current opportunities.[22]

Active Management of Opportunities in the ROG Matrix

In the real-options growth matrix, projects move over time from the bot-

[22]The optimal mix of strategic versus operational investment categories would depend on three relationships, based on an expanded NPV criterion. The first would maximize the combined expanded NPV of all investment categories. As noted, the expanded NPV is defined as the net present value plus the value of the growth opportunities (PVGO). A second relationship specifies the interdependencies and sets the growth constraints for the next investment opportunities based on investment in prior periods via the growth (spawning) matrix. The third relationship specifies the initial endowment of investment opportunities of each category.

tom (left) to the top (right) of the matrix as they develop from a technology or from an idea stage to commercialization, as illustrated via the linkages (and arrows) in figure 2.6. Projects, however, do not passively follow a predetermined trajectory from "question marks" to become "stars" or end up as "cash cows" or "dogs." Active development of a firm's growth options involves proactive planning and flexibility to react to adverse market movements or capitalize on favorable opportunities. As an opportunity develops, its value increases (as does the size of the circle in figure 2.6). As various sorts of uncertainties resolve themselves either unfavorably or favorably over time, the investment may accordingly end up in a less desirable region or in a more desirable region. Figure 2.6 illustrates valuation of a two-stage R & D investment opportunity, discussed in more detail in box insert 2.5.

As soon as the firm invests in R & D (the compound option in region 4), the development trajectory starts at the bottom left of the option space, starting in stage I with a negative NPV (-30) on the horizontal axis and a PVGO of 37 on the vertical axis in the ROG matrix. This R & D investment creates a growth option to make an investment in the second stage having a positive NPV of 26 and a PVGO component of 11 that creates a total expanded value of 37. Such investment opportunities in general tend to move upwards. They might move to the left as time passes if management makes the wrong decisions or simply waits passively, as waiting generally implies erosion of option value. As we move out of stage I, the underlying asset value of this compound option (a completed commercialized project) would move upwards, ending to the left or right as technical and other uncertainties are resolved unfavorably or favorably and as management succeeds or fails to adapt its strategy effectively to these changes.

As shown in the right panel of figure 2.6, the project is guided to move to the upper regions of the matrix and enter the commercialization phase. If R & D is unsuccessful, however, the subsequent investment need not take place, limiting the downside value to zero. Thus, if research fails, only the relatively small up-front R & D investment is lost. This represents the option premium or price that must be paid to acquire and develop the growth option.

Embedding Competitive Portfolio Strategies

The firm must of course select the markets it will serve and the development of its investment strategy in light of its industry and competitive environment. There are two main competitive portfolio strategies: diversification and focus. The economic logic behind a broadly diversified

FIGURE 2.6 R & D INVESTMENT IN THE REAL-OPTIONS GROWTH
(ROG) MATRIX

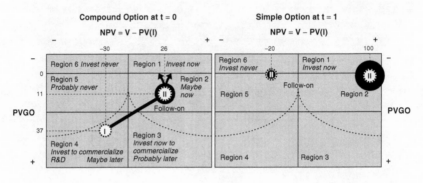

Investment Opportunity	NPV Metric	PVGO Metric	Total Value	Strategy
t = 0:				
Stage I: R&D Investment				
Exercise price, $I_0 = 30$				
Underlying asset value: follow-on option value on $V_0 = \$100$ million	-30	37	$+7$	Invest now
Time to expiration (years), $\tau = 0$				
Risk-free rate, $r = 0.08$				
Stage II: Follow-on commercial project				
Exercise price, $I_1 = 80$; $PV(80) = 74$				
Underlying asset: $E(V_1) = \$120$ million;				
$PV(120) = 100$	$100 - 74 = 26$	11	$+37$	Maybe later
Time to expiration, $\tau = 1$ year				
Uncertainty up = 1.6, down = 0.8				
t = 1:				
Expected underlying asset value:				
$E(V_1) = \$120$ million				
Value of follow-on project				
when nature moves up	$180 - 80 = 100$	0	$+100$	Invest now
Value of follow-on project				
when nature moves down	$60 - 80 = -20$	0	0	Invest never

strategy is that competitive advantages in certain industries are based
on the existence of economies of scale and scope across products or technologies. These economies of scope may come from products that share
common production facilities or components. They may also result from
technical knowledge strengthened by learning effects (as in software) or

Box 2.5 Option Valuation: An Example

A high-tech company has an exclusive opportunity (a license or patent) to build a plant to produce a new product. This commercial investment opportunity has a (gross) project present value of $V_0 = 100$. What is really of interest in a world of uncertainty is not the value of the *immediate* investment per se, but rather the value of the *opportunity* to invest. The opportunity to invest provided by the proprietary license or patent allows management the *flexibility to defer* investment for a year and invest *only* if conditions (e.g., demand or prices) are favorable. As we follow the expected trajectory of the project, we are faced with significant uncertainty. Suppose that this opportunity involves an expenditure over one year of $I_1 = 80$ and that the (gross) value of expected future cash inflows from production, V, fluctuates in line with random fluctuations in demand, say to $V^+ = 180$ or $V^- = 60$ (with equal probability) by the end of the period.[1]

The total value of this investment opportunity (expanded NPV or NPV^*), seen as a call option, can be obtained from the end-of-period expected values (with expectations taken over risk-neutral or certainty-equivalent probabilities, here $p = 0.4$ and $1 - p = 0.6$), discounted at the risk-free rate (here $r = 0.08$):[2] NPV^* or $C = [0.4 \times (180 - 80) + 0.6 \times 0] / 1.08 = 37$. The value of this premium depends on various sources of uncertainty, the value of the underlying asset, interest rates, and the life of the real option.

How can management decide whether or not to invest in R & D to develop a new proprietary technology? To answer this question we introduce an R & D stage in the decision process. Now the firm faces the decision about whether to make the R & D expenditure in the first place in order to acquire the proprietary option to proceed with commercialization in the second stage. The table at the bottom of figure 2.6 illustrates this two-stage R & D investment opportunity, which requires an immediate, stage-I investment outlay of $I_0^I = 30$ (a compound growth option). Despite high costs and no expected cash inflows during the first stage, management intuitively feels the necessity of the investment to develop the new technology and possibly enhance the company's market position. Investing now in the pioneer R & D creates strategic value by generating opportunities to invest in future commercial projects.

Based on a naive DCF analysis, the standard total net present value of this pioneer R & D venture is NPV (stage I) + NPV (stage II). Here, $NPV^I = -I^I = -30$. The follow-on commercial project (stage II) has an NPV of 26 in year zero. If the firm were to commit to both stages right now, the total expected net project value would be negative.[3] However, the appropriate decision rule for such a growth option to be exercised should not be based only on its static NPV. When its

continued . . .

Box 2.5 continued

total value, including its potential growth option value, is positive, management should start the option development process.

The cost of first-stage R & D is the price that must be paid to acquire a growth option on the commercial project. Is the value of the acquired option, however, worth the required investment cost? Using options valuation, the value of the second-stage commercialization (growth) option in year zero is $Option^{II} = 37$ rather than $NPV^{II} = 26$, as given by conventional DCF.[4] Thus, the total strategic value (or expanded NPV) of the entire R & D venture is $NPV^* = NPV^I + Option^{II} = -30 + 37 = +7\ (> 0)$, which makes the R & D investment worthwhile.

Notes

[1]We use the same example in a later chapter. The project is expected to generate a $t = 1$ value of $E(V_1) = 0.5 \times 180 + 0.5 \times 60 = 120$; discounted at the opportunity cost of capital, assumed to be $k = 20\%$ (for the last stage of production), this results in a (gross) project present value of $V_0 = 100$. The firm would thus be willing to make an *immediate* investment outlay of $I_0 = 80$ in return for the higher present value of expected cash inflows, $V_0 = 100$. In the absence of managerial flexibility, the traditional (static or passive) net present value, $NPV = V_0 - I_0 = 100 - 80 = 20\ (> 0)$, would justifiably recommend project acceptance.

[2]The risk-neutral probabilities (that would prevail in a risk-neutral world where any asset is expected to yield the risk-free rate) can be obtained from

$$p = \frac{(1 + r)\,V - V^-}{V^+ - V^-} = \frac{(1.08)100 - 60}{180 - 60} = 0.4$$

where V^+ and V^- are the end-of-period up and down values. Note that if there are no options or other asymmetries (nonlinearities), applying this risk-neutral probability measure (p) would give the same present value as traditional DCF valuation:

$$V_0 = \frac{p \times V^+ + (1 - p)\,V^-}{1 + r} = \frac{0.4 \times 180 + 0.6 \times 60}{1.08}$$
$$= \frac{q \times V^+ + (1 - q)\,V^-}{1 + k} = \frac{0.5 \times 180 + 0.5 \times 60}{1.20} = 100,$$

where q is the actual probability (of up demand moves), k is the risk-adjusted opportunity cost of capital, p is the risk-neutral probability, and r is the risk-free rate. Risk-neutral probabilities are explained in chapter 3.

[3]The follow-on commercial project (stage II) requires an outlay of $I^{II} = 80$ in year 1 and has an expected value of $E(V_1) = 120\ (= 0.5 \times 180 + 0.5 \times 60)$. This gives a time-zero second-stage value of $NPV^{II} = 100 - 74 = 26$ (after discounting $E(V_1) = 120$ at the opportunity cost of capital, $k = 20\%$, and the known investment outlay of $I^{II} = 80$ at the risk-free rate, $r = 8\%$. Thus, if the firm were to commit to both stages right now, the total expected net project value would amount to $NPV = NPV^I + NPV^{II} = -30 + 26 = -4\ (< 0)$.

[4]The option value equals $(0.4 \times \text{Max}\,(180 - 80, 0) + 0.6 \times 0)) / 1.08 = 37$, where 0.4 is the risk-neutral probability.

from complementary effects and network externalities between products. For instance, the technological knowledge Microsoft gained with the development of its operating system created an advantaged strategic position for Microsoft to market their major software products such as Word, Excel, and PowerPoint and later also helped in marketing their Internet and e-mail programs. In high-tech industries, firms are often acquired in part or primarily because of the growth option value generated by their capabilities or resources.

Firms may, alternatively, follow a focus strategy, if competitive advantage is based on commitment to and specialization in a single market or product. One focus strategy is product specialization, but the company can also be geographically focused or customer specialized or can pursue a particular niche. When selecting which markets to serve, a firm must consider not only potential cost economics and demand, but also the type and reaction of competition. When demand is not sufficient to accommodate many firms, it may be far more profitable for the firm to position itself as a focused seller in a low-demand segment than to serve several markets with stiff competition.

Although standard real-options theory suggests that it is preferable to leave options open or "wait and see," competitive or strategic elements can change this view. With competition, the value of a project can be potentially increased by moving as quickly as possible through the introduction stages. To continue with our numerical example, suppose that the simple option (mentioned in figure 2.6 and in box insert 2.5) is now available to two competitors. Figure 2.7 illustrates such a competitive game in the normal form (right matrix). Consider the resulting values either at the end of each tree branch or in the payoff table (firm A, firm B) in the following four investment-timing scenarios: (i) when both firms decide to wait, they equally share the value of the deferral option, resulting in an equal payoff of 18.5 for each firm; (ii)/(iii) when one firm (A or B) invests first (while the other waits), it preempts its competitor, appropriating the full NPV of 20 for itself; and (iv) when both firms invest immediately (simultaneously), they share equally the total NPV ($\frac{1}{2} \times 20$), resulting in an equal value payoff of 10 for each firm.

In the matrix shown in the left of figure 2.7, we represent competitive strategies and strategic moves with split (shared) circles. In the presence of competition, we not only need to draw the strategy of the firm but also the strategy of its competitors and examine how they affect each other. Under such conditions, managing an options portfolio is no longer an internal value-optimization problem under uncertainty, but a strategic game against competitors. In the value-payoff structure of figure 2.7, an equilibrium outcome is reached in the lower right box. Firm A's payoff

FIGURE 2.7 A SHARED OPTION IN THE REAL-OPTIONS GROWTH (ROG)
MATRIX

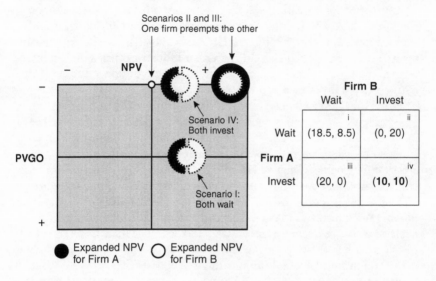

from pursuing an immediate investment commitment strategy (lower row)
exceeds its payoff from a wait-and-see strategy (upper row), regardless of
which strategy firm B chooses (20 > 18.5 in left "wait" column, 10 > 0
in right "invest" column). That is, firm A has a *dominant strategy* to invest, regardless of the decision of its competitor. Firm B here also has a
dominant strategy to invest. These forces result in a Nash equilibrium in
the lower right cell, where both firms receive their second-worst payoff of
10, an example of the well-known *prisoners' dilemma*. The paradox, of
course, is that the equilibrium outcome (10, 10) is worse for both firms
than when both choose to defer (18.5, 18.5). If the two firms could coordinate their investment strategy, they could share the flexibility benefits of
the wait-and-see option, potentially avoiding the inferior "panic equilibrium" in which everybody rushes to invest prematurely.

Under competition, restricting one's freedom to choose may sometimes have important strategic or commitment value. For instance, in
classical war games, by "burning one's bridges" one eliminates the opportunity to retreat and therefore increases the commitment to stay and
fight to the end. Similarly, when a firm has no option to retreat, it may actually be able to prevent competitive entry because potential rivals would
not want to risk a war of attrition. A focus strategy can be seen in this
light. Commitment to a strategy that limits the firm's options can some-

FIGURE 2.8 POLAROID VERSUS KODAK'S SHARED OPTION IN REAL-
OPTIONS GROWTH MATRIX

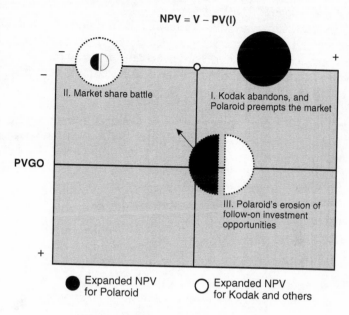

times make the firm better off. Inflexibility is valuable if the firm's commitment can alter the rival's strategy.

Dixit and Nalebuff (1991) refer to the example of Polaroid versus
Kodak. Polaroid focused its resources on the instant photography business, and created a dominant market position in this business. In 1976,
Eastman Kodak announced its entry into the market with a new instant
film camera. Enjoying a monopoly for almost three decades, Polaroid
was committed to deter any potential rival in its market and mounted a
reciprocating response. Figure 2.8 illustrates this strategic example in the
real-options growth matrix. It revisits the competition between two
firms, but in another strategic context. If Kodak enters, both firms end up
in a market share (and legal) battle with a negative payoff. Polaroid
would prefer to continue to develop its instant photo market alone while
Kodak follows or waits (scenario I). Both firms regard concurrent investment in this market as the worst scenario since it will result in intense rivalry
and a bitter market share and legal battle (scenario II). This situation
would result in a payoff in the "invest never" region. A bad scenario for
Polaroid would be to make no further investment and wait while Kodak

invests heavily, eroding Polaroid's follow-on investment opportunities (scenario III). This may involve permanent abandonment of the opportunity (with an expanded NPV of 0).

This example illustrates the idea behind the commitment value of Polaroid's focused portfolio strategy, which supposed its rival would back down to avoid a market share battle. Actually, in 1990 the courts ruled against Kodak for patent infringement, and Kodak was forced to withdraw its instant film camera from the market.

Of course such a bet on a single market was risky. Polaroid regained its dominance over the instant photography market, but the business was subsequently eroded by the development of portable videocassette recorders and one-hour minilabs for conventional film. As the value of its growth options in the instant film camera market seemed to be eroding (III in figure 2.8), Polaroid needed to explore new markets to generate further growth. The company began to broaden its strategy into video and conventional film.

2.5. Conclusions

Although various strategic paradigms take a different view of whether the sources of competitive advantage and value creation are internal or external to the firm, we think that both the resource-based view and the industry and competitive analysis framework can benefit from a closer linkage with quantification tools from corporate finance. Analysis of complex strategic problems may benefit from the insights obtained from all of the paradigms we have discussed, depending on their economic context.

The "competitive forces" approach is appropriate in cases where excess profits derive from limitations on competition, achieved through raising rivals' costs and exclusionary behavior. The sources of competitive advantage and excess profits here lie at the level of the industry and in the firm's strategic behavior. The competitive forces approach views concentrated industries as attractive in that market positions can be shielded behind entry barriers.

Strategic conflict based on game theory makes two important contributions for strategic management. First, it provides a consistent framework for framing complex strategic problems. Second, it is useful in obtaining insights about the structure of interaction between the players, and in understanding the existing possibilities and consequences of rivalry.

The resource-based view has a different orientation. It views excess profits as stemming from specific resources and capabilities within the firm. It thus tends to steer a value-creating strategy toward creating distinctive and difficult-to-imitate advantages. Projects with an add-on strategic value can be found when the firm invests in its own resource position and directly or indirectly makes it more difficult for others to catch up. The firm can use blocking mechanisms to influence the acquisition cost or the user revenues of other firms with a weaker position.

The dynamic capabilities variant is particularly relevant to developing new capabilities in a changing environment. It recognizes that value-augmenting strategic change is difficult and costly, and it generally occurs incrementally. Hence distinctive competences and capabilities generally cannot be acquired, but must be built over time. From this perspective, strategy involves choosing among and committing to long-term paths or trajectories of competence development. The "window of opportunity" to change strategic direction is typically present when the "design" is more fluent, manufacturing routines have not yet been developed, and the firm has not yet committed capital. Path dependencies and technological opportunities mark the road ahead. Developing growth options and developing a strategic position to acquire their benefits are enabled in part because of policies pursued and experiences and efficiencies acquired in earlier periods.

The new synergy focus is directed towards creating value by establishing core businesses with related resources and capabilities and cross-project and cross-time effects (compound option effects) in a changing environment. When there are interproject and intertemporal synergies between projects, careful portfolio planning is paramount. In particular, in volatile and evolving industries, portfolio strategies have to be flexible to enable the firm to adjust to an uncertain and changing competitive and technological landscape. For instance, in the information technology and pharmaceutical industries, acquisitions are undertaken for their potential strategic growth option value that enables the firm to bet on several evolving technologies in the industry.

The new framework for strategic portfolio planning proposed here combines the best features of the BCG growth-share matrix with modern valuation. Analysis of complex portfolio-planning problems may benefit from insights obtained through real-options thinking and competitive considerations, depending on their economic context. In an uncertain environment, a real-options approach may better reveal the flexibility value in a portfolio strategy. Each project or business unit in a strategic investment program can be seen as a necessary link in generating other options, leading to cross-time synergies between projects that extend over the long term.

Opportunities cannot be considered in a vacuum, however, as competitors may negatively affect the value of an option. In a competitive context, game theory becomes important for portfolio planning. Key questions for portfolio planning in this context include: Can the firm use first-mover advantages to preempt opportunities? What is the impact of investment in first-stage R & D on the strategic ability to invest in future follow-on options? Which investments justify cooperation and may increase the total "pie" if the firms cooperate (when it is legal to do so), and when should a firm compete to try to capture a larger piece of the pie for itself? The proper integration of the portfolio-planning framework from strategic management with corporate finance may help in subjecting the strategic planning process and managerial intuition to the more rigorous quantitative analysis of modern finance.

Suggested Readings

Grant, R. M. "The Resource-Based Theory of Competitive Advantage: Implications for Strategy Formulation." *California Management Review* 33 (1991): 114–35.

———. *Contemporary Strategy Analysis.* Oxford: Blackwell Business, 1995.

Luehrman, T. A. "Strategy as a Portfolio of Real Options." *Harvard Business Review* 76 (1998): 89–99.

Porter, M. E. *Competitive Strategy.* London: Macmillan, 1980.

Shapiro, A.C. "The Theory of Business Strategy." *Rand Journal of Economics* 20 (1989): 125–37.

Teece, D. J., G. Pisano, and A. Shuen. "Dynamic Capabilities and Strategic Management." *Strategic Management Journal* 18 (1997): 509–34.

Wernerfelt, B. "A Resource-Based View of the Firm." *Strategic Management Journal* 5 (1984): 171–80.

Chapter 3

Corporate Real Options

Necessity never made a good bargain.
— Benjamin Franklin (1706–1790)

3.1. Introduction

How important is intuition or flexibility in making optional decisions?
Box 3.1 provides interesting thoughts on decision-making by important
people. Options thinking has had a profound influence on economic
thought and business practice. Options have become a fundamental part
in global capital markets in recent years, though they have been in use
for centuries. Options contracts were already written by Romans and
Phoenicians on cargo transported by ships. In Holland, there was an active derivatives market in the seventeenth century in tulip bulbs.

However, it was not until the early 1970s, when Nobel laureates
Robert Merton and Myron Scholes conducted their seminal work in pricing options, that options developed into liquid traded contracts in financial markets. In their 1973 article, *The Pricing of Options and Corporate
Liabilities,* Myron Scholes and the late Fischer Black put forth the now
famous Black-Scholes model. This laid the foundation for options and
derivatives pricing, expanding the scope of options by considering equity
as an "option on the firm." The value of the firm itself depends on its options to develop "real" assets, for which Stewart Myers (1977) coined the
term *real options.*

Real options refers to choices on whether and how to proceed with
business investments. Real-options analysis helps management decide on
investments that might be delayed, expanded, abandoned, or repositioned.
A venture capitalist deciding to finance the next stage in a start-up, a retail chain that has to decide how and where to expand, or a multinational
company deciding whether to abandon an unprofitable division or to
shift operations to a plant in another country, all involve real-options decisions under uncertainty. Real-options theory, developed to cope with an
uncertain future, offers new insights into corporate finance and strategy.
Indeed, real options theory is already having a substantial influence on
corporate practice and market performance (see box insert 3.2).

This chapter provides an overview of common recurring corporate real options and reviews the basic principles of quantifying their value to capture important strategic dimensions that are at the core of strategic planning and investing under uncertainty. The chapter is organized as follows. Section 3.2 discusses the nature of options and the valuation principles underlying option pricing. Section 3.3 describes various common corporate real options and reviews related literature. In section 3.4, two extended pedagogical numerical examples illustrate the basic valuation principle applied in R & D and mining programs. Section 3.5 presents an in-depth case application of an oil field concession, and discusses the advantages and limitations of applying real-options valuation in practice. Section 3.6 provides a summary.

3.2. Options Valuation

In the current highly volatile and competitive business environment, the horizon over which cash flows can be estimated confidently is shrinking, making it essential for firms to be more flexible in their investment programs. The future is uncertain, and as the dynamic investment path unfolds, the firm's management can learn, adapt, and revise future investment decisions in response to unexpected market developments. An evaluation of projects in a dynamic environment is often more complex than standard (DCF) analysis may suggest, which implicitly assumes a static view of investment decisions and projected cash flow scenarios.[1] A real-options framework adds a dynamic perspective to the traditional valuation approach by incorporating the value of flexibility and growth opportunities in an uncertain environment.[2]

Increasingly, option valuation is being used as a tool to value corporate real options. Treating business opportunities as a collection of cor-

---

[1]The standard NPV methodology has obvious shortcomings in analyzing investment opportunities whose value derives from future growth options. NPV implicitly assumes such investment decisions are a now-or-never proposition; it does not take into account the value of a wait-and-see approach, which allows one to alter planned investment decisions as uncertainty is resolved over time.

[2]A number of papers have addressed the importance of managerial flexibility. Baldwin (1982) examines sequential investment strategies and interdependencies with future investment opportunities. She observes that if firms with market power wish to compensate for the loss in the value of future opportunities that result from undertaking a project now, they must require a positive premium over NPV. Myers (1987) suggests considering strategic investment opportunities as growth options, while Kester (1984) discusses qualitatively strategic and competitive aspects of growth opportunities. Dixit and Pindyck (1994), Trigeorgis (1988, 1995, 1996a), Kemna (1988), Sick (1989), Smit (1996), and others discuss many corporate options and provide various expositions of the real-options approach to investment.

BOX 3.1 THOUGHTS ON DECISION-MAKING BY IMPORTANT PEOPLE

Stripped down to its essentials, business is about one thing: making decisions. We're always deciding something — from the small and the daily (which emails to answer, what meetings to have) to the macro and the strategic (what product to launch and when) to the intensely personal (what job to take, whom to hire, whom to marry). But what does it take to make a "good" decision? Is it about going by facts and percentages — or about following your gut instinct? Does time produce better decisions, or does pressure make you decide not only faster but also more wisely? And finally, is better decision making something that you can learn? We asked 11 decisive leaders, inside and outside of business, to answer these and other related questions. Does their advice help? You decide.

To make good decisions, you need confidence in your judgment.
Ed Koch, Mayor of
New York City, 1978–89

I make bad decisions all the time. But I've been successful because I've developed a process for identifying and changing those decisions quickly. I approach every decision with an eye to the long-term outcome.
Pamela Lopker, Chairman and
President, QAD Inc., CA

For those big decisions — Should I marry this person? Should I follow that career? Should I sell my company? When should we go public? — let patterns develop in your mind. Let clues and evidence emerge from your environment. This approach to decision making requires time, patience, and another key ingredient: courage. It takes courage to listen to your inner wisdom. But once you hear that wisdom, making a decision becomes fairly easy.
W. Brian Arthur, Professor,
Santa Fe Institute, New Mexico

I've learned a lot about decision making by watching how a machine plays chess. In 1996, Deep Blue played Gary Kasparov, the world chess champion. Deep Blue won the first game but lost the match. A human uses a combination of knowledge, strategy, and intuition to make chess decisions. A machine relies on brute computational power and on an ability to examine a tremendous amount of data. On average, the human mind can manage three or four positions per second. Deep Blue can evaluate 200 million alternatives per second. So the machine has a huge advantage. But Deep Blue also had weaknesses, and they centered on its inability to be flexible.

continued . . .

Box 3.1 continued

An interesting thing happened when Deep Blue met Kasparov for the rematch. While we had refined Deep Blue so that it could make decisions and play more like a human, Kasparov had refined his strategy so that he could play better against standard computer-chess programs. In game six, Deep Blue surprised Kasparov by sacrificing a knight to gain strategic advantage. Kasparov, who hadn't planned for such a decision, realized how inflexible his own strategy had become.

> *Chung-Jen Tan,* Senior Manager,
> Applications Systems,
> IBM's Thomas J. Watson
> Research Center, New York;
> Tan manages IBM's Deep Blue
> computer-chess project

Intuition offers a way to integrate and synthesize, to weigh and balance information. If I have to make a big decision, I listen to what others think. But ultimately, I listen to my intuition. I postpone a decision until I wake up one morning and know where my gut is going.

> *Deborah Triant,* CEO and
> President, Check Point Software
> Technologies Inc., CA

Nothing can paralyze a decision-making process more than uncertainty can. The big decisions that have failed at Shell didn't fail because of our operations or because of project management; they failed because we misunderstood the external world. That's why, when we're on the verge of a big decision, we do scenario planning.

> *Roger Rainbow,* VP, Global
> Business Environment, Shell
> International Ltd., London

The crux of making good decisions isn't doing things right — it's making sure that you focus on the right things.

> *Chris Newell,* Executive Director,
> the Lotus Institute,
> Lotus Development Corp., MA

By transforming the art of decision making into a science, you can save time, money, and frustration.

> *Buz Mertes,* VP, Loss Management
> and Policy Servicing, GE Capital
> Mortgage Insurance Corp.,
> North Carolina

continued ...

Box 3.1 continued

Once you make a decision, you'd better be able to communicate it.
Jerry Seeman, Senior Director of
Officiating, National Football
League, New York

When making a decision, don't listen to your intuition. Intuition will lead you astray; it's drastically overrated. The desire to follow intuition reflects the mythology of people who don't want to think rationally and systematically. They tell stories about how their intuition guided them through a decision, but they don't understand how or why. Often, when you hear about intuition, what you're really hearing is a justification of luck. Intuition might be fine for the small decisions in life — like what kind of ice cream to buy. But when you get to the biggies, you need a more systematic thought process.

You go through a systematic process of identifying all of the factors and weighing them for each alternative. You do a little arithmetic, and your analysis says to pick A over B. But your intuition says to pick B over A. So what do you do?

Most people will go on their intuition — which raises the question, Why did you do all that work in the first place? One of these two options is wrong. So postpone your decision until you can determine why your intuition is out of sync with the systematic analysis. That's the purpose of systematic analysis: to inform your intuition, to make you consider all of the options, and to help you make a wise decision.
Max Bazerman, Professor,
Kellogg School of Management,
Northwestern University

One of the biggest pitfalls in decision making is not creating enough alternatives. You can make a decision in order to solve a problem — or you can make a decision in order to exploit an opportunity.
Howard Raiffa,
Professor Emeritus, Harvard
Business School

Source: Excerpts from Muoio 1998.

porate real options has enriched modern corporate resource allocation and planning during the last two decades. The techniques derived from option pricing can be used to help quantify management's ability to adapt its future plans to capitalize on favorable investment opportunities or to respond effectively to undesirable developments in a dynamic environment by cutting losses. Before cataloguing the different types of real options, we first discuss the basic nature and valuation principles of options.

Box 3.2 Optional Investing and Market Performance

Orthodox investment theory suggests that firms should invest in a project as soon as its NPV is positive. Insights from option-pricing theory suggest something quite different: that it will often make sense for firms to invest in a project only when its NPV is very large. In fact, that is what usually happens in practice. Most bosses do their basic NPV sums, but add in a margin to help them feel comfortable.

However, the new "real options" theory allows bosses to set them on a more rational basis than gut instinct. The theory also explains why firms often respond slowly to changes in tax, interest rates or demand — all of which, orthodox theory suggests, should elicit an instant response.

The theory will be most useful in areas where the uncertainties are relatively apparent. The sums are already being churned over in the computers of some oil firms, for instance. There is one main risk in developing an oil field — a change in the oil price. Property developers, electric utilities and drug companies are also investigating how to apply the theory in practice.

The theory is likely to prove a big advance on the old NPV method. Though its aim is to improve company decision-making by showing how bosses can learn from financial markets, it can also help people in financial markets to understand firms better. Projects that a firm has not yet invested in may be at least as valuable to it as the ones that are going ahead — especially in a volatile market. Might bosses boost their firms' share price by telling analysts about all the lucrative things they are not doing?

Source: The Economist Newspaper limited, London, January 8, 1994.

3.2.1. Basic Nature of Options

An option gives its holder the right, but not the obligation, to buy a specific asset. Options represent rights; consequently, the payoff to an option can never be less than zero, regardless of the underlying asset price. As a result, the value of an option can never be negative. Options come in two basic types: calls and puts. A call option gives its owner the right to buy an asset at a prespecified price (exercise price) in a specified period. The writer or seller of the option has an obligation to deliver the asset if the option is exercised, and receives in return the exercise price. This is a zero-sum game, since the gain to one party is a loss to the other side.

For example, consider a call option to buy one share of Philips at $40 on or before March 15, 2004. Suppose that the owner will hold the option until maturity. The decision to exercise it or not depends on whether

Philips' share price would exceed $40 at maturity. This will depend on the resolution of uncertainty about Philips' stock price in the meantime. If Philips' stock trades at $55 at maturity, the call option will be in-the-money and will be exercised. Excluding the premium that is paid up front, the payoff from exercising the call option at maturity will be $15. On the other hand, if the stock price at maturity ends up at $20, the option will be out-of-the-money and worthless.

A put option, by contrast, gives the right to sell an asset in exchange for receiving a specified exercise price on a prespecified date. When the holder of a put option exercises, he or she sells the underlying asset to the writer for the exercise price. Options can be either European or American. A European option can be exercised only at the maturity date. An American option can also be exercised at any date before the maturity date. Many options traded in financial markets are of the American type (except for options on an index), whereas nontraded or over-the-counter options are often European.

The holder of an option is typically not entitled to receive any dividends that the underlying asset pays over the life of the option. To receive the dividends, the call option holder must exercise the option. A trade-off is involved, since exercising a call option early involves costs: the option is lost and the time value of money from delaying paying the exercise price is lost. For this reason it is never optimal to exercise early an American call option on a non-dividend-paying asset. In such a case, the value of an American call will equal the value of a European call.

The holder of a put option receives the exercise price when the option is exercised and the time value of money provides a reason to exercise the put option early. A counteracting force is that the option is lost. Here, there is no dominance of either one of the two effects, so the decision to exercise early must be evaluated in each specific case. While dividends provide an incentive to exercise calls early, dividends are an additional reason not to exercise puts early. Exercising a put early means that you forgo dividends, since you sell the underlying asset.

Real options are in some ways analogous to financial options. Consider the example of an oil field concession. Similar to an American call option, the concession gives the oil company the right to develop the field during a specific period, with an exercise price equal to the investment outlay needed to install the oil production facilities. The value of this timing flexibility depends on the prices of (futures contracts in) oil. Also, similar to dividends, the company misses an operational cash flow that would have been received if the option to develop the oil field was exercised early. Option pricing can support management to determine the value of acquiring the oil field concession and provides guidelines if and when to exercise the option to develop.

3.2.2. FROM FINANCIAL TO REAL-OPTIONS VALUATION

In 1973 Fischer Black and Myron Scholes published their option-pricing model, introducing a valuation principle that laid the foundation for option theory and introduced the idea that corporate securities can be viewed as options on the firm's value. Black and Scholes demonstrated that a financial call option is similar to (a dynamic strategy in) a levered position in the underlying share. However, the share of a firm with a leveraged capital structure is itself an option. The equity of a leveraged firm is a call option on the firm's overall asset value with an exercise price equal to the promised payment on the debt, having expiration at the maturity of the debt. The idea that the value of a leveraged firm can be viewed as a set of nested options is illustrated in figure 3.1. Consider the position of the shareholders of a leveraged firm that pays no dividends on equity, E, and has issued a single zero-coupon debt, D.[3] On the debt maturity, if the value of the firm exceeds the promised principal, $V \geq B$, the shareholders will repay the debt in full ($D = B$). However, if the value of the firm turns out to be lower than the debt principal ($V < B$), the shareholders are only liable for the funds invested in the firm and would exercise their option to default. The shareholders' claim cannot be worth less than zero. Because of this limited liability, the firm's assets would be surrendered to the bondholders ($D = V$), and the equity value would be bounded below by zero.[4]

Application of option theory actually just starts here. The value of the firm itself can be seen as a package of embedded corporate real options. Most firms have real options to later expand production, abandon a project for its salvage value, reposition its assets, and so on. Option pricing can help value these options. To understand the valuation of such options presupposes an understanding of the basics of valuation in corporate finance. Corporate finance theory posits that firms create value by investing in those projects for which the market (present) value of expected cash inflows, V, exceeds the required investment outlays, I. The process of real asset valuation attempts to determine what a project would be worth *if it were traded* in the financial markets.

An estimation of the market value of an option can in principle be obtained by creating a project equivalent in the market.[5] This equivalent dy-

[3]Mason and Merton (1985) provide a discussion of many operating and financing options, and integrate them in a project-financing application of a hypothetical, large-scale energy project.
[4]Brealey and Myers (2003) distinguish various agency games that management and shareholders may play at the expense of the bondholders. The value of equity with the option to default depends on the firm's value ($+$), the debt principal ($-$), debt maturity ($+$), business risk ($+$), and interest rates ($+$). Shareholders may be tempted to play political games to influence these parameters at the expense of the bondholders.
[5]Financial option pricing models are typically based on arbitrage arguments in financial markets. The arbitrage relation is based on the construction of a hedge by taking positions

FIGURE 3.1 CORPORATE SECURITIES AS OPTIONS ON THE FIRM'S VALUE

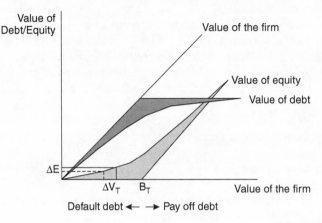

| | | Payoff at Maturity | |
		$0 \leq V \leq B$	$V \geq B$
Shareholder Position	Call Option	0	$(V - B)$
Bondholder Position	Risk-Free Bond +	B	B
	Put Option	$-(B - V)$	0
Value of the Firm		V	V

The shareholder's wealth, E, at maturity is $E = \text{Max [fulfill debt } (V - B)$, default $(0)]$. The value of risky debt, D, is equivalent to the price of a risk-free bond with the same terms, minus the price of a put option, P, written on the value of the firm. At maturity, the bondholders would receive the promised principal, B, or, in case of bankruptcy, the remaining value of the firm (if $V < B$). $D = \text{Min [value of the firm } (V)$, promised principal $(B)]$.

namic portfolio strategy, consisting of a position in the underlying asset partly financed with a risk-free loan, can be constructed such that in every future state over the next period it has the same payoff as the option, so it should have the same current value as the option. Valuation of some types of real options, particularly found in natural resources, may closely resemble the no-arbitrage valuation of financial options. The replication argument can be justified if a financial instrument is traded with similar risk characteristics as the project. This is the case, for example, if the underlying state variable is the price of a commodity, as in

in the underlying asset and the risk-free asset. Black and Scholes (1973) demonstrated that hedging a financial option requires a dynamic strategy with adjustments made over time, depending on changes in the market price of the underlying asset. European options can be hedged almost perfectly, which allows pricing them with good accuracy, assuming a good estimation of volatility.

Brennan and Schwartz's valuation of a mine (1985a, 1985b) or Paddock, Siegel, and Smith's (1988) oil-leasing valuation. In section 3.4 we illustrate this replication argument in the valuation of a gold mine license and in the valuation of an oil-gas field. The value of the license is estimated by using a financial instrument (futures on gold or oil prices, respectively) whose probabilistic behavior is close to that of the developed project.

In other settings, option valuation by replication may be a bit stretched. For instance, valuation of an investment opportunity to build a facility to produce nanotubes is less directly analogous to financial option pricing. If a similar plant is not traded on financial markets, option valuation cannot take advantage of a traded asset or dynamic replication strategy that drives the value of flexibility. This would present a fundamental problem in applying the arbitrage argument for financial options, but for real-options valuation it does not. Real options — in contrast to financial derivatives — are not traded in arbitrage-free financial markets, but present themselves in imperfect real markets. An estimation of the real asset's value *as if the asset were traded* is sufficient for the valuation objective of corporate finance, namely to enhance the market value for the firm. Real-options valuation is still applicable provided we can find a reliable estimate for the market value of the asset. We can oftentimes use the discounted cash flow (DCF) approach to estimate the underlying project value (the gross present value of operating cash flows) as if the project were traded. Real-options valuation can then help us determine the value of the option *relative* to the estimated value of the underlying (developed) project. Both the DCF and the option valuation rest on the assumption of market completeness, i.e., that existing traded securities are sufficient for dynamic spanning of the underlying asset. That is, the firm's decisions should not significantly expand the investor's opportunity set in a way that acceptance of the project would change its value.[6] Later box insert 3.3 illustrates the use of both replication and risk-neutral valuation principles in the case of the real option to invest by a high-tech firm holding a one-year license.[7] The appendix at the end of this chapter discusses these ideas in more detail, and shows that the binomial approach in many steps converges to the Black-Scholes model. Sections 3.4.2 and 3.5 illustrate the use of the certainty-equivalent valuation principle and replication arguments in the case of a mine concession (a pedagogical example) and an oil field concession (a real-life application).

---

[6]From a practical perspective, it does not seem likely that the typical projects would significantly change required returns in financial markets.
[7]This is essentially the same example used in box insert 2.5 in Chapter 2, but in more detail.

Box 3.3 Numerical Valuations Example: A License by a High-Tech Firm

Consider the capital investment opportunity described in figure 3.2. A high-tech company has a proprietary opportunity (a license or patent) to build plant capacity for producing a new product that involves making an expenditure of $I_0 = \$80$ million (in present value terms). Suppose that the (gross) value of expected future cash inflows from production, V, may fluctuate in line with the random fluctuation in demand, say to $V^+ = \$180$ or $V^- = 60$ million (with equal probability, $q = 0.5$) by the end of the period (e.g., due to uncertainty over the product standard). Consequently, the project is expected to generate a $t = 1$ value of $E(V_1) = 0.5 \times 180 + 0.5 \times 60 = \$120$ million; discounted at the opportunity cost of capital, assumed to be $k = 20\%$ (for the last stage of production), this results in a (gross) project present value of $V_0 = 100$ million. The firm would thus be willing to make an *immediate* investment outlay of $I_0 = \$80$ million in return for the higher present value of expected cash inflows, $V_0 = \$100$ million. In the absence of managerial flexibility, the traditional (static or passive) net present value, $NPV = V_0 - I_0 = 100 - 80 = \$20$ million (> 0), would justifiably recommend project acceptance.

What is really of interest in a world of uncertainty, however, is not the value of the *immediate* investment per se, but rather the value of the *opportunity* to invest (i.e., the option to wait to invest for one period). The NPV does not properly capture the dynamics and active management of investment under uncertainty, except indirectly (and inadequately) through the adjustment of discount factors. From the perspective of NPV, high (market) risk calls for a high required return by the capital markets and a low market value for the project considered for immediate investment. Real options introduce a new insight with respect to the effect of uncertainty on investment opportunity value that runs counter to this traditional thinking about the role of risk. High (total) risk can have a positive influence on the value of real options.

Figure 3.3 shows that the *opportunity* to invest provided by the proprietary license or patent is more valuable than an *immediate* investment *commitment* since it allows management the *flexibility to defer* investment for a year and invest *only if* developments (e.g., demand or prices) are favorable (worth $V^+ - I = 180 - 80 = 100$ million at the license's expiration at $t = 1$), or to back out with limited loss (0) under unfavorable developments. The *opportunity to invest* provided by the license is thus analogous to a *call option* on the value of the developed (completed) project (V), with an "exercise price" equal to the required outlay, $I = 80$ million. The basic idea enabling determination of the current value of a call option is that one can

continued . . .

Box 3.3 continued

form a portfolio consisting of buying a particular number, N, of shares of the underlying asset, V, or a correlated traded security, S (e.g., stock of an unlevered company exclusively operating in the same business as the completed project, say, with current price of $20 expected to move up to $36 or down to $12 next period); and borrowing an appropriate amount, $B, at the riskless rate, such that it would exactly replicate the future returns of the option in any state of nature over next period. Since the option and this equivalent portfolio (effectively, an appropriately levered position in the asset) would provide the same future returns, they must sell for the same current value. Thus, we can value the option by determining the cost of constructing its equivalent replicating portfolio. From appendix 3.1,

$$N = (C^+ - C^-)/(S^+ - S^-)$$
$$= (100 - 0)/(36 - 12) = 4.167 \text{ million shares (in the similar security);}$$

and

$$B = (NS^- - C^-)/(1 + r)$$
$$= (4.167 \times 12 - 0)/1.08 = \$46.3 \text{ million (in the risk-free asset).}$$

That is, we can replicate the return to the call option by purchasing N (= 4.167 million) shares in a twin financial security having the same risk characteristics as the underlying asset at the current price, S (= $20), and borrowing the amount $B (= $46.3 million) at the riskless rate, r. The cost of this portfolio, and hence the value of the option, must then be: $C = NS - B = (4.167)20 - 46.3 = \$37$ million.

Note from $C - NS = -B$ that having the option and selling N shares of the twin security provides a constant amount ($B) or riskless hedge over the next period regardless of whether the asset value moves up or down, which "squeezes" risk out of the problem (that constant amount should then be discounted back at the risk-free rate, regardless of the investor's risk attitude). The option is valued *relative* to the underlying asset as if risk did not matter or the world were risk-neutral. This motivates use of a shorter alternative route compared to the portfolio replication approach described, that of risk-neutral valuation. To value the investment opportunity in this way we need to determine risk-neutral or certainty-equivalent probabilities, which then allow discounting at the riskless rate, r. The risk-neutral probabilities are the probabilities that would prevail in a risk-neutral world (where any asset is expected to yield the risk-free rate of return), obtained from

$$p = \frac{(1 + r)V - V^-}{V^+ - V^-} = \frac{(1.08)100 - 60}{180 - 60} = 0.4,$$

continued . . .

Box 3.3 continued

where V^+ and V^- are the end-of-period values in the up $(+)$ and down $(-)$ states. If there are no options or other asymmetries (non-linearities), applying this risk-neutral probability (p) would give the same present value as traditional DCF valuation:

$$V_0 = \frac{p \times V^+ + (1-p)V^-}{1+r} = \frac{0.4 \times 180 + 0.6 \times 60}{1.08}$$
$$= \frac{q \times V^+ + (1-q)V^-}{1+k} = \frac{0.5 \times 180 + 0.5 \times 60}{1.20} = \$100 \text{ million}$$

where q is the actual probability (of up demand moves), k is the risk-adjusted opportunity cost of capital, p is the risk-neutral probability and r is the risk-free rate. When there are options present, the risk profile changes, e.g., we can limit downside losses. The risk-neutral or certainty-equivalent valuation captures the changes in the risk profile in an appropriate manner.

The value of the above investment opportunity (expanded NPV or NPV^*), seen as a call option, can thus be obtained from the end-of-period expected values with expectations taken over the risk-neutral or certainty-equivalent probabilities (here $p = 0.4$ and $1 - p = 0.6$), discounted at the risk-free rate (here $r = 0.08$):

NPV^* or $C = [0.4 \times 100 + 0.6 \times 0] / 1.08 = \$37$ million

This confirms the answer obtained by portfolio replication above. Note that if one naively used traditional NPV or decision tree analysis, determining the expected value using the actual probabilities and discounting back at the cost of capital ($k = 20\%$), the current value of the investment opportunity (including the value of the option to wait) would be

$[0.5 \times 100 + 0.5 \times 0] / 1.20 = \$41.67$ million.

This is different from the value estimated from options pricing. It overestimates the value of the option because it uses the constant 20% discount rate required of securities comparable in risk to the *naked* (passive/inflexible) project or its twin security, although the presence of flexibility has dramatically altered the structure of the flexible project's payoffs. To see why $41.67 million given by the traditional approach is not correct, simply refer back to the portfolio replication argument. Would anyone be willing to pay $41.67 million for the license? The answer is no because any prospective buyer could instead purchase $N = 4.167$ million shares of the "twin security" at its current price of $20 per share for a total cost of $83.33 million, while

continued . . .

Box 3.3 *continued*

financing the remaining part of that purchase by borrowing $B =$ \$46.3 million at the riskless rate. Next year the investment will be worth \$100 million or 0:

$$NS^+ - (1 + r)B = 4.167 \times 36 - 1.08 \times 46.3 = 100,$$
$$NS^- - (1 + r)B = 4.167 \times 12 - 1.08 \times 46.3 = 0.$$

Thus, one would be able to exactly replicate the payoff of the investment in any state of the world for an out-of-pocket expense of \$37 million. Clearly, one would not pay \$41.67 million for an opportunity that can be replicated for \$37 million. Therefore, the value of this investment opportunity must be \$37 million, as given by the options approach. The error in the traditional approach arises from the use of a single (or constant) risk-adjusted discount rate. Asymmetric claims on an asset do not have the same riskiness (and hence expected rate of return) as the underlying asset itself. Real options corrects for this error by transforming the probabilities.

3.3. Overview of Common Real Options

Real-options valuation provides a helpful tool for making strategic investment decisions. First, it enhances net present value (NPV) to capture managerial decision flexibilities. Second, it enables taking a complex uncertain managerial situation and reducing it to a simpler analytical structure made up of basic types of real options.

Table 3.1 provides an overview of the basic types of real options analyzed in the literature.[8] It includes the option to defer investment in new uncertain markets, keeping open the possibility of abandoning the project by defaulting on planned staged outlays. Other types of options include the option to expand or contract capacity, the option to abandon either whole businesses or production facilities for salvage value, the option

[8]Applications of real-options concepts can be found in various areas. As noted by Trigeorgis (1993b), early applications are found in natural resource investments, such as mining (e.g., Brennan and Schwartz 1985a, 1985b), offshore petroleum leases (e.g., Paddock, Siegel, and Smith 1988; Kemna 1993), forestry development and minerals (e.g., Morck, Schwartz, and Stangeland 1989; Trigeorgis 1990a), due to available commodity market prices. Real-options applications have also been seen in land development (e.g., Titman 1985; Quigg 1993, 1995; Capozza and Sick 1992; Williams 1993; Grenadier 1996), flexible manufacturing (e.g., Kulatilaka 1988, 1993), government subsidies and regulation (e.g., Mason and Baldwin 1988; Teisberg 1993), research and development (e.g., Nichols 1994), venture capital (e.g., Sahlman 1988), strategic acquisitions (e.g., Smith and Triantis 1994), environmental policy (e.g., Hendricks 1991; Cortazar, Schwartz, and Salinas 1994; Edleson and Reinhardt 1995), and many other fields.

FIGURE 3.2 STATIC NPV (NO SURPRISE OR FLEXIBILITY TO DEVIATE FROM EXPECTED SCENARIO): INVEST NOW

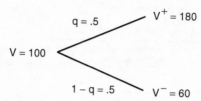

Investment: $I = 80$
Discount rate: $k = .20$
Risk-free rate: $r = .08$
Actual probability: $q = .5$

$$p = \frac{(1 + r)V^+ - V^-}{V^+ - V^-} = 0.4$$

(Gross) Project value:

$$V_0 = \frac{p \times V^+ + (1 - p)V^-}{1 + r} = \frac{0.4 \times 180 + 0.6 \times 60}{1.08}$$

$$= \frac{q \times V^+ + (1 - q)V^-}{1 + k} = \frac{0.5 \times 180 + 0.5 \times 60}{1.20} = 100$$

Invest now (commitment value): NPV = V − I = 100 − 80 = 20 (> 0)

FIGURE 3.3 PROPRIETARY OPPORTUNITY (LICENSE): WAIT TO INVEST UNDER UNCERTAINTY

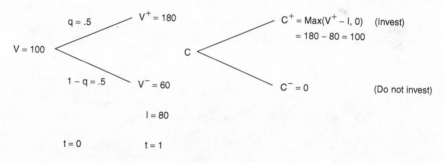

Opportunity to invest provided by license (call option):

$$C = \frac{p \times C^+ + (1 - p) \times C^-}{1 + r} = \frac{.4 \times 100 + .6 \times 0}{1.08} = 37$$

TABLE 3.1
Common Corporate Real Options

Category	Description
Operational flexibility	
Option to defer (simple option)	Management holds a lease on (or the option to buy) valuable land or natural resources. It can wait to see if output prices justify constructing a building or plant, or developing a field.
Growth option (compound option)	An early investment (e.g., R & D, lease on undeveloped land or oil reserve or strategic acquisition) or a strategic investment is a prerequisite or a link in a chain of interrelated projects, opening up future growth opportunities (e.g., a new generation product or process, oil reserves, access to a new market, stengthening of core capabilities, strategic positioning investments).
Option to abandon	If market conditions decline severely, management can abandon current operations permanently and realize on secondary markets the resale value of capital equipment and other assets.
Options to expand, contract, or extend the life of a facility	If market demand turns out to be more favorable than expected, management may increase capacity or accelerate resource utilization. Management may also extend production if the life of the product is longer than expected. Conversely, management may reduce the scale of operations.
Option to temporarily shut down the production process	If operations are less favorable than expected, management may temporarily halt and then start up again.
Option to switch (e.g., raw materials, final products)	If prices or demand changes, management may change the product mix of the facility ("product flexibility"). Alternatively, the same outputs can be produced by different production processes or inputs ("process flexibility").
Financial flexibility	
Option to default	If profits are less favorable than expected and the value of the firm declines below the promised bond repayments, the firm can go bankrupt. With this option to default, the liability of equity holders is limited to the equity invested in the firm.
Staged financing	If the firm's performance is less favorable than expected, the venture capitalist has the option to exit early.

Source: Trigeorgis 1996a.

Typical Industries	Relevant Research
All natural resource extraction industries, real estate development, farming, paper products	Tourinho 1979 Titman 1985 McDonald and Siegel 1986 Paddock, Siegel and Smith 1988 Ingersoll and Ross 1992
All industries that involve sequential investment processes (e.g., pharmaceuticals, electronics, oil, chemicals etc.)	Myers 1977 Kester 1984, 1993 Trigeorgis 1988 Pindyck 1988 Chung and Charoenwong 1991 Smit 1996
Capital-intensive industries with tangible assets, such as airlines and railroads, financial services, and new product introductions in uncertain markets	Myers and Majd 1990 Kemna 1988
Facilities planning and construction in cyclical industries; fashion apparel; commercial real estate	McDonald and Siegel 1985 Trigeorgis and Mason 1987 Pindyck 1988 Kemna 1988
Natural resource industries such as mine operations	Brennan and Schwartz 1985a, 1985b

Product switches
   Any goods sought in small batches or subject to volatile demand, e.g., consumer electronics, toys, specialty paper, machine parts, automobiles
Input switches
   All feedstock-dependent facilities, e.g., oil, electric power (oil/gas), crop switching, sourcing.
	Margrabe 1978
	Kensinger 1987
	Kulatilaka 1988, 1995a
	Aggarwal 1991
	Kamrad and Ernst 1995
	Kogut and Kulatilaka 1994

All levered firms	Black and Scholes 1973 Mason and Merton 1985
Start-up ventures. Small firms operating in uncertain growing or emerging markets, requiring sequential investments.	Trigeorgis 1993b Sahlman 1988 Willner 1995

to switch inputs or outputs, and the option to temporarily shut down (not operate during a given period). We extend the analysis to staged (compound) growth options, such as in R & D or with a pilot project.

A brief description of each option follows.[9] We follow a discrete-time exposition due to its relative simplicity, transparency, and usefulness in practical decision making. The binomial option valuation approach developed by Cox, Ross, and Rubinstein (1979) is a useful vehicle in this regard.[10]

3.3.1. THE (SIMPLE) OPTION TO DEFER

In the case of simple proprietary options, when the commercial prospects are uncertain, firms may have an incentive to wait to invest until the market develops sufficiently, rather than investing immediately and killing their option to "wait and see" (e.g., McDonald and Siegel 1986; Dixit and Pindyck 1994). The option to defer is particularly important when making an irreversible investment decision under uncertainty.[11] If management cannot disinvest and recover the initial expenditures if events turn out worse than expected, the investment timing decision should be taken with caution and the project should be deferred until it earns a sufficient premium over NPV. In such a case a deferrable investment opportunity can be viewed as a call option that has as underlying asset the present value of expected cash inflows from the completed and operating project, V_t, with exercise price the necessary investment outlays, I. Figure 3.4 illustrates this analogy. The curve in figure 3.4 represents the current market value of the option to defer. At maturity (i.e., when no further delay is possible), the value of this option would equal its NPV when positive, or zero if management abandons the project:

$$\text{Expanded NPV} = \text{Max}[\text{net present value } (V_t - I), \text{abandon } (0)]. \quad (3.1)$$

We might ask whether it is always desirable to delay investment under uncertainty. Besides the advantage of a wait-and-see strategy, project deferral can involve some disadvantages in certain situations. For example, if a project has a specified life (e.g., due to patent expiration), the firm would forgo early operating cash inflows when the plant is not in operation (Trigeorgis 1990b, 1991a). We can treat this effect as analogous to

[9]We here focus on valuing only equity-financed projects. It should be noted that valuation of a leveraged firm requires recognition of the nested options in its capital structure.

[10]However, it is important to notice that option-pricing theory extends this method to derive pricing formulas when the uncertainty in the stock price is more complex than in the examples presented here.

[11]McDonald and Siegel (1986) examine the optimal timing of initiating a project, noting that deferment of an irreversible investment decision creates valuable flexibility. Pindyck (1988) analyzes the option to invest in irreversible capacity under product price uncertainty, while Dixit (1989) considered the timing of a firm's entry and exit decisions.

FIGURE 3.4 THE (SIMPLE) OPTION TO DEFER

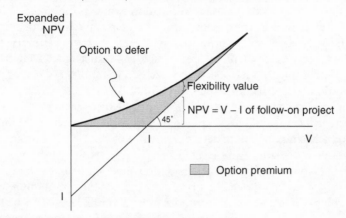

Project	Variable	Call Option
Present value of expected cash flows	V	Stock price
Present value of investment outlays	I	Exercise price
Length of deferral time	T	Time to maturity
Time value of money	r	Risk-free rate
Volatility of project's returns	σ^2	Variance of stock returns

dividends. In other circumstances, strategic considerations make it imperative for a firm to invest early on, giving up the "option premium" of postponement in order to preempt investment by competitors or otherwise influence the equilibrium outcome.[12]

Box insert 3.3 provides a numerical example of the option to defer embedded in the license of a high-tech firm. The information underlying the NPV and options analysis is summarized in figures 3.2 and 3.3, respectively. From this example, at maturity: if demand is high $(+)$: $C^+ = \text{Max}[V - I, 0] = 180 - 80 = 100$, or if demand is low $(-)$: $C^- = \text{Max}[60 - 80, 0] = 0$, so NPV^* or $C = [0.4 \times 100 + 0.6 \times 0] / 1.08 = 37$ million. Clearly, the value of the proprietary *opportunity* to invest provided by the license exceeds the passive NPV of an immediate investment commitment $(37 > 20)$. Since an early investment commitment would sacrifice the value of the option to wait, this lost option value would be an additional

[12]Trigeorgis (1991a) uses quantitative option-pricing techniques to examine early investment that may preempt competitive entry and determines the value of deferring an investment under random competitive entry. Ang and Dukas (1991) incorporate incomplete information. Kulatilaka and Perotti (1998) examine how an early investment decision that results in a cost advantage can influence the production decisions of a firm's competitors and the product's market price. Smit and Ankum (1993) combine the real-options approach of investment timing with basic principles of game theory and industrial organization. Williams (1993) and Grenadier (1996) model real estate development strategies.

investment opportunity cost, justifying investment only if the value of cash inflows, V, actually exceeds the required outlay, I, by a positive premium.

The above analysis is appropriate for *proprietary* investment opportunities. Many investment opportunities with high barriers of entry for competitors, such as a patent for developing a product having no close substitutes, or a unique know-how of a technological process or market conditions that competitors are unable to duplicate for at least some time, are examples of such proprietary real options. The (proprietary) option to wait is particularly valuable in resource extraction industries, farming, paper products, and real estate development due to the high uncertainties, long investment horizons, and limited competitive erosion. However, in high-tech industries such as computers or consumer electronics, competitors can substantially influence a firm's opportunity. At a minimum, exogenous competitive entry may introduce a dividend-like effect on such a growth option's value that may justify early exercise (discussed next); endogenous competitive interactions can add further complications that require a game-theoretic treatment (discussed from chapter 4 onward).

Option to Defer under Exogenous Competition

The value of a firm's investment opportunities is sometimes affected by exogenous competitive value erosion. Examples of such *shared real options* include the opportunity to introduce a new product impacted by introduction of close substitutes or to penetrate a new geographic market without barriers to competitive entry. For example, the introduction of the multimedia compact disk developed by Sony (and Philips) in 1995 faced exogenous competitive erosion from companies like Toshiba, Time Warner, and Matsushita (with the Super-Density Disk). Similarly, Texas Instruments' entry into digital TV with its digital light processing technology for high-quality big-screen television, developed over a decade for over $500 million faced anticipated competitive erosion with substitute products by Sony, Fujitsu, and Sharp.

Figure 3.5 presents an example of such an investment opportunity that is *shared* with competition. Suppose for simplicity that the incumbent and its competitors participate equally in the collective opportunities of the industry, sharing both the necessary investment outlay for developing the technology of $I = 80$ million as well as the total market value of cash inflows ("size of the pie"), $V = 100$ million. Thus, the project value for the incumbent firm next period may be either $(V^+)' = \frac{1}{2} \times 180 = 90$ million or $(V^-)' = \frac{1}{2} \times 60 = 30$ million. The *shared opportunity* to invest in the project with exercise price half the total investment outlay, $I' = 40$ million, seen as a call option, is now worth: $C' = [0.4 \times \text{Max}(90 - 40, 0) + 0.6 \times 0] / 1.08 = 18.5$ million (or half of 37 million found in the previous example of the proprietary option of figure 3.3).

FIGURE 3.5 SHARED OPPORTUNITY: INVEST NOW IF EARLY
COMMITMENT CAN PREEMPT COMPETITION

A. Impact of *exogenous* competitive entry (substitutes): reduced option
value (50% cash flow "dividends")

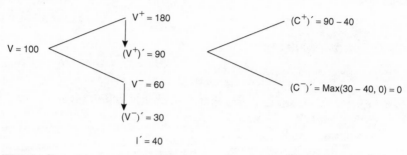

Wait (call option with "dividends"):

$$C' = \frac{0.4 \times (90 - 40) + 0.6 \times 0}{1.08} = 18.5$$

B. *Invest now/exercise early* (e.g., build excess plant capacity) to
preempt competitive erosion or capture cash flow "dividends"

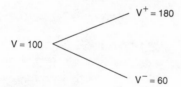

Invest now: $V - I = 100 - 80 = 20 \ (> 18.5)$.

    The option value of the incumbent would be eroded by exogenous competitive entry, analogous to a dividend yield (here at 50%), that tends to reduce the value of its option. Incumbent firms may have an incentive to commit to invest early to be able to protect against such exogenous competitive value erosion and preempt competitors from exercising their shared rights.[13] A firm anticipating competitive entry may commit excess production capacity early on to preempt competition, receiving the immediate NPV

---

[13]Dixit (1979, 1980) discusses the role of early investment in entry deterrence, while Spence (1977) shows that existing firms in an industry facing competitive threat should carry excess capacity so as to expand output and reduce prices when entry is threatened, thereby preempting competitive entry. Spence (1979) finds that constraints on growth and the timing of entry place firms in asymmetrical positions concerning investment, with those firms in the most advantageous positions preempting the market to some degree.

value of $100 - 80 = 20$ million rather than the shared option value of 18.5 million. In the absence of such exogenous competitive value erosion, the firm might prefer to wait until future price or demand uncertainty is resolved. The more complicated case of deciding when to initiate a deferrable investment when competition is endogenous is addressed in subsequent chapters.

3.3.2. Options to Expand or Contract

Once a project is undertaken, management may have the flexibility to alter it in various ways at different times during its life. The flexibility to expand or contract a project's scale can be quite valuable. When a firm buys vacant, undeveloped land, or when it builds a small plant in a new geographic location to position itself to develop a large market, it essentially acquires an expansion option. Figure 3.6 depicts the case of an opportunity to build excess production capacity, if it turns out that the product is more enthusiastically received in the market than originally expected.

Figure 3.6 Value of a Project That Has Options to Expand or Contract Production Capacity

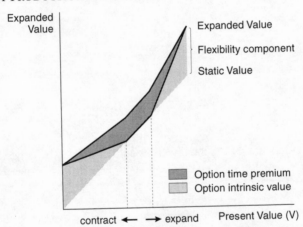

Project	Variable	Call option (expand)	Put option (contract)
Fraction of project value (e% or c%)	e% (c%) of V	e% Stock price	c% Stock price
PV of extra investment outlays	I_1'	Exercise price	-
Present recovery value	R_c	-	Exercise price
Length of deferral time	T	Time to maturity	Time to maturity
Time value of money	r	Risk-free rate	Risk-free rate
Volatility of project's returns	σ^2	Variance	Variance

An option to expand the scale of production by $e\%$ is analogous to a call option, C, on (a fraction $e\%$ of) the value of a project. If demand is high, management can expand capacity (by $e\%$ of the value of the base capacity). The exercise price is the value of the extra investment outlay, $I_1{}'$, required to build additional plant capacity (or expand scale). At maturity,

Option to expand: $C = \text{Max}[\text{NPV of expansion } (eV - I_1{}'), 0]$. (3.2)

Analogous to the option to expand a project is the option to contract the scale of a project's operation by forgoing planned future expenditures if the product is not as well received in the market as initially expected. The option to contract can thus be seen as a *put option* on the part of the project that can be contracted, with an exercise price equal to the part of planned expenditures that can be canceled. If demand turns out to be weaker than originally expected, management can operate below capacity or even reduce the scale of operations (by $c\%$), thereby saving part of the variable costs (or recovering a resale value), R_c, from contracting. The option to contract by $c\%$ is analogous to a put option, P, on (a fraction $c\%$ of) the value of the project:

Option to contract: $P = \text{Max}[\text{NPV of contraction } (R_c - cV), 0]$. (3.3)

The expanded NPV of a project with both options at maturity would equal the static NPV plus Max[NPV of expansion $(eV - I_1{}')$, NPV of contraction $(R_c - cV)$, retain base-scale capacity (0)].

Let us return to the basic example of the previous section where project value V may fluctuate in line with the random fluctuation in demand, to $V^+ = 180$ million or $V^- = 60$ million by the end of the period. Suppose that in our example (assuming that the project was started in year 0) management has the option to invest an additional $40 million outlay (e.g., in excess production capacity and increased advertising expenditures) one year after the initial investment (that is, $I_1{}' = \$40$ million), which would increase by half the scale and value of the facility (i.e., an expansion factor $e = 50\%$). Then in year 1 management has the flexibility either to maintain the same scale of operation (i.e., receive project value, V, at no extra cost) or expand the scale and project value by 50% by paying the additional cost, whichever is highest.

In addition, also in one year, suppose that as an alternative to making the full investment outlay necessary to maintain the current scale of operations, management has the option to halve the scale ($c = 50\%$) and value of the project, and recover $35 million ($R_c = \$35$ million). This may be the case, for example, if part of the investment cost necessary to maintain the base scale of the project's operation can be saved.

What is the value of each of these options? Clearly, if conditions are as expected, management would maintain base capacity. If market conditions next year turn out unfavorably, management may find it valuable to exercise its option to contract the scale of the project's operation. If conditions are better than expected, management would exercise its option to expand. At maturity,

$\text{Max}[0, (eV - I_1'), (R_c - cV)]$

If +: $\text{Max}[0, (0.5 \times 180 - 40), (35 - 0.5 \times 180)] = 50$
(expand by 50%);

If −: $\text{Max}[0, (0.5 \times 60 - 40), (35 - 0.5 \times 60)] = 5$
(contract to half the scale).

Management will exercise its option to expand if market conditions turn out favorably (+), and contract when conditions are unfavorable (−). The value of the investment opportunity (including the value of options) then becomes:

Expanded NPV = static NPV + value of the options;
$NPV_0^* = 100 + [0.4 \times 50 + 0.6 \times 5]/1.08 = 121.3$ million.

The value of the expansion and contraction flexibility increases the static project value by 21.3%.

The options to expand and contract capacity may be particularly valuable in the case of new product introductions in uncertain markets. These options, which will be exercised only if future market developments turn out different than expected, can make an otherwise unprofitable (based on static NPV) base-case investment worth undertaking. Consideration of options to expand or contract are important when management makes capacity decisions and can position the firm to adjust to a changing market more readily than competitors, for example, when it buys vacant land or builds-in excess plant capacity from the outset. The flexibility to contract may also be important in choosing among technologies or plants with a different construction-to-maintenance mix. Management may find it preferable to build a plant with lower initial construction costs and higher maintenance expenditures in order to acquire the flexibility to contract operations by cutting down on maintenance if the market conditions turn out less favorably than anticipated.

3.3.3. The Option to Abandon for Salvage or Switch Use

Once a project is undertaken, management may also have the flexibility to abandon the project in exchange for its salvage value or value in its best alternative use before the end of its useful life. The flexibility to stage investments can provide great benefits to a firm if markets have substantial demand uncertainty. At an extreme, the firm can abandon operations, divisions, or entire businesses. For example, if a project involves valuable real estate that can be sold if the plant is shut down, abandonment may allow management to avoid incurring the fixed costs of continuous operation and receive the value in the next-best use.

FIGURE 3.7 THE OPTION TO ABANDON PRODUCTION CAPACITY

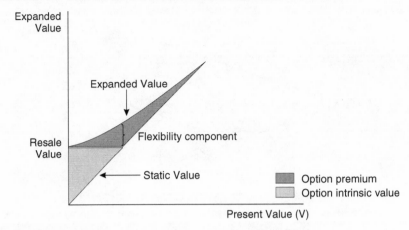

Project	Variable	Put option (abandon)
PV of cash inflows	V	Stock price
Resale value	A	Exercise price
Length of deferral time	T	Time to maturity
Time value of money	r	Risk-free rate
Volatility of project's returns	σ^2	Variance

Figure 3.7 illustrates the expanded present value of a project with an option to abandon. The straight line represents the present value of operating cash inflows, while the total of both shaded areas reflects the abandonment option. The current expanded present value equals the sum of these components, captured by the curve. At maturity (with no further delay of the abandonment decision), the value of the project equals the present value of cash flows, V, plus the intrinsic value of the option:

Expanded present value =
static value V + Max[abandon $(A - V)$, continue].   (3.4)

The resale value in figure 3.7, A, is certain. However, in an actual situation, as market conditions and the value of the project changes, the plant resale value in the secondary market would also fluctuate. Let the project's value in its best alternative use, A (or the *salvage value* for which it can be abandoned), fluctuate over time as shown in figure 3.8.[14]

The project's salvage value ($A = 90$) is currently below the project's value in its present use ($V = 100$); otherwise management would have

[14]We assume here for simplicity that the project's value in its current use and in its best alternative use (or salvage value) are perfectly positively correlated. In fact, the option to switch use would be even more valuable the lower the correlation between V and A.

FIGURE 3.8 FLUCTUATIONS OF SALVAGE VALUE UNDERLYING OPTION TO
SWITCH USE

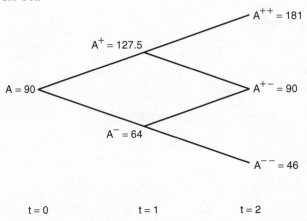

$t = 0$ $t = 1$ $t = 2$

switched use immediately. However, salvage value has a smaller variance;
thus if the market keeps moving up, it would not be optimal to abandon
the project early for its salvage value, but if it moves down, management
may find it desirable to do so (e.g., in year 1 exchange the present use
value of $V_1^- = 60$ for a higher alternative use value of $A_1^- = 64$). In other
words, the option to abandon the project early in exchange for its *salvage
value* translates into the equityholders' option to choose the maximum of
the project's value in its present use, V, or its value in its best alternative
use, A, that is, $E = \text{Max}(V, A)$:

$E^+ = \text{Max}(V^+, A^+) = \text{Max}(180, 127.5) = 180 = V^+$ (continue);
$E^- = \text{Max}(V^-, A^-) = \text{Max}(60, 64) = 64 = A^-$ (abandon).

The presence of two (partially correlated) stochastic processes compli-
cates the risk-neutral valuation of this option. Even when the two processes
are perfectly correlated, the risk-neutral probabilities for the two processes
are not the same, because their variances differ. Dimensionality can be reduced by expressing one asset relative to the other (as a numeraire). The
basic guideline is that the project is undertaken when its value from continuing is larger than the salvage value, and abandoned otherwise. When the
ratio of project value to salvage value is larger than 1, the project is continued, and otherwise is abandoned. The option to switch can be rewritten as
a call option on this ratio with an exercise price equal to 1. To construct a
binomial tree of the ratio of these two values requires an estimation of their
relative volatility.[15] As such the value of this option on the ratio is

---

[15]This relative volatility is a function of the volatilities of the two processes for the project
and salvage value.
$\hat{\sigma} = \sqrt{\sigma_V^2 + \sigma_A^2 - 2\rho\sigma_V\sigma_A}$.

$$E_0 = [pE^+ + (1 - p)E^-]/(1 + r) =$$
$$[0.6 \times 0.41 + 0.4 \times 0]/1.08 = 0.23. \tag{3.5}$$

The value of the option to switch is the value of the above call option on the ratio multiplied with the initial value of the project, $0.23 \times 100 = 23$.

The option to abandon, or switch use, has significant value in capital-intensive industries involving large tangible assets and can be especially valuable in new product introductions in highly uncertain markets, particularly in projects that can easily switch among alternative uses or be traded in secondary markets. Bjerksund and Ekern (1990) and Kemna (1993) value an oil field with the option to abandon operations. Brealey and Myers (2003, chap. 21) illustrate the importance of the flexibility to abandon in the example of launching a new product involving the choice between two alternative technologies for its production facilities.[16] Myers and Majd (1990) value the option to abandon as an American put option, with the underlying value being the present value of the net operating cash inflows. The exercise price is the salvage or resale value in the secondary market.

3.3.4. The Option to Temporarily Shut Down

In some circumstances, it may be desirable to temporarily suspend production. For instance, if cash revenues are not sufficient to cover variable operating costs and the costs of switching between the operating and idle modes are relatively small, it may be better to suspend operations (e.g., see McDonald and Siegel 1985). Brennan and Schwartz (1985a, 1985b) examine this real option in the context of a mine operation.

The above (relative) volatility of the returns of the ratio is 25% in this example. As the processes are perfectly correlated, ρ is equal to 1. For positively correlated processes, the reduced risk in downside states and large potential in upside states is reflected in a lower volatility than the volatilities for the project and salvage value, which are 59% and 33% respectively in this example. The size of the upside movement u is thus 1.28, and $d = 0.78$. The risk-neutral probability of the ratio is therefore

$$p = \frac{(1 + r) - d}{u - d} = \frac{(1 + 0.08) - 0.78}{1.28 - 0.78} = 0.6.$$

[16]Technology A is a specialized, custom-designed technology for high-volume production and low cost per product. However, if demand is sluggish, this equipment is worthless. Technology B involves standard machine tools with higher labor costs, but the tools can be sold for salvage value if product demand is low. The technology A alternative will have a higher value in a standard NPV analysis of the production facilities, because it has the lowest costs at the planned production volume. However, because of the commercial uncertainty of new product launches, management would be reluctant to invest in technology A; technology B has an abandonment flexibility advantage if demand proves disappointing.

Consider evaluating the production policy of a gold mine when there is uncertainty in gold prices. Suppose for simplicity that in each period the operating cash flow equals the quantity produced, Q, times the spot price of gold, S_t, minus variable costs c, that is, $CF_t = Q(S_t - c)$. If there are no additional costs involved, the operating cash flow from the option to produce cannot be worth less than zero. Management may temporarily shut down production in periods of low prices if the contribution margin from operations becomes negative, that is, if $S_t - c < 0$. That is, CF = Max[quantity × (price − variable costs), 0].

Valuation, starting from the right in figure 3.9, would proceed backward in time. Suppose the mine has a fixed operating life of two periods. At the end, in states C, D, or E, project value, V, would equal the maximum of the residual operating value (i.e., the final cash flow, CF) and the nonoperating value (zero). Stepping backward in time, the value of the mine in the first period would equal the expected value of the future operating and nonoperating values plus the cash flow of the current period.

Generally, there may be costs involved in shutting down or (re)opening a mine. Because of the shutdown option, the mine can never be worth less than its nonoperating value minus the costs of shutting down operations. Equivalently, a nonoperating mine can be reopened as soon as the operating value, V_o, minus the cost of reopening, exceeds the nonoperating or closure value, V_c. The curves in figure 3.10 represent the value of a

FIGURE 3.9 OPTION TO TEMPORARILY SHUT DOWN THE PRODUCTION PROCESS

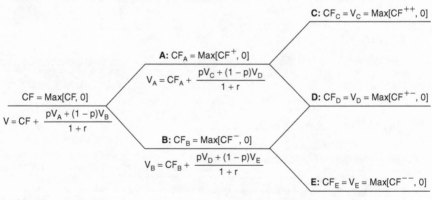

Notes:
Q: Quantity of the reserves
S: Spot price
F: Fixed costs = 0, c: variable costs
CF: Operating cash inflow, CF = QS − Qc
u, d: Dynamics in gold prices

FIGURE 3.10 OPTION TO TEMPORARILY SHUT DOWN AND REOPEN A MINE

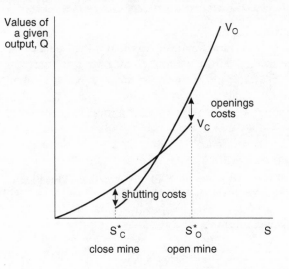

Notes:
S: Price
V_o: Value of an operating mine
V_c: Value of a closed or nonoperating mine
Expanded V_o = Max[operating value, nonoperating value − shutting costs]
Expanded V_c = Max[nonoperating value, operating value − opening costs]

Source: Brennan and Schwartz 1985a.

mine that temporarily suspends production in periods of low prices. The values shown in the figure include switchover costs.

How much should the gold price drop before management should shut down operations, and how much should it increase again before it becomes lucrative to reopen the mine? To answer these questions, one must determine the trigger prices of gold, S^*, that would trigger temporary closing and reopening of the mine. Because it is costly to shut down and reopen the mine, these trigger prices are not equal and there is a "delay" (hysteresis) region during which the mine should remain closed down or reopened. As shown by Brennan and Schwartz (1985a, 1985b) and illustrated in figure 3.10, management would shut down operations as soon as the gold price drops below the closing trigger price, S^*_c. Whenever the gold price exceeds the reopening trigger price, S^*_o $(> S^*_c)$ management should restart the production process. Thus the presence of significant switching costs introduces a delay effect in the timing of switches.

3.3.5. Options to Switch Inputs or Outputs

When the prices or quantities of raw materials (inputs) or end products (outputs) are uncertain, flexibility in the production (conversion) process can be quite valuable. An example of the option to switch outputs is provided by a flexible manufacturing system. As noted by Baldwin and Trigeorgis (1993), such systems may provide product flexibility, producing a mix of existing products with little setup time between component types. Alternatively, they may provide product design flexibility, producing new products more economically or quickly in response to a changing market demand. Process flexibility can be achieved by technology, by maintaining relationships with various suppliers, or by maintaining production facilities in various locations. In the latter case, management can switch production to the lowest-cost producing facilities as the relative costs, local market conditions, or exchange rates change over time. Product flexibility, enabling management to switch between different products, is important when the firm directs its strategy toward a broad product line. This option is valuable in industries such as automobiles, consumer electronics, and pharmaceuticals.[17]

A classic example of switching inputs is an electricity power station that runs on a coal-burning system (e.g., see Kemna 1988). In deciding to convert the power station to a gas-burning system, there are two alternatives: a system that works solely on gas, or a more expensive, flexible system that can burn either gas or coal. This latter system can provide valuable built-in flexibility to switch from the current input to the cheapest future input when relative prices fluctuate. Essentially, management would have the option of switching one risky asset for another. The firm should be willing to pay a premium for such flexible technology. The value of switching flexibility must be weighted against the incremental investment cost of the more flexible technology. Figure 3.11 illustrates the input costs for the flexible gas-and-coal producing alternative (with changing gas prices and a relatively stable coal price).

Process flexibility is important in natural resource industries such as mining operations, oil extraction, electricity generation, the chemical industry, and crop switching.

---

[17]The option to switch has been examined by Margrabe (1978), Kensinger (1987), Kulatilaka (1988, 1993), Triantis and Hodder (1991), and others.

FIGURE 3.11 OPTION TO SWITCH INPUTS WITH CHANGING GAS PRICES

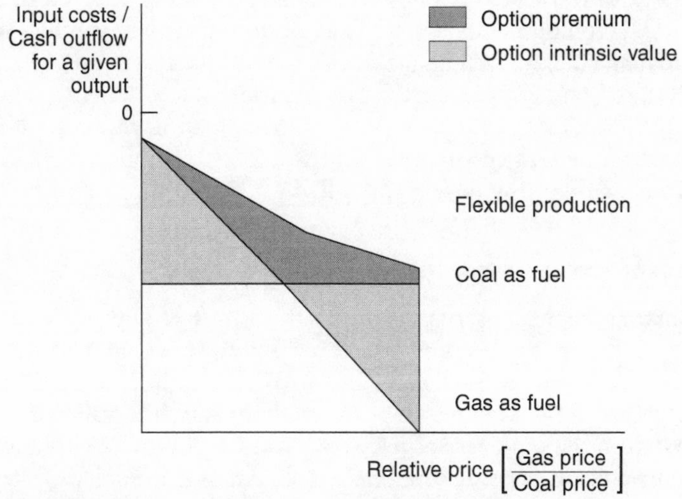

Underlying Value	Variable	Call Option
Relative Price	P_A / P_X	Stock price
Equal to 1	X	Exercise price
Length of deferral time	T	Time to maturity
Time value of money	r	Risk-free rate
Relative volatility of exchange option as function of volatilities of the two assets	σ^2	Variance of stock returns

$$\hat{\sigma} = \sqrt{\sigma^2_A + \sigma^2_X - 2\rho\sigma_A\sigma_X}$$

3.4. Prototype Examples: Valuing an R & D Program and a Mine Concession

In this section we present two extended prototypical real-options valuation applications. In the first example, we consider the value of investing in R & D and subsequent stages of commercialization. This multistage R & D investment decision can be viewed as a compound option (or option on an option). The second example considers the valuation of a gold mine license, where the current project value can be benchmarked and estimated using a traded financial instrument (gold futures) whose probabilistic behavior is close to that of the producing mine. The valuation of a license to develop the mine is treated analogously to the valuation of a (simple) call option.

The next section will present an actual "soup to nuts" implementation of the real-options valuation in exploration investments. It describes the valuation of the staged development of an oil field concession of a block on the Dutch continental shelf. The development program is flexible in that management may change the amount of investment as uncertainty is resolved over time. At its core is the valuation of a producing field, based on replication using crude oil futures. The valuation results confirm that exploration investments in "speculative blocks" are more valuable than otherwise similar low-uncertainty blocks.

3.4.1. VALUING A RESEARCH AND DEVELOPMENT PROGRAM

Our first example concerns how to analyze an R & D program available to a high-tech company, and which technology development strategy to pursue. As noted, R & D programs involve multiple contingent stages and thus should not be treated as isolated projects. The value of potential profits from the commercial projects that may follow from the research stage must be properly incorporated in determining the value of the underlying research program. Hence, the analysis requires explicit consideration of the project's various stages, from research and product development to future commercialization.

Figure 3.12 shows the structure and timing of cash flows of an R & D project available to a high-technology company. Suppose the project involves a two-year R & D phase, followed by expected cash inflows over the four-year period of commercialization. The R & D phase requires an immediate capital outlay of $15 million, and an outlay of $50 million in year 1. The follow-on commercial project has expected cash inflows over the four-year period of $CF_3 = \$200$ million, $CF_4 = \$500$ million, $CF_5 = \$700$ million, and $CF_6 = \$200$ million, and requires an outlay of $I_2 = \$1,200$ million as of year 2. Even though the R & D program appears to have a low return on investment, it may be profitable to develop the new technology to enhance the company's future market position.

What would the value of the R & D program be if management were to commit to both stages immediately? Its value at the beginning of commercial phase, V_2, discounted at an opportunity cost of capital $k = 15\%$, is $1,127 million, and its NPV_2 therefore would equal $1,127 million − $1,200 million = − $73 million (as of $t = 2$). Based on the expected scenario of a passive NPV analysis (that assumes commitment to both stages), the commercialization project itself does not appear to be profitable. Calculating the present value as of $t = 0$, using an opportunity cost of $k = 15\%$, results in a $852 million value for the technology. The present value of the (known) investment outlays for the entire program, discounted at the risk-free rate of 4% assuming no systematic risks, equals $1,109

FIGURE 3.12 CAPITAL OUTLAYS FOR R & D PROJECT TO DEVELOP A
NEW TECHNOLOGY, AND EXPECTED CASH INFLOWS FROM THE
POTENTIAL FOLLOW-ON COMMERCIAL PROJECT

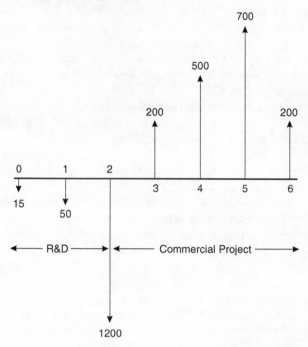

million for the commercial stage and $63 million for the R & D stage. Thus, if the firm were to commit to both stages of the program right now, the total expected net value loss would amount to $NPV_0 = V_0 - I_0 = \$852$ million $- (\$1109$ million $+ \$63$ million$) = -\$320$ million.

However, the firm does not have to commit to both stages immediately. Investing in R & D derives strategic value from generating the opportunity to commercialize later under the right circumstances, but implies no obligation to invest in the future commercial project. In other words, R & D is analogous to an option, in the sense that it creates a valuable future opportunity without committing the company to making the complete investment right now.

Is this technology strategy worth pursuing? We must consider two decisions: Should the R & D be undertaken now, and if so, should the technology be commercialized after R & D results are known? (e.g., see Kolbe, Morris, and Teisberg 1991). The opportunity to invest in the commercialization project is like a call option with time to maturity $T = 2$ years, and an exercise price of $1,200 million. The underlying asset is the current (time-zero) value of a claim on the commercial project's expected future cash inflows of $852 million. Suppose that uncertainty during the R & D phase results in a yearly increase or decline with multiplicative up and down factors, $u = 1.5$ or $d = 0.67$. The dynamics in the time series of commercial project values (V) are illustrated in the event tree of figure 3.13.

As with decision tree analysis, we first value the option at the end of the tree at year 2 and work backward, using risk-neutral binomial option valuation. At the end of the R & D phase, management must decide whether to commercialize the technology. The worst possible outcome for the commercialization stage will be zero if the new technology is not implemented. Thus, at year 2, the value of the option would equal the higher of (a) the NPV of commercialization ($V^{++} - \$1{,}200$ million); or (b) not implementing the technology (zero). As of year 2 this results in a net commercialization value of $717 million [$= 1{,}917 - 1{,}200$] in the case events turn out favorable, or a zero net value in the case of abandonment of the program (see the end nodes of the option valuation tree of figure 3.14). Under risk-neutral binomial option valuation, the current value of this claim can be determined from its expected future up and down values discounted at the risk-free interest rate ($r = 4\%$), with expectations taken over the risk-neutral probabilities ($p = 0.45$). Stepping back in time (to $t = 1$) results in a zero value in the low state and a ($0.45 \times \$717$ million $+ 0.55 \times 0$) / $1.04 = \$310$ million option value in the high state. Finally, as of year zero, the value of this growth option equals ($0.45 \times \$310$ million $+ 0.55 \times 0$) / $1.04 = \$134$ million.

After valuing the option to invest in commercialization, we can now consider the first question: should the R & D program be undertaken in the first place? Investment in the R & D program can be viewed as acquiring (and potentially exercising) a compound option (or option on an option). The underlying value of the R & D investment is the subsequent commercialization option, which has a value of $134 million. The exercise price of the R & D compound option is the present value of the R & D

FIGURE 3.13 DYNAMICS IN THE VALUE OF THE COMMERCIAL PROJECT (IN $ MILLIONS)

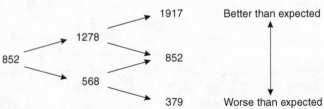

FIGURE 3.14 NET VALUE OF THE OPTION TO INVEST IN THE
COMMERCIAL PROJECT (IN $ MILLIONS)

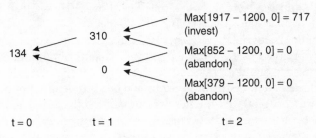

outlays, which equals $63 million. The worst possible outcome will be zero if management decides not to develop the new technology in the first place. The value of the R & D program therefore equals Max[0, $134 million − $63 million] = $71 million.

Expanded NPV = −$320 million + $391 million = $71 million.

In this case, management is justified to invest in R & D to prove the new technology and position itself to take advantage of a future growth option, despite the negative NPV of its expected cash flows (−$320 million). Management should recognize that a wider range of possible outcomes does in fact increase the option value of commercialization.

3.4.2. VALUING A MINE CONCESSION (LICENSE) USING CERTAINTY-EQUIVALENT VALUATION

Following the classic example of Brennan and Schwartz (1985), consider a firm that must decide whether to invest in a gold mine. The decision to develop the mine is irreversible, in that after development, management cannot disinvest and recover the expenditure. To keep matters simple, suppose that development and extraction can be started immediately, requiring an investment outlay, I, of $4.5 million. There are no variable extraction costs. The gold reserves (14,000 ounces) and the production profile, Q_t, over time t, is known ahead of time: production in year 1, Q_1, is expected to be 4,000 ounces, and production in year 2, Q_2, 10,000 ounces.

Uncertainty over the value of the project is closely related to the dynamics in gold prices. Currently, gold is priced at $300 per troy ounce; next year, the price will change. For simplicity, we assume two possible end-of-period prices after one period: price increasing (with a multiplicative factor $u = 1.5$) to $S^+ = 450, or price decreasing (with a multiplicative factor $d = 0.67$) to a value of $S^- = 200. Both prices are equally likely (with actual probability $q = 0.5$). In the subsequent year ($t = 2$), prices may rise or decrease again, and the same multiplicative factors will apply. Table 3.2 summarizes the possible gold prices (S), extraction quantities (Q), and the resulting operating cash flows, $CF = QS$.[18] Suppose further that the riskless interest rate r is 4% per year.

Given the size of the investment outlay, the current gold price, and the dynamics in gold prices, is this a good investment? Should management invest now, or should it wait and see how the gold prices will develop? For an immediate investment decision, we need to determine the opportunity cost of capital and the net present value (NPV). The required return can be estimated from a traded financial instrument (gold) whose probabilistic behavior is close to that of the completed project (i.e., a producing mine). With a spot gold price of $300 per ounce, the implied market-required return, k, for the same risk can be derived from the expected gold prices over the next one-year period, or it can be derived from the expected gold prices over a two-year period:

$$300 = \frac{0.5 \times \$450 + 0.5 \times \$200}{1 + k} =$$
$$\frac{0.25 \times \$675 + 0.5 \times \$300 + 0.25 \times \$133}{(1 + k)^2}. \tag{3.6}$$

The expectation of future gold prices given above has an implied required rate of return equal to $k = 8.33\%$. The computation below shows that the present value of the expected cash inflows equals $4.2 million. The NPV of the gold mine is $4.2 million $-$ $4.5 million $=$ $-$0.3 million; therefore, management would not invest in such a project right now.

$$NPV = \frac{0.5 \times 1.80 + 0.5 \times 0.80}{1.0833}$$
$$+ \frac{0.25 \times 6.75 + 0.5 \times 3.00 + 0.25 \times 1.33}{(1.0833)^2} - 4.5$$
$$= 4.2 - 4.5 = -\$0.3 \text{ million}. \tag{3.7}$$

An alternative approach to valuing the mine is to replicate the cash flows with an equivalent "twin" traded security rather than using the twin security's required return. Consider the position of the company that owns the producing mine. The company's position is long in gold. The company could offset this position and realize the value of the field today if management could sell short gold futures that exactly match the mine's production profile over time. This particular project is lucrative for the corporation's shareholders if the value of the covered position exceeds the investment outlay required for the project.

[18]Again, variable (extraction) costs are assumed negligible. Some of the numbers in table 3.1 are rounded.

TABLE 3.2
Quantities, Prices, and Operating Cash Inflows of a Mine in Various
States

Period	State (nature)	Probability q	Gold Price per Ounce, S	Quantity Q	Cash Inflows (QS) CF (millions)
0	Current		$300		
1	High	0.5	$450	4,000	$1.80
1	Low	0.5	$200	4,000	$0.80
2	High, high	0.25	$675	10,000	$6.75
2	High, low / Low, high	0.5	$300	10,000	$3.00
2	Low, low	0.25	$133	10,000	$1.33

Consider, for instance, the dollar revenue of the mine at $t = 2$, which equals the production times the market price in two years, $10,000S_2$. The company can offset the price risk of this cash flow by selling future contracts short for 10,000 ounces of gold, with a futures price (set at $t = 0$ for delivery at $T = 2$) F_2 and a dollar revenue $10,000F_2$ at $t = 2$. Since it can offset the risk of gold prices, this hedged position, $Q_2(F_2)$, provides a certainty equivalent, CEQ_2, of the uncertain operating cash flow at $t = 2$. This certainty-equivalent cash flow equals the expected cash flow minus a risk premium (RP). The present value of this certainty-equivalent cash flow can then be determined using the risk-free rate, r, as the appropriate discount-rate:

$$NPV = \frac{Q_1F_1}{1 + r} + \frac{Q_2F_2}{(1 + r)^2} - I \tag{3.8}$$

What is the price of a long-term (futures) contract traded in an arbitrage-free financial market? The futures price, F_T, equals the current spot price of gold, S_0, plus the interest accrued until maturity T of the contract, that is, $F_T = S_0 (1 + r)^T$.[19] Equations 3.9 and 3.10 show the present value of the certainty-equivalent cash flows using the (theoretical) futures prices, $F_T = S_0(1 + r)^T$, where T is the time to maturity of the contract.

[19]This assumes no convenience or dividend-like yield. Suppose that this relation does not hold and that the futures price is higher. Should this happen, a "cash and carry" arbitrage opportunity is available if traders short the contract and simultaneously buy the gold. At maturity, the gold is delivered, covering the short position in the futures contract. Hence, traders are unlikely to be willing to serve this "free lunch" for the company by selling futures.

$$NPV = \frac{Q_1 S_0 (1 + r)}{1 + r} + \frac{Q_2 S_0 (1 + r)^2}{(1 + r)^2} - I \qquad (3.9)$$

$$= (Q_1 + Q_2)S_0 - I = 14{,}000 \times \$300 - \$4.5 \text{ million} = -\$0.3 \text{ million}.$$

$$(3.10)$$

Equation 3.10 illustrates that we can replicate the cash flows of the mine with a gold "cash and carry" strategy. In other words, owning the mine is equivalent to owning a portfolio of gold. We are able to replicate the cash flows directly if we buy 14,000 ounces of gold (the total amount of the reserves) today and sell 4,000 ounces at $t = 1$ and 10,000 ounces at $t = 2$. The current market value of this strategy and the gross value of the mine, therefore, equals $14{,}000 \times \$300 = \$4.2$ million; the NPV of the mine equals $4.2 million − \$4.5 million = −\$0.3 million.

Interestingly, both the NPV and the certainty-equivalent valuation approaches resulted in the same answer (−\$0.3 million). What is happening? In the NPV method, the risk adjustment was carried out in the denominator through an appropriate risk-adjusted discount rate, k. In the certainty-equivalent approach, the adjustment for risk was made in the numerator, allowing the certainty-equivalent cash flows then to be discounted at the risk-free rate, r.

As a variation to the above certainty-equivalent approach, we could instead calculate the (artificial) risk-neutral probability, p, of possible gold price up (and down) movements, which would enable us to calculate the CEQ from the dynamics of gold prices.[20] The risk-neutral probability is the one that would prevail if the underlying asset (in a risk-neutral world) were expected to earn the risk-free return: $pS^+ + (1 - p)S^- = (1 + r)S$. This risk-neutral probability (or equivalent martingale measure), p, differs from the actual (true) probability, q. The risk-neutral probability is given by equation 3.12 (see Trigeorgis and Mason 1987), where S^+ and S^- are the possible gold prices in the up and down states next period, and r is the risk-free interest rate.

$$S_0 = \frac{q \times S^+ + (1 - q)S^-}{1 + k} = \frac{p \times S^+ + (1 - p)S^-}{1 + r} = \frac{CEQ}{1 + r}, \qquad (3.11)$$

where

$$p \equiv \frac{(1 + r)S_0 - S^-}{S^+ - S^-}. \qquad (3.12)$$

---

[20]Because of the ability to replicate the mine with a specific gold position, the value of the mine license is independent of investor risk attitudes, and hence it is the same as if investors were risk-neutral.

In the computation below we apply the risk-neutral valuation of equation 3.11 to the above mine, using the risk-neutral probability from equation 3.12:

$$p = \frac{(1 + 0.04)300 - 200}{450 - 200} = 0.45.$$

The resulting valuation once again gives the same project value of −$0.3 million:

$$NPV = \frac{0.45 \times 1.80 + (1 - 0.45) \times 0.80}{1.04} +$$
$$\frac{0.45^2 \times 6.75 + 2(0.45 \times 0.55)3.00 + (1 - 0.45)^2 \times 1.33}{1.04^2} - 4.5$$
$$= 4.2 - 4.5 = -\$0.3 \text{ million.}$$

So far, the certainty-equivalent approach based on replication of cash flows or properly discounting them at the required risk-adjusted return has resulted in the same answer. We next examine situations in which NPV does not give the right answer. Capital investments are not usually a now-or-never proposition. Suppose that management can buy a one-year license that enables it to wait for a year and observe how gold prices develop before making an investment commitment in the project. If gold prices drop and the value of the mine declines below the required investment outlay, management can allow the license to expire. Figure 3.15 illustrates how this option to defer alters the shape (distribution) of the value of the mine. At a high gold price ($S^+ = 450$), the value of the mine equals $6.3 million ($Q \times S^+ = 14{,}000 \times \$450$). At that value, management would invest $4.5 million and the NPV would equal $6.3 million − $4.5 million = $1.8 million. At a low price ($S^- = 200$), management would decide not to invest, as the value of the project would be only $2.8 million ($< \$4.5$ million). In this case, management would allow the license to expire (abandoning the project), and the value would be truncated to zero.

FIGURE 3.15 ASYMMETRY IN THE DISTRIBUTION OF PROJECT VALUE DUE TO FLEXIBILITY (VALUES IN $ MILLIONS)

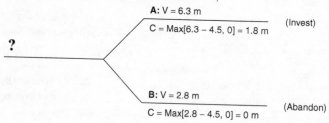

As noted, the standard NPV framework, which determines the present value of the *expected* cash inflows and then subtracts the present value of *expected* capital outlays, does not give the right answer in such cases. Under uncertainty, management has the flexibility to revise the investment decision as uncertainty over gold prices and the value of the project gets resolved. The future investment decision is based on future gold prices, information that is not yet known. Decision tree analysis (DTA) can in principle capture this decision flexibility that is not handled well by static NPV. However, to find the appropriate discount rate (cost of capital) along each branch (gold price state) at different times is not an easy task. As in a call option, the risk of the license changes each time the underlying mine value changes; the risk of the license is reduced if the price of gold — and hence the value of the mine — increases. Moreover, the risk profile is affected by the presence and optimal exercise of managerial options (e.g., to abandon). An option-based approach uses decision nodes (rather than passive event nodes) in modeling such flexibility, with risk-neutral valuation capturing changes in the risk profile in an appropriate manner. As with DTA, the valuation problem can be solved recursively, starting with future values and working backward along the tree. The resulting "certainty equivalent" values can then be consistently discounted at the risk-free rate, r. The value of the license determined in this way equals

$$V_0 = \frac{p \times C^+ + (1 - p)C^-}{1 + r} =$$

$$\frac{0.45 \times 1.8 + (1 - 0.45) \times 0}{1.04} = \$0.78 \text{ million}, \tag{3.13}$$

where C^+ and C^- denote the values of the option (license) in the up ($+$) and down ($-$) states next period (at $t = 1$). Note that the \$4.5 million investment cost is incurred in the up state (C^+) but not in the down state (C^-). Based on the expanded NPV criterion, the value of the license to invest has the following components:

Expanded NPV = (passive) NPV + flexibility (or option) value
\$0.78 million = $-$\$0.3 million + \$1.08 million.

The difference between the expanded NPV and the standard (passive) NPV [0.78 million $-$ ($-$0.3 million)] is the flexibility option value. The risk-neutral valuation method used above is originally based on the ability to replicate the value of the mine's cash flows. In this case, management can create a gold portfolio in the financial markets that replicates the future payoff of the mine license. In order to truncate the resulting payoff, it combines this gold portfolio with the risk-free asset. The position in gold in the replicating portfolio, N (the option's *delta* or hedge ratio), equals the spread in the value of the license ($1.8 million − 0) divided by the spread in gold prices ($450 − $200).

Table 3.3 shows that a synthetic license can be created, consisting of a position of $N = 7,200$ ounces in gold and a risk-free payment of $1.44 million that exactly replicates the future truncated payoff of the mine (0 or $1.8 million) at $t = 0$. If at the end of the period the gold price is low ($S^- = $200), the value of this replicating portfolio equals 7,200($200) − $1.44 million = 0. If the price is high ($S^+ = $450), the value of the synthetic license equals 7,200($450) − $1.44 million = $1.8 million. These are exactly the cash flow consequences of owning the actual mine license.

Since the actual license and the replicating portfolio (synthetic license) have the same future payoff in each gold price state, the value of the license today must be the cost of constructing this replicating portfolio. Equation 3.14 estimates the value of the license using the position in gold ($N = 7,200$) multiplied by the current gold price ($S_0 = $300) and the present value of the risk-free loan ($1.44 million / 1.04 = $1.38 million). This results in a $0.78 million value, exactly the same as found earlier when using the risk-neutral probabilities under the risk-neutral binomial valuation method:

Value of license = $N S_0 + B$ = 7,200 × $300 − $1.38 million = $0.78 million.

$$(3.14)$$

It is worth noting that in the valuation of the above gold mine we could use directly the principle of replicating future project cash flows. However, in other cases, such as in the R & D example above, an implementation problem with carrying out the replication argument of standard option pricing may arise because a correlated financial instrument may not exist. Nevertheless, the certainty-equivalent approach can still be applied for valuing the contingent claim (investment opportunity), provided there is a corresponding valuation (estimate) for the underlying asset (relative valuation). The issue is to determine the market value of the project to a firm *if it were traded* in the financial markets, which is a standard assumption in capital budgeting (e.g., see Mason and Merton 1985).

TABLE 3.3
Replication of Mine Project Value (License) with a Gold Position

	Low Price ($200)	High Price ($450)
7,200 ounces of gold	$1.44 million	$3.24 million
Loan repayment (risk-free)	($1.44 million)	($1.44 million)
Project value (license)	0	$1.8 million

3.5. An In-Depth Case Application: Valuing Offshore Oil Concessions in the Netherlands

This section describes an in-depth case application concerning the valuation of a complex capital project: the staged development of an oil field concession in the Netherlands.[21] The development of a license area in the Dutch continental shelf consists of sequential investments in test drilling, evaluation drilling, and production capacity. The program is flexible in that management may change the amount of investment as uncertainty over the value of the project is resolved over time. The investment for test and appraisal wells in the exploration phase, while typically yielding a low return, is the first link in the chain of subsequent investment decisions.

The value of developing oil reserves is estimated by reference to a financial instrument whose probabilistic behavior is close to that of the completed project. At the core lies the valuation of a producing field, based on replication using Brent crude oil futures. For the valuation of exploration investments, geological and geophysical data also provide probability distributions for the amount of reserves that might be found in different "block types." The valuation results based on these data reveals the relative attractiveness of exploration investments in uncertain blocks, as well as the influence of quantity and price uncertainty on the value of exploration licenses.

The section is organized as follows: section 3.5.1 discusses the various stages in offshore development on the Dutch continental shelf and the government's percentage of total revenues. Section 3.5.2 presents the valuation model based on a dynamic replication strategy using oil futures and the valuation results using different geological distributions. Section 3.5.3 provides gained insights and concluding remarks.

3.5.1. Stages of Offshore Petroleum Development on the Dutch Continental Shelf

For companies willing to develop reserves, there are two stages at which state licenses are required. The first stage requires an exploration license. In the exploration stage, initial geological studies and geophysical surveys identify the prospects within a block. Test and appraisal drillings are done in order to prove economically exploitable reserves. If these tests are successful, a production stage follows. A production license is then required for development of the field and the extraction of hydrocarbons.

---

[21]This section is based on Smit 1997.

The Exploration Phase

The decision to start the exploration phase is determined by the probability of finding exploitable reserves, by oil price levels, by technical capabilities, and by investment outlays. In this phase, management must decide if the hydrocarbon expectations of the prospects justify investment by means of exploration wells and possibly subsequent appraisal wells. Each well requires an investment on the order of $10 million.

The exploration license conveys an exclusive right to explore the block, and carries a maximum maturity of ten years. In rounds of exploration license applications, firms compete with each other by offering different proposals for exploitation. On the basis of seismic tests and drilling commitments, an exploration license is granted. Management must decide within six years whether to apply for a development license, or return 50% of the block (of about 400 km^2) to the state.

The Production Phase

Once economically exploitable reserves are proven, a company is entitled to request a production license or concession, and start building production capacity. Production licenses are granted for a period of 40 years. Normally, it takes several years to build capacity before starting production, requiring investments in drilling production wells and installing production, storage, and transport facilities. Depending on the existing infrastructure, additional investments may also be required for offshore facilities, such as pipelines and storage, pumping, and tanker-loading facilities. As this stage requires the largest capital expenditures, this is where option value is most important. Management must determine whether and when it is optimal to invest in production facilities, given the quantity of reserves and the uncertainty of oil prices.

On average, the state captures 50% to 80% of the total revenues of a producing field. The state's receipts consist mainly of

1. *Royalties.* These are computed according to a percentage of the revenues from oil and gas produced under the license.
2. *State participation.* An arrangement exists in which the state and the oil companies are jointly involved in the recovery and sale of oil and natural gas. For the Dutch government, Energy Control Netherlands (EBN) is entitled to take a 50% participation in the exploitation of oil and gas discoveries. As compensation, EBN will refund 50% (the participation share) of exploration costs and investments incurred in the past.

3. *State profit share.* In addition to the state participation, there is a state profit share. To support exploitation of marginal reserves, fields with low operating costs per barrel are taxed more heavily than fields with high operating costs per barrel.

4. *Dutch corporate income tax* (at a rate of 35%).

At the production phase of the investment program, uncertainty regarding the quantity of reserves is resolved and the production profile for the field's useful life is determined.

Nested Options and Resolved Uncertainty

The sequence of project stages can be viewed as a set of nested call options. The various contingent decisions are illustrated in the decision tree shown in figure 3.16. Management has the following contingent decisions (□) or options:

The option to start test drilling. Geological and geophysical studies help to identify prospective locations for drilling. Based on these prospects, management can apply for an exploration license and start test drilling.

The option to invest in appraisal wells. If oil is found during test drilling, further drilling can ascertain whether the reserves are large enough and hence suitable for commercial production.

The option to invest in development. Following the exploration phase and having determined the amount of exploitable reserves in a field, the firm has to decide whether to exploit the field and start development, or abandon operations.

The abandonment option. At the end of the project's life, management must incur certain abandonment costs. Total expenses for dismantling may require more than $18 million. However, management has the option of shutting down production early to avoid incurring additional fixed costs. There is no option value to temporarily shut down (mothballing) in the North Sea, since there is very rapid deterioration of pipelines and facilities. Final abandonment of production will take place when the value to continue (and abandon later) falls below the value of immediate abandonment.

At the same time, different types of uncertainty or risk are resolved in different stages (O in figure 3.16).

Uncertainty in the quantity of reserves. Test drilling for exploration wells maximizes information on the geological section and helps re-

FIGURE 3.16 DECISION TREE FOR THE OFFSHORE OIL DEVELOPMENT
PROJECT

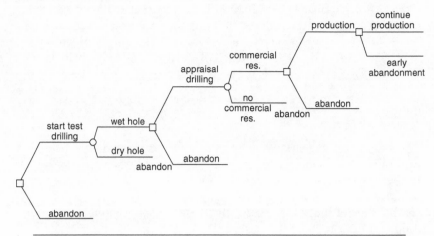

Note: Management has the following contingent decisions (□) or options: The option to start test drilling, to invest in appraisal wells, to invest in development, and to abandon. At the same time, price and quantity uncertainty (○) evolves over the life of the project.

solve the uncertainty with respect to the presence of hydrocarbons. Evaluation drilling by means of additional appraisal wells can ascertain the size of the accumulation of reserves in the well.

Uncertainty in oil prices. After the uncertainty of the quantity of reserves is (partly) resolved, the risk of the project is dominated by fluctuations in oil prices. The quantity of reserves found in combination with the range of future oil prices determines whether the field is suitable for commercial exploitation.

The uncertainty or risk of the project evolves over the life of the project, changing after each branch. The initial decision to invest in test drillings can be reached by first looking at the future consequences. Naturally, better-informed decisions can be made after uncertainty is resolved over time. For example, the decision to invest in production facilities is contingent on the quantity of reserves found during the exploration phase and the oil price at that time. The idea is to begin with each potential quantity of reserves and oil prices at the terminal nodes in the decision tree, and determine the optimal decision to make at each of these points working backward. We start solving at the right side of a more complex and detailed tree, valuing a producing field, and then work backward in time to value the exploration phase.

3.5.2. Valuation Based on Replication in Financial Markets

This section discusses the valuation principle in the context of exploration investments. At its core is the valuation of a producing field, based on replication using Brent crude oil futures. The values of producing fields with different reserves and a geological probability distribution of the potential reserves provide the basis for the exploration investment decisions.

Valuing a Producing Field

The real-options valuation of a producing field is based on formulating a portfolio in the financial markets with the same risk characteristics as the project.[22] Consider the position of an oil company that owns a producing field, which is long in oil. The company can offset this position and realize the value of the field immediately by selling short an oil futures portfolio that matches the field's production over time.

Estimating Brent Crude Futures Prices

At the International Petroleum Exchange (IPE) in London (and other such futures markets) Brent crude oil futures trade with expiration dates up to six months only. To value the field, we therefore use "hypothetical long-term futures" to offset the long-term position of the field. What would the price of these long-term futures contracts be if they were to be traded? In arbitrage-free markets, the futures price would equal the current spot price of Brent crude oil plus the interest accrued until maturity of the contract.[23]

Actually, the price of the hypothetical oil futures contract cannot be as exact. Traders have additional storage costs or production benefits of physically holding oil, compared to holding a futures contract. For example, to avoid shortages in various industries, oil inventories can conve-

---

[22]As noted, firms create value by investing in those projects for which the market value of cash inflows exceeds the required investment outlay. Therefore, the process of real-asset valuation attempts to determine what a project would be worth if it were to be traded in the financial markets.

[23]Suppose that this relation does not hold and, for example, the price of an oil futures contract with a 10-year maturity is higher. If this happens, a "cash-and-carry" arbitrage opportunity is available if traders short this futures contract and simultaneously buy the Brent crude. Ten years later, the oil is delivered to cover the short position in the long-term futures contract for more than the current spot price and 10 years of accrued interest. Hence, traders would not be willing to serve this "free lunch" for the company by selling this overpriced futures contract. Likewise, the corporation would not be willing to sell the futures contract for a lower price.

niently be held for long periods. The benefits and costs of having a physical inventory of oil instead of a futures contract are referred to as the "convenience yield" in the futures market. The cash-and-carry relationship of equation 3.15 gives the hypothetical futures price from the available Brent crude spot price, increased at the risk-free rate of interest less an (estimated) convenience yield. In this relationship, the hypothetical futures prices, F, cannot be exceedingly high relative to the spot price, S.

$$F_t = S_t(1 + r - \delta_t)^{T-t}. \tag{3.15}$$

Inverting this relationship gives

$$\delta_t = (1 + r) - {}^{(T-t)}\sqrt{\left(\frac{F_t}{S_t}\right)}, \tag{3.16}$$

where δ_t is the convenience yield, $T-t$ is the time to maturity of the futures contract, and r is the risk-free interest rate.

To estimate the long-term futures price, F_t, we need an estimate of the convenience yield. The current implied convenience yield can be estimated by inverting the relationship between three-month Brent crude futures and the current spot price given by equation 3.16. Figure 3.17 shows the time series (monthly data) for implied convenience yields estimated in this fashion for a moving window from January 1991 to December 1993. The short-term (three-month) convenience yield is shown on a yearly basis. The convenience yield is not deterministic, and so it is hard to estimate. In an extreme case, the futures price can be so far below "full carry" that the spot price can exceed the futures price. Then the market is in backwardation, expressing the high demand for immediate

FIGURE 3.17 THE CONVENIENCE YIELD δ (IN %) OF THREE-MONTH BRENT CRUDE FUTURES FROM JANUARY 1, 1991 TO DECEMBER 1, 1993

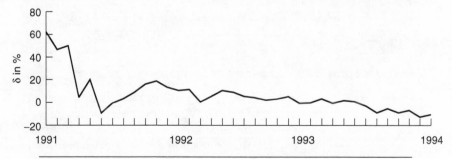

Note: The time series (monthly data) for implied convenience yield was estimated for a moving window. The short-term (three-month) convenience yield is expressed on a yearly basis.

oil (as, for example, in January 1991 at the end of the Gulf War). The average convenience yield in this period was 7%. For simplicity, the long-term futures prices (up to 20 years) can be estimated using a constant 7% long-term convenience yield and a 7% long-term interest rate. The oil price, S_0 (as of March 4, 1994) was $14 per barrel.

Estimating the Volatility in Oil Prices

Estimating oil price volatility is essential to determine the flexibility value of an operating field. After uncertainty in quantity is resolved in the exploration phase, uncertainty regarding the operating field is dominated by oil price volatility. How would one make an estimate of oil price volatility for the next 20 years of the field's development? In principle, there are two methods: One prospective method might be based on calculating the implied volatility resulting from the market prices of call options on Brent crude oil futures traded on the International Petroleum Exchange. Unfortunately, long-term options contracts are not traded, so the method is not applicable. A second method is to calculate the standard deviation from the time series of spot oil prices and use this historical standard deviation as an estimate for the volatility of Brent crude futures prices. Figure 3.18 illustrates the weekly Brent crude oil price per barrel (in dollars) from February 19, 1988 to January 7, 1994. During this period, the increase in prices was a result of the uncertain market supply of crude oil during the Gulf War.

Table 3.4 presents the yearly standard deviation of Brent crude oil returns estimated in different sample periods using weekly data. The standard deviation of the different time series varies from 41.17% in 1988 to 23.34% in 1993. To allow for this estimation variability and its influence on the value of the flexible investment program, we later perform a sensitivity analysis on volatility. In the valuation that follows, the base-case standard deviation is set at 22%, based on the low volatility of the time series in 1992 and 1993. To incorporate sensitivity to this parameter, the field is valued using 15% and 30% standard deviations.

Reserve Valuation with Continuous Production

Consider first the valuation of a hypothetical producing field without taking into consideration any of the options described earlier. At this phase of the investment program, uncertainty regarding the quantity of reserves has been resolved and the production profile is expected to follow a specified pattern over the field's useful life. For this producing field, the oil price dynamics result in a closely related dynamic movement of the operating cash inflow.

FIGURE 3.18 BRENT CRUDE OIL PRICE IN US$ PER BARREL

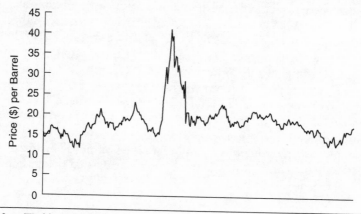

Note: Weekly Brent crude oil price FOB in U.S.$ per barrel from February 19, 1988 to January 7, 1994. During this period, the increase in price is a result of the uncertain market supply of crude oil during the Gulf War.

TABLE 3.4
Yearly Standard Deviation of Oil Returns

Year	SD
1988	41.17%
1989	26.56%
1990	27.00%
1991	39.41%
1992	17.38%
1993	23.34%
Over total period (including Gulf War)	41.40%
Over total period (excluding Gulf War)	32.11%

Note: Numbers show the yearly standard deviation of Brent crude oil returns estimated in different sample periods using weekly data. The standard deviations of the different time series vary from 41.17% in 1988 to 17.38% in 1992 and 23.34% in 1993. To allow for this estimation variability and its influence on the value of the flexible investment program, we perform a sensitivity analysis on volatility.

Future oil prices and the linked gas prices are assumed to follow a lognormal process, which is modeled in discrete time by a multiplicative binomial process (see Cox, Ross, and Rubinstein 1979). In each subperiod of one year, prices may increase by a multiplicative up factor u, or decline by a down factor d. A yearly base-case standard deviation in returns of 22% per year implies a 25% increase ($u = 1.25$) or a 20% decline ($d = 0.80$) per year in spot and future prices. Equations 3.17, 3.18, and 3.19 are used to estimate the series of future oil prices over the 324-year life of the entire project (exploration and production phase). In the following valuation process, the risk-neutral probability, p, is based on a dynamic replication strategy using futures in Brent crude oil partly financed with a risk-free loan. This risk-neutral probability is adjusted for the convenience yield, δ, as shown below.

$$u = e^{\sigma}, d = \frac{1}{u}. \tag{3.17}$$

$$uS_t = S_{t+1}^+. \tag{3.18}$$

$$dS_t = S_{t+1}^-. \tag{3.19}$$

$$p = \frac{(1 + r - \delta)S_t - S_{t+1}^-}{S_{t+1}^+ - S_{t+1}^-}, \tag{3.20}$$

where p is the risk-neutral probability and r is the risk-free interest rate.

Assuming a fixed production profile, the uncertainty of the yearly cash flows of the field is driven by the prices, not the quantity produced, of Brent crude oil. For each state (potential) oil price, S, the net operating cash inflow is estimated from the reserves produced yearly, Q_t, times the current spot price, S_t, minus the operating costs, the state participation, royalties, profit share, and corporate taxes.

In this fashion, an oil-price-related movement results in a series of potential operating cash flows. The reserve valuation procedure for the operating field works recursively, starting at the terminal nodes of the tree and working backward in time to the beginning of the production phase. In the final production period (at $t = 32$), the state project value equals the operating cash flow CF_s. For each state oil price S, equation 3.21 is used to sum the state project cash inflows when stepping backward in time.

$$V_t = CF_t + \frac{pV_{t+1}^+ + (1 - p)V_{t+1}^-}{1 + r}, \tag{3.21}$$

where V is the project value under continuous production.

The Option to Abandon Operations Early

We now consider the hypothetical producing field with an additional twist. At the end of the economic life of the project, management is required to pay for dismantling the platform and other production facilities. Total expenses for restoring the environment may require $18 million.[24] Furthermore, management has the option of shutting down production early if the remaining operating value becomes negative and exceeds the abandonment costs. This flexibility is particularly valuable for small undeveloped reserves and during periods of low oil prices.

The basis for the valuation of this field is the binomial valuation tree resulting from the recursive valuation procedure for the operating field without any of the options. Equation 3.22 subtracts the costs at the end of the project's life for restoring the environment. When stepping back again in the tree using equation 3.23, the adjusted state project value, V^*, equals the maximum of the operating value V and the nonoperating value from immediate abandonment (equal to the breakdown costs A, with $A < 0$).

At the end of the
life of the well:
$$V_T^* = A \quad \text{for} \quad Q_T = 0. \tag{3.22}$$

Early
abandonment:
$$V^* = \text{Max}\left[A, \frac{pV^+ + (1-p)V^-}{1+r} \right] \text{for} \quad Q_t > 0. \tag{3.23}$$

V^* = value of the reserves including the option to abandon early, and A = abandonment costs (assumed to be 15% of the investment outlay in production facilities).

The Option to Develop

Consider now the valuation of a similar field in an earlier phase. The field is still undeveloped, and management must decide if and when to invest millions of dollars to bring it into production. To commence production, the firm must invest in the installation of offshore platforms, including pipelines and storage, pumping, and tanker-loading facilities. In this case, EBN and the company must spend $120 million for small reserves while investing $130 million for a higher production field ($Q > 60$ million barrels). Since this decision stage requires the largest outlay, the default option value is very important. When is it optimal (if at all) to invest in production

[24] A tax relief has already been granted by means of deduction.

facilities, given the quantity of reserves, in light of the uncertainty in oil prices?

An undeveloped field in this stage can be viewed as similar to a call option. The underlying asset is the value of a completed, operating field (including the option to abandon). In equation 3.24, the present value of the investment outlay in production facilities, I, is equivalent to the exercise price. If in time the operating field value exceeds the investment outlay, management would invest and the undeveloped net field value would equal $NPV^* = V^* - I$. However, due to uncertainty in oil prices, the NPV may turn out to be negative. In this case, however, management may decide not to invest, and the net value would be zero.

Besides the wait-and-see advantage, deferment has certain disadvantages. For example, management would receive the net operating cash inflow with delay. Again, the question is, What would this call option on the Brent crude futures position be worth if it were traded in the financial markets? The investment opportunity value, NPV^*, equals

$$NPV^* = \text{Max}\left[V^* - I, \frac{p \times NPV^+ + (1 - p)NPV^-}{1 + r}, 0 \right], \qquad (3.24)$$

where NPV^* = net present value including the value of flexibility, and I = investment outlay for development.

Table 3.5 illustrates the valuation results for 10 undeveloped fields, ranging from proven reserves of 10 million barrels to an undeveloped field of 100 million barrels. In particular for small (low-NPV^*) fields the option characteristics of development and abandonment are important. Because of these option characteristics, the greater the volatility of oil prices, the larger the value of the oil reserves.

Valuing Exploration Drillings

Next consider the valuations that take place in the exploration phase. During the exploration phase, the geological distribution of the reserve quantity is updated twice: test drillings indicate the presence of reserves, while appraisal drillings provide additional information about the quantity of reserves. The value of an appraisal drilling is made only after a strike. Figure 3.19 presents an example of the two-step valuation procedure for a block with a large probability of finding a small quantity of reserves. Starting from the values of the producing fields shown on the right, the value of appraisal drilling is calculated by using the quantity distribution conditional on a strike. The procedure continues by working backward to the value of exploration drilling, using the probability of a strike.

TABLE 3.5

Reserve Valuation (NPV*) at Different Quantities of Proven Reserves (in $millions)

	10	20	30	40	50
σ = 15%	0.000	1.261	7.973	18.326	25.458
σ = 22%	0.151	2.595	10.762	19.653	27.149
σ = 30%	0.476	4.406	14.183	23.438	29.460

	60	70	80	90	100
σ = 15%	34.984	40.664	46.690	55.847	68.972
σ = 22%	36.630	42.239	48.156	57.270	70.276
σ = 30%	39.557	45.336	51.740	61.404	74.545

Note: Reserve valuation results for 10 undeveloped fields, ranging from proven reserves of 10 million barrels to an undeveloped field of 100 million barrels, at various volatility levels. The investment outlay for development is estimated at $120 million for $Q \leq 60$ million barrels and at $130 million for $Q > 60$ million barrels. The costs for dismantling facilities are assumed to be 15% of the investment outlay. The long-term futures prices are estimated using a constant 7% long-term convenience yield and a 7% long-term riskless interest rate. The oil price as of March 4, 1994, was $14 per barrel.

First consider the valuation of an undeveloped field where the firm has just proven the existence of oil and gas in the license area. For exploration drillings, production facilities could be leased from specialized drilling contractors (e.g., Schlumberger) at some daily rate. Geological expectations must justify a further investment of $10 million in appraisal wells in order to estimate the quantities more exactly.

The uncertainty regarding the quantity of oil or gas reserves is unrelated to the overall economy, and is therefore nonsystematic. Because this uncertainty can be fully diversified, we can estimate the value of an undeveloped field discounting at the risk-free rate while using the actual probabilities of the distribution to form value expectations. In order to estimate the value of a new well as in equation 3.25, the quantities of reserves and the corresponding values of the producing fields, including any options, shown in table 3.5, represent the potential values at the end of the exploration phase. First, these (producing and nonproducing) conditional NPV*s are multiplied by the actual probability of finding the corresponding quantity, conditional on exploration drilling resulting in a strike. Second, the expected value is discounted back for two years of

FIGURE 3.19 DECISION TREE FOR A "SURE SMALL QUANTITY" TYPE BLOCK

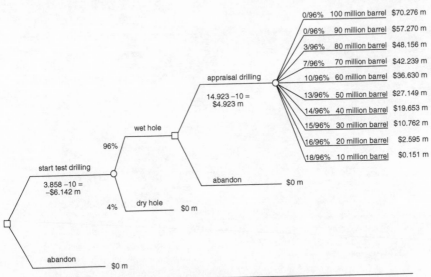

Note: This figure summarizes the valuations that take place in the exploration phase. Starting from the values of the producing fields shown on the right, the value of appraisal drilling is calculated by using the quantity distribution conditional on a strike. The procedure continues by working backward to the value of exploration drilling, using the probability of a strike. Even though the probability of finding oil and gas reserves for this type of block is high, it is not attractive to commence exploration drilling.

appraisal drilling using the risk-free interest rate. Finally, the expected value of the well is determined by summing these expected discounted values:

$$V^{strike} = \frac{\sum \left\{ P(Q) = x \,|\, Q > 0 \right\} NPV_Q^*}{(1 + r)^{T-t}}, \tag{3.25}$$

where $\{P(Q) = x \mid Q > 0\}$ is the probability conditional on quantity Q after a strike; V^{strike} is the value of the exploration program after a strike; and $T - t$ is the two-year time lag between drilling appraisal wells and production.

For example, in table 3.5, the estimated value of a 40-million-barrel well is equal to $19.653 million (Quantity = 40, σ = 22%). In figure 3.19, the probability of finding a quantity of 40 million barrels is 14% and the probability of finding oil is 96%, so the conditional probability of finding 40 million barrels (after a strike) equals 14% / 96%. The expected value of finding this quantity is 0.14 / 0.96 (19.653) = $2.866 million, and the present value of a 40-million-barrel well equals $2.866

million $/ (1.07)^2 = \$2.503$ million.[25] The expected value of the field after a strike is calculated by summing the expectation of the present values of these wells over the total geological distribution, taking discrete steps of 10 million barrels (e.g., 10, 20 . . . 100). This results in a \$14.923 million value for this block. The appraisal drillings require an investment of \$10 million; hence management would continue to drill for appraisal wells (\$14.923 million − \$10 million > 0).

Finally, in the second step of the valuation procedure, equation 3.26 helps estimate the value of the option to start exploration drilling:

$$V^{exp} = \frac{P(Q = 0) \times 0 + P(Q > 0)\left\{ \text{Max}(V^{Strike} - I^{ap}, 0) \right\}}{(1 + r)^{T-t}}, \qquad (3.26)$$

where V^{exp} = value of the exploration phase; I^{ap} = investment outlay of \$10 million for appraisal drilling; $T - t$ = three-year time lag between exploration drilling and drilling appraisal wells.

The NPV after the required appraisal drillings equals \$14.923 million −10 million = \$4.923 million; the cumulative probability of finding oil is 96%. Therefore, the option value to invest in exploration drillings equals $0.96(14.923 - 10) / 1.07^3 = \$3.858$ million. Estimating the outlay for exploration drillings at \$10 million, the NPV of exploration drillings turns out to be negative: \$3.858 million − \$10 million = −\$6.142 million. Even though the probability of finding oil is high, it is not attractive to start exploration drilling in this "Sure Small Quantity" type block.

Expectation Curves

Extensive geological and geographical research has been conducted in the North Sea. To gain an insight into potential reserves and to find the best locations for drilling, the Rijks Geologische Dienst (RGD), EBN, and the large oil corporations map the soil structure of the blocks. How does geological uncertainty influence the value of a block? For this case, figure 3.20 describes the cumulative distribution of reserves for three hypothetical block types (expectation curves obtained from Shell 1988), that are representative of blocks in the continental shelf. The vertical axis represents the cumulative probability of finding the corresponding quantity of reserves. For example, the "Either Dry Well or Strike" block has a 55% cumulative probability of finding 40 million barrels or more. This cumulative probability is calculated by starting at a quantity of 100 million barrels and summing the probabilities, taking discrete steps of 10 million

---

[25]See also panel A, table 3.5, at Quantity = 40, $\sigma = 22\%$.

FIGURE 3.20 CUMULATIVE DISTRIBUTION OF OIL RESERVES BY BLOCK
TYPE

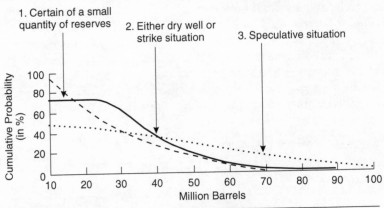

Note: Expectation curves for three hypothetical block types that are representative
of blocks in the Dutch continental shelf. The vertical axis represents the cumulative
probability of finding the corresponding quantity of reserves for each block type. All
three distributions have the same expected quantity of reserves (equal to 35 million
barrels).

barrels. All three distributions have the same expected quantity of reserves (equal to 35 million barrels).

1. The first block has a large probability of finding an exploitable
quantity of reserves (96% cumulative probability). For example,
this might be the case if the block is adjacent to blocks with small
proven reserves.
2. The second type of block has a 25% chance of finding a dry well
or a 75% cumulative probability of finding a commercially exploitable quantity of reserves.
3. The "speculative" third block has a 56% cumulative probability
of finding oil or gas. If a well is found, there still remains great uncertainty regarding the quantity of the reserves.

Table 3.6 provides the expected values of the other blocks using the
values of the completed field shown in table 3.6, for σ = 15%, 22%, and
30%. Panel A in table 3.6 refers to the "Sure Small Quantity" type block,
panel B considers the "Either Dry Well or Strike" type block, and panel
C considers the "Speculative" block.

It can be confirmed from table 3.6 that the volatility of oil prices has a
positive influence on the value of the investment program. But more interesting is that exploration investments are more valuable in a "Speculative" block than in a "Sure Small Quantity" block. The base-case NPV

of the "Sure Small Quantity" block equals −$6.124 million. The NPV of the "Either Dry Well or Strike" type block equals −$3.001 million, and the NPV of the "Speculative" type block equals $0.225 million. The exploration investments in the speculative block are more effective in resolving the uncertainty than the exploration investments in a certainty situation because there is more risk involved. Therefore, management's flexibility to change the implicit investment scenario will be more valuable for the more uncertain blocks.

Even if current oil prices were to rise substantially (to $20), the speculative block would continue to offer the highest NPV ($12.635 million). However, there is a nonlinearity in the value of blocks with respect to oil price changes. At higher oil prices, intermediate reserves and eventually small reserves become commercially attractive for development. As a result, the "Sure Small Quantity" block ($6.351 million) and the "Either Dry Well or Strike" block ($10.290 million) become relatively more valuable as oil prices rise.

3.5.3. Main Insights

This case application illustrates a stage-by-stage valuation of the development of an oil field concession block on the Dutch continental shelf. The experience gained from this actual implementation provides various insights regarding (1) the advantages and limitations of option valuation, (2) the factors that affect offshore decisions, and (3) adopting and implementing option valuation in practice.

Advantages and Limitations of Option Valuation

For the practical application of real-options valuation, it is important to point out both its advantages and limitations. The following points offer some insights:

1. Implementing real-options valuation and estimating the boundaries of some input parameters is a potential limitation in evaluating the worth of a concession. Hard-to-estimate parameters, such as volatility in oil prices, sensitize the valuation results. Complicating the model with additional variables does not necessarily result in a better valuation or more accurate answers.[26] With higher complexity, much of the intuition of viewing projects as real options may be sacrificed. For this kind of application, more complex and

---

26. For example, the above analysis does not take into account currency exchange risk, tax carrybacks, and other such effects.

TABLE 3.6
Valuation Results for Oil Field on Dutch Continental Shelf (in $millions)

Quantity (in million barrels)	Probability	σ = 15%	σ = 22%	σ = 30%
Panel A. The "Sure Small Quantity" Block				
100	0%	0.000	0.000	0.000
90	0%	0.000	0.000	0.000
80	3%	1.274	1.314	1.412
70	7%	2.590	2.690	2.887
60	10%	3.183	3.333	3.599
50	13%	3.011	3.211	3.484
40	14%	2.334	2.503	2.985
30	15%	1.088	1.469	1.936
20	16%	0.184	0.378	0.641
10	18%	0.000	0.025	0.078
Cumulative probability of finding reserves	96% Present value of the well at $t = 3$	13.664	14.923	17.024
Option to invest in exploration at $t = 0$		2.872	3.858	5.504
NPV of the exploration phase at $t = 0$		−7.128	−6.142	−4.496
Panel B. The "Either Dry Well or Strike" Block				
100	0%	0.000	0.000	0.000
90	2%	1.301	1.334	1.430
80	4%	2.175	2.243	2.410
70	5%	2.368	2.460	2.640
60	11%	4.482	4.692	5.067
50	15%	4.447	4.743	5.146
40	18%	3.842	4.120	4.913
30	13%	1.207	1.629	2.147
20	7%	0.103	0.212	0.359
10	0%	0.000	0.000	0.000
Cumulative probability of finding reserves	75% Present value of the well at $t = 3$	19.924	21.432	24.114
Option to invest in exploration at $t = 0$		6.076	6.999	8.641
NPV of the exploration phase at $t = 0$		−3.924	−3.001	−1.359

Table 3.6 continued

Quantity (in million barrels)	Probability	σ = 15%	σ = 22%	σ = 30%
Panel C. The "Speculative" Block				
100	5%	5.379	5.481	5.813
90	6%	5.226	5.359	5.746
80	8%	5.826	6.009	6.456
70	8%	5.074	5.271	5.657
60	8%	4.365	4.571	4.936
50	8%	3.177	3.388	3.676
40	5%	1.429	1.533	1.828
30	4%	0.497	0.671	0.885
20	2%	0.039	0.081	0.137
10	2%	0.000	0.005	0.015
Cumulative probability of finding reserves	56% Present value of the well at $t = 3$	31.013	32.367	35.149
Option to invest in exploration at $t = 0$		9.605	10.225	11.496
NPV of the exploration phase at $t = 0$		−0.395	0.225	1.496

Note: The expected value of the exploration investment is calculated by taking the expectation of values of a completed field (shown in table 3.5) over the total geological expectation curve (shown in figure 3.20). The valuation results show that exploration investments for speculative blocks are more effective in resolving the inherent uncertainty, and hence are more valuable, than for otherwise similar low-uncertainty blocks.

technical models do not necessarily add accuracy to the valuation results, and may lose other important features, such as accessibility of the methodology, tractability of the model, economic insights, and intuition.

2. Other staged investments, such as R & D or a venture capital investment,[27] can be valued using a similar stage-by-stage valuation. In this particular implementation, we use the concept of replicating future cash flows. The estimated value of a producing field is directly based on its relationship with oil futures. However, an implementation problem arises due to the lack of observable quotes for long-dated forward prices on futures markets. We thus impute reasonable approximations for forward prices. An insufficient number of observable quotes of a related financial instrument is a general

[27]See, for instance, Fried and Hisrich (1994) Lerner 1994 for stages in venture capital investment decision-making.

implementation weakness (e.g., in the valuation of R & D programs). However, the methodology can still be applied as long as there is a corresponding reliable valuation for the underlying asset.

3. A major advantage of real-options analysis over NPV analysis is that it highlights an appropriate procedure for analyzing geological and oil price uncertainty and management's ability to react to it. In the analysis of the production phase, EBN uses a good, fair, and bad scenario analysis. Each of these scenarios assumes a managerial commitment to a certain investment plan. At first sight, the observed hurdle rate of this scenario (20%) seems exceedingly high. However, this can be explained by viewing the production phase as an option. Using this high hurdle rate, EBN requires a premium over the standard NPV and implicitly defers the project in periods of low prices. Option valuation represents a superior tool for capturing managerial flexibility.

Factors That Affect Offshore Investment Decisions

The option pricing methodology, when properly applied, can be useful in the project evaluation process.[28] Quantitative techniques complement the strategic thinking process; they do not replace it. In order to believe a project's positive NPV, management has to think *why* a particular block is more valuable for this company than for its competitors. Typical value drivers in the offshore development include whether the investment decision exploits an inherently attractive opportunity that is due to a lucky strike, (exclusive) geological information, or synergistic effects with other prospects; low investment cost because the block is near a company-owned pipeline or production facility; and finally, good timing due to high oil prices.

Thinking in terms of options impacts strategic planning in this particular area. Real-options implementation illustrates that geological and oil price uncertainty is important in the valuation of the exploration phase. The valuation results show that exploration investments in speculative blocks are more effective in resolving the inherent uncertainty, and hence are more valuable, than otherwise similar low-uncertainty blocks. This

[28]No methodology can capture all the factors that affect the investment decisions, but for many investment selection criteria in corporate finance the problem is that they are too narrow. A firm's strategy arguably involves more than just making money for its shareholders: firms also have a public responsibility in terms of employment, the environment, and so on. For example, there are large undeveloped fields that are not exploited because of the potential ecological damage to an important natural area. It should be clear that value creation is a healthy goal and a proper criterion from the financial management perspective, but other disciplines may also impose their own limitations.

result, which may seem surprising, hinges on the fact that if the exploration phase fails, the enormous follow-on investment for the production phase need not be made. In other words, if the block turns out dry, then only the relatively small exploration investment is lost. On the other hand, more can be gained in a speculative block if it has exceptionally high values in the production phase.

The observed strategies of large oil companies support the idea that exploration investments are more effective, and hence more valuable, in more uncertain areas. The reserves on the Dutch continental shelf are relatively small, although their magnitude is fairly certain due to extensive seismic and geological research. Recently, large exploration firms have decided to leave the Dutch continental shelf and explore unknown and uncertain areas in the Soviet Union and China, where there are believed to be opportunities for larger discoveries. However, if oil prices were to rise substantially the smaller and more certain reserves at the Dutch continental shelf would become commercial to develop.

Valuation and Presentation

Complicated methods are not easily adopted in practice. Complex investment problems have to be simplified to make the analysis accessible for management. To make things easier to understand, we used a discrete-time binomial valuation process. Working backward from the production phase, decision makers can trace the values and intuit from the model the relative magnitude of values in the different project phases. In addition, the discrete-time calculations also have an advantage in the tractability of the model to changes in taxes, geological distributions, and other parameters.

In order to present this approach as a practical aid to corporate planners, it is useful to develop appropriate user-friendly software with simulation capabilities.[29] Given the diversity of investment problems inherent in the blocks, spreadsheets can only provide a prototype for evaluating alternatives. Practitioners will need to adjust the spreadsheets to the particular geological expectations and requirements of their own prospects.

Given the increasing attention paid by corporations to option-pricing application and implementation issues, the practical use of real-options analysis looks promising. Real-options concepts and tools have been applied in internal (pilot) studies by leading firms in the oil industry, such as British Petroleum, Shell, and Amoco Netherlands Petroleum Company.

---

[29]For this case application a Microsoft Excel spreadsheet was used. The total workbook (of 320 kb) consisted of three worksheets; an input sheet, a graphic sheet, and a calculation sheet (of FD columns by 170 rows).

Various other industries have analogous sequential investment programs. Real-options applications have been used at Merck (pharmaceuticals) and have been under consideration at Philips (consumer electronics) for evaluating product development programs, among others.

3.6. Summary and Conclusions

This chapter provided an overview of corporate real options and the basic valuation principles involved in real-options analysis. We discussed commonly recurring options, such as the option to defer, the option to expand or contract capacity, the option to abandon, the option to switch inputs or outputs, and the option to temporarily shut down. We have also noted that firms have nested options embedded in their financial structure.

Extended numerical examples illustrated the valuation of a license on an R & D program and a mine concession. We pointed out the shortcomings of traditional NPV when management has flexibility to adapt its future contingent decisions based on the evolution of major uncertainties. We have seen that risk-neutral option valuation or a certainty-equivalent-based approach is superior to traditional DCF or decision tree analysis. It combines the use of decision nodes (rather than passive event nodes) to model flexibility choices while being more careful to price risk correctly in each branch (state) of the tree as the project's risk profile changes. When implementing this real-options valuation in natural resources, management can make use of the concept of replicating future cash flows, given that the value of a producing oil field can be linked directly to oil futures. Lack of a correlated financial instrument (e.g., futures or forward contracts) may pose a practical implementation problem in many cases, but the basic methodology can still be applied provided there exists a corresponding estimate for the underlying asset.

Before leaving this chapter, a word of caution is in order. Real-life projects are often more complex, and may involve a collection of interacting real options (see Trigerorgis 1993a). The valuation of flexible projects should be based on an expanded NPV criterion that captures the flexibility value of the combined portfolio of these options. There may be option interactions, in that the combined value of a collection of such real options may differ from the sum of separate or stand-alone option values. Sometimes there may be a synergistic effect, but the combined value typically is less than the sum of the parts. For instance, the option to abandon for salvage value may not add much in the presence of the option to default held by the shareholders of a leveraged firm. If the firm declares bankruptcy, most of this value will go to the bondholders. The moral of the story here is to value the package of embedded options as a combination, rather than applying ready-made tools (e.g., the Black-Scholes formula) on separate components.

Suggested Readings

Brennan, M., and E. Schwartz. "Evaluating Natural Resource Investments." *Journal of Business* 58, no. 2 (1985): 135–57.

Cox, J. C., S. A. Ross, and M. Rubinstein. "Option Pricing: A Simplified Approach." *Journal of Financial Economics* 7 (1979): 229–63.

Smit, H. T. J. "Investment Analysis of Offshore Concessions in the Netherlands." *Financial Management* 26, no. 2 (1997): 5–17.

Trigeorgis, L. *Real Options: Valuing Managerial Flexibility and Strategy in Resource Allocation.* Cambridge: MIT Press, 1996.

Appendix 3.1

Binomial Option Valuation

The Basic Valuation Idea: Option Replication and Risk Neutrality

The basic idea enabling the pricing of options is that one can construct a portfolio consisting of buying a particular number, N, of shares of the underlying asset (e.g., common stock) and borrowing against them an appropriate amount, $\$B$, at the riskless rate, that would exactly replicate the future returns of the option in any state of nature. Since the option and this equivalent portfolio (effectively, an appropriately levered position in the stock) would provide the same future returns, to avoid risk-free arbitrage profit opportunities they must sell for the same current value. Thus, we can value the option by determining the cost of constructing its equivalent replicating portfolio, that is, the cost of a *synthetic* or homemade option equivalent.

Suppose that the price of the underlying stock (currently at $V = \$100$) will move over the next period either up to $V^+ = 180$ (i.e., with a multiplicative up parameter, $u = 1.8$) or down to $V^- = 60$ (with a multiplicative down parameter, $d = 0.6$), with probabilities q and $(1 - q)$, respectively, that is,

$$
\begin{array}{c}
V \\
100
\end{array}
\begin{array}{c}
\overset{q}{\nearrow} V^+ = 180 \\[10pt]
\underset{1-q}{\searrow} V^- = 60.
\end{array}
$$

The value of the option over the period would then be contingent on the price of the underlying stock. Assuming $I = \$80$ (and $r = 0.08$),

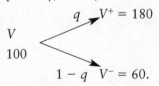

$$
\begin{array}{c}
C
\end{array}
\begin{array}{c}
\overset{q}{\nearrow}
\begin{array}{l}
C^+ = \text{Max}(V^+ - I, 0) \\
\quad = 100
\end{array} \\[14pt]
\underset{1-q}{\searrow}
\begin{array}{l}
C^- = \text{Max}(V^- - I, 0) \\
\quad = 0
\end{array}
\end{array}
$$

where C^+ and C^- are the values of the call option at the end of the period if the stock moves up or down, respectively.

Suppose now we construct a portfolio as described above, consisting of (a) buying N shares of the underlying stock at its current price, V, financed in part by (b) borrowing an amount of $B at the riskless interest rate (e.g, selling short Treasury bills), for a net out-of-pocket cost of $NS - B$. That is,

Call option $\approx$ Buy N Shares at V & Borrow B at r (3.A.1)
or $C \approx (NV - B)$.

After one period, we would need to repay the principal amount borrowed at the beginning (B) with interest, or $(1 + r)B$ for certain. The value of this portfolio over the next period will thus be

$$N V - B \quad \begin{array}{c} \xrightarrow{\quad q \quad} N\,V^+ - (1 + r)B \\[2ex] \xrightarrow{\quad 1-q \quad} N\,V^- - (1 + r)B \end{array}$$

If the portfolio is to offer the same return in each state at the end of the period as the option, then

$$\begin{array}{c} \nearrow\ N\,V^+ - (1 + r)B = C^+ \\[2ex] \searrow\ N\,V^- - (1 + r)B = C^- \end{array}$$

Solving these two equations (conditions of equal payoff) for the two unknowns, N and B, gives

$$N = (C^+ - C^-)/(V^+ - V^-) \tag{3.A.2}$$
$$= (100 - 0)/(180 - 60) = 0.83 \text{ shares;}$$

$$B = (V^- C^+ - V^+ C^-)/[(V^+ - V^-)(1 + r)] \tag{3.A.3}$$

$$= (N\,V^- - C^-)/(1 + r)$$
$$= (0.83 \times 60 - 0)/1.08 = \$46.$$

The number of shares of the underlying asset that we need to buy to replicate one option over the next period, N, is known as the option's *delta* or *hedge ratio*, and is simply obtained in the discrete case as the difference (spread) of option prices divided by the spread of stock prices. That is, we can replicate the return to the option by purchasing N (= 0.83) shares of the underlying stock at the current price, V, and borrowing the amount $B (= \$46)$ at the riskless rate, r.

When substituted back into equation 3.A.1, $C = NV - B$, equations 3.A.2 and 3.A.3 finally result in

$$C = [pC^+ + (1 - p)C^-]/(1 + r) \tag{3.A.4}$$
$$= [0.4 \times 100 + 0.6 \times 0]/1.08 = \$37,$$

where

$$p = [(1 + r)V - V^-]/(V^+ - V^-) \tag{3.A.5}$$
$$= [1.08 \times 100 - 60]/(180 - 60) = 0.4$$

is a transformed or *risk-neutral probability,* that is, the probability that would prevail in a risk-neutral world where investors are indifferent to risk.

Risk-Neutral Valuation
Intuitively, equation 3.A.1 can be rearranged into $NV - C = B$, that is, creating a portfolio consisting of (*a*) buying N shares of the underlying stock and (*b*) selling (writing) one call option would provide a certain amount of $(1 + r)B = \$50$ next period, regardless of whether the stock moves up or down:

$$N V^+ - C^+ = (1 + r)B$$
$$.83(180) - 100 = 50$$

$$N V - C = B$$
$$.56(100) - 37 = 46$$

q

$1-q$

$$N V^- - C^- = (1 + r)B$$
$$.83(60) - 0 = 50$$

Through the ability to construct such a *riskless hedge,* risk can effectively be "squeezed out" of the problem, so that investors' risk attitudes do not matter. Therefore, we can equivalently — and more conveniently — obtain the correct option value by *pretending* to be in a *risk-neutral world* where risk is irrelevant. In such a world, all assets (including stocks, options, etc.) would earn the risk-free return, and so *expected* cash flows (weighted by the risk-neutral probabilities, p) could be appropriately discounted at the risk-free rate.

Denoting by $R^+ \equiv u - 1 = V^+/V - 1$ ($= 0.80$ or 80%) the return if the stock moves up (+), and by $R^- \equiv V^-/V - 1$ ($= -0.40$ or -40%) the down ($-$) return, the risk-neutral probability, p, can be alternatively obtained from the condition that the *expected* return on the stock in a risk-neutral world must equal the riskless rate, that is,

$$pR^+ + (1 - p)R^- = r.$$

Solving for p yields

$$p = (r - R^-)/(R^+ - R^-)$$
$$= [0.08 - (-0.40)]/[0.80 - (-0.40)], \text{ or} \tag{3.A.5'}$$
$$= [(1 + r) - d]/(u - d) = (1.08 - 0.6)/(1.8 - 0.6)$$
$$= 0.4.$$

Similarly, the expected return on the option must also equal the risk-free rate in a risk-neutral world, that is,

$$[pC^+ + (1 - p)C^-]/C - 1 = r,$$

resulting in above equation 3.A.4.

A number of points are worth reviewing about the above call option valuation. It provides an exact formula for the value of the option in terms of V, I, r, and the stock's volatility (spread). With no dividends, $C > V - I$, so an American call option should not be exercised early; when dividends are introduced, early exercise may be justified, however. The motivation for the pricing of the option rests with the absence of arbitrage profit opportunities, a strong economic condition.

The actual probability of up and down movements, q, does not appear in the valuation formula. Moreover, the value of the option does not depend on investors' attitudes toward risk or on the characteristics of other assets — it is priced only relative to the underlying asset, V.

The value of the option can be equivalently obtained in a risk-neutral world (since it is independent of risk preferences). Actually, p is the value probability q would have in equilibrium if investors were risk neutral. As the above valuation formula confirms, in such a risk-neutral world — where all assets are expected to earn the riskless rate of return — the current value of the option can be obtained from its expected future values (using the risk-neutral probability, p), discounted at the risk-free interest rate.

A put option can be valued similarly, except that we would need to *sell* (instead of buy) shares of the underlying stock, and *lend* (instead of borrow) at the riskless interest rate (i.e., buy government bonds), that is,

Put option ≈ *Sell N* shares at V & *Lend $B* at r.

The hedge ratio, or delta, for a put option is simply the delta of the corresponding call option minus 1, giving $0.83 - 1 = -0.17$ in the above example (with the minus sign indicating *selling*, rather than buying, 0.17 shares of the underlying stock). Applying equation 3.A.3 in the case of a similar put option where $P^- = A - V^- = 100 - 60 = 40$, the amount to lend is given by

$$B = (N\,V^- - P^-)/(1 + r)$$
$$= (-0.17 \times 60 - 40)/1.08 = -\$46.3. \qquad (3.A.6)$$

Thus, to replicate a put option, we need to sell 0.17 shares of stock at $V = \$100$ and lend (minus sign in B) $46.3 at the riskless rate (i.e., buy Treasury bills with that face value). Thus, the current value of the put option should be

$$P = N\,V - B = (-0.17)(100) - (-46.3) = \$29.6. \qquad (3.A.7)$$

The General Multiplicative Binomial Approach

The general multiplicative binomial option pricing approach was popularized by Cox, Ross, and Rubinstein (1979). It is based on the replication argument described above, except that the underlying stock price follows a multiplicative binomial process over successive periods described by

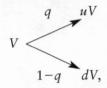

where the stock price at the beginning of a given period, V, may increase (by a multiplicative factor u) with probability q to uV or decrease with complementary probability $(1 - q)$ to dV at the end of the period. Thus u and d represent the (continuously compounded or logarithmic) rate of return if the stock moves up or down, respectively, with $d = 1/u$. (Since riskless borrowing at the rate r is also available, to avoid riskless arbitrage profit opportunities, $u > (1 + r) > d$.)

In our earlier notation, $V^+ \equiv uV$ and $V^- \equiv dV$ with $d = 1/u$, or alternatively

$$u \equiv V^+/V = 1 + R^+, \tag{3.A.8}$$

where R^+ is the up $(+)$ return, and

$$d \equiv V^-/V = 1 + R^-, \tag{3.A.8'}$$

where R^- is the down $(-)$ return.
Thus, expressions 3.A.2, 3.A.3, 3.A.4, and 3.A.5 would now become

$$N = [C^+ - C^-]/[(u - d)V], \tag{3.A.2'}$$
$$B = [dC^+ - uC^-]/[(u - d)(1 + r)], \tag{3.A.3'}$$
$$C = [pC^+ + (1 - p)C^-]/(1 + r), \tag{3.A.4'}$$

and

$$p = [(1 + r) - d]/(u - d) \tag{3.A.5'}$$
$$= (1.08 - 0.6)/(1.8 - 0.6) = 0.4.$$

This valuation procedure can be easily extended to multiple periods. If the time to expiration of the option, τ, is subdivided into n equal subintervals, each of length $h \equiv \tau/n$, and the same valuation process is repeated starting at the expiration date and working backward recursively, the general binomial pricing formula for n periods would be obtained:

$$C = \sum_{j=0}^{n} \{n!/\, j!(n - j)!\} p^j (1 - p)^{n-j} \mathrm{Max}(u^j d^{n-j} V - I, 0) / (1 + r)^n.$$

The first part, $\{n!/\, j!(n - j)!\}\, p^j\, (1 - p)^{n-j}$, is the binomial distribution formula giving the probability that the stock will take j upward jumps in n steps, each with (risk-neutral) probability p. The last part, $\mathrm{Max}(u^j d^{n-j} V - I, 0)$, gives the value of the call option with exercise cost I at expiration conditional on the stock following j ups each by $u\%$, and $n - j$ downs each by $d\%$ within n periods. The summation of all the possible (from $j = 0$ to n) option values at expiration, multiplied by the probability that each will occur, gives the expected terminal option value, which is then discounted at the riskless rate over the n periods.

If we let m be the minimum number of upward moves j over n periods necessary for the call option to be exercised or finish in the money (i.e., $u^m d^{n-m} V > I$, or by logarithmic transformation m is the smallest nonnegative integer greater than $\ln(I/Vd^n)/\ln(u/d)$), and break up the resulting term into two parts, then the binomial option-pricing formula can be more conveniently rewritten as

$$C = V\Phi[m; n, p'] - \{I/(1 + r)^n\}\, \Phi\,[m; n, p], \qquad (3.A.9)$$

where Φ is the complementary binomial distribution function (giving the probability of at least m ups out of n steps):

$$\Phi\,[m; n, p] = \sum_{j=m}^{n} \{n!/\, j!(n - j)!\}\, p^j\, (1 - p)^{n-j},$$

and

$$p' \equiv [u/(1 + r)]p,$$

with p and m as defined above.

One may initially object to this discrete period-by-period binomial valuation approach, since in reality stock prices may take on more that just two possible values at the end of a given period, while actual trading in the market takes place almost continuously and not on a period-by-period basis. However, the length of a "period" can be chosen to be arbitrarily small by successive subdivisions.

As the length of a trading period, h, is allowed to become increasingly smaller (approaching 0) for a given maturity, τ, continuous trading is effectively approximated. In the continuous-time limit, as the number of periods n approaches infinity, the multiplicative binomial process approximates the log-normal distribution or *smooth* diffusion Wiener process.

By choosing the parameters $\{u, d, \text{ and } p\}$ so that the mean and variance of the continuously compounded rate of return of the discrete binomial process are consistent in the limit with their continuous counterparts, the stock price will become log-normally distributed and the (complementary) binomial distribution function, $\Phi[.]$, will converge to the (cumulative) standard normal distribution function, $N(.)$. Specifically, by setting

$$u = \exp(\sigma\sqrt{h}),$$

$$d = 1/u, \hspace{6cm} (3.A.10)$$

$$p = \tfrac{1}{2} + \tfrac{1}{2}(\mu/\sigma)\sqrt{h},$$

where $\mu \equiv \ln r - \tfrac{1}{2}\sigma^2$, τ is the time to option expiration, n is the number of subperiods, and $h \equiv \tau/n = dt$ is the subinterval or length of a small trading period (typically expressed as a fraction of a year). Cox, Ross, and Rubinstein (1979) show that as $n \to \infty$, $\Phi[m; n, p'] \to N(x)$, so that the above binomial formula converges to the continuous-time Black-Scholes formula:

$$C = V N(x) - I(1 + r)^{-\tau} N(x - \sigma\sqrt{\tau}), \hspace{3cm} (3.A.11)$$

where $x \equiv \ln(V/I(1 + r)^{-\tau})/\sigma\sqrt{\tau} + \tfrac{1}{2}\sigma\sqrt{\tau}$.

For example, if $\tau = 3$ months $= 0.25$ years and $n = 12$ steps, a discrete multiplicative binomial process with $u = 1.1$ and weekly intervals ($h = \tau/n = 0.02$ years) would be consistent in the limit with a lognormal diffusion process with annual standard deviation, $\sigma = \ln(u)/\sqrt{h} = \ln(1.2)/\sqrt{0.02} = 0.66$, or 66%.

Chapter 4

Games and Strategic Decisions

In war the will is directed at an animate object that reacts.
— Karl Von Clausewitz, *On War*

4.1. Introduction

In 1944 mathematician John von Neumann and economist Oskar Morgenstern published their seminal book, *Theory of Games and Economic Behavior.*[1] With the development of game theory, a formal analysis of competitive interactions became possible in economics and business strategy, though its scope and influence was soon extended in fields as diverse as political science, litigation, and even evolutionary biology. For a motivating piece on game theory, its ability to accommodate win-win situations, and its practical usefulness, see box insert 4.1, "It's Only a Game — but a Very Useful One."

Firms often make investment decisions for strategic reasons. What distinguishes strategic investment decisions from other types of decisions is that these investments are made in a context where the firm must take into account the reaction of other players and its potential positive or negative effect on its own value. Firms take deliberate actions that have implications for other firms. Knowledge of a competitor's likely reaction can improve a firm's ability to pursue a better competitive strategy. Anticipation of a competitor's response is an essential element in designing a competitive strategy. See box insert 4.2 for a discussion of the usefulness of anticipating one's opponent in practice and for a discussion of various benefits of game theory in cooperating, negotiating, signaling, and so on.

This chapter provides an overview of basic principles of game theory and strategic decisions that are essential for our understanding of strategic options. Game theory can help determine what a competitor's reaction might be and what kinds of actions might trigger positive or negative competitive responses. For a more compact though comprehensive overview of game theory and its impact on daily decisions see box insert 4.3.

[1]This chapter in part uses concepts developed in Bierman and Fernandez 1998; Dixit and Nalebuff 1991; and Tirole 1990.

Box 4.1 It's Only a Game — but a Very Useful One

Managers have much to learn from game theory — provided they use it to clarify their thinking, not as a substitute for business experience.

For old-fashioned managers, business was a branch of warfare — a way of "capturing markets" and "making a killing." Today, however, the language is all about working with suppliers, building alliances, and thriving on trust and loyalty. Management theorists like to point out that there is such a thing as "win-win," and that business feuds can end up hurting both parties.

But this can be taken too far. Microsoft's success has helped Intel, but it has been hell for Apple Computer. Instead, business needs a new way of thinking that makes room for collaboration as well as competition, for mutual benefits as well as trade-offs. Enter game theory.

Stripped to its essentials, game theory is a tool for understanding how decisions affect each other. Until the theory came along, economists assumed that firms could ignore the effects of their behavior on the actions of rivals, which was fine when competition was perfect or a monopolist held sway, but was otherwise misleading. Game theorists argue that firms can learn from game players: no card player plans his strategy without thinking about how other players are planning theirs.

Economists have long used game theory to illuminate practical problems, such as what to do about global warming or about fetuses with Down's syndrome. Now business people have started to wake up to the theory's possibilities. McKinsey, the consultancy, is setting up a practice in game theory. Firms as diverse as Xerox, an office-equipment maker, Bear Stearns, an investment bank, and PepsiCo, a soft-drinks giant, are all interested.

The game theorists have already notched up some significant practical successes. The Federal Communications Commission used the theory to help design its $7 billion auction of radio spectrum for mobile phones — and hundreds of mobile-phone companies also used the theory to formulate their bids.

Source: The Economist Newspaper limited, London, June 15, 1996.

BOX 4.2 BENEFITS OF GAME THEORY: ANTICIPATING YOUR RIVAL

Anticipating your opponent: It's key to any sport or business. But unlike sports, where there's a winner and loser, you can have win-win and lose-lose situations in business. When the competition views your actions as beneficial or at least nonthreatening, it's less likely to retaliate. Conversely, seeing your competitors' actions in the same light can avert a costly price war. Visualizing and anticipating your competitor's moves are the venue of a branch of mathematics called game theory — the study of competitive interaction. Companies use it to anticipate their competitors' reactions in order to improve their own decisions.

Last March, the Federal Communications Commission completed the largest application of game theory — the $7 billion auction of wireless personal communication services.

Game theory helps firms better assess their own negotiating position. They can also learn how to change the game they're playing rather than just play the existing one.

Having game theory in your corporate "bag of tricks" can mean the difference between success and failure. "Our company only gets to bid on deals once in a generation," said Dallas Luby, executive vice president and chief marketing officer at Stamford, Conn.–based General Re Corp., a property/casualty reinsurer. "We want the best information possible."

Game theory also can help firms look beyond the traditional roles of competitors, customers and suppliers, says Barry J. Nalebuff, management professor at the Yale School of Management and author of a book on game theory, *Co-opetition* (co-authored by Adam M. Brandenburger, business strategy professor at the Harvard Business School). Too often, firms "leave out complementors." "Sometimes, what you do helps me," Nalebuff added. An example is the development of a new airplane. They are "too expensive for one firm to have/develop alone. Airlines share the development cost." It's important to note, however, that firms must avoid collusion.

Another reason game theory is catching on is that firms don't want to be at a competitive disadvantage because they failed to use the tool. At General Re, "Game theory is a significant part of senior management education," Luby said. The real benefit of game theory is finding areas of cooperation, Luby adds. It helps answer the question: "What's everybody's motivation in the game?"

Like bids in an auction (e.g., the FCC auction), the actions firms take are also interpreted by their competitors as signals. They convey what's important to the company. "Firms may give false signals" to confuse competitors, [Avinash] Dixit (a Professor at Princeton) said.

continued ...

Box 4.2 *continued*

"But other firms will not give much weight to signals that can easily be mimicked." Game theory helps sensitize companies to such actions as false signaling. "It safeguards you from being taken advantage of," Dixit said.

So what's in store for game theory? "There will be more cooperation between buyer and seller than you've ever seen before," Luby said. As a result, "more and more people are going to use game theory." Game theory will continue to grow because of the importance added value plays in business today, Nalebuff says. It "helps companies define their added value.'"

And firms will have "to give up old habits such as thinking that business is war and that they must beat the competition," Nalebuff added. "This is true for card games and sports, but not in business."

Source: Excerpts from "Let Game Theory Begin: Anticipating Your Rival," by Gerald A. Achstatter. Reprinted from *Investors Business Daily,* January 25, 1996, by permission.

BOX 4.3 GAME THEORY: OVERVIEW AND ITS IMPACT ON DAILY SITUATIONS

Game theory studies interactive decision-making, where the outcome for each participant or "player" depends on the actions of all. If you are a player in such a game, when choosing your course of action or "strategy" you must take into account the choices of others. But in thinking about their choices, you must recognize that they are thinking about yours, and in turn trying to take into account your thinking about their thinking, and so on.

It would seem that such thinking about thinking must be so complex and subtle that its successful practice must remain an arcane art. Indeed, some aspects such as figuring out the true motives of rivals and recognizing complex patterns do often resist logical analysis. But many aspects of strategy can be studied and systematized into a science — game theory.

A Theory Is Born

This science is unusual in the breadth of its potential applications. Unlike physics or chemistry, which have a clearly defined and narrow scope, the precepts of game theory are useful in a whole range of activities, from everyday social interactions and sports to business and economics, politics, law, diplomacy and war. Biologists have recog-

continued . . .

Box 4.3 continued

nized that the Darwinian struggle for survival involves strategic interactions, and modern evolutionary theory has close links with game theory.

Game theory got its start with the work of John von Neumann in the 1920s, which culminated in his book with Oskar Morgenstern. They studied "zero-sum" games where the interests of two players were strictly opposed. John Nash treated the more general and realistic case of a mixture of common interests and rivalry and any number of players. Other theorists, most notably Reinhard Selten and John Harsanyi, who shared the 1994 Nobel Memorial Prize with Nash, studied even more complex games with sequences of moves, and games where one player has more information than others.

The Nash Equilibrium

The theory constructs a notion of "equilibrium," to which the complex chain of thinking about thinking could converge. Then the strategies of all players would be mutually consistent in the sense that each would be choosing his or her best response to the choices of the others. For such a theory to be useful, the equilibrium it posits should exist. Nash used novel mathematical techniques to prove the existence of equilibrium in a very general class of games. This paved the way for applications. Biologists have even used the notion of Nash equilibrium to formulate the idea of evolutionary stability. Here are a few examples to convey some ideas of game theory and the breadth of its scope.

The Prisoner's Dilemma

In Joseph Heller's novel *Catch-22,* allied victory in World War II is a foregone conclusion, and Yossarian does not want to be among the last ones to die. His commanding officer points out, "But suppose everyone on our side felt that way?" Yossarian replies, "Then I'd certainly be a damned fool to feel any other way, wouldn't I?"

Every general reader has heard of the prisoner's dilemma. The police interrogate two suspects separately, and suggest to each that he or she should fink on the other and turn state's evidence. "If the other does not fink, then you can cut a good deal for yourself by giving evidence against the other; if the other finks and you hold out, the court will treat you especially harshly. Thus no matter what the other does, it is better for you to fink than not to fink — finking is your uniformly best or 'dominant' strategy." This is the case whether the two are actually

continued . . .

Box 4.3 continued

guilty, as in some episodes of *NYPD Blue,* or innocent, as in the film *L.A. Confidential.* Of course, when both fink, they both fare worse than they would have if both had held out; but that outcome, though jointly desirable for them, collapses in the face of their separate temptations to fink.

Yossarian's dilemma is just a multi-person version of this. His death is not going to make any significant difference to the prospects of victory, and he is personally better off alive than dead. So avoiding death is his dominant strategy.

John Nash played an important role in interpreting the first experimental study of the prisoner's dilemma, which was conducted at the Rand Corporation in 1950.

Real-World Dilemmas

Once you recognize the general idea, you will see such dilemmas everywhere. Competing stores who undercut each other's prices when both would have done better if both had kept their prices high are victims of the dilemma. (But in this instance, consumers benefit from the lower prices when the sellers fink on each other.) The same concept explains why it is difficult to raise voluntary contributions, or to get people to volunteer enough time for worthwhile public causes.

How might such dilemmas be resolved? If the relationship of the players is repeated over a long time horizon, then the prospect of future cooperation may keep them from finking; this is the well-known tit-for-tat strategy. A "large" player who suffers disproportionately more from complete finking may act cooperatively even when the small fry is finking. Thus Saudi Arabia acts as a swing producer in OPEC, cutting its output to keep prices high when others produce more; and the United States bears a disproportionate share of the costs of its military alliances. Finally, if the group as a whole will do better in its external relations if it enjoys internal cooperation, then the process of biological or social selection may generate instincts or social norms that support cooperation and punish cheating. The innate sense of fairness and justice that is observed among human subjects in many laboratory experiments on game theory may have such an origin.

Mixing Moves

In football, when an offense faces a third down with a yard to go, a run up the middle is the usual or "percentage" play. But an occasional long pass in such a situation is important to keep the defense honest. Simi-

continued . . .

Box 4.3 continued

larly, a penalty kicker in soccer who kicks exclusively to the goalie's right, or a server in tennis who goes exclusively to the receiver's forehand, will fare poorly because the opponent will anticipate and counter the action. In such situations it is essential to mix one's moves randomly, so that on any one occasion the action is unpredictable.

Mixing is most important in games where the players' interests are strictly opposed, and this happens most frequently in sports. Indeed, recent empirical studies of serving in tennis grand slam finals, and penalty kicks in European soccer leagues, have found the behavior consistent with the theory.

Commitments

Greater freedom of action seems obviously desireable. But in games of bargaining, that need not be true because freedom to act can simply become freedom to concede to the other's demands. Committing yourself to a firm final offer leaves the other party the last chance to avoid a mutually disastrous breakdown, and this can get you a better deal. But a mere verbal declaration of firmness may not be credible. Devising actions to make one's commitments credible is one of the finer arts in the realm of strategic games. Members of a labor union send their leaders into wage bargaining with firm instructions or mandates that tie their hands, thereby making it credible that they will not accept a lower offer. The executive branch of the U.S. government engaged in international negotitations on trade or related matters can credibly take a firm stance by pointing out that the Congress would not ratify anything less. And a child is more likely to get the sweet or toy it wants if it is crying too loudly to hear your reasoned explanations of why it should not have it.

Thomas Schelling pioneered the study of credible commitments, and other more complex "strategic moves" like threats and promises. This has found many applications in diplomacy and war, which, as military strategist Karl von Clausewitz told us long ago, are two sides of the same strategic coin.

Information and Incentives

Suppose you have just graduated with a major in computer science, and have an idea for a totally new "killer app" that will integrate PCs, cell phones, and TV sets to create a new medium. The profit potential is immense. You go to venture capitalists for finance to develop and market your idea. How do they know that the potential is

continued ...

Box 4.3 continued

as high as you claim it to be? The idea is too new for them to judge it independently. You have no track record, and might be a complete charlatan who will use the money to live high for a few years and then disappear. One way for them to test your own belief in your idea is to see how much of your own money you are willing to risk in the project. Anyone can talk a good game; if you are willing to put enough of your money where your mouth is, that is a credible signal of your own true valuation of your idea.

This is a game where the players have different information; you know the true potential of your idea much better than does your prospective financier. In such games, actions that reveal or conceal information play crucial roles. The field of "information economics" has clarified many previously puzzling features of corporate governance and industrial organization, and has proved equally useful in political science, studies of contract and tort law, and even biology. The award of the Nobel Memorial Prize in 2001 to its pioneers, George Akerlof, Michael Spence, and Joseph Stiglitz, testifies to its importance. What has enabled information economics to burgeon in the last twenty years is the parallel development of concepts and techniques in game theory.

Aligning Interests, Avoiding Enrons

A related application in business economics is the design of incentive schemes. Modern corporations are owned by numerous shareholders, who do not personally supervise the operations of the companies. How can they make sure that the workers and managers will make the appropriate efforts to maximize shareholder value? They can hire supervisors to watch over workers, and managers to watch over supervisors. But all such monitoring is imperfect: the time on the job is easily monitored, but the quality of effort is very difficult to observe and judge. And there remains the problem of who will watch over the upper-level management. Hence the importance of compensation schemes that align the interests of the workers and managers with those of the shareholders. Game theory and information economics have given us valuable insights into these issues. Of course we do not have perfect solutions; for example, we are just discovering how top management can manipulate and distort the performance measures to increase their own compensation while hurting shareholders and workers alike. This is a game where shareholders and the government need to find and use better counterstrategies.

continued . . .

4.2. The Rules of the Game

Game theory is concerned with the strategic impact of investment decisions in situations where firms are aware that their strategy affects the value of the investment opportunities of other firms. Evaluation of an investment opportunity in a strategic context and actual determination of its value presupposes a clear description of the structure of the game. A *game* is characterized by four dimensions: the players, the actions available to them, the timing of these actions, and the payoff structure of each possible outcome. The context of the investment problem also helps determine what constitutes a game. Real-life strategic decisions are complex: there may be many incumbents and potential entrants, whose payoffs are not always obvious. To apply game theory in strategic decision making, management needs to know the possible actions and timing available to each rival (e.g., invest in a new technology or not, enter a new geographical market), and the payoff from choosing each action. Although to an outsider these concepts may seem difficult to estimate, competitors within an industry may often have reliable estimates of technological options, investment costs, or the profitability of their competitors.

Game theory can be helpful in analyzing strategic investment decisions for several reasons. First, following the rules of game theory can help reduce a complex strategic problem into a simple analytical structure consisting of four dimensions.[2] Second, game theory is a helpful valuation

---

[2] These four dimensions are: (1) identification of the players, (2) the timing or order in which the players make their decisions, (3) the available actions and information set, and (4) the payoff structure attached to each possible outcome.

tool for strategic decisions because it encompasses a solution concept that can help in understanding or predicting how competitors will behave, and it also provides an equilibrium strategy and values for the strategic decisions. The basic dimensions and rules for structuring and solving games are described below.

The Players

Decision makers are like "players" in a game. Outside factors that also affect the outcome of a decision maker's actions, like the outcome of a technology or demand for an entrant's product, collectively called *state of the world,* can also be considered as a "player." In games under uncertainty the actions of players depend not only on their belief about the competitors' strategies, but also on such exogenous events or "states of the world." Nature chooses the state of the world at random without regard to the players' actions.

The Timing or Order of the Play

Understanding how decisions are interdependent is essential in a game of strategy. The players in a game can choose among a set of actions at certain points in time, called decision nodes. The timing or order of the play and the interactions of decisions can arise in two ways. If players make their decisions one after another having first observed the earlier player's action, we have a *sequential-move* game. For example, when a pioneer invests early on in a new market, it faces a sequential game vis-à-vis potential followers. In this case, the firm must look ahead to see how its pioneering investment will affect its competitors and how they will react, for example, whether they will back down or retaliate with higher investment at a later stage, and how these reactions will affect the pioneer's own value and future actions in turn.

In other strategic situations it may make sense for firms to take *simultaneous* actions. In a *simultaneous-move* game all players make their investment decisions at the same time, so no player has an advantage of observing the other's action before making its own. When two competing firms face a simultaneous investment decision, each must be aware that there is another active player, which is similarly aware of the potential choices of the other firm. In a simultaneous game it is not sufficient to merely take notice of the opponent's position. The strategist must also consider that the opponent's strategic thinking process simultaneously has an impact on its own position (Dixit and Nalebuff 1991).

Of course real-life games might involve a combination of simultaneous and sequential games. Consider a pioneer who enters a new market.

When the market proves itself, the firm is likely to face competition from entrants who will install additional capacity. The investment decisions in capacity would form a sequential game. However, once capacity is installed, competition might shift to prices. The players would then face a simultaneous price-setting game.

Available Actions and Information Set

Players face different choices or actions, and have different information sets on which these decisions or actions are based. The information set consists of all information available to a player at a given time on which it bases its actions. At each decision node the information set may be different. Relying on the information known at each decision point, a player chooses that action which provides the highest value (or utility). A *pure strategy* is a contingent plan of the optimal actions of the player *for each* information set. A strategy includes potential actions at decision points that might actually not be reached during the game.

In games of *perfect information* the players know all previous decisions of all the players in each decision node. In games with *complete* information, the complete structure of the game, including all the actions of the players and the possible outcomes, is common knowledge. In real-life applications in business strategy, it may be unclear to each player where his or her rivals are at each point. Firms may be unsure about some issues: Will my rival back down or reciprocate? Will he believe my threat or not? In games of *incomplete* information players have asymmetric information about outcomes or payoffs. In games with *asymmetrical* information, firms do not have the same information about their opponent or the environment in which they are playing. In R & D investment games, for instance, firms may have incomplete information about the quality or success of each other's research effort, while in a game with imperfect information the firms do not know if or how much their rivals have invested in R & D.[3] A problem that commonly arises in certain games of incomplete information, like auctions, is overestimating the worth of an asset and overbidding in order to win a competitive game. Box insert 4.4 discusses this winner's curse in the context of e-commerce auctions.

Payoff Structure

Each sequence of possible actions by the players results in an outcome for each player. By choosing the right actions, each firm pursues a strategy

---

[3]A game of *incomplete* information can be structured as a game of *imperfect* information by introducing uncertainty or "nature," which chooses the "type" of each player.

Box 4.4 E-commerce Auctions and the Winner's Curse

In this age of e-commerce overdo, it's often proclaimed that online auctions are the ideal way to match buyers and sellers — fast, frictionless, and perfectly fair. But auctions aren't a perfect form of commerce — far from it. They're prone to two fundamental flaws: winner's curse, which hurts buyers; and collusion, which usually hurts sellers. While it's possible to minimize both flaws through clever design of auction mechanisms, it's not clear that Internet auctioneers are paying the subject much attention.

Winner's curse is the bane of clueless newbies on auction sites like eBay's. It's what people suffer when they win an auction by overestimating how much something is worth and therefore bidding too much. It's a sucker's game, yet it's part of daily business in online consumer auctions. Collecting money from newbies who overbid because they're ill-informed is "part of the business plan," says one message poster on AuctionWatch.com's site. "Started an item at $9 & it closed at $366+!!!" brags another.

Paul Klemperer, an Oxford University economist who specializes in the economics of auctions, illustrates winner's curse to his students by auctioning off a jar with an undisclosed number of pennies. The students bid a little below their estimate of the jar's contents to leave a profit. Every time, though, the hapless winner of the jar is the student who overestimates the number of pennies by the greatest amount, and therefore overpays by the most.

The soundest way to dodge winner's curse is to gather more information about the true value of what's being sold. That's one of eBay's strengths: Bidders can study past auctions of like items. And they can find out more about sellers by reading feedback about them. But if there's still uncertainty, bidders often watch the behavior of fellow bidders. That's where things get really complicated. If few others are bidding, does that mean the object isn't worth much — or are you in line for a bargain? Is your rival in a bidding war knowledgeable, or just crazy?

Collusion is especially easy when there are few buyers or sellers, as in many business-to-business auctions. Businesses don't even need to break the law. If a few companies are competing for a customer's business, they could tacitly agree that it's in their mutual interest to charge the same high price and share the business. If one supplier defected from the group by dropping its price, its rivals could punish it by dropping their own prices.

Source: Excerpts from "Online Auctions: How 'Winner's Curse' Could Undermine This E-commerce Channel," by Peter Coy. Reprinted from March 20, 2000 issue of *Business Week* by special permission, copyright © 2000 by the McGraw-Hill Companies, Inc.

that maximizes its value.[4] Identifying an objective such as profits or share-holders' value is important in predicting a company's optimal choice.[5] A player chooses the optimal or best set of actions at each decision node to maximize her payoff or value. An example of a payoff structure is given in the two-by-two table in figure 4.1.

Solving the Game

A *solution concept* is a methodology for predicting player behavior in-tended to determine the optimal decisions along each trajectory. Like fi-nance theory, standard game theory assumes that players behave rationally, that is, decision makers choose their actions based on inter-nally consistent criteria. The rationality of each player is accepted as common knowledge: every player is aware of the rationality of the other players and acts accordingly.[6] Once the structure of the game is under-stood, the strategies of the players and the solution of the game can be de-termined. The set of best actions a player chooses at each stage forms his strategy. The player determines at the start of the game what to do in later stages of the game in each state of nature, given the other players' possible actions.

The solution of the game should form a Nash equilibrium (we later discuss different equilibrium refinements), named after Nobel Prize win-ner John Nash. A *Nash equilibrium* is a set of strategies such that no player can do better by unilaterally changing her position or strategy. In a Nash equilibrium, each player follows her best response to the other players' strategy. Box insert 4.5 provides an intuitive discussion of Nash equilibrium, a discussion (questioning) of the rationality assumption, and alternative explanations for auction overbidding.

Finding a Nash equilibrium depends on the order of the play, that is, on whether firms move simultaneously or sequentially. Dixit and Nale-buff (1991) catalogue the following rules as a practical guide for solving a game.

---

[4]Following standard finance theory we assume value-maximizing firms. However, some sit-uations might require a utility preference for each player over all possible outcomes of the game.

[5]If, for example, we know the company's management pursues profit, we can assume it will choose the higher-profit alternative.

[6]This rationality assumption imposes an important limitation in situations where pride and irrationality cannot be ignored. However, apparent irrationality and the reputation of being irrational or unpredictable can make good strategic rational sense. One can turn a "reputa-tion of irrationality" to its advantage. For instance, a firm that has a reputation for going straight into a "war of attrition" with any contestant imposes a credible threat on competi-tors who might think twice before entering this market.

Box 4.5 Nash Equilibrium, (Ir)rationality, and Auction
Overbidding

A third of the way into *A Beautiful Mind,* the recent film about mathematician John Nash, a sexy blonde and four brunettes walk into a
bar, batting their eyelashes. After a bit of ogling, Nash and his num-
ber-minded friends decide to compete for the blonde. Then Nash has
second thoughts. If everyone goes for the same woman, he says, we'll
just end up blocking each other out and offending the rest of the
women. The only way for everyone to succeed is to ignore the blonde
and go for the brunettes instead.

The scene is an attempt to illustrate Nash's most important contribution to game theory — the Nash equilibrium. Nash showed that
in any competitive situation — war, chess, even picking up a date at a
bar-if the participants are rational, and they know that their opponents are rational, there can be only one optimal strategy. That theory won Nash a Nobel Prize in economics. The math behind it is
flawless and has transformed the way people think about evolution,
arms races, stock markets, and tick-tack-toe. There's only one problem: People aren't rational.

A breakthrough came when economists factored in altruism and
skepticism. The players knew that their decisions didn't always make
sense — and that their opponents weren't always rational, either — and
that made their optimal strategy distinctly different from what Nash
predicted. "You can never know what somebody else is thinking,"
Thomas R. Palfrey, a professor at Cal Tech, says. "All you can do is
try to guess what they're thinking. And they're trying to guess what
you're thinking, too." To model this behavior, Palfrey mixed a little
statistics in with the theory behind the Nash equilibrium. Strategic
mistakes and errors are part of the new formula, but the reasoning is
the same as Nash's. There's still a single best strategy: Palfrey calls it
the quantal response equilibrium.

In 1998, not long after Palfrey and McKelvey's ideas coalesced, Palfrey started running model auctions to test the theory. For years in
economic circles, a controversy had raged over the subject of overbidding. Why is it that people in auctions routinely pay more than they
should? Some economists, like Glenn Harrison of the University of
South Carolina, thought that bidders simply value the joy of winning
more than the satisfaction of getting an object for less than it's worth —
especially when it's not worth much to begin with. Others, like Daniel
Friedman at the University of California at Santa Cruz, thought overbidding might be the result of an aversion to risk: Most bidders would
rather bid too high than run the risk of losing the item altogether.

To see who was right, Palfrey had a group of students join a series
of computer auctions using real money. The experiment banged the

continued . . .

Box 4.5 continued

gavel on the overbidding debate. Risk aversion and random mistakes pushed the bids higher — even in auctions for inexpensive objects. When overbidding was riskier than underbidding, the students were less likely to overbid. To Palfrey, bidders are like people in a parking lot faced with feeding the meter or potentially paying a parking ticket: They'll feed the meter even if the attendant only comes by once a year. "The more risk averse you are in an auction, the higher you bid," Palfrey says. And the more bidders overbid, the more their high bids begin to snowball.

Source: Excerpts from Abrams 2002.

1. *Find dominant strategies.* For simultaneous-move games, we should first consider whether a player has a strategy or course of action that outperforms all others regardless of what the other player does. That is, whatever actions his opponents take, the player cannot improve his payoff or value by choosing any other strategy. When a dominant strategy exists, solving the game becomes simplified; the firm should pursue its dominant strategy without taking consideration of the rivals' moves. Similarly, a *dominated strategy* is a strategy that is always worse than any other strategy, regardless of what the other players do. So whatever actions its opponents take, the firm can always improve its outcome by not choosing the dominated strategy.

2. *Eliminate dominated strategies.* Although the dominant strategies of all players might not be transparent at once, the strategies that are dominated should be excluded. One should proceed by successive elimination of dominated strategies. At each stage, elimination of dominated strategies for a player at a previous stage might uncover dominated strategies for other players and finally lead to finding dominant strategies for all players. When a dominant strategy exists, all other strategies are dominated. If there is no dominant strategy for a player but there is one for a competitor, one should find the best response to the dominant strategy of that competitor.

3. *Find Nash equilibrium in pure strategies.* Not all games can be solved through the elimination of dominated strategies. By using the simplification of eliminating dominated strategies, a simultaneous-move game can be reduced to its simplest form. Even when there are no dominant strategies, cell-by-cell inspection and reasoning can lead to a Nash equilibrium. Since in a Nash equilibrium each player's strategy is the best response to the strategies of his rivals,

to choose his best strategy a player must form a belief about the strategies the other players will adopt. As each player will base his beliefs on the strategies that are optimal for the other players, the strategies adopted by these players should lead to a Nash equilibrium, representing the best response of each player to the other's optimal moves.[7]

4. *Find Nash equilibrium in mixed strategies.* Sometimes there may be no Nash equilibrium in pure strategies, but optimal actions may depend on the probability of an event occurring. In a *mixed strategy*, players assign probabilities to their actions, and in a *mixed equilibrium* they randomize over their actions so that all players are indifferent between these actions. In a practical sense this captures the value of being "unpredictable," or preventing others from exploiting any systematic pattern in your behavior. To be unpredictable, one should act so as to make others indifferent about their actions. The value of being unpredictable in a mixed strategy is best observed in repeated games. Being unpredictable makes sense in repeated zero-sum games where the gain of one firm is the other firm's loss. This is not so obvious for games where players have common interest. In such cases mixing the strategies can lead to inferior outcomes for both parties. For an intuitive illustration of mixed strategies from the field of sports, see box insert 4.6.

5. *Use backward induction for solving sequential games.* Finding a dominant strategy is a useful approach in a simultaneous game. However, when the game is sequential a dominant strategy might not be optimal because the nature of competition changes with the order of the game. In a sequential game where your rival moves first, you still always choose the dominant strategy. However, when you move first, your rival's move is not given and can be influenced by your move. Your rival will observe your choice and then take her action. This creates an opportunity for you to influence her behavior. Thus, in sequential-move games each player should anticipate the competitor's responses and use that information in determining her own best current move. This must therefore be solved by *backward induction.* We must anticipate where the initial position or choices will ultimately lead to, and use this information to calculate the best current choice by "reasoning back" given optimal future behavior. In *finite* sequential-move games, the decisions end after a

---

[7]Unfortunately, more than one pure Nash equilibrium may exist in a game. In such situations, one must predict which equilibrium is the most likely outcome of the game. In coordination games there might be a *focal point* equilibrium, representing a natural or intuitive preference because of an asymmetry in the game that is common knowledge.

Box 4.6 Mixed Strategies: Game Theory and Sports

In strategic situations, you want to keep the other guy guessing. This goes for baseball, soccer, football, chess, you name it. If your opponent knows your strategy, you're done. (Unless you're Woody Hayes and just want to settle it like men.) If you never throw deep, the DBs creep to the line. If you never throw to first, Rickey cruises into second. You know, in the shootout, since the goalie is always jumping to the left or right, guys and gals should sometimes kick to the center. It's wide open! But I know why they don't. (Hint: They're men, or they act like them.)

Economics professors teach Matching Pennies in game theory courses around the world (much like soccer is played around the world). Rajah and Clemente each have a penny they can place heads up (H) or tails up (T). Rajah wants to avoid matching. Clemente wants to match. Rajah throws fastball. Clemente thinks fastball, Clemente wins. Clemente thinks curve, Clemente loses. So, what should Rajah do? If he always plays H, then Clemente will figure it out and also play H. Therefore, Rajah should randomize 50-50 between H and T (taking the quality of the pitches out of the equation for now). If Rajah does this, it doesn't matter what Clemente does — he'll win half the time. If Clemente plays H, half of the time Rajah is playing H, so Clemente wins, and half of the time Rajah is playing T, so Clemente loses. If Clemente plays T, he also wins half the time and loses half the time.

Now, let's apply this logic to soccer. Two players, a goalie we'll call Gehrig, and a kicker Koufax. In watching the World Cup (or at least the highlights), you may have noticed that Koufax seems to have two options. Left or right. Gehrig has the same two options. Computing the probability of a goal gets a little more difficult here. It depends upon Koufax's skill level. Koufax may be able to score with incredibly high probability, even if Gehrig guesses correctly. How? By lofting the ball into the upper corner. However, a lesser player aiming for the corner may either miss high or hit low.

We're going to summarize all of this information by letting Q be the probability that Koufax scores even if Gehrig guesses correctly. Q stands for quality. A dead guy has a Q of 0, and Pelé a Q of 1. The rest of us are in between. As with Rajah and Clemente above, the equilibrium of this matchup is for Koufax to play left half the time and right half the time. So, if left and right are the only options, then the probability of a goal is $(1+Q)/2$. If $Q = \frac{1}{2}$, the probability of a goal equals $\frac{3}{4}$.

You might be tempted to say that it doesn't take game theory to say that (*a*) better players score more often, and (*b*) the players should randomize. True enough. But, here's where the game theory earns its

continued . . .

Box 4.6 continued

keep. We're going to show you that these soccer players' massive egos prevent them from playing an even smarter strategy.

The question is why the heck doesn't Koufax kick the ball into the center of the net? If Gehrig is jumping left or right, that means that the center is open. Let's expand the game and find out what's up. We'll assume that if Gehrig plays C (for center) and Koufax goes with either L or R, Koufax scores. But, if Koufax and Gehrig both play C, Koufax loses every time. After all, Gehrig is just standing there, like Bill Buckner, only he stops the ball.

Now, if Gehrig always chooses L or R, then Koufax can just play C, score for sure, and make Gehrig look foolish. In that case, Gehrig would want to play C sometimes as well. And Koufax should randomize so that Gehrig doesn't know whether to play L, C, or R. And, since Koufax would have three options instead of two, the chances that Gehrig could match would be reduced. So, why don't we see kicks in the center of the net? The answer: ego.

Source: Excerpts from Page 1998.

finite number of steps. These games can in principle be solved completely. Starting at the end-node payoffs, we can determine the outcome of the game for each player and the equilibrium paths. A backward induction process works through the complete tree to determine the optimal set of actions for each firm. The equilibrium paths take into account the future consequences as the valuation process works backward in time.

6. *Find a subgame perfect equilibrium.* A subgame is a game within the total game.[8] A *subgame perfect equilibrium* is a set of strategies for each player such that any of the strategies is also a Nash equilibrium for every subgame of the game (Selten 1965). The equilibrium set of strategies in a multistage game under uncertainty can be found by backward induction within a binomial valuation tree, starting with the end-node payoff (equilibrium state net project) values for a given competitive structure and working back through the tree. This is illustrated later in chapter 6. For each subgame, the competitive strategy of each firm consists of mapping the information set about its competitor's actions. A player may sometimes use a *threat* in an attempt to get another player to believe he will em-

[8]A subgame is a subset of the initial game with the following properties: (1) as a game, a subgame begins with one initial node; (2) once players begin playing a subgame, they continue playing the subgame for the rest of the game; (3) all information sets of the subgame are information sets of the initial game (Selten 1965).

ploy a specific strategy. Backward induction should utilize only *credible threats* and ignore *noncredible threats*. For a threat to be credible, it must be in the player's interest to carry out the threat (and so typically involves a cost or a partially irreversible decision). 7. We add another rule. *Use real options or certainty-equivalent valuation in backward induction for sequential games under uncertainty.* In option games the expected utility commonly used in game theory is now replaced by *real-options value*. In solving for equilibrium in the overall multistage game under uncertainty, we move backward over strategic choice branches using game theory analysis and move backward over random moves using certainty-equivalent binomial tree option valuation. This involves using appropriate risk-neutral probabilities to calculate the option value at each branch. In this way traditional game theory analysis can be married with (binomial) option pricing. This new approach makes it possible to value complete strategies in a competitive context in a fashion that is consistent with both modern economics and finance theory.[9]

4.3. A Taxonomy of Basic Games

Table 4.1 provides a taxonomy of basic games and metaphors, a description of strategic investment analogues, and some illustrative examples and applications. In the classic "prisoners' dilemma" two prisoners accused of a crime are worse off if they both confess than if they do not, but the fear of the other prisoner's confessing puts pressure for both to do so even though not confessing is preferable for both. Obviously, here both firms are better off to collaborate or coordinate. In a strategic investment analogue in an innovation race, firms under competitive pressure have an incentive to invest prematurely (e.g., to win the patent first and avoid

---

[9]This relies on the basic finance valuation principle that a firm creates value by investing in projects for which the market (present) value of expected cash inflows, V, exceeds the required investment outlays, I. The objective is to determine what a project would be worth if it were traded in the financial markets (Mason and Merton 1985). The current value of an investment opportunity or strategy, C, is determined from its future up and down values (C_u and C_d) discounted at the risk-free interest rate (r), with expectations taken over risk-neutral (or certainty-equivalent) probabilities (p):

$$C = \frac{pC_u + (1-p)C_d}{1+r}.$$

In complete markets in which there exist portfolios of securities that replicate the dynamics of the present value of the project caused by changes in equilibrium state profits, the risk-neutral probabilities can be obtained from $p = (1 + r - \delta - d)/(u - d)$. Here, u and d represent the up and down multiplicative factors, and δ any dividend-equivalent yield or opportunity cost of delaying investment.

TABLE 4.1
Taxonomy of Game-Theory Metaphors and Investment Applications

Game-Theory Metaphor	Description/Investment Analogy	Examples/Applications
"Prisoners' Dilemma" (fig. 4.1) Two people (players) are arrested as suspects for a crime. The police puts the suspects in different cells to avoid communication. A suspect is to be released if he admits they did it. If one refuses to confess, he will receive the most severe punishment. If neither confesses, both will get a lower punishment. The paradox is that the equilibrium outcome where both confess is worse for both prisoners, compared to the situation where neither confesses.	**Innovation Race (Symmetric)** Each of two innovative firms (players) faces two possible actions: invest early or wait. Competitive pressure to be the first (e.g., to acquire a patent) induces firms to invest early, receiving their second-worst payoff. If the two firms could coordinate their investment strategy they could share the flexibility benefits of the wait-and-see option, avoiding the inferior panic equilibrium where they rush to invest prematurely.	In high-tech industries like consumer electronics, firms often get into innovation races, even forming strategic partnerships to acquire a first-mover or time-to-market advantage, that erode the value of wait-and-see flexibility from deferring investment. A noted example is the intensely competitive race in memory chip development. In February 1997 Hitachi, Mitsubishi Electric, and Texas Instruments announced they would jointly develop a 1 gb DRAM. NEC, which has been co-operating loosely with ATT spin-off Lucent Technologies and Samsung, announced in June 1997 that it developed a 4 gb DRAM.
"Grab the Dollar" (fig. 4.2) Each of two players has two possible actions: grab the dollar or wait. In the complete information (symmetric) version of the game, a player wins the dollar if he is the only one who grabs, but loses if both players try to grab the dollar. The payoff is similar to the prisoners' dilemma game, but both players recognize that they have a negative payoff if they both play tough.	**Innovation Race (Asymmetric)** In a strategic context the market prospects are favorable only if one of the players invests, whereas simultaneous investment results in a battle with a negative expected payoff. Either one player captures the market (dollar) or the other, but when they both enter, they both loose in the resulting battle. In many emerging, high-growth industries, the possibility of each firm pursuing independent innovative activities to capture the product standard may trigger a simultaneous similar investment by competitors that results in such a market battle.	Under competitive pressure to be the first (e.g., in a patent race) competitors may rush to make parallel innovation investments simultaneously, with one or both sides potentially getting hurt. For instance, Novell was hurt due to competition in networking products; Apple lost its lead as a user-friendly computer with the development of Microsoft's Windows, while in the 1980s Philips was hurt by losing the race against Matsushita over the VCR standard.

"Burning the Bridge" (fig. 4.3)

Two opposing armies are asked to occupy an island between their countries, connected by bridges to both. Each army would prefer to let the island go to its opponent rather than fight. Army 1, which moves first, occupies the island and burns the bridge behind it (signaling its commitment to fight). Thus army 2 has no option but let army 1 keep the island, because it knows that army 1 has no choice but fight back if attacked. The paradox of commitment is winning the game by reducing your options (burning the bridge behind).

Product Standard/Preemption

Each firm (player) has two possible actions: high irreversible investment commitment or more flexible, low-cost investment. The value of early/heavy commitment is that it may set the product standard or signal to competing firms reduced future profitability of their options in this market. If a pioneer firm makes an early, large-scale irreversible R & D investment in a new market, its competitors could view this as a threat to their future profit base and decide to stay out or enter the market later on a reduced scale to avoid a market share battle.

Being the first in the market enables a firm to capture a larger share of the market putting followers at a strategic disadvantage. For instance, in cellular phones the early introduction of new models by Nokia preempted a significant market share (compared to larger competitors). Major competitors like Philips (who formed a partnership with Lucent Technologies) could not catch up and left this market. In extreme cases, the pioneer can capture the product standard early on. For instance, Intel preempted 80% of the microprocessor market with its Pentium microchip that became the product standard. This forced competitors like Digital to retreat from the market, even though Digital's Alpha chip was three to four times as powerful as the Pentium chip at a fraction of the cost.

"The Market for Lemons"

Games with information asymmetry present themselves in many situations. One of the most well known is the market for "lemons" (Akerlof 1970). Information asymmetry over quality may result in pooling (averaging) of quality by buyers and an adverse selection problem since sellers would have an incentive to offer lower than average quality due to the information asymmetry.

Signaling Games (fig. 4.4)

With information asymmetry in R & D, firms may try to signal their quality by investment. In the example in section 4.3.3 each firm (player) faces two possible actions: high irreversible investment commitment or more flexible, low-effort investment. The value of early/heavy commitment is that it may signal research quality to competing firms and therefore reduced future profitability of their options in this market.

Examples of games with information asymmetry can be found in R & D intensive industries, e.g., electronics or information technology. Firms try to signal their intention to change the game to their advantage. To establish credibility, firms use commitment or reputation. For instance, Intel established a reputation of suing every player that is developing similar technology. The lemons problem can be found in many markets, varying from financial markets to markets for used vehicles.

"Battle of the Sexes"

A couple must choose between going to a movie or to a play. The couple prefers going somewhere together rather than separate, although one prefers the movie and the other the play. The couple would be better off to collaborate, sometimes going to a movie and other times to a play.

Standardization Game

Two (alliances of) firms must choose between product standard A or standard B. Everyone would be better off with one standard (avoiding a "war of attrition"), but for one firm standard A would be the best, while for the other firm the best would be standard B. Collaboration is the best long-term outcome.

In the standardization of the high-density disk, on one side was an alliance between Toshiba and Time Warner, who had jointly developed a Super Density disk; on the other side was an alliance between Philips and Sony with their Multi-Media Compact Disk. In this high-density CD battle, both sides recognized that the launch of more than one system would result in confusion and major capital waste, particularly for the losing company as well as the consumers. A standardization agreement resulted in increased productivity and expanded markets for both.

being preempted), which results in an erosion of flexibility value. The payoff in this competitive game may be positive, but less than had players followed a (coordinated) wait-and-see strategy. A similar strategic context is present in the "grab the dollar" game, but here firms obtain a negative payoff when they end up investing simultaneously. The "grab the dollar" game describes a situation where the current market prospects are favorable only if one of the players invests, but simultaneous investment results in a battle with a negative expected payoff. The first player "captures the dollar" (e.g., the patent), but when both firms enter the market, they end up losing in a battle. A dominant firm has an advantage in this simultaneous game. The "burning the bridge" game explains how a firm can use the threat of a battle where it has no flexibility to retreat (via commitment) if it has a first-mover advantage and can make the first investment commitment to capture a large portion of the market. The paradox of *commitment* here is winning the game by "killing" one's options ("burning the bridge" behind, leaving no option but fight). Of course, instead of fighting for a leading position in the market, firms may sometimes find it beneficial to follow an accommodating strategy to avoid a market battle. The "battle of the sexes" game illustrates that in certain cases firms have an incentive to align their strategies and cooperate, accommodating each other rather than fighting.

The following sections illustrate these ideas with a series of business examples, ranging from a (symmetric) decision to launch an R & D project (faced by two comparable competitors), to an asymmetric game involving different degrees of R & D effort and the possibility of complete preemption, to a game of R & D competition versus collaboration via joint R & D ventures or strategic alliances.[10]

4.3.1. Time to Launch under Competition (Symmetric Innovation Race)

Consider first the example of an innovation race involving a shared R & D option between two consumer electronics firms, Philips (P) and Sony (S). Each firm plans to develop an interactive CD technology and expects subsequent commercialization applications. The total market value (NPV-pie) from immediate investment (whether by a single firm or shared equally among the two firms) is $400 million. The additional value of the flexibility to "wait and see" under demand uncertainty (had there been no competition) is $200 million. This results in a total (shared) opportunity value (option pie or expanded-NPV) of $600 million if the two firms could fully appropriate the flexibility value of waiting.

[10]See Dixit and Nalebuff 1991 for various applications of standard games.

FIGURE 4.1 INNOVATION RACE: COMPETITIVE PRESSURE TO BE FIRST
INDUCES FIRMS TO INVEST PREMATURELY, EVEN THOUGH THEY COULD
BOTH BE BETTER OFF TO WAIT ("PRISONERS' DILEMMA")

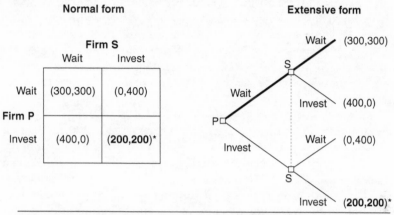

Note: Payoff in each cell is for (firm P, firm S).
Strategies of firm P: Wait (upper row) or Invest (lower row)
Strategies of firm S: Wait (left column) or Invest (right column)

This strategic situation can be represented in *normal form* in a two-by-
two table. Figure 4.1 summarizes the payoffs (firm P, firm S) in four
investment-timing scenarios: (1) when both firms invest immediately (simultaneously) they equally share the total NPV ($\frac{1}{2} \times 400$), resulting in a
(200, 200) value payoff for each firm; (2)/(3) when one firm (P or S) invests first while the other waits, it preempts its competitor and captures
the full NPV value (400) for itself, resulting in a payoff of (400, 0) or (0,
400), respectively; and (4) when both firms decide to wait, they equally
share the value of the investment option ($\frac{1}{2} \times 600$), resulting in a (300,
300) payoff.

Games can also be described in *extensive form* in a treelike represen-
tation. The extensive form exhibits a tree of the game and specifies the
order of the decisions and events, and the information and choices available to each player at each stage in the game. In figure 4.1 the connecting
line between the nodes of firm S indicates that player S has the same information whether player P is investing or waiting, and is called player
S's *information set* (this can also be represented by an oval around the
subgame).

To make an optimal decision, a player must generally foresee how its
opponent(s) will behave. To decide which strategy to adopt, it must form
a belief about the strategies other players are expected to adopt. The
choices that a player is likely not to make are dominated by better
choices.

In the example of figure 4.1, firm P's payoff from immediate investment (lower row) exceeds its payoff from a wait-and-see strategy (upper row), regardless of which strategy firm S chooses (400 > 300 in left "wait" column, 200 > 0 in right "invest" column). The wait-and-see strategy for firm P is purely *dominated* by the strategy to invest now, regardless of the timing decision of its competitor. Firm S also has a *dominant* strategy to invest regardless of firm P's decision (200 > 0 and 400 > 300). As noted, pure *dominated strategies,* that is, actions that always give a payoff to a player lower than any other action, whatever the other players do, should be eliminated.

The above value-payoff structure results in a *Nash equilibrium* outcome in the lower right cell, where both firms invest (200, 200). In a Nash equilibrium (*) each player makes an optimal decision in light of the other player's optimal decisions. Neither firm can improve by making a unilateral move. Any deviation will lead back to the equilibrium outcome. Thus, both firms receive their second-worst payoff of (200, 200), an example of the well-known *prisoners' dilemma*.[11]

If an action of a player is to be taken with certainty, it is called a *pure strategy*. In the above example both firms have a *pure strategy equilibrium* to invest. In contrast, when there is an expectation that the player might choose between actions (investing or waiting) with a certain probability, a *mixed strategy* results. The payoff of a mixed strategy is estimated by taking the expectation of the corresponding payoffs weighted by the probabilities. A pure strategy is a special case of a mixed strategy with a probability of 1 of a certain action. Not all games have a pure strategy equilibrium, but a *mixed-strategy equilibrium* always exists, so games can be solved with mixed strategies when no pure strategy equilibrium exists.

4.3.2. ASYMMETRIC INNOVATION RACE AND PREEMPTION

Let us revisit the above innovation race between the two firms, Philips (P) and Sony (S), but in another strategic context. If both firms invest, they end up in a market share battle with a negative payoff. Suppose now that firm P has an edge in developing the technology, although it has limited (financial or other necessary) resources at the time. Competitor S may take advantage of this resource weakness and try to win the race to the market. Each firm can choose how intense an effort to make in develop-

---

[11]In the classic prisoners' dilemma, two prisoners accused of a crime are worse off if they both confess (200, 200) than if they do not (300, 300), but the fear of the other prisoner's confessing (0, 400) puts pressure for both to do so even though not confessing is preferable for both. Obviously, here both firms are better off to collaborate or coordinate and fully appropriate the option value of waiting (300, 300).

ing this innovative technology (see Dixit and Nalebuff 1991). Less effort is consistent with a (technological) follower strategy involving lower development costs, but is more flexible (safe) in case of unfavorable developments. More effort corresponds to a (technological) leader strategy involving higher development costs that could result in earlier product launch and a first-mover cost advantage.

Figure 4.2 illustrates the resulting payoffs if the competitor chooses a (technological) leader or follower strategy (high or low R & D investment) when they are in an asymmetric power position. In this payoff table, both sides regard a high-cost R & D battle as their worst scenario: for firm S because it is likely to loose an all-out race, and for firm P because it would incur large costs. Suppose that this situation results in a (−$100 million, −$100 million) payoff.

The next-worst scenario for each competitor is to make a low-cost investment while its competitor chooses a high-cost R & D strategy. This entails spending money with little chance of success, resulting in a payoff of only $10 million. Under firm S's technological leader strategy, it develops its interactive CD technology by making a high-cost investment ($200 million), while firm P follows with a low-cost follower strategy. In the best scenario for firm P, both firms avoid an intense innovation race and make a low-cost investment, with firm P more likely to win due to its

FIGURE 4.2 SIMULTANEOUS INNOVATION RACE WITH HIGH VERSUS LOW R & D INVESTMENT COST (ASYMMETRIC "GRAB THE DOLLAR" GAME)

		Firm S	
		Low (follower)	High (leader)
Firm P	Low (follower)	($200 m, $100 m)	($10 m, $200 m)*
	High (leader)	($100 m, $10 m)	(−$100 m, −$100 m)

Note: Payoff in each cell is for (firm P, firm S).
Strategies of firm P: Low-cost R & D (upper row) or high-cost R & D (lower row)
Strategies of firm S: Low-cost R & D (left column) or high-cost R & D (right column)

technological edge and lower cost (resulting in a payoff of $200 million for P, $100 million for S).

Consider the equilibrium implications of an asymmetric payoff structure as that of the "grab the dollar" game in figure 4.2.[12] Firm P's payoff for pursuing a low-cost R & D strategy (upper row) exceeds the payoff of a high-cost strategy (lower row), no matter which strategy firm S chooses (200 > 100 and 10 > −100). Thus, Firm P has a dominant strategy to pursue low-cost R & D. Knowing this, firm S will pursue a high-cost R & D strategy (since 200 > 100). The Nash equilibrium (*) outcome of this R & D rivalry game is given by the top right cell (10, 200), where firm P receives its second-worst payoff. Firm P would follow a flexible, low-cost strategy, while firm S would follow the high-cost R & D strategy.

In a dynamic or *sequential game*, a player can choose its strategy after observing its opponent's actions. Consider a similar situation (as the simultaneous innovation race of figure 4.2), but with the difference that firm P would make its R & D investment before firm S would have to decide which strategy to follow. Which R & D strategy should firm P follow, given that it can observe its opponent's prior action? Management must now recognize that its investment decisions will directly influence competitive behavior, as illustrated in the sequential game of figure 4.3. This *sequential game* is presented in extensive form. The threat of a market battle could actually now work in firm P's favor.

As noted, such a sequential game can be solved by backward induction: we first consider all different possible future actions, and then "reason back" to consider the value of these actions today. Firm P should anticipate its competitor's response, and use this information to determine its own best current move. If firm P pursues a flexible low-cost strategy (making a small R & D investment), firm S will respond with a high-cost investment, and firm P's payoff will be $10 million. However, if P pursues a high-cost R & D strategy, firm S can be expected to respond with a low-cost strategy (since 10 > −100), in which case P's payoff will be $100 million. Therefore, firm P would invest heavily in R & D, signaling a credible commitment to the high-cost R & D strategy (with the competitor responding with a low-cost strategy). With such a strategic timing move, equilibrium forces would result in a more desirable payoff for firm P ($100 million) than that of the earlier (simultaneous) game ($10 million). The value of a heavy R & D investment commitment is that it can pose the threat of a battle to signal to competitors the reduced profitability of their options in the market so they would stay out or enter

[12]This is an asymmetrical variant of the "grab the dollar" game, in that both firms have a negative payoff if they both make a high-cost R & D investment, and there is a positive payoff if only one of them follows a high-cost strategy. Only firm S has a dominant position in playing this game, reflected in its higher payoff.

FIGURE 4.3 SEQUENTIAL INVESTMENT GAME WITH HIGH VERSUS LOW
R & D INVESTMENT COST ("BURNING THE BRIDGE")

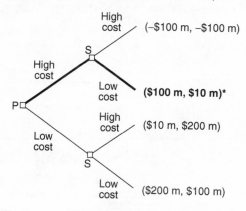

on a reduced scale to avoid a catastrophic market share battle. As in "burning the bridge" behind, the paradox of heavy commitment can win the game here by reducing or eliminating one's flexibility.

4.3.3. SIMULTANEOUS INNOVATION RACE WHEN THE OPPONENT'S CAPABILITIES ARE UNKNOWN

So far we have looked at situations of *complete information,* where all players know everything about everybody else. In reality this is often not the case. A distinction can be made between imperfect information and incomplete information. Under *imperfect information* a player must make decisions without knowing enough (i.e., without having full information) about what its opponent's actions or strategies have been (or will be). Under *incomplete information* the firm does not know its rivals' precise characteristics or type. In the above innovation race between the two firms, P and S, if firm S does not know if or how much its rival has spent on R & D (high-cost or low-cost investment), it has imperfect information. Firm S has incomplete information if it does not know its rival's cost or the type of its R & D capability.

Tirole (1988, 174) remarks that the distinction between incomplete and imperfect information is somewhat semantic. Imperfect information can be modeled as incomplete information by introducing "nature" in the game, choosing the characteristics or the type of firm P and then assuming that firm S is not informed about the nature's choice concerning its opponent's type. Let us revisit the two-player R & D investment game under *incomplete information* depicted in figure 4.4. Firm S is of a specific type N (i.e., having Normal research capabilities). Firm P has complete

FIGURE 4.4 SIMULTANEOUS INNOVATION GAME WITH HIGH VERSUS
LOW R & D INVESTMENT COST UNDER INCOMPLETE INFORMATION
(FIRM P CAN BE OF NORMAL OR SUPERIOR TYPE)

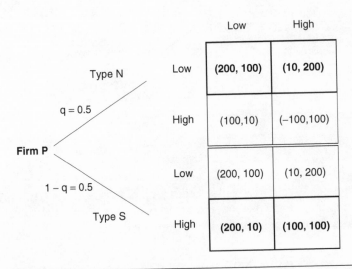

Note: Type N: Normal research capabilities; type S: Superior research capabilities.

information about firm S. There is, however, incomplete information about
the research capabilities of firm P. Firm P can be one of two possible types:
N (Normal research capabilities) or S (Superior research capabilities).

While firm P knows what kind of technology it has and the quality of
its research capabilities (knows its own type), firm S does not and assigns
equal probabilities to both types ($q = 0.5$). In figure 4.4 the upper two-
by-two matrix box presents the strategic game payoffs if firm P has Normal research capabilities and the lower matrix if it has Superior
capabilities. A natural generalization of the Nash equilibrium concept to
games of incomplete information is a *Bayesian equilibrium*. In a *Bayesian
equilibrium* each player correctly anticipates the strategy for each of the
types of the other player. If firm P has Normal research capabilities the
low-cost R & D strategy is purely dominant for firm P (since $200 > 100$
and $10 > -100$). By contrast, if firm P has Superior capabilities, it will
pursue the high-cost R & D strategy (since $200 = 200$ and $100 > 10$).
This game can be solved easily since both cases (types of firm P) have a
dominant strategy. The investment problem from firm S's perspective
now boils down to an opponent who is expected to pursue a high-cost
R & D strategy if it has superior capabilities or a low-cost strategy if it has

Normal capabilities, with equal probabilities. The expected payoff for the low-cost strategy for firm S is $0.5 \times 100 + 0.5 \times 10 = \$55$ million, while the expected payoff for the high-cost strategy is $0.5 \times 200 + 0.5 \times 100 = \$150$ million. Firm S will thus follow the high-cost strategy (since $150 > 55$).

4.4. Competitive Reactions in Quantity versus Price Competition

The design of strategy may involve strategic investment decisions in new plants or innovation activity. It may also involve decisions on the right quantity to produce, setting of prices, and the addition of services and quality features that can differentiate the firm's products and services in the marketplace. Attention must be paid on the effect of the firm's own strategic choices on the behavior of its competitors. Industrial organization has a history of model development for strategic choices. The Cournot quantity competition and Bertrand price competition in a duopoly market structure are the best known. Both models focus on the short term in that they reflect the profitability of competitive tactics today. Dynamic considerations, such as making a strategic investment in cost-efficient R & D or building market share today to enhance profits tomorrow, can be treated as advanced refinements of these models in a multistage framework.

4.4.1. QUANTITY COMPETITION

One of the first models of oligopoly was developed in 1838 by Augustin Cournot. In the Cournot competition model firms choose quantities or capacity. Consumer demand in the marketplace determines the price. Cournot developed this model to explain how firms in a duopoly structure choose their capacity in order to maximize profits. The standard Cournot model is a one-stage game, assuming firms will not revise the production capacity often. OPEC, for example, makes decisions concerning the quantity of oil production, and the market determines the price. Other examples include the competition for the development of a new superplane between Airbus and Boeing, and the competition in memory chips.

Consider a duopoly competition between a European (firm A) and a U.S. company (firm B) in a new generation of nanotechnology that just moved to commercial-scale production. The two high-tech firms are expected to enter the market simultaneously. Because with the new commercial-scale process the marginal costs of nanotubes are becoming substantially lower, once a facility is built, it is profitable to run it at a high utilization rate. What should the size of the capacity of the European manufacturing facility and the U.S. manufacturing facility be?

The strategic choice for each firm i is the capacity it puts on the market, Q_i. Price is not a strategic choice but the result of supply and demand for the new generation of commercial-scale nanotechnology. The clearing market price, P, is the price at which customers will buy the total production in the market, $Q_A + Q_B$. Suppose this price is given by the following inverse demand function:

$$P = \theta - (Q_A + Q_B). \tag{4.1}$$

Suppose the demand parameter θ is constant and equal to 17.5 (in chapters 6 and 7 we will allow demand uncertainty by making this a stochastic variable). Q_A and Q_B are the production capacities of firm A and firm B, respectively. Consistent with this inverse demand function, each firm's capacity decision is a strategic choice. If one firm increases its production of nanotubes, it would reduce the equilibrium market price and thereby affect its competitor's profits as well. Suppose that the unit variable cost is $c_i = 5$, and the total variable production cost for each firm i ($i = A$ or B) is given by

$$C(Q_i) = c_i Q_i. \tag{4.2}$$

Total variable costs, $C(Q_i)$, are increasing with the size of production Q_i. How much should each firm plan to produce? The gross project value (profit value), V_i, and the net present value, NPV_i, can be determined from the present value of the expected cash flows (or profits). The size of the plant to produce the new generation nanotubes would depend on the value-maximizing output. The profits of each firm i ($i = A, B$) depend on the output of that firm and its competitor's. The annual operating profits for each firm i are given by

$$\pi_i(Q_A, Q_B) = PQ_i - C(Q_i) = [17.5 - (Q_A + Q_B)]Q_i - 5Q_i. \tag{4.3}$$

Suppose each firm i ($i = A$ or B) acts as if it were a monopolist facing an inverse demand function in which the production of its competitor is treated as given:

$$P = (17.5 - Q_j) - Q_i. \tag{4.4}$$

Table 4.2 shows the profits for firm A (panel A) and firm B (panel B), respectively, as a function of the firm's production and that of its competitor. The profit entries are based on possible production combinations of the two rivals presented in the columns and rows. For instance, a production combination where firm A produces two units of nanotubes and firm B produces four units is shown in the fifth row and third column of table 4.2. At this production level for both companies, the market price equals $17.5 - (4 + 2) = 11.5$ per unit. Firm A's profit of $(11.5 - 5) \times 2 = 13$ is shown in panel A, while firm B's profit of $(11.5 - 5) \times 4 = 26$ is

TABLE 4.2

Profits for Firm A and Firm B under Cournot Quantity Competition

Panel A. Firm A's Profit

		Firm A's Production									
		0	1	2	3	4	5	6	7	8	9
Firm B's Production	0	0.0	11.5	21.0	28.5	34.0	37.5	39.0	38.5	36.0	31.5
	1	0.0	10.5	19.0	25.5	30.0	32.5	33.0	31.5	28.0	22.5
	2	0.0	9.5	17.0	22.5	26.0	27.5	27.0	24.5	20.0	13.5
	3	0.0	8.5	15.0	19.5	22.0	22.5	21.0	17.5	12.0	4.5
	4	0.0	7.5	13.0	16.5	18.0	17.5	15.0	10.5	4.0	−4.5
	5	0.0	6.5	11.0	13.5	14.0	12.5	9.0	3.5	−4.0	−13.5
	6	0.0	5.5	9.0	10.5	10.0	7.5	3.0	−3.5	−12.0	−22.5
	7	0.0	4.5	7.0	7.5	6.0	2.5	−3.0	−10.5	−20.0	−31.5
	8	0.0	3.5	5.0	4.5	2.0	−2.5	−9.0	−17.5	−28.0	−40.5
	9	0.0	2.5	3.0	1.5	−2.0	−7.5	−15.0	−24.5	−36.0	−49.5

Panel B. Firm B's Profit

		Firm A's production									
		0	1	2	3	4	5	6	7	8	9
Firm B's Production	0	0.0	0.0	0.0	0.0	0.0	0.0	0.0	0.0	0.0	0.0
	1	11.5	10.5	9.5	8.5	7.5	6.5	5.5	4.5	3.5	2.5
	2	21.0	19.0	17.0	15.0	13.0	11.0	9.0	7.0	5.0	3.0
	3	28.5	25.5	22.5	19.5	16.5	13.5	10.5	7.5	4.5	1.5
	4	34.0	30.0	26.0	22.0	18.0	14.0	10.0	6.0	2.0	−2.0
	5	37.5	32.5	27.5	22.5	17.5	12.5	7.5	2.5	−2.5	−7.5
	6	39.0	33.0	27.0	21.0	15.0	9.0	3.0	−3.0	−9.0	−15.0
	7	38.5	31.5	24.5	17.5	10.5	3.5	−3.5	−10.5	−17.5	−24.5
	8	36.0	28.0	20.0	12.0	4.0	−4.0	−12.0	−20.0	−28.0	−36.0
	9	31.5	22.5	13.5	4.5	−4.5	−13.5	−22.5	−31.5	−40.5	−49.5

shown in panel B. For each level of output of the competitor j, firm i ($i =$ A or B) can determine how much it should produce in order to maximize its profits. Given that firm A produces two units, firm B should produce five units. Firm B will gain 1.5, while firm A will lose 2, since the equilibrium price decreases due to the increased world production.

Reaction Curves and Cournot Nash Equilibrium

When choosing its production quantity, a firm may not know the production quantity to be chosen by its competitor. However, it may be able to determine which quantity to choose for each quantity the other firm might choose in order to maximize its profits or value. The reaction or best-response curve displays the optimal quantity of one firm at different quantity levels chosen by its competitor. This curve assigns to every output level of one firm, the best or value-maximizing output for the other. The reaction functions for quantity competition are shown in figure 4.5, with the equilibrium being marked at the intersection of the two reaction curves.

In quantity competition the slope of the reaction curves is negative or downward-sloping. If a firm decreases the quantity it puts on the market, its rival will increase its own quantity in order to maximise its profit. A decline in total quantity supplied drives up the market price, which raises the profit margin per unit, making it worthwhile to produce more units.

Under complete information, each firm knows the reaction curve of its competitor and knows that its competitor knows its own reaction curve. A firm will choose that quantity which is optimal given the optimal quantity chosen by its competitor. This results in an equilibrium at the cross-section of the two reaction curves. In the example of figure 4.5, both firms will produce four units. The market price will be 9.5, so each firm

FIGURE 4.5 DOWNWARD-SLOPING REACTION CURVES UNDER COURNOT QUANTITY COMPETITION

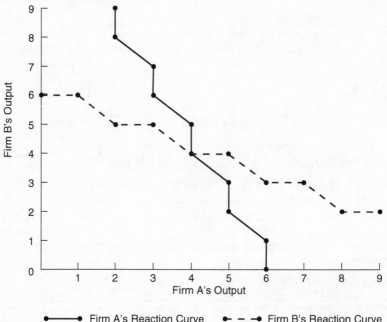

will make a profit of 18. This outcome constitutes a *Cournot-Nash equilibrium*, as it is not optimal for either firm to deviate by changing its output from this equilibrium level.

Nonetheless, the total production of eight units is not the optimal outcome from an industry point of view. Competitive pressures make it impossible to maximize (joint) total industry profits, and the two firms give up part of the potential profits they would have gained had they acted as a monopolist. If the firms could cooperate, they would each produce three units, which would yield a combined profit for both firms of 19.5 (an increase of 1.5). However, under competition and given that the other firm produces three units, each firm would have an incentive to try to produce five units. To continue this cycle, when its competitor would produce five units, the firm's optimal response would be to produce two units. Finally, in equilibrium, both firms will end up producing four units and forgoing the extra profit of 1.5.

Another way to derive a reaction curve is to use iso-profit curves. An iso-profit curve gives the combinations of output that will generate the same level of profit (iso-profit) for each firm. For instance, the combination of output that results in a level of zero profit is given by:

$$[\theta - Q_A + Q_B] - c_i Q_i = 0. \tag{4.5}$$

This iso-profit curve is shown in the left panel of figure 4.6. There is a different iso-profit curve for each level of profit. The parabolic iso-profit curves drawn above are combinations with a higher quantity for the competitor (firm B), and consequently a lower profit for firm A. The iso-profit curves closer to the axis correspond to a higher profit for firm A.

FIGURE 4.6 COURNOT-NASH AND STACKELBERG EQUILIBRIUMS UNDER QUANTITY COMPETITION (DOWNWARD-SLOPING REACTION CURVES)

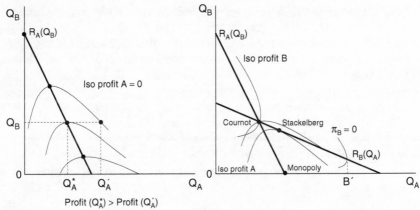

The iso-profit curve with the highest level of profit for firm A is found when firm B produces an output of zero.

Firm B has similar iso-profit curves, with the difference that the output of firm A is measured along the vertical axis while the output of firm B is measured along the horizontal axis. Since both firms are symmetrical in costs in this case, the parabolic iso-profit functions of firm B are just "rotated" versions of the ones of firm A.

The solid line $R_A(Q_B)$ in figure 4.6 depicts graphically firm A's reaction function. It shows firm A's profit maximizing output for each level of output produced by firm B, Q_B. Interestingly, the reaction curve intersects all the tops of the iso-profit curves for firm A. The reaction function presented in figure 4.6 allows for continuous scaling of production, but is otherwise similar to the one in figure 4.5. Firm A's optimal reaction to a given production quantity of firm B is the output where firm A maximizes its own profits. The idea is to get to the highest level of profit, that is, reach the iso-profit curve that is closest to the horizontal axis for each given level of output of the competitor.

In Cournot quantity competition the two firms choose that pair of outputs which correspond with the intersection of the two reaction curves. In a Cournot-Nash equilibrium each firm reacts optimally to the other firm's expected action (as expressed by its reaction function, R), that is, $Q_A^* = R_A(Q_B^*)$ and $Q_B^* = R_B(Q_A^*)$. Thus, the Nash equilibrium Cournot quantities, Q_A^* and Q_B^*, are on the intersection of the reaction functions of both firms, as shown in the right-hand panel of figure 4.6.

First-Mover Advantage: Stackelberg Leadership

In 1934 Heinrich von Stackelberg developed a model that shows the advantage of being the first mover. In the Stackelberg model of a duopoly, two firms choose their outputs *sequentially*. Revisiting our example of building capacities in nanotubes, we consider the same inverse demand function and profit functions for the two firms as given in equations 4.1 and 4.3. Suppose now the European firm (firm A) has a lead and can commercialize production of nanotubes with a large facility before the U.S. company (firm B) can begin commercial-scale production. How much capacity should the European facility have, given the expected market size? How much capacity should the U.S. company build?

Suppose the timing of these capacity investment decisions influences neither market demand nor the cost structure of the firms. The capacity decisions will be different than in the previous case, as the firms will not make their choices simultaneously. In this *sequential* strategic situation, a *Stackelberg leader/follower* equilibrium can result. Firm A can make an aggressive commitment in capacity to preempt the market and force its competitor to retreat. That commitment is credible if the facility is costly and built before firm B can start. When firm B decides to make the decision to install capacity, its management will already observe production of firm A's capacity.

Firm B will drive prices down if it builds according to the Cournot capacity; instead, it will build a smaller facility. In the Stackelberg duopoly model, firm B's decision on how much to produce is rather simple to determine, as it knows the production of firm A. The reaction curve as given in the previous section in the Cournot model will give that output which yields the highest profits. Firm A should take into account the effect of the follower's output choice on its own profit, as the decision of the follower will affect the market price. Under complete information, firm A knows the reaction curve of firm B and will use this information in maximizing its own profits. When considering its own capacity choice, firm A will anticipate the corresponding output of firm B and the resulting equilibrium market price. In table 4.3, for each output of firm A the corresponding output of firm B is given as derived from its reaction curve (as well as the profits for both).

The opportunity to move first gives an incentive to increase nanotube capacity and force others in the industry to scale back. The increased nanotube production due to increased capacity will result in lower market prices. Lower prices would lower the return on the capacity investment planned by competition. The new equilibrium reflects this outcome, with increased market share for firm A and decreased market share for firm B.

As firm A has the advantage to choose capacity first, it will produce six units, which will yield a profit of 21. Firm B has no other choice than to produce three units, which will result in a profit of 10.5. Being the first mover in this case proves to be very profitable, with profits being 10.5 higher than the follower's. Total industry output is higher than in the (simultaneous) Cournot model, reducing overall profits, but the first mover gets a larger share of the pie. For the Stackelberg leader/follower market

TABLE 4.3
Output Decisions and Profits in Duopoly under Cournot Competition

Firm A's output	0	1	2	3	4	5	6	7	8	9
Firm B's output	6	6	5	5	4	4	3	3	2	2
Profits for firm A	0.0	35.5	11.0	13.5	18.0	17.5	21.0	17.5	20.0	13.5
Profits for firm B	39.0	33.0	27.5	22.5	18.0	14.0	10.5	7.5	5.0	3.0

shares to be stable, firms must find it costly to alter this quantity. Early investment commitment permanently shifts the location of the firm's best response curve by altering its underlying cost or revenue structure. The commitment of the first mover will be credible if it changes its course of action in its favor and the outlay of the manufacturing facility for nanotube production is costly to reverse.

In this way firm A may preempt its competitor and capture a significant share of the market by setting large capacity early on. Given that the follower will observe the leader's prior action, the Stackelberg quantity leader will choose that action on the follower's reaction function, $R_B(Q_A)$, which will maximize its own profit value, that is, Max $V_A(Q_A, R_B(Q_A))$.[13] The Stackelberg leader outcome is shown in figure 4.6 as the point where firm A's iso-profit curve closest to the horizontal axis is just tangent to firm B's reaction curve, and corresponds to the highest level of profit given the reaction of its competitor.

Entry Deterrence

The leader could even earn monopoly profits in the short run while facing the threat of competitive entry later on. In case the leader has a first-mover cost advantage or realized demand is low, the leader may choose an early action (e.g., a high enough quantity — above profit-break-even ($\pi_B = 0$) point B' in the right panel of figure 4.6 — on the follower's reaction curve such that it would become unprofitable for the follower to operate ($\pi_B(Q_A, Q_B) < 0$, or net of the required outlay, $NPV_B < 0$), preempting its entry and earning monopoly profits (π_m). The monopoly outcome lies on an iso-profit curve with a higher level of profit than the Stackelberg leader outcome.

4.4.2. PRICE COMPETITION

Now suppose instead that firms set their own prices and consumers determine the quantities sold. In 1883 Joseph Bertrand developed a price-competition duopoly model to determine the profits of a company based on this type of competitive setting. In this framework, firms may be inclined to lower prices to get a larger share of the market. Under Bertrand price competition, price settings are complements (as in ticket pricing by

---

[13]In quantity competition, an aggressive firm that invests early acting as a Stackelberg leader can acquire a larger share of the market. Under price competition, a Stackelberg price leader would choose a price on the competitor's reaction function that maximizes its profit value. In the case of an accommodating price leader there need not be a first-mover advantage, as both firms can set higher prices than when they invest at the same time.

FIGURE 4.7 BERTRAND-NASH AND STACKELBERG EQUILIBRIUMS UNDER
PRICE COMPETITION (UP-SLOPING REACTION CURVES)

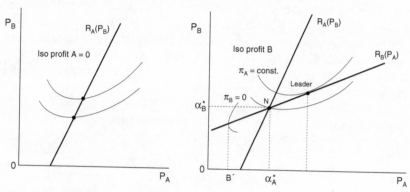

airlines). If one firm sets a low price, so will the other; prices will be "bid down," hurting the profit margins of both firms.[14]

Assume for simplicity that the demand for the product is linear in prices, as follows:

$$Q_i(P_i, P_j) = \theta - bP_i + dP_j. \tag{4.6}$$

The quantity sold by firm i is a negative function of its own price (P_i) and is higher for a higher price charged by its competitor (P_j). The coefficients b and d ($b > 0$, $d > 0$ assuming demand substitutes) capture the sensitivities of the quantity sold to the firm's own and its competitor's price settings, respectively.

Airline ticket pricing is a classic example of price competition, even though consumers may have different preferences for each airline. If an airline raises its price for a ticket to a particular destination, some customers may switch to another airline, while others will prefer to pay a higher price with the same airline. An airline that lowers its price will gain some new customers who, until the price dropped, were not in the market for this destination, as well as attract some customers from its rivals. Other examples include price competition in soft drinks between Coca-Cola and Pepsi, in detergents between Unilever and Procter and Gamble, and in cigarettes.

The reaction curves under price competition are upward sloping, as shown in figure 4.7. If an airline lowers its ticket price, its rival does best by lowering its price also. It may not match the markdown in full. By

---

[14]Firms may instead try to differentiate their products with marketing investments to avoid competition in prices.

lowering its own price, the competitor prevents some of its customers from leaving. However, a lower price means a lower profit margin, so it is often not worth matching the price drop fully but only partially to preserve some margin on the existing customer base.

The market equilibrium prices for Bertrand price competition are shown in figure 4.7, along with the reaction curves of the two rivals. The Bertrand equilibrium prices P_i^*, P_j^* are determined from the intersection of the reaction curves of the two firms. If both companies want to make best responses to the other's price, which itself is a best response to their own price, the intersection of the two reaction curves is the only possible profit-maximizing combination of prices.

4.4.3. TYPE OF COMPETITIVE REACTION: STRATEGIC SUBSTITUTES VERSUS COMPLEMENTS

The essence of competitive strategy is to anticipate your competitor's moves. The type of competition in the industry is of crucial importance for properly anticipating the competitor's response. The two basic models of duopoly competition discussed above, price competition and quantity competition, imply opposite types of competitive responses. This distinction was first made by Jeremy Bulow, John Geanakoplos, and Paul Klemperer in their article "Multimarket Oligopoly: Strategic Substitutes and Complements."[15] Figure 4.8 summarizes the two qualitatively different cases of competitive reaction (see also Tirole 1990, 327). Panel A (left) shows competitive reactions that are strategic substitutes — such as in quantity competition — involving downward-sloping reaction curves $(-)$, while panel B (right) illustrates strategic complement reactions — such as in price competition — with upward-sloping reaction functions $(+)$.

The classic example of a strategic substitute action is a company's choice of production quantity, shown in the left panel of figure 4.8. When a leading firm increases its quantity on the market (e.g., capturing a larger market share via economies of scale or a learning cost advantage), its rival responds by decreasing its output and market share in order to maximise its profit. Thus, the best response to a competitor's move in a strategic substitutes game is to do the opposite. An action (output level) of the first-moving firm substitutes for the action (output level) of its competitor. Since the competitor's reaction is contrary to the leader's action, we refer to this as *contrarian* competitive reactions. When a rival increases output, the firm's profits fall. The firm can improve them somewhat by reducing its own output, but the profits are still lower. On the other hand, if a competitor lowers its capacity, the firm's profits rise and

[15]For an accessible description, see Morton 1999.

FIGURE 4.8 CONTRARIAN VERSUS RECIPROCATING COMPETITIVE
REACTIONS (STRATEGIC SUBSTITUTES VS. COMPLEMENTS)

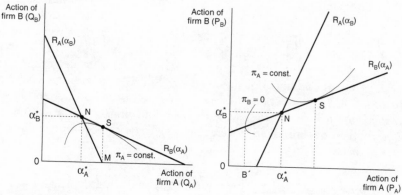

A. Contrarian competition/substitutes; down-sloping reaction curves $R_i(\alpha_i)$ e.g., Quantity competition, $(\alpha_i = Q_i)$

B. Reciprocating competition/complements; up-sloping reaction curves, $R_i(\alpha_i)$ e.g., Price competition, $(\alpha_i = P_i)$

will rise further if it increases its own capacity. For each firm in quantity competition, lower quantity goes hand in hand with lower profits, and higher quantity with higher profits.

The right panel of figure 4.8 depicts upward-sloping reaction functions characterizing strategic complement actions in price competition. Consider again the example of airline tickets. If an airline raises its price, its rival could improve its profits by partially matching the price increase. It could steal some customers away and serve them at a higher margin than before if it matches part of the price increase. If the airline lowers its price, it would be matched by a low price by the competitor (and lower profit margins for both). Both firms may thus be better off if instead the leading firm sets a higher price that the follower can also adopt.

In contrast to quantity competition, the best response in a price competition game is to reciprocate by imitating the original move of your rival. We refer to this as *reciprocating* competitive reaction. In a price competition game, a lower price induces a lower price, while raising prices causes the other company to raise prices; competitors' prices move in the same direction. The pattern of profit changes is also different from quantity competition. Firm actions (price changes) and profits move together, that is, industry prices and profits rise or fall in tandem.

As noted, strategic substitutes or complement reactions are typical in industries characterized by quantity or price competition, respectively. A relevant question is, Which makes sense in a given situation? In general, the demand curve may have both a price component as well as a quantity component. In price competition the company chooses to set the price component of the demand curve. In airlines, cigarettes, or soft drinks, competitors choose the price at which they sell their products. The Bertrand price model pertains to markets where capacity is sufficiently flexible that firms can meet all demand if they change their prices. In a Cournot quantity game, a company chooses what quantity (or capacity) to put on the market, and it is up to market demand to determine the price. Quantity competition more naturally arises in industries where firms set their investment and production decisions in advance and have higher cost for inventories. In such a setting, prices will adjust more quickly than quantities, so price changes will not steal consumers away from others.

4.5. Two-Stage Games: Strategic Value of Early Commitment

We now move to strategic two-stage games. A value-creating strategy may be directed first toward building competitive advantage through an early strategic investment commitment in the first stage, followed by subsequent cash-generating commercial investments in a later stage. An early investment commitment in R & D or a pilot plant in a new market, for example, may seem unattractive based on its direct measurable cash flows when considered in isolation, but may entail substantial strategic value from improving the firm's long-term strategic position (e.g., via reducing operating costs in a later stage or preempting competitive entry).

Understanding the type of competition a firm is likely to face and how to influence it can significantly improve strategic decision making. What makes a strategic investment decision, such as R & D or an advertising campaign, interesting is that the forces in the environment are interactive, that is, competitors are likely to respond. Before making a strategic investment decision, it is crucial to understand in which way a rival will respond, given the competitive setting of the market. Expanding capacity may cause a rival to build less capacity under quantity competition or might even deter competitive entry in some circumstances. However, in a different competitive setting, early strategic investment can be a disadvantage, for example, if advertising is answered by more advertising or if retaliating competition reacts aggressively under price competition.

Clearly, the benefit of a strategic investment will partially depend on its impact on the future position of the firm vis-à-vis its competitor and the type of competitive reaction. An important question is, Would the rival's reaction benefit or hurt the firm and would it intensify or lessen competitive pressures in the industry? Fudenberg and Tirole (1984) have developed an interesting framework for business strategies to capture such strategic interactions. A competitor's response to a strategic investment decision is likely to depend on two dimensions: the type of competitive (re)actions — strategic substitutes or complements — and whether the strategic investment is tough or accommodating. Fudenberg and Tirole's framework helps determine what a competitor's reaction will be and what kinds of initial action might generate positive or negative feedback.

4.5.1. DIRECT VERSUS STRATEGIC EFFECTS OF INVESTMENT COMMITMENT

Following Fudenberg and Tirole, assume that firm A can make a first-stage strategic capital investment, K_A, such as in R & D or in advertising/goodwill. The value (V_i) of second-stage operating profits (π_i) for firm i in each state of nature (for $i = A$ or B) depends on the strategic investment of the pioneer firm, K_A, as well as on the firm's ability to appropriate the benefits when investing in subsequent investment opportunities, which is a function of competitive reaction.

Firm A $\qquad V_A(K_A, \alpha_A^*(K_A), \alpha_B^*(K_A))$ (4.7)

Firm B $\qquad V_B(K_A, \alpha_A^*(K_A), \alpha_B^*(K_A))$

Here

K_A = first-stage strategic capital investment of pioneer firm A (potentially influencing second-stage operating costs, c, if in R & D, or market demand, θ, if in goodwill);

$\alpha_i^*(K_A)$ = optimal (*) second-stage action of firm i (Q_i in quantity competition if R & D, or P_i in price competition if goodwill), in response to first-stage strategic investment (K_A);

$V_i(\ )$ = present value of operating profits (π_i) for firm i in the second stage of the market, given K_A and the optimal actions of both firms.

Firm A must decide whether or not to make an upfront strategic investment commitment, K_A, while each firm must decide whether and when to invest in the second stage and select an optimal action (Q or P), taking the competitor's reaction into account. The strategic investment commitment itself has, in addition to the usual direct cost and benefits, a strategic effect on second-stage competition. For example, an R & D investment that lowers the operational cost of a new factory or technology involves a direct initial capital outlay, K_A, a direct long-run operating cash-flow benefit from a follow-on commercial investment, and a strategic impact due to the change in the competitor's behavior. Sometimes competitive strategies are directed at hurting competitors' future profits so that they accept a smaller market share or even exit the industry.

Pioneer firm A, for example, may invest in a strategic project in order to deter entry by making firm B's entry unprofitable ($NPV_B < 0$), thereby earning monopoly profits in the first stage of the market. The incremental impact of firm A's strategic investment (dK_A) on firm B's second-stage profit value (dV_B) is generally given by

$$\frac{dV_B}{dK_A} = \frac{\partial V_B}{\partial K_A} + \frac{\partial V_B}{\partial \alpha_A} \frac{d\alpha_A^*}{dK_A}. \tag{4.8}$$

To deter entry, firm A must take a tough stance that would hurt its competitor (i.e., $dV_B/dK_A < 0$). If entry deterrence is not feasible or desirable (e.g., if it is too costly), firm A may find it preferable in some cases to follow an accommodating strategy. Firm A's incentive to make the strategic investment then depends on the impact of its incremental investment (dK_A) on its own value from second-stage operating profits, that is,

$$\frac{dV_A}{dK_A} = \frac{\partial V_A}{\partial K_A} + \frac{\partial V_A}{\partial \alpha_B} \frac{d\alpha_B^*}{dK_A}, \tag{4.9}$$

$$\left(\begin{array}{ccc} \text{commitment} & = & \text{direct} + \text{strategic} \\ \text{effect} & & \text{effect} \quad \text{effect} \end{array} \right)$$

where

K_A = first-stage strategic investment outlay of pioneer firm A;

$\alpha_i^*(K_A)$ = optimal (*) second-stage action of firm i (e.g., Q_i in quantity competition, or P_i in price competition), in response to first-stage strategic investment (K_A);

$V_i(\ )$ = present value of operating profits (π_i) for firm i in the second stage of the market, given K_A and the optimal actions of both firms.

It is a prerequisite for an accommodating strategy that firm A's strategic investment must result in a positive commitment value ($dV_A/dK_A > 0$). Equation 4.9 confirms that the commitment effect consists of two components. The total impact of an upfront strategic investment in a more cost-efficient technology, for example, is the sum of the direct and strategic effects. The first term in equation 4.9 captures the direct effect of an incremental strategic investment on firm A's own second-stage profit value, with the competitor's reaction constant. The strategic effect results from the impact of firm A's strategic investment on competitor firm B's optimal second-stage action (e.g., B's output decision), $d\alpha_B^*/dK_A$, and *its* resulting indirect impact on firm A's profit value. Whether firm A should make the strategic investment or not depends, in addition to the direct influence on its own profit value, on whether the indirect strategic effect via the competitor's reaction is positive or negative.

4.5.2. STRATEGIC EFFECT, TOUGH OR ACCOMMODATING POSITIONS, AND TYPE OF COMPETITION

A strategic investment commitment can change the rival's expectations and thereby the firm's own actions. To be credible, a strategic commitment should be costly to reverse and change the best course of action for the firm. If the rival is not convinced that the firm's incentives have changed, or if the commitment can be readily reversed at little cost, it will not have much impact and the strategies will stay basically the same. It is typically hard to reverse investments in R & D or advertising and recover expenditures. Other moves, such as a promise or threat to invest when a player can reverse its decision or cancel it without penalties, are less likely to be perceived as credible commitments. In such cases, the best-response curves will move less or perhaps not at all. True commitments that are costly to reverse alter firm incentives permanently.

A strategic investment commitment can significantly alter the firms' strategic position in the industry. Strategic commitments come in two types: A commitment can either hurt or benefit the competitor. Which type is strategically beneficial depends on what kind of competition exists in the industry. In a price competition game where reactions are reciprocating, you get what you give: accommodating strategic investments are returned with nice behavior, aggressive ones with aggressive behavior. In quantity competition games where reactions are contrarian, aggressive behavior is met with a soft response. A tough or accommodating position could either lessen or increase competitive pressure depending on the type of competition prevailing in the industry at the time.

The sign of the strategic effect in equation 4.9 depends on (1) whether firm A's strategic investment (K_A) would hurt ($-$) or benefit ($+$) its competitor's second-stage profit value, that is, whether A takes a *tough* or *accommodating* position vis-à-vis its competitor (for instance, depending on whether the benefits of the strategic investment are proprietary or shared);[16] and (2) whether competitor B's reaction to firm A's action, $R_B(\alpha_A)$,

---

[16]A *tough* position depends on the firm's ability to appropriate the benefits of its strategic investment so as to hurt its competitor ($dV_B/dK_A < 0$). An example would be a first-mover proprietary cost advantage in the form of lower relative production costs in the later operating stage. Such a cost advantage may be the result of a learning process that is difficult to imitate and is not expected to be eliminated by subsequent technological developments. The position of the pioneering firm is *accommodating* if the resulting benefits are shared and benefit its competitor ($dV_B/dK_A > 0$). That may be the case if the benefits of testing, opening

is *reciprocating,* as often happens in price competition, or *contrarian,* as is often the case in Cournot-type quantity competition. That is,[17]

Sign of the strategic effect ($-$ or $+$) =
whether investing results in a tough ($-$) or accommodating ($+$) position
$\times$ whether competitive actions are contrarian ($-$) or reciprocating ($+$).

Let us first examine the contrarian reactions under quantity competition more closely. Suppose a company faces a strategic investment in an innovation that substantially lowers cost for the next generation of nanotubes. The company wants to build more capacity. Its reaction curve will shift out as it produces more nanotubes. We know from the preceding discussion of quantity competition in section 4.2 that the rival's best response would be to scale back production. Recall that in a quantity competition game, profits move with market share. The pioneer firm would have a positive strategic effect at the expense of the competitor who will earn lower profit [($-$) tough $\times$ ($-$) contrarian].

A strategic investment commitment may have a different impact in a price competition game. Suppose a company pursues a strategic advertising campaign accompanied with charging a lower price than it did before, at each price level its rival would charge. In addition to the direct effects of this campaign on the firm's profits, the advertising campaign will shift its reaction curve down (to lower prices). Lower prices will hurt its competitor, who will reciprocate by (partially) lowering its price. A negative strategic effect will result [($-$) tough $\times$ ($+$) reciprocating].[18]

---

up the market, or developing a more cost-efficient technology are diffused to all firms in the industry. In this case, both firms can have lower costs — a *shared* cost advantage.

[17]Following Fudenberg and Tirole (1984), if we assume that the (second-stage) actions of each firm are of a reciprocal nature so that $\partial V_A / \partial \alpha_B$ has the same sign as $\partial V_B / \partial \alpha_A$, and use

$$\frac{d\alpha_B^*}{dK_A} = \frac{d\alpha_B^* d\alpha_A^*}{d\alpha_A dK_A} = R'_B(\alpha_A^*) \times \frac{d\alpha_A^*}{dK_A},$$

where $R'_B(\alpha_A^*)$ denotes the slope of firm B's reaction function to A's action, the sign of the strategic effect is

$$sign \frac{\partial V_A d\alpha_B^*}{\partial \alpha_B dK_A} = sign \frac{\partial V_A d\alpha_A^*}{\partial \alpha_B dK_A} \times sign(R'_B(\alpha_A^*)).$$

Thus, the sign of the strategic effect is crucially dependent on the sign of the slope of the reaction functions (i.e., whether they are downward sloping or upward sloping), depending on contrarian or reciprocating competition, i.e., on whether the actions are strategic substitutes or complements.

[18]On the other hand, an investment resulting in a higher price than it did before would shift up its best-response curve. The higher prices that result would improve the profitability of the competitor and generate a positive strategic effect [($+$) accommodating $\times$ ($+$) reciprocating].

While the preceding discussion expands the strategic effect of various types of investment commitment, the commitment itself usually also has a direct cost as well as a direct benefit. A discounted cash-flow analysis solely based on the incremental cash flows of the direct effect that naively ignores competitor responses can over- or underestimate the value of strategic investments. Because the direct and strategic effects can be either positive or negative, a careful expanded NPV analysis is required to determine the proper signs and magnitudes, and whether the company will benefit from the strategic move.

Consider, for example, the new manufacturing facility that can produce nanotubes with a more cost-efficient process that would substantially lower prices. Internal corporate estimates for the European firm suggest that greater price differential between the rivals' products will enable the company to enhance its market share by 50%. Missing here, though, is an assessment of the reaction of the competitor. It is unlikely that the U.S. competitor will keep its prices constant in the face of this challenge. The competitor will likely drop its price (at least in part) in response to this lower price. The strategic effect will here be negative $[(-)$ tough $\times (+)$ reciprocating]. As a result, a standard DCF calculation of the new manufacturing facility will likely overestimate the market share and value of this strategic investment. This type of problem requires an expanded NPV analysis of the total value from the new manufacturing facility. It should incorporate not only the direct effect on the company's profits, but also the negative strategic effect resulting from a likely drop in the competitor's price.

A simplistic view of strategic investments based on standard NPV analysis presupposes that only the direct effect matters and that the strategic effect is negligible. This can lead to gross valuation errors and wrong strategic decisions. In the preceding discussion, the strategic investment has no effect on the reaction curve of the rival. Only the firm's own reaction curve is shifted. When the reaction curves of rivals also shift as a result of our strategic investment, the strategic effect might get even more amplified and can overwhelm the direct NPV in many cases.

Often, the benefits of a strategic investment are shared with competitors and might affect a rival's reaction curve. Suppose, for example, that the up-front investment in R & D for a new cost-efficient nanotechnology for commercial production cannot be kept proprietary but is diffused to the industry. Figure 4.8 shows the shifted competitive reaction curves when the shared cost-efficient technology changes the cost structures of both firms. In this case both reaction functions shift outward, further amplifying the strategic effect. An R & D investment commitment with shared benefits might be interpreted as an accommodating stance to a rival who might increase capacity, leading to declining profit margins for both. The strategic reaction effect would be negative [(+) accommodating × (−) contrarian]. Similarly, panel B shows a strategic investment commitment under price competition that shifts both reaction curves upwards, for example, due to a broad advertising campaign directed at customer education that benefits everyone in the industry. The strategic reaction effect would be positive [(+) accommodating × (+) reciprocating], and would get amplified by the upward shift in both firms' reaction curves.

4.6. Summary and Conclusions

Understanding competitors' behavior and how to affect it can significantly improve managerial decisions of strategic investments in oligopolistic markets. When your competitors' behavior has an impact on your profit and value, it is crucial to manage the competitive relationship to your advantage. The combined options and games approach developed in this book can be a valuable tool of analysis to support the overall corporate strategy. These tools are meant to supplement the strategic thinking process and executive's intuition and experience with a more rigorous analysis.

Competitive interaction can sometimes get complicated and sophisticated. Complex real-life strategic investment problems must be simplified to their basic components to make the analysis more feasible. Game theory (supplemented with options analysis) helps doing this. We can take a complex strategic problem and reduce it to a simpler analytical structure with five dimensions: (1) identification of the players, (2) appropriate order in which the players make their decisions, (3) the set of actions and information set, (4) the payoff structure attached to each possible outcome, and (5) the backward induction solution procedure.

In oligopolistic markets, game theory can be applied to model the impact of a firm's decision on competitors and determine equilibrium outcomes and competitive strategies. The examples we provided are relatively simple, but they represent a critical building block for understanding more elaborate situations. While these games may seem simplistic in many regards, they illustrate fundamental points about how competition works in these settings. More elaborate strategies can be built based on these insights, so it is important to understand these basic ideas.

The combined options and game theory perspective is particularly relevant for innovative oligopolistic industries (e.g., pharmaceuticals or consumer electronics) facing high research and development costs in multiple stages in a technologically uncertain and competitive environment. The war of attrition in video systems, the coordination game of the CD technology, or the adversarial and accommodating strategies for the high-density disk are just a few examples of games that corporations face in daily life. Firms can make early strategic investments in R & D to improve their competitive position and their ability to develop and capitalize on growth opportunities in the industry. Patents and proprietary use of information can limit the exploitation of similar opportunities by competitors. In cases of differentiated products under contrarian, quantity-type competition (e.g., in pharmaceuticals), competition is likely to retreat. However, we saw that it is not always wise to compete aggressively.

An important aspect of corporate strategy is knowing when to compete aggressively and when to coordinate strategies with competition or support rivals. If you know whether competitors' actions are strategic substitutes or complements and you understand whether your strategic position is tough or accommodating, you can predict your competitors' response. This allows managers to avoid harmful competitive reactions and take advantage of profitable opportunities and competitive dynamics. For instance, when the product is homogeneous and competitive response is reciprocating, as in price competition in the airline, tobacco, or food industries, adversarial strategies may result in price wars and erosion of profit margins for all sides. Such competitive pressures could be avoided with more accommodating strategies in these cases.[19]

A word of caution is in order here. Game theory assumes rationality on the part of all players in a game. As we have noted (see box insert 4.5), that may not always be the case. It is common for people to act in imperfectly rational ways. There are many unexplained phenomena — even assuming rationality — that we only now begin to understand. Alternating (or randomizing) between two losing strategies, for example, may lead to a winning result! There are other phenomena we do not currently understand at all. Many times psychology can take dominance over rationality (as we all experience many times in our daily lives). Still, in business and economic decisions, the assumption of rationality may be a good starting point for gaining a better understanding of the world around us.

---

[19]Coordination and gains from sharing information may result in higher profits for all under certain circumstances. Firms can also work together to achieve more innovation and growth. Firms can cooperate in R & D via standardization agreements, joint R & D ventures, or other forms of strategic alliances. A potential drawback is that while these ventures may strengthen the firm's position, they may sometimes also help to build up new competitors. We will revisit these issues via a more rigorous analysis in later chapters.

Appendix 4.1

A Chronology of Game
Theory Developments[*]

0–500 C.E.

The Babylonian Talmud, a compilation of ancient law and tradition set down during the first five centuries C.E., serves as the basis of Jewish religious, criminal, and civil law. One problem discussed in the Talmud is the following marriage contract problem: a man has three wives whose marriage contracts specify that in the case of his death they receive 100, 200, and 300, respectively. The Talmud gives apparently contradictory recommendations. Where the man dies leaving an estate of only 100, the Talmud recommends equal division. However, if the estate is worth 300, it recommends proportional division (50, 100, 150), while for an estate of 200, its recommendation of (50, 75, 75) is a complete mystery. This has baffled scholars for two millennia. In 1985, it was recognized that the Talmud might anticipate the modern theory of cooperative games. Each solution corresponds to the nucleolus of an appropriately defined game.

1713

James Waldegrave provided the first known minimax mixed-strategy solution to a two-person game. Waldegrave wrote a letter about a two-person version of the card game *le Her* to Pierre-Remond de Montmort, who in turn wrote to Nicolas Bernoulli about the Waldegrave solution. Waldegrave's solution is a minimax mixed-strategy equilibrium, though he expressed concern that a mixed strategy "does not seem to be in the usual rules of play" for games of chance.

1838

Publication of Augustin Cournot's *Researches into the Mathematical Principles of the Theory of Wealth*. In chapter 7, "On the Competition of

---

[*]A more complete chronology is provided by Walker 1995.

Producers," Cournot discusses the special case of duopoly and utilizes a solution concept that is a restricted version of the Nash equilibrium. In the first edition of his book *The Descent of Man and Selection in Relation to Sex,* Charles Darwin gives the first (implicity) game-theoretic argument in evolutionary biology. Darwin argued that natural selection will act to equalize the sex ratio.

1881

Publication of Francis Ysidro Edgeworth's *Mathematical Psychics: An Essay on the Application of Mathematics to the Moral Sciences.* Edgeworth proposed the contract curve as a solution to the problem of determining the outcome of trading between individuals. In a world of two commodities and two types of consumers, he demonstrated that the contract curve shrinks to the set of competitive equilibriums as the number of consumers of each type becomes infinite.

1913

The first 'theorem' of game theory was put forth, asserting that chess is strictly determined, that is, either white or black can force a win or at least a draw. This theorem was published by E. Zermelo (and is referred to as Zermelo's Theorem).

1921–27

Emile Borel published four notes on strategic games, giving the first modern formulation of a mixed strategy along with finding the minimax solution for two-person games with three or five possible strategies. Initially he maintained that games with more possible strategies would not have minimax solutions, but by 1927 he considered this an open question, as he had been unable to find a counterexample.

1928

John von Neumann proved the minimax theorem, stating that every two-person zero-sum game with finitely many pure strategies for each player is determined. That is, when mixed strategies are admitted, this game has precisely one rational payoff vector. von Neumann also introduced the extensive form of a game.

1944

Theory of Games and Economic Behavior by John von Neumann and Oskar Morgenstern is published. Besides expounding two-person zero-sum theory, this book provided seminal work in cooperative games transferable utility (TU), coalitional form and stable sets. The book's account of axiomatic utility theory led to widespread adoption of the theory within economics.

1950

Contributions to the Theory of Games I, vol. 1, edited by H. W. Kuhn and A. W. Tucker is published. In January 1950 Melvin Dresher and Merrill Flood carry out, at the Rand Corporation, an experiment that introduced the prisoners' dilemma. The famous story associated with this game is due to A. W. Tucker, "A Two-Person Dilemma" (memo, Stanford University). Howard Raiffa also independently conducted unpublished experiments with the prisoners' dilemma.

1950–53

In four papers between 1950 and 1953 John Nash made seminal contributions to both noncooperative game theory and to bargaining theory. In two papers, "Equilibrium Points in N-Person Games" (1950) and "Noncooperative Games" (1951), Nash proved the existence of a strategic equilibrium for noncooperative games — the Nash equilibrium — and proposed the "Nash program," in which he suggested approaching the study of cooperative games via their reduction to noncooperative form. In his two papers on bargaining theory, "The Bargaining Problem" (1950) and "Two-Person Cooperative Games" (1953), Nash founded axiomatic bargaining theory, proved the existence of the Nash bargaining solution, and provided the first execution of the Nash program.

1952–53

The notion of the core as a general solution concept was developed by L. S. Shapley and D. B. Gillies. The core is the set of allocations that cannot be improved upon by any coalition.

1955

One of the first applications of game theory to philosophy is R. B. Braithwaite's *Theory of Games as a Tool for the Moral Philosopher.*

1961

The first explicit application to evolutionary biology is by R. C. Lewontin in *Evolution and the Theory of Games.*

1962

In *College Admissions and the Stability of Marriage,* D. Gale and L. Shapley examine whether it is possible to match *m* women with *m* men so that there is no pair consisting of a woman and a man who prefer each other to the partners with whom they are currently matched.

1967–68

In a series of three papers, "Games with Incomplete Information Played by 'Bayesian' Players," *Parts I, II and III,* John Harsanyi developed the theory of games of incomplete information. This laid the theoretical groundwork for information economics that has become one of the major themes of economics and game theory.

1972

The International Journal of Game Theory is founded by Oskar Morgenstern. The concept of an Evolutionarily Stable Strategy (ESS) is introduced to evolutionary game theory by John Maynard Smith in an essay "Game Theory and the Evolution of Fighting." The ESS concept has since found increasing use within the economics (and biology) literature.

1973

In the traditional view of strategy randomization, the players use a randomizing device to decide on their actions. John Harsanyi is the first to break away from this view with his paper "Games with Randomly Disturbed Payoffs: A New Rationale for Mixed Strategy Equilibrium Points." For Harsanyi nobody really randomizes. The appearance of randomization is due to the payoffs not being exactly known to all; each player, who knows his own payoff exactly, has a unique optimal action against his estimate of what the others will do.

A major impetus for the use of the ESS concept is the publication of J. Maynard Smith and G. Price's "The Logic of Animal Conflict."

1977

S. C. Littlechild and G. F. Thompson apply the nucleolus to the problem of cost allocation in "Aircraft Landing Fees: A Game Theory Approach." They use the nucleolus, along with the core and Shapley value, to calculate fair and efficient landing and takeoff fees for Birmingham airport.

1982

David M. Kreps and Robert Wilson, in "Sequential Equilibrium," extend the idea of a subgame perfect equilibrium to subgames in the extensive form that begin at information sets with imperfect information. They call this extended idea of equilibrium *sequential.*

1982

Publication of *Evolution and the Theory of Games* by John Maynard Smith.

1984

Publication of *The Evolution of Cooperation* by Robert Axelrod.

1985

For a Bayesian game the question arises as to whether it is possible to construct a situation for which there is no set of types large enough to contain all the private information that players are supposed to have. In their paper, "Formulation of Bayesian Analysis for Games with Incomplete Information," J.-F. Mertens and S. Zamir show that it is not possible to do so.

1988

One interpretation of the Nash equilibrium is to think of it as an accepted (learned) "standard of behavior" that governs the interaction of various agents in repetitions of similar situations. The problem then arises of how agents learn the equilibrium. One of the earliest works to attack the learning problem was Drew Fudenberg and David Kreps's "A Theory of Learning, Experimentation and Equilibrium," which uses a learning process where players occasionally experiment by choosing strategies at random in the context of iterated extensive form games. Evolutionary game models are commonly utilized within the learning literature.

1994

The Central Bank of Sweden Prize in Economic Science in Memory of Alfred Nobel is awarded to John Nash, John C. Harsanyi, and Reinhard Selten for their contributions to game theory.

Part II

Competitive
Strategy and Games

Chapter 5

Simple Strategic Investment Games

*Any intelligent fool can make things
bigger, more complex . . . It takes . . .
a lot of courage . . . to move in the
opposite direction.*
— Albert Einstein

5.1. Introduction

In April 1997 Microsoft agreed to buy WebTV Networks, a startup company that delivered Internet information directly to television sets for $425 million, even though the company's plans did not call for WebTV to become profitable until after its third year of operation. WebTV attracted nine major financiers in several rounds of financing, indicating that both Microsoft and the market recognized its future growth-option value. Since WebTV's founding two years earlier, investors had earned more than a 14-fold return. The acquisition was part of Microsoft's strategy to define the technology for the coming era of digital television and to embed its technology in nearly every consumer electronics device.

This chapter presents a simple options and games framework that addresses questions such as, "How much is a strategic option such as Microsoft's future growth opportunities worth?" And, given anticipated competitive reactions, "How does one analyze such strategic options in a dynamic, interactive competitive environment?" More generally, what logic should managers use in evaluating investments under uncertain conditions, especially when conventional approaches (NPV) to this problem are unsuitable?

To address these questions we develop simple numerical examples that integrate option theory with principles from game theory and strategic management theory, allowing us to *quantify* flexibility in simple terms and demonstrate its relevance in practical cases from high-tech industries. We recognize there are many complications in reality that are different from our stylized examples, but believe that these can serve as a starting basis for a more rigorous strategic analysis. We cast our model in a realistic setting, for example, by discussing the nature of first-mover advantage via its impact on the value of growth options, and illustrate the mechanisms at work in the phenomena we observe.

The chapter is organized as follows. Section 5.2 presents a road map for analyzing competitive strategies with the analysis made increasingly complicated at successive stages. One-stage and two-stage strategic investment problems are discussed in section 5.3, and sections 5.4 and 5.5, respectively. Section 5.6 examines the effect of cooperation. Section 5.7 provides a summary and concludes.

5.2. A Road Map for Analyzing Competitive Strategies

This chapter illustrates the different features and richness of our framework in a detailed but simple way. Table 5.1 helps provide a road map by showing how the analysis starts simple and becomes complicated in successive stages, and provides an overview of the structure of this chapter. To introduce different aspects into the analysis one at a time, we start with simple one-stage investment decisions (options) under uncertainty (first when proprietary and then under endogenous competition), and then extend the analysis to two-stage (compound) option games (again first with no competition, and then with endogenous competition in the last stage only, and finally in both stages). We find it instructive to follow the following step-by-step thought experiment, starting with one-stage strategic investments.

1. Consider a high-tech company holding a one-year license (or a patent expiring in a year) giving it a simple proprietary option to invest in commercial production of a new product (a single-stage investment) this year or wait until next year when demand uncertainty will be clarified. What is the value of this license?
2. What is the impact on the value of the option to wait represented by the license when competitive entry can take part of total market value away from the incumbent, while early strategic investment by the incumbent can preempt competitive entry altogether (avoiding competitive value erosion), reverting back to capturing the full market value for itself?

Turning to two-stage strategic investments:

3. Stepping back in time to an earlier stage in the decision process of the high-tech company, should it make the R & D expenditure in the first place in order to acquire a proprietary option to proceed with the commercialization investment in the second stage (introduced in number 1 above)? Similarly, how can we think about valuing an infrastructure investment, a strategic investment to gain a foothold in a new market, a strategic acquisition, or other multistage growth options?

4. What is the impact on the firm's first-stage R & D strategy of facing (endogenous) competition in production (stage 2) that can influence asymmetrically the equilibrium production outcome and its profit value? Can the optimal competitive R & D strategy be different depending on whether the strategic R & D investment creates proprietary or shared benefits? How does it differ when competitive responses are opposite (aggressive vs. accommodating) from strategy under complement or reciprocating responses (that may increase the total "pie" if the firms cooperate but may reduce it if they get into intensified rivalry or a price war)? We suggest that the firm may be better off to make the strategic R & D investment in some cases (e.g., when there are proprietary benefits when competitive reactions are contrarian or shared benefits when competitive reactions are reciprocating) but not in others (e.g., shared benefits when competition is contrarian or proprietary benefits when competition is reciprocating).

5. Besides the firms competing in production in the second stage, what is the impact of their also competing in R & D (in the first stage) in a *sequential* investment timing game (e.g., an innovation race) whereby the first mover can achieve a time-to-market advantage that may preempt its competitor and "win all"? But then what if both competitors end up making a similar investment *simultaneously* such that one is badly hurt or both are left worse off?

6. What are the benefits instead of cooperating in the first stage via a joint R & D venture (in a simultaneous investment game), as many computer and other high-tech firms do today (while they may still compete in the last stage of commercial production)? Do the benefits of sharing the R & D costs and more fully appropriating jointly the option value of waiting under demand uncertainty outweigh any potential competitive advantage that a first mover might achieve under a competing strategy?

Table 5.1 distinguishes between these one-stage and two-stage investment problems and their varieties. The one-stage option problem and the impact of endogenous competitive entry are introduced in section 5.3. In section 5.4 we start our discussion of two-stage strategic investments as compound growth options (e.g., proprietary R & D). In section 5.5 we add the complication of endogenous competitive dynamics in the second (production) stage depending on the nature of competitive reactions (contrarian vs. reciprocating) and the type of investment (proprietary or shared); then we examine endogenous competition in the first stage as well, for example, competition in R & D or innovation races and strategic alliances. Section 5.6 examines the effect of cooperation in first-stage

TABLE 5.1
Successive Stages of Analysis: Option Games, Related Literature, Problem
Description, Implications, and Practical Examples/Applications

Type of Option Game	Relevant Research	Problem Description
One-stage games with no competition (proprietary option). See section 5.3.	McDonald and Siegel 1986; Brennan and Schwartz 1985a, 1985b	Investment *opportunities* can be viewed as simple proprietary options to invest. For example, a high-tech company holding a one-year license (or a patent expiring in a year) giving it an option to decide whether to invest in commercial production of a new product this year or wait until next year when demand uncertainty will be clarified
One-stage games with endogenous competitive reactions (shared options). See section 5.3.	Dixit 1979, 1980; Spence 1977, 1979; Kester 1984; Baldwin 1987a; Trigeorgis 1988; Ghemawat and del Sol 1998; McGahan 1993b; Smit and Ankum 1993	A *game-theoretic* treatment becomes necessary when shared opportunities face a competitive loss. Firms have incentives to invest earlier than one otherwise would to preempt anticipated competitive entry (strategic games against competition)
Two-stage options with no competition. See section 5.4.	McGrath 1997; Bettis and Hitt 1995; Bowman and Hurry 1993	Investments in growth options, for example the analysis of R & D opportunities in order to acquire a proprietary option to proceed with the commercialization investment in the second stage
Two-stage games with endogenous competition in stage 2. See section 5.5.	Dasgupta and Stiglitz 1980; Appelbaum and Lim 1985; Daughety and Reinganum 1990; Spencer and Brander 1992; Kulatilaka and Perotti 1998	First-stage R & D strategy facing (endogenous) competition in production (stage 2) that can influence asymmetrically the equilibrium production outcome and the incumbent's profit value
Two-stage games with endogenous competition in both stages. See section 5.5.	Appelbaum and Lim 1985; Spencer and Brander 1992	Endogenous competition via strategic investments in the first stage affects the value in the second stage
Competition vs. cooperation in stage 1 (joint R & D ventures). See section 5.6.	Kogut 1991	Cooperation competition in the first stage affects the value in the second stage

Implications	Examples/Applications
Incentive to delay investment under uncertainty (as found in resource extraction industries)	In 1990 Digital faced a timing decision as to when to commercialize its Alpha microprocessor chip and decided to wait in light of uncertain demand resulting from uncertainty about which product standard would prevail. Similarly, in 1995 Sony had to decide when to commercialize the Multi-Media CD, developed in cooperation with Philips, under uncertainty over the future product standard and competitive moves.
Timing is a tradeoff between commitment and flexibility value. Competitors face a timing game where investment may pre-empt competitors from exercising their shared rights	The commercialization decision of Digital's Alpha chip was greatly influenced by Intel's decisions regarding its Pentium processor; similarly, Philips and Sony's strategy to commercialize the digital video disk was affected by competitive decisions by Toshiba and Time Warner. The introduction of the Multi-Media Compact Disk developed by Sony (and Philips) in 1995 faced competitive erosion from companies like Toshiba, Time Warner, and Matsushita (with the Super-Density Disk). Similarly, Texas Instruments' entry into digital TV with its digital light processing technology for high-quality big-screen television, developed over a decade for over $500 million, faced anticipated competitive erosion with substitute products by Sony, Fujitsu, and Sharp.
Negative NPV of the first stage can be justified for its growth option value	In April 1997 Hewlett-Packard agreed to buy Verifone, the leading maker of credit card authorization devices, for $1.15 billion (although Verifone's 1996 earnings of just $39.3 million gave a negative NPV) for its growth potential to dominate the emerging electronic commerce business. In the same month, Microsoft bought WebTV Networks, maker of set-top boxes that bring the Internet to TV sets, at a price of $425 million, despite its losing over $30 million in the past year alone.
Competitive strategy based on the *type* of investment *(proprietary* vs. *shared)* and the *nature* of competitive *reaction (reciprocating* vs. *contrarian)*	Cooperation in (second-stage) production and services among many leading Japanese and US firms: IBM and Toshiba jointly manufacturing liquid-crystal display panels; GE supplying components to Toyota, while Toyota helps distribute GM's Cavalier through its dealership network in Japan; Mitsubishi and Dupont launching a joint polyethylene manufacturing venture; Sumitomo and Exxon cooperating in oil and gas development in China.
Trade-off between cooperation and competition	Race in memory chip development: In February 1997 Hitachi, Mitsubishi Electric, and Texas Instruments announced they would jointly develop a 1 gb DRAM. NEC, which has been cooperating loosely with ATT spin-off Lucent Technologies and Samsung, announced in June 1997 that it had developed a 4 gb DRAM, the largest-capacity memory chip ever developed, putting NEC in the lead in the intensely competitive memory chip technology race.
Evolution of cooperation in technology intensive industries	In 1995 the alliance of Philips and Sony (which developed the Multi-Media CD) came to agreement with the alliance of Toshiba and Matsushita (which developed the Super-Density Disk) to set a common industry standard for the new-generation high-density CD (the digital video disc). Other examples involve joint R & D ventures, especially among U.S. and Japanese firms: Toshiba and IBM shared the $1 billion cost of developing a 64 mb and 256 mb memory-chip facility outside Nagoya using IBM's know-how in chemical mechanical polishing (the technology was to be transferred back to an IBM plant in Virginia in 1997).

R & D (joint R & D ventures) on the value of such pioneering strategies. Section 5.7 provides a summary and conclusion.

5.3. One-Stage Strategic Investments

In general, we can distinguish between two basic types of decision problems that a firm's management may face: (1) *games against nature*, in which management's problem is to optimize in the face of random fluctuations in demand or prices (and hence in project value, V), most typical in perfectly or highly competitive markets; and (2) *strategic games against competition*, in which each firm's investment decisions are made with the explicit recognition that they may invite competitive reaction that would in turn impact the value of its own investment opportunity, generally found in less competitive or oligopolistic markets.

Simple Proprietary Options: A License by a High-Tech Firm

In 1990 Digital faced a timing decision as to when to commercialize its Alpha microprocessor chip and decided to wait in light of uncertainty in demand, which would depend on which product standard would prevail. Similarly, in 1995 Sony had to decide when to commercialize the digital video disc (Multi-Media CD), developed in cooperation with Philips, under uncertainty over the future product standard and competitive moves.

Consider again the capital investment opportunity shown in figure 3.1, reproduced here as figure 5.1.[1] A high-tech company has an exclusive opportunity (a license or patent) to build plant capacity for producing a new product that involves making an expenditure of $I_0 = \$80$ million (in present value terms). The (gross) value of expected future cash inflows from production, $V_0 = 100$ million, may fluctuate in line with the random fluctuation in demand, say to $V^+ = 180$ million or $V^- = 60$ million (with equal probability, $q = 0.5$) by the end of the period (e.g., due to uncertainty over the product standard). The *opportunity to invest* provided by the license is thus analogous to a *call option* on the value of the developed (completed) project (V), with an "exercise price" equal to the required outlay, $I_0 = 80$ million.

The value of this investment opportunity can be obtained from the end-of-period expected values with expectations taken over risk-neutral probabilities (here $p = 0.4$ and $1 - p = 0.6$), discounted at the risk-free rate (here $r = 0.08$): the expanded net present value NPV^* or $C = [0.4 \times 100 + 0.6 \times 0] / 1.08 = \$37$ million. The value of the proprietary option exceeds the passive NPV of an immediate investment commitment of 100

[1]This example is similar to the one used in chapter 3.

FIGURE 5.1 PROPRIETARY OPPORTUNITY (LICENSE):
WAIT TO INVEST UNDER UNCERTAINTY

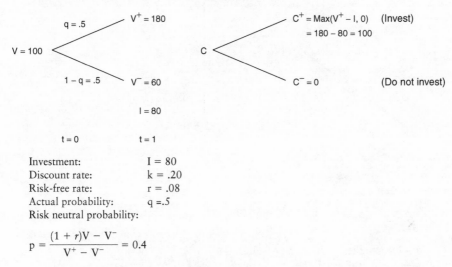

Investment: $I = 80$
Discount rate: $k = .20$
Risk-free rate: $r = .08$
Actual probability: $q = .5$
Risk neutral probability:

$$p = \frac{(1 + r)V - V^-}{V^+ - V^-} = 0.4$$

Opportunity to invest provided by license (call option):

$$C = \frac{p \times C^+ + (1 - p) \times C^-}{1 + r} = \frac{.4 \times 100 + .6 \times 0}{1.08} = 37$$

− 80 (i.e., 37 > 20 million). However, a firm anticipating competitive entry can commit early to preempt competition and avoid competitive erosion in a way analogous to capturing a dividend-like benefit.

Endogenous Competitive Reactions

In the earlier example of chapter 3, the impact of competitive entry was assumed to be *exogenous:* Management still faced an *optimization problem* in that it had to incorporate the anticipated impact of competitive erosion on its own investment decision (requiring a dividend-like adjustment in option value), but could ignore any reciprocal effects of that decision on the competitor's actions. Exogenous competition can actually be thought of as a special case of endogenous competition when the firm's actions do not affect those of other firms.

If, however, each competitor's decisions depend on the other's moves, then a more complex *game-theoretic* treatment becomes necessary.[2] The

[2]There is a considerable literature on endogenous timing of investment and preemption, e.g., Anderson and Engers 1994, and Holden and Riis 1994. Dixit (1979, 1980) discusses the role of early investment in entry deterrence, while Spence (1977) shows that existing firms in an industry facing competitive threat should carry excess capacity so as to expand

FIGURE 5.2 SIMULTANEOUS INVESTMENT TIMING GAME: COMPETE AND
INVEST PREMATURELY (PRISONERS' DILEMMA)

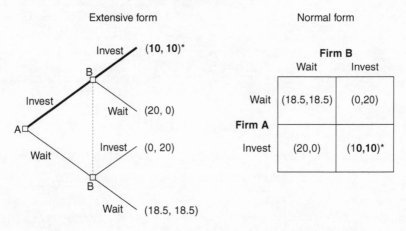

commercialization decision of Digital's Alpha chip was in fact greatly influenced by Intel's decisions regarding its Pentium processor; similarly,
Philips and Sony's strategy to commercialize the digital video disc was affected by competitive decisions by Toshiba and Time Warner, and vice
versa. Investing earlier than one otherwise would to preempt anticipated
competitive entry was a simple case of such *strategic games against competition.* More generally, instead of the optimization relying solely on option valuation techniques, the investment opportunity values at the end
nodes in a binomial option tree are replaced by the equilibrium outcomes
of competitive investment subgames.

Figure 5.2 illustrates such a game both in *extensive* form (tree to the
left) and in normal form (value-payoff table to the right). Consider the resulting values either at the end of each tree branch or in the payoff table
(firm A, firm B) in the following four investment-timing scenarios: (1) when
both firms invest immediately (simultaneously), they equally share the
total NPV ($\frac{1}{2} \times 20$) resulting in a (10, 10) value payoff for each firm; (2)/
(3) when one firm (A or B) invests first while the other waits, it preempts
its competitor, appropriating the full NPV (20) for itself and resulting in
a payoff of (20, 0) or (0, 20), respectively; and (4) when both firms decide
to wait, they equally share the value of the defer option ($\frac{1}{2} \times 37$), resulting in a (18.5, 18.5) payoff.

---

output and reduce prices when entry is threatened, thereby preempting competitive entry.
Spence (1979) finds that constraints on growth and the timing of entry place firms in asymmetrical positions concerning investment, with those firms in the most advantageous positions preempting the market to some degree.

In the value-payoff structure of figure 5.2 a Nash equilibrium outcome is reached. Firm A's payoff from pursuing an immediate investment commitment strategy (lower row) exceeds its payoff from a wait-and-see strategy (upper row), regardless of which strategy firm B chooses (20 > 18.5 in left "wait" column, 10 > 0 in right "invest" column); that is, firm A has a *dominant strategy* to invest, regardless of the timing decision of its competitor. Firm B also has a dominant strategy to invest, resulting in a Nash equilibrium (*) in the lower right cell, where both firms receive their second-worst payoff of (10, 10), an example of the prisoners' dilemma. The paradox, of course, is that the equilibrium outcome (10, 10) is worse for both firms, compared with the situation when both choose to defer (18.5, 18.5). If the two firms could coordinate their investment strategy, they could share the flexibility benefits of the wait-and-see option, potentially avoiding the inferior "panic equilibrium" in which everybody rushes to invest prematurely.[3] In section 5.6, we will return to examine how cooperation may improve the situation.

An important aspect in exercising options in the competitive game is the intrinsic value $(V - I)$ of the option or the value of immediate exercise (investment). The exercise cost (I) is likely to be idiosyncratic to each firm. Exercising the option to launch a new Windows-based package, for instance, is going to be less expensive for Microsoft than for another firm, by virtue of its dominance in desktops. The exercise price ratio is therefore not "half" of the total investment outlay for all players, but instead an idiosyncratic value that is dependent on the cost of the project beyond the cost incurred. The value of the underlying cash flows, V, is also likely to be idiosyncratic, as firms may earn a higher benefit because of reputation or other effects. The uncertainty each firm faces is likely to be idiosyncratic as well. Higher firm-specific uncertainty increases the value of a firm's growth options, increasing its incentive for waiting in the trade-off between strategic commitment and flexibility.

First-movership may provide differing advantages depending upon the quality and market power of the mover, the imitability (proprietary nature) of the incumbent's position, the time lag of the follower, learning, buyers' switching costs, and network externalities. If the technology or position of the firm is more (less) difficult to protect, the erosion effect could be higher (lower). In high-tech industries, a firm may preempt competition and capture a significant share of the market by setting the product standard early on. Time-to-market may be an important source of advantage that may establish a sustainable strategic position for the organization. Intel preempted 80% of the microprocessor market with its

[3]This observation has been analyzed extensively in the literature on investment under incomplete information, e.g., Hendricks and Kovenock 1989.

Pentium microchip that became the product standard, forcing competitors like Digital to retreat from the market, even though Digital's Alpha chip was three to four times as powerful as the Pentium chip at a fraction of the cost. Network externalities can also influence the strategic game between firms in the choice of technologies. In the competition in video between VHS, Betamax, and V2000, the early mover developed a large installed base and became the product standard. First-mover advantage can of course be influenced by the reputation of the firm and buyers' switching costs, in cases where buyers develop brand-specific know-how that is not fully transferable if they switch (as in document processing). In some cases there may be second-mover advantages, typically present in two-stage games where the follower can benefit from the pioneer's first-stage strategic investment (discussed in section 5.4).

Securing an early-mover advantage may enable a firm to capture a larger share of the market. Whether the early-mover advantage can be sustained depends on subtle ways of the industry context. Switching costs and network externalities may suppress competition in a later stage of the market (Klemperer 1987). In the next section we endogenize this behavior and trade-offs. We next turn to multistage strategic decisions.

5.4. Two-Stage (Compound) Options: The Case of Proprietary R & D

The distinction between one-stage and two-stage option games or simple and compound options is important because most strategic opportunities involve path-dependent sequential investments. Many multistage strategic investments appear to have a negative NPV when considered in isolation, although they may have substantial growth option value. In April 1997 Hewlett-Packard agreed to buy Verifone, the leading maker of credit card authorization devices, for $1.15 billion (although Verifone's 1996 earnings of just $39.3 million gave a negative NPV) for its growth potential to dominate the emerging electronic commerce business. In the same month, Microsoft bought WebTV Networks, maker of set-top boxes that bring the Internet to TV sets, at a price of $425 million, despite its losing over $30 million in the previous year alone. Again, this "negative NPV" acquisition can be justified for its growth option value as part of Microsoft's strategy of dominating the Internet.

What is the value of such a strategic acquisition or of an R & D venture that may result in uncertain future commercialization opportunities? How can management decide whether or not to invest in R & D to develop a new proprietary technology, or how much to bid for a strategic acquisition? Such investments often involve high initial costs and highly uncertain, contingent and remote cash inflows. Figure 5.3 illustrates a

FIGURE 5.3 TWO-STAGE INVESTMENT (E.G., R & D/INFRASTRUCTURE/ GROWTH OPTION)

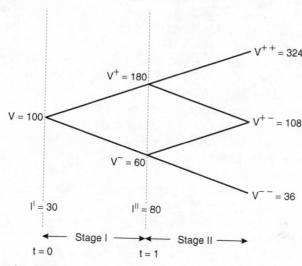

$$NPV = NPV^I + NPV^{II}$$
$$= -30 + \left(\frac{-80}{1.08} + \frac{.5 \times 180 + .5 \times 60}{1.20}\right)$$
$$= -30 + (-74 + 100) = -30 + 26 = -4\,(< 0)$$

$$NPV^* = NPV^I + \text{Option}^{II} = -30 + \left(\frac{.4 \times (180 - 80) + .6 \times 0}{1.08}\right)$$
$$= -30 + 37 = +7\,(> 0)$$

two-stage R & D project with an immediate, stage-I investment outlay of $I^I = 30$ million. Despite high costs and no expected cash inflows during the first stage, management intuitively feels the necessity of the investment to prove the new technology and enhance the company's market position if that market (or a spin-off product) develops. Investing now in the pioneer R & D venture derives strategic value from generating growth opportunities to invest in future commercial projects.

Based on naive DCF analysis, the standard total net present value of this pioneer R & D venture is $NPV = NPV$ (stage I) + NPV (stage II). Here, $NPV^I = -I^I = -30$ million. The follow-on commercial project (stage II) requires an outlay of $I^{II} = 80$ million (the same as in earlier examples) in year 1 and is expected to generate a value of subsequent cash inflows at that time of $E(V_1) = 120$ million (= $0.5 \times 180 + 0.5 \times 60$). This gives a time-zero second-stage value of $NPV^{II} = 100 - 74 = 26$ million (after discounting $E(V_1) = 120$ million at the opportunity cost of capital, $k = 20\%$, and the known investment outlay of $I^{II} = 80$ million at the risk-free rate, $r = 8\%$). Thus, if the firm were to commit to both stages right now, the total expected net project value would amount to $NPV = NPV^I + NPV^{II} = -30 + 26 = -4$ million (< 0). Since commitment to this two-stage investment is expected to result in negative NPV, a naive finance executive may recommend rejecting the R & D venture altogether.

However, top management may realize that it has an *option* (not a commitment) to invest in the second stage. The negative NPV (cost) of first-stage R & D is the price that needs to be paid to acquire a growth option in the commercial project: the more uncertain the technology or the more volatile the future market demand, the higher the value of this option will be. That is so because the firm is asymmetrically positioned since it will invest in the follow-on commercial project (stage II) *only if* project value *at that time* turns out to exceed the required investment outlay of $I^{II} = 80$ million, but it has no obligation to proceed otherwise (truncating downside value to 0 rather than receiving $60 - 80 = -20$ million, as might implicitly be factored into the expectation underlying a naive application of NPV). Is the value of the acquired option, however, worth the required investment cost? Using options valuation, the value of the second-stage commercialization (growth) option is $Option^{II} = (0.4 \times \text{Max} (180 - 80, 0) + 0.6 \times 0) / 1.08 = 37$ million (rather than $NPV^{II} = 26$ million, as given by conventional DCF). Thus, the total strategic value (or expanded NPV) of the entire pioneer R & D venture is $NPV^* = NPV^I + Option^{II} = -30 + 37 = +7$ million (> 0), which makes the R & D investment worthwhile.

It is important to recognize that different stages may have distinctly different risk characteristics: the first stage explores and creates options that can be exploited in the second stage. There is a distinction between uncertainties that investment can resolve via learning and those that cannot (e.g., see Dixit and Pindyck 1994). The firms in the one-stage games of our framework face *market uncertainty* over operating cash flows that result primarily from uncertainties in demand or prices of factors of production. These uncertainties are largely exogenous to the firm. This creates an incentive in simple options to delay until more information is revealed that the project is clearly profitable. Of course, this depends on the context in that even attractive demand conditions may not generate favorable option value in cases where adoption rates are slow and commercialization costs are high (see McGrath 1997). Two-stage games additionally include exploratory options involving firm-specific uncertainties (that may or may not be reduced by investment). These include technical, strategic, and organizational uncertainties.[4]

---

[4]The uncertainty of "technical success" relates to the outcome of the R & D effort. Examples include investment in clinical testing in order to resolve side effects in the development of a new drug.

5.5. Two-Stage Investments with Endogeneous Competition

As noted above, with an early strategic investment the firm may acquire options to capitalize on follow-on investment opportunities or may enhance its relative competitive position in a later stage of the market by deterring entry or otherwise influencing the behavior of its competitors. In section 5.5.1 we introduce endogenous competition in the last stage (production) that may have a different impact depending on whether they are contrarian (strategic substitute) or reciprocating (strategic complement) competitive reactions. In section 5.5.2 endogenous competition may take place in the strategic investment (first) stage as well as in the production (second) stage.

5.5.1. COMPETITION IN LAST (PRODUCTION) STAGE: CONTRARIAN VERSUS RECIPROCATING COMPETITION

Sometimes competitive strategies are directed at hurting competitors' future profits so that they accept a smaller market share or exit the industry, creating proprietary (monopoly) profit opportunities for an incumbent. On other occasions, for example if entry deterrence is not feasible or desirable (e.g., if it is too costly) or if competition is such that retaliation is likely and potentially very damaging, an incumbent may find it preferable to follow an accommodating strategy.

As discussed in chapter 4, a key factor in determining an appropriate competitive strategy is whether the strategic investment makes the firm more "tough" (that is, whether it can appropriate the resulting benefits for itself and hurt its competitors), or "accommodating" (i.e., whether the resulting advantage can be shared with and benefit its rivals) in a later stage. A second factor, relating to how a firm expects its competitors to react to its action, is whether firms' reactions are contrarian (strategic substitutes) or reciprocating (strategic complements), that is, whether the competitors' reactions are opposite or whether they are similar to the (aggressive or accommodating) actions of the first firm.

As also noted, often capacity decisions and setting quantities are regarded as contrarian. A larger quantity produced by one firm (e.g., capturing a larger market share via economies of scale or a learning cost advantage) would result in a lower equilibrium (profit-maximizing) quantity by its competitor. Competitive actions under price competition are typically reciprocating, in that the more of the action (price) one firm chooses, the more its competitor will also optimally choose. Here, a reduction in price by one firm would be matched by a profit-maximizing price cut by the competitor (and lower profit margins for both). Microchip prices, for instance, generally start out higher and then shrink rapidly due to intense price competition. Prices on the standard 16-megabyte chips fell 80% in 1996 alone. Similar price wars have often been disastrous in the food, tobacco, and airline industries. In these circumstances, firms may be better off if one of the firms sets a higher price that competitors can follow, resulting in a larger pie for all.

Consider a two-stage game with endogenous competitive reactions in the second (production) stage among two otherwise similar competitors. Similar to the example in figure 5.3, firm A (alone) can make a first-stage strategic investment of $I_A^I = 30$ million (e.g., in R & D); this may be followed by a production investment of $I^{II} = 80$ million by either competitor. When both firms decide to invest, the shared investment outlay made by each firm is half the total cost assumed in the previous proprietary R & D example (i.e., $I_A^{II} = \frac{1}{2} \times 80 = 40$ million).

Here, since a first-stage strategic investment is made only by one of the competitors, it may influence asymmetrically their relative competitive position and market value outcomes (V_A, V_B) at time 1, depending on two main factors.

1. The *type* of investment *(proprietary vs. shared)*: if the strategic (e.g., R & D) investment generates a competitive advantage with proprietary benefits (making the pioneer firm tough), the pioneer captures most (here we assume $s = \frac{2}{3}$) of the total market value ("pie") in the second stage. On the other hand, if the strategic investment benefits are diffused to the industry and become shared with competitors (an accommodating stance), each firm captures an equal part (here $s = \frac{1}{2}$) of the total value. The size of the pioneer's market share, s, depends on the context of the industry and is related to the presence of first- versus second-mover advantages. A pioneer firm may develop a new technology but fail to become the market leader if it cannot achieve sustainable competitive advantage in the second stage, for example, when it lacks complementary assets needed to commercialize the product. On the other hand, an early mover may affect the pace of technological development or establish a product standard with network externalities that may increase the market share, s, of the firm.

2. The *nature* of competitive *(re)action* (contrarian or reciprocating).[5] In the case of contrarian competition, firms have an incentive to

---

[5] As discussed in chapter 4, strategic substitute versus complement actions are typical in industries characterized by quantity vs. price competition, respectively. An interesting question is, When can one expect quantity or price competition? Cournot quantity competition more naturally arises in industries where firms set their investment and production decisions in advance and face higher cost for holding inventories. Firms first choose capacity (inflexible) and in a later stage choose production (quantity) to fill capacity. Here prices will adjust more quickly than quantities, with competitors expected to match any price change

make strategic investments (e.g., in R & D or marketing campaigns) to improve their competitive position and ability to appropriate future benefits for themselves. The total market value ("pie") is assumed to be given (a zero-sum game), so a firm with a proprietary competitive advantage captures more share and value at the expense of competition (here $s = \frac{2}{3}$ vs. $\frac{1}{3}$). When firms reciprocate (or their actions are strategic complements), on the other hand, an early strategic investment by a firm resulting in a proprietary advantage that would hurt its competitors may provoke intensified rivalry and a price war that in the end may damage the profit margins of both firms, so the total market value may decline (here we assume by a $\frac{1}{4}$). The total market "pie" may instead be enlarged (say by $\frac{1}{4}$) when firms are accommodating. That would likely be the case when the investment benefits are shared. For example, an R & D innovation that is diffused to the industry or a marketing campaign focusing on the overall benefits of the industry's products (rather than the firm's specific brand) may increase overall demand and market value. An accommodating behavior does not necessarily presuppose cooperation or implicit collusion. For example, if one firm takes the initiative to keep a high price and has flexibility to revise its decision periodically (in a dynamic pricing rivalry or repeated game), accompanied with an announced policy to match the competitor's price in the following period, firms can maintain prices above (single-period) competitive levels (and enlarge the market pie) without any communication, implicit collusion, or cooperation. The resulting equilibrium here is equivalent to that of cooperation or collusion, even though firms make pricing decisions independently.[6]

---

in order to meet their planned production, so price changes would not take business away from competitors. By contrast, Bertrand price competition pertains to markets where capacity is sufficiently flexible that firms can meet all demand at their chosen price. It is more applicable when firms' products are homogeneous or undifferentiated, believing that they can take business away from competitors if they cut prices. In some cases, Cournot and Bertrand competition may take place over different stages: competitors may choose capacities in the first stage, and then compete on price given the chosen capacities (resulting in a Cournot equilibrium in quantities).

[6]A decision by a firm to set a high price has little risk or cost since if competition does not follow, it can revise its price back down. Moreover, the competitor can recognize that itself is better off in the long term to follow with the higher prices (even if the first period appears unprofitable). The above tit-for-tat strategy of matching the competitor's price in the next period is robust, allowing the firm to do well in the long run; it is nice (never the first to defect), provocable (immediately punishing a defecting rival by matching its price next period), and forgiving (will go back to cooperative outcome if rival returns). In other cases

FIGURE 5.4 COMPETITIVE STRATEGIES DEPENDING ON TYPE OF
INVESTMENT (PROPRIETARY VS. SHARED) AND NATURE OF COMPETITIVE
REACTION (CONTRARIAN VS. RECIPROCATING)

COMPETITION (B)

	Contrarian/ Strategic Substitutes (fixed market value) e.g., Quantity competition	Reciprocating / Strategic Complements (altered market value) e.g., Price competition
Proprietary (capture most of total market value)	i **committing and offensive** Preemptive commitment (+) effect	ii **flexible and inoffensive** Non-provoking (–) effect
Shared (share total market value)	iii **flexible and offensive** Vulnerable (–) effect	iv **committing and inoffensive** Cooperative commitment (+) effect

PIONEER (A)

As mentioned in chapter 4 and illustrated in figure 5.4, we can distinguish four different competitive investment strategies, depending on whether the resulting benefits of the strategic R & D investment are proprietary or shared and whether competitive reactions are reciprocating or contrarian.

Proprietary Investment When Firms' Actions Are Contrarian

R & D may generate a high strategic value if the technology can be kept proprietary (e.g., well protected by patents or by its install base), creating a comparative advantage for the pioneer firm and forcing competitors to retreat. For example, suppose that R & D generates a proprietary advantage that makes the pioneer firm stronger, hurting its competition in the

---

firms may actually find it preferable to cooperate (e.g., by utilizing network investments) to increase the total value of growth opportunities in the industry. They can follow an accommodating strategy, working together to build networks or to share costs to achieve more overall industry growth. Although cooperation or implicit collusion is another way to justify an enlarged market pie, it is a different issue and is not necessary for the strategic complementarity argument above.

second stage by capturing a larger share (⅔) of the market; if the competitor's reactions are contrarian, it will back down, accepting a lower share (⅓). In figure 5.5, panel A, the subgame to the left concerns investment in follow-up production capacity (in stage 2), and illustrates the competitive dynamics when demand and total project value are high (V^+ = 180). When both competitors invest in production capacity (lower right box), the value payoffs are (80, 20). Pioneer firm A generates a competitive advantage via its early proprietary strategic investment that allows it to capture ⅔ of total value by making a $I_A^{II} = \$40$ million production capacity investment ($NPV_A{}^+ = ⅔ \times 180 - 40 = 80$). The competitor only captures $NPV_B{}^+ = 20 (= ⅓ \times 180 - 40)$. Similarly, in the situation where both firms choose to wait, pioneer firm A appropriates a larger portion of the next-stage growth option value, \$81 million, while firm B gets \$25 million; this results in a (81, 25) value payoff (upper-left box).[7] In the off-diagonal boxes, each firm regards preempting the other and capturing the entire market value ($NPV^+ = 180 - 80 = \$100$ million) as its most preferred outcome, (0, 100) or (100, 0). Under high demand, each firm has a dominant strategy to invest, regardless of its competitor's decision (for firm A, 100 > 81 and 80 > 0; for firm B, 100 > 25 and 20 > 0), even though both firms would be better off to wait. The Nash equilibrium (*) is the bottom right, invest-invest outcome (80, 20).

Now consider the low-demand case ($V^- = 60$ million) to the right of figure 5.5, panel A. Even if one of the firms were to invest alone, this would result in a negative value ($NPV^- = 60 - 80 = -\$20$ million). If both firms wait, firm A would appropriate the full wait-and-see option value, resulting in payoffs (10, 0). In this wait-and-see scenario, firm A's dominant market power would enable it to preempt competitive entry in case

---

[7]If both firms wait, the competitive dynamics of the next-period subgames are as follows: firm A captures a larger market share ($\frac{2}{3} V$) at a very high level of demand ($V^{++} = 324$) and preempts the full value at lower, intermediate demand ($V^{+-} = V^{-+} = 108$), while both firms defer at very low levels of demand ($V^{--} = 36$). At $V^+ = 180$ the option values therefore are:

$$OPTION_A^+ = \frac{0.4 \times (\frac{2}{3} \times 324 - 40) + 0.6 \times (1 \times 108 - 80)}{1.08} = 81;$$

$$OPTION_B^+ = \frac{0.4 \times (\frac{1}{3} \times 324 - 40) + 0.6 \times 0}{1.08} \approx 25.$$

Similarly, at $V^- = 60$ the option values are:

$$OPTION_A^- = \frac{0.4 \times (1 \times 108 - 80) + 0.6 \times (0)}{1.08} = 10; OPTION_B^- = \frac{0.4 \times 0 + 0.6 \times 0}{1.08} = 0.$$

FIGURE 5.5 PROPRIETARY STRATEGIC BENEFITS WHEN COMPETITOR
REACTIONS ARE CONTRARIAN OR RECIPROCATING

A. Proprietary benefits ($\frac{2}{3}$) of strategic investment when competitor
reactions are contrarian (fixed size): invest in R & D (offensive strategy
to preempt)

High demand ($V^+ = 180$)   Low demand ($V^- = 60$)

		Firm B					Firm B	
		Wait	Invest				Wait	Invest
		i	ii				i	ii
Wait		(81, 25)	(0, 100)		Wait		(10, 0)*	(0, −20)
Firm A		iii	iv		**Firm A**		iii	iv
Invest		(100, 0)	(80, 20)*		Invest		(−20, 0)	(0, −20)

$$NPV_A^* = -30 + \left(\frac{0.4 \times 80 + 0.6 \times 10}{1.08}\right) = -30 + 35 = 5;$$

$$NPV_B^* = 0 + \left(\frac{0.4 \times 20 + 0.6 \times 0}{1.08}\right) = 7$$

$$I_A^I = 30; I_A^{II} = 40; I^{II} = I_A^{II} + I_B^{II} = 80 \text{ (if pre-emption } I_A^{II} = I_B^{II} = 80)$$

i OPTION$_A$ =

$$\frac{0.4 \times (1 \times 324 - 40) + 0.6(1 \times 108 - 80)}{1.08}$$

$$= 81$$

i OPTION$_A$ =

$$\frac{0.4 \times (1 \times 108 - 80) + 0.6 \times (0)}{1.08} = 10$$

ii NPV$_A$ = 0
iii NPV$_A$ = 180 − 80 = 100
iv NPV$_A$ = $\frac{2}{3}$ × 180 − 40 = 80
   NPV$_B$ = $\frac{1}{3}$ × 180 − 40 = 20

ii NPV$_A$ = 0
iii NPV$_A$ = 60 − 80 = −20
iv NPV$_A$ = $\frac{2}{3}$ × 60 − 40 = 0
   NPV$_B$ = $\frac{1}{3}$ × 60 − 40 = −20

next period's demand develops favorably to an intermediate level.[8] Both
firms have a dominant strategy to defer under low demand, with firm A
capturing the full growth option value.

To summarize, during the second stage (as of $t = 1$), both firms will invest in case of high demand and defer otherwise. In case of high demand
($V^+ = 180$ million), firm A captures a larger share in Nash equilibrium

[8]At an intermediate level of demand ($V^{-+} = 108$) total market value is sufficiently low that
the competitor's value would be negative ($NPV_B = \frac{1}{3} \times 108 - 40 = -4$) if they both invest, while firm A's NPV would still be positive ($NPV_A = \frac{2}{3} \times 108 - 40 = 32$). Consequently, firm A has a dominant strategy to invest, while firm B defers, resulting in a Nash
equilibrium where firm A preempts with a ($108 - 80 = 28$, 0) payoff.

FIGURE 5.5 *continued*

B. Proprietary strategic investment (⅔) when competitor actions are *reciprocating* (−¼): do not invest in R & D (inoffensive strategy to avoid intensified rivalry and price war)

High demand ($V^+ = 180$)

		Firm B: Wait	Firm B: Invest
Firm A	Wait	i (61, 25)	ii (0, 100)
	Invest	iii (100, 0)	iv **(50, 5)***

Low demand ($V^- = 60$)

		Firm B: Wait	Firm B: Invest
Firm A	Wait	i **(10, 0)***	ii (0, −20)
	Invest	iii (−20, 0)	iv (−10, −25)

$$NPV_A^* = -30 + \left(\frac{0.4 \times 50 + 0.6 \times 10}{1.08}\right) = -30 + 24 = -6 (< 0)\ ;$$

$$NPV_B^* = 0 + \left(\frac{0.4 \times 5 + 0.6 \times 0}{1.08}\right) \approx 2$$

iv $NPV_A^+ = \frac{2}{3} \times (\frac{3}{4} \times 180) - 40 = 50$; $NPV_B^+ = \frac{1}{3} \times (\frac{3}{4} \times 180) - 40 = 5$

iv $NPV_A^- = \frac{2}{3} \times (\frac{3}{4} \times 60) - 40 = -10$; $NPV_B^- = \frac{1}{3} \times (\frac{3}{4} \times 60) - 40 = -25$

($NPV_A^+ = 80$ million) due to its proprietary R & D advantage, while in case of low demand ($V^- = 60$ million) its dominant position again enables it to preempt the full growth option value ($Option_A^- = 10$ million). Using binomial option valuation, the current value of firm A's investment opportunity one period earlier (at $t = 0$) is given by: $Option^{II} = (p \times NPV_A^+ + (1 - p) \times Option_A^-)/(1 + r) = (0.4 \times 80 + 0.6 \times 10)/1.08 =$ 35 million. Thus, as can be confirmed from the calculations at the bottom of panel A, figure 5.5, the total strategic or expanded NPV of firm A's proprietary R & D investment under second-stage endogenous competition is $NPV_A^* = NPV^I + Option^{II} = -30 + 35 = +5$ million (> 0). Thus, the pioneer should make the strategic R & D investment.

The above confirms that an early R & D investment may be warranted if it generates a proprietary advantage that makes the firm tough and hurts its competition in a later stage; when the competitor's reaction is contrarian, it may follow a share-retreat strategy with the pioneer expanding its market share as demand grows. If demand turns out sufficiently low that the competitor's profit value would be negative, the pioneer can preempt competitive entry and earn monopoly profits.[9]

Proprietary Benefits When Competitors' Actions Are Reciprocating

Consider now the case that the competitor would reciprocate rather than retreat. Unlike the previous case of competition that creates incentives to take an offensive stance to increase one's ability to preempt a larger share of the market, here a tough stance (via a proprietary strategic investment) when competitors' actions are reciprocating (strategic complements) may instead result in intensified rivalry, a decline in total market value and reduced profit margins.

In May 1997 Microsoft announced an all-out attack into the lucrative heavy-duty corporate computing market, traditionally a mainframe task performed by IBM, Sun Microsystems, and Oracle. This was a high-risk strategy for Microsoft: if successful, it could have a sweeping impact on business computing, just as its Windows software had on PCs. But its competition, already having made heavy investments, did not seem ready to retreat; instead it was poised to *reciprocate* and fight to the end: "Every major corporation needs its Vietnam, and this will be Microsoft's," responded an IBM executive (*New York Times,* May 19, 1997). Such intense price competition had already been taking place in networking products. In January 1997 Intel moved aggressively into this market, forcing competitors to reduce their prices; in April 1997 Intel announced it would invest even more, as this was a "very high priority" on its list of growth areas. Novell, maker of computer networking software, got hurt as a result, announcing in May 1997 that it was cutting 18% of its workforce "in response to competitive pressures in the market for networking products" (*New York Times,* May 29, 1997).

How would our analysis of a proprietary technological innovation be different if competitor actions were instead reciprocating? Suppose that generating a proprietary competitive advantage via a strategic investment will again enable firm A to capture ⅔ of stage-2 total value, but now it will invite a tough reaction by a reciprocating competitor such that total market value will decline (e.g., due to price competition) by ¼ (to ¾V). This game is illustrated in figure 5.5, panel B. The decline in total market value as a result of intensified rivalry offsets the advantage of capturing a bigger share due to the proprietary advantage of the strategic investment for firm A. The end share for firm A is now ⅔ × (¾V) = ½V, while firm B receives ⅓ × (¾V) = ¼V. Consider the subgame under high demand

---

[9]This proposition is well understood in the industrial organization literature (see, for instance, Stackelberg 1934). Here, proprietary advantage also may not be necessary.

($V^+ = 180$ million) at the left of figure 5.5, panel B. When both firms decide to invest, firm A receives an NPV of $\frac{1}{2} \times 180 - 40 = 50$ million and firm B receives $\frac{1}{4} \times 180 - 40 = 5$ million, whereas if they both choose to wait, firm A retains a growth option value of 61 million and firm B of 15 million.[10] However, both firms again have a dominant strategy to invest under high demand (50, 5). The competitor is worse off, but the damage is not enough to preempt its entry under high demand. The values under low demand ($V^- = 60$ million) are similar, resulting in a similar wait-wait equilibrium outcome (10, 0). As is shown in the calculations at the bottom of panel B in figure 5.5, $NPV_A^* = -30 + (0.4 \times 50 + 0.6 \times 10) / 1.08 = -30 + 24 = -6$ million (< 0). *To avoid such a potentially damaging rivalry, a firm may therefore be better off deciding not to invest if its investment will provoke an all-out war.*[11] In the 1980s Philips, which collaborated with Sony in the development of the VCR standard, learned the hard way, losing out to Matsushita and switching over to the standard that prevailed.

Shared Benefits When Competitors' Actions Are Reciprocating

A decade later the same players followed a different strategy, choosing to adopt a common, industry-wide standard for the high-density CD. These players seemed to realize that when firms' actions are reciprocating, it may be better to follow an accommodating strategy that enhances the total value for the industry. Another example of an investment with shared benefits is Mobil placing a goodwill ad in the *New York Times* educating the public about the benefits of oil refining for society in general (rather than its specific products).

In the example shown in figure 5.6, panel A, the strategic investment brings shared benefits for the competitor, who is ready to reciprocate.

---

[10]The competitive dynamics of the second-period subgames are similar to those in footnote 7: Firm A captures a larger market share under intense rivalry ($\frac{2}{3} \times \frac{3}{4} V$) at a very high level of demand ($V^{++} = 324$) and preempts at lower, intermediate demand ($V^{+-} = V^{-+} = 108$), while they both defer at very low levels of demand ($V^{--} = 36$). For example, at $V^+ = 180$ the option values equal

$$\text{OPTION}_A = \frac{0.4 \times (\frac{1}{2} \times 324 - 40) + 0.6 \times (1 \times 108 - 80)}{1.08} = 61;$$

$$\text{OPTION}_B = \frac{0.4 \times (\frac{1}{4} \times 324 - 40) + 0.6 \times (0)}{1.08} \approx 15.$$

[11]This result, already known in IO (e.g., see Fudenberg and Tirole 1984), is again confirmed from a combined real-options and game theory perspective. Although not necessary, proprietary technology is more likely to strengthen the pioneer and weaken the competitor, provoking a reciprocating response.

The higher prices attained result in higher profit margins for both and an enlarged total market value by ¼ (to $\frac{5}{4}V$), shared equally by both firms. Under high demand, both firms will invest to receive $\frac{1}{2} \times (\frac{5}{4} \times 180) - 40 = 73$, resulting in a symmetric Nash equilibrium outcome of (73, 73); under low demand, both firms will choose to wait, obtaining (10, 10).[12] Investment in the strategic project with shared benefits is thus justified in this case: The total strategic value of the pioneer R & D venture for firm A is $NPV_A^* = -30 + (0.4 \times 73 + 0.6 \times 10) / 1.08 = -30 + 33 = +3 \, (> 0)$.

Shared R & D can bring a strategic advantage when firms whose actions are reciprocating can share a larger market value. This may be due to option value benefits (e.g., appropriating the option value of waiting under demand uncertainty), or due to sharing strategic benefits such as avoiding price rivalry or a war of attrition among competing standards when the firms' actions are reciprocating.[13]

Experimental research shows that cooperation based on reciprocity can be a successful strategy. Box insert 5.1 describes a tournament organized by Robert Axelrod (see also his book *The Evolution of Cooperation,* 1984), involving a repeated prisoners' dilemma. A reciprocating strategy called "tit for tat" turns out to be the winning strategy.

Shared Investment When Competitors' Actions Are Contrarian

In a different competitive landscape, however, sharing technological innovation may result in a vulnerable strategic position for the pioneer if a competitor can take advantage of its accommodating stance and the gen-

---

[12]The growth option values for the subgames under high demand ($V^+ = 180$) and low demand ($V^- = 60$) for both firms A and B are as follows:

$$\text{OPTION}^+ = \frac{0.4 \times (\frac{1}{2} \times \frac{5}{4} \times 324 - 40) + 0.6 \times (\frac{1}{2} \times \frac{5}{4} \times 108 - 40)}{1.08} = 75;$$

$$\text{OPTION}^- = \frac{0.4 \times (\frac{1}{2} \times \frac{5}{4} \times 108 - 40) + 0.6 \times (0)}{1.08} \approx 10.$$

[13]There are many dimensions that can affect the value of the firm's options, including the possibility of collaboration or collusion. Collusion (that helps increase the market pie) focuses on the more transparent dimensions of strategy. If prices are easy to observe, firms would be more reluctant to try to manipulate prices. However, there are other dimensions that are harder to monitor (e.g., quality or service) which firms may try to compete on. In the case of collusion, to work effectively, there must be some mechanism to punish those deviating from the agreement. Although we presented the investment example here in a two-stage game, the real-life setting is likely a repeated game where short-term considerations in one play may be offset by gains (or losses) in the long term.

FIGURE 5.6 SHARED BENEFITS OF STRATEGIC INVESTMENT WHEN
COMPETITOR ACTIONS ARE RECIPROCATING OR CONTRARIAN

A. Shared strategic benefits (½) when competitor reactions are
reciprocating (+ ¼): invest in strategic project (share expanded pie
from accommodating stance)

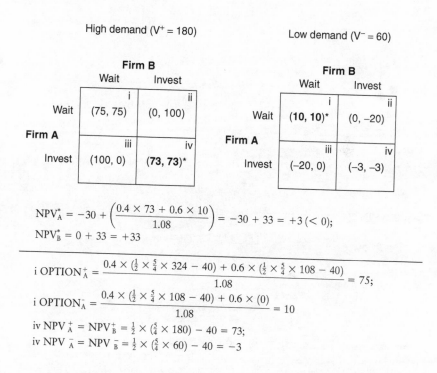

$$\text{NPV}_A^* = -30 + \left(\frac{0.4 \times 73 + 0.6 \times 10}{1.08} \right) = -30 + 33 = +3 \, (< 0);$$
$$\text{NPV}_B^* = 0 + 33 = +33$$

$$\text{i OPTION}_A^+ = \frac{0.4 \times (\frac{1}{2} \times \frac{5}{4} \times 324 - 40) + 0.6 \times (\frac{1}{2} \times \frac{5}{4} \times 108 - 40)}{1.08} = 75;$$
$$\text{i OPTION}_A^- = \frac{0.4 \times (\frac{1}{2} \times \frac{5}{4} \times 108 - 40) + 0.6 \times (0)}{1.08} = 10$$
$$\text{iv NPV}_A^+ = \text{NPV}_B^+ = \frac{1}{2} \times (\frac{5}{4} \times 180) - 40 = 73;$$
$$\text{iv NPV}_A^- = \text{NPV}_B^- = \frac{1}{2} \times (\frac{5}{4} \times 60) - 40 = -3$$

erated shared knowledge. In May 1997, one week after Intel announced
its next-generation microprocessor, the Pentium II, Digital sued Intel,
claiming remarkable similarities with its Alpha chip; Digital had revealed
the Alpha design to Intel during their failed negotiations on licensing
Alpha technology for Intel's next-generation chip in 1990–91. In an independent suit in 1997, Fujitsu agreed to pay compensation to IBM in a
decade-old suit for allegedly copying IBM products.

In our valuation example where the benefits of the strategic investment
are shared, a competitor whose actions are contrarian can take advantage of the pioneer's accommodating position and capture half of total

FIGURE 5.6 *continued*

B. Shared strategic benefits when competitors are contrarian (1): do not invest in R & D (avoid subsidizing aggressive competitor)

High demand ($V^+ = 180$)   Low demand ($V^- = 60$)

	Firm B	
	Wait	Invest
	i	ii
Wait	(53, 53)	(0, 100)
	iii	iv
Invest	(100, 0)	(50, 50)*

Firm A

	Firm B	
	Wait	Invest
	i	ii
Wait	(5, 5)*	(0, –20)
	iii	iv
Invest	(–20, 0)	(–10, –10)

Firm A

$$NPV_A^* = -30 + \left(\frac{0.4 \times 50 + 0.6 \times 5}{1.08}\right) = -30 + 21 = -9\,(<0);$$
$$NPV_B^* = 0 + 21 = 21$$

$$\text{i OPTION}_A^+ = \frac{0.4 \times (\frac{1}{2} \times 324 - 40) + 0.6 \times (\frac{1}{2} \times 108 - 40)}{1.08} = 53;$$

$$\text{i OPTION}_A^- = \frac{0.4 \times (\frac{1}{2} \times 108 - 40) + 0.6 \times (0)}{1.08} = 5$$

$$\text{iv NPV} = \tfrac{1}{2} \times 180 - 40 = 50;$$
$$\text{iv NPV} = \tfrac{1}{2} \times 60 - 40 = -10$$

market value (assumed given). Consider the symmetric subgame under high demand ($V^+ = 180$ million) at the left of figure 5.6, panel B: when both firms decide to invest, they both receive an NPV of $\frac{1}{2} \times 180 - 40 = 50$ million, whereas if they both choose to wait, they each receive a growth option value of 53 million.[14] However, both firms have a dominant strategy to invest early regardless of the other's action, resulting in the symmetric Nash outcome of (50, 50). Under low demand, the firms would be better off to wait, obtaining (5, 5). The calculations in panel B

---

[14] The values in this case are

$$OPTION_A^+ = \frac{0.4 \times (\frac{1}{2} \times 324 - 40) + 0.6 \times (\frac{1}{2} \times 108 - 40)}{1.08} = 53;$$

$$OPTION_A^- = \frac{0.4 \times (\frac{1}{2} \times 108 - 40) + 0.6 \times (0)}{1.08} = 5.$$

Box 5.1 Tit for Tat: Cooperation Based on Reciprocity

Evolutionary biologists have had considerable trouble explaining the evolution of co-operative behavior. The problem is that co-operation can always be exploited by selfish individuals who cheat. It seems that natural selection should always favor the cheats over the co-operators. Co-operation involves doing and receiving favors and this means that the opportunity to cheat and not return a favor is a very real possibility. Trivers (1971) tackled this problem and developed the theory of reciprocal altruism based on the idea that co-operation could evolve in species clever enough to discriminate between co-operators and cheats. The concept is summarized in the saying "you scratch my back and I'll scratch yours." Trivers' theory of reciprocal altruism is particularly successful in explaining human behavior because reciprocal altruism is a major part of all human activities.

As a first means of eliciting reciprocity we use displays of generosity, gratitude, sympathy and sincerity. These "guarantors" of reciprocity typically operate at the family, friend, and local community levels. If they fail to generate appropriate reciprocity we employ moralistic aggression in the form of sermons and lectures designed to bully all the cheats back into line. Moralistic aggression is the number one weapon of religions around the world. The strength and weakness of religions lies in their promise of "reciprocation after death." The sky is offered but how can we tell if it is true? Religions have found that moralistic aggression of the hell-fire-and-damnation variety is needed to calm such doubts and keep the flow of altruism coming their way.

Robert Axelrod was interested in finding a winning strategy for repeated prisoner's dilemmas games. He conducted a computer tournament where people were invited to submit strategies for playing 200 games of prisoner's dilemma (Axelrod and Hamilton 1981). The result of the tournament was that the simplest of all strategies submitted attained the highest average score. This strategy, called *tit for tat* by its submitter Anatol Rapoport, had only two rules. On the first move co-operate. On each succeeding move do what your opponent did the previous move. Thus, *tit for tat* was a strategy of co-operation based on reciprocity.

The results of Axelrod's tournament were published and people were invited to submit programs for a second tournament. From an analysis of the 3 million choices made in the second competition, four features of *tit for tat* emerged:

1. Never be the first to defect
2. Retaliate only after your partner has defected
3. Be prepared to forgive after carrying out just one act of retaliation

continued . . .

Box 5.1 *continued*

4. Adopt this strategy only if the probability of meeting the same player again exceeds ⅔.

According to Axelrod, *tit for tat* is successful because it is "nice," "provokable" and "forgiving." A nice strategy is one which is never first to defect. In a match between two nice strategies, both do well. A provokable strategy responds by defecting at once in response to defection. A forgiving strategy is one which readily returns to co-operation if its opponent does so; unforgiving strategies are likely to produce isolation and end co-operative encounters.

Source: Excerpts from *Tit for Tat,* by Chris Meredith, [The Slab] Australian Broadcasting Co., 1998.

---

of figure 5.6 confirm that this results in a negative total strategic value for the pioneer's R & D venture: $NPV_A^* = -30 + (0.4 \times 50 + 0.6 \times 5) / 1.08 = -30 + 21 = -9$ million (< 0).

There is less competitive advantage for a pioneer firm to single-handedly make a costly strategic investment when the resulting benefits will be shared with competition without reciprocity. A competitor whose actions are contrarian can take advantage of the pioneer's accommodating position and capture part of the shared benefits of the pioneer's strategic investment, without sharing in the cost. The pioneer may in some cases be better off to avoid subsidizing the creation of such shared opportunities for competition if it believes they may eventually be used against it.

We turn next to two-stage games with endogenous reactions in the first (strategic) stage.

5.5.2. COMPETITION IN INNOVATION INVESTMENT: TIME-TO-MARKET RACES AND STRATEGIC ALLIANCES

An additional dimension is introduced when either of the two firms can make independent, noncooperative strategic R & D investments in the first stage (as well as compete in the second, production stage). In this case firms may feel competitive pressure to rush into an innovation or patent race.[15]

---

[15]Grossman and Shapiro (1986, 1987) and Reinganum (1985) discuss R & D in a competitive context, while Dasgupta and Stiglitz (1980) and Fudenberg et al. (1983) discuss patent races. In a Poisson-type patent race it is often assumed that a firm's probability of making a discovery and obtaining a patent depends on its R & D expenditures. These models show

Suppose that technological investment by both firms now increases total market value (say by ¼), while the other parameters remain the same as in the proprietary investment case when firms' actions are *contrarian*. We consider first the situation where the firms invest sequentially in R & D with the first mover obtaining a competitive time-to-market advantage (e.g., a patent). We then examine the situation where both may invest *simultaneously* in R & D with equal market power.[16]

Figure 5.7, panel A, shows the case of *sequential* R & D. There are four scenarios.

Scenario i. If the two firms invest in R & D in sequence, with firm A investing before firm B, the first mover obtains a competitive time-to-market advantage that allows it to capture ⅔ of the total (expanded) market value in each demand state. The follower's payoff equals ⅓ × (⅝ × 180) −40 = 35 million in case of high demand, and −15 million in low demand — preferring instead to wait (0). At low demand, the technology leader (firm A) also prefers to wait a period (preempting competitive entry in case demand later increases), appropriating growth option value of 20 million,[17] while capturing a greater market share in case of high demand (⅔ × ⅝ × 180) − 40 = 110 million. The total strategic value for the follower therefore equals $NPV_B^* = NPV^I + Option^{II}$ (Shared) = $-30 + (0.4 \times 35 + 0.6 \times 0) / 1.08 = -17$ million (< 0); for the leader, $NPV_A^* = -30 + (0.4 \times 110 + 0.6 \times 20) / 1.08 = 22$ million (> 0). Being the first mover confers a significant strategic advantage in this case.

Scenarios ii and iii. If an early innovator's (either firm A or firm B) R & D investment preempts the competitor's entry and establishes the industry standard, the winner's value is 145 million (= ⅝ × 180 − 80) in case of high demand, or a growth option value of 20 million under low demand. Consequently, the total strategic value of winning the product standard equals $NPV^* = -30 + (0.4 \times 145 + 0.6 \times 20) / 1.08 = 35$ million, resulting in (35, 0) or (0, 35) payoffs, respectively.

Scenario iv. When both firms decide to defer investment in R & D, they share the growth option value symmetrically. At a high level of next-period demand they will both invest simultaneously ($NPV^+ = -30 + 73$

---

that uncertain R & D may be more valuable. As in real-options theory, this result is based on an inherent value asymmetry. In a "winner takes all" game, the firm benefits from the high upside potential, while on the downside it does not matter how far behind it finishes in the patent race because the patent will be worthless anyway.

[16]Timing games are well understood in the industrial organization literature, particularly that on endogenous timing of investment and preemption (e.g., Anderson and Engers 1994; or Holden and Riis 1994). This section illustrates the timing issues properly incorporating the option value of waiting under uncertainty.

[17]$OPTION_A = \dfrac{0.4 \times (1 \times \frac{5}{4} \times 108 - 80) + 0.6 \times 0}{1.08} = 20.$

FIGURE 5.7 BOTH FIRMS CAN MAKE STRATEGIC (E.G., R & D)
INVESTMENT IN THE FIRST STAGE, ENHANCING MARKET VALUE ($\frac{5}{4}$):
R & D COMPETITION

A. Sequential R & D investment race: invest to preempt (($\frac{2}{3}$) first-mover or time-to-market advantage)

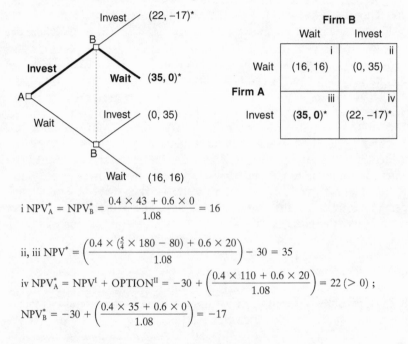

i $\text{NPV}_A^* = \text{NPV}_B^* = \dfrac{0.4 \times 43 + 0.6 \times 0}{1.08} = 16$

ii, iii $\text{NPV}^* = \left(\dfrac{0.4 \times (\frac{5}{4} \times 180 - 80) + 0.6 \times 20}{1.08}\right) - 30 = 35$

iv $\text{NPV}_A^* = \text{NPV}^I + \text{OPTION}^{II} = -30 + \left(\dfrac{0.4 \times 110 + 0.6 \times 20}{1.08}\right) = 22\ (>0)\ ;$

$\text{NPV}_B^* = -30 + \left(\dfrac{0.4 \times 35 + 0.6 \times 0}{1.08}\right) = -17$

B. Simultaneous R & D investment battle: invest prematurely (prisoners' dilemma)

		Firm B	
		Wait	Invest
		i	ii
	Wait	(16, 16)	(0, 35)
Firm A		iii	iv
	Invest	(35, 0)	(**2, 2**)*

iv Both firms invest simultaneously (share equally expanded benefits):

$\text{NPV}_A = \text{NPV}_B = \dfrac{0.4 \times (\frac{1}{2} \times \frac{5}{4} \times 180 - 40) + 0.6 \times 10}{1.08} - 30 = 32 - 30 = 2$

= 43 million), while at a low level both will choose to abandon (NPV^- = 0), resulting in a payoff of (16, 16) for each firm.[18]

Since firm A can make its R & D investment decision before firm B, to decide which timing strategy to follow it must recognize how its decision will influence its competitor's behavior. If firm A pursues a wait-and-see approach, while firm B rushes to make an R & D investment (receiving 35 rather than 16 from waiting), firm A's payoff will be 0. However, if firm A pursues an early technological investment commitment strategy, firm B will choose to wait (receiving 0 rather than −17 if it also invests with a delay), in which case A's payoff will be 35. Thus, firm A will invest immediately to signal a credible commitment to the market and deter competition. The equilibrium outcome in this case is (35, 0).

In reality, the value of an option is likely to be idiosyncratic to each firm, due to differences in firm-specific uncertainty, exercise costs, option expiration, even discount rates and the cost of capital. Hence the different, firm-specific value of the growth options introduces an asymmetry where a firm with lower firm-specific uncertainty, exercise cost, or maturity may exercise its options early and invest first, while another may rationally choose to wait.

In the literature on patent races, success of R & D depends on how long it takes to achieve usable outcomes (the hazard rate of R & D success), who wins the race (which depends on the number of participants), and the degree to which a winner can appropriate the resulting advantage (Dasgupta and Stiglitz 1980). These factors can to some extent be influenced by investment: the hazard rate of success, and hence the chance of winning the race, may be increased by increasing R & D intensity.

In practice we often see firms rushing into innovation races and forming strategic partnerships to acquire a first-mover or time-to-market advantage. Consider, for example, the race in memory chip development: In February 1997 Hitachi, Mitsubishi Electric, and Texas Instruments announced they would jointly develop a 1 gb DRAM. NEC, which has been cooperating loosely with ATT spin-off Lucent Technologies and Samsung, announced in June 1997 that it had developed a 4 gb DRAM, the

---

[18]At $t = 2$ both firms invest at high demand ($V^{++} = 324$) and wait (abandon) at low demand. At $t = 1$,

$$NPV^+ = \frac{0.4 \times (\frac{1}{2} \times \frac{5}{4} \times 324 - 40) + 0.6 \times (\frac{1}{2} \times \frac{5}{4} \times 108 - 40)}{1.08} - 30 = 73 - 30 = 43;$$

$$NPV^- = \frac{0.4 \times (\frac{1}{2} \times \frac{5}{4} \times 108 - 40) + 0.6 \times \text{Max}(\frac{1}{2} \times \frac{5}{4} \times 36 - 40, 0)}{1.08} - 30 = 10 - 30$$

$$= -20 < 0 \quad \text{(choose 0)}.$$

Thus, growth option value (at $t = 0$): $\dfrac{0.4 \times (43) + 0.6 \times 0}{1.08} = 16.$

largest-capacity memory chip ever developed, putting NEC in the lead in the intensely-competitive memory chip technology race.

Under competitive pressure to be the first (e.g., in a patent race) competitors may rush to make parallel innovation investments *simultaneously*, with one or both sides potentially getting hurt. Novell was hurt due to competition in networking products, Apple lost its lead as a user-friendly computer with the development of Microsoft's Windows, while in the 1980s Philips was hurt from losing the race against Matsushita over the VCR standard.

Let us revisit the numerical example of the investment-timing game above, but with the twist that the competing firms (or alliances) can invest *simultaneously* in R & D, as shown in figure 5.7, panel B. This involves larger total expenditures in the first stage ($I_A + I_B = 60$ million), while the two firms share total market value symmetrically: 72.3 ($= \frac{1}{2} \times \frac{5}{4} \times 180 - 40$) under high demand or 10 under low demand. The total strategic value for each firm now is $NPV^I + Option^{II}$ (Shared) $= -30 + (0.4 \times 72.5 + 0.6 \times 10) / 1.08 = 2$.

In many emerging, high-growth industries, the possibility of each firm pursuing independent R & D activities to capture the product standard may trigger a simultaneous similar investment by competitors that, as in a prisoners' dilemma, can make both firms worse off [(2, 2), compared to a scenario of waiting (16, 16)]. Without a first-mover advantage, this simultaneous game provides a lower value-payoff for firm A (2 million) than in the above sequential game (35 million).[19]

The strategic moves by Microsoft to gain an advantage in its battle with Netscape over who would be the Internet standard bearer may be seen in this light. The purchase of WebTV might help Microsoft outflank its rivals, including Oracle and Sun Microsystems as well as Netscape. A reciprocating reaction, however, came from Oracle and Netscape. In May 1997 Oracle gave a boost to its strategy of developing a network computer as an alternative to the PC (dominated by Microsoft Windows software and Intel chips), announcing a majority investment in Navio Communications, established by Netscape to develop Internet software for consumer electronics; Navio also made deals with Hewlett-Packard, Sun Microsystems, and others threatened by Microsoft.

---

[19]The situation triggering simultaneous investment by competition has been extensively studied in the investment cascade literature (e.g., see Hendricks and Kovenock 1989).

5.6. Cooperation in the First Stage: Joint R & D Ventures

Given that independent R & D investments by each competitor may lead to a race that may damage one or both sides, an interesting question is whether two firms (or alliances) should pursue independent, competing R & D activities or cooperate in the first stage via a joint research venture, competing only in the second stage of commercial production and sales.

Figure 5.8 illustrates the valuation of first-stage cooperation via a joint research venture. Cooperation via joint R & D has the following implications for competitive R & D strategies:

Joint R & D may have a beneficial impact on value (NPV) by providing the same R & D benefits while sharing the R & D costs among the cooperating firms (15 versus 30, if equally shared among two firms). The value of investing immediately in the joint R & D venture for each firm is $32 + -15 = +17$ million (> 0).[20] A joint R & D venture not only provides a mechanism to share the scale economies in R & D, but may sometimes enhance them as the parties may bring different complementary skills, thereby lowering the total investment costs.

It may enable the two firms to more fully appropriate the flexibility value from waiting under demand uncertainty. If both firms above choose to wait to invest and appropriate the option value of waiting (16) plus save (make only) half of the R & D costs (15) in case of high demand next period, the option value in the joint venture is worth $16 + (0.4 \times 15 + 0.6 \times 0) / 1.08 = 22$ million.[21] With R & D cooperation, there is no sacrifice of flexibility value from an attempt to preempt the market as under direct R & D competition.

It is known that risk reduction can be achieved through organizational mechanisms, but organizations may also benefit from uncertainty. Joint ventures may serve as platforms for possible future development, where uncertainty might have a positive impact on the value of the venture.[22]

---

[20]This equals 2 (from the simultaneous investment of figure 5.7, panel B) plus half the saved expenditures (15). Alternatively, if both invest simultaneously (cooperatively),

$$NPV_A = NPV_B = \frac{0.4 \times (\frac{1}{2} \times \frac{5}{4} \times 180 - 40) + 0.6 \times 10}{1.08} - 15 = 32 - 15 = 17.$$

[21]The value if invest at $t = 1$ under high demand equals $73 - 15 = 58$, so that the option value of waiting (at $t = 0$) is

$$\frac{0.4 \times (58) + 0.6 \times 0}{1.08} = 22.$$

[22]Chi (2000) provides an interesting discussion on joint venture options. Kogut (1991) provides empirical evidence that joint ventures can be motivated by the option to expand in new markets and technologies where the option to expand is more valuable. The evidence

FIGURE 5.8 COOPERATE IN TECHNOLOGY INVESTMENT (INNOVATION): JOINT R & D VENTURES

	Firm B	
	Wait	Invest
Wait (Firm A)	i (22, 22)*	
Invest (Firm A)		iv (17, 17)

i. OPTION $= 16 + \dfrac{0.4 \times 15 + 0.6 \times 0}{1.08} = 22$

iv. NPV $= 2 + 15 = 17$

To achieve these benefits the firm must give up the possibility of gaining a first-mover advantage via preempting its competitor (the R & D investment in the preemptive sequential game is worth 35 million, while the joint R & D option is worth 22 million). However, at the same time joint R & D ventures may have a beneficial strategic effect in high-tech industries, and the strong position of the alliance may result in a first-stage "technology shakeout" of inferior and dominated technology.[23]

Most of the new product introductions in electronics have been based on product standardization agreements in R & D. In 1995 the alliance of Philips and Sony (which developed the Multi-Media CD) came to agreement with the alliance of Toshiba and Matsushita (which developed the Super-Density Disk) to set a common industry standard for the new-generation high-density CD (the digital video disc); the computer industry encouraged the two sides to coordinate, avoiding the major waste of capital and confusion that would have resulted from the launching of multiple systems (as happened a decade earlier when the two sides com-

---

also shows that strategic factors, such as market concentration, influence the creation of joint ventures. Kogut (1991) hypothesizes that the timing of the acquisition is triggered by a product market signal, indicating an increase in the venture's valuation. The results show that unexpected increases in the value of the venture and the degree of market concentration significantly affect the likelihood of an acquisition.

[23]Besides the above benefits, alliances and joint ventures may suffer from several drawbacks. An alliance often forces parties to exchange considerable information and independent firms may lose control over proprietary information. In addition, the governance structure of the alliance may not provide a formal mechanism for decision making. Finally, agency costs can arise, because the benefits of the alliance are split among two or more firms, giving rise to free-rider problems.

peted against each other, with the Philips alliance losing out). Other examples involve joint R & D ventures, especially among U.S. and Japanese firms: Toshiba and IBM shared the $1 billion cost of developing a 64 mb and 256 mb memory-chip facility outside Nagoya using IBM's know-how in chemical mechanical polishing (the technology was to be transferred back to an IBM plant in Virginia in 1997). Canon and Hewlett-Packard shared laser engine printer technology, even though they competed fiercely with their end products around the world. Kodak and archrival Fuji have for years collaborated on joint research on a new advanced photo system (see also box insert 5.2).[24]

The above models are based on stylized bimatrix rivalry (or coordination) games and simple strategic interactions. Among other simplifications, option parameters (e.g., exercise price, firm-specific volatility, or option maturity) are assumed given. Of course there are many complexities in reality that present more richness than our stylized models, including option parameters that can be influenced by competitive behavior. The timing of entry and the nature of competitive advantage, for example, may better be captured by endogenizing some of these option parameters. For instance, it may be possible to some extent to influence a competitor's option value by investments that increase entry barriers (increasing the option exercise price for competition). The exercise cost or exercise capacity of a firm may also depend on what other organizational assets and resources the firm has. The value of the underlying cash flows (V) is also likely to be idiosyncratic, as firms may earn a premium because of reputation or other effects. Further, beyond the technical uncertainty of the innovative (R & D) process, organizational and strategic uncertainties may also be subject to influence.[25] Dynamic capabilities may also be idiosyncratic.[26]

---

[24]Recently we also have witnessed a cooperation trend in production and services among many leading Japanese and U.S. firms: IBM and Toshiba jointly manufacturing liquid-crystal display panels; GE supplying components to Toyota, while Toyota helps distribute GM's Cavalier through its dealership network in Japan; Mitsubishi and Dupont launching a joint polyethylene manufacturing venture; Sumitomo and Exxon cooperating in oil and gas development in China, etc.

[25]Strategic uncertainty relates to competitive interaction, first- or second-mover advantages, and market entry and preemption. There may also be uncertainty concerning the intensity of competition among incumbent producers, or about new entrants, depending on the contestability of the market.

[26]Dynamic capabilities that enable a firm to adapt fast can be a source of sustainable competitive advantage. Different firms may have different capabilities, which evolve over time

Box 5.2 How Can Companies Collude?

In theory, companies cannot strategically collude; the prisoners' dilemma tells us as much. In the prisoners' dilemma, a famous specimen of game theory, two suspected criminals are interrogated separately by the police. Both know that if they both say nothing they will each be sentenced to a year in prison; if they both confess they will each be jailed for five years; and if one confesses but the other says nothing, the confessor will be released and the other will be jailed for seven years. Collectively, the best strategy is to say nothing, thus minimizing time in jail. Yet for each individual, it is rational to confess, in the hope of immediate release — or, at the least, of not suffering a seven-year sentence. So both confess, yielding the worst outcome — a collective total of 10 years in prison.

Similarly, collusion in the long run should break down as players will have an incentive to cheat. Yet in fact many companies have colluded in the long run. So how do they go about it? Based on a study of over 7,000 cases of collusion over the past five years across a broad spectrum of industries, I have found that four factors are needed to make collusion work — the "four Cs." These are communication, constraints, co-ordination and confusion. They are managed using "facilitators," which ensure that the Cs can survive in the long run — that is, that companies can strategically collude. The ultimate goal for colluders is a covert cartel. A cartel is a publicly known agreement among companies selling substitutes (for example, Opec). A covert cartel is the same thing, except that the public is unaware of the arrangement; even in countries lacking laws against collusion, for obvious reasons it may not be desirable for consumers, or even employees, to know that such an arrangement exists. Unless the colluders manage the four Cs carefully, using the right doses of Fs, the cartel will break down. Price wars, research and development wars or marketing wars will then be likely to ensue. The four Cs framework can be seen as a substitute for a competitive strategy model which assumes that competitors are independent players (like Michael Porter's five competitive forces model).

Source: Excerpts from "Mastering Marketing 3: How Do Companies Collude," by Philip Parker, *Financial Times,* September 28, 1998.

5.7. Summary and Conclusions

Strategic competitive interactions clearly influence the value of a sequential investment plan under uncertainty, as was illustrated in this chapter by practical examples from high-tech industries. The chapter discussed a simplified options and games framework for analyzing various competitive strategies in increasing complexity, allowing us in principle to *quantify* flexibility and identify those strategic factors that affect total value. The option game models have similar benefits and problems as the applied game theory literature generally. The analysis prescribes what the players should do, assuming they behave rationally. It is part of a framework for sensible guidance, but it does not cover all the angles for successful strategic behavior. Concepts from management theory can provide additional insights in many complications that affect the value of growth options by examining the conditions differentiating one firm's situation and option value from another's, for example relating to the nature of first-mover advantage. Complementing quantitative options models developed in finance with game theory principles from economics and the qualitative organizational insights from strategic management theory provides a richer framework that can help us better understand the strategic mechanisms at work in the phenomena we observe in high-tech and other dynamic industries.

In the analysis of one-stage option games under uncertainty, we discussed the trade-off between the flexibility/learning value from waiting under demand uncertainty against competitive erosion and preemptive commitment effects. On one hand, a *flexibility effect* arises from management's ability to wait to invest until demand develops sufficiently. On the other hand, a *competitive value erosion effect* may arise when *exogenous* competitive entry can take part of total market value away from the incumbent firm. A *preemptive commitment effect* is important when investing early can preempt anticipated competitive entry.

Extending the analysis to two-stage or compound option games (e.g., R & D, market positioning, or strategic acquisitions), we recognized that

---

in a path (or history) dependent way. The benefits of dynamic capabilities are limited when learning is incremental and technology is proprietary and hard to codify. When one firm tries to improve its operations, its success is likely to be based on its own past activities and those of its rival. The value of dynamic capabilities may also depend on the stage in the development process. A "window of opportunity" will typically present itself in the early stage when the design is more fluent, manufacturing routines have not yet been developed, and the firm has not yet committed capital. In the later stage a specialized design may emerge as network externalities or learning effects dominate. In this later, more rigid stage, the firm may not be able to adapt existing capabilities as effectively.

an early strategic investment commitment may not only result in future commercialization or growth opportunities but may also influence the competitor's future behavior in desirable or potentially damaging ways. A pioneer, for example, may use a first-stage R & D investment to gain a strategic advantage via lower future operating costs or an expanded market share when competitive reactions are contrarian (strategic substitutes). In other cases, however, an early investment commitment may create a strategic disadvantage if it reduces the firm's ability to respond toward aggressive competitors who can exploit shared benefits resulting from the strategic investment, or if it provokes a retaliating response and intense rivalry that may badly damage both competitors when competitive actions are reciprocating (strategic complements).

We have seen that the impact (sign) of the strategic commitment effect may differ, depending on the nature of competitive reaction (reciprocating or contrarian) and on whether the benefits of R & D are proprietary or shared. In particular, a *proprietary* R & D investment commitment may result in a *preemptive commitment effect* (+ impact), making the firm tougher in the second stage via a proprietary advantage if competitive actions are *contrarian*. However, *a provoking effect* (−) may arise when competition reciprocates with an aggressive response. When the benefits of R & D are shared, the above competitive effects may reverse (under contrarian vs. reciprocating reactions). A *shared* R & D may result in a *cooperative commitment effect* (+) when the R & D benefits are diffused to the entire industry. On the other hand, a *vulnerability effect* (−) may arise when the firm loses competitive advantage by spillovers to one's competitors.

We also examined the case of competition in technological innovation (e.g., R & D) between two competitors during the first stage, as in the case when each firm strives to acquire the product standard. Tempted by the potentially high payoffs of acquiring the dominant product standard or being left with nothing (a "winner takes all" situation with a call-option asymmetry), firms may be trapped in a patent or innovation race in an effort to preempt each other. Such competitive pressure may result in a "prisoners' dilemma" with an inferior "panic" equilibrium outcome in which everybody rushes into R & D prematurely, sacrificing the flexibility benefits of a wait-and-see strategy.

Interesting implications can be drawn concerning the nature of first-mover competitive advantage, depending upon the quality and market power of the mover, the imitability (proprietary nature) of the incumbent's position, the time lag of the follower, buyers' switching costs, learning, and network externalities. In many high-tech industry contexts innovation leadership is based on timing advantage. A firm or an alliance that can bring new products faster to the market can enjoy a significant advantage. In addition, the quality of its products and its organizational capabilities are often idiosyncratic to the firm and can be a comparative advantage in the strategic exercise of the firm's options. The factors affecting each firm's growth options may be idiosyncratic to that firm, generating significant interfirm asymmetries that can explain differences in exercise and timing behavior (e.g., first-mover or follower timing). For example, a firm with lower firm-specific uncertainty, exercise (investment) cost, or option maturity (e.g., anticipating earlier competitive entry) may exercise its options early, while another may rationally choose to wait. The exercise cost or exercise capacity of a firm may depend on what other organizational assets and resources the firm already has in place.

A joint research venture enabling the firms to cooperate in R & D during the first stage may be a way to avoid the prisoners' dilemma. Joint research can have a beneficial impact compared to direct R & D competition for several reasons: (a) it can achieve the same research (and subsequent commercialization) benefits with lower (shared) R & D costs by each firm; (b) it may enable the cooperating firms to more fully appropriate the flexibility (option) value from a wait-and-see approach under technological or demand uncertainty, avoiding the competitive pressures of an innovation race to preempt the market. To achieve these benefits, the firm may have to give up the possibility to gain a first-mover advantage on the other members of the alliance. At the same time, joint R & D ventures may have a more positive strategic effect in high-tech industries, and the stronger position of the alliance may result in a "technology shakeout" of inferior and dominated technology by rivals.

Our analysis in this chapter was deliberately simplified.[27] Nonetheless, the simple option games we examined here provide valuable insights for certain strategic contexts by endogenizing strategic interactions. Of course, there are many complexities in reality that present more richness than these stylized examples. Beyond technical exploration and market demand or price uncertainties, there may also be substantial strategic uncertainty. Strategic uncertainty relates to issues of competitive interaction,

---

[27]For example, we did not consider situations when rivals are more than two. The analysis would provide similar results with a limited number of players but as the number of players increases, the reaction of players and equilibrium results become less predictable. More than two competitors may also limit the strategic effect from preemption, and jumps in value would be smaller. More competitors introduce more volatility (more smaller changes) in firm value. As the number of firms increases, the market structure tends to change from oligopoly to perfect competition, where the individual strategic impact of competitors becomes negligible, but might still be captured via an exogenous "dividend" effect.

first- or second-mover advantages, and market entry. There may also be uncertainty concerning the intensity of competition between incumbent producers, or about new entrants, depending on the contestability of the market. Of course, it is important to recognize that the appearance of entirely new kinds of competitors or entirely new technologies can significantly modify the game at play.

In the new uncertain competitive landscape that high-tech and other dynamic industries are facing today, it becomes essential for firms to be more flexible in their investment programs, allowing management to change the amount, rate, timing, or scale of investment in response to new, unexpected developments and competitive moves. However, this flexibility must be balanced against the strategic value of early commitment. We have shown in this chapter via simple examples how the integration of real options, game-theoretic industrial organization, and strategic management concepts provides a useful framework for analyzing the trade-off between strategic adaptability and commitment in such a dynamic competitive environment.

Chapter 6

Flexibility and Commitment

The power to constrain an adversary
depends upon the power to bind oneself.
— Thomas Schelling

6.1. Introduction

In an environment of high uncertainty, firms have an incentive to defer irreversible investment. However, early investment can be used to gain strategic advantages (e.g., see Spence 1977, 1979; Dixit 1979, 1980; Baldwin 1987a; Kulatilaka and Perotti 1998).[1] As we have noted, a value-creating strategy can be directed first toward generating competitive advantage through an early strategic investment, followed by subsequent commercial projects in later stages. Pioneering strategies often involve a sequence of interdependent investment decisions. An early investment in R & D or a pilot plant in a new market may entail strategic value by improving the firm's competitive position if it decides to invest in commercialization.[2]

We have seen in chapter 4 that proper evaluation of strategic investments requires explicit recognition of the importance of a firm's ability to use investments to influence the ex post market outcomes. As a consequence, the *flexibility value effect* from postponing irreversible investments must be traded off against the *commitment effect* from precommitting investments to gain strategic advantages. Here we review the different investment strategies based on the strategic effect of an up-front strategic investment and the form of competition.

In each strategy, the incremental *flexibility value* of the base case is traded off against the incremental *commitment value* of the strategic investment. The value of a strategy is based on the *expanded* or *strategic*

---

[1]Kulatilaka and Perotti (1998) make the point that the first mover gets a larger market share. An increase in uncertainty increases the first mover's market share and the relative value of early investment.

[2]Grenadier and Weiss (1997) model optimal investment strategies when a firm is confronted with a sequence of technological innovations, while Williams (1993) and Grenadier (1996) model exercise strategies in real estate development. McGahan (1993a) models the effect of incomplete information about demand on preemption.

NPV criterion that incorporates both the early commitment effect on value from a firm's ability to influence its future competitive position, and the flexibility effect from strategic investment:

Expanded (strategic) net present value (NPV^*)
= [direct (static) NPV + strategic value] + flexibility value.   (6.1)

The combination of the incremental direct NPV (net of the required investment outlay) and the total strategic value resulting from an early strategic investment commitment is referred to as the *net commitment value.* As noted in chapter 4, the total strategic value consists of a *strategic reaction value* (reflecting the impact of competitor's reaction on profit value for a given market structure) and the *strategic preemption value* from deterring competitive entry and changing the market structure altogether (e.g., from Cournot-Nash equilibrium in the base case to a Stackelberg leader/monopoly in quantity competition under the strategic investment alternative).

Although an early strategic investment would necessarily sacrifice flexibility value, it may have either a positive or negative net commitment value (depending on the sign of the strategic value). Figure 6.1 reviews the various competitive strategies, depending on the effect of the first-

FIGURE 6.1 SIGN OF THE STRATEGIC EFFECT AND COMPETITIVE STRATEGIES FOLLOWING A TOUGH OR ACCOMMODATING POSITION UNDER CONTRARIAN OR RECIPROCATING COMPETITION

COMPETITION

		Contrarian (down-sloping reaction/ strategic substitutes) e.g., Quantity competition	*Reciprocating* (up-sloping reaction/ strategic complements) e.g., Price competition
	Tough e.g., proprietary investment (hurt competition)	i **committing and offensive** Invest (+ strategic effect) (Monopoly profits or Nash Cournot competition)	ii **flexible and inoffensive** Don't invest / wait (– strategic effect) (Nash Price competition)
PIONEER	**Accommodating** e.g., shared investment (benefit competition)	iii **flexible and offensive** Don't invest / wait (–strategic effect) (Nash Cournot competition)	iv **committing and inoffensive** Invest (+ strategic effect) (Leader-follower / accommodation or Nash Price competition)

stage strategic investment (whether firm A takes a *tough* or an *accommodating* position) and the form of competition (whether competition reacts in a *reciprocating* or in a *contrarian* fashion).

Under contrarian competition, the firm has an incentive to invest in a strategic project if its benefits are proprietary or it increases the firm's ability to preempt a larger share of the market. In reciprocating competition a strategic investment may result in lower prices via intensified rivalry. In such cases it may be appropriate to invest in strategic projects, creating shared opportunities to "soften" competitive reaction in the later stage of the market.

The different competitive strategies are summarized below.

Committing and Offensive Strategy (Tough Position with Contrarian Competition). An offensive strategic investment, for example an R & D project, can generate a proprietary advantage and make the firm tough, hurting its competition in the second stage. Under contrarian (e.g., quantity) competition, competition will retreat and the pioneering firm can expand its share and gain leadership as the industry grows. At lower demand the competitor's profit value is negative, and the pioneer may even enjoy monopoly rents.

Flexible and Offensive Strategy (Accommodating with Contrarian Competition). Under contrarian competition, the new entrant may take advantage of the pioneer's accommodating position and capture most of the shared benefits of its R & D investment. There is no strategic advantage to precommit investment. In order to prevent the creation of valuable shared opportunities for competition, the firm should maintain an offensive posture via its option (flexibility) to wait to invest. In case future demand grows, two identical competitors would choose to invest simultaneously (Cournot-Nash equilibrium). If demand declines, both would abandon the market.

Flexible and Inoffensive Strategy (Tough with Reciprocating Competition). A tough position via a strategic investment (e.g., goodwill investment) may hurt competition but can invite a tough reaction by a reciprocating competitor, resulting in intensified rivalry (e.g., price competition in the airline industry). To avoid such intense (and potentially damaging) second-stage competition, the firm will not invest in an early strategic investment, staying flexible and inoffensive. If demand develops later, both firms can invest, resulting in Nash price equilibrium.

Committing and Inoffensive Strategy (Accommodating with Reciprocating Competition). Now suppose that early strategic (e.g., goodwill) investment will also benefit the demand for the competitor, who is ready to reciprocate. The pioneering firm should invest in the strategic goodwill project and be accommodating in a later stage of the market, avoiding price competition and reaping shared benefits. Through maintaining high prices and higher profit margins, both firms can enjoy more profitable follow-on investments. The pioneer firm may act as a Stackelberg leader, with the competitor following suit. Compared to the base case, a strategic goodwill investment has positive strategic reaction and coordination effects but a flexibility loss (negative flexibility effect).

This chapter develops further our integrated real-options and game-theoretic framework for analyzing strategic investments in a more rigorous fashion. The basic setup involves a two-stage game in which the option value of R & D depends on endogeneous competitive reactions. We consider a sequence of investment decisions by one of two firms involving a first-stage strategic investment commitment that can influence its strategic position (relative future production costs or market share) vis-à-vis its competitor in the second stage, and subsequent productive investment (commercialization) decisions by either firm. This setup illustrates the trade-off between the flexibility value of waiting and the strategic commitment value of early investment.

Section 6.2 describes the basic two-stage investment game, the equilibrium quantities, prices and payoff values, and the valuation process. Section 6.3 presents numerical examples to illustrate the different competitive strategies under contrarian versus reciprocating competition. Section 6.4 provides a summary and conclusions. Derivations are given in the appendix.

6.2. The Basic Two-Stage Game

Consider the case of an R & D investment for the development of a new, cost-efficient technological process versus the base case of no R & D investment and continuing to use the existing technology. The basic problem in its simplest form is illustrated by the two-stage game presented in figure 6.2. The alternative actions of a single pioneer firm (firm A) to make a first-stage strategic investment or not at time 0 are reflected by the tree branches (shown by squares, □). If the strategic investment is made, the second-stage market outcomes are influenced by this investment (using

FIGURE 6.2 THE TWO-STAGE GAME IN EXTENSIVE FORM UNDER DIFFERENT MARKET STRUCTURES

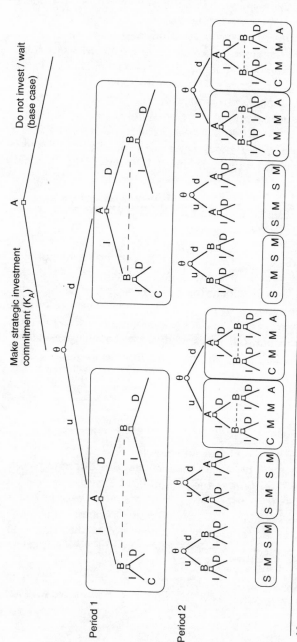

Notes: A or B (□) represents a decision to invest (I) or defer (D) by firm A or B. θ (O) represents the state of market demand or nature's up (u) and down (d) moves.

The combination of competitive decisions (A or B) and market demand moves (θ) may result in one of the following market structure game outcomes:

C: Cournot Nash quantity / price competition equilibrium outcome

S: Stackelberg leader (S^L) / follower (S^F) outcome

M: Monopolist outcome

A: Abandon (0 value)

D: Defer / stay flexible (option value)

the new technology). If the strategic investment is not made, the two firms are identical (using the existing technology). The resolution of *market demand uncertainty* (shown by circles), reflected by nature's (θ) up (u) or down (d) moves, can influence competitive strategies and result in a range of potential investment opportunity values over time.

At time 1 (the second stage) the market opens and the market structure is assumed to result in a duopoly, where either of two competing firms (A or B) may make subsequent commercial investments. Thus, in the second stage, each firm faces a timing option for installing production capacity. To accommodate various market structure possibilities, the second stage itself is assumed to consist of two periods (1 and 2). Given market demand up or down moves, $\theta\{u, d\}$, in each period during the second stage, each competitor's actions to invest in production capacity (I) or defer (D) investment in the commercial project are represented by the tree branches, A {I, D} and B {I, D}. When both firms decide to invest simultaneously (I, I), the game ends in a Cournot Nash equilibrium (C); when both firms choose to defer (D, D) under low realizations of demand, nature (θ) moves again and the game is repeated; finally, when one firm invests first, acting as a Stackelberg leader (S^L) — or in some cases a monopolist (M) — market demand is revealed again and the competitor may then decide to invest later — as a Stackelberg follower (S^F) — or to abandon (A).

The different sets of actions of the two firms result in project value payoffs at the end of each branch (node) in the binomial valuation tree, representing the equilibrium outcomes of different competitive market structure games. If the first-stage strategic investment is made, the end node market outcomes are influenced by this investment (relative to the base case).

6.2.1. EQUILIBRIUM QUANTITIES, PRICES, AND PAYOFF VALUES

In this section we describe the equilibrium payoff values *at the end* of the last stage of our investment problem. These terminal equilibrium payoff values are a nonlinear function of the evolution of exogenous market demand (θ). For example, for high levels of demand the early investor captures a greater market share than new entrants; for intermediate levels of demand the early investor may delay or deter potential entrants and capture Stackelberg leadership or monopoly rents; for very low levels of demand the early investor may not find it profitable to invest in the follow-on commercial project. The different market structure games in the commercialization stage (see bottom of figure 6.2 and table 6.1) are as follows.[3]

Cournot Quantity or Bertrand Price Competition (C)

If both firms decide to invest (I) in the same period (*simultaneously*) without observing each other's actions, a Cournot-Nash equilibrium is reached when each firm reacts optimally to the other firm's expected action (as expressed by its reaction function, R), that is, $\alpha_A^* = R_A(\alpha_B^*)$ and $\alpha_B^* = R_B(\alpha_A^*)$. Thus, the Cournot Nash equilibrium actions (or Bertrand prices), α_A^* and α_B^*, are on the intersection of the reaction functions of both firms, shown as outcome C in figure 6.2 (and in figure 6.5). These Nash equilibrium actions can be obtained by substituting the expression for $R_j(\alpha_i)$ into $R_i(\alpha_j)$, or by equating the reaction functions $R_A(\alpha_B)$ and $R_B(\alpha_A)$, and solving for the optimal actions α_A^* and α_B^*.

Stackelberg Leadership (S)

If one firm invests first in a commercial project and its competitor invests at a later period (e.g., if the follower faces relatively higher operating costs that require waiting until demand has risen more, or if a lag is involved for the follower to set up plant capacity), a Stackelberg leader/follower game can result. Given that the follower will observe the leader's prior action, the Stackelberg quantity (or price) leader will choose that action on the follower's reaction function, $R_B(\alpha_A)$, which will maximize its own profit value, that is, Max $V_A(\alpha_A, R_B(\alpha_A))$.[4] The Stackelberg outcome is shown in figure 6.2 (and in figure 6.5) as point S, where firm A's highest iso-profit curve (π_A = constant) is just tangent to firm B's reaction curve, and corresponds to a higher profit value than the Cournot Nash equilibrium.

---

[3] The symbols C, S, M, A, D at the bottom of figure 6.2 refer to the different market structure games described herein (and summarized in table 6.1). As noted, the state payoff values at the end of the second stage are the outcomes of different market structure games depending on the state of demand (θ), each firm's actions (invest, do not invest/defer), and their timing (simultaneous or lagged, at $t = 1$ or 2).

[4] In contrarian quantity competition, an aggressive firm that invests early, acting as a Stackelberg leader, can acquire a larger share of the market. Under reciprocating price competition, a Stackelberg price leader would choose a price on the competitor's reaction function that maximizes its profit value. In the case of an accommodating price leader, there need not be a first-mover advantage, as both firms can be better off setting higher prices than when they invest at the same time.

Monopoly (M)

In some cases, the leader may choose an early action (e.g., a high enough quantity) on the follower's reaction curve such that it would become unprofitable for the follower to operate ($\pi_B(Q_A, Q_B) < 0$, or net of the required outlay, $NPV_B < 0$), preempting its entry and earning monopoly profits (π_m). The monopoly outcome is shown as point M in panel A of figure 6.2 (and in figure 6.5), and lies on a higher iso-profit curve than the Stackelberg and Cournot outcomes.

Do Not Invest/Defer (D) or Abandon (A)

Management, of course, has the option not to invest or to wait if market demand (θ) is low and undertaking the project would result in a negative value. By deferring investment, management keeps alive the opportunity that demand may improve and the project may become profitable in a future period. In case the firm does not invest up until the very last stage, or if it decides to abandon, the value of follow-on investment is truncated to 0.

In the appendix to this chapter (see also chapter 9) we describe a model that allows closed-form analytic expressions for quantifying the equilibrium quantities (Q^*), profits (π^*), and state net project values (NPV^*) at the end states (nodes) under the various market structures (e.g., Cournot, Stackelberg, or monopoly). The second part of the appendix derives equilibrium prices (P^*) when assuming Bertrand-type price competition. The equilibrium quantities and profit values for the various market structures under quantity competition are summarized in table 6.1. The equilibrium prices for the different market structures under reciprocating price competition are summarized in table 6.2. The equilibrium path to reach these terminal values depends on the evolution of market demand and the outcome of the competitive subgames in the two stages.

6.2.2. Valuation of Competitive Strategies

The equilibrium set of strategies is found by backward binomial valuation, starting with the end-node payoff (equilibrium state net project) values of a given competitive structure summarized in table 6.1 and working back through the tree of figure 6.2. In each case above, the competitive strategy of each firm consists of mapping the information set about its competitor's actions and the development of market demand (u or d moves in θ) to an optimal investment action by the firm. The current value of a claim on project value, C, is then determined from its future up and

TABLE 6.1
Equilibrium Quantities, Profits, and State Project Values for Various Market Structures under Contrarian Quantity Competition in the Second Stage

Action[a] (A, B)	Market Structure C/M/S/A/D	Equilibrium Quantity Q_i^*	Equilibrium Profit[b] π_i^*	State Project Value[c] NPV_i	Demand State θ_t
(DI, DI) (II, II)	Cournot Nash (C)	$\dfrac{(\theta_t - c_i)(2 + q_i) - (\theta_t - c_j)}{(2 + q_i)(2 + q_j) - 1}$	$\dfrac{(\theta_t - 2c_i + c_j)^2}{9}$	$\dfrac{(\theta_t - 2c_i + c_j)^2}{9k} - I$	$\geq 3\sqrt{kI} + 2c_i - c_j$
(DI, DD) (II, DD)	Monopolist (M)	$\dfrac{\theta_t - c_i}{2 + q_i} \;\; (Q_j = 0)$	$\dfrac{(\theta_t - c_i)^2}{4} \;\; (\pi_j \leq 0)$	$\dfrac{(\theta_t - c_i)^2}{4k} - I$	$< 3\sqrt{kI} + 2c_j - c_i$
(II, DI)	Stackelberg leader (S^L)/ Monopolist (M)	$\dfrac{(\theta_t - c_i)(2 + q_j) - (\theta_t - c_j)}{(2 + q_i)(2 + q_j) - 2}$	$\dfrac{(\theta_t - 2c_i + c_j)^2}{8}$	$\dfrac{(\theta_t - 2c_i + c_j)^2}{8k} - I'$	$\geq 4\sqrt{kI} + 2c_j - c_i$ $(< 4\sqrt{kI} + 2c_j - c_i)$
(DI, II)	Stackelberg follower (S^F)	$\dfrac{(\theta_t - c_j)(2 + q_i) - (\theta_t - c_i)}{(2 + q_i)(2 + q_j)}$	$\dfrac{(\theta_t - 2c_j + c_i)^2}{16}$	$\dfrac{(\theta_t - 2c_j + c_i)^2}{16k} - I$	$\geq 4\sqrt{kI} + 2c_j - c_i$
(DD, DD)	Abandon (A)	0	0	0	
Period 1					
(I, I)	Cournot Nash (C)	$\dfrac{(\theta_t - c_i)(2 + q_i) - (\theta_t - c_j)}{(2 + q_i)(2 + q_j) - 1}$	$\dfrac{(\theta_t - 2c_i + c_j)^2}{9}$	$\dfrac{(\theta_t - 2c_i + c_j)^2}{9k} - I$	
(I, D)	Monopolist (M) / Stackelberg leader (S^L)	$\dfrac{\theta_t - c_i}{2 + q_i}$	$\pi_m = \dfrac{(\theta_t - c_i)^2}{4}$	$\dfrac{pV_u^* + (1 - p)V_d^*}{1 + r} - I + \dfrac{\pi_m}{1 + k}$	
(D,D) (D, I)	Defer (D)	0	0	$\dfrac{pNPV_u^* + (1 - p)NPV_d^*}{1 + r}$	

[a] During period 1, (A, B) means that firm A took action while A competitor from B took action B.

[b] Calculated from $\pi_i = P_i Q_i - C(Q_i)$, assuming for simplicity $q_i = q_i = q = 0$.

[c] Determined in the last stage from $NPV_i = \text{Max}(\pi_i/k - I, 0)$, where I is required outlay and k the risk-adjusted discount rate. In the first period, it may be determined from future expanded (strategic) net present values (NPV^*) in the up and down states using backward binomial risk-neutral valuation.

down state values (C_u and C_d) discounted at the risk-free interest rate (r), with expectations taken over the risk-neutral or "certainty-equivalent" probabilities (p):[5]

$$C = \frac{pC_u + (1 - p)C_d}{1 + r} \tag{6.2}$$

The market demand parameter θ is assumed to follow a multiplicative binomial process (or random walk) in complete markets, moving up to $\theta_u \equiv u\theta$ or down to $\theta_d \equiv d\theta$ over each period.[6]

As noted, the incremental value of making the strategic R & D investment (vs. the base case of no R & D investment) may have both a direct effect on the innovating firm's profit value via lowering its own future production costs as well as an indirect or strategic effect via altering the competitor's equilibrium production quantity.[7]

Base Case Illustration

To illustrate how the valuation works, consider the game where pioneer firm A can make a first-stage strategic R & D investment that results in a deterministic operating cost advantage in the second stage (commercialization). We assume that pioneer firm A can enhance its relative competitive position by making an early R & D investment of $K_A = 100$ in a more cost-efficient technological process. In the second stage, either firm A or firm B can invest $I = 100$ in follow-up production capacity (commercialization projects), depending on subsequent random demand moves (where initial demand is $\theta_0 = 17.5$ and can move up or down with binomial parameters $u = 1.25$ and $d = 1/u = 0.80$). The risk-free interest rate (r) is 10% (while the risk-adjusted discount rate in the last stage is $k = 13\%$). If firm A chooses not to make the R & D investment (base case)

---

[5]We here adopt the assumption of complete markets with portfolios of securities that replicate the dynamics of the present value of the project caused by changes in equilibrium state profits. In such complete markets, the risk-neutral probabilities can be obtained from

$$p = \frac{(1 + r - \delta) - d}{u - d},$$

where u and d represent the multiplicative up or down moves in market demand, r is the risk-free interest rate, and δ is the constant asset (dividend-like) payout yield (equal to $k / (1+k)$ for a perpetual project, where k is the risk-adjusted discount rate).

[6]In chapter 9, θ follows a continuous-time random walk or geometric Brownian motion.

[7]The total strategic value in equation 6.1 consists of this *strategic reaction value* (reflecting the impact of competitor's reaction on profit value via incremental changes in equilibrium quantity for a given market structure) and of a *strategic preemption value* from changing the market structure altogether, e.g., from Cournot-Nash equilibrium in the base case (staying with the existing, costlier process) to a Stackelberg leadership or monopoly equilibrium under the strategic investment alternative.

TABLE 6.2
Equilibrium Prices for Different Market Structures under Reciprocating
Price Competition in the Second Stage

Action[a] (A, B)	Market Structure N/M/S/A/D	Equilibrum Price,[b] p_i^* (for $q_i = q_j = 0$)
(DI, DI) (II, II)	Nash price competition (N)	$\dfrac{2b(\theta_{i,t} + bc_i) + d(\theta_{j,t} + bc_j)}{4b^2 - d^2}$
(DI, DD) (IL, DD)	Monopolist (M)	$\dfrac{\theta_t + c(b - d)}{2(b - d)}$
(II, DI)	Stackelberg price leader (S^L)	$\dfrac{2b(\theta_{i,t} + bc_i) + d(\theta_{j,t} + bc_j - dc_i)}{4b^2 - 2d^2}$
(DD, DD)	Abandon (A)	
Period 1		
(I, I)	Nash (N)	$\dfrac{2b(\theta_{i,t} + bc_i) + d(\theta_{j,t} + bc_j)}{4b^2 - d^2}$
(I, D)	Stackelberg price leader (S^L)/ Monopolist (M)	$\dfrac{2b(\theta_{i,t} + bc_i) + d(\theta_{j,t} + bc_j - dc_i)}{4b^2 - 2d^2}$
(D, D) (D, I)	Defer (D)	

[a]During period 1, (A, B) means that firm A took action A while competitor firm B took action B.

[b]Given this equilibrium price, firm i's corresponding profit can be calculated from $\pi_i = (P_i - c_i)Q_i$ (assuming $q_i = q_j = 0$), while the second-stage state net present values from $NPV_i = \mathrm{Max}\,(\pi_i/k - I, 0)$, where I is the required outlay and k the risk-adjusted discount rate. Period 1 values may be determined from future expanded (strategic) net present values (NPV^*) in the up and down states using backward binomial risk-neutral valuation.

the two firms would have symmetric second-stage operating costs, based on the old technology, of $c_A = c_B = 5$.

Figure 6.3 illustrates the valuation results (state project values) for the base case alternative of no R & D in both periods during the commercialization stage of this simplified basic game. The optimal competitive strategies are derived by utilizing the project payoff values summarized in table 6.1. For example, in the subgame at the bottom of figure 6.3 when demand

FIGURE 6.3 THE BASE CASE (NO STRATEGIC R & D INVESTMENT): TWO-STAGE GAME IN EXTENSIVE FORM UNDER DIFFERENT MARKET STRUCTURES

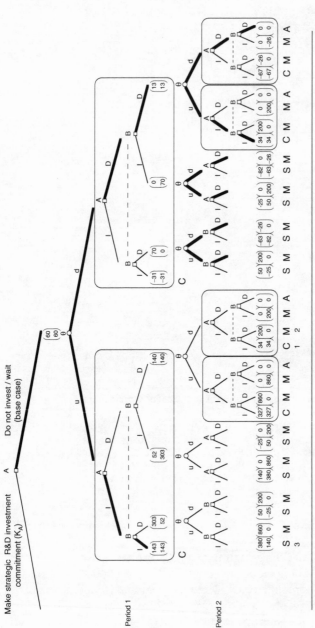

Notes: A or B (□) represents a decision to invest (I) or defer (D) by firm A or B. θ (O) represents the state of market demand or nature's up (u) and down (d) moves.

The combination of competitive decisions (A or B) and market demand moves (θ) may result in one of the following market structure game outcomes:

C: Cournot Nash quantity / price competition equilibrium outcome

S: Stackelberg leader (S^L) / follower (S^F) outcome

M: Monopolist outcome

A: Abandon (0 value)

D: Defer / stay flexible (option value)

is up ($\theta = u$) and both firms defer (D, D) and then moves down and both firms invest (I, I), the resulting Cournot-Nash equilibrium value at end node 1 (C) (see appendix equation 6.A.7 or the first row in table 6.1)[8] is

$$NPV_A = \frac{(\theta_t - 2c_A + c_B)^2}{9k} - I = \frac{(17.5 - 2(5) + 5)^2}{9(0.13)} - 100 = 34.$$

When $\theta = u$ in period 2, the Cournot-Nash equilibrium value is 327. The expected equilibrium value one step earlier (in period 1) is then obtained from these values using equation 6.2 (with $p = 0.41$):

$$\frac{0.41(327) + 0.59(34)}{1.10} = 140.$$

The other values shown in the two boxes of figure 6.3 in period 1 of the commercialization stage are derived similarly. Note that if $\theta = u$ (left box), each firm has a dominating strategy to invest in production capacity (I) regardless of the other's actions (for each firm $303 > 140$ if the competitor defers and $143 > 52$ if it invests), resulting in a symmetric Cournot-Nash equilibrium outcome of (143, 143). For $\theta = d$ (right box), however, both firms may choose to defer and obtain (13, 13). Finally, from the backward binomial risk-neutral valuation of equation 6.2, the expected equilibrium value for the base-case (no R & D) strategy at $t = 0$ is

$$NPV_A^* = \frac{0.41(143) + 0.59(13)}{1.10} = 60.$$

The base case value of no R & D investment is (by construction) symmetric for both firms, that is, (60, 60) for firm (A, B). By way of an overview, the later table 6.5 summarizes the breakdown of total value into various components for each of the cases we examine. In the above base case (column 1), total value (60) consists of a base case NPV of 37 and a flexibility value of 23.

---

[8] In end node 2 (M) next to it, when firm A invests and firm B defers, firm A's monopoly (net) profit value (from equation 6.A.11 with $q = 0$ or second row in table 6.1) is

$$\frac{(\theta_t - c)^2}{4k} - I = \frac{(17.5 - 5)^2}{4(0.13)} - 100 = 200.$$

In end node 3 (S), when $\theta = u$ and firm A invests while firm B defers (I, D) but then decides to invest in the next period (2) if θ moves up, the resulting Stackelberg leader equilibrium value for firm A is given by (see the appendix equation 6.A.12 or third row in table 6.1):

$$NPV_A = \frac{(\theta_t - 2c_A + c_B)^2}{8k} - I' = \frac{(17.5 \times 1.25 - 2(5) + 5)^2}{8(0.13)} - 100 = 380.$$

6.3. Numerical Examples of Different Competitive Strategies under Contrarian versus Reciprocating Competition

In this section we illustrate different competitive strategies with numerical examples. First, we examine an R & D game under contrarian quantity competition. Later we analyze a goodwill-price competition game that involves reciprocating reactions. In both competitive environments, the ability of the firm to enjoy proprietary benefits influences its strategic investment decision. The two numerical examples result in opposite strategic effects and different optimal competitive strategies for shared and proprietary investments.

6.3.1. COMPETITIVE R & D STRATEGIES UNDER QUANTITY COMPETITION

Firm A's ability to use the R & D investment to gain a strategic advantage depends on the extent to which the benefits of R & D can be made proprietary to the firm. When firm A decides to make a strategic R & D investment, two different strategies can result depending on whether the resulting cost benefits of the second-stage commercialization project are proprietary (asymmetric costs) or shared (symmetric).

Proprietary Investment: Committing and Offensive Strategy (Positive Strategic Effect)

Consider first the case where making a strategic R & D investment results in a *proprietary* operating cost advantage for firm A during commercialization. Specifically, suppose the second-stage operating cost for firm A is reduced from 5 to 0 ($c_A = 0$) if it invests in R & D (with sure success) while for firm B it remains at 5 ($c_B = 5$) — as compared to the base case ($c_A = c_B = 5$) when neither firm invests in R & D. This upfront R & D investment commitment makes the pioneer firm stronger in the second stage, preempting market share under quantity competition.

Panel A of figure 6.4 summarizes the valuation results for the first period of the commercialization phase (stage 2) for the proprietary R & D case (the right branch of the tree is the base case of figure 6.3).[9] The tree

_____

[9]Due to space considerations, figure 6.4 does not show the last period of the second-stage game, which incorporates the equilibrium values for the Cournot (C), Stackelberg leader/follower (S), or monopoly (M) games (summarized in table 6.1) in the various states shown in figure 6.1. These were illustrated in detail for the base case alternative of no R & D in figure 6.3. All the numerical values shown in figure 6.4 are, nevertheless, the expected values derived from backward binomial option valuation based on the entire multistage game and the equilibrium payoff values of table 6.1.

Box 6.1 Contrarian (Cournot Quantity) Competition and Timing of Investments in the Production of Memory Chips

Demand for memory chips has grown exponentially, driven by the increased demand for personal computers and the embedding of the technology in other consumer electronics devices, such as cellular phones and televisions. The timing of investment is critical in this industry. New factories require an immense capital investment, which may quickly become obsolete as technology changes rapidly in this innovative environment. The industry is characterized by Cournot quantity competition, where firms chose their capacity and then the market clears the price. Capacities are strategic substitutes: if one firm expands capacity, its competitors will install less. When value is more idiosyncratic for one firm, the exercise game becomes asymmetrical where the better-positioned firm exercises its options early preempting the market.

In the beginning of the 1980s much of the chip-industry was concentrated in the United States. Declining prices in 1984 led many chip producers such as Intel and Texas Instruments to reduce their investment and postpone expansion options. Instead, Japanese firms like Toshiba, NEC, and Onki Electric precommitted capital in new plants, preempting the shared growth opportunities in the industry. By the late 1980s, Japanese firms captured 80% of the world chip market, while American firms held only 15%. A subsequent substitution of capacity occurred in the 1990s. In the economic downturn that brought the Japanese economy into a recession, the Japanese chipmakers deferred their expansion options in new chip factories. South Korean competitors, such as Hyundai, Samsung, and Goldstar Electron, reacted aggressively with increased investment commitment. By 1994 the South Koreans captured 36% percent of the market, and Samsung became the largest producer in the world.

Sources: based partly on Besanko, Dranove, and Shanley 2000; and "Silicon Duel: Koreans Move to Crab Memory-Chip Market from the Japanese," *Wall Street Journal,* March 14, 1995, A1, A8.

FIGURE 6.4 COMPETITIVE INVESTMENT STRATEGIES IN THE R & D
EXAMPLE: PROPRIETARY VERSUS SHARED INVESTMENT UNDER
CONTRARIAN QUANTITY COMPETITION

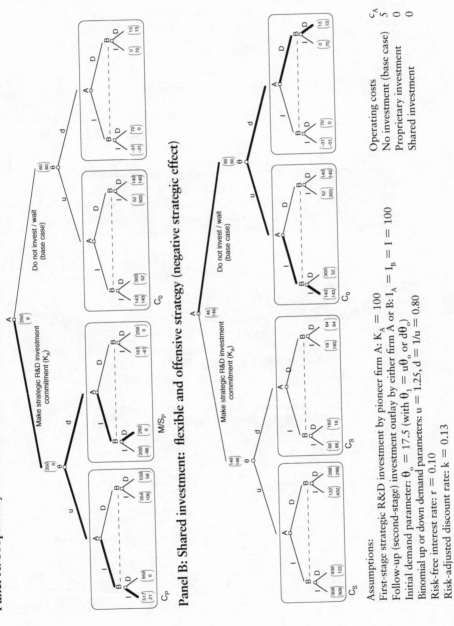

Panel A: Proprietary investment: committing and offensive strategy (positive strategic effect)

Panel B: Shared investment: flexible and offensive strategy (negative strategic effect)

Assumptions:
First-stage strategic R&D investment by pioneer firm A: $K_A = 100$
Follow-up (second-stage) investment outlay by either firm A or B: $I_A = I_B = I = 100$
Initial demand parameter: $\theta_0 = 17.5$ (with $\theta_1 = u\theta_0$ or $d\theta_0$)
Binomial up or down demand parameters: $u = 1.25$, $d = 1/u = 0.80$
Risk-free interest rate: $r = 0.10$
Risk-adjusted discount rate: $k = 0.13$

	c_A	c_B
Operating costs		
No investment (base case)	5	5
Proprietary investment	0	5
Shared investment	0	0

is solved by backward induction in a similar fashion as in the base case.[10] The highlighted (bold) branches along each tree indicate the optimal actions along the equilibrium path. In this case, firm A may use the up-front R & D investment to strengthen its strategic position in the second stage. Pioneer firm A should make the R & D investment in stage 1. It should then make a follow-on commercialization investment (I) in the second stage regardless of demand. For high levels of demand the pioneer captures a greater market share than the competitor in a Nash equilibrium. For lower levels of demand the early investor will deter the potential entrant and gain Stackelberg leadership.

The asymmetry introduced in the relative operating costs from the strategic R & D investment clearly influences each firm's reaction function and the end-node equilibrium payoff values. In panel A of figure 6.5, the proprietary R & D investment causes firm A's reaction function to shift to the right, changing the base-case Cournot equilibrium outcome from C_0 to C_p and increasing firm A's relative market share.[11]

Shared Investment: Flexible and Offensive Strategy (Negative Strategic Effect)

Panels B in figures 6.4 and 6.5 illustrate the symmetric shared case, where R & D by firm A results in a more cost-effective technology that both competitors can exploit ($c_A = c_B = 0$). The R & D expenditure strengthens the competitor's strategic position and enhances its incentive to respond aggressively in the future. As a consequence, R & D creates a strategic disadvantage for firm A. In panel B of figure 6.5, firm B's reaction function shifts to the right as well, which increases both firms' quantities

[10]Consider first the subgame (in the second box) concerning investment in follow-up production capacity, following a decision by firm A to invest in R & D (K_A) and a downward demand realization ($\theta = d$). In this case, a production capacity investment (I) by firm A dominates deferral (D) since it results in a higher net value for firm A's follow-up project regardless of whether competitor B decides to invest (I) or defer (D). Knowing that firm A has a dominating strategy to invest, firm B would defer (obtaining 0 rather than -86). Thus firm A would earn monopoly profits, resulting in net present values of (293, 0) for the follow-up projects of firms A and B, respectively. However, if $\theta = u$ as in the first box, total market demand would be sufficient for a Cournot-Nash equilibrium outcome where both firms, regardless of the other's actions, have dominant strategies to invest (I) in subsequent commercialization projects, resulting in values of (517, 21). Using backward binomial valuation results in expected gross investment opportunity values of (350, 8) when firm A invests in R & D. Net of the required outlay of $K_A = 100$, this results in an expanded net present value (*NPV**) for firm A of 250. Since the base case alternative of no R & D results in values of (60, 60), firm A should make the R & D investment (250 > 60), increasing its expanded NPV by 190 (= 250 − 60) relative to the base case.

[11]The equilibrium quantity (Q^*) and profits (π^*) are shown in the table at the bottom of figure 6.5 for the Cournot, Stackelberg leader, and monopoly market structures.

with equal market share. As a result, the opposite competitive strategy results for the shared case (compared to the proprietary one), as shown in panel B of figure 6.4. Firm A should not invest in R & D but should rather retain a flexible wait-and-see position, attaining the base case equilibrium values of (60, 60). Investing in R & D may create a strategic disadvantage for firm A by paying the cost of creating valuable investment opportunities for competition or by enhancing the competitor's ability and incentive to respond aggressively in the future (resulting in a value of 51 versus 60 from waiting with an incremental NPV^* of -9).

Value Components

It is useful here to identify and quantify the different value components that make up total value and identify the sign of the strategic effects. As noted, for each R & D strategy, the *commitment effect* from precommitting investment must be traded off against the *flexibility value effect* from postponing irreversible investment. Although an early strategic R & D investment may reduce option or flexibility value, it may have a high or low net commitment value, depending on the strategic effects. The sign of these strategic effects may be positive or negative, depending on whether the benefits are proprietary or shared. The total commitment value of R & D can be broken down into a *direct value* from direct reduction in future operating costs, a *strategic reaction value* reflecting the impact of competitor's reaction on profit value for a given market structure, and a *strategic preemption value* from deterring competitive entry and causing a change in the market structure altogether.

Consider, for example, the case that market demand develops favorably (for $\theta_1 = u\theta_0 = 21.88$), resulting in simultaneous second-stage investment by both firms and Cournot quantity Nash equilibriums (highlighted leftmost branch (I, I)). The Nash equilibrium values in this case are shown in the table of figure 6.5. Table 6.3 (and the last row of Table 6.4) shows the strategic interactions for the proprietary and shared investment.

The Direct Effect. The incremental direct effect of the strategic R & D investment is the change in profit value compared to the base-case of no R & D investment, with the competitor's reaction constant. If competing firm B would maintain its quantity at $Q_B = 5.633$ as in the base case, firm A would expand production to $Q_A = 8.125$ if the advantage is proprietary, resulting in a direct profit value of 507.6.[12] Thus, the incremental direct effect from the R & D investment, determined as the strategic investment profit value when the competitor does not change its productive decision (507.6) minus the base-case profit value (243 = 31.6/0.13, from the table of figure 6.5 under C_0), equals 264.

Strategic Reaction Effect. The strategic effect of firm A's R & D

FIGURE 6.5 REACTION FUNCTIONS AND EQUILIBRIUM COURNOT, STACKELBERG, AND MONOPOLY OUTCOMES UNDER THE NO STRATEGIC R & D (BASE CASE), PROPRIETARY, OR SHARED R & D INVESTMENT CASES ASSUMING QUANTITY COMPETITION

Panel A. Proprietary Investment ($c_A = 0$, $c_B > 0$)

Panel B. Shared Investment ($c_A = c_B = 0$)

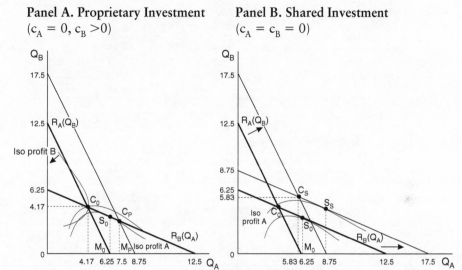

Notes: The demand for each firm (i = A, B) is of the form $P_i(Q_A, Q_B, \theta_t) = \theta_t - (Q_A + Q_B)$ with $\theta_0 = 17.5$ ($u = 1.25$, $d = 0.8$), and the total variable production cost for firm i is of the form $c(Q_i) = c_i Q_i$.

If no strategic R & D investment: base-case costs $c_A = c_B = c = 5$ (base-case Cournot Nash equilibrium at C_0).

If proprietary R & D investment: $c_A = 0$ ($c_B = 5$), R_A shifts to right (at $C_P Q^*_A\uparrow$, $Q^*_B\uparrow$) and $V_A\uparrow$.

If shared R & D investment: $c_B = c_A = 0$, R_B (and R_A) shift right (at $C_S Q^*_B\uparrow$) and $V_B\downarrow$.

Pioneer Firm A	Cournot Nash Outcome			Stackelberg leader			Monopoly	
	C_0 base	C_p propriet.	C_s shared	S_0 base	S_p propriet.	S_s shared	M_0 base	M_p propriet.
Quantity (Q^*_A)	$\frac{1}{3}(\theta_t-c)$	$\frac{1}{3}(\theta_t+c_B)$	$\frac{1}{3}\theta_t$	$\frac{1}{2}(\theta_t-c)$	$\frac{1}{2}(\theta_t+c_B)$	$\frac{1}{2}\theta_t$	$\frac{1}{2}(\theta_t-c_A)$	$\frac{1}{2}\theta_t$
base demand								
(θ_0=17.5)	4.167	7.5	5.833	6.25	11.25	8.75	6.25	8.75
up ($\theta_1=u\theta_0$ =21.875)	5.625	8.958	7.292	8.438	13.438	10.938	8.438	10.938
Profit (π^*_A)	$\frac{1}{9}(\theta_t-c)^2$	$\frac{1}{9}(\theta_t+c_B)^2$	$\frac{1}{9}\theta_t^2$	$\frac{1}{8}(\theta_t-c)^2$	$\frac{1}{8}(\theta_t+c_B)^2$	$\frac{1}{8}\theta_t$	$\frac{1}{4}(\theta_t-c_A)^2$	$\frac{1}{4}\theta_t^2$
base demand								
(θ_0=17.5)	17.361	56.25	34.028	19.531	63.281	38.281	39.063	76.563
up ($\theta_1=u\theta_0$ =21.875)	31.641	80.252	53.168	35.596	90.283	59.815	71.191	119.629

Note: C_0, C_p, C_s are the Cournot Nash, and S_0, S_p, S_s the Stackelberg equilibrium outcomes for the zero, proprietary, or shared investment cases; M_0 and M_p are the base case and proprietary monopoly outcomes. $R_j(Q_i)$ is the reaction function of firm j given the quantity of firm i (Q_i), i = A, B. Q^*_i and V^*_i fluctuate with the state of demand θ_t.

TABLE 6.3
The Strategic Reaction Effect (when Demand Develops Favorably)
under Contrarian Quantity Competition

Investment Type	Operating Costs (c_A^*, c_B^*)	Quantities Q_A^*	Q_B^*	Profit π_A^*
No investment (base case)	$c_A = 5, c_B = 5$	5.63	5.63	31.6
Proprietary investment	$c_A = 0, c_B = 5$	8.95	3.96	80.3
Shared investment	$c_A = 0, c_B = 0$	7.29	7.29	53.2

Investment Type	Direct Effect	Strategic Reaction	Commitment (direct + strat.)	NPV_A^*
No investment (base case)				143
Proprietary investment	264	+110	374	517
Shared investment	264	−98	166	309

Note: c_A, c_B are the second-stage operating costs (influenced by the first-stage strategic investment) for firm A, B.

investment results from the indirect impact on firm A's profit value of the reaction in the competitor's productive decision ($\partial V_A / \partial \alpha_B \times d\alpha_B^* / dK_A$). For high states of demand firm A captures a larger market share in equilibrium as a result of firm A's proprietary R & D investment. The strategic reaction effect in the proprietary investment case has a positive value of +110 (= total profit − direct profit value = 80.3/0.13 − 507.6) as a rresult of firm A's tough position (since the strategic R & D investment reduces firm A's costs via a proprietary advantage that supports enlarged production) and the submissive productive reaction of competitor B.[13]

Table 6.3 also illustrates the strategic reaction effect for the shared investment case that ends in this particular Nash equilibrium ($u\theta_0$ = 21.88). By contrast to the proprietary case above, the negative strategic reaction value is −98 (= 53.2/0.13 − 507.6) as a consequence of firm A's accommodating position and the competitor's aggressive (contrarian) reaction to enlarge its share from $Q_B = 5.625$ to 7.292 (= Q_A).

Strategic Preemption Effect. With a proprietary R & D investment, firm A may even deter entry and gain Stackelberg leader or monopoly

[12]From the reaction function of equation 6.A.5 in the appendix, with $q_i = 0$ and $Q_B = 5.633$ (constant as in base case), $R_A(Q_B) = \frac{1}{2} (\theta_t - c_A - Q_B) = \frac{1}{2} (21.88 - 0 - 5.633) = 8.125$. The direct profit to firm A for a proprietary investment ($c_A = 0$, $Q_A = 8.125$) is given by $\pi_A = [(\theta_1 - c_A) - Q_B]Q_A - Q_A^2 = [21.875 - 0 - 5.625]8.125 - 8.125^2 = 66$, giving a profit value of $V_A = \pi_A/k = 66/0.13 = 507.6$. A similar result is obtained for the shared investment.

TABLE 6.4
Second-Stage Equilibrium State Project Values (NPV*) and Strategic Effects for Different Market Structures and States of Demand (θ) for the Base Case and Proprietary R & D Investment Case

Panel A. Base Case

θ	Market Structure (Static)	Quantity Q^*_A	Profit π^*_A	NPV_A	Market Structure (Dynamic)	Flexibility Value	Base Case NPV^*_A
8.96	Nash	1.32	1.7	−87	Defer	87	0
11.20	Nash	2.07	4.3	−67	Defer	67	0
14.00	Nash	3.00	9.0	−31	Defer	43	13
17.50	Nash	4.17	17.4	34	Nash	0	34
21.88	Nash	5.63	31.6	134	Nash	0	143

Panel B. Proprietary Strategic Investment

θ	Market Structure (Dynamic)	Q^*_A	π^*_A	Direct Value	Strategic Reaction Value	Preemption Value	Commitment Value	Flexibility Loss	NPV^*_A
8.96	Monop./Stackelberg	4.48	20.1	99	42	7	148	(87)	61
11.20	Monop./Stackelberg	5.60	31.4	128	64	27	218	(67)	151
14.00	Monop./Stackelberg	7.00	49.0	163	76	84	323	(43)	293
17.50	Monop./Stackelberg	7.50	56.3	208	91	180	479	0	513
21.88	Nash	8.96	80.3	264	110	0	374	0	517

profits in intermediate states of demand. However, if the cost advantage is shared, the two firms are identical and firm A cannot deter entry. Table 6.4 shows the equilibrium actions (Q^*_A), profits (π^*_A), commercial project values (NPV^*_A), and the various value components in different states of demand (θ) for the base case and for the proprietary strategic investment case. Under the proprietary investment, while for high demand $(\theta = 21.88)$ a Cournot-Nash equilibrium outcome results, medium demand (e.g., $\theta = 17.5$) may result in a monopoly or a Stackelberg leader/follower game, and low demand $(\theta = 8.96)$ induces both firms to defer. As can be seen from the last row of table 6.4 (for $\theta = 21.88$), high demand involves only a strategic reaction effect, but no strategic preemption value or flexibility value loss since both the base case and the proprietary investment case involve the same market structure where it is optimal for both firms to invest immediately (Cournot Nash equilibrium). When demand drops to $\theta = 17.5$, there is an additional strategic preemption effect (180) because of a change in the market structure (from Nash equilibrium in the base case to a monopoly).

The Flexibility Effect. The high-demand states involved no flexibility value loss compared to the (static) Cournot Nash equilibrium base case. However, for lower states (e.g., if $\theta = 8.96$) there is also flexibility value loss (87) since firm A would invest earlier under the proprietary investment (becoming a monopolist or Stackelberg leader) compared to a dynamic base-case alternative where the firm would defer.

We can best see the interplay between the loss of flexibility value and the net commitment value of a strategic R & D investment using initial (time-zero) unconditional values, as shown in table 6.5 (panel A for the proprietary and panel B for the shared investment cases). The values in Table 6.5 are obtained after applying the backward binomial valuation process using these conditional equilibrium values (e.g., for the various strategic effects) for each θ, weighted with the appropriate risk-neutral probabilities and discounted to the beginning at the risk-free rate. Table 6.5 shows the breakdown of total value into its various components when the R & D investment is proprietary (panel A) or shared (panel B). Panel A confirms that if firm A makes a proprietary R & D investment $(K_A = 100)$ in a new, more cost-efficient technology the total expanded NPV will be 250, whereas in the base-case of waiting (staying with the old, costlier technology) it is 60 (37 for base-case NPV plus 23 in flexibility value). By investing in R & D, firm A generates a net commitment

[13]The total commitment value (direct effect + strategic effect = 264 + 110) is thus 374 (for $\theta = 21.88$). Since this is the incremental value resulting from the strategic investment that incorporates competitor's reaction above the base case, the proprietary investment's NPV^* is base-case NPV + commitment value = 143 + 374 = 517.

TABLE 6.5
Breakdown of Value Components for the Strategic R & D Investment versus the Base Case when the Investment Is Proprietary or Shared

Panel A. Proprietary Strategic Investment

	Base Case (no investment, use old technology)	K_A	Strategic Direct	Strategic Reaction	Proprietary R & D Investment (new technology)	Δ(proprietary −base case)
NPV	37	−100	+186	+82	205	+168
Strategic preemption	0				45	+45
Net commitment value						+213
Flexibility value	23				0	−23
Total expanded NPV	60				250	+190

ΔNPV^* = net commitment value + flexibility value
= $[-K_A$ + (direct value + strategic reaction value + strategic preemption value)] + flexibility value
= $[-100 + (86 + 82 + 45)] - 23 = -213 - 23 = -190 > 0$ (invest).

Panel B. Shared Investment

	Base Case No investment	K_A	Strategic Direct	Strategic Reaction	Shared R & D Investment	Δ(proprietary −base case)
NPV	37	−100	+186	−72	51	+14
Strategic preemption	0				0	0
Net commitment						+14
Flexibility value	23				0	−23
Total expanded NPV	60				51	−9

ΔNPV^* = net commitment value + flexibility value
= $[-100 + (186 - 72)] - 23 = +14 - 23 = -9 < 0$ (don't invest).

value of $+213$, consisting of a direct value of $+186$ from direct reduction in future operating costs, a strategic reaction value via an incremental change in the competitor's output of $+82$, and a strategic preemption effect of $+45$ from deterring competitive entry in certain states of demand. This net commitment value of $+213$ more than compensates for the loss in flexibility value of 23 from giving up the option to wait (base case), resulting in an incremental value (difference between the expanded NPVs of the R & D investment alternative of 250 and the base case of 60) of 190 (> 0) that makes investment in R & D worthwhile. In the shared case (panel B) both the sign of the strategic reaction effect (-72) as well as of the difference between the net commitment value and the flexibility loss ($14 - 23 = -9$) get reversed, so that it becomes preferable to wait rather than invest in R & D.

6.3.2. GOODWILL/ADVERTISING STRATEGIES UNDER PRICE COMPETITION

Consider now a large one-time advertising expenditure or goodwill investment in an environment of reciprocating competition where price settings by competing firms are reciprocating (strategic complements).[14] A good example may be the airline or the cigarette industry, where a price reduction by one firm is met by similar price cutting by its competitor (see box 6.2 on p. 283). The strategic investment in such a case develops market demand and creates goodwill for subsequent investments (reflected in larger demand for the product). The basic assumptions are similar to the earlier example.

The pioneering firm can achieve a proprietary or a shared advantage via the strategic goodwill investment. For example, a large company-focused advertising campaign can enhance market share through customer loyalty and reputation. In other cases, the benefits may be shared with competitors as a public good of the entire industry. For example, a product-focused goodwill investment to promote a new technology or to open up the market via customer education (e.g., an advertising campaign about cellular phones when they were first introduced) or obtaining regulatory approvals benefiting the entire industry can result in a larger market demand for both firms. In some cases it may be better to follow an accommodating strategy and set higher prices that competitors can follow, sharing the benefits of the enlarged market pie.

Figure 6.6 shows the equilibrium outcomes for the different market structure games under the proprietary or shared investment cases when

[14]Firm A can make a first-stage goodwill investment of $K_A = 85$, while either firm can invest $I = 100$ in either period during the second stage. Both firms face symmetric costs of $c_A = c_B = c = 1$. The firm's own and cross price sensitivity parameters in demand equation 6.A.16 in the appendix are $b = 2$ and $d = 1$.

FIGURE 6.6 EQUILIBRIUM BERTRAND NASH, STACKELBERG, AND
MONOPOLY OUTCOMES UNDER THE NO INVESTMENT (BASE CASE),
PROPRIETARY, OR SHARED INVESTMENT CASES, ASSUMING
RECIPROCATING PRICE COMPETITION (UP-SLOPING REACTION CURVES)

Panel A. Proprietary Investment
$(\theta_A = 12, \theta_B = 9)$

Panel B. Shared Investment
$(\theta_A = 12, \theta_B = 12)$

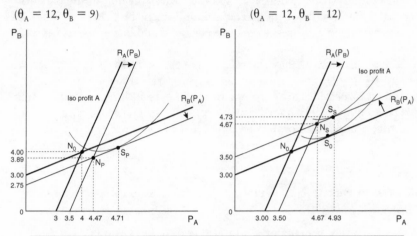

Notes: The demand for each firm i is of the form $Q_i(P_i,P_j,\theta_{i,t}) = \theta_{i,t} - bP_i + dP_j$, where $\theta_0 = 10$ ($u = 1.25$, $d = 0.80$), $b = 2$, $d = 1$, while the total variable production cost is given by $c(Q_i) = c_iQ_i$, with $c_i = 1$ ($i = A, B$).

If no strategic investment: base-case demand $\theta_A = \theta_B = \theta = 10$ (base-case Bertrand Nash equilibrium at N_0).

If proprietary investment/tough position: $\theta_A = 12$ $\theta_B = 9$, R_A and R_B shift to right (at N_p $P_A^* \uparrow, P_B^* \downarrow$) and $V_A \downarrow$.

If shared investment/accommodating position: $\theta_B = \theta_A = \theta' = 12$, R_A shifts right and R_B shifts to the left (at N_s $P_A^* \uparrow$ and $P_B^* \uparrow$) and $V_A \uparrow$.

	Nash Price Outcome			Stackelberg Price Leader			Monopoly	
Pioneer Firm A	N_0 base-case	N_p propriet.	N_s shared	S_0 base case	S_p propriet.	S_s shared	M_0 base	M_p propr.
Price (P_A^*) base demand	$\frac{1}{3}(\theta+2c)$	$\frac{1}{15}(4\theta_A+\theta_B+10c)$	$\frac{1}{3}(\theta+2c)$	$\frac{1}{14}(5\theta+9c)$	$\frac{1}{14}(\theta_A+\theta_B+9c)$	$\frac{1}{14}(5\theta'+9c)$	$\frac{1}{2}(\theta_A+c)$	$\frac{1}{2}(\theta'+c)$
($\theta_0 = 10$)	4	4.467	4.667	4.214	4.714	4.929	5.5	6.5
up ($u\theta_0 = 12.5$, $u\theta' = 15$)	4.833	5.417	5.667	5.107	5.732	6	6.75	8
Profit (π_A^*) base demand								
($\theta_0 = 10$)	18	24.036	26.889	18.08	26.929	27.009	40.5	60.5
up	29.389	39.014	43.556	29.520	43.624	43.750	66.125	98

Note: N_0, N_p, N_s are the Bertrand Nash, and S_0, S_p, S_s the Stackelberg equilibrium outcomes for the zero, proprietary, or shared investment cases; M_0 and M_p are the base case and proprietary monopoly outcomes. $R_j(P_i)$ is the reaction function of firm j given the price of firm i (P_i), $i = A, B$. P^*_i and V^*_i fluctuate with the state of demand θ_t.

there is price competition (characterized by upward-sloping reaction curves). In the base-case the (firm-specific) initial demand parameters are identical ($\theta_A = \theta_B = 10$). In the left panel a goodwill investment will place firm A at a competitive advantage by increasing its demand to $\theta_A = 12$ while reducing firm B's demand to $\theta_B = 9$, changing the base-case Nash equilibrium outcome from N_0 to N_p with lower profits. In the panel on the right the benefits of the strategic commitment by firm A are shared. As a consequence, this results in larger demand and higher prices for both competitors ($\theta_A = 12$ and $\theta_B = 12$).

The offensive strategies observed earlier for shared and proprietary investments under contrarian quantity competition would be reversed under reciprocating price competition. The resulting accommodating strategies can be determined using the two-stage game of figure 6.2 and the price competition project payoff values of table 6.2, as shown in figure 6.7.

Proprietary Investment: Flexible and Inoffensive Strategy (Negative Strategic Effect)

The proprietary benefits of a strategic goodwill investment would help develop a larger market share, placing competition at a disadvantage compared to the base-case alternative. To avoid a retaliating response from the reciprocating competitor, firm A will pursue the base case strategy. This example is illustrated in panel A (top) in figure 6.7. From a similar backward valuation process as applied earlier, the expected value of the investment opportunities for the two firms equals (55, 55) for the base case of no strategic investment. If future market demand is favorable ($\theta = u$), both firms will have a dominant strategy to invest with Nash price equilibrium values of (126, 126). If market demand is unfavorable, however, both firms may be better off to wait, resulting in expected values of (14, 14).[15]

---

[15]The same expected values are obtained if both firms defer, or if a mixed Nash equilibrium results. Note that each firm would be better off to invest, given that the other would defer. However, if both firms invest they will end up worse off (-16, -16). It may thus be preferable for both to defer and obtain (14, 14). Alternatively, if each firm chooses to appear unpredictable, a symmetric mixed Nash equilibrium would result with investment probabilities equal to 0.39 and expected equilibrium values (14.8, 14.8).

FIGURE 6.7 COMPETITIVE INVESTMENT STRATEGIES IN THE
GOODWILL/ADVERTISING EXAMPLE: PROPRIETARY VERSUS SHARED
INVESTMENT UNDER RECIPROCATING PRICE COMPETITION

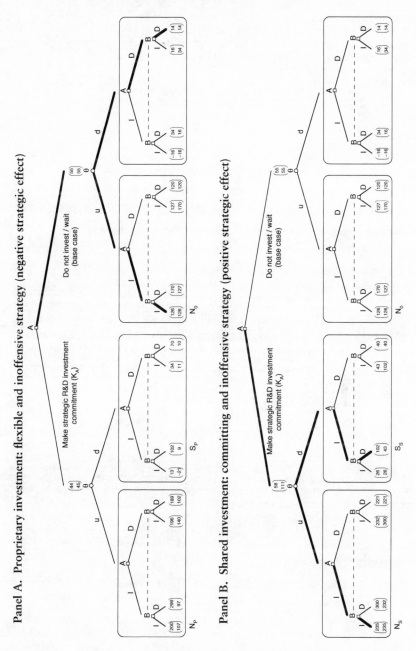

FIGURE 6.7 *continued*

Assumptions:
First-stage strategic investment by pioneer firm A: $K_A = 85$
Follow-up (second-stage) investment outlay by either firm A or B: $I_A = I_B = I = 100$
Operating costs for either firm A or B: $c_A = c_B = c = 1$
Own and competitor price sensitivity parameters: $b = 2, d = 1$
Binomial up or down demand parameters: $u = 1.25, d = 1/u = 0.80$
Risk-free interest rate: $r = 0.10$
Risk-adjusted discount rate: $k = 0.13$

Initial demand parameter	θ_A	θ_B
No investment (base case)	10	10
Proprietary investment	12	9
Shared investment	12	12

Shared Investment: Committing and Inoffensive Strategy (Positive Strategic Effect)

In this case pioneer firm A has the ability to use a strategic investment to create a shared advantage and generate larger demand for both. As illustrated in lower panel B in figure 6.7, the committing but inoffensive strategy results in (143, 111) expected values for the growth opportunities, with a $143 - 85 = 58$ expanded NPV for the shared strategic investment of firm A.[16] A high level of demand results in a symmetric Nash price equilibrium, whereas for a low level of demand, firm A may become a Stackelberg leader.

[16]In the case of strategic investment, if $\theta = u$ both firms have a dominating strategy to invest, resulting in symmetric Nash equilibrium values of (235, 235). If $\theta = d$, there are multiple equilibria. To focus on the strategic effect, we use the focal point equilibrium (I, D) (the same as in the corresponding proprietary investment case). In this case firm A has a dominating strategy to invest knowing that firm B is better off to defer (43) than to also invest (26), resulting in Stackelberg values of (102, 43). Backward valuation then gives

$$NPV_A^* = \frac{0.41(235) + 0.59(102)}{1.1} - 85 = 143 - 85 = 58$$

and

$$NPV_B^* = \frac{0.41(235) + 0.59(43)}{1.1} = 111.$$

Box 6.2 Observed Firm Behavior: Reciprocating (Price) Competition and Advertising Retaliation in the Cigarette Industry

Retaliatory behavior via advertising and price competition is observed in the U.S. cigarette industry. The cigarette industry is an oligopolistic market characterized by reciprocating competitive reactions. Advertising expenditures are often *tough,* as they are used to differentiate a firm's product in order to gain market share. This invites a retaliating *tough* campaign from rivals, forcing firms to invest heavily in advertisements. In some cases, the initial event is not initiated by one of the main rivals but by a third party. For instance, in the late sixties regulation banned cigarette advertisement from television. Initially the cigarette industry protested, thinking that this would hurt their profitability. But in the subsequent period the reduced burden of intense advertising increased their earnings, showing that a large proportion of their advertising expenditures was defensive (Dixit and Nalebuff 1993).

Pricing in the U.S. cigarette industry is characterized by reciprocating competition. The accompanying figure shows the stock price performance of several cigarette producers. In the cigarette industry, when the dominant firms such as RJR Nabisco and Philip Morris announce their intention to raise the prices of their cigarettes, it seems within days the other cigarette producers follow. The dominant firms were *soft* or accommodating to their competitors who followed. During the first half of the twentieth century this industry exhibited coordination in prices, which made firms in the industry highly profitable.

Smaller producers sometimes think they can gain more by taking the risk of changing the competitive landscape and break the implicit price coordination. In the first half of the 1980s, Liggett and Myers made a move that could be considered *tough* toward its larger competitors. The firm differentiated its cigarettes and introduced a discount cigarette that sold directly at a 30% discount in grocery stores. The sales tripled largely due to the increase in share as a result of the success in discount cigarettes. However, the decision to go after this discount niche-market had an impact on the premium market, inviting a *retaliating* reaction by the larger competitors. In a reciprocating tit-for-tat fashion the large competitors introduced their own line of discount cigarettes, and Ligett's market share declined from 90% in the beginning of the 1980s to 15% by the end of the 80s, forcing Liggett to further drop prices to 30% under the discount cigarettes.

In the beginning of the 1990s the cigarette market could be divided into three segments: a premium segment, a discount tier, and a deep discount tier. Much of the growth in the lower segments came at the expense of growth in the premium brands. This substitution effect

continued . . .

Box 6.2 continued

explains Philip Morris's decision to cut prices on their main brand, Marlboro, by 20% in 1993 to combat a decline in market share. Other manufacturers, including RJR, were forced to follow suit. RJR has put a firm figure on the cost of the price war when it announced that the operating income of its U.S. tobacco unit, before amortization of trademarks and goodwill, was $900 million lower in 1993 than the $2.11 billion in 1992.

Following this price war, coordination in cigarette prices was subsequently restored. However, in the next period the cigarette industry faced large legal claims that reduced stock prices.

Source: Based partly on Dixit and Nalebuff 1991; and Besanko, Dranove and Shanley 2000.

Chronology of events

1. Coordination period. Coordination in prices shows a superior performance for the larger cigarette producers over the S&P 500 index and the smaller producers.
2. The price war in the beginning of the 1990s due to reciprocating competition resulted in a general decline in the prices of cigarette producers, while the S&P 500 index shows a steady increase in value.
3. Coordination returns. Philip Morris's market value rises.
4. Spin-off of RJ Reynolds from RJR Nabisco.
5. Large claims resulted in a decline in stock prices for the cigarette industry while the S&P 500 remained stable.

TABLE 6.6
The Strategic Reaction Effect (when Demand Develops Favorably)
under Reciprocating Price Competition

Investment Type	Demand Parameter (θ_A, θ_B)	Prices		Profit
		$\overline{P^*_A}$	P^*_B	π^*_A
No investment (base case)	$\theta_A = 10, \theta_B = 10$	4.83	4.83	29
Proprietary investment	$\theta_A = 12, \theta_B = 9$	5.42	4.67	39
Shared investment	$\theta_A = 12, \theta_B = 12$	5.67	5.67	43

Investment Type	Direct Effect	Strategic Reaction	Commitment (direct + strat.)	NPV^*_A
No investment (base case)				126
Proprietary investment	85.5	-11.5	74	200
Shared investment	85.5	$+23.5$	109	235

Note: θ_A, θ_B are the second-stage demand (influenced by the first-stage strategic investment) for firm A, B.

Value Components

Table 6.6 illustrates the strategic interactions for the proprietary and shared investment cases under reciprocating Nash price competition when $\theta = u$. The direct effect in each case is 85.5 $[= (40 - 29) / 0.13]$. Compared to the offensive strategies of the R & D example, the inoffensive strategies under reciprocating competition result in a reversal of the sign of the strategic reaction effect (-11.5 for the proprietary and $+23.5$ for the shared investment) and in opposite investment strategies, compared to the contrarian quantity competition case.

The trade-off between the flexibility effect and the net commitment value of a strategic goodwill investment is shown in table 6.7 (panel A for the proprietary and panel B for the shared investment cases). To avoid intense price competition, firm A would not make a strategic investment if the benefits are proprietary since a hurt competitor will retaliate, but would do so if the benefits are shared and the competitor will respond positively to an accommodating pricing strategy.

6.4. Summary and Conclusions

Strategic competitive interactions clearly influence the value of a sequential investment plan under uncertainty. The standard NPV decision rule should be expanded by adding a strategic as well as a flexibility value

TABLE 6.7
Breakdown of Value Components for the Strategic Investment under Reciprocating Competition When the Investment Is Proprietary or Shared

Panel A. Proprietary Strategic Investment

	Base Case (no investment)	K_A	Strategic Direct	Strategic Reaction	Proprietary Strategic Investment	Δ(proprietary −base case)
NPV	38	−85	−50	−6	−3	−41
Strategic collusion	0				47	+47
Net commitment value						+6
Flexibility value	17				0	−17
Total expanded NPV	55				44	−11

ΔNPV^* = net commitment value + flexibility value
= [$-K_A$ + (direct value + strategic reaction value + strategic collusion value)] + flexibility value
= [−85 + (50 − 6 + 47)] −17 = 6 − 17 = −11 < 0 (don't invest).

Panel B. Shared Investment

	Base Case (no investment)	K_A	Strategic Direct	Strategic Reaction	Proprietary Strategic Investment	Δ(proprietary −base case)
NPV	38	−85	+50	+14	17	−21
Strategic collusion	0				41	+41
Net commitment value						+20
Flexibility value	17				0	−17
Total expanded NPV	55				58	13

ΔNPV^* = net commitment value + flexibility value
= [−85 + (50 + 14 + 41)] −17 = 20 − 17 = +3 > 0 (invest).

component to capture these effects. In general, the expanded NPV of a strategic investment is influenced by two main effects.

1. *The flexibility effect:* this arises from management's ability to wait to invest until demand develops sufficiently. A strategic investment commitment, although it can improve the firm's strategic position and enhance the value of its future growth opportunities, sacrifices flexibility value arising from management's ability to wait to invest until demand develops sufficiently. From an options perspective, the value of flexibility increases with the level of interest rates, time to maturity, and market demand uncertainty. However, because the market structure may change altogether (e.g., from a simultaneous-move Cournot Nash equilibrium to a monopoly or leader-follower Stackelberg equilibrium) as uncertainty increases, the flexibility value may actually be lower.

2. *The net commitment effect:* early strategic investment commitment may not only result in direct incremental future cash flows (the direct NPV), but it may indirectly also affect value by influencing the competitor's reaction (strategic reaction effect) and the resulting competitive equilibrium, in some cases even changing the market structure entirely by deterring entry by rivals (strategic preemption effect). The nature of industry competition (reciprocal or contrarian) may thus critically influence the optimal investment strategy. In some cases, an early investment commitment may be a strategic disadvantage if it reduces the firm's ability to respond toward aggressive competitors who can exploit shared benefits from the strategic investment, or if it provokes a retaliating response and intense rivalry when competitive actions are reciprocating.

Although an early strategic investment necessarily reduces option or flexibility value, other things constant, it may have a high or low (even negative) net commitment value, depending on the strategic effect. The sign of the strategic effect itself may be positive or negative, depending on whether the benefits are proprietary or shared, and may be opposite for reciprocating (e.g., price) competition than for contrarian (e.g., Cournot quantity) competition.

Using a combination of real-options valuation with basic game-theoretic principles from industrial organization, we can distinguish various competitive investment strategies, depending on whether competitive actions are reciprocating or contrarian and whether the resulting benefits are proprietary or shared.

1. *When competitive actions are contrarian and the benefits of strategic investment can be appropriated by the pioneering firm at*

the expense of its competitors, the firm should commit to an offensive strategy. Commitment makes the firm tougher in the second stage by creating a proprietary advantage when investing in follow-on projects. If competitive actions (e.g., quantities) are contrarian (strategic substitutes), competition will retreat in the later stage and the pioneering firm can become a leader as demand grows.

2. *When the benefits of strategic investment commitment are shared and competition is contrarian, rivals would respond aggressively, and the firm should not invest immediately but rather follow a flexible and offensive strategy.* By delaying strategic investment, it prevents its competition from exploiting the shared benefits to grow at its own expense.

3. *When the benefits of strategic investment can be appropriated by the firm at the expense of competitors and rivals may reciprocate with an aggressive response, the firm should follow a flexible and inoffensive strategy.* The firm should avoid committing to the strategic investment to preserve its resources and flexibility and avoid intensified price competition in the later stage of the market.

4. *When the strategic investment benefits both the firm and its competitors, and rivals would reciprocate with an accommodating position (e.g., maintaining high industry prices), the pioneer should follow a committing and inoffensive strategy.* It may invest in goodwill to appear inoffensive in the later stage, avoiding intense price competition that would hurt the entire industry. Through maintaining higher prices, both firms may enjoy more profitable follow-on investments.

The optimal competitive strategy thus depends not only on the stance of the pioneer firm (tough or accommodating) and the type of investment (proprietary or shared), but also on the nature of competitive reaction (reciprocating or contrarian). The marriage of real-options valuation with game-theoretic industrial organization principles enables simultaneously the determination of different market structure equilibrium games in the various states of demand (nodes) within the binomial option valuation tree, as well as proper accounting of the interdependencies among the early strategic commitment and sequential investment (along with competitive quantity or price setting) decisions in a dynamic competitive environment.

Appendix 6.1

Reaction Functions, Equilibrium Actions, and Values in Different Market Structures under Quantity or Price Competition

Quantity Competition

This appendix develops an analytical derivation of the reaction curves and the equilibrium outcomes for the Cournot, Stackelberg, and monopoly models. Specifically it derives the equilibrium quantities (Q^*) and net project values or expanded NPV (NPV^*) for the various market structures under quantity competition. Exogeneous uncertainty in future market demand is assumed to be characterized by fluctuations in the demand parameter, θ_t. In the second-stage game, we assume for simplicity a linear inverse demand function of the form

$$P(Q, \theta_t) = \theta_t - (Q_A + Q_B), \qquad (6.A.1)$$

where θ_t is the demand shift parameter, assumed to follow a lognormal diffusion process (or a multiplicative binomial process in discrete time). Q_A and Q_B are the quantities produced by firms A and B, respectively, and $P(Q)$ is the common market price as a function of total quantity ($Q = Q_A + Q_B$). The initial investment represents the fixed costs, while the total variable costs depend on the size of production. The total variable production cost for firm i ($i = A$ or B) is given by

$$C(Q_i) = c_i Q_i + \tfrac{1}{2} q_i Q_i^2, \qquad (6.A.2)$$

where c_i and q_i are the linear and quadratic cost coefficients (or the fixed and variable coefficients of the marginal cost function, $c_i + q_i Q_i$) for firm i. The second-stage annual operating profits for each firm i are given by

$$\pi_i(Q_i, Q_j, \theta_t) = P Q_i - C(Q_i) = [(\theta_t - c_i) - Q_j]Q_i - (1 + \tfrac{1}{2} q_i) Q_i^2. \qquad (6.A.3)$$

The gross project value (profit value), V_i, and the net present value, NPV_i, from the second-stage investment for firm i, assuming perpetual annual operating cash flows (profits) and a constant risk-adjusted discount rate k in the last stage, are obtained from[17]

$$V_i = \frac{\pi_i}{k},\qquad\qquad\qquad\qquad\qquad\text{(6.A.4)}$$

and

$$NPV_i = V_i - I = \frac{\pi_i}{k} - I.\qquad\qquad\qquad\text{(6.A.4')}$$

Under quantity competition, the reaction function of each firm is downward sloping. Maximizing firm i's (i = A, B) own profit value over its quantity given that its competitor produces Q_j (setting $\partial V_i/\partial Q_i = 0$), each firm's reaction function is given by.[18]

$$R_i(Q_i) = \frac{\theta_t - c_i - Q_j}{2 + q_i}.\qquad\qquad\qquad\text{(6.A.5)}$$

If both firms make a *simultaneous* production capacity investment in the second stage (I, I), a Cournot-Nash equilibrium outcome results. The equilibrium quantities, Q^*_A and Q^*_B, are obtained by equating (being at the intersection of) the reaction functions of the two firms:

$$Q^*_i = \frac{(\theta_t - c_i)(2 + q_i) - (\theta_t - c_i)}{(2 + q_i)(2 + q_j) - 1}.\qquad\qquad\text{(6.A.6)}$$

In the case that firm i's early strategic investment reduces its cost (c_i) below its competitor's (c_j), then $Q^*_i > Q^*_j$. If we simplify by setting $q_i = q_j = q = 0$, this asymmetric Cournot-Nash equilibrium quantity for firm i reduces to $Q^*_i = \frac{1}{3}(\theta_t - 2c_i + c_j)$. (For example, if firm A's early strategic investment makes $c_A = 0$, $Q^*_A = \frac{1}{3}(Q_t + c_B) > \frac{1}{3}(Q_t - 2c_B) = Q^*_B$). Substituting back into profit value equations 6.A.3 and 6.A.4, again assuming $q_i = q_j = 0$, gives the Cournot-Nash equilibrium profit value for firm i (i = A, B) as follows:

---

[17]For simplicity, we assume zero taxes and depreciation so that the operating cash flows are equivalent to operating profits.

[18]As illustrated in the example of figure 6.5 (with $q_i = 0$), if pioneering firm A's early strategic investment (K_A) would create a first-mover cost advantage (reducing c_A below c_B, say to 0) that would result in proprietary benefits and make the firm tougher, it would increase its intercept and shift its reaction curve out to the right, increasing its equilibrium quantity (Q^*_A) while reducing that of its competitor (Q^*_B) — moving from Cournot equilibrium outcome C_0 to C_p. By contrast, if firm A would take an accommodating position resulting in shared benefits with its competitor (e.g., also reducing the competitor's cost c_B, say to 0), firm B's reaction curve would also shift to the right, increasing its equilibrium output (Q^*_B) to that of outcome C_s.

$$V_i^* = \frac{(\theta_t - 2c_i + c_j)^2}{9k}.$$

(6.A.7)

In case the pioneering firm does not make an early strategic investment and both firms invest simultaneously in the second stage, a symmetric Cournot-Nash equilibrium may result if the firms are otherwise identical ($Q_A^* = Q_B^* = Q^*$, with $c_A = c_B = c$ and $q_A = q_B = q$), yielding (if $\theta_t > c$)

$$Q_i^* = \frac{(\theta_t - c)}{(3 + q)}$$

(6.A.8)

and

$$V_i^* = (1 + \tfrac{1}{2}q)\frac{(\theta_t - c)^2}{(3 + q)^2 k}.$$

(6.A.9)

(If $q = 0$, the symmetric Cournot equilibrium quantity simplifies to $Q_i^* = \tfrac{1}{3}(\theta_t - c)$ and $V_i^* = (\theta_t - c)^2 / 9k$.) Note that each firm i will eventually be profitable, net of its second-stage outlay I, if demand is such that its NPV, determined from equations 6.A.4′ and 6.A.7 above, is positive (in this case if $\theta_t \geq 3\sqrt{kI} + 3c_i - c_j$). If demand is too low for either firm to operate profitably, they will both wait, whereas if $\theta_t < 3\sqrt{kI} + 2c_i - c_j$, firm j will be unprofitable ($NPV_j < 0$) and firm i can earn monopoly profits.[19] It can be seen from equation 6.A.5, with $Q_j = 0$, that the value-maximizing quantity for a monopolist firm i (points M in figure 6.2, where $q_i = 0$) is given by

$$Q_i = \frac{\theta_t - c_i}{2 + q_i} \qquad \text{(with } Q_j = 0\text{)}.$$

(6.A.10)

The monopolist firm can then set a monopolist price $[\theta_t(1 + q_i) + c_i] / (2 + q_i)$, and enjoy monopoly profit value of

$$V_i = \frac{(\theta_t - c_i)^2}{(4 + 2q_i)k} \qquad \text{(with } V_j = 0\text{)}.$$

(6.A.11)

In case firm i invests first and firm j defers investment until next period (I, D), the follower will set its quantity having first observed the leader's output according to its reaction function, $R_j(Q_i)$, as in equation 6.A.5. The Stackelberg leader i will then maximize $V_i(Q_i, R_j(Q_i))$ over Q_i, taking the follower's reaction function $R_j(Q_i)$ as given, resulting in equilibrium quantity and profit value (assuming for simplicity that $q_i = q_j = 0$) for the Stackelberg leader given by

[19] It is assumed that the last stage is infinite (steady state) and the possibility of re-entry is precluded.

$$Q_i = \frac{(\theta_t - c_i)(2 + q_i) - (\theta_t - c_j)}{(2 + q_i)(2 + q_j) - 2} \tag{6.A.12}$$

and

$$V_i = \frac{(\theta_t - 2c_i + c_j)^2}{8k}. \tag{6.A.13}$$

Substituting the leader's optimal quantity from equation 6.A.12 into the follower's reaction function in equation 6.A.5 gives the Stackelberg follower's quantity and profit value (assuming $q_i = q_j = 0$):

$$Q_j = \frac{(\theta_t - c_i)(2 + q_i) - (\theta_t - c_i)}{(2 + q_i)(2 + q_j)} \tag{6.A.14}$$

and

$$V_j = \frac{(\theta_t - 2c_j + c_i)^2}{16k}. \tag{6.A.15}$$

As expected, the follower's equilibrium quantity and profit value are lower than the leader's ($Q_j < Q_i$, $V_j < V_i$). Further, if demand is low ($\theta_t < 4\sqrt{kI} + 2c_j - c_i$) the Stackelberg follower will be unable to cover its investment outlay I ($NPV_j < 0$) and will not enter; the Stackelberg leader's profit value can therefore improve (from that of equation 6.A.13) to the monopoly profit value shown in equation 6.A.11 (with $q_i = 0$). The equilibrium quantities and profit values (assuming $q_i = q_j = 0$) for the various market structures above under contrarian quantity competition are summarized in table 6.1.

Price Competition

In this part we present the analytical derivation of the reaction functions and equilibrium outcomes for the various market structures under price competition. We again assume for simplicity that the demand for the good is linear in prices:

$$Q_i(P_i, P_j, \theta_{i,t}) = \theta_{i,t} - bP_i + dP_j. \tag{6.A.16}$$

The quantity sold by firm i is a function of its own price (P_i) as well as that of its competitor (P_j). The coefficients b and d ($b > 0$, $d > 0$ assuming demand substitutes) capture the sensitivities of the quantity sold to the firm's own and its competitor's price settings, respectively. The total variable cost is again of the form assumed in equation 6.A.3. The profits of each firm i ($i = A$ or B) are then given by

$$\pi_i(P_i, P_j, \theta_{i,t}) = (P_i - c_i)(\theta_{i,t} - bP_i + dP_j). \tag{6.A.17}$$

The reaction function of each firm i is again obtained by maximizing its profit value $V_i(P_i, P_j) \equiv \pi_i / k$ over its own price P_i. Setting $\partial V_i / \partial P_i = 0$, gives[20]

$$R_i(P_j) = \frac{(\theta_{i,t} + dP_j)(1 + bq_i) + bc_i}{b(2 + bq_i)}. \tag{6.A.18}$$

A company engaged in price competition has a best (profit-maximizing) response to competitor price changes according to its reaction function. Substituting the expression for $R_j(P_i)$ in place of P_j in equation 6.A.18 gives the general asymmetric Nash equilibrium price expression:

$$P_i^* = \frac{2b(\theta_{i,t} + bc_i) + d(\theta_{j,t} + bc_j)}{4b^2 - d^2}. \tag{6.A.19}$$

If firm i does not make an early strategic investment and both firms invest simultaneously in the second stage, a symmetric Bertrand equilibrium price will result if the firms are otherwise identical ($P_i^* = P_j^* = P^*$, with $\theta_{i,t} = \theta_{j,t} = \theta_t$, $c_i = c_j = c$ and $q_i = q_j = q = 0$):

$$P^* = \frac{\theta_t + bc}{2b - d}. \tag{6.A.20}$$

The Nash price equilibrium quantity and profit value for firm i can be generally obtained by substituting P_i^* and P_j^* from equation 6.A.19 back into the quantity and profit expressions in equations 6.A.16 and 6.A.17, respectively. For example, in the symmetric Nash equilibrium case with $q = 0$, the equilibrium quantity (Q^*) and profit value (with $\pi^* = (P^* - c)Q^*$), respectively, become

$$Q^* = \frac{b[\theta_t - c(b - d)]}{2b - d} \tag{6.A.21}$$

and

$$V^* = \frac{b[\theta_t - c(b - d)]^2}{(2b - d)^2 k}. \tag{6.A.21'}$$

Both firms will have a positive Nash equilibrium quantity and earn positive profits if $\theta_t > c(b - d)$. However, to cover their investment outlay (I) and earn a positive NPV, V^* must be larger than I. This would require a

---

[20]The slope of this reaction function, given by $R_i'(P_j) = d(1 + bq_i) / b(2 + bq_i)$, is positive and is affected by the competitor's response coefficient d. These upward-sloping reaction functions, illustrated in figure 6.6, lead to reciprocating price competition, where a low price setting by one firm would be matched by its competitor.

higher demand, namely $\theta_t > c(b - d) + (2b - d)(kI/b)^{1/2}$. Otherwise, both firms would prefer to wait instead.

In case firm i invests first and firm j defers until next period (I, D), the leader will choose the price that maximizes its own profit value, using the reaction function of the follower. Maximizing $V_i(P_i, R_j(P_i))$ over P_i, given $R_j(P_i)$, gives a Stackelberg leader price (for $q_i = q_j = 0$):

$$P_i = \frac{2b(\theta_{i,t} + bc_i) + d(\theta_{j,t} + bc_j - dc_i)}{4b^2 - 2d^2}. \tag{6.A.22}$$

Note that the above Stackelberg leader price may exceed the Nash equilibrium price of equation 6.A.19. Substituting this into the follower's reaction function from equation 6.A.18 would give the Stackelberg follower's price. In case the leader invests first (I, D) and demand is low such that it becomes uneconomical for the follower to operate profitably, the leader can improve by earning monopoly profits.

Chapter 7

Value Dynamics in Competitive R & D Strategies

Research is what I'm doing when I don't know what I'm doing.
— Wernher von Braun (1912–1977)

7.1. Introduction

This chapter aims to gain a deeper understanding of the dynamics in the value of competitive R & D strategies. Stocks in dynamic, innovative, and growth industries exhibit a behavior distinguishably different from that in other, more stable industries. Higher volatility, discontinuities, and value asymmetries characterize the market value of innovative firms. These value dynamics can be attributed in part to the corporate real-options characteristics and the strategic and competitive interactions these firms experience. The implicit leverage of multistage growth options amplifies the impact of uncertainty, while the strategic positioning of a firm and its ability to capitalize on its growth opportunities is vulnerable to the introduction of new technologies and competitive entry that can modify the industry market structure.

We discuss a dynamic options and games valuation analysis to better understand the value dynamics of R & D strategies in an uncertain, competitive environment. This topic is important because conventional DCF-based approaches (e.g., NPV) are inadequate to explain the dynamics in the value of R & D investment strategies (see box insert 7.1 on p. 324).

An R & D investment opportunity depends on the resolution of several sources of uncertainty. In early stages, there may be technical uncertainty concerning the outcome of each firm's R & D effort. Later on, there is market demand uncertainty once the product is launched in the market. Both of these uncertainties may influence the investment decision of each competing firm. The optimal decision of each firm depends on the degree of (complete or incomplete) information about the resolution of the other firm's technical R & D uncertainty (R & D success or failure). In case of asymmetric information, each firm also faces a decision to signal information or not. As an alternative (to R & D) for reducing future production costs, learning experience cost effects may also be an important factor influencing the timing of R & D investment and subsequent capacity commitment in a competitive context.[1] Moreover, each firm can decide to invest in R & D independently (i.e., compete in R & D), or alternatively, both firms may choose to invest in R & D jointly (collaborate via a joint research venture). We derive economic implications to help explain the economics of strategic investment behavior of innovative firms under uncertainty and provide some insight about their value dynamics. We develop propositions for the value characteristics of competitive R & D strategies depending on uncertainty in market demand and the stochastic outcome of the R & D effort, on the proprietary or shared nature of R & D benefits, on imperfect or asymmetric information with signaling, learning or experience cost effects, and on R & D competition versus cooperation via a joint research venture.

The remainder of the chapter is organized as follows. Section 7.2 reviews the literature. Section 7.3 reviews the basic two-stage R & D investment game within an integrated real-options and industrial organization framework. Section 7.4 deals with valuation of R & D strategies for proprietary versus shared investments and illustrates value discontinuities with critical demand zones and other sensitivity results. A comparative statics investigation is carried out in section 7.5 with respect to technical R & D uncertainty, stochastic reaction functions, and asymmetric information. Section 7.6 examines the impact of learning cost effects, while section 7.7 examines the trade-off between competition versus cooperation in R & D. The last section concludes and discusses various implications.

7.2. Literature on R & D Options

R & D investment has been analyzed extensively in the industrial organization literature. Recently a number of researchers in financial economics have studied the R & D process as a contingent claim on the cash flow value (e.g., Baldwin 1987a; Berk, Green, and Naik 1998; Childs and Triantis 1999; Grenadier and Weiss 1997; Myers and Howe 1997; Schwartz 2001; and Schwartz and Moon 2000). These approaches value R & D using a continuous-time option model where uncertainty is resolved during investment. Often there are three types of uncertainty modeled: technical uncertainty associated with the success of the R & D process itself; an exogenous chance of obsolescence during or after the development process; and market uncertainty about the value of the project on completion of the R & D.

---

[1]We later expand the results of Majd and Pindyck (1993) by comparing the effect of learning with an extra strategic benefit to a cost-saving R & D investment in an interactive competitive setting.

Based on nonlinearity of the options payoff, various real-options models have developed implications of general interest for the value dynamics of R & D. Multistage ventures such as R & D are in particular skewed in value and returns, because the implicit option leverage makes growth option value sensitive in a varying degree to changes in its underlying value (see Myers and Howe 1997; Berk, Green, and Naik 1998).[2] Jumps in value may result, for example, from catastrophic events (Schwartz 2001). Although there is no risk premium earned per se due to nonsystematic technical uncertainty, idiosyncratic uncertainty can dramatically alter the risk and value of the venture as a whole.

Contrary to standard real-options analysis, the literature that focuses on the intersection of real options with game theory finds that option value may be eroded because competitive forces provide an incentive to invest early. Garlappi (2002) models R & D in an interactive competitive setting and analyzes the impact of competition on the risk premiums of ownership claims to R & D ventures engaged in a multi-stage patent race. Miltersen and Schwartz (2003) study an optimal stopping time problem of R & D investment in which firms learn in competitive markets, in the sense that investments take time and information is revealed while investing, so that it becomes optimal to abandon an investment before completion.

Our focus here is on the relative strategic position and value asymmetries in the product market, where the strategic context of R & D creates heterogeneity between firms that makes it natural for one firm to exercise its expansion option before another. We derive economic implications to help explain how the value characterisitics of competitive R & D strategies depend on the degree of technical and market uncertainty, and the degree of R & D cooperation via a joint research venture.

A number of the results are interesting. First, contrary to standard option analysis, the value of an R & D investment opportunity may not increase monotonically with demand uncertainty (or with maturity and other option parameters). Strategic preemption may cause value discontinuities (e.g., higher variability may shift demand below the critical demand

---

[2]Novy-Marx (2003) argues that firms in general preserve their option value because competition is limited due to heterogeneity. Firms delay capacity investment, and the option component embedded in the firm value introduces skewness in returns that may vary over the business cycle. In his model, firms can add capacity quickly in response to rising demand, but cannot adjust capacity as quickly to falling demand due to the irreversible nature of investment. As a result, increasing supply attenuates positive demand shocks, which are only partially translated into prices, while negative demand shocks are translated into prices more fully.

investment threshold into a different zone where it may be unprofitable for the competitor to operate), further enhancing nonlinearity and asymmetry.[3] The sign and magnitude of this strategic effect on R & D value may depend on the proprietary or shared nature of the investment, on technical R & D uncertainty, on the degree of incomplete information, on the existence of learning effects, and on the willingness to compete or form joint research alliances. Second, we confirm that the effect on R & D value for proprietary investments can be the opposite compared to shared investments. Third, the presence of technical R & D uncertainty in the outcome of each firm's R & D effort can reduce the strategic (preemption) value of R & D (since R & D may fail) and mitigate the value discontinuity due to preemption. Fourth, under incomplete information about the outcome of the competitor's R & D effort, signaling strategies (about when to truthfully inform the competitor or not) can be devised in a way that benefit the innovator as well as the competitor. Fifth, if a firm can alternatively reduce future production costs via learning experience effects, there may be an incentive to invest early; however, there is also an extra strategic preemption benefit of early R & D investment since preemption can eliminate the competitor's learning advantage. Finally, in the R & D stage, besides reducing (sharing) research costs, collaboration in R & D enables firms to more fully appropriate the flexibility value from waiting and avoid the competitive pressure to invest prematurely (the prisoners' dilemma), even if it leads to potential sacrifice of strategic (e.g., preemption) value. The implications of this framework can be measured against observed firm behavior using data on the competitors' relative market performance and their corresponding risk profiles.

7.3. The Basic Two-Stage R & D Game

This section describes the two-stage competitive R & D investment game under demand uncertainty, assuming a duopoly market structure. Each of two competitors faces a decision as to whether and when to make an R & D investment as well as follow-on commercialization investment decisions. The firms compete in the commercialization stage, and may also

---

[3]Higher uncertainty generally increases the deferral or flexibility value that is lost when making an early R & D investment commitment, but it may either increase or decrease strategic value (from influencing a competitor's equilibrium output), possibly by a higher amount; a jump in value may even result as uncertainty increases, shifting from one demand zone (e.g., Cournot-Nash equilibrium) to another (e.g., Stackelberg or monopoly), depending on initial demand.

compete (or collaborate) in the research stage. The type of competition in each of the two stages affects the equilibrium production, optimal investment strategy, and upfront R & D investment value.[4]

Consider again an R & D investment by firm A (or B) involving the development of a new, cost-efficient technological process that can influence the firm's relative competitive position (vis-à-vis firm B) via lowering its operating costs $(c_A < c_B)$ in a later stage of the market. The value of firm A's strategic R & D investment (requiring an outlay K_A) is determined relative to the base case of no R & D (i.e., continue using the existing technology, with $c_A = c_B$). In addition to market demand uncertainty, the innovation strategy here may also involve technical uncertainty in that with probability η_i or $(1 - \eta_i)$ the R & D effort by firm i $(i = A, B)$ may succeed or fail. This technical R & D uncertainty is unrelated to market movements and is therefore of a nonsystematic nature (i.e., it is not priced).

The alternative actions by each firm i $(i = A, B)$ to make the strategic R & D investment (K) or to defer (D) are shown by the tree branches in the first stage (panel A) of figure 7.1. Either firm A or firm B can decide to make a strategic R & D investment (shown by squares, □). If both firms decide to invest simultaneously (K_A, K_B), technical uncertainty is resolved with probability of R & D success η_A or η_B, possibly resulting in asymmetric future production costs $(c_A \neq c_B)$. Under low demand realization (low commercialization potential) both firms may choose to defer (D, D), maintaining symmetrical costs, whereas only one firm alone may invest in R & D (K, D or D, K) at intermediate levels of demand.[5]

The commercialization-phase (stage 2) market structure is also assumed to result in a duopoly under quantity competition, where either of the two competing firms (A or B) may invest (I) in subsequent production capacity (using either the existing or the new technology from R & D) or defer investment (D) during either of two subperiods (1 and 2). The dynamics of market demand in the second stage are represented by nature's (θ) random up (u) or down (d) moves, according to the linear demand function

$$P(Q, \theta_t) = \theta_t - (Q_A + Q_B), \tag{7.1}$$

[4]In subsequent sections we investigate how the outcome of these games and therefore R & D value is influenced by the proprietary or shared nature of the R & D investment, by technical R & D uncertainty and asymmetric information/signaling, learning cost effects, and the possibility of collaboration in the R & D stage.
[5]The first-stage R & D game may thus result in a second-stage commercialization phase (panel B of figure 7.1) with asymmetrical production costs (e.g., at K, D or D, K with R & D success), with lower but symmetric costs (e.g., at K, K when both succeed in R & D), or with the same base-case costs of the existing technology (e.g., at D, D, or in case of technical R & D failure at K, K, K, D or D, K).

where θ_t is the demand shift parameter, P is the market price, and Q_i is the production quantity of firm i (i = A, B).[6] The resolution of *market demand uncertainty* θ in the second stage is shown by circles (O) in figure 7.1 (panel B). The second-stage (commercialization) game is similar to the first-stage duopoly (R & D) game described earlier, except for the two subperiods that allow for potential investment timing differences among the firms. When both firms decide to invest (produce) *simultaneously* in the second stage (I, I), without observing each other's actions, the game ends in a Cournot-Nash equilibrium (C); when both firms choose to defer (D, D) under low realizations of demand, nature (θ) moves again and the game is repeated; finally, when one firm invests first in a *sequential* game, acting as a Stackelberg leader — or in some cases a monopolist (M) — market demand is revealed again and the competitor may then decide to invest later — as a Stackelberg follower — or to abandon (A).

The strategic impact of R & D investment is captured via changing asymmetrically the second-stage production cost structure (i.e., the relative operating costs, c_A vs. c_B) and through its impact on equilibrium payoff values and resulting competitive reactions in the two-stage game of figure 7.1. In the next sections we examine (*a*) proprietary versus shared cost advantages from the R & D investment; (*b*) complete versus imperfect information concerning the success of each competitor's R & D effort; (*c*) learning cost effects where either firm can achieve future cost reduction by investing in production capacity early (besides reducing future costs through innovation by making a first-stage R & D investment); and (*d*) competing in R & D versus cooperating via a joint R & D venture. By way of an overview, table 7.1 summarizes the breakdown of total value into various components for each of the cases we examine.

7.4. Critical Demand Zones/Sensitivity

We next analyze the effect of dispersion of R & D benefits on the critical demand zones triggering invest or defer decisions under different market structures, and examine its influence on the flexibility and strategic components of R & D value. To simplify the discussion, consider again the simplest form of the game (presented in chapter 6) where only one of the two firms (pioneer firm A) can make a first-stage strategic R & D investment. This results in a deterministic operating cost advantage in the second stage (commercialization). The general first-stage R & D game of figure 7.1 is then reduced to the special case of a single R & D investment

---

[6]The results are robust to different specifications of the functional form of the demand and cost functions (e.g., an iso-elastic demand curve of the form $P = \theta Q^{-1/\eta}$).

FIGURE 7.1 THE BASIC TWO-STAGE INVESTMENT GAME INVOLVING R & D
AND COMMERCIALIZATION PHASE UNDER DIFFERENT MARKET
STRUCTURES

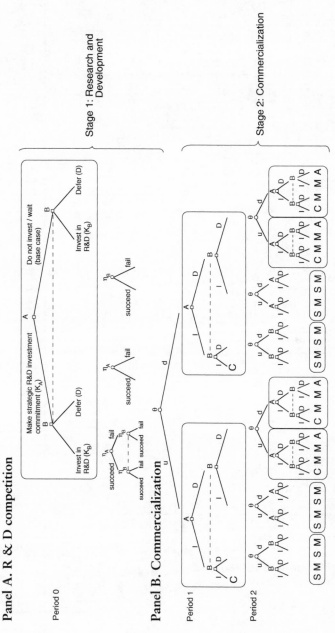

Notes: A or B (□) represents a decision to invest (I) or defer (D) by firm A or B.
θ (○) represents the state of market demand or nature's up (u) and down (d) moves.
The combination of competitive decisions (A or B) and market demand moves (θ) may result in one of the following market structure game outcomes:
C: Cournot Nash quantity competition equilibrium outcome
S: Stackelberg leader (S^L) follower (S^F) outcome
M: Monopolist outcome
A: Abandon (0 value)

TABLE 7.1
Summary (Overview) of the Breakdown of Value Components for the Strategic R & D Investment of Firm A in Different Cases

	Basic Game (sections 7.2 and 7.3)			Uncertain R & D ($\eta = 50\%$) (section 7.4)			Learning ($\gamma = 10\%$) (section 7.5)		Cooperation (vs. competition) (section 7.6)	
	(1) Base Case (no R & D)	(2) Proprietary R & D (K = 100)	(3) Shared R & D	(4) Complete Information (proprietary)	(5) Imperfect Information	(6) Signaling	(7) Base Case	(8) Proprietary Uncertain R & D	(9) R & D Competition (K = 100)	(10) R & D Cooperation (K = 50)
1 Direct		186	186	93	93	93	111	37	93	83
2 Strategic reaction		82	−72	41	31	44	−45	15	−16	−32
3 Strategic preemption		45	0	22	34	28	0	44	11	0
4 Net commitment value (1+2+3−K)		213	14	56	58	65	66	−4	−12	6
5 Flexibility value	23	0	0	12	9	6	0	0	17	25
6 Base case NPV	37	37	37	37	37	37	37	103	37	37
Total Expanded NPV (4+5+6)	60	250	51	105	104	108	103	99	42	68

decision by firm A (only), without any technical R & D uncertainty or learning effects.

As in Chapter 6, we assume here that pioneer firm A can enhance its relative competitive position by making an early R & D investment of K_A = 100 in a more cost-efficient technological process. In the second stage, either firm A or firm B can invest $I = 100$ in follow-up production capacity (commercialization projects), depending on subsequent random demand moves (where initial demand is $\theta_0 = 17.5$ and can move up or down with binomial parameters $u = 1.25$ and $d = 1/u = 0.80$). The risk-free interest rate (r) is 10% (while the risk-adjusted discount rate in the last stage is $k = 13\%$). If firm A chooses not to make the R & D investment (base case), the two firms have symmetric second-stage operating costs, based on the old technology, of $c_A = c_B = 5$.

When only one of the firms (firm A) decides to make a strategic R & D investment, two different strategies can result depending on whether the resulting cost benefits of the second-stage commercialization project are proprietary (asymmetric costs) or shared (symmetric). Consider first the case where making a strategic R & D investment results in a *proprietary* operating cost advantage for firm A during commercialization. Specifically, suppose the second-stage operating cost for firm A is reduced from 5 to 0 $(c_A = 0)$ if it invests in R & D (with sure success) while for firm B it remains at 5 $(c_B = 5)$ — as compared to the base case $(c_A = c_B = 5)$ when neither firm invests in R & D. This up-front R & D investment commitment makes the pioneer firm stronger in the second stage, pre-empting market share under quantity competition.

In this setup, the second-stage investment payoff is a nonlinear function of exogenous demand (θ) as a result of changes in the subgame outcomes. Figure 7.2 shows how the value in the commercialization stage for firm A $(NPV^*_A$ as of $t = 1)$ varies with market demand θ and the resulting subgame equilibriums. Panel A shows the critical demand zones for the base case of no R & D, while panels B and C illustrate the shared and proprietary cases, respectively. In each case, each firm's decision to invest or defer depends on two critical or threshold market demand parameters, θ^*_{INVEST} and θ^*_{DEFER}, separating the spectrum of demand states into three demand zones. In the base case of no R & D (panel A), for example, if market demand θ exceeds θ^*_{INVEST} $(= 16)$, at the intersection of the curves whereby firm A invests or defers given that firm B invests, both firms have a dominant strategy to invest, resulting in a Cournot-Nash equilibrium market structure. If θ declines below θ^*_{DEFER} $(= 12)$, at the intersection of the invest/defer and defer/defer curves, both firms have a strictly dominant strategy to defer. In between there is an unpredictable (mixed equilibrium) zone with no pure dominant strategy when

FIGURE 7.2 FIRM A'S EXPANDED NPV (NPV*$_A$) IN THE COMMERCIALIZATION
STAGE (AT $t = 1$) VERSUS MARKET DEMAND (θ) ILLUSTRATING CRITICAL
DEMAND ZONES FOR THE VARIOUS COMPETITIVE STRATEGIES

Panel A. Base Case (No R & D Investment)

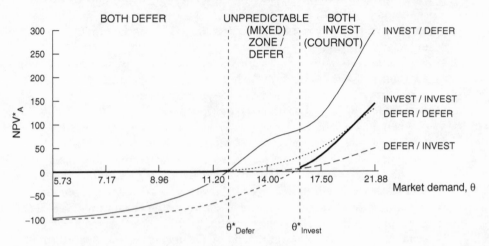

Panel B. Shared Benefits of R & D Investment

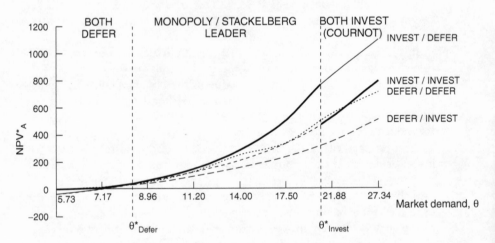

FIGURE 7.2 *continued*

Panel C. Proprietary Benefits of R & D Investment

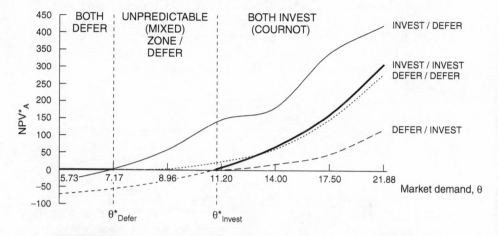

Parameter values: investment: $K_A = 100$, $I_A = I_B = 100$; interest rates: $r = 0.10$, $k = 0.13$; demand uncertainty: $u = 1.25$, $d = 0.8$; no technical R & D uncertainty: $\eta_A = 100\%$; no learning: $\gamma = 0\%$.

A. Base-case costs: $c_A = 5$, $c_B = 5$;

B. Proprietary R & D costs: $c_A = 0$, $c_B = 5$;

C. Shared R & D costs: $c_A = 0$, $c_B = 0$.

firms are symmetric.[7] In the shared R & D case (panel B) there are three similar demand zones, except that the critical θ values are lower. Both firms would again invest (Cournot) if θ exceeds 10.8, whereas both will defer if θ declines below 7.1. The lower threshold value for θ^*_{INVEST} compared to the base case (10.8 vs. 16) reflects the incentive of both firms to invest earlier due to the lower costs resulting from the shared R & D investment; similarly, with lower costs, the region of demand over which both firms would wait is reduced ($7.1 < 12$).

In panel C, where the benefits of R & D are proprietary for the pioneer firm resulting in an asymmetric cost advantage, the mixed (unpredictable) zone is replaced by a larger zone where the pioneer dominates

---

[7]In this "unpredictable" (or mixed equilibrium) zone, investing by one firm would result in a higher value (compared to the base case where both firms defer) if the competing firm defers or the first-moving firm becomes a Stackelberg leader (I, D > D, D), but would result in a lower value if the competitor simultaneously decides also to invest, leading to Cournot-Nash equilibrium (I, I < D, D). The firms may equivalently choose to defer.

as a Stackelberg leader or monopolist. Here R & D improves the firm's strategic position via lower relative future production costs, expanding market share and preempting competitive entry. For θ below θ^*_{INVEST} (= 20.8) and above θ^*_{DEFER} (= 8.5), the NPV of the competitor turns negative, giving firm A the ability to preempt competitive entry and become a Stackelberg leader or monopolist. Since firm A's proprietary R & D limits firm B's output and incentive to invest, the critical value θ^*_{INVEST} required for both firms to invest in the proprietary case is higher than in the base case and the shared investment cases (20.8 > 16 > 10.8). Given firm A's cost advantage, NPV^*_A in the proprietary case is also higher than in the other cases (for a given θ).

We next consider the effect of the degree of shared cost benefits on the strategic and flexibility values of the first-stage R & D investment. Figure 7.3 presents the sensitivity of firm A's value (NPV^*_A at $t = 0$) to the degree of shared cost benefits to competitor B (at an initial demand of $\theta_0 = 17.5$), with c_B ranging from 0 to 5. Point A corresponds to the base case of no R & D. Point B at 100% ($c_B = 0$) corresponds to the special case of a fully shared cost advantage ($NPV^*_A = 51$ as in table 7.1, column 3), while with 0% shared benefits ($c_B = 5$) the fully proprietary case of point C obtains ($NPV^*_A = 250$ as in table 7.1, column 2). The shared R & D investment results in symmetric Cournot-Nash equilibriums in the second-stage. The initial gradual increase in the value of firm A's R & D investment (moving from B toward C, as the degree of shared cost advantage declines) is due to the positive strategic reaction effect as firm A gets a relatively larger market share (in Cournot-Nash equilibrium) as a result of its greater proprietary cost advantage. As the R & D investment becomes more exclusive, firm A can preempt competitive entry at lower demand, changing the market structure from Cournot-Nash equilibrium (at high θ) to Stackelberg leadership or monopoly. The resulting preemption effect thus causes a jump in value (at about 60% or $c_B = 2$). The further gradual increase is a result of added strategic reaction value in Cournot equilibrium at higher levels of demand.

Figure 7.4 shows sensitivity of NPV^*_A to changes in market demand uncertainty u (panel A) and to the time interval or separation (panel B) for the proprietary R & D case. Compared to the base case of no R & D (lower curve in panel A), where project value increases monotonically with demand uncertainty as expected from standard option theory, the competitive interaction resulting from firm A's R & D investment (top curve) causes the sensitivity of value to demand uncertainty to vary non-monotonically (i.e., there is a jump when u exceeds 1.19). Given that at initial demand ($\theta_0 = 17.5$) firm A is in the Stackelberg leadership zone due to its proprietary R & D investment (figure 7.2, panel C), low changes in demand (left region with u below 1.19) maintain Stackelberg leader-

FIGURE 7.3 SENSITIVITY OF FIRM A'S TOTAL PROJECT VALUE (NPV^*_A)
TO THE DEGREE OF SHARED COST BENEFITS TO COMPETITOR B (WITH
c_B FROM 0 TO 5)

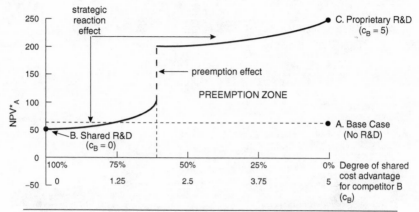

Parameter values: investment: $K_A = 100$, $I_A = I_B = 100$; interest rates: $r = 0.10$, $k = 0.13$; base demand: $\theta_0 = 17.5$; demand uncertainty: $u = 1.25$, $d = 0.8$; no technical R & D uncertainty: $\eta_A = 100\%$; no learning: $\gamma = 0\%$.

NPV^* = base-case NPV + $[-K_A +$ (direct value + strategic reaction value + preemption value)] + flexibility value

A. Base case $(c_A = 5, c_B = 5)$: $37 + [0] + 23 = 60$;

B. Shared R & D $(c_A = 0, c_B = 0)$: $37 + [-100 + (186 - 72)] + 0 = 37 + 14 = 51$ (< 60; do not invest);

C. Proprietary R & D $(c_A = 0, c_B = 5)$: $37 + [-100 + (186 + 82 + 45)] + 0 = 37 + 213 = 250$ (> 60; invest in R & D).

ship for firm A. But with higher demand uncertainty (beyond the critical level $u = 1.19$), competition may enter despite higher costs if demand realization turns out high (i.e., if $\theta_1 = u\theta_0$), changing the market structure from Stackelberg to Cournot-Nash equilibrium and causing a decline in strategic value and in NPV^*_A.[8]

Panel B shows the sensitivity of NPV^*_A to the time interval (separation or lag) between the R & D and the follow-on commercialization investments. From option theory, the length of time that the project outlays can

---

[8]This result about a nonmonotonic impact of uncertainty is in contrast to earlier findings in the option literature. The nonmonotonicity in the results depends on the initial parameters and particularly on the initial demand zone and how far away θ_0 is from θ^*_{INVEST} or θ^*_{DEFER}. As a result, precise estimation of demand is important in deciding on an investment strategy.

FIGURE 7.4 SENSITIVITY OF FIRM A'S PROPRIETARY R & D INVESTMENT
VALUE (NPV^*_A) TO MARKET DEMAND UNCERTAINTY (PANEL A) AND TO
THE TIME INTERVAL (SEPARATION) BETWEEN STRATEGIC R & D INVEST-
MENT AND FOLLOW-ON COMMERCIALIZATION INVESTMENT (PANEL B)

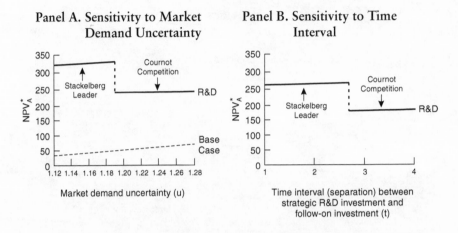

Panel A. Sensitivity to Market Demand Uncertainty

Panel B. Sensitivity to Time Interval

Parameter values: investment: $K_A = 100$, $I_A = I_B = 100$; base-case costs: $c_A = 5$,
$c_B = 5$; proprietary R & D costs: $c_A = 0$, $c_B = 5$; interest rates: $r = 0.10$, $k = 0.13$;
base demand: $\theta_0 = 17.5$; no technical R & D uncertainty: $\eta_A = 100\%$; no learning: $\gamma = 0\%$; panel B demand uncertainty: $u = 1.25$, $d = 0.8$.

be deferred makes an investment opportunity more valuable. However, if
there is competitive interaction, the sensitivity of value to option maturity time may again change nonmonotonically. Although the expanded
NPV for a proprietary investment by firm A increases gradually with separation time, it may drop suddenly when the time interval increases beyond a critical level (about three periods in panel B of figure 7.4), resulting
in a change in market structure from Stackelberg leadership to Cournot
duopoly competition).[9]

---

[9]According to real-options theory, a higher interest rate (*r*) also influences flexibility value
positively; however, it generally also translates into a higher required return (discount rate)
and a lower market value upon investment, other things constant. Similar to figure 7.4,
there may again be a jump when market structure changes (from Stackelberg to Cournot if
$\theta_1 = u\theta_0$).

7.5. Technical R & D Uncertainty, Stochastic Reaction Functions, and Asymmetric Information with Signaling

Competitive R & D strategies can be affected by many determinants that are uncertain or cannot be directly observed. Technical uncertainty of the success of the R & D effort is one such critical dimension in assessing the strategic position of the firm and the valuation of its R & D strategy. Uncertainty may also take the form of incomplete information if rivals are not aware of each other's R & D success or cannot observe the innovations of competitors and their precise costs. In a multiperiod game a firm's behavior may reveal some of its private information, or alternatively, firms may wish to signal their innovation success as a commitment to a certain technology or market for preemptive purposes. This section continues the previous comparative statics analysis by extending the basic analysis to incorporate technical R & D uncertainty, first under complete or symmetric information, and then under imperfect or asymmetric information (using stochastic reaction functions), with and without signaling.

7.5.1. TECHNICAL R & D UNCERTAINTY (UNDER SYMMETRIC INFORMATION)

The proprietary R & D investment (similar to the one discussed in chapter 6, panel A of figure 6.4, or column 2 in table 7.1) can be seen as a special case of assuming sure R & D success under complete (symmetric) information within a more general model that allows technical R & D uncertainty. In addition to market demand uncertainty in the second stage, we now allow for technical uncertainty in the first stage in that with probability η or $(1 - \eta)$ the R & D effort may succeed or fail.[10]

Figure 7.5, panel A, illustrates the sensitivity of firm A's R & D investment value (NPV_A^*) to the probability of firm A's R & D success (η_A) and its resulting expected cost $E(c_A)$. The earlier proprietary R & D case corresponds to point A $(NPV_A^* = 250$ in column 2 of table 7.1), illustrating the extreme case of sure R & D success $(\eta_A = 100\%$ and $c_A = 0)$. Point B $(NPV_A^* = -40)$ illustrates the other extreme case of sure R & D failure and no cost reduction $(\eta_A = 0\%$ and $c_A = 5)$,[11] while point C illustrates the case that R & D has a 50% probability of success or failure (with $E(c_A) = 0.5 \times 5 + 0.5 \times 0 = 2.5$). With technical R & D uncertainty, the

---

[10]Because technical uncertainty is nonsystematic, we can estimate the expected value of the strategic R & D investment using the actual probabilities (0.5) while discounting at the risk-free rate $(r = 0.10)$.

[11]For point B, $NPV_A^* = $ Base case value $- K_A = 60 - 100 = -40$.

FIGURE 7.5 SENSITIVITY OF NET PROJECT VALUE OF FIRM A'S
PROPRIETARY INVESTMENT TO TECHNICAL R & D UNCERTAINTY
(PANEL A) AND TO IMPERFECT (INCOMPLETE) INFORMATION (PANEL B)

Panel A. Sensitivity to Technical R & D Uncertainty (Probability of R & D Success)

Panel B. Perfect Information, Imperfect (No) Information, and Signaling under R & D (with 50% probability of success)

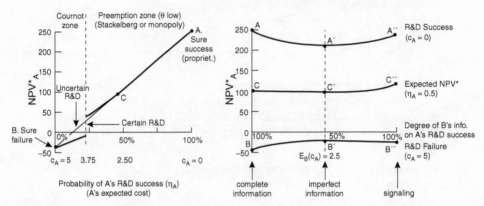

Parameter values: investment: $K_A = 100$, $I_A = I_B = 100$; interest rates: $r = 0.10$, $k = 0.13$; base demand: $\theta_0 = 17.5$; demand uncertainty: $u = 1.25$, $d = 0.8$; no learning: $\gamma = 0$; panel B technical R & D uncertainty: $\eta_A = 50\%$. Cost of signaling R & D success by firm A is lower than cost for B ($c_B = 4.5$ at 100%, $c_B = 4.75$ at 75%, $c_B = 5$ at 50%).

NPV* = base-case NPV + [$-K_A$ + (direct value + strategic reaction value + strategic preemption value)] + flexibility value

A. Sure success ($\eta_A = 100\%$):
    $37 + [-100 + (186 + 82 + 45)] + 0 = 250$

B. Sure failure ($\eta_A = 0\%$):
    $37 + [-100] + 23 = -40$

C. Uncertain success ($\eta_A = 50\%$):
    $37 + [-100 + (93 + 41 + 22)] + 12 = 105$
C. Perfect information:
    $37 + [-100 + (93 + 41 + 22)] + 12 = 105$
C'. Imperfect information:
    $37 + [-100 + (93 + 31 + 34)] + 9 = 104$
C''. Signaling:
    $37 + [-100 + (93 + 44 + 28)] + 6 = 108$

expected value of firm A's R & D varies linearly (from point A to C to B) with firm A's probability of R & D success (η_A from 100% to 0%).

This is in contrast to the case of certain (successful) R & D where the innovating firm can attain a sure cost advantage over its competitor; above a given "threshold" cost advantage ($c_A = 3.75$), firm A can preempt competition (entering a preemption zone under low demand) so that the NPV_A^* curve exhibits a discontinuity (jump in value). With technical R & D uncertainty (with the same expected cost reduction, or mean-preserving spread), the chance of R & D failure mitigates the strategic preemption effect so that an increasing expected cost advantage exhibits a smoother increase in R & D value. Effectively, under technical R & D uncertainty the preemption effect (discontinuity) is averaged out (linearized) in the first-stage R & D value.[12]

The introduction of technical R & D uncertainty results in less commitment (strategic reaction and preemption) value for firm A because it involves a sure up-front expenditure with a probability $(1 - \eta_A)$ that R & D may fail and both firms may end up with equal (symmetric) operating costs. While net commitment value declines (from 213 in point A, to 56 in C, and -100 in B) with a lower probability of success (from $\eta_A = 100\%$ to 50% to 0%), option or flexibility value increases (from 0 to 12 to 23) but to a lower degree.

7.5.2. IMPERFECT/ASYMMETRIC INFORMATION AND STOCHASTIC REACTION FUNCTIONS

Often firms have to make R & D investment decisions under imperfect information, without being able to observe all the important strategic factors, such as the success of their rivals' R & D efforts and their precise cost functions. Although an innovator would know (ex post) whether its innovation succeeded or not, its rival may not know this with certainty and may have to design a strategy based on its expectation of the rival's behavior and costs. In this example we examine the dynamics in R & D value under incomplete information when private information is revealed over time as the rival exhibits the behavior of a successful (or failing) innovator.

In panel B of figure 7.5 we consider these information effects on the value of R & D strategies. Panel A of figure 7.5 is actually a special case of the more general model depicted in panel B where firm B has complete information over the success of firm A's R & D effort (corresponding to points A, B, and C on the vertical axis). Under full symmetric (complete) information, competitor B knows whether firm A's R & D effort has succeeded or

---

[12]If successful in its R & D, firm A preempts with a cost advantage of $c_A = 0$ vs. $c_B = 5$, while if its fails, it cannot preempt. By taking the expectation the discontinuity is averaged out.

not, and therefore uses firm A's actual ex post costs in its reaction function (i.e., $c_A = 5$ if R & D of firm A failed and $c_A = 0$ if it succeeded).

Under imperfect or asymmetric information, firm A still has complete (private) information about its own R & D success and uses its actual cost in its reaction function. However, in simultaneous Cournot competition where firm B does not know whether firm A's cost is low ($c_A = 0$) or high ($c_A = 5$), it now faces a stochastic reaction function (using firm A's expected quantity), maximizing its expectation of profit values over firm A's being a low- or high-cost type, contingent on firm A's success or failure.[13] This results in the equilibrium values for firm A (NPV_A^*) shown in panel B of figure 7.5 under imperfect information (at the midpoint where $\eta_A = 50\%$, obtaining points A', B', C').

In case of sequential investment in a Bayesian (separating) equilibrium, firm B can observe firm A's quantity choice in the prior period and can infer whether firm A is a low-cost or a high-cost type (reducing to the complete information case).[14] The change in value in the first half along the three curves in panel B of figure 7.5 represents the impact of imperfect information under R & D uncertainty in case of R & D success (upper curve AA'), failure (lower curve BB'), and the expected value using 50% probability of success (middle curve CC').[15] In case firm A's R & D actually succeeds (upper curve with $c_A = 0$), firm A's value declines as firm B's information on A's R & D success becomes more incomplete. This results from overestimation by firm B of firm A's actual cost (essentially using $E_B(c_A) = 2.5$ rather than 0), which would lead firm B to set a higher quantity under contrarian competition, hurting firm A's profit and value (NPV_A^* at A' is lower than at A). By contrast, in case of actual R & D failure (lower curve), the value of firm A's R & D investment (NPV_A^*) is higher with less complete (imperfect) information (NPV_A^* at B' > B).[16] Interestingly, these opposite biases (i.e., the value reduction due to firm B's overestimation of firm A's cost under R & D success and the value increase due to the opposite effect in case of failure) are

---

[13]Since firm A's expected quantity is linear in firm A's expected cost, the Cournot equilibrium values are equivalently obtained by using firm B's perceived *expected* cost of firm A. For instance, if firm B has no information whatsoever whether firm A's effort succeeded or not (using $\eta_A = 50\%$), firm B's estimation of firm A's cost would be $E_B(c_A) = 0.5(5) + 0.5(0) = 2.5$.

[14]The incentive compatibility conditions that firm A will not set a misleading quantity are satisfied.

[15]Note that the case of a 100% probability of R & D success (point A in panel A of figure 7.5) corresponds to the special case of complete information (vertical axis) on the upper curve of panel B (point A), while 50% (point C) and 0% (point B) correspond to the initial points on the middle (C) and lower curves (B) of panel B (on the vertical axis).

[16]If firm A's R & D fails ($c_A = 5$), firm B will essentially underestimate firm A's actual cost and set a lower quantity using firm A's expected cost (2.5 rather than 5), resulting in higher values for A (NPV_A^* at B' > B).

approximately averaged out when determining the expected value of firm A's R & D investment with $\eta_A = 50\%$ (middle line at $C' = 104$ versus 105 at C). The breakdown of value components under complete versus imperfect information (with $\eta_A = 50\%$) is given in columns 4 and 5 of table 7.1. If we compare the effect on the value components of the case of complete versus incomplete information, we see that the value of flexibility and strategic reaction become less important due to the "averaging out" of these opposite effects in firm B's response, effectively from using firm A's expected rather than actual costs. As we move from point C (perfect, complete information) to C' (imperfect information), there is a negative effect on strategic reaction (31 vs. 41) and on flexibility value (9 vs. 12), which is roughly offset by the higher strategic preemption value (34 vs. 22) because firm B (by essentially using its expectation of Firm A's cost) may stay out even when firm A's R & D fails if demand is low.

7.5.3. SIGNALING EFFECTS

Under asymmetric (imperfect) information, firm A may have an incentive to provide (partial or misleading) information over the success of its R & D efforts. If its R & D efforts were successful, firm A would have an incentive to communicate/signal this to firm B to induce it to set a lower quantity and soften second-stage competition.[17] By contrast, firm A has an incentive not to inform firm B in case its R & D efforts are failing, so that Firm B, in maximizing its expectation of profit value, would in effect use firm A's expected cost (2.5) in its reaction function rather than the actual cost (0) under simultaneous Cournot competition. At first glance, firm A appears to have an incentive to always tell its competitor that its R & D effort is successful, whether it actually succeeds or not. Of course this is not credible, as firm B knows this and would not be fooled. If firm A always informs in case of R & D success but keeps silent in case of failure, firm B will infer that no information (silence) implies that firm A's R & D actually failed and will increase quantity competition accordingly (in a repeated game).[18]

It might in fact be better for firm A to inform (tell the truth) in some cases while keeping silent in others (never explicitly lying). Firm A can follow an implicit signaling rule conditioned on the outcome of its R & D effort (success or failure) as well as on the level of market demand θ and the resulting market structure (deviating from the "rule" whenever there are overriding preemption/strategic benefits from telling the truth over

---

[17]Firm B would essentially adjust its expectation of firm A's cost from $E_B(c_A) = 2.5$ to 0, causing a shift in firm B's reaction function to the left and increasing firm A's market share under a Cournot-Nash equilibrium.

[18]Firm A may try to fool firm B into believing that its R & D is a success even when it is failing, but this is not credible without costly signaling.

keeping silent).[19] Signaling credibly R & D success is costly. The innovative firm must disclose sufficient specific details about its R & D innovation (e.g., through the process of registering its patents or through a public announcement to the market) that allow firm B to also benefit somewhat, partially reducing its own costs (from 5 to 4.5).[20]

In figure 7.5 (panel B), the rising right part of the upper curve under R & D success (A'A'') reflects an increasing reaction effect for firm A who sets a higher quantity due to its distinct relative cost advantage, despite firm B's cost decrease from 5 to 4.5 ($c_A = 0$, $c_B = 4.5$). NPV_A^* at A'' (with signaling) is less than at A (no signaling) because of this signaling cost. If R & D fails (at B''), firm A keeps silent at high levels of demand, appropriating the benefit of imperfect information under Cournot competition which is reflected in the relatively flat right part of the lower curve (B'B''). Comparing the case of asymmetric information with signaling to imperfect information (with no signaling) summarized in columns 6 and 5 of table 7.1, strategic reaction value is now significantly higher (44 vs. 31), while preemption value is lower (28 vs. 34) as a result of firm B's entry in case of R & D failure. Nevertheless, both firms benefit from this signaling scheme. For firm A the expected NPV^* of 108 at C'' (average of values at A'' and B'') with signaling is higher than in the case without signaling (104 at C'). Firm B benefits from going along with this scheme as well, with either success or failure of R & D, since its smaller market share in a Cournot equilibrium when not informed is offset by its lower cost when it is informed. When firm A informs in case of success, firm B benefits from the lower cost (4.5 vs. 5); in case of failure under low demand, firm B benefits from knowledge of firm A's actual higher cost (5) and increasing its own quantity accordingly.

---

[19]A simple version of the basic signaling "rule" is

Signal success (tell the truth) in case of R & D success under high demand:
$E_B(c_A) = 0$ $(c_B = 4.5)$

Keep silent in case of R & D success under low demand:
$E_B(c_A) = 2.5$, except when firm B is follower (uses $c_A = 0$)

Keep silent in case of R & D failure under high demand:
$E_B(c_A) = 2.5$, except when firm B is follower (uses $c_A = 5$)

Signal failure (tell the truth) in case of R & D failure under low demand: $E_B(c_A) = 5$.
[20]We assume here that firm B cannot discover this conditional signaling rule (e.g., firm A may have superior or lead information on market demand), although it may choose to respond to all signals as being truthful or ignore them altogether (using firm A's expected cost of 2.5 instead, except when it is a follower and can infer whether firm A is a low-cost or high-cost type). We do not investigate here the case where firm B discovers the signaling rule through repetition; in any case, firm B is shown to be better off following the rule as well.

7.6. Learning Experience Cost Effects

Experience is an important determinant of efficiency and lower costs. The learning curve encapsulates a cost advantage that flows from accumulated experience and know-how. Besides reducing future production costs via making a strategic R & D investment in an innovative new production process, firms can alternatively achieve cost reduction by investing earlier or heavier in production capacity (e.g., see Majd and Pindyck 1987). With learning, the marginal cost of firm i ($i =$ A, B) is assumed to decline exponentially with cumulative production $\Sigma Q_{it}(= Q_{it} + \Sigma Q_{it-1})$ at a learning rate γ, converging to a floor level c_i^F according to

$$c_i(Q_{it}) \equiv c_i^F + c_i^L e^{-\gamma \Sigma Q_{it}}. \tag{7.2}$$

The rate of learning, γ, can be estimated by measuring how fast the operational cost declines when cumulative production increases. The learning rate is likely to be firm-specific, as different organizations and processes embody different levels of experience and know-how. Learning and experience curve effects are particularly significant if intricate or complex tasks must be performed, as in shipbuilding, airplane manufacturing, consumer electronics, or the design and production of software.

Clearly there is an important trade-off between waiting, or the value of flexibility to adapt to change, and early investment to take advantage of cumulative experience and the benefits from learning (even without R & D precommitment). Figure 7.6 shows the impact of a higher learning rate on the value of firm A's investment when both firms can experience learning cost effects under complete information in different cases. Panel A illustrates the base case of no strategic R & D with learning. Point B, for example, shows that learning at a rate of $\gamma = 10\%$ increases firm A's value to 103 due to future production cost savings, compared to the base-case value of 60 with no learning effects (point A). As higher learning favors early investment, it results in an erosion of flexibility value (from 23 at point A to 0 at B when ∂ increases from 0 to 10%) while it increases direct NPV value due to cost savings (from 0 to 111, as seen in column 7 of table 7.1). NPV_A^* generally rises more steeply at first with a higher learning rate because the cost savings rise more than the flexibility loss.[21]

This analysis is based on the symmetrical case of identical firms facing simultaneous investment opportunities. Seizing a first-mover advantage

[21]The curve changes in a nonsmooth fashion (exhibiting a small down jump at a critical rate of $\gamma^* = 4.5\%$) because of changes in subsequent period subgames, such as switching from (Defer, Defer) to (Invest, Invest) and a resulting prisoners' dilemma–type loss under low demand as production costs drop (below a critical level) with a higher learning rate.

FIGURE 7.6 VALUE OF FIRM A's PROPRIETARY CERTAIN R & D (PANEL B)
AND UNCERTAIN R & D (PANEL C) VERSUS THE BASE CASE OF NO R & D
(PANEL A) WITH LEARNING EXPERIENCE COST EFFECTS BY BOTH FIRMS

**Panel A. Base Case (no R & D)
with Learning ($c_A = c_B = 5$)**

**Panel B. Proprietary Certain R & D
with Learning ($c_A = 2.5$, $c_B = 5$)**

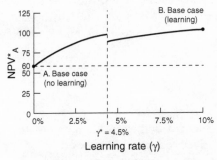
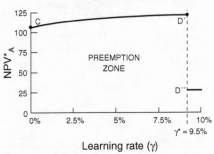

Panel C. Proprietary Uncertain R & D with Learning ($E(c_A) = 2.5$, $c_B = 5$)

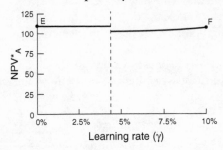

Parameter values: investment: $K_A = 100$, $I_A = I_B = 100$; interest rates: $r = 0.10$, $k = 0.13$; base demand: $\theta_0 = 17.5$; uncertainty: $u = 1.25$, $d = 0.8$.

Panel B. proprietary R & D costs: $c_A = 2.5$, $c_B = 5$; no technical uncertainty: $\eta_A = 100\%$.

Panel C. costs: R & D success $c_A = 0$, $c_B = 5$; R & D failure $c_A = 5$, $c_B = 5$; technical uncertainty: $\eta_A = 50\%$; $E(c_A) = 2.5$.

Initial total marginal cost $c_i = 5$ ($= c_i^F + c_i^L$), with a learning-cost component $c_i^L = 4$ and a fixed (floor) cost $c_i^F = 1$ for each firm ($i = A, B$).

NPV* = base-case NPV + $[-K_A$ + (direct value + strategic reaction value + strategic preemption value)] + flexibility value

A. Base case ($\gamma = 0\%$): 37 + (0) + 23 = 60

B. Base case learning ($\gamma = 10\%$):
    37 + (111 − 45 + 0) + 0 = 103

C. Certain R & D with $c_A = 2.5$ ($\gamma = 0\%$):
    37 + [−100 + (93 + 41 + 22)] +12 = 105

E. Uncertain R & D with $E(c_A) = 2.5$ ($\gamma = 0\%$):
    37 + [−100 + (93 + 41 + 22)] + 12 = 105

F. Uncertain R & D with learning ($\gamma = 10\%$):
    103 + [−100 + (37 + 15 + 44)] + 0 = 99 (< 103; do not invest in R & D).

is important in this context, as the market leader accumulates more experience and gains a cost advantage. As costs continue to decline, it becomes increasingly more difficult for imitators to catch up. When we additionally consider R & D precommitment, the total value of the R & D strategy depends not only on the pioneer's learning benefits; its strategic preemptive value is also dependent on the cumulative production and learning rate of the rival. The R & D pioneer may lose preemption value when the rival can more fully exploit a learning cost advantage.

Panel B of figure 7.6 shows the case when firm A makes a proprietary R & D investment with certain success ($\eta_A = 100\%$) that reduces its cost to $c_A = 2.5$ (rather than to 0 as assumed earlier) with additional learning cost savings at a rate $\gamma\%$ (by both firms). Since the learning benefits are relatively higher for firm B (with firm A's cost starting at $c_A = 2.5$ while B's at $c_B = 5$, with both assumed to decline at the same rate), the rate of increase in NPV_A^* is slower. Further, while at a low learning rate firm A can preempt firm B given its initial strategic cost advantage from its R & D, beyond a critical learning rate ($\gamma^* = 9.5\%$) firm B can no longer be preempted due to its relatively stronger offsetting operating/production cost advantage, resulting in a large downward jump in firm A's value from D' to D''.

R & D uncertainty is already known to affect the total flexibility and commitment value. In this context uncertainty has side effects: only if the pioneer's R & D succeeds is there a preemptive effect; however, the higher cost advantage (50% in $c_A = 0$ or $c_A = 5$ instead of $c_A = 2.5$) is sufficient for a preemptive effect that spans a larger demand zone. If R & D fails and there is no preemptive effect, the firm may still benefit from learning experience effects, while the learning advantage of firm B is eroded compared to the previous case.

Panel C of figure 7.6 illustrates the value of firm A's making an *uncertain* proprietary R & D investment with success probability $\eta_A = 50\%$ that reduces its cost to $c_A = 0$ (assuming firm B has perfect information), with learning by both firms. Since $E(c_A) = 2.5$, the value with no learning in the uncertain R & D case (point E in panel C) is the same ($NPV_A^* = 105$) as in the certain R & D case (point C in panel B). In case its R & D fails, firm A can still take advantage of learning experience effects. In case of firm A's R & D success, higher learning benefits firm B relatively more. This results in a more flattened value for firm A.[22] At a high learning rate beyond a critical threshold (e.g., at point F with $\gamma = 10\%$), firm A may find it optimal to wait rather than invest in R & D ($NPV_A^* = 99$ with uncertain

---

[22]In case of R & D failure, the two firms have symmetric costs and learning benefits (as in the base case of panel A in figure 7.6), but in case of success firm A here does not derive further benefits from learning. In panel B above, firm A derives learning benefits in case of R & D success as well (with $c_A = 2.5$ instead of 0).

R & D at F, exceeding 103 with no R & D at B); under R & D uncertainty firm A cannot attain high preemption value, while it can potentially benefit more from future production with learning instead of investing in R & D. Compared to the certain R & D case in panel B (mean-preserving spread), the effect of technical R & D uncertainty is to reduce the impact of preemption (jump); it results in lower value due to the inability to take advantage of a strong preemption effect when learning is low (see preemption zone in panel B for $\gamma^* = 9.5\%$), although it may have relatively higher value at higher learning rates (e.g., at $\gamma = 10\%$ $F > D''$). Compared to the base case in panel A, the impact of learning is to reduce the incentive to make a strategic R & D investment; without (or with less) learning, firm A would have invested in R & D instead (e.g., with $\gamma = 0\%$, $NPV_A^* = 105$ at E vs. 60 at A).

The breakdown of value components for uncertain proprietary R & D with learning cost effects is shown in column 8 of table 7.1 (to be contrasted to column 4 without learning). In general, the learning cost effect has the following influences on value when firm A makes the strategic R & D investment:

1. It has a negative impact on the direct value of the NPV^* for firm A through earlier larger production by firm B. The direct value of making an upfront strategic R & D investment under learning by either firm declines since the strategic investment could result in a relatively smaller cost reduction for firm A.[23]

2. The strategic reaction value of the R & D investment of firm A declines with learning, compared to the situation without learning (15 for $\gamma = 10\%$ vs. 41 for $\gamma = 0\%$), since the larger production of firm B results in a lower quantity for firm A. That is, the R & D investment has a smaller impact on competitor B's reaction, because firm B's cost declines with production under learning. Interestingly, the presence of learning enhances the strategic preemption value of firm A (44 for $\gamma = 10\%$ vs. 22 for $\gamma = 0\%$) because of the increased difference between the Cournot and the Stackelberg leadership equilibrium values. In the case of learning, the Cournot-Nash equilibrium values of firm A decline when firm B learns. Thus, under learning, preemption with a strategic investment is valuable, as it prevents the competitor from taking advantage of the learning experience cost effects.

3. Learning cost effects erode flexibility value (12 for $\gamma = 0$ vs. 0 for $\gamma = 10\%$ at point F, where learning results in Cournot-Nash equilibriums in both states). Under learning, either firm has an incentive

---

[23]This can be seen by comparing the direct values of 37 for $\gamma = 10\%$ at point F of figure 7. 6 (or column 8 of table 7.1) vs. 93 for $\gamma = 0\%$ at point E (column 4 with $\gamma = 50\%$).

to invest earlier rather than wait. In essence, instead of responding to firm A's strategic R & D investment with its own R & D to reduce its cost, firm B can alternatively achieve similar cost reduction by intensifying its productive (commercialization) investment.

7.7. Competition versus Cooperation in R & D

Let us now revisit the question of whether it is better for the two firms to pursue independent, competing R & D activities or whether to cooperate in the first stage via a joint research venture (sharing the R & D costs) and compete instead only in the second stage of commercial production. In the competition case the firm that seizes initiative can gain a comparative advantage. As in patent races, this analysis highlights the often critical advantage that goes to the first innovator, providing insight on how the magnitude of the advantage affects the incentive to innovate. However, when the two firms cooperate in R & D, there may be regions of coordination and mutual benefit from timing investment under demand uncertainty and more fully appropriating the embedded option value. We assume that instead of both firms independently investing 100 in R & D, they can now contribute $K_A = K_B = K/2 = 50$ each in a joint research venture. Table 7.1 shows the components of value for proprietary R & D under technical R & D uncertainty in case of R & D cooperation (column 10) versus first-stage R & D competition (column 9).[24] As noted earlier, joint research has the following three influences on value compared to first-stage competition in R & D.

1. It has a beneficial impact on direct NPV and net commitment value by achieving the same cost savings during commercialization (second-stage production) with a lower first-stage R & D expenditure by each firm (50 vs. 100).
2. It enables the two firms to more fully appropriate the flexibility value from waiting (25 vs. 17). There is no sacrifice of flexibility value in this case from an attempt to preempt the market as under direct R & D competition.
3. On the negative side, it results in potential sacrifice of strategic preemption (from 11 to 0) and strategic reaction value (from -16 to -32) because α firm can no longer acquire a competitive advantage via an early R & D investment. The second-stage game in this case is symmetrical and does not allow the potentially high Stackelberg leadership or monopoly profits that enhance strategic value if one firm invests earlier.

---

[24]In case the R & D benefits are shared, it might be better to wait and benefit from the R & D investment of the competitor or cooperate via a joint research venture.

FIGURE 7.7 DEMAND ZONES FOR FIRST-STAGE R & D COMPETITION
(PANEL A) AND COOPERATION VIA A JOINT R & D VENTURE (PANEL B)

Panel A. Demand Zones for R & D Competition

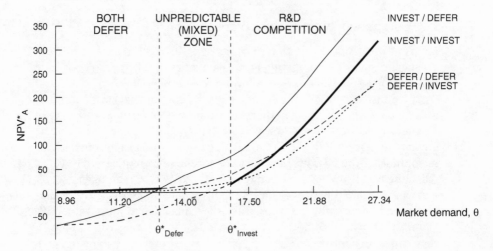

Panel B. Cooperation via Joint Research Venture

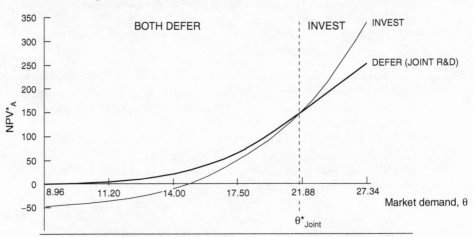

Parameter values: investment: $K_A = K_B = 100$, $I_A = I_B = 100$; interest rates: $r = 0.10$, $k = 0.13$; base demand: $\theta_0 = 17.5$; demand uncertainty: $u = 1.25$, $d = 0.8$; technical R & D uncertainty: $\eta_A = \eta_B = 50\%$; base-case production costs $c_A = c_B = 5$; cost of proprietary R & D in case of success by firm i ($i = A$, B), $c_i = 0$.

Figure 7.7 graphically illustrates the valuation results for different demand zones in these two cases of R & D competition (panel A) versus cooperation (panel B). The analysis incorporates technical R & D uncertainty (with success probability $\eta = 50\%$) and proprietary benefits from monopoly rents in case a firm's R & D succeeds or the competitor's R & D effort fails. As can be seen from figure 7.7 (panel A), first-stage R & D competition again involves three critical demand zones. At low demand, both firms are better off to defer R & D due to its low commercialization potential. At intermediate levels of demand, there is an unpredictable (mixed equilibrium) zone. Here, the R & D investment is lucrative if only one firm invests but if both firms invest the R & D investment strategy turns out to have a negative or low NPV^*. At higher demand (above $\theta^*_{INVEST} = 16$) the possibility (threat) of each firm pursuing independent R & D activities triggers a simultaneous similar investment by its competitor that, like in a prisoners' dilemma, makes both firms worse off compared to the base-case scenario of waiting.[25] In the case of cooperation (panel B), there are only two demand zones with a single, higher investment threshold ($\theta^*_{JOINT} = 21$). By cooperating, the two firms can avoid the prisoners' dilemma (in the region between θ^*_{INVEST} and θ^*_{JOINT}) and can jointly coordinate their actions against exogenous demand uncertainty, more fully appropriating the flexibility value from waiting. Thus the investment threshold (and the defer zone) is larger.

Comparing the two cases presented in the two panels above leads to several interesting observations. Very high states of demand result in Cournot-Nash equilibriums where both firms invest simultaneously, so that there is no preemption advantage from competing in R & D. Thus the joint R & D strategy is more appealing (compare the values for Invest/Invest in panel A versus Invest in panel B for each given θ) because there is no advantage from preemption. The situation is more dynamic at intermediate levels of demand: firms may follow a competing R & D strategy due to high potential profits resulting from high strategic preemption and reaction effects. A firm may acquire monopoly profits as a result of early investment due to a proprietary cost advantage or in case the competitor's R & D effort fails. At lower market demand, simultaneous investment by both firms may result in negative values in case of R & D competition due to the prisoners' dilemma; the higher flexibility value (option value of waiting) resulting from coordination in a joint research venture may compensate for the strategic preemption and reaction value benefits of R & D competition.

---

[25] The Defer/Defer equilibrium outcome (60, 60) actually has a higher value than Invest/Invest (42, 42).

7.8. Summary and Conclusions

A combination of real-options valuation with basic game-theoretic principles has a number of implications for strategic investment behavior. Contrary to standard option valuation, we find that the value of an R & D investment opportunity may no longer increase monotonically with option parameters because strategic preemption may cause value discontinuities. A jump in value may result as uncertainty increases, when the equilibrium trajectory shifts from one demand zone (e.g., Cournot-Nash equilibrium) to another (e.g., Stackelberg or monopoly), influencing the competitor's equilibrium production decisions. The sign and magnitude of this effect on R & D value depends on the proprietary or shared nature of the investment, on technical R & D uncertainty, on the degree of incomplete information, the existence of learning effects, and on the firm's willingness to compete or form joint research alliances. Our comparative statics analysis enabled us to develop a number of implications for competitive R & D strategies:

1. In the case of a proprietary R & D investment under quantity competition, the firm should follow an aggressive R & D strategy to become stronger in the second stage. Under quantity competition, its competitor will retreat in the later stage and the pioneering firm can become a leader as demand grows.

2. When the benefits of R & D are shared and competition would respond aggressively, the firm should not invest immediately but rather follow a flexible wait-and-see strategy. By delaying R & D investment, it can prevent its competition from exploiting the resulting shared benefits to grow at the firm's own expense.

3. Technical uncertainty in the outcome of R & D generally enhances the flexibility value of waiting and reduces the strategic preemption and commitment value of R & D (compared to the situation of certain proprietary R & D). That is, with the same expected cost reduction, sure R & D success leads to higher preemption value (discontinuity).

4. Under imperfect information where the competitor in effect uses the expected cost of the pioneer in its stochastic reaction function in case of simultaneous Cournot competition, the value of flexibility and strategic reaction become less important due to "averaging out" in the competitor's response of opposite biases from misestimating firm A's actual cost. When signaling is possible, by providing (partial) information over the success of its R & D efforts, the pioneer firm can enhance the strategic reaction and commitment values of R & D. If its R & D efforts are successful, the firm would be tempted to com-

municate this to its competitor if demand is sufficiently high, resulting in Cournot competition to induce the competitor to set a lower
quantity and soften second-stage competition (but may keep silent
under low demand); if its R & D fails, firm A may keep silent under
high demand (but tell the truth under low demand). Through such a
signaling rule contingent on the state of demand and different market
structure outcomes, firm A can be better off with signaling (while
firm B is not expected to improve by ignoring the signal).

5. Learning cost effects trigger earlier investment via reducing future production costs, thereby eroding flexibility value. Learning or
cost experience effects by both firms have the following influences
on the value of a strategic R & D investment: (a) they have a negative impact on direct NPV and on the strategic reaction value for
the pioneer firm because the competitor builds up production volume more quickly and benefits more from learning once it enters;
(b) the strategic preemption value of R & D investment is higher
under learning since preemption can eliminate the competitor's learning advantage; (c) learning erodes flexibility value since either firm
has a cost-driven incentive to invest earlier rather than wait.

6. When the firms can cooperate in R & D via a joint research venture during the first stage, we have the following three influences on
value compared to direct competition in R & D: (a) a joint research
venture enables the cooperating firms to more fully appropriate the
flexibility value from waiting. There is no sacrifice of flexibility
value from the pressure to preempt the market as under direct R & D
competition; (b) joint research has a beneficial impact on direct NPV
and commitment value compared to R & D competition by achieving the same cost savings during second-stage production with a
lower (shared) first-stage R & D expenditure by each firm; (c) on the
negative side, joint research results in sacrifice of potential strategic
value because the firm, by accepting symmetry, gives up the possibility of acquiring a competitive advantage (e.g., preempting competition) via an early R & D investment.[26]

---

[26]These results do not depend on the particular functional forms assumed for the demand
and cost functions (i.e., the above implications are quite robust). For instance, with a more
convex, iso-elastic demand function the basic results regarding the value discontinuity due
to preemption are still valid, though more pronounced. The strategic effects due to the proprietary nature of R & D benefits, technical R & D uncertainty, or information asymmetries
are also preserved but are more amplified under an iso-elastic demand, for similar reasons.
If we compare a certain cost reduction, other things equal, we observe a similar but larger
discontinuity due to the preemption effect of the certain cost reduction. Imperfect information has a positive effect on R & D value: in case of R & D success the leader will preempt,
even if the competitor has incomplete information, while if R & D fails, the competitor will

Box 7.1 In R & D, The Next Best Thing to a Gut Feeling

The tendency of Japanese companies to take advantage of innovations devised in the U.S. is almost automatically attributed to Japan's
lower capital costs and its supportive government-industry alliances.
But it's often overlooked that from the very start U.S. corporations
put their emerging technologies at an enormous disadvantage because of the techniques they use to evaluate payoffs. The rigid equations and models currently used unfortunately have replaced the
instinct and intuition that once guided U.S entrepreneurs.

The fundamental test used in most U.S. companies is: Does the return exceed the cost of capital over the life of the project? To find the
answer companies subject the project to a variety of discounted cash
flow measures.

Dozens of assumptions go into this methodological overkill. Many
of the assumptions aren't reliable. Some are tenuous at best. And if
it's a long-term project that would take, say, 10 years to commercialize (five years being the outer limits of American corporations' horizon), the distant estimates are considered highly speculative and are
heavily discounted. Even the "terminal value," the value of the plant
and other assets upon commercialization, is assumed to be zero.
When all is said and done, the payoff estimates produced by the
quantitative analyses are usually too low. They stand little chance of
beating that ultimate yardstick — the cost of capital. Nine out of 10
projects, on average, fail the test.

Perhaps the most fundamental problem with the current techniques is that they fail to take into account the consequences of not
pursuing a technology. An auto maker may give up on ceramic en-
gines, because technically they seem unfeasible. But a rival who makes
prosaic ceramic parts with the aim of one day using the knowledge to
build a ceramic engine — as the Japanese are doing — can quickly change
the competitive balance.

How to get American companies to act on their intuition again?
There is a new technique that will go a long way toward that. It
deserves wide attention, for it comes closest to simulating the old-
fashioned gut feeling.

Designed after well-developed stock-options theories, the technique works something like this: Suppose there are two emerging

continued ...

be preempted if it uses its expected cost in its reaction function. Similarly, under learning,
the cost advantage is typically sufficient to preempt the competitor (so that the competitor
cannot take advantage of learning). However, for a lower cost advantage of R & D or if R
& D fails, learning by the competitor results in a similar but larger impact due to the higher
production implied by more convex demand.

Box 7.1 continued

technologies, X and Y, that have some bearing on the company's main business. The X may involve a well-understood technology and a market. The Y may involve a wide range of possible outcomes and new markets but with, say, 40% chance of technical failure. The benefits of X are easily quantifiable, and hence salable to top management for funding. The Y is unsalable because it's unquantifiable, even though it seems more promising.

Instead of ignoring Y, the company commits small amounts to develop the technology, in effect taking a "call option" on the underlying technology. The option allows R & D people to explore its technical possibilities, market opportunities, development costs and competitors' strategies. If these don't become clear within the time period of the option, the option is allowed to "expire."

The loss is limited to the small initial funding (the value of the R & D option), just as in the stock option. "The important thing to realize is that the initial expenditures are not directed so much as an investment as they are toward creating an option," says William Hamilton of the University of Pennsylvania's Wharton School, who has co-authored a paper on options valuations of R & D with Graham Mitchell, director of planning at GTE Laboratories in Waltham, Mass.

R & D options, fundamentally, help identify the unapparent outcomes that may be the most important reasons for undertaking the investment. Consider:

- In 1984, W.R. Grace decided to invest in a new technology for catalytic converters for the automobile aftermarket. The discounted-cash-flow analysis — which used a generous "terminal" value — showed that it was an "attractive" project. What looked like a sure-fire technology now can't compete on price. "We didn't accurately predict the price-performance requirement we needed in the aftermarket," says Peter Boer, chief technical officer.

Grace would have dropped the project, except that other opportunities for that technology intervened. The recent clean-air legislation has created applications in cogeneration plants, in planes to reduce ozone emissions, and in utilities to control emissions. Suppose the automotive catalyst technology had been given a thumbs-down by the quantitative techniques, but the other downstream markets loomed on the horizon. Could Grace have overturned the negative signal and invested in the automotive catalyst anyway? "I don't think I would have been able to communicate that to the finance people," says Mr. Boer.

continued . . .

Box 7.1 continued

- In the early 1980s, General Electric initially ignored the emerging magnetic resonance imaging (MRI) technology for medical diagnosis. The MRI market was unclear. And most important, it would have cannibalized the market for GE's existing CT diagnostic machine, which uses X-rays. GE overruled the directive of the discounted-cash-flow technique, as it realized that if it didn't cannibalize the CT market, someone else was going to. Walter Robb, director of GE's R & D, says he doesn't have much use for quantitative techniques now. "The challenge is to find 30 projects a year that will pay off not by NPV (net present value) but by the seat of our pants," he says.

- It's the downstream rewards that are allowing the pharmaceutical company Merck & Co. to plan extensive automation. When it considered the idea first for a drug packaging and distribution plant, the labor savings didn't justify the investment. Moreover, with no prior experience with robots, Merck also wasn't certain about the technical success.

"It was a tricky thing to convince the management. But options valuation allowed engineers to articulate a whole range of outcomes and their benefits," says Judy Lewent, chief financial officer at Merck. The management agreed to take an "option" on automating the plant, and results from the pilot project since early this year have clarified the potential future benefits to the point that the company is now willing to expand automation to its diverse manufacturing operations.

- US West, a telecommunications concern in Denver faced with fast-changing technologies in its industry, also has taken the options approach. It's pursuing technologies — that it otherwise wouldn't be able to justify — aimed at making its cellular phones and paging devices more user-friendly. "Our company doesn't have the maturity and experience to act on gut feelings," says David Sena, strategic technology planner of US West, a company spawned in 1984 by the AT&T breakup.

The options technique needs refining (how to calculate the value of an R & D option is a subject of debate, for instance). But it is the first clear mechanism for R & D people to communicate with their finance men.

Part III

Applications
and Implications

Chapter 8

Case Applications

Trust, but verify.
— Ronald Reagan

8.1. Introduction

We have seen that in a dynamic environment strategic adaptability has become essential for firms to respond appropriately to competitive moves and other changes in the marketplace. Real-options and games applications have been receiving increased attention among major U.S. and international corporations and governmental agencies, among leading consulting firms, and business schools.[1] Real-options valuation is being applied in a variety of contexts, ranging from R & D, new ventures, natural resource investments, land development, leasing, flexible manufacturing, government subsidies and regulation, corporate acquisitions and divestitures, foreign investment, and strategy. Similarly, game theory is being applied to a broad range of industries, such as consumer electronics, airlines, pharmaceuticals and health care, telecommunications, strategic acquisitions and joint ventures, energy and environmental protection, various areas involving contract design and negotiations, and to fields as varied as politics, biology, and sports. In the subsequent sections we provide various examples and applications involving options and games.

In its issues of August 12 and September 30, 1989, the *Economist* although refraining from quoting company names, mentioned that options-based methods were either being used or were being seriously considered in many practical industrial applications, and that there were management consulting firms working on developing these tools. Use of real-options valuation has indeed been considered or adopted by a host of companies in a range of industries, such as British Petroleum and Shell Oil in the oil business, the RTZ Corporation and Newmont Mining in the natural resource industry, Digital Equipment Corporation and Cray

---

[1] In a large survey conducted by Graham and Harvey (2001) 392 CFOs answered a questionnaire, showing that 26.6 % of the firms are using real options "always or almost always" (table 2, p. 198).

Research in the mainframe and supercomputer businesses, Ford and several Japanese competitors in the automobile industry, and many others.

In terms of real-options applications in R & D, many high-tech companies invest heavily to develop technologies that may result in a wide range of possible outcomes and new potential markets, but with a high probability of technical or market failure. In the pharmaceutical industry, for example, on average it costs $360 million and takes a decade to bring a drug to market, and once the drug reaches the market, it faces a 70% chance of failing to earn the cost of invested capital. Such investments are hard to sell to top management on financial grounds because their benefits are remote and hard to quantify, even though they seem promising in terms of growth potential. Instead of ignoring these technologies, the company can make a capital commitment in stages, effectively taking a call option on the underlying technology (or future applications). The initial outlay is not made so much for its own cash flows, but rather for its growth option value. The *Wall Street Journal* in its May 21, 1990, issue made reference to a number of companies that have used real-options analysis.[2]

In 1984, W. R. Grace made an investment in a new technology for automotive catalytic converters. Although that market proved uncompetitive on price, new applications arose in cogeneration plants and in utility emission control as a result of the Clean Air Act. In the early 1980s, General Electric at first ignored the emerging magnetic reasonance imaging (MRI) technology for medical diagnosis. The market at that time was unproven, and the project seemed unjustified based on DCF analysis. Besides, the new technology would have cannibalized GE's existing X ray–based CT diagnostic machine. Nevertheless, eventually top management overruled NPV on strategic grounds and saw the project to success. The *Wall Street Journal* quoted Walter Robb, director of GE's R & D, as saying: "The challenge is to find 30 projects a year that will pay off not by NPV but by the seat of our pants."

"Our company doesn't have the maturity and experience to act on gut feelings," said David Sena, strategic planner at U.S. West, a telecommunications company. The firm has adopted the options approach, investing in technologies intended to make its cellular phones and paging devices more user friendly, that otherwise would not be justified.

Digital Equipment Corporation in the late 1980s used options analysis to value a proposal to build a semiconductor fabrication facility. The strategic planning and analysis group identified and valued several inherent strategic options that made the project's strategic (expanded) NPV more than twice the traditional NPV estimate of $20 million. Technology impact options, giving management the ability to consolidate the tradi-

[2]See the article by A. K. Naj (1990) and relevant excerpts from box insert 7.1.

tional manufacturing activities of two plants into one as a result of increased system functionality designed into the new advanced silicon chips to be fabricated, were valued at $8 million. In addition, strategic technology options (providing flexibility to reequip a facility to quickly ramp up a new manufacturing process technology if called for by the competitive environment) and options to expand capacity were estimated at an additional $13.6 million.

In its June 7, 1999, issue, *Business Week* refers to a number of other companies from a variety of industrial sectors, which have benefited from real-options analysis. In natural resources, Anadarko Petroleum used real-options analysis to justify making a high bid for a lease in the Gulf of Mexico with vast but unproven (uncertain) reserves. Anadarko bid more because the range of possible reserves was so broad. Michael Cohran, vice president for worldwide exploration, commented: "Most people looked at it and just saw the minimum case." Anadarko won the lease and subsequently announced a major oil and gas discovery in that field. Similarly, Chevron used real options to form its 1997 bid for the huge Elk Hills Naval Petroleum reserve in California. The Tennessee Valley Authority used real-options analysis to reach a decision to contract out for 2,000 megawatts of power rather than building extra plants of its own. On the manufacturing side, Hewlett-Packard decided to build more costly but more versatile components for the option to use them in different products. It also used real options to reverse its earlier policy of customizing its inkjet printers for foreign countries at the factory and instead decided to ship partially assembled printers and do the customization in the foreign country. This reduced the previous misestimation of foreign demand and, despite the higher customization costs, resulted in a $3 million savings per month from more effective matching of foreign demand and supply. In the airline manufacturing industry, both Airbus Industrie and Boeing have used real-options analysis to price the generous options they had been extending (in the past for free) to airlines for purchasing, changing, or canceling orders the last minute. Further on the contractual side, Cadence Design Systems in California used real options to value intellectual-property licenses and gave away its model to customers Intel and Toshiba for use in their negotiations. The feedback was said to be fantastic. For more details on exploiting uncertainty and the use of real options in practice, see box insert 8.1.

Merck is an interesting case of a company that has recognized the importance and explicitly adopted the use of both real-options and game theory. Merck recently embarked on extensive automation, starting with a drug-packaging and distribution plant, even though technical success was uncertain and projected labor savings did not seem to justify the investment. "It was a tricky thing to convince the management. But options

Box 8.1 EXPLOITING UNCERTAINTY: REAL OPTIONS IN PRACTICE

"Real-options theory" in a nutshell says that when the future is highly uncertain, it pays to have a broad range of options open. Real-options analysis rewards flexibility — and that's what makes it better than today's standard decision-making tool, "net present value." NPV calculates the value of a project by predicting its payouts, adjusting them for risk, and subtracting the investment outlay. But by boiling down all the possibilities for the future into a single scenario, NPV doesn't account for the ability of executives to react to new circumstances — for instance, spend a little up front, see how things develop, then either cancel or go full speed ahead.

Real-options analysis persuades companies to create lots of possibilities for themselves — for instance, by doing spadework on several projects at once. As events unfold, many options won't be worth pursuing. But a few could be blockbusters.

Rapid change has exposed the weaknesses of less flexible valuation tools. Experts have developed rules of thumb that simplify the formidable math behind options valuation, while making real options applicable in a broader range of situations. And consulting firms have latched on to the technique as the Next Big Thing to sell to clients.

Hewlett-Packard has experimented with real options since the beginning of the 1990s. Example: In the 80s, HP customized inkjet printers for foreign markets at the factory, then shipped them in finished form in warehouses. Customizing at the factory is cheaper than customizing in the field. But HP kept guessing wrong on demand and ending up with, say, too many printers configured for French customers but not enough for Germans.

Executives realized that it would be smarter to ship partially assembled printers and then customize them at the warehouse, once it had firm orders. True, local customization costs more. But even though production costs rose, HP saved $3 million a month by more effectively matching supply to demand, says Corey A. Billington, who directs HP's Strategic Planning & Modeling group.

Increasing the cost of production — anathema to your average engineer — was in effect the price HP paid for the option to delay configuration choices until the optimal time. Since then, more units of HP have gotten the real-options treatment. Right now, the corporation is calculating the value of having inkjet mechanisms that work in products from different divisions. Building in such flexibility costs extra. HP's answer: Quantify the value of the flexibility to HP as a whole, and then create incentives for the division managers to do what's in the best interests of the company.

continued . . .

Box 8.1 continued

The earliest applications [of real options] were in oil, gas, copper, and gold, and companies in those commodity businesses remain some of the biggest users. Chevron Corp. used real options in forming its 1997 bid for Elk Hills Naval Petroleum Reserve, a federal property in California. Anadarko Petroleum Corp. of Houston says real-options analysis gave it the confidence to outbid others for a tract in the Gulf of Mexico called Tanzanite that has proved rich in oil and gas. Anadarko paid more because Tanzanite's range of possible reserves was so broad. Says Michael D. Cochran, vice president for worldwide exploration: "Most people looked at it and just saw the minimum case."

What's hot now is the extension of real options beyond commodities — into biotechnology, pharmaceuticals, software, computer chips, and similar fields. This requires some innovation. The underlying asset of the option is no longer a traded product such as oil, whose going price can be plugged easily into a formula. Now, the asset that you get with the call option is something that's not traded — for example, a factory that hasn't even been constructed yet. Its present value must be estimated from projections of its future cash flows.

That's not a simple calculation, to be sure, but it gives better answers than the methods that most companies use today to make major investment decisions. Strictly speaking, net present value theory says that companies should fund every project whose expected return exceeds the corporate cost of capital. But Treasury Secretary Lawrence H. Summers in his past life as a Harvard University economist, noted that companies set hurdle rates for proposals that are far higher than their cost of capital. That's a vote of no confidence in NPV.

Real-options analysis helps decide when to kill projects that aren't working — following the Silicon Valley tradition of "fail fast." Equally important, it helps decide when to keep projects alive. According to McKinsey & Co., a strict NPV analysis would have had Apple Computer Inc. quit the personal-computer business in 1995–96 because it wasn't earning its cost of capital. But real-options analysis says that a period of losses can be a worthwhile price to pay for keeping alive an enterprise that might earn big bucks in the future. Indeed, today Apple is making money and its market share is on the rise. One reason Silicon Valley is embracing real options is that the method abets collaboration between companies. Technology has become so complex that no company can supply everything it needs internally. A company creating an electronic product may need to acquire up to 15 intellectual-property licenses. That can be enormously time-consuming, notes Adriana G. Chiocchi, division counsel for worldwide services at Cadence Design Systems Inc. in San Jose, Calif. "If one deal takes months and you have 15 deals to do — hello?

continued . . .

Box 8.1 continued

You're not going to be getting a lot of projects out." So Chiocchi's team has designed an options-based method for valuing licenses. It gave its model away to customers Intel Corp. and Toshiba Corp. for use in their negotiations, hoping for it to catch on as a standard. Says Chiocchi: "The feedback was fantastic."

More and more companies are embracing real options. The Tennessee Valley Authority used them in a 1994 decision to contract out for 2,000 megawatts of power instead of building its own plants. In some cases, the TVA paid for options to buy power but never exercised them. That seems like a waste. On the other hand, power-purchase options are a more efficient buffer against unexpected demand than, say, building a nuclear power plant that might not be needed, says Larry Taylor, vice-president for bulk power trading. "It has been phenomenally successful at saving money, and keeping the rates down," he says.

Airbus Industrie uses the theory to calculate the value of the options that it gives to airlines to change or cancel orders at the last minute. Today, airlines don't know how much such options are worth compared with, say, a lower price per plane. So they can't weigh the trade-offs or easily compare deals offered by Airbus and archrival Boeing Co.

A new generation of business analysts is starting to be schooled in options thinking. Already, the major consulting firms are recruiting students versed in the field. Competing in the New Economy with inflexible management tools is like playing basketball in ski boots. Real-options analysis lets you kick off those clunkers and sprint down the floor.

Source: Excerpts from "Exploiting Uncertainty: The Real-Options Revolution in Decision-Making," by Peter Coy. Reprinted from June 7, 1999 issue of *Business Week* by special permission, copyright © 1999 by the McGraw-Hill Companies, Inc.

Who has Opted for Real Options — and Why

Hewlett-Packard

HP wants to keep its component costs as low as possible. But it also wants its components to be versatile, to give it the option of using them in different products. That raises their cost. Real options help weigh the trade-off between higher cost and flexibility.

Cadence Design Systems

This Silicon Valley outfit uses real-options valuation methods to break logjams in negotiations over computer chip design licenses.

continued . . .

Box 8.1 continued

Contracts are easier to hammer out when buyers and sellers speak the same real-options language.

Airbus Industrie

Airbus and its rival Boeing both offer generous options to airline customers to cancel or change orders. But airlines don't know how much those options are worth — compared with, say, a price cut. Airbus explains their value using real-options analysis.

Anadarko Petroleum

Real options gave Anadarko the confidence to bid high for a lease in the Gulf of Mexico, where the potential was vast but uncertain. It won 100% of the Tanzanite lease and last July announced a "major oil and gas discovery" there.

---

valuation allowed engineers to articulate the whole range of outcomes and their benefits," said Judy Lewent, Merck's chief financial officer. After management was convinced to take an option on automating the plant and the results were promising, it was later willing to expand automation to its other operations.

In their R & D activities, pharmaceutical companies like Merck often enter into collaborative agreements with smaller biotechnology companies or universities in order to gain access to early-stage research projects. (Several Japanese companies recently attracted media attention by going as far as developing such relationships on American university campuses.) Because of small chances of making it to market and long development horizons, cash flows are remote and highly uncertain (a 40–60% standard deviation for biotechnology stocks is not uncommon). To control risk and preserve its abandonment options, financing by the larger pharmaceutical company is often staged as a series of contingent progress "installments," with an early payment giving the right to make further investments (e.g., in clinical trials or commercialization). Merck was recently examining project "Gamma," involving the acquisition of new technologies from a small biotech firm (for product development, scale-up of the manufacturing process, product commercialization), which would position Merck to enter a desirable new market. Merck's Financial Evaluation and Analysis Group knew it could not rely on traditional DCF approaches and chose to use option analysis. Their option analysis is summarized in box insert 8.2. The option value Merck arrived at was significantly higher than the $2 million required up-front investment (a small amount compared to Merck's $1 billion annual research budget). On a different occasion, Merck used options thinking to justify the $6 billion acquisition of Medco, a company that managed prescription drug benefits for over 30 million Americans through various employer-sponsored plans. Merck saw the acquisition as an option to gain access to Medco's information technology that stored detailed information on over 30 million patients, consistent with its strategy of getting closer to its ultimate customers. In commenting on their experiences with options analysis, Merck's CFO Judy Lewent said: "When you make an initial investment in a research project [or a platform acquisition like Medco], you are paying an entry fee for a right. . . . To me, all kinds of business decisions are options" (Nichols 1994). Indeed, building and using their options-based planning models was viewed as having created a valuable new capability for the company.

The Merck CFO also recognized the need to use game theory to better understand other aspects of their acquisition of Medco. "When you are in a situation like this, with many players, I think it is instructive to use game theory analysis . . . game theory forces you to see a business situation from two perspectives: yours and your competitor's." She also understood in a broader context when it makes sense to compete and when to cooperate. "On the business end, we also think that sharing information can be more productive than hiding it. And I believe that business is more productively done in an expanding market than in a shrinking market. When we came out with our antihypertensive Vasotec, Bristol-Myers Squibb had already launched Capoten. Both drugs have roughly the same method of action. The strategy that we adopted was not to cannibalize the Capoten markets. Rather, we wanted to go after the tenfold additional patients who were on older, less safe and effective medicine. In that way, we could expand the market for both companies." In terms of knowing when to support a rival versus when to compete aggressively, Lewent said: "The paradox is that we perform in both modes at the same time." For the new pharmaceutical paradigm based on options valuation and game theory, see box insert 8.2, "Options and Games at Merck."[3]

Turning to other game theory applications, various examples from daily life and various disciplines, including economics, business, and politics, are provided in Dixit and Nalebuff 1991. Other economists have used game theory to understand many practical problems, such as how to deal with global warming or with fetuses with genetic disorders.[4] In its June 15, 1996, issue, the *Economist* mentions companies as diverse as Xerox in office equipment, Bear Stearns in investment banking, and PepsiCo in soft drinks as being interested in the use of game theory. Even at General Re

---

[3]This is based on the article by Nancy Nichols (1994).
[4]In another application, McGahan (1994) discusses capacity commitments in the introduction of the compact disk.

BOX 8.2 OPTIONS AND GAMES AT MERCK

Risk, complexity, and uncertainty define the business environment of the 1990s. While there is broad agreement about the need to manage within an ever-changing context, few have suggested a framework for managing risk or a set of tools to help cope with uncertainty. Yet that is precisely what Judy Lewent, CFO of Merck &Co., Inc., and her 500-member finance team have developed to deal with the high-stakes nature of the pharmaceutical industry. [On average, it costs $359 million and takes ten years to bring a drug to market. Once there, seven out of ten products fail to return the cost of the company's capital.]

"To me, all kinds of business decisions are options," says Judy Lewent. "I believe strongly that financial theory, properly applied, is critical to managing in an increasingly complex and risky business climate. I think that finance departments can take the nuances, the intuitive feelings that really fine business people have and quantify them. In that way, they can capture both the hard financials of a project and the strategic intent.

"When you are in a situation like this [involving the acquisition of another company like Medco], with many players, I think it is instructive to use game theory analysis. Game theory suggests one optimal strategy if the game ends after one play. However, since this particular game won't be over in one play, game theory forces you to see a business situation over many periods from two perspectives: yours and your competitor's.

"Tremendous spillover benefits arise as a result of scientists' propensity to publish and exchange ideas, particularly at the discovery stage; yet this in no way diminishes the highly competitive nature of the research process.

"On the business end, we also think that sharing information can be more productive than hiding it. And I believe that business is more productively done in an expanding market than in a shrinking market. "When we came out with our antihypertensive Vasotec, Bristol-Myers Squibb had already launched Capoten. Both drugs have roughly the same method of action. The strategy that we adopted was not to cannibalize the Capoten markets. Rather, we wanted to go after the tenfold additional patients who were on older, less safe and effective medicine. In that way, we could expand the market for both companies.

"*How do we know when to support a rival and when to compete more aggressively?* The paradox is that we perform in both modes at the same time. For example, we formed joint ventures such as The Du Pont Merck Pharmaceutical Company and the Johnson & Johnson

continued . . .

Box 8.2 continued

Merck Consumer Pharmaceuticals Co. We brought together organizations with distinctly different strengths in a financial framework that helps each party achieve its strategic objectives. The agreements also help each partner diversify risk by sharing future investment and financial gain. The downside is that while we strengthen our own position with these 50% owned ventures, we are also building new competitor companies.

"But the most interesting aspect of this is to think about the nature of innovation in the drug industry. What exactly does it take to have the kind of scientific breakthrough necessary to create a new drug, one with significant therapeutic value? That intangible element of insight makes all the difference in our industry."

Source: Excerpts from Nichols 1994.

Option Analysis at Merck

Pharmaceutical companies frequently enter into business relationships with small biotechnology companies or universities in order to gain access to early-stage research projects. Analyzing the strategic value of such projects, however, can be difficult. Because of the prolonged development phase of any pharmaceutical product (often up to a decade before the first commercial sale) and the extreme difficulty of predicting cash flows and market conditions far into the future, net-present-value techniques may not capture the real strategic value of the research.

As a result, the business agreements are often structured so that the larger pharmaceutical company will make an up-front payment followed by a series of progress payments to the smaller company or university for research. These contingent progress payments give the pharmaceutical company the right — but not the obligation — to make further investments: for instance, funding clinical trials or providing capital for manufacturing requirements. This is known as an option contract.

The financial Evaluation and Analysis Group at Merck was recently presented with just such an option contract — I'll call it Project Gamma. Merck wanted to enter a new line of business that required the acquisition of appropriate technologies from a small biotech company called Gamma: product development, scale-up of the manufacturing process, coordination of regulatory requirements, and product commercialization. Under the terms of the proposed agreement, Merck would make a $2 million payment to Gamma over a period of three years. In addition, Merck would pay Gamma royalties

continued . . .

Box 8.2 continued

should the product ever come to market. Merck had the option to terminate the agreement at any time if dissatisfied with the progress of the research.

When it came to analyzing the strategic value of Project Gamma, the finance group could not rely on traditional techniques. Project returns were difficult to model both because of the high degree of uncertainty regarding the size and profitability of the future market segments and because sales were not expected to commence until the latter part of decade. But here was a project that clearly had option characteristics: an asymmetrical distribution of returns present or, in other words, an overwhelming potential upside with little current downside exposure. The group therefore, chose to use option analysis.

Two factors determine a project's option value. The first factor is the length of time the project may be deferred. Clearly, the longer Merck had to examine future developments, the more valuable the project would be. With more time, Merck would be able to collect more information and therefore make a better investment decision. The second factor that drives option value is project volatility. The high degree of uncertainty in terms of project returns increases a project's value as an option because of the asymmetry between potential upside gains and downside losses. In this case, Merck's downside loss potential was limited to the amount of the initial investment, and substantial upside potential existed.

Merck's finance group used the Black-Scholes option-pricing model to determine the project's option value. Five factors that influence an option's price are used in the Black-Scholes model. The finance group defined those factors as follows:

- The exercise price is the capital investment to be made approximately two years hence.

- The stock price, or value of the underlying asset, is the present value of the cash flows from the project (excluding the above-mentioned capital investment to be made and the present value of the up-front fees and development costs over the next two years).

- The time to expiration was varied over two, three, and four years. The option could be exercised in two years at the earliest. The option was structured to expire in four years because Merck thought that competing products, making market entry unfeasible, would exist by then.

continued . . .

Box 8.2 continued

- A sample of the annual standard deviation of returns for typical biotechnology stocks was obtained from an investment bank as a proxy measure for project volatility. A conservative range for the volatility of the project was set at 40% to 60%.

- A risk-free rate of interest of 4.5% was assumed. This figure roughly represents the U.S. Treasury rate over the two to four year period referred to in the time to expiration of the model.

The option value that the Financial Evaluation and Analysis Group arrived at from the above factors showed that this option had significantly more value than the up-front payment that needed to be invested.

Source: Reprinted by permission of *Harvard Business Review* from "Scientific Management at Merck: An Interview with CFO Judy Lewent," by Nancy A. Nichols, January–February 1994, pp. 88–99. Copyright © 1994 by the Harvard Business Review School Publishing Corporation; all rights reserved.

Corp., a property/casualty reinsurer in Connecticut, "Game theory is a significant part of senior management education," according to vice president and chief marketing officer Dalas Luby. The Federal Communications Commission's $7 billion auction of radio spectrum for mobile phones in March 1995 is the largest quoted example of application of game theory. From their angle, hundreds of mobile-phone companies also relied on game theory to decide how much to bid in that same auction.

Robert Gertner and Marc Knez (1999) provide an illustration of the use of game theory supplemented with scenario analysis to understand competition in microchips. Box insert 8.3 describes a case application of the competition between Advanced Micro Devices (AMD) and Intel regarding microprocessors, analogous to a prisoners' dilemma. In 1997, AMD launched its K6 microprocessor, aimed to capture leadership of the fast microprocessors market away from Intel. AMD feared that Intel would respond by launching a similar or superior chip and use its brand name to drive AMD out of the high-end microprocessor segment. However, with the development of the low-cost PC market, the risk was reduced since AMD could produce alternative versions of the K6 chip (in the same plant) for the low-end market. But this depended on Intel staying out of the low-end segment. Thus, AMD needed to view the situation from Intel's perspective in deciding whether to enter the low-end segment or wait. The simple strategic scenario analysis described in box insert 8.3 suggests that AMD had good reason to believe that Intel would delay, increasing its own expected payoff from launching the K6 chip. In fact Intel

Box 8.3 Case Application of Competition between AMD and Intel in Microchips

The field of strategy is long on conceptual frameworks and relatively short on formal tools that support strategic decision-making. Game theory and scenario analysis, for example, provide valuable techniques for modeling the business environment but each fails to capture all the relevant variables. Thus game theory focuses on competitors' strategies at the expense of the big picture; scenario analysis, on the other hand, sketches the big picture but misses the strategic details. To show how this tool works, we present a case study of the competition between AMD and Intel in the microchip market.

In 1997, Advanced Micro Devices (AMD) introduced its K6 microprocessor. Its aim was to capture leadership of the market for fast microprocessors, a position held at the time by Intel. The primary risk to AMD was that Intel would quickly introduce a comparable or superior chip and, with its brand equity, drive AMD out of the high-end chip segment. This risk was dampened by the emerging cheap PC market. While the K6 chip was aimed at the high-end market, alternative versions (made in the same plant) could be sold in the low-end market. However, this low-end "hedge" depended on Intel staying out of the low-end segment. Our strategic scenario analysis will focus on the uncertainty surrounding Intel's decision to enter the low-end segment or not.

The key to strategic reasoning in general, and the application of strategic scenario analysis in particular, is for the decision-maker to take the perspective of other players in an effort to predict how they will behave. In this case, decision-makers at AMD needed to take Intel's perspective. So in what follows we develop a simple scenario game to capture the trade-offs Intel had to make when deciding whether to enter the low-end segment. The results of that analysis in turn provide a foundation for the judgments AMD had to make about the likelihood of significant low-end market share. In our game, Intel has to decide whether to bide its time in the low-end segment, with the option of introducing its Celeron chip at some later time, or to introduce the Celeron without delay. Besides Intel, there are two other sets of players: the competition — AMD and National Semiconductor (NS), which will surely introduce low-end chips immediately; and the major PC manufacturers — NEC, Compaq, IBM, Toshiba, DEC and others.

Intel faces many critical uncertainties in making its "wait/introduce" decision. The most important are: (i) the demand for cheap PCs; (ii) the quality of its competitors' low-end chips; and (iii) whether its brand equity is strong enough to overcome its second-mover

continued . . .

Box 8.3 continued

disadvantage if it waits. Intel's uncertainties are linked to those faced by the PC manufacturers and the competition. The PC manufacturers will have to decide whether to buy the AMD/NS chips or Intel's. AMD and NS face capacity and pricing decisions that will depend on whether Intel has entered the low-end market. For simplicity we focus on a single structural uncertainty — cheap PC demand — and a single strategic uncertainty — PC makers' purchase decisions. The next step in any scenario analysis is to determine the minimum number of states that each scenario variable can assume. The idea is to choose as many states as will lead to qualitatively different outcomes. In many situations two or three states will suffice; "average," "more successful than expected," and "failure" may capture the essence of the uncertainty. So while there is a continuum of alternative demand outcomes, we assume there are only two: "high" or "low." Similarly, for the PC makers we assume a 60/40 versus a 40/60 split, where Intel retains either 60 per cent or 40 per cent of the market. Note that the PC makers have mixed motives in their purchase decisions. The demand for their product is likely to be higher if they use an Intel chip, but the price of competitors' chips is likely to be lower. The decision will come down to the price/performance trade-offs and the strength of Intel's brand equity.

The simplified description of the game generates eight initial scenarios, four under each of the possible Intel actions. The next step is to eliminate scenarios that are either implausible or internally inconsistent. Beginning with those that arise under "introduce," 1 and 3 are relatively implausible. If Intel enters with a low-end chip that is comparable to the competition's low-end chip, its competitors should be able to capture at least 60 per cent of the market, whether demand is high or low. Hence, we are left with two scenarios under "introduce," whereby Intel gets 60 per cent of either a large or small market for cheap PCs. Under the "wait" decision, all four scenarios are plausible, conditional on Intel actually introducing its low-end chip after observing the level of demand for cheap PCs. However, it will not be optimal for Intel to introduce its low-end chips if demand for cheap PCs turns out to be low. Hence scenarios 7 and 8 are not internally consistent from a game theoretical perspective. This leaves us with two scenarios to consider under "wait," whereby Intel gets either 40 per cent or 60 per cent of the cheap PC market under conditions of high demand. From this simple scenario analysis we see that Intel's downside risk from introducing is simply that the market for cheap PCs does not materialize — the "stuck with no market" scenario. Of course, the upside is that the market does materialize — the "capture the market right away" scenario. If Intel waits, the risk is

continued . . .

Box 8.3 continued

that demand will be high and the PC makers will commit to buying from the competition, which will give Intel a second-mover disadvantage — the "take what's left" scenario. Alternatively, many PC makers may switch to Intel as soon as it enters because of its brand equity — the "wait and take the market" scenario. As in most entry decisions, the benefit of waiting is the option value of observing whether demand is high or low before committing assets to enter. The value of this option depends on the degree of second-mover disadvantage. In Intel's case, that disadvantage is relatively low. It knows it will be able to capture significant market share with its brand equity (provided it has a competitive chip). The question is to what extent profits will be dissipated through price competition. The next step is to take the model beyond its role of explaining the strategic structure of the competitive environment and to use it to provide insights into the decision itself. The way to do this is to analyze each scenario in detail and determine pay-offs for each player. This can then be used, like our simple entry game example, to predict competitors' behavior and to determine which course of action is most profitable.

In 1997 Intel decided not to introduce a low-end chip for the emerging cheap PC market. Subsequently, the demand for cheap PCs grew rapidly. Intel was forced to introduce an underperforming chip in early 1998, leaving 80 per cent of the low-end chip market to its competitors (mostly AMD). Andy Grove, the company's chairman, commented that the cheap PC boom was "broader and more profound" than he had anticipated the previous autumn. From AMD's perspective, Intel's delayed entry opened a critical window of opportunity. AMD had time to establish a strong position in the low-end market that could support its attempts to enter the more lucrative high end — Intel's dominant market. Ignoring the obvious criticism of hindsight bias, our simple strategic scenario analysis suggests that AMD had good reason to bet that Intel would delay, increasing AMD's expected pay-offs from the K6 chip. This Intel example is an abbreviated description of a complete strategic scenario analysis.

Source: Excerpts from Gertner and Knez 1999.

decided not to introduce a low-end microprocessor for the emerging cheap PC market. As the demand for cheap PCs grew rapidly, Intel was forced to introduce an inferior chip in early 1998, leaving 80% of the low-end chip market to its competitors (mostly AMD). Andy Grove, Intel's chairman, admitted that the cheap PC growth was "broader and more profound" than anticipated. Intel's delayed entry enabled AMD to establish itself as a leader in the low-end market. This position could also

Box 8.4 California's Electricity Crisis as a Game of Chicken

It's hard to imagine, but the California electricity crisis has gotten even uglier of late. "They are the biggest snakes on the planet Earth," Governor Gray Davis recently said of the state's power suppliers, adding not long after: "If they do not cooperate I'll have no choice but to sign a windfall-profits tax or seize plants."

Power companies are hardly taking the threats lying down. Increasingly, they seem intent on making sure state officials know there's a limit to how much they can be pushed around.

No mystery. As the California electricity crisis enters its second summer, the situation seems to be disintegrating into a giant game of chicken. Politicians are trying to pressure producers to cut prices and lower the roughly $5.5 billion tab they claim they're owed from previous power sales. The generators want to avoid being hit with wholesale price caps or dragged into court for price-gouging, a prospect that seems more likely every day. The result is continued uncertainty — and the distinct possibility that many new power plants might not get built.

Therein lies the rub. Even if power companies are overcharging or otherwise gaming the market to their own benefit, as many have alleged, the state's politicians and regulators have little choice but to work with them to solve the state's power problems. Producers, too, clearly have little long-term interest in exiting what remains one of the country's largest power markets. This is a game of chicken neither side can win.

Source: Excerpts from "California's Giant Game of Chicken," *Business Week,* June 18, 2001.

provide a platform for it to attempt to penetrate the more lucrative high-end segment, Intel's home domain.

The next two box inserts illustrate applications of game theory in other business or economic situations. Box insert 8.4 explains California's electricity crisis and the stand-off between the state and its power suppliers and their exchange of threats as a "game of chicken" that neither side can win but which will result in blocking or delaying building of new plants.

Box insert 8.5 uses game theory to explain self-inflicted wounds by some of the smaller German telecoms, who seemed to play poker in launching third-generation (3G) high-speed mobile services, as their strategies seem to depend on predictions of their rivals. "Many analysts say we should pull out," says one European executive with a German business. "And we have to look at shareholders' interests. But it is also a competition game and we don't want to help our rivals (by eliminating competition). If we pull out now, we won't get the best out of assets we already have.

BOX 8.5 GAME THEORY AND GERMAN TELECOMS: PREDICTING RIVAL'S BEHAVIOR, OR WHO WILL BLINK FIRST?

Six top telecoms players will need to decide this year whether to show their hand in Germany, Europe's largest telecoms market, in what is becoming the highest stake poker game on the continent.

Having gambled $46 billion on new-generation mobile licenses last year and seen share prices crash, executives admit they risk throwing good money after bad.

But the German market is governed by game theory, where strategies hinge partly on predictions about the behavior of rivals.

The key protagonists are Vodafone Group Plc., Deutsche Telekom, KPN Telecom, BT's wireless demerger MM02, French-owned Orange and the Telefonica Moviles-Sonera joint venture.

Despite mounting calls from analysts and investors for some of the smaller operators to shut up shop and head for home, all six insist they are on track to launch a third generation (3G) of high-speed mobile phone services around 2003.

"Many analysts say we should pull out," says one European executive with a German business. "And we have to look at shareholders' interests. But it is also a competition game and we don't want to help our rivals (by eliminating competition). "If we pull out now, we won't get the best out of assets we already have. We have to defend the value of the license."

Industry experts and company insiders have long predicted a shake-out among the four smaller German operators, which are backed by Dutch, British, French and Spanish groups. They account for just 20% of a market dominated by the twin might of Deutsche Telekom and Vodafone, and their businesses are not deemed big enough to ensure a lucrative future.

"Everything turns on what will happen in the mobile market," says one industry source close to a German operator. "And the trigger could be Germany. It's clear there will be not six, five or four (3G) German networks. There will probably be three."

In the meantime, partly because of the technological uncertainties over 3G services, analysts value some German assets at less than zero.

Source: Excerpts from "Who Will Blink First in German Telecoms Poker?" *Business World,* Reuters, January 3, 2002.

We have to defend the value of the license." Industry experts and company insiders have long predicted a shakeout among the four smaller German operators. "It's clear there will be not six, five or four (3G) German networks. There will probably be three." Meanwhile, analysts assign some German assets a negative value.

Many other companies have not been fortunate in recognizing the strategic value of proving a new technology, of preserving corporate capabilities serving as an infrastructure for the creation, preservation, and exercise of corporate real options, or have misestimated the strategic reaction of competitors. In 1986, Ford conceded small-car development in the United States to Mazda, and along with it gave up invaluable technological expertise and capabilities that could be applied elsewhere. RCA also conceded to the Japanese the development of VCR technology, from which later sprang CD players, video cameras, and a range of other applications. Erosion of in-house technological expertise resulting from "passive" partnerships has inflicted companies like Boeing and many others. Even without quantitative analysis, conceptual options and games or strategic thinking could have helped many of these companies. More games and options applications are given below.

The rest of the chapter is organized as follows. Section 8.2 discusses product launch scenarios and strategic games in consumer electronics. Section 8.3 applies options and games to an acquisition strategy known as "buy-and-build." Section 8.4 describes a "soup-to-nuts" implementation in the case of European airport expansion and discusses specific implementation issues. The last section provides concluding comments.

8.2. Strategic Games in Consumer Electronics

This section discusses product launch applications in consumer electronics. Philips has developed many innovative products, and has often been engaged in market and technology battles, as well as in standardization agreements and joint ventures with large Japanese competitors.

8.2.1. WINNER TAKES ALL VERSUS STRATEGIC ALLIANCES IN THE LAUNCH OF VIDEO RECORDER SYSTEMS

In consumer electronics, firms like Philips, Sony, Matsushita, and Toshiba have a history of competing in the development of technologically innovative products, such as CD players, CDi, Walkman, 100 Hz TV, and the high-density disk. Innovative strategies are often accompanied by high commercial as well as technological risk. Such strategies also require close contact with customers and careful monitoring of competition. It is possible that firms may compete in one product and cooperate on another, or compete in commercialization and cooperate on R & D. Strategic alliances with some competitors that use mutual agreements over standardization can help win a battle in the competition between different systems.

Firms often perceive that they have a strategic incentive for taking a tough competitive position. In the development of video recorders there were three systems: the V2000, Betamax, and VHS. In the battle for a standard video technology, Philips, Sony, and JVC competed fiercely. Later, the same firms cooperated on technology for the development of the CD player. A more recent case is the development by Philips of the digital cassette DCC against the competing minidisk technology by Sony.

Consider the battle for developing a technology standard in the video recorder market. In the late seventies, the introduction of three types of video recorders resulted in intense rivalry among the key players. Philips launched the V2000 system to compete with Sony's Betamax and JVC's VHS system. Instead of following a single standard, Philips decided to make the V2000 system incompatible with VHS tapes, believing that the advantage of reversible tapes and better slow-motion pictures was sufficient to win substantial market share. The aggressive position taking by these players resulted in an intense market share battle in the video recorder market.

Figure 8.1 illustrates a stylized evolution of the market share battle between Sony, JVC, and Philips. Uncertainty concerning Philips' market share compared to the other systems is reflected by the states of nature (o). The branches in bold-type in the upper part of the tree illustrate the historic path of actions actually taken by the players involved and the resolved uncertainty.

The market for consumer video recorders grew rapidly. Sony with its Betamax system and JVC with VHS were already involved in a market share battle before Philips introduced the V2000. Philips decided not to make its system compatible with the existing VHS system. Unfortunately for Philips, however, its claimed technical advantage was not translated commercially into a larger market share. The existing systems had already developed a large captive market supported with software (movies).

It was clear from the beginning that only one of the systems could win, and that in the end only one could become the standard in the market. The other firms eventually would have to switch to this system. Hence, each player must have believed it had a good chance of winning in order to be willing to participate in this battle.

The situation can be viewed as an optimal stopping problem against competition with uncertainty over the future value of the product standard. A "war of attrition" game such as this is more likely to occur in an industry in which economies of scale are important. Fighting is costly because it may lead to low or negative profits and R & D outlays may not be recovered. The object of the battle is to induce the rival to give up. The winning firm acquires the standard, and the losers are left wishing they had never entered the fight. Figure 8.2 illustrates the war of attrition for the video recorder market. The game ends when one of the players has either quit or switched to another system. In the rectangle, the historic path

FIGURE 8.1 TIMING PRODUCT LAUNCH UNDER COMPETITION

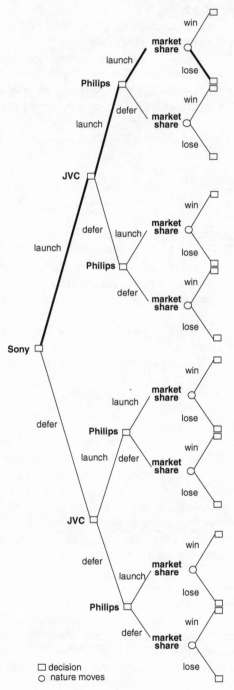

FIGURE 8.2 WAR OF ATTRITION GAME

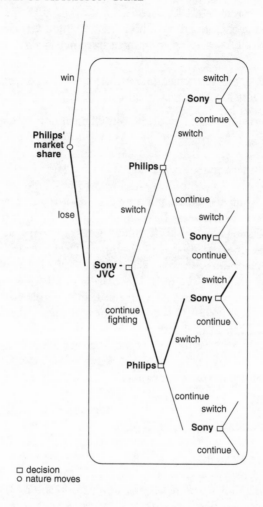

followed is represented by the bold-type branches. Philips suffered intense competition and a low market share as unfavorable information was revealed, and in the end it switched to the VHS system. The VHS system by JVC (Matsushita) became the market standard.

By contrast, in the subsequent development of the CD technology a decade later, Philips recognized that the CD player would be more successful if other firms would be willing to produce CDs and CD players with the same standard. Philips and Sony exchanged licenses to acquire an install base for the CD player. The joint development of the CD turned out to be a success, resulting in a range of subsequent growth opportunities. It appears that the development of the CD has been a far greater success than initially expected. In 1995, total sales for the entire market using this technology came to about $50 billion. Three billion CDs and about 110 million pieces of CD-carrying equipment have been sold annually.

8.2.2. The Competition versus Coordination Game of the High-Density Disk

By 1995, the storage capacity of the old CD technology had become insufficient for current requirements. Many applications for computers, multimedia, movies, and computer games came to require more storage capacity. Consider the battle and coordination game in the development of the high-density disk. Initially it seemed as if it would end up in a technological war, but instead it ended up in a coordination game. On one side was an alliance between Toshiba and Time Warner, who had jointly developed the super density disk (SDD). On the other side were Philips and Sony with their Multi-Media Compact Disk (MMCD). With new compression techniques and the use of two layers, the storage capacities of the new-generation disks would increase tenfold (to more than 7 gb). The new technology was expected to result in valuable growth opportunities in audio CD, CD-ROM (information storage), digital video disc (DVD), and other CD applications.

Both sides claimed victory in advance, hoping to enhance the commitment value of their own technology (see chapter 7, section 7.4). Both made advance announcements of the launch of their high-density players and disk, listing the computer producers who had chosen their system, emphasizing the success of their R & D efforts, even providing misleading information about the capabilities of each other's systems.[5]

The game below captures the dilemma of each side whether to compete or to cooperate. Each side had to choose between two competitive strategies: (1) Take an accommodating stance that may benefit the other with standardization agreements and compromises; or (2) take a tough position developing one's own technology as exclusive as possible and avoid creating valuable opportunities for the competition. Figure 8.3 gives the four possible outcomes in a two-by-two game. Suppose that both sides regard as their worst outcome (1) taking accommodating position when competition takes a tough stance. An example would be sharing one's technology while competition takes advantage of this shar-

---

[5]For example, Toshiba announced that its competitor, Philips, would not develop a rewritable CD version. Philips called this untrue: "Of course we are working on that. However, we have to protect the copyright first before we launch the product." In this aggressive situation, managers made tough statements, e.g., "We are in a state of war" (NRC, May 7, 1995).

FIGURE 8.3 THE TWO-BY-TWO COMPETITION VERSUS COORDINATION
GAME (PRISONERS' DILEMMA)

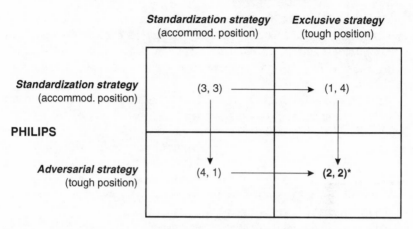

COMPETITION

ing and enhances their own technology. In this situation the tough side is going to win and receive its highest payoff (4). Call this outcome (1, 4) or (4, 1). The second-worst outcome (2, 2) is the situation in which both sides pursue exclusionary technological strategies and develop competing products independently. This would result in intense competition. After a couple of years, uncertainty over the winning system will be resolved. The case in which both sides decide to follow accommodating strategies and make agreements on a single standard results in a higher (3, 3) payoff.

The situation described above is analogous to the prisoners' dilemma. A tough position in product development dominates an accommodating strategy for each side, regardless of whether its competitor takes an accommodating or an aggressive position (4 > 3 and 2 > 1). Without coordination, both sides will play tough, resulting in a moderate (2, 2) payoff. However, by recognizing that a standardization agreement may lead to a preferable (3, 3) outcome, the two sides will have an incentive to be accommodating. A standardization agreement may result in increased productivity and expanded markets for both. In the case of the high-density disk, both sides recognized that the launch of more than one system would result in confusion and major capital waste, not only for the losing company but also for consumers. A "technical working group" representing the leading firms in the computer industry investigated the competing systems and found that both the MMCD of Philips and Sony and the SDCD of Toshiba fulfilled the requirements. The computer industry, which would also benefit if the two alliances agreed on one standard, encouraged the two sides to negotiate and coordinate. Subsequently, the competitive moves of the two sides reported in the press changed from tough to accommodating.[6]

The above examples illustrate the use of options and games in better understanding competitive behavior under uncertainty in oligopolistic markets. The war of attrition in video systems, the coordination game of CD technology, and the adversarial and accommodating strategies for the high-density disk are just a few examples of games that corporations face in real life.

As we saw, an important aspect in corporate strategy is whether to co-ordinate strategies with competition and support rivals, or to compete against them aggressively. Patents and exclusive use of information can prevent the creation of valuable opportunities for competitors that take a hostile posture. Under contrarian competition, an aggressive strategy may induce rivals to retreat from the market. However, when competitive re-sponse is reciprocating, adversarial strategies may result in erosion of profit margins for both sides. Instead, gains from sharing information, coordinating activities, and higher productivity can exceed the loss in premium from an exclusionary strategy. With an accommodating strat-egy, firms can work closely together and improve innovation. Firms often cooperate in both R & D and in joint venture programs. For example, Philips formed joint ventures with competitors like Matsushita Electron-ics. A downside was that while these ventures strengthened Philips's po-sition, Philips was also helping build up new competitors.

8.3. Buy-and-Build Platform Acquisition Strategies

In 1996, HAL Investments, a European private equity investor, agreed to buy Pearle Benelux, a leading optical chain in Belgium and the Nether-lands. HAL subsequently made further acquisitions in Belgium and the Netherlands as well as in Germany, Austria, and Italy, all within the same industry. These transactions are part of an acquisition strategy known as "buy and build," in which an equity investor initially undertakes a "plat-form" acquisition in an industry and then leverages core competencies or efficiencies onto follow-on acquisitions in a broadened geographical base. The goal of this strategy is targeted industry consolidation. In con-trast to standard roll-ups and quick-restructuring strategies, which aim to turn investments around in two to three years, a buy-and-build acqui-

---

[6]The vice president of Philips made accommodating statements about coming to one stan-dard. The outcome would be a new standard for the next 20 years. The expectations were that over five years 200 million pieces of CD-carrying equipment would be sold yearly. Multimedia sales would represent 10% of total sales.

sition is a longer-term sequential strategy with a typical planning horizon of at least five years.

Other prominent private equity firms such as Hicks, Muse, Tate & Furst, Warburg Pincus, and Golder Thoma Cressey Rauner (GTCR) — as well as specialized publicly traded funds — also provide capital in active pursuit of industry consolidations. These investors recognize that pricing the first of an expected series of acquisitions requires a "dynamic" analysis of the target's synergistic growth potential. A traditional net present value (NPV) analysis of a set of forecasted cash flows from a single transaction does not capture the full value of a platform acquisition, since much of this value derives from the option to build on the initial acquisition by expanding either organically (internally) or through further acquisitions. Another potentially serious limitation of traditional NPV analysis is its failure to explicitly consider the effect on an acquisition's value of competitive responses by other companies within the industry.

This section develops a framework for assessing the value generated by both the option-like as well as the competitive game-theoretic characteristics of an acquisition strategy. It treats an acquisition strategy as a package of corporate real options actively managed by the firm in a context of competitive responses and changing market conditions. This framework can help management in answering several questions that are important for a successful acquisition strategy: How valuable are the growth opportunities created by the acquisition? When is it appropriate to grow organically and when are strategic acquisitions the preferred route? How is the industry likely to respond and how will that affect the acquisition value? Our framework makes it possible for such strategic considerations to be analyzed in a rigorous fashion.

8.3.1. Classifying Acquisitions Based on Options and Games

In quantifying the value of a buy-and-build strategy, acquisitions are viewed as links in a chain of interrelated investments in which the early investments are prerequisites and set the path for the ones to follow. Moreover, these synergies can fluctuate as the business environment changes. The relevant question in strategic investment planning is, How does the strategic portfolio of acquisitions create value, particularly when the environment changes?

The flexibility of a sequential or staged acquisition strategy can provide great benefits to the investor when there is major uncertainty about the consolidation. Once uncertainty about the success of the first stage of the consolidation is resolved, management can expand its program or simply decide not to proceed with the next stage (i.e., not exercise the real option or sell the company to another player). This option can be seen as an "exchange" option in which the value to the buyer is traded or exchanged against a future price or value.[7] However, there is an important element missing — namely, the competitive setting. Few investment opportunities, whether they are organic investments or acquisitions, exist in a vacuum. Other players in the industry can be expected to react in some way. For example, acquisition of the target could set off a series of acquisitions by competitors, thereby preventing the firm from carrying out its plan of follow-on bids. Or the initial acquisition could have the opposite effect of discouraging would-be competitors and solidifying the firm's first-mover status. Options and games allow for a proper assessment of the flexibility value of an acquisition strategy in an interactive competitive setting.

Classifying acquisitions based on their real-options characteristics, as discussed in chapter 1 and shown in figure 8.4, helps focus managerial attention on their embedded strategic and growth option value.[8] The investor must first ascertain the value characteristics of the target. Investment opportunities that realize their benefits primarily through an expected stream of earnings (or operating cash inflows) are classified as *simple* options, requiring a relatively simple analysis. Examples might include a divestiture of an unwanted division or a late-stage follow-on acquisition in a mature industry that generates cash inflows but has no potential for synergistic follow-on acquisitions.

Other investment opportunities will have significant growth option value. A firm acquired by a strategic buyer, a seed financing by a venture capitalist, or a platform acquisition by a private equity investor all create the possibility of follow-on investments at the time of the initial deal. A platform acquisition in a buy-and-build strategy provides a foothold in a new sector, and derives a significant part of its value from follow-on investment opportunities. In this sense, the platform acquisition is better seen as an option on an option, or as a first stage in a sequence of interrelated investment opportunities. The earlier investments effectively incorporate options to proceed to the next stage if doing so then appears beneficial. This is a multistage or *compound* option because it is the first link in a chain of synergistic growth opportunities, perhaps involving access to new geographical markets or a strengthening of core capabilities. For instance, Merrill Lynch's acquisition of Mercury Asset Management provided a platform for the global expansion of Merrill's asset management business.

---

[7]For a numerical model of the exchange option in a financial context, see Margrabe, 1978.
[8]For an extensive discussion of the classification of investment opportunities as growth options and the drivers of growth option value, see Kester (1984). Smith and Triantis (1994) provide a good analysis of strategic acquisitions as real options.

FIGURE 8.4 THE REAL-OPTIONS APPROACH TO CLASSIFYING
ACQUISITIONS

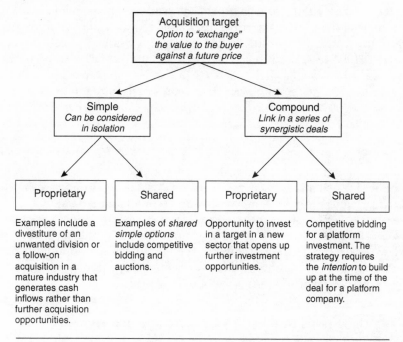

Source: Based on Kester 1984 and Trigeorgis 1996a.

Another important aspect of the valuation of targets concerns the firm's ability to appropriate the opportunity — which depends on whether and the extent to which the option is "shared" with competitors. This situation arises, for example, when multiple bidders make an offer on a publicly traded firm or when the target is offered at an auction. It is the interaction among competitors that makes strategic investment decisions different from other types of decisions. Historically, it has been very difficult for financial buyers to compete for high-quality companies when there are a large number of strategic buyers in the marketplace. However, recently we have seen financial buyers competing with strategic buyers on some transactions. The competitive aspect of shared options makes it difficult for strategic and financial buyers to avoid paying for at least part of the synergies. An important step in understanding the ability of the firm to appropriate the potential value creation is to distinguish between drivers of value that are idiosyncratic to the firm and those that competitive bidders in the marketplace also possess. To create value requires that the firm possesses unique resources and capabilities that make it impossible for competitors to duplicate the value-creating strategy of the firm.

Game theory can also help provide a useful road map, helping buyers to evaluate the likely competitive responses and their impact on the acquisition strategy. For instance, in 1999, Hicks, Muse, Tate & Furst acquired Hillsdown, the British foods and furniture conglomerate. In the battle for Hillsdown, Hicks outbid a British venture capital firm, Candover Investments. Both players' bids represented substantial premiums above the prevailing market price. Hicks, Muse, Tate & Furst made an initial bid of 127 pence per share and subsequently raised its offer to 147 pence to acquire control of the company. The investor justified this high price on the basis that it provided a platform for developing the food business in Europe. This transaction is an example of a *shared compound* option. In such a bidding context, the investment opportunity is shared forcing bidders to take competitors into account, and ultimately to pay for at least a portion of the synergies that a competitor could have realized. The investment is also a compound option insofar as it can be viewed as a first step on a path of synergistic deals — an option whose value depends on uncertain market developments, consolidation strategies, and synergistic opportunities of other players.

8.3.2. Growth Option Value in a Buy-and-Build Strategy

In a buy-and-build strategy, the investor acts as an industry consolidator with the aim of transforming several smaller companies into an efficient large-scale network. The initial platform acquisition generates options for further acquisitions. Additional value can be created through the consolidation of synergistic acquisitions as operations become integrated, cost efficiencies are realized, and market share increases. Financial buyers then have several exit strategies available, including sale to a strategic buyer or a larger financial buyer, or an initial public offering. One of many buy-and-build examples is the acquisition of DuPont's connector systems unit (later renamed Berg Electronics) by Hicks, Muse, Tate & Furst in 1993. The buy-and-build strategy included seven follow-on acquisitions, whereby Berg improved its efficiency in marketing and distribution. In 1996 Berg went public and was eventually acquired by Framatome in 1998, providing a generous return to its shareholders.

The platform acquisition target should be a respected company to provide a secure foothold for future growth opportunities and to generate a compound growth option value. It should preferably have a leadership role in quality or service, or some other characteristic differentiating its production process or product, which can be successfully leveraged onto further acquisitions. In a bidding situation, the acquisition of a good platform company may require a substantial premium, and the deal can appear to have a low NPV based on expected cash inflows considered in isolation. For instance, the 1999 acquisition of Hillsdown required a substantial premium over its market value. The value of an acquisition critically depends on the strategic plans of the buyer and may have significant strategic value when considered as a first step in a series of investments. The value of a target to a buy-and-build investor can be significantly different from its value trading in the financial markets on a stand-alone basis. The synergistic opportunities of the investment, and the premium that must be paid to acquire the target company, are significant components of value and should be incorporated in the valuation analysis.

In this view, an individual acquisition is a component of a strategic investment plan. Its value should thus be based on the expanded NPV criterion. This starts with the stand-alone value and takes into account not only *potential* synergistic effects but also management's flexibility to alter planned investment decisions as future market conditions change, as well as the strategic impact of competitive interactions:

Expanded NPV = (stand-alone value of platform − price) +
value of future (shared) synergistic opportunities.　　　　　　(8.1)

To determine the value of an acquisition requires first estimating its stand-alone value. Next, a real-options analysis can help assess the value of any synergistic opportunities, arising mainly from the flexibility to adapt the strategy when market conditions turn out differently than expected. Finally, principles of game theory can be used to assess the likely effect of competitors' responses on the eventual value of the acquisition. For instance, there can be value erosion in a shared compound option if other buyers bid up the price or if the industry responds by expanding capacity and reducing market power.

Stand-Alone Value

The stand-alone value can be estimated directly or indirectly. A direct approach is to use the market value before any merger negotiations. The indirect method involves first estimating the total company value by discounting the net free cash inflows of the company at the weighted average cost of capital (after taxes) and then subtracting the (market) value of debt to arrive at the value of the equity. This value can be subjected to a "reality test" using competitor earnings multiples.

Added Value of Synergistic Opportunities

The consolidation strategy is based in part on cost advantages that can be gained when one entity can support profitable activities less expensively in combination than separately. One of the key drivers of synergistic value in a buy-and-build strategy is building size in a fragmented market. Highly fragmented markets with no dominant players are ripe for consolidation. Through resulting economies of scale, the consolidation strategy aims at market share leadership, with investment timing and pricing policies that enable the firm to create facilities of efficient scale. In sectors with economies of scope, important competencies or technologies cut across geographic boundaries. These cost advantages can result from producing and selling multiple products related by a common technology, product facilities, or network. Another source of value is the contribution of the private equity investor, who provides strategic input regarding acquisitions, financing, and exit.

Having entrusted these functions to the investor, the target company's management can focus on growth, integration, and improving margins. The elusive value of synergistic opportunities requires an estimate of the cost efficiencies gained through consolidation of the sector based on a relative analysis of profitability, market position, and size. The *average synergistic effect* is measured by the ratio of the acquisition value to the buyer to the acquisition price (or to the acquisition value considered in isolation when ignoring any competitive bidding effects). For instance, suppose that the potential *available acquisitions* have a present value of €750 million, which could be increased by 10% as a result of cost and marketing efficiencies following the platform acquisition. The average synergistic effect is then 1.10, and the added value of synergistic opportunities is as follows:

Expected value of synergies = (average synergistic effect − 1) × PV
of available acquisitions
= (1.10 − 1) × 750
= 75 million.

The above analysis is based on expected synergies assuming the firm is committed to a predetermined path of future follow-on acquisitions. However, the future synergistic benefits, just like future demand in the industry, are highly uncertain, requiring flexibility or the option to adapt the strategy if the path evolves differently than expected. As mentioned earlier, the opportunity to acquire the target is like an exchange option on the buyer's future value (with exercise price equal to the acquisition price). The acquisition can also be seen as providing a call option on the average synergistic effect (the ratio of the buyer's value to the acquisition

FIGURE 8.5 STAGED DECISIONS FOR A BUY-AND-BUILD STRATEGY

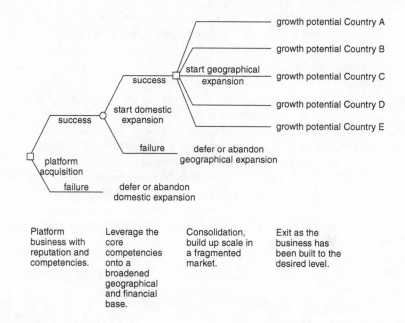

price) with a time to maturity equal to the horizon of the buildup, and with exercise price calibrated to one.[9] A firm will continue to consolidate as long as the net synergies of the acquisition at that time are sufficiently valuable (synergistic effect greater than one). However, if sector developments turn out worse than expected, the net synergistic value would be zero as management can decide not to build up.

To assess the flexibility value we have to *look forward* to how the industry might evolve and then *reason back* to when follow-on acquisitions are undertaken. This is analogous to the backward induction principle of option valuation discussed in chapter 3. The value dynamics of the synergistic effect can be modeled with a binomial tree over the life of the option. At each branch we would assess the synergistic effect (ratio of buyer value to acquisition price) according to favorable or unfavorable developments in the sector. Starting at the end of the tree and working backwards, the option tree would assign values to outcomes such as undertaking the acquisition immediately, waiting to see how the market evolves, or forgoing any follow-on acquisitions. With a backward induction process the estimated option effect would be higher than the

---

[9]The exercise price is equal to 1, while the "dividend yield" is the yield on the buyer value and the "interest rate" is the yield on the price.

net synergistic effect (which is 10% in our example) since it accounts for flexibility.

A compound option valuation is more complex in that it may involve a collection of interacting sequential options. Further follow-on acquisitions in several geographical locations could increase cash flows as a result of cost and marketing efficiencies. Figure 8.5 presents a simplified structure of the value of future synergistic opportunities. Future follow-on acquisitions can be undertaken (i.e., options can be exercised) after market indications are received as to the likely potential speed of consolidation and as uncertainty about the success of the buildup strategy is resolved over time. Starting from the potential acquisition opportunities of each country shown on the right of figure 8.5, the investor can estimate the value of the options portfolio in the consolidation. Suppose that this procedure of working backward results in a value of future synergistic opportunities of €125 million. The net synergistic effect of the potential acquisitions was 10% (in our earlier example), which when applied to the available acquisition pool of €750 million (ignoring any competitive interaction effects) result in an expected value of synergistic opportunities of €75 million. The additional flexibility value therefore equals €125 − €75 = €50 million.

Suppose that the expected yearly incremental operating cash inflows of the platform, discounted at the weighted average cost of capital, are worth €450 million, and that the price of acquiring the platform is €500 million. The expanded NPV of the strategy would be calculated as follows:

Expanded NPV = (platform value considered in isolation − price)
+ expected value of synergies + flexibility value
= (450 − 500) + 75 + 50
= 75 million.   (8.1)

8.3.3. Competition in a Buy-and-Build Strategy

When competing firms can affect each other's behavior, it is useful to expand the valuation analysis using game theory. In an integrated options and games treatment, the synergistic option value at the end of each branch in the binomial option tree equals the equilibrium outcome of a simultaneous investment subgame. Each subgame provides the possible payoffs to each firm.[10] This can involve a zero-sum game (when two firms face a shared investment opportunity) in which the value for the players

---

[10]In solving the overall game, the valuation process uses game theory analysis and moves backward over random moves using binomial spanning, resulting in a subgame-perfect equilibrium. In this sense the model marries strategic IO analysis with option pricing as in chapters 5 and 6.

of the game is in strict conflict — that is, the gain of one player is the other player's loss. Alternatively, there may be opportunities for cooperation among firms that can increase the total market. On the other hand, more extreme (intense) forms of competition can end up shrinking the players' share of the total economic pie.

The Bidding Game

Buy-and-build investors do not like to admit that they pay a premium for synergies. However, the competitive forces of shared opportunities make it difficult for the buy-and-build investor to undertake acquisitions without paying for at least some of the synergies. Indeed, in most industries we typically see firms paying a premium to acquire a target. Consider a situation in which two firms engage in a bidding contest for a follow-on acquisition. In the classic bidding contest between two equally dominant players, competitive pressure to acquire the target induces the two firms to bid and pay a premium, "killing" (at least in part) the synergistic option value. When two firms enter into the bidding contest simultaneously and their synergistic effects are equal, they might be forced to pay a premium equal to the total synergistic value in order to capture the target opportunity. In case of a *proprietary investment opportunity*, on the other hand, a single bidding buyer can capture the value of the synergy option without having to pay a premium at all. Obviously, there is a range of intermediate possibilities between these two extremes.

Of course, in reality the players will not likely be exactly "symmetric"; one of them will have a stronger market position. The organizational capabilities and bundles of corporate real options, like uncertainty itself, will be different for each firm. As a result, the value of a platform acquisition may be different for each buyer, depending on the firm's other resources and assets. Exercising the option to expand, for instance, is going to be more valuable for a consolidator than for another player when the consolidated firm is a market leader by virtue of its size, earlier acquisitions, and complementary assets.[11]

A bidding game in an acquisition can arise when various bidders assign different values than the market currently does. In the battle for Hillsdown, as we have mentioned, Hicks, Muse, Tate & Furst outbid Candover Investments. Both players' bids exceeded the prevailing market price. The value to Candover, backing a management buyout team,

---

[11]In some cases companies may learn about their competencies by undertaking investments, so that an acquisition may be even more valuable (hence command a higher price) in the case of a less well-established firm with potentially more to learn. See Bernardo and Chowdhry 2002.

FIGURE 8.6 TIMING STRATEGIES OF FOLLOW-ON INVESTMENTS UNDER
ASYMMETRIC COMPETITION

NPV FROM IMMEDIATE INVESTMENT

	Low NPV	*High NPV*
Dominant	Low commitment value and high flexibility value favor postponement [i] No threat of preemption	High commitment value and low flexibility value favor early investment [ii] No threat of preemption Position increases the ability to acquire market share
Weak	Low value enhances deferment until the market develops sufficiently [iii] Threat of complete preemption	Early investment to prevent erosion of value [iv] Risk of preemption, NPV might become negative

MARKET POSITION OF CONSOLIDATED FIRM (row labels: Dominant / Weak)

Source: Smit and Ankum 1993.

stemmed in part from the commitment of management. Hicks viewed
Hillsdown as a platform to develop the food business in Europe.

Preemption Value of Investment Timing Strategies

As noted, contrary to options theory, game theory shows that it is not always preferable to "keep options open." Sometimes a player can seize a
first-mover advantage by making an early preemptive investment commitment (i.e., exercising the option "prematurely"). Recognizing this
trade-off allows us to shed light on — and in some cases even quantify —
the value of a first-mover competitive advantage, depending upon the
quality and market power of the platform and the generic or proprietary
nature of the opportunity. In many industry contexts the synergies are
sometimes based on a timing advantage. A firm or an alliance that can
consolidate first can enjoy a significant cost advantage. In addition, the
quality of a firm's products and its organizational resources and capabilities are often distinctive (if not unique) assets — assets that can prove to
be a source of comparative advantage in the strategic exercise of the
firm's acquisition buildup options. The factors affecting growth options
may also be different for each firm, generating significant differences in
exercise and timing behavior. For example, a firm with less acquisition

buildup variability or a lower investment cost — or one that anticipates earlier competitive entry — is likely to exercise its options early.

When competitors' relative market power and asset base differs, their investment timing strategies are likely to differ as well, as shown in figure 8.6.[12] In cases where expansion opportunities have relatively low net present value from immediate investment but are characterized by high uncertainty and relatively larger flexibility (option) value, the most valuable strategy is likely to be postponement. If the consolidated company has established a dominant position in its industry, there is little threat of preemption by a competitor. The company can safely postpone the investment and decide to invest later if the market develops favorably, or if the weaker competitor invests first. On the other hand, follow-on projects with a relatively high net present value (from immediate investment) will likely have a high opportunity cost of deferment (in the form of either missed cash inflows during the deferment period or potential competitive damage), inducing a dominant firm to invest early. If the consolidated company has a weak position in the market relative to its competitors, however, undertaking the follow-on projects immediately will not likely sustain a large net present value (due to competitive vulnerability). Only later, if the market develops sufficiently, will it be appealing to make the next investment. If the firm has a weak market position and the investment appears to have a positive net present value, the company may consider expanding immediately if early investment can preempt competition or help create a sustainable cost advantage. However, because of its weak position, the firm must be mindful that a stronger competitor might come in and erode its investment value.

Reaction Value of Tough versus Accommodating Strategies

In a buildup, the company must decide if it should expand through internal organic growth or through acquisitions. This decision could have a different market response and reaction value. As noted, a key factor in determining an appropriate competitive growth strategy is whether it involves the firm taking a tough stance toward competition (in the sense of increasing market share at the expense of its competitors) or an accommodating stance (if the resulting value creation can be shared with and benefit its rivals).[13] A second important factor is how the competitor is expected to react to such a tough or accommodating stance. This may depend on industry characteristics, specifically on whether competitive

[12]A numerical real-options and games model for competitive investment timing can be found in Smit and Ankum 1993.
[13]This discussion of reciprocating and contrarian competitive reactions is based on the framework of chapters 4 and 6.

FIGURE 8.7 DIFFERENT COMPETITIVE STRATEGIES FOLLOWING
"BUY" OR "BUILD" EXPANSION IN A VALUE-ENHANCEMENT OR
VALUE-PREEMPTION GAME

COMPETITION

	Contrarian Value-preemption game e.g., Quantity competition	Reciprocating Joint value enhancement e.g., Price competition
Tough Build: Growth by organic expansion and hurt competition	i Invest early to preempt favorable investment opportunities (win-lose)	ii Don't invest / wait since capacity expansion creates a tough position and can trigger a reciprocating reaction and price war (lose-lose)
Accommodating Buy: Growth through acquisitions and benefit competition	iii Don't invest / wait if competitors can take advantage of the consolidation strategy (lose-win)	iv Firms can increase the total size of the pie if they are accommodating to each other, jointly exploiting the synergetic effects of the consolidated firm (win-win)

GROWTH STRATEGY (label to the left, between the Tough and Accommodating rows)

actions tend to be reciprocating or contrarian — that is, whether the competitors' reactions are similar (playing fair when treated fairly) or opposite (taking advantage of the other's accommodating stance). In chapters
5 and 6 we distinguished various competitive investment strategies according to the competitive stance (tough or accommodating) and the nature of the competitive reaction (reciprocating or contrarian).

Figure 8.7 recaps the four different competitive strategies in the context of an acquisitions buildup. When overall growth in the market is
limited, growth by a particular firm is possible only by taking business
away from competitors (tough stance) or by making acquisitions that
jointly exploit economies of scale (accommodating). In this context, a
firm can increase the total size of the economic pie only if it "accommo-
dates" its competitors through acquisitions that more fully utilize the
benefits and cost efficiencies of cooperation in a consolidated entity. By
contrast, the pie can shrink if a firm plays tough by pursuing an organic
growth strategy that would be perceived as a threat to its competitors'
market share, thereby inviting retaliation and defensive reactions. In mature industries, in particular, this could result in intensified price competition or a "war of attrition" for larger market shares (a lose-lose situation).
When facing the risk of intense competition, strategic acquisitions seem

to be the preferred route since they accomplish synergies expressed through a quick increase in market share while minimizing the potential for price wars within the sector (win-win).

The competitive landscape may be different in times of higher growth, when there is greater opportunity for profitable capacity expansion. In these conditions, the industry investment opportunities faced by competitors give rise to what might be viewed as a value-capture game. With higher industry growth, organic capacity expansion by one firm is less likely to take place at the expense of a competitor's existing capacity, thus limiting the risk of intensified competition. The optimal route in these circumstances can be to seize an advantage by taking the initiative. An aggressive buildup strategy can generate a first-mover advantage, with the first-moving firm taking a tough position. If the competition retreats, the expanding firm can gain market share and become an industry leader as the sector grows. The total strategic value of a buy-and-build platform may thus consist of a *strategic preemption value* from timing investment opportunities versus other players and a *strategic reaction value* reflecting the impact of the market's response on profits.[14]

Revisiting our earlier simple example, suppose that the consolidating firm seizes the initiative in a fragmented and growing market and moves before any of its competitors with an early and aggressive acquisition and organic growth program. Suppose that exercising the options "prematurely" erodes flexibility value. Other consolidators observe this strategy and may choose to stay out altogether or enter later. Suppose that this *strategic preemption value* is estimated at €60 million, while incumbents would expand capacity at a reduced scale to avoid a market-share battle, generating a *strategic reaction value* of €25 million (based on an estimation of incremental profits compared to a base-case sequential strategy). The expanded NPV with the additional strategic value component would then be calculated as follows:

Expanded NPV = (stand-alone value of platform − price)
+ (expected value of synergistic opportunities + flexibility value)
+ strategic value   (8.7)
= (450 − 500) + (75 + 0) + (60 + 25)
= 110 million.

By reducing the likelihood of competitive intrusion, the strategic (commitment) value of €85 million more than offsets the loss in flexibility value of €50 million in the sequential strategy.

[14]A numerical analysis of different components of value where the investment decisions interact with the production or pricing decisions was presented in chapters 6 and 7.

In summary, this section has described a framework for applying real options and games to acquisitions strategy planning and valuation. Although the approach can be used in pricing all kinds of strategic corporate acquisitions, it was discussed with particular relevance to the case of a buy-and-build strategy. Such a strategy aims to achieve consolidation of a fragmented industry through a series of synergistic deals, complemented in some cases by organic growth. Options and games can be used in practice to *shape* the strategic thinking process. One advantage is the extent to which it is consistent with and reinforces the intuitive strategic logic underlying much buy-and-build investing. The valuation components of a strategy should also be consistent with the strategy's underlying logic and design. Perhaps this type of analysis might help us better understand the restructuring of fragmented markets as well as justify (part of) the substantial takeover premiums in certain acquisitions.

8.4. Infrastructure Investment: The Case of European Airport Expansion

Infrastructure provides a platform and creates the strategic context for a firm's growth opportunities to flourish. A firm's infrastructure investment, whether strengthening its core capabilities or accessing new geographical locations, sets the path for investments to follow. Thus, such investments shape the strategic position of the enterprise.

Although the nature of infrastructure investments depends on the business context, their defining characteristic is that they generate follow-on investment opportunities. For the firm, development of infrastructure can include investment in land, distribution, communication, human capital, or technology, any one or all of which help create the necessary platform for the growth potential of the firm. Such growth opportunities are often contingent on follow-on investments and can therefore be seen as a bundle of real options. Few of such investment opportunities, whether they are capacity expansions or network investments, exist in a vacuum. By integrating real-options valuation with game theory principles, we can make a more complete assessment of the strategic growth option value in an interactive competitive setting.

Although infrastructure investment is an area of general interest, its valuation is not well understood. Here, we examine infrastructure as an option game in which infrastructure generates a strategic position in the industry in a capacity expansion game. A new element in the analysis is the valuation of sequential expansion subgames by a firm instead of a focus on a single project. Capacity expansion is not a one-time opportunity, but a repeated game where "lumpy" expansion investments are made as uncertainty gets resolved over time. The valuation of a firm's growth opportunities (PVGO) herein is estimated as the sum of the outcomes of repeated expansion subgames along an equilibrium path in the overall game. We focus on European airport expansion, taking a detailed look at a specific application while validating our more general option games approach.[15]

For simplicity and accessibility, we present this application of a sequential exercise game in discrete time.[16] We explain developments in the European airport industry by considering the infrastructure of each airport as a firm-specific asset (platform) that generates a set of sequential expansion options in a context of competitive responses and changing market conditions. However, limited overall growth or local growth restrictions might foreclose exercising certain expansion options. When local growth becomes restricted for large airports, growth is still possible by investment in regional airports or international strategic network acquisitions that can create value by jointly exploiting economies of scale or other competencies.

Our discussion is organized as follows. Section 8.4.1 describes infrastructure investment and developments in European aviation. Section 8.4.2 presents the valuation approach for infrastructure investment strategies. Section 8.4.3 discusses an implementation for expansion of Schiphol airport. The last section summarizes the insights gained and discusses relevant implications.

8.4.1. INFRASTRUCTURE INVESTMENT AND AVIATION DEVELOPMENTS

To understand the growth and strategic option value of infrastructure investment, we must again consider the investor's ability to appropriate the value of growth opportunities. By nature, benefits that result from infrastructure are dispersed across divisions and potentially external players. For instance, there are corporate, network, and regional benefits associated with infrastructure. Corporate growth opportunities result from the fact that infrastructure is a firm-specific asset, in the sense that it can create an

---

[15]Although our approach is applied here to a specific case, it can be generalized to infrastructure investments in the context of other industries. For instance, it can be applied in the context of corporate infrastructure, platform, or R & D investments in volatile high-tech industries, such as information technology, electronics, and pharmaceuticals.

[16]For this kind of applied option games, more complex continuous-time models would not necessarily add significantly to the accuracy of valuation results. Such models might lose other important features of a discrete-time approach, such as the accessibility of the valuation methodology, tractability of values in the model, and the modularity to embed the many strategic features necessary for a realistic setting.

advantaged strategic position to expand. Examples of infrastructure investment with corporate benefits are projects in physical infrastructure, such as distribution, service, information technology, communication, and transportation systems; human capital infrastructure; and social infrastructure. In short, infrastructure can be viewed as a platform for creating future growth for the enterprise.[17]

Other infrastructure investments may require a network or alliance to develop shared opportunities. For instance, transport and distribution operations can gain cost efficiencies with more efficient network connections between firms. The same is true in high-tech industries, where alliances often make value-increasing "preinvestments" to develop and position a common technology standard. Investment infrastructure in new markets and network investments among firms cannot be considered in isolation. Firms must seek out opportunities to complete the investments collaboratively and utilize complementary competencies. Network infrastructure investment, for instance, can be particularly important when innovation entails novel connections between previously unconnected industries, markets, or technologies.

In addition to corporate or network opportunities, infrastructure investments can further promote or induce growth in a region. Infrastructure investments that generate regional benefits include investments in marine ports, airports, railroads, or electricity networks that further promote growth opportunities in the area. Governments play a key role here, both because they make the regulations and often because they provide the infrastructure. A part of the growth option value of these investments does not flow to the investor but is shared with other players in the region where the investment is made.

Airport infrastructure investments may generate corporate as well as network and regional growth opportunities. Many airport investments, such as runways or terminals, are large and lumpy so that investment decisions require an important trade-off between the values of flexibility and precommitment. For example, in providing a rationale for its capacity expansion with the proposed Terminal 5, Heathrow (London) alludes to the competitive interaction (commitment value) associated with their corporate and regional growth opportunities: "Without a fifth terminal (Terminal 5) at Heathrow, the world's busiest international airport, many travelers will be forced to use rival continental airports to connect between flights. Transfers account for a third of Heathrow's business, and losing this could have a damaging effect not only on BAA [British Airports Authority], but also on the national and local economies. If airlines

---

[17]See Kulatilaka, Balasubramanian, and Stork 1996 for the analysis of IT infrastructure investments.

are denied the opportunity to grow at Heathrow many of them will choose Paris, Frankfurt or Amsterdam to expand their business — not other UK airports" (Terminal 5 BAA, 1999).

Our framework focuses on the associated corporate and network benefits of airport infrastructure to analyze the implications for the development of the European aviation industry structure. Infrastructure is idiosyncratic for each airport and growth opportunities arise from the interplay of infrastructure, uncertain development of demand, and environmental restrictions. Several new developments in aviation have affected the positions and expansion strategies of European airports, and will continue to do so in the coming decades, necessitating a new, more dynamic approach to long-term planning.

First, increasing passenger demand has resulted in global growth in aviation. The number of flights within Europe is expected to continue to grow during the coming decades despite the development of new and efficient transportation alternatives, such as the expansion of the TGV (Train à Grande Vitesse, or high-speed train) network and the channel tunnel.

Second, a small number of European mainports (as the main airports are called) and many smaller airports characterize the industry structure. Airports face significant uncertainty in demand growth due to changes in the overall economy and potential alliances of their home carriers. An unexpected decline in the level of growth could motivate airports to defer their expansion plans. Furthermore, blocking, which occurs when environmentalists create obstacles that can severely limit the profit stream from airport growth opportunities, can prevent some airports from further expansion.

Third, European airports are starting to form efficient, star-shaped, "hub and spoke" networks. These networks are expected to influence the relative competitive positions of European airports. A hub-and-spoke system in Europe would make it possible to increase the frequency and variety of destinations relative to the current "point-to-point" system. The advantage of this system is that a central or hub airport connects many spoke destinations, thus using capacity more efficiently. In such a star-shaped network, the central hub (often a mainport) functions as a pivot point. Numerous smaller airports at the end of the spokes feed the hubs. Demand could bring some airports prosperity, but others could face lower demand for intercontinental flights.

Fourth, there has been a strong tendency recently to deregulate aviation. Deregulation will create new connection opportunities, while increased competition will support efficiency and concentration. Low-seating-occupancy flights, high costs, and expansion of the network have already forced airline companies to cooperate so that they can better exploit

economies of scale and scope. At a global level, governments are liberal-
izing the rules for airlines and the frequency of their schedules, and guidelines for foreign companies within the European Union are becoming less
restrictive. The unification brought about through the European Mone-
tary Union (EMU) also strengthens this liberalization tendency, making it
possible for Europe to become a border-free area.

Fifth, governments in some countries are limiting their roles as airport
owners. Airport infrastructure is traditionally supported and regulated
by the government, since these investments are a prerequisite for the
growth in production and services in a country. Several European airports are still fully government-owned, e.g., Aéroports de Paris (ADP)
(which includes Orly and Roissy–Charles de Gaulle), while some airports
have plans to go public in the near future (e.g., Schiphol at Amsterdam).
Others, such as British Airports Authority (BAA) (includes the three London airports Heathrow, Gatwick, and Stanstead among others)[18] or Fraport
(Frankfurt), are already public companies. Whether the airport stock is
traded or not can affect the growth potential that is considered one of the
benefits of investment decisions.

Concentrated ownership of a government-owned airport imposes discipline. Further, the government's primary interest may be different than
the shareholders of traded airports. When the government is the major
shareholder of an airport, the induced and dispersed regional growth
could play a more important role in the airport's investment decisions.
The more restricted airports are forced to go public to seek international
growth through networks and cooperation. But when the airport is publicly traded, its shareholders play a "value maximizing game" and are
particularly interested in the corporate and international network growth
opportunities for the airport. In some cases, publicly traded shares could
avoid the regulations against joining with foreign airports. Such a development could contribute to increased network and cooperation benefits
in European aviation. For instance, government-owned Schiphol airport
imposes restrictions on mergers and stakes by other parties.

8.4.2. INFRASTRUCTURE VALUATION AS AN OPTIONS GAME

We subsequently value infrastructure investment by an airport in a competitive context as an options game. In the infrastructure investment options game below, we use a two-step procedure. We first trace the value
dynamics in a binomial event tree, without any of the expansion opportunities. Then we determine the "value added" of the infrastructure-
related expansion options (PVGO) in a competitive setting. The PVGO is

---

[18]In July 1987 British Airports Authority (BAA) was floated.

estimated as the present value of the expansion values of the subgames along the equilibrium growth path. As we shall see, the strategic position of the airport and its growth option value will depend on the infrastructure and the timing of the expansion investments under competition.

The Value of Assets in Place

We first determine the value of assets in place. We begin the analysis with a "catchment area," which is defined here as a "local market" for flights. For instance, nearby airports (airport A and airport B) can compete for local or transfer passengers in a certain area. Suppose a catchment area is characterized by a duopoly. Q_A and Q_B are the yearly demands (measured in flights) for airports A and B, respectively (with $Q_M = Q_A + Q_B$). Current demand for airport i (i = A or B) equals the current market share, $s_{i,0}$, times total demand: $Q_i = s_{i,0} Q_M$.[19]

To determine the value of assets in place, consider first the value dynamics event tree of airport i (i = A or B), $V_{i,t}$, without any of the expansion opportunities, government restrictions, or competitive interactions. The total operating cash flow, $TCF_{i,t}$, equals demand, $Q_{i,t}$, multiplied by the average operating cash flow per air transport movement, $CF_{i,t}$, that is $TCF_{i,t} = Q_{i,t} CF_{i,t}$. Demand ($Q_{i,t}$) is uncertain and is assumed to follow a binomial process. This results in a series of potential operating cash flows, $TCF_{i,s,t} = Q_{i,s,t} CF_{i,t}$. Using a binomial option framework, we first calculate the risk-neutral probability, p, from the tree values (of TCFs), without any of the options and competitive interactions:

$$p = \frac{(1 + r)TCF_t - TCF_{t+1}^-}{TCF_{t+1}^+ - TCF_{t+1}^-}. \tag{8.2}$$

Here, TCF_{t+1}^+ and TCF_{t+1}^- are the next-period total operating cash flows under uncertain demand in the up (+) or down (−) states, and r is the risk-free interest rate. The certainty-equivalent (CEQ) value can be calculated using these probabilities. The NPV and the certainty-equivalent valuation approaches result in the same valuation for the event tree (without options and competitive interactions). However, the use of certainty equivalents facilitates correct valuation in each branch (state) of the tree when expansion options and competitive interactions are also incorporated.[20]

---

[19]This can easily be adjusted in other applications. For instance, prices could be set according to the linear demand function: $P(Q, \theta_t) = \theta_t - (Q_A + Q_B)$, where θ_t is the demand shift parameter, P is the market price, and Q_i the production quantity of airport i (i = A, B).

[20]This is the traditional "as if traded" argument used for valuing real options as discussed in Mason and Merton 1985.

In the valuation of assets in place for the current infrastructure (without any of the expansion opportunities), most European airports face growth restrictions. The free cash flow in the base case is truncated due to full-capacity or environmental restrictions, Q_{max}.

$$Q_i = \text{Min } [Q_{max}, Q]. \tag{8.3}$$

At the end nodes (at time $= T$), the gross project value (without any competitive interactions or restrictions), $V_{i,T}$, is obtained assuming perpetual annual operating cash flows subsequently and a constant risk-adjusted discount rate, k_i, from

$$V_{i,T} = \frac{TCF_{i,T+1}}{k_i - g_{i,T}}, \tag{8.4}$$

where $V_{i,T}$ is the project value at the terminal time for airport i, k_i is the weighted average cost of capital for airport i, $g_{i,T}$ is the constant growth rate, and $TCF_{i,T+1}$ is the total operating cash flow at time $T + 1$. We need to estimate the opportunity cost of capital only at the last stage. In the backward valuation, we can then consistently discount the resulting certainty-equivalent values at the risk-free rate, r. When stepping backward in time to the current state, we calculate the value by taking the expectation of the future up and down states using the risk-neutral probabilities, p, that is, $(pV^+ + (1 - p)V^-)/(1 + r)^{\Delta t}$, and summing (the present value of) these expected net total cash inflows for the period in-between the nodes.

Competitive Equilibrium Expansion (PVGO)

Suppose that investment in such a bundle of development opportunities creates additional capacity $\Delta Q_{i,t}$, measured in flights per year. The cash-flow value of additional expansion, $\Delta V_{i,t}$, is the present value of the total cash flow ($\Delta TCF_{i,t}$) from the incremental expansion capacity. This additional capacity $\Delta Q_{i,t}$ can be temporarily underutilized until demand has grown sufficiently. In standard real-options theory, the option to expand would be analogous to a call option, C_i, on this added cash-flow value ΔV_i. The exercise price would be equal to the extra investment outlay, I_i, required to build additional capacity. In each period, management has an option to invest to expand capacity (I) if demand is high or defer investment (D) if demand is low. This results in a (nonlinear) payoff: $C_i = \text{Max } [\Delta V_i - I_i, 0]$. However, in an option-game valuation, the incremental value of a lumpy (or indivisible) expansion investment $\Delta V_i - I_i$ involves competitive interactions, introducing a discontinuity in this nonlinear option payoff.

We simplify the analysis by ignoring situations in which there are more than two rivals. Figure 8.8 shows a (two-period) example of the repeated expansion game in extensive form. The two airports play a repeated expansion game, where in each period they may expand simultaneously by making a lumpy investment. Either of the two competing airports (A or B) can invest (I) in subsequent capacity (building on the opportunities generated by their infrastructure investment), or defer investment (D). The alternative actions by each airport i (i = A, B) to make the expansion investment or to defer (D) are shown by squares ($\square$) along the tree branches in figure 8.8.

Consider the resulting total value creation (expanded NPV) of an expansion opportunity, $C_{Q_{i,t}}$, at the end of each tree branch in the subgame of figure 8.9, under the four investment-timing scenarios: (1) when both airports invest simultaneously (N), sharing the additional aircraft traffic, ΔQ_N, resulting in an equal payoff for capacity expansion for each firm in a symmetrical game ($C_N = \Delta V_N - I$). (2)/(3) when one airport (A or B) invests first and the other waits, with the first mover (L) preempting the market growth in flights from its competitor. The value creation for the leader equals $C_i = \Delta V_{iL} - I_i$, whereas the value of waiting/not investing equals 0; (4) when both airports decide not to invest in a period (A), with the value created in that period being zero.

In figure 8.9 circles ($\bigcirc$) show the resolution of market demand (traffic) uncertainty in this two-period example. After the first expansion game, demand (Q_i) moves again, and the game is repeated.[21] The solution concept for predicting player behavior invokes finding the optimal decisions in each subgame. For each subgame, we can first identify pure dominant strategies, that is, those actions that always give a higher payoff to a player than any other action, whatever the other player does. In a Nash equilibrium in pure strategies, neither firm can improve by making a unilateral move. The investment opportunity value at the end of each branch in the binomial option tree would equal the Nash equilibrium outcome of a simultaneous investment subgame.

Backward induction using these subgames results in a subgame perfect equilibrium trajectory. In solving for equilibriums in the overall (super)game, the valuation process of the strategic choices uses standard game theory analysis. The process moves backward over random demand moves, using the associated risk-neutral probabilities to calculate values at the beginning of each branch. The expansion option value in equilibrium for airport i at time t ($PVGO_{i,t}$) is calculated by adding to the expectation of the following period's growth value (using risk-neutral

---

[21]Earlier decisions to expand can affect the value in the second expansion subgame. Although figure 8.8 presents a two-period example, the tree can be expanded in a multiperiod setting to include more periods and nodes, thus increasing the complexity and accuracy of the model.

FIGURE 8.8 TWO-PERIOD EXAMPLE OF THE EXPANSION GAME
(IN EXTENSIVE FORM)

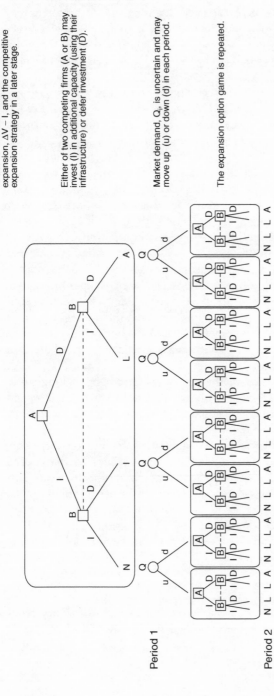

An upfront strategic infrastructure investment K affects the value of expansion, ΔV – I, and the competitive expansion strategy in a later stage.

Either of two competing firms (A or B) may invest (I) in additional capacity (using their infrastructure) or defer investment (D).

Market demand, Q, is uncertain and may move up (u) or down (d) in each period.

The expansion option game is repeated.

Period 1

Period 2

The firm may gain an advantageous strategic position as a result of a better infrastructure (or create such a position by making a strategic infrastructure investment K). The market structure is assumed to result in a duopoly, where either of two competing firms (A or B) may invest (I) in additional capacity (using their infrastructure) or defer investment (D). The incremental value of an additional lumpy unit of capacity, $\Delta V - I$, depends on the development of demand (Q_i) (u or d) and the investment decision in the previous period by the firm and its competitor (D or I). Starting at the terminal nodes, the valuation works backwards in time to the top, summing the state value creation and taking expectations over the future growth option values.

The value of the investment opportunity, C, in each "state of the world," is the outcome of an investment subgame:

Simultaneous expansion, N. If both firms decide to invest in expansion (I) in the same period (simultaneously), the value creation of the expansion for firm A or B equals $C = \Delta V_N - I$

Sequential expansion, L. If one firm invests first in an expansion project and its competitor invests in a later period, the value of the expansion for the leader equals $C = \Delta V_L - I$ (with $\Delta V_L > \Delta V_N$); the value for the follower at that state equals 0.

Do Not Invest/Defer (D) or Abandon (A). Management has the option not to invest or to wait if market demand (Q_i) is low and undertaking the project would result in a negative value. The value C equals 0.

probabilities) the cash-flow value creation at the current expansion sub-game, $C_{i,t}$:

$$PVGO_{i,t} = \text{Max}\left[0, \frac{pC^+_{i,t+1} + (1 - p)C^-_{i,t+1}}{(1 + r)^{\Delta T}}\right] + C_{i,t}. \qquad (8.5)$$

Numerical Example of Valuing Growth Opportunities (PVGO)

To illustrate the valuation of growth opportunities, consider the example of a two-staged game in figure 8.9. The growth opportunities (PVGO) comprise of local expansion (in stage 1) and further geographical growth (in stage 2). We assume that competitors have the same relative competitive position. Either airport A or airport B can invest in sequential capacity expansion depending on subsequent random demand moves.[22]

The first expansion subgame of figure 8.9 involves local expansion. The additional value of this incremental capacity, C_A or C_B, depends on the timing of capacity installation by the airport relative to its competitor resulting in C_N = €400 million, C_L = €580 million, C_F = €241 million and C_D = €421 million. The optimal competitive strategies are derived by utilizing the project payoff values. For example, in the subgame of the first stage of figure 8.9, each airport has a dominating strategy to invest in production capacity (I) regardless of the other's actions (for each airport 580 > 421 if the competitor defers and 400 > 241 if it invests), resulting in a (symmetric) Nash equilibrium outcome of a €400 million incremental value of expansion for the airport.

When facing growth restrictions in future periods, the option of further investment at complementary regional or international airports becomes more significant. Although harder to estimate, the incremental values of international expansion shown in the two boxes of figure 8.9 can be derived similarly. Note that if $Q = u$ (left box), each airport has a dominating strategy to invest in production capacity (I) regardless of the other's actions (for each airport 700 > 450 if the competitor defers and 425 > 250 if it invests), resulting in a symmetric Nash equilibrium outcome of (425, 425). The other subgames can be solved similarly. For $\theta = d$

---

[22]In this setting we assume that the players know or have complete information about the competitor's investment. In many applications this may not be the case. The analysis can be extended to the case in which there is uncertainty about the type of competition and the payoff. An important aspect of sequential games with incomplete information is that firms can extract information from their opponents' prior moves, resulting in a Bayesian equilibrium. Firms may have learned in a competitive (game) setting, while the resolution of uncertainty itself may involve learning.

FIGURE 8.9 NUMERICAL EXAMPLE OF THE
TWO-PERIOD EXPANSION GAME

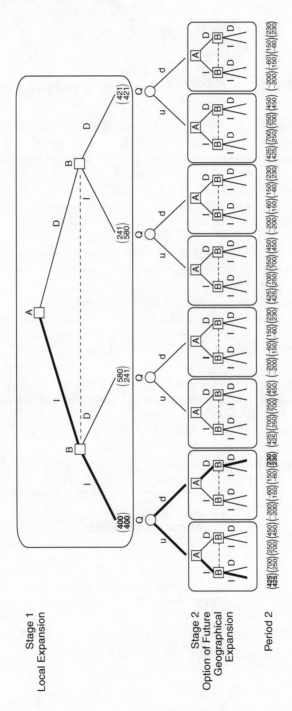

FIGURE 8.9 *continued*

Local Expansion: the value creation of the expansion for firm A or B equals

$$C = \Delta V_N - I = \frac{\Delta Q_N CF}{k - g} - I = \frac{75.000 \times 600}{0.08 - 0.03} - 500 \text{ million} = 400 \text{ million under simultaneous expansion}$$

$$C = \Delta V_L - I = \frac{\Delta Q_L CF}{k - g} - I = \frac{90.000 \times 600}{0.08 - 0.03} - 500 \text{ million} = 580 \text{ million under sequential expansion (leader)}$$

$$C = \frac{p(uV_F - I) + (1 - p)(dV_F - I)}{1 + r} = \frac{0.64(1.07 \times 720 - 500) + 0.36(1 \times 720 - 500)}{1 + r} = 241 \text{ million under sequential expansion (follower)}$$

$$C = \frac{p(uV_N - I) + (1 - p)(dV_N - I)}{1 + r} = \frac{0.64(1.07 \times 900 - 500) + 0.36(1 \times 900 - 500)}{1 + r} = 421 \text{ million when both defer}$$

Parameter Values (for airport A and B): $\Delta Q_N = 75.000$; $\Delta Q_L = 90.000$; $Q_F = 60.000$; $I = 500$ million; $CF = 600$; $k = 8\%$; $g = 3\%$; $r = 4.5\%$; $u = 1.07$; $d = 1$; $p = 0.64$.

Future Geographical Expansion: the value creation of the expansion equals

high demand (u)	low demand (d)
$C_N = \Delta V_N - I = 425$ million	$C_N = \Delta V_L - I = -200$ million
$C_L = \Delta V_N - I = 700$ million	$C_L = \Delta V_L - I = -60$ million
$C_F = 250$ million	$C_F = 150$ million
$C_D = 450$ million	$C_D = 230$ million

The value of the investment opportunity, in each state of the world, is the outcome of an investment subgame. Starting at the terminal nodes, the valuation works backwards in time to the top, summing the state value creation and taking expectations over the future growth option values. This results in

$$PVGO_A^* = 400 + \frac{0.64(425) + 0.36(230)}{1.045^4} = 697 \text{ million.}$$

(right box), however, both airports may choose to defer important decisions (or invest at lower scale) and obtain (230, 230) as growth option value.

The additional value of these growth opportunities depends on the development of demand and the timing of capacity installation by competition. The highlighted (bold) branches along each tree indicate the optimal actions along the equilibrium path. In this example local expansion will generate €400 million and further geographical growth opportunities may create additional value (equal to the expectation over 230 million and 425 million after four years). To estimate the present value of growth opportunities, PVGO, we sum the option value of the expansion subgames along the equilibrium path. Suppose that the implied risk-neutral probability, p, estimated from the event tree in values, equals 0.64 and the risk-free interest rate equals 4.5% per year (over the four years of stage 1). From the backward binomial risk-neutral valuation of equation 8.5, the expected equilibrium growth option value then equals

$$PVGO = \text{local expansion} + \text{option value of future geographical expansions}$$

$$PVGO_A^* = 400 + \frac{0.64(425) + 0.36(230)}{1.045^4} = \text{€}697 \text{ million.}$$

If the value of assets in place equals €2.6 billion, the breakdown of total value into the two components in a symmetrical game equals €2.6 billion + €697 million = €3.3 billion of total asset value.

Subgame Equilibrium Paths

The combined options and games analysis for the European airport expansion is shown in figure 8.10 for a three-period game in normal form. As noted, the investment opportunity value at the end of each branch in the binomial options tree now equals the equilibrium outcome of a simultaneous investment subgame. First, consider the symmetrical game, in which the airports have an equal strategic position to expand. The equilibriums in pure strategies of a symmetrical subgame appear in the left column of figure 8.10.

At paths with high demand, expansion investment has a positive expected payoff, regardless of the expansion strategy of the competitor. With a pure dominant strategy to invest, the payoff of airport A's expansion strategy (total lower row) exceeds its payoff from a regular investment strategy (total upper row), regardless of which strategy airport B chooses (left-hand "defer" column or right-hand "expansion" column). That is, $\Delta V_L - I_A > 0$ and $\Delta V_N - I_A > 0$. A Nash equilibrium in pure strategies for this investment rivalry subgame results in the lower right cell, with a value creation equal to $C_A = C_B = \Delta V_N - I_i$.

At low demand paths (e.g., following the path $S_1 \Rightarrow S_3 \Rightarrow S_6 \Rightarrow S_{10}$ in figure 8.10), expansion will result in a negative value regardless of the competitor's strategy. That is, $\Delta V_L - I_i < 0$ and $\Delta V_N - I_i < 0$, which may give management an incentive not to invest (with $C_A = C_B = 0$) or defer. The payoff from pursuing a regular strategy in the total upper row (and left-hand column for airport B) exceeds the airport's payoff from an expansion strategy in the total lower row (and right-hand column for airport B). A pure Nash equilibrium for this subgame results in the values in the upper left-hand cell, which show that both airports would follow a regular (defer) strategy with no value creation from expansion. An intermediate level of demand, however, cannot justify expansion in both airports. In this unpredictable zone a mixed equilibrium is used.

The value payoff in panel A of figure 8.11 confirms that the option subgame of investing in additional capacity, C, is a nonlinear function of the evolution of exogenous market demand and exhibits discontinuities due to competitive interactions. For very low and very high demand growth paths, the subgame has a Nash equilibrium in pure strategies. In low demand, no one builds, whereas for high levels of demand, everyone builds. Note that for intermediate-demand growth trajectories, lumpy investment means that there will be no Nash equilibriums in pure strategies.

As noted, infrastructure investment can modify the position of the enterprise and enhance the scale and value of the airport's growth opportunities.[23] Consider the case where airport A modifies its infrastruc-

---

[23]Recall that the (incremental) value of an asymmetrical equilibrium position where airport A has a modified infrastructure, compared to a symmetrical equilibrium position, involves two components: a direct effect on airport A's own expansion value, and a strategic effect resulting from the impact of airport A's strategic investment on competitor airport B's investment decision and its resulting indirect impact on airport A's profit value. An upfront infrastructure modification investment (K_A) can change the subgame values and the equilibrium strategies. The value of airport A's infrastructure depends on the impact of its incremental investment (dK_A) on its own value from operating profits of future potential expansion, i.e.,

$$\frac{dV_A}{dK_A} = \frac{\partial V_A}{\partial K_A} + \frac{\partial V_A}{\partial Q_B}\frac{dQ_B^*}{dK_A}$$

(commitment effect = direct effect + strategic effect)
where

K_A = upfront strategic infrastructure investment
$Q^*_i(K_A)$ = optimal (*) action of airport i in response to upfront strategic investment (K_A);
$V_i(\ )$ = present value of operating profits for airport i in a later stage of the game, given K_A and the optimal actions of both airports.

FIGURE 8.10 THE TWO-BY-TWO SIMULTANEOUS SUBGAME IN EACH
STATE AND THE NASH EQUILIBRIUMS FOR DIFFERENT DEMAND
REGIONS

**Panel A. Repeated Investment Subgame Embedded in a Dynamic
Option Analysis**

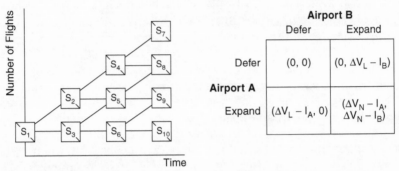

The investment opportunity value at the end of each branch in the binomial option tree
equals the Nash equilibrium outcome of a simultaneous investment subgame. Backward induction of the subgames results in a subgame perfect equilibrium.

ture resulting in a better competitive position vis-à-vis airport B. The equilibriums in pure strategies for the asymmetrical subgame appear in the
second column of figure 8.10. This modification will in turn alter the subgame-perfect equilibrium demand regions, particularly the intermediate
region of demand growth trajectories where the airport with the better
infrastructure would have the ability to preempt growth. In this intermediate demand region, airport A, which has a superior infrastructure, may
have a pure dominant expansion strategy—the lower row exceeds its
payoff from a wait-and-see strategy (upper row), regardless of the actions
of the competitor: $\Delta V_L - I_A > 0$ and $\Delta V_N - I_A > 0$. The NPV of the
competitor can turn negative, making it optimal for airport B to defer. A
new pure Nash equilibrium for this investment rivalry subgame results in
the lower left-hand cell, which shows that the airport with the better infrastructure absorbs growth with a value creation of $\Delta V_{AL} - I_A$ for airport
A and a value creation of zero for airport B.

Panel B of figure 8.11 illustrates the nonlinear value payoff of such an
asymmetrical option-game. For high levels of demand, the better-infra-
structure airport captures a greater market share than its competitor
does. At intermediate levels of demand, the leader may choose an early
preemptive action that would make it unprofitable for the follower to ex-

FIGURE 8.10 *continued*

Panel B. Subgame Equilibrium for Different Demand Trajectories

Trajectories of Demand	Symmetrical Game		Asymmetrical Capture Game	
	Payoff structure (for both)	Nash equilibrium	Payoff structure	Nash equilibrium
High	$\Delta V_L - I > 0$ and $\Delta V_N - I > 0$	Everyone builds	$\Delta V_L - I_i > 0$ and $\Delta V_N - I_i > 0$ for both	Everyone builds (better infrastructure allows to build faster)
Intermediate	$\Delta V_L - I > 0$ and $\Delta V_N - I < 0$	Disequilibrium	$\Delta V_L - I_i > 0$ and $\Delta V_N - I_i > 0$ while $\Delta V_N - I_i < 0$ for other	Better infrastructure preempts growth
Low	$\Delta V_L - I < 0$ and $\Delta V_N - I < 0$	No one builds	$\Delta V_L - I_i < 0$ and $\Delta V_N - I_i < 0$	No one builds

FIGURE 8.11 NONLINEAR PAYOFF OF EXPANSION OPTION COMPARED
TO EXOGENOUS DEMAND, ILLUSTRATING THE EQUILIBRIUM DEMAND
ZONES FOR THE SYMMETRICAL GAME (PANEL A) OR WHEN ONE
AIRPORT HAS A BETTER INFRASTRUCTURE (PANEL B)

Panel A. Payoff of Expansion in a Symmetrical Subgame (equal infrastructure)

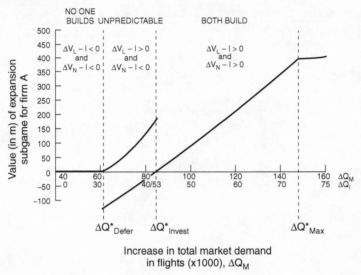

pand at high scale. For very low levels of demand, neither infrastructure
can make it profitable to build.

8.4.3. IMPLEMENTATION IN THE CASE OF SCHIPHOL AIRPORT

We next take a detailed look at a European airport expansion to high-
light important features of the approach. We consider the growth options
and restrictions that have been implemented at Schiphol Airport in the
Netherlands. The first section a shows the valuation results of assets in
place and growth options. In the next section, we present the strategy results involving an expansion game for airport growth. It illustrates a
growth strategy as an optimization of sequential modules of investment
under demand uncertainty and competitive interaction in which high-
growth paths trigger large-scale investment and network expansion. We
analyze the implications for the expansion of European airports and the
development of the European industry structure.

FIGURE 8.11 *continued*
**Panel B. Payoff of Expansion in an Asymmetrical Subgame
(airport A has a better infrastructure)**

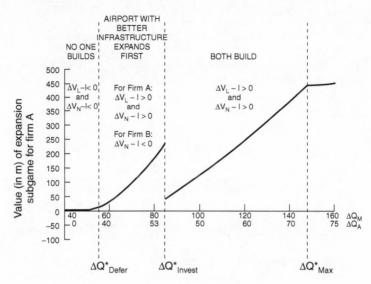

Increase in total market demand
in flights (x1000), ΔQ_M

Notes: Parameter values for panel A: $\Delta Q_N = \frac{1}{2}\Delta Q_M$; $\Delta Q_L = \frac{2}{3}\Delta Q_M$; $Q_F = \frac{1}{3}\Delta Q_M$; $\Delta Q_{max} = 75.000$; CF = 600; k = 8%; g = 3% (in CF); r = 4.5%; u = 1.07; d = 1; p = 0.64; $I_A = I_B = 500$ million. Parameter values for panel B: $I_A = 450$ million; $I_B = 500$ million.

Sensitivity of subgame equilibrium value, C, to demand shows an option-like payoff with competitive interactions. The symmetrical game shown in panel A has a Nash equilibrium in pure strategies at low demand (no one builds) and high demand (everyone builds). For intermediate growth trajectories, there is no Nash equilibrium in pure strategies. A maximum capacity restriction limits the upside potential. Panel B shows that differences in existing infrastructure and expansion opportunities change the relative strategic positions of the airports, causing the game to become asymmetrical. The airport with a better infrastructure can preempt growth at intermediate and high-growth trajectories.

Valuation Results

The horizon (end nodes) in the expansion game for airport growth is the year 2020. The analysis encompasses two phases: between years 2000 and 2020, industry experts believe that liberalization in the European aviation market will result in competitive capacity expansion. After 2020, "the hand will have been played" in Europe, and industry analysts expect that operational cash flows at Schiphol will grow at a constant (low) rate.

FIGURE 8.12 HYPOTHETICAL "STATES OF THE WORLD" AS NUMBER OF FLIGHTS
(IN THOUSANDS) FROM 2000 TO 2020 FOR SCHIPHOL AIRPORT (PANEL A) AND
ROLLBACK PROCEDURE FOR A FLEXIBLE EXPANSION STRATEGY (PANEL B)

Panel A. Extrapolation of Flights (including network expansion)

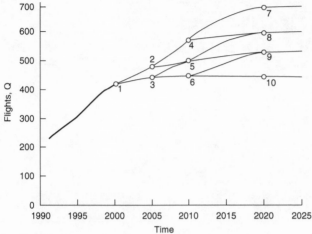

Panel B. Flexible Expansion Strategy

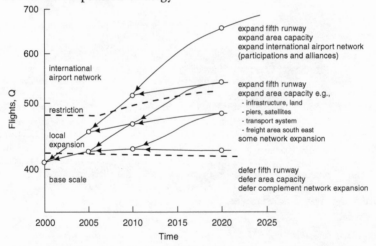

Notes: We use a binomial process for the valuation of flexible growth. The extrapolation of demand is a series of potential "states of the world" for Schiphol Airport until the year 2020, expressed in air transport movements (further divided in local and transfer passengers, and freight),
shown in panel A. After 2020, projections are that demand will grow at a constant rate. These projections are used to estimate volatility in demand.

Panel B presents the strategy results for capital allocation decisions. The lower line represents
the threshold for expansion of runway and area capacity, while the line in the middle presents the restriction for growth. The upper line represents the growth option for investment in a network of complement airports under the assumption that the noise restriction is not imposed on regional airports.

In panel A of figure 8.12 the projection of demand from S_0 into the future is mapped into a binomial forward process. In the figure the number of nodes is limited to link up with the schematic option game tree presented in figure 8.10. This projection is based on the historical pattern of demand for Schiphol Airport from 1958 to 2000, extrapolated by modeling uncertainty until the year 2020.[24] To estimate the uncertainty of flights, we project a set of trajectories or scenarios in the future and back out implied uncertainty embedded in the various growth trajectories.

The number of nodes in this projection is limited to preserve the intuition of scenario analysis, but can be converted to a shorter subperiod for sufficient accuracy in the valuation. The uncertainty in demand growth implied in the event tree results in (average) binomial parameters $u = 1.07$ and $d = 1$ when we convert the subperiods to a yearly basis.[25] We used the historical volatility of growth in flights for a reality check on average growth and volatility that is implied in the projection. The historical volatility over the period 1990–2000 was lower, about 7%, but a higher volatility is justified if we consider the changing environment in European aviation.

The average operating cash inflows (per flight), CF_t, are both directly and indirectly related to air transport traffic, $Q_{i,s,t}$. The direct component of CF_t results from (the average) amount of local passenger traffic, transfer passengers and freight, multiplied by the appropriate tariffs, plus payments for landing rights minus operating costs and regular investments. The indirect portion of the cash inflow, $CF_{i,t}$, per flight results from landside activities, such as real estate leases for retail and customers, and is estimated as a proportion of the direct $CF_{i,t}$. The estimated operational cash flow per flight after corporate taxes during 2001 equals €550.[26]

Once the volatility of demand in air transport movements and the operating cash flows are determined, the event tree in values can be constructed. The total operating cash flow, $TCF_{i,t}$, is determined from demand, $Q_{i,t}$, multiplied by the average operating cash flow per air transport movement, $CF_{i,t}$: $TCF_{i,t} = Q_{i,t} CF_{i,t}$. The value dynamics of assets in place requires an estimation of the maximum capacity. In higher-demand states, maximum capacity is reached (using equation 8.3) when

[24]Source: NV Luchthaven 1988, chap. 1.

[25]We traced the value dynamics from the event tree, and for simplicity we used constant binomial up and down parameters for the subperiods. Alternatively, we could back out implied binomial parameters for each subperiod.

[26]The cash flows per flight are likely to be time and state dependent. Transfer passengers and freight follow a closely related pattern in which, at a higher level of demand, the proportion of transfer passengers increases compared to the number of local passengers. For network expansion opportunities (at high trajectories of demand) the proportion of landside activities increases.

growth exceeds 425,000 flights. Starting with values at the terminal
nodes of the tree, using a constant growth model (equation 8.4), the valuation of assets in place works recursively in time. For this particular set
of input variables,[27] the backward binomial valuation of assets currently
in place results in an estimated value of €2.6 billion (in the year 2000).

The preceding valuation involves a symmetrical equilibrium. However, regulatory restrictions can severely limit the upside potential of
Schiphol Airport, causing the subgames for local expansion to become
asymmetrical at intermediate and higher states of demand. In addition to
the restricted local expansion, the valuation of growth opportunities requires an estimation of the regional growth opportunities as well as international network potential.

Although hard to estimate, the incremental value of international expansion that derives from leverage of Schiphol's core competencies (e.g., "Air-
portCity" concept) onto follow-on acquisitions, causes important favorable
asymmetries in the expansion subgames at higher trajectories of demand.
The total sum of the estimated values for (restricted) local, regional, and international expansion subgames equals €720 million (as of 2000).[28]

If we include local, regional, and international expansion options, the
total company value estimated as the value of assets in place plus PVGO,
equals €2.6 billion + €720 million = €3.3 billion. If we subtract the
(market) value of debt (€0.9 billion), the value of (total) equity is €2.4 billion (as of the year 2000).[29]

Strategy Results and Industry Implications

In the above valuation procedure, the pattern of expansion-related outlays is not treated as a static scenario, but is instead adjusted according to
the level of growth. Panel B of figure 8.12 provides a schematic summary
of the strategy implications for capital allocation resulting from this valuation.

In 2000, the quantity of air transport movements was 423,000 flights
per year. Without expansion, demand would reach full capacity immedi-

---

[27] $Q_0 = 423,000$ and can move up or down with binomial parameters $u = 1.07$ and $d = 1$ per year, max capacity (without expansion) is $Q_{max} = 425,000$. The average investment to sustain assets in place equals €100 million per year. The risk-free interest rate (r) was 4.5%, while the weighted average cost of capital (k), applied at the end nodes, equals 8.5% and declines in the end nodes with excess demand. The risk-neutral probability, p, equals 0.64.

[28] Of the total investment of €300 million per year, we assume that €100 million is used to sustain assets in place and €200 million is for growth opportunities.

[29] This valuation can of course easily be recalculated with updated input parameters if Schiphol would go public in the future.

ately and the cash flows would become truncated.[30] The lower line in figure 8.12, panel B shows the "local expansion" threshold above which the local expansion options would get exercised. Continuous growth from S_1 to S_2 triggers sequential investment until Schiphol's expansion reaches the limits of environmental restrictions (460,000 flights by 2003), as shown by the restriction line in figure 8.12, panel B. Examples of important local expansion projects involve infrastructure investments in land, the five-runway system, and the expansion of Terminal West, which should help to preempt growth in the capture game for transfer passengers in the same catchment area. At lower paths, for example from S_1 to S_3, management might find it better to defer several investment decisions (i.e., would have a dominant strategy to defer).

To reach higher levels of growth, the airport group should become less dependent on the location and avoid capacity restrictions by setting up strategic alliances and forming joint ventures in international airports. The upper, or "network growth options," line represents further growth opportunities due to expansion at regional and international airport networks.[31]

Of course, one must take into account the trade-off between flexibility and competitive pressure of investment commitment for different types of investment strategies. For instance, at the time that management was pondering building a (large scale) complement airport in the North Sea as an expansion option for Schiphol (Amsterdam), BAA (London) officially expressed its concerns that the large scale of this project would affect its own growth opportunities in London. This enormous up-front investment for Schiphol would generate strategic commitment value but sacrifice flexibility value. It might preempt future growth in the industry, and once made the investment will be very hard to recover. By contrast, the current strategy seems to be a more flexible one where management may adjust sequential investments according to the level of growth.[32]

The valuation of Schiphol Airport can be subjected to a "reality test" by comparing it with the value of assets and growth options of other

[30]The maximum capacity in 2000 is 45 million passengers per year and 170 gates.

[31]Examples of investment in regional airports include real estate investment in Rotterdam Airport and Lelystad and terminal expansion at Eindhoven Airport. Examples of international growth opportunities include the new Terminal 4 of John F. Kennedy International Airport in New York, a participation in Brisbane Airport, and the cooperation agreement with Fraport (Pantares).

[32]An additional complication in the valuation arises when the growth option value is path dependent. In that case, the growth option value at any point in time depends not only on the current level of demand, but also on the history of trajectories of demand for the firm and the firm's competitors. A growth strategy is typically path dependent if projects are irreversible and require time to build, or when the infrastructure development process involves mutually exclusive projects of considerable scale, which makes it difficult to switch between strategic paths without costs.

TABLE 8.1

Stock Prices, Earnings, and Values of Current Operations versus Growth
Opportunities for the Airports of British Airports Authority (BAA),
Frankfurt, Copenhagen, Zurich, and Vienna (estimated September 2001)

Airport	Value per Share		Total Value of Traded Shares				PVGO/P
	(1) Share Price	(2) Earnings per Share	(3) Market Value of Equity	(4) Capitalized Value of Earnings Using Various Discount Rates			(5) Growth Options to Equity
			(€millions)	10%	11%	12%	((3 − 4) / 3)
London	£5.51	£ 0.31	9,413	5,292	4,811	4,410	44%–53%
Frankfurt	€25.5	€1.42	2,298	1,279	1,163	1,066	44%–54%
Zurich	SF 150	SF 8.7	493	286	260	564	42%–52%
Vienna	€32.2	€3.2	676	676	615	564	0%–17%
Copenhagen	DK 489	DK 38	597	463	421	386	22%–35%

Notes: The table presents the implicit market valuation of the growth prospects for
a number of European airports by adjusting the stock price for the value generated
by continued current operations of assets in place under a no-growth policy (Kester
1984). The value of the firm equals the value of debt plus the value of equity (=
value of debt + [value of assets in place + growth option value]). The market equity value prices the firm's "bundle of growth options." The first column presents the
average stock price as of September 2001. The earnings per share (second column)
is the average analyst forecast next period. Column 3 presents total traded equity.
The earnings are discounted under a no-growth and full-payout policy (as an annu-
ity) using various discount rates. The last column shows the value of growth opportunities as a proportion of the stock price of European traded airports: (equity
value–asset value) / equity value.

competing airports. Table 8.1 shows the implied value of the growth opportunities embedded in the stock prices of traded competing airports,
namely BAA (which includes a network of airports), Fraport (Frankfurt),
UZAZ (Zurich), VIA (Vienna), and CPH (Copenhagen), as of September
2001. The table confirms that the market clearly appreciates the growth
opportunities of publicly traded airports. The implied growth option
value as a proportion of the stock price (PVGO/equity) ranges between
40% to 50% for large airports such as BAA (London network) and
Frankfurt. The estimated PVGO-to-equity ratio for Schiphol is about
720 million/2.4 billion or 30%.

The valuation of assets in place embedded in the equity of €1.7 billion
(total value of assets in place − debt = 2.6 − 0.9 = 1.7) and the present

value of growth opportunities of €720 million for Schiphol Airport thus appears consistent with the value components of public airport stocks presented in table 8.1. The airports of London and Paris (not traded) seem to sustain their positions as mainports in Europe. London has the largest airports, but Paris's Roissy–Charles de Gaulle has the advantage of considerable growth options emanating from its infrastructure. Heathrow and Schiphol may reach their boundaries for growth in the next two decades. Frankfurt is also restricted. The airports of Frankfurt and Amsterdam aspired to first become Eurohubs and then grow into mainport status.

There are several insights from competitive strategies for the development of the European airport industry. Location, relative size, prior infrastructure, the quality and strategic position of the home carrier, and complementary assets, can make exercising the expansion option more valuable for a mainport than for a smaller player. These also introduce asymmetries into the expansion game. The market share of European airports seems to be affected by a concentration trend due to the value asymmetries that enable larger airports to grow more rapidly than smaller airports. This concentration trend, if continued, should result in a limited number of large European mainports, with many smaller airports.

Figure 8.13 shows the development of aircraft movements, passengers, and freight. The larger airports in particular have shown a significant increase in aircraft movements, passengers, and freight, as illustrated by the steeper slope of the higher curves compared to the lower curves in figure 8.13. In the coming decades most intercontinental and European flights will be concentrated at the largest airports. Following this concentration trend, many of the smaller airports will follow a market-niche strategy of feeding the hubs at the end of a spoke. A few airports will emerge as mainports (big), some as Eurohubs (medium), while most of them will be spokes (small).

Idiosyncratic growth restrictions may also be natural reasons for airports to seek cooperation with other airports. A cooperation strategy may involve strengthening the position of domestic regional airports that are part of a group, or it may involve becoming part of an international network. For instance, BAA has a network of regional airports in the United Kingdom, that is, Heathrow, Gatwick, Stansted, Southampton, Glasgow, Edinburgh, and Aberdeen, and has equity stakes in airports outside the United Kingdom.

8.5. Conclusions and Implications

Since the value of strategic acquisitions and infrastructure derives from enhancement of the strategic position of an enterprise, acquisitions, infrastructure, and network investments require careful scrutiny and more sophisticated competitive analysis than suggested by standard DCF

FIGURE 8.13 DEVELOPMENT OF MARKET SHARE OVER TIME
ILLUSTRATING THE GROWTH OF THE LARGER AIRPORTS IN FLIGHTS
(PANEL A), PASSENGERS (PANEL B), AND FREIGHT (PANEL C) IN THE
PERIOD 1991–2000

**Panel A. Development of Flights (in thousands) of Largest European
Airports**

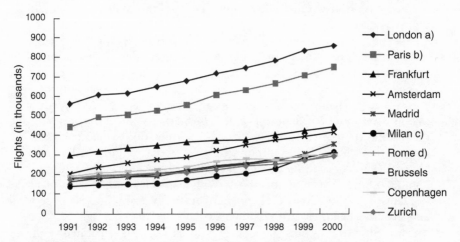

**Panel B. Development of Passengers (in thousands) of Largest
European Airports**

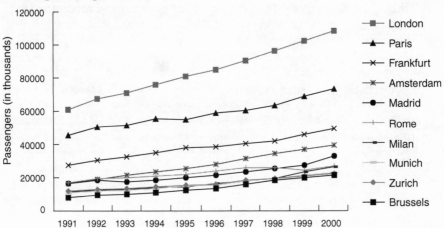

FIGURE 8.13 *continued*

Panel C. Development of Freight (in thousands of tons) of Largest European Airports

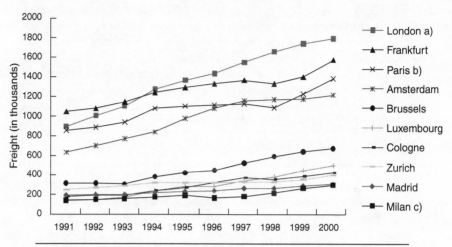

a) Heathrow, Gatwick, Stansted b) Orly, Charles de Gaulle c) Linate, Malpensa
d) Fiumicino, Ciampino

analysis. The options and games approach helps explain the future competitive developments in an industry by using a dynamic analysis. Firms can make platform acquisitions or corporate infrastructure investments to increase their future ability to capture growth opportunities in the industry.

In the case of buy-and-build acquisitions, the approach can be used to guide the strategic thinking process. Options and games can be used in the pricing and competitive bidding of platform acquisitions aimed to achieve consolidation in a fragmented industry. In growing industries, the series of synergistic deals can also be complemented by organic growth. In mature industries, strategic acquisitions seem to be the preferred route since they can accomplish synergies through a speedy increase in market share while minimizing the potential for price wars within the sector.

In the case of capacity expansion, an airport's prior infrastructure, size, governmental growth restrictions, and home carrier are generating significant competitive asymmetries that can help explain differences in the valuation, exercise, and timing of expansion options. The larger airports or mainports, which have infrastructures that enable them to absorb high growth, are expected to solidify or enhance their positions. The result will be a structure in which many smaller airports will support a limited number of European mainports. At the same time, to achieve higher growth, local expansion limitations and the influence of globalization may motivate some airports to devise network strategies that can more fully utilize economies of scale and derive network benefits.

Valuation of an acquisition or infrastructure expansion strategy should be consistent with that strategy's underlying logic and design. Analytical methods like real-options techniques and game theory can complement the strategic thinking process in an intuitive and dynamic way. A combined real-options and games framework can help guide managerial judgment in deciding whether, when, and under what conditions it would be appropriate to invest. It can also help management decide whether to compete or to cooperate with other players.

Suggested Readings

Amram, M., and N. Kulatilaka. *Real Options: Managing Strategic Investment in an Uncertain World.* Boston: Harvard Business School Press, 1999.

Smit, H. T. J. "Acquisition Strategies as Option Games." *Journal of Applied Corporate Finance* 14, no. 2 (2001): 79–89.

———. "Infrastructure Investment as a Real Options Game: The Case of European Airport Expansion." *Financial Management*, 32, no. 4 (2003): 27–57.

Chapter 9

Continuous-Time Models and Applications

9.1. Introduction and Overview

This chapter provides a synthesis of continuous-time analytical work on competitive strategy, and discusses some more applications.[1] This introductory section provides a brief overview of relevant literature. Section 9.2 presents a continuous-time version of the discrete-time model we developed earlier in chapters 6 and 7 that incorporates asymmetric costs and managerial flexibility in output decisions to explain how one firm may gain a competitive advantage over another. Competitive advantage is modeled here through asymmetric costs arising from a strategic technological (e.g., IT infrastructure) investment.[2] This results in a more natural competitive

---

[1]Models combining game theory and options are typically based in continuous time and are developed from a theoretical perspective. Often, researchers assume that firms have the same costs or produce only one unit forever (if they are active in the market), and that the inverse demand curve is generic. For a good discussion focusing exclusively on continuous-time models involving game theory with options, see Huisman 2001. Although interesting theoretical issues are investigated through these continuous-time models, the models are not readily applicable for practical valuation purposes. In practice, firms are not generally homogeneous. The underlying stochastic variables are seldom likely to follow a geometric Brownian motion, in particular for applications other than in natural resources. The firm must choose not only the optimal timing of an expansion but also the optimal capacity to install. It is much easier to handle asymmetries between competitors and to define alternative stochastic processes with a discrete time approach. Such an approach is thus better suited for the practical application of the options-game approach to investments in real markets. The resulting analysis is also more accessible for corporate managers, since it does not require in-depth knowledge of stochastic calculus and differential equations.

[2]We here model competitive advantage via differential costs, although a similar analysis would carry through if firms faced the same costs but differentiated products, e.g., in terms of higher quality or service. In this case, the firm facing lower demand for its product would need to incur additional costs (e.g., in production, advertising, or distribution) in order to achieve the same revenues. These indirect costs reduce profits similar to a direct production cost disadvantage. Thus, the resulting strategic equilibrium is the same whether competitive advantage is modeled via lower costs or higher revenue due to product differentiation. The firm with the competitive advantage (and higher profits) enters first.

equilibrium, with the lower-cost firm entering first.[3] As benchmark cases the synthesis encompasses the investment decision of a monopolist (McDonald and Siegel 1986) and the symmetric competition model of Dixit and Pindyck (1994). Section 9.3 discusses strategic interactions and the timing of investment, and considers innovation with uncertainty over completion and time delays. Section 9.4 discusses analytical extensions under incomplete information about the competitor's threshold entry level and cost, and other applications from patent races, exit and debt restructuring, takeovers, and so on. Section 9.5 discusses more general equilibrium competitive entry strategies under imperfect competition and asymmetric information.

As noted, the basic net present value (NPV) rule, which suggests an investment should be accepted if its NPV is positive, fails when a firm has an option to defer investment under uncertainty. The opportunity to invest is analogous to a call option on the project. The optimal trigger value at which a monopolist firm should invest must be well above the investment cost (i.e., there should be a large positive NPV) due to the option value to "wait and see" (McDonald and Siegel 1986; Dixit and Pindyck 1994). Investing early would sacrifice this option premium. However, if there is (a threat of) competition, whereby each firm's payoff is affected by the actions of other players, competitive interaction can again change the optimal investment criterion. Trigeorgis (1991a), for example, shows that a firm anticipating future competitive entry at a specified time will invest earlier for preemptive reasons. In the early industrial organization literature, Spence (1977, 1979) argues that strategic signaling considerations may provide firms with an incentive to commit capital early in order to deter entry or expansion by rivals. Dasgupta and Stiglitz (1980) find that an incumbent firm can preempt potential competitors by spending excessive amounts on R & D, and that a monopolist would delay innovation, whereas the threat of competition may induce a firm to innovate earlier. Dixit (1979, 1980) also provides various treatments of strategic

---

[3]In most models of competitive strategy using real options, costs are assumed to be zero or symmetric (see, e.g., Dixit and Pindyck 1994; Grenadier 1996). With symmetric firms, however, equilibrium is indeterminate in an intermediate range of demand. Grenadier (1996) suggests that some artificial random mechanism (e.g., flip of a coin) must be used to decide which of two identical firms will invest first. Dixit and Pindyck (1994) also place a zero probability of a joint investment in this intermediate demand region. However, Huisman and Kort (1999) and Huisman (2001) point out that if the demand level is between the two entry thresholds, there is a strictly positive probability of joint investment. Fudenberg and Tirole (1985) also support this point. In a more recent paper, Grenadier (2001) recognizes that there is a positive probability of joint investment in this intermediate demand region. In any case, using asymmetric costs enables a more natural and realistic identification of the strategic equilibrium, as the lower-cost firm would enter first. Asymmetric costs can arise from imperfections in either the input or the output markets.

investments (such as building excess capacity) designed to preempt competitive entry. Spatt and Sterbenz (1985) analyze preemption under learning and the influence of the number of competitors on market equilibrium. As we shall see, competitive threat can erode the value of the option to wait and induce investment near the zero-NPV value threshold.

The use of game theory in combination with real options can provide a useful framework for analyzing investment opportunities in the case of imperfect competition. Smit and Ankum (1993) analyze competitive investment timing via a simple option game. Dixit and Pindyck (1994, 309–16) consider two competitors who can strategically time their investment decisions (for given output choices) and show that the first firm would enter earlier (and the second firm later) than if there is no threat of competition. Smit and Trigeorgis (1997) analyze two-stage games where investment opportunity value depends on endogenous competitive interactions and study under what situations a firm that can optimally choose its timing and output decisions may be justified in making a strategic investment early and when it should wait. Kulatilaka and Perotti (1998) show that in a Cournot duopoly setting where a first mover can gain a strategic advantage by investing in a strategic growth option, the market share and value of early investment increases more with higher demand uncertainty than the value of waiting (since profits are convex in demand). Perotti and Kulatilaka (1999) consider a Stackelberg growth option when a firm has a first-mover advantage and also conclude that higher demand uncertainty justifies earlier exercise of the growth option. Perotti and Rosetto (2002) show that firms may pursue different competitive entry strategies, depending on the degree of strategic advantage that investing in the growth opportunity provides. If the strategic advantage acquired via the investment is small, the firm becomes a leader but is induced to invest prematurely to preempt its competitor. If the advantage is high, the firm can enter at the optimal time without fear of preemption, as if it were a monopolist. Pawlina and Kort (2001) examine the impact of investment cost asymmetry on the value and exercise strategies of firms under imperfect competition. If the cost asymmetry is small, the firms invest jointly, but if it is high, the lower-cost firm preempts its competitor. If the cost asymmetry is sufficiently large, the firms enter sequentially.

Weeds (2002) derives optimal investment strategies for two firms that compete for a patent that may help explain strategic delay in patent races and shed some light on the role of first versus second movers. Mason and Weeds (2002) consider more general strategic interactions with externalities that may justify why investment might sometimes be speeded up under uncertainty. Finally, Weeds (2000a, 2000b) considers innovation with uncertainty over completion and time delays that can explain phenomena like faster exit ("reverse hysteresis") and delayed commercialization (sleeping patents). We review Weeds's work and its implications regarding strategic investment timing under uncertainty in section 9.3.

Lambrecht and Perraudin (2003) consider entry exercise strategies with preemption effects under incomplete information about the competitor's entry threshold and investment amount, which can help explain why firms in practice may delay their entry beyond the break-even investment threshold. In section 9.4 we discuss their framework in more detail, along with three applications from Lambrecht (2000, 2001, 2002) that explain strategic sequential investments and sleeping patents, firm exit, product market competition and debt restructuring, and takeovers and restructuring activity.

In other applications, Williams (1993) and Grenadier (1996) develop continuous-time models for exercise strategies in real estate development. Grenadier uses his equilibrium framework to explain development cascades and overbuilding in real estate markets. Grenadier (1999) considers more general equilibrium exercise strategies under asymmetric information, while Grenadier (2001) provides a general solution approach for equilibrium investment strategies in a Cournot-Nash oligopolistic setting. He shows that the Nash equilibrium exercise strategies are the same as those obtained in an artificial perfectly competitive equilibrium with a modified demand function. Thus one can leverage on the continuous-time results under perfect competition to obtain results for an imperfectly competitive setting. We provide an overview of Grenadier's work in section 9.5.

9.2. Continuous-Time Version of Smit-Trigeorgis Framework

In this section we consider a continuous-time version of the Smit-Trigeorgis framework involving two firms facing an investment opportunity in an uncertain market.[4] Each firm's investment generates a profit stream that depends on the two firms' relative cost structure and output decisions, and on whether the other firm has entered the market. Uncertainty is modeled via random fluctuations in demand. The value of the investment thus depends on product demand, marginal costs, the relative timing of investment, and the actions of the competing firms.[5] The analysis proceeds

---

[4]This section is partly based on Joaquin and Butler 2000, which in turn is based on Smit and Trigeorgis 1997. There is an important difference between Joaquin and Butler 2000 and our approach, however. In Joaquin and Butler 2000 the demand is deterministic, while the exchange rate is stochastic. In our approach, the (inverse) demand curve parameter θ_t is stochastic, while there is no multiplicative stochastic shock like exchange rate uncertainty.

[5]In our model, firms can adjust their output levels in response to (or in order to strategically influence) market entry by competing firms. The strategic investment timing model of Dixit and Pindyck (1994, 309–16) assumes a fixed level of output, which limits a firm in a duopoly to op-

as follows. Section 9.2.1 discusses the investment opportunity available to the two firms and derives the equilibrium output and values. Section 9.2.2 discusses the entry decisions of the follower and the leader. Section 9.2.3 discusses equilibrium entry and critical demand thresholds. Section 9.2.4 considers the two important benchmark cases of symmetric competition and monopoly.

9.2.1. EQUILIBRIUM OUTPUT AND VALUES

This section discusses the equilibrium output (Q_i), profits (π_i) and project value payoffs (V_i) for various market structures under quantity competition. These will serve as building blocks of subsequent analyses of equilibrium under endogenous competition. Again, consider two firms having the option to invest in commercial production in the last stage using a given technology (e.g., IT infrastructure). Commercial production requires an initial investment I. Exogenous uncertainty in future market demand is assumed to be characterized by fluctuations in the demand parameter, θ_t. The output can be sold at a common unit market price, P_t, determined by the inverse linear demand function

$$P_t(Q_T) = \theta - Q_T. \tag{9.1}$$

Q_T is total industry output ($= Q_i + Q_j$, with Q_i and Q_j being the quantities supplied by firms i and j), and θ_t is the stochastic demand shift parameter assumed to follow the lognormal diffusion (or geometric Brownian motion) process:

$$\frac{d\theta}{\theta} = \alpha dt + \sigma dz, \tag{9.2}$$

where $d\theta$ is the change in the stochastic demand variable θ over a small time interval dt, α is the constant growth rate (drift) of θ, σ is the constant instantaneous standard deviation in the drift rate, and dz is an increment of a standard Wiener process.[6]

The variable production cost function for firm i is given by

$$C_i(Q_i) = c_i Q_i, \tag{9.3}$$

---

timally respond to potential competitive entry via a combination of output and timing decisions. An irreversible investment will optimally be made earlier if the firm has the extra flexibility to adjust its output level and thereby influence favorably the market share dynamics.

[6]An alternative modeling approach to the price process in equation 9.1, instead of treating the demand parameter θ as stochastic (which may lead to negative prices if θ drops

where Q_i is the output flow and c_i is the (positive) constant marginal production cost for firm i.[7] One firm can have a lower unit cost than the other, reflecting a competitive advantage in the input or product markets, or by making a strategic investment (e.g., in IT infrastructure) in the first stage. The lower-cost firm, which would naturally become the leader or first entrant, is denoted by the subscript L and the higher-cost firm (follower) by subscript F, that is, $c_L < c_F$.[8]

Firm i's second-stage instantaneous operating profit flow at time t is given by

$$\pi_i(Q_i) = PQ_i - c_iQ_i = [(\theta - Q_T) - c_i]Q_i. \tag{9.4}$$

The gross project value (profit value), V_i, and the net present value, NPV_i, from the second-stage investment for firm i, assuming perpetual subsequent operating cash flows (profits), a constant equilibrium risk-adjusted discount rate k, and a profit growth rate α in the last stage (resulting in a below-equilibrium return shortfall or "dividend yield" $\delta = k - \alpha$),[9] are obtained from[10]

$$V_i = \frac{\pi_i}{\delta}, \text{ and } NPV_i = V_i - I. \tag{9.5}$$

Under quantity competition, the reaction function of each firm is downward sloping. Maximizing firm i's own profit value over its quantity given that its competitor produces Q_j (setting $\partial V_i / \partial Q_i = 0$), each firm's reaction function is given by

---

below Q_T or may lead to a discount rate for profit flow which may depend on θ) is to consider a multiplicative stochastic demand shock Y (with θ being a constant), i.e.,

$$P_i(Q_T) = Y_t(\theta - Q_T), \tag{9.1'}$$

where Y_t follows a geometric Brownian motion with $Y_0 = 1$. The price then follows the same process (GBM) as Y with the same parameters. However, we choose to maintain the same price process assumption for consistency with the discrete-time treatment of earlier chapters (where it was much simpler treating θ as the stochastic variable).

[7] The above demand and cost functions (with the quadratic cost term set to 0) are the same as in chapters 6 and 7.

[8] Differential costs can be determined endogenously through firm's decisions to invest in research and development. R & D can lead to competitive advantage in areas such as technology and technological processes, supply chain management, information systems, human resources, and organizational capital. This is the approach taken in the two-stage strategic model of chapters 6 and 7. In this model, R & D investment in an initial stage influences the firm's competitive position in the second stage.

[9] δ can also be seen to equal $r - \hat{\alpha}$ where $\hat{\alpha} \equiv \alpha - RP$ is the risk-neutral drift rate in demand θ, α is the actual growth rate in θ, and RP is an appropriate risk premium. The discount rate actually depends on θ since value is the expectation of discounted profit flow, which is quadratic in θ. The exact value function is derived in appendix 9.2. For expositional simplicity (and consistency with the discrete-time formulation used in earlier chapters) we assume in the text that δ is constant and the following value function holds: $V_i = \pi_i / \delta$.

[10] For simplicity, we assume zero taxes and depreciation so that the operating cash flows are equivalent to operating profits.

$$R_i(Q_j) = \frac{\theta - c_i - Q_j}{2}. \tag{9.6}$$

If both firms make *simultaneous* production capacity investments in the second stage (I, I), without observing or having knowledge of each other's actions, a (asymmetric) Cournot-Nash duopoly equilibrium outcome (C) will result.[11] Once the competitor enters, the two firms (the leader L and the follower F) have the following (interacting) profit functions:

$$\pi_{ic}(Q_i; Q_j) = \left[[\theta - (Q_i + Q_j) - c_i]Q_i\right], \tag{9.7}$$

where i = L or F. At Cournot-Nash equilibrium (C), each firm's output must be optimal given the other firm's output. The (asymmetric) Cournot equilibrium outputs, obtained (simultaneously) by maximizing π_{iC} above with respect to Q_i (or by equating the reaction functions of the two firms), is given by

$$Q_{ic} = \begin{cases} \dfrac{\theta - 2c_i + c_j}{3} & \text{if } \theta - 2c_i + c_j > 0 \\ 0 & \text{if } \theta - 2c_i + c_j \le 0 \end{cases} \tag{9.8}$$

where i = L, F. If firm i's early strategic investment reduces its cost (c_i) below its competitor's (c_j), then $Q_i > Q_j$. Firm i's associated instantaneous (duopoly) profit flow is given by

$$\pi_{ic} = \frac{(\theta - 2c_i + c_j)^2}{9}. \tag{9.9}$$

The (asymmetric) Cournot-Nash equilibrium project value for firm i can be simplified to[12]

---

[11]It is the information structure rather than the sequencing that is important here. Even if the firms move sequentially in time, as long as they have imperfect information or no knowledge of the other's choice when selecting their own strategy, the same Cournot-Nash equilibrium will result as in the simultaneous-move Cournot game.

[12]This is a simplification. The exact value function for firm i in Cournot-Nash equilibrium actually is (see appendix 9.2, equation 9.A2.3 with $n = 9$)

$$V_{ic} = \frac{1}{9}\left[\frac{\theta^2}{\delta'} - \frac{2\theta K_i}{\delta} + \frac{K_i^2}{r}\right], \tag{9.10'}$$

where $K_i = 2c_i - c_j$, $\delta = r - \hat{\alpha}$, $\delta' = r - 2\hat{\alpha} - \sigma^2$. The discount rate actually depends on θ, with the quadratic θ term being discounted at δ', the linear term at δ, and the constant term at the risk-less rate r. For expositional simplicity (and consistency with the discrete-time framework used in earlier chapters) we assume a constant discount rate δ and that the following value function holds: $V_i = \pi_i/\delta$.

$$V_{ic} = \frac{(\theta - 2c_i + c_j)^2}{9\delta}. \tag{9.10}$$

In case the pioneering firm does not make an early strategic investment and both firms invest simultaneously in the second stage, a *symmetric* Cournot-Nash equilibrium (S) in which the two firms share the market equally may result if the two firms are otherwise identical (i.e., $c_i = c_j = c$), yielding

$$Q_S = \frac{(\theta - c)}{3}, \text{ and } \pi_S = \frac{(\theta - c)^2}{9} \text{ (if } \theta > c). \tag{9.11}$$

Note that each firm i will eventually be profitable, net of its second-stage outlay I, and will enter if demand is high enough such that its NPV, determined from equation 9.10 above, is positive, that is, if $\theta_t \geq \theta_F^*$ where $\theta_F^* \equiv 3\sqrt{\delta I} + 2c_i - c_j$. If demand is too low for either firm to operate profitably, namely if $\theta_t < \theta_L^*$ where $\theta_L^* \equiv 2\sqrt{\delta I} + 2c_i - c_j$, they will both wait. In an intermediate demand region, $\theta_L^* < \theta_t < \theta_F^*$ or $2\sqrt{\delta I} + 2c_i - c_j \leq \theta_t < 3\sqrt{\delta I} + 2c_i - c_j$, the high-cost firm j will be unprofitable ($NPV_j < 0$) and will delay entry (until $\theta_t > \theta_F^*$), enabling firm i to (temporarily) earn monopoly profits.[13] It can be seen from equation 9.6 with $Q_j = 0$, assuming $c_i < \theta$, that the value-maximizing quantity for a monopolist firm i (M), is given by

$$Q_{iM} = \frac{(\theta - c_i)}{2} \text{ (with } Q_j = 0) \tag{9.12}$$

(and zero otherwise). Before the entry of a competitor, the first entrant (firm i) can set a monopolist price $(\theta + c_i)/2$ and enjoy a temporary monopoly (M) profit:[14]

$$\pi_{iM} = \frac{(\theta - c_i)^2}{4}. \tag{9.13}$$

The case where the two firms make their investments *sequentially* such that one firm observes the other's moves, leading to a Stackelberg leader-follower equilibrium, can be derived similarly (see appendix 9.3).[15] Generally, the evolution of entry dynamics consists of two stages. In the first stage, the low-cost firm (leader) enters and earns a temporary monopoly

---

[13]It is assumed that the last stage is infinite (steady state) and the possibility of reentry is precluded.

[14]The subscript M indicates a monopolist.

[15]We suppress the Stackelberg equilibrium (and relegate it to appendix 9.3) since in timing games even with one firm entering earlier, the Cournot-Nash outcome may still be the most likely equilibrium. Fudenberg and Tirole (1991, 74–76) point out that there is a problem of "time consistency" with the Stackelberg equilibrium, because the leader quantity in Stackelberg is not a best response for the follower production. If firms can repeat the quantity choice game, there is an incentive for the leader to reduce production, creating an incentive for the follower to adjust the production again, converging to the Cournot-Nash outcome.

profit. In the second stage these excess profits induce the entry of the second firm (follower). The market is subsequently shared by the two firms in a Cournot-Nash equilibrium (in perpetuity). The resulting dynamic game is solved by backward induction, that is, first reasoning forward and then solving backward.

9.2.2. STRATEGIC ENTRY DECISIONS

We discuss next, in turn, first the follower's decision to be a late entrant (given an earlier entry by the low-cost firm), and then the leader's decision to enter first (given the possibility of later competitive entry).

The Follower's Decision to Enter Later

Consider the decision of firm j to enter in the last stage, with its output set optimally at the Cournot-Nash equilibrium duopoly level given in equation 9.8,[16] assuming the low-cost firm, firm i, has already invested earlier. Assuming that the time-t demand level θ_t follows the geometric Brownian motion of equation 9.2, the investment opportunity can be seen as a contingent claim whose value V depends on the current level of demand θ_t or price level $P_t(\theta_t)$ and the equilibrium (duopoly) profit. By Ito's Lemma, the change in the value of the investment opportunity (see appendix 9.1) satisfies

$$dV = (\alpha\theta V_\theta + \tfrac{1}{2}\sigma^2\theta^2 V_{\theta\theta} + V_t)\, dt + \sigma\theta V_\theta dz, \tag{9.14}$$

where $V_\theta = \partial V/\partial\theta$, $V_{\theta\theta} = \partial^2 V/\partial\theta^2$, and $V_t = \partial V/\partial t$. Thus, the investment opportunity value V must satisfy the following general differential equation:[17]

$$\tfrac{1}{2}\sigma^2\theta^2 V_{\theta\theta} + \hat{\alpha}\theta V_\theta - rV + V_t + \left[\frac{(\theta - 2c_j + c_i)^2}{9}\right] = 0, \tag{9.15}$$

where $\hat{\alpha} = \alpha - RP$ or $r - \delta$, with $\hat{\alpha}$ being the risk-adjusted growth rate in demand θ. The first part is the standard differential equation for the option value of waiting (without cash flow) for a single firm (derived in appendix 9.1; see also McDonald and Siegel 1986 or Dixit and Pindyck 1994). The last term in brackets represents firm j's instantaneous cash (profit) flow in Cournot-Nash duopoly equilibrium from equation 9.9. Before entry, the second (cash flow) term drops out, so the follower value

---

[16]Assuming $\theta - 2c_i + c_j > 0$, equilibrium duopoly output levels are positive for both firms.
[17]This follows from the standard replication argument of Black and Scholes (1973) and Merton (1973). It can also be obtained from the consumption-CAPM or by using the risk-neutral valuation argument of Cox and Ross (1976).

is simply the option value of waiting. After entry (in the duopoly phase), the first (option value) term drops out, leaving only the cash flow term in perpetuity (static NPV). If the equilibrium duopoly output is earned in perpetuity, the value is time-independent (so $V_t = 0$). The solution to equation 9.15 is then simplified to[18]

$$V_{jc}(\theta) = A_j\theta^{\beta_1} + B_j\theta^{\beta_2} + \left[\frac{(\theta - 2c_j + c_i)^2}{9\delta}\right], \tag{9.16}$$

where $\delta = r - \hat{\alpha}$, the constants A_j and B_j are to be determined from the relevant boundary conditions, and β_1 and β_2 are, respectively, the positive and negative roots of the fundamental quadratic equation (see McDonald and Siegel 1986; or Dixit and Pindyck 1994, 141–43):

$$\beta_1 = \tfrac{1}{2} - \frac{r - \delta}{\sigma^2} + \sqrt{\left(\frac{r - \delta}{\sigma^2} - \tfrac{1}{2}\right)^2 + \frac{2r}{\sigma^2}} \; (> 1); \tag{9.17}$$

$$\beta_2 = \tfrac{1}{2} - \frac{r - \delta}{\sigma^2} - \sqrt{\left(\frac{r - \delta}{\sigma^2} - \tfrac{1}{2}\right)^2 + \frac{2r}{\sigma^2}} \; (< 0).$$

If there are barriers to further competitive entry by other firms, both firms will maintain the same output level in perpetuity, so the last term of equation 9.16 can fully capture the value to firm j given that the other firm (firm i) has already invested. That is, $A_j = B_j = 0$ for firm j as a Cournot duopolist (C) (see also equation 9.10):

$$V_{jc}(\theta) = \frac{(\theta - 2c_j + c_i)^2}{9\delta}. \tag{9.18}$$

The value of firm j as a Cournot duopolist above is the expected capitalized value of its perpetual Cournot duopoly profits (π_{jC}).[19]

Suppose firm j has not yet invested in the project, but considers doing so at an optimal time by investing an amount I. If the current level of demand is θ, then the net value of undertaking the project immediately is given by its net present value

---

[18]Again, this is using the simplified value function assuming a constant discount rate. The more accurate expression is

$$V_{jc}(\theta) = A_j\theta^{\beta_1} + B_j\theta^{\beta_2} + \frac{1}{9}\left[\frac{\theta^2}{\delta'} - \frac{2\theta K_i}{\delta} + \frac{K_i^2}{r}\right]. \tag{9.16'}$$

[19]Again, the more accurate expression is

$$V_{jc} = \frac{1}{9}\left[\frac{\theta^2}{\delta'} - \frac{2\theta K_j}{\delta} + \frac{K_j^2}{r}\right], \tag{9.18'}$$

where $K_i = 2c_i - c_j$, $\delta = r - \hat{\alpha}$, $\delta' = r - 2\alpha - \sigma^2$.

$$NPV_{jc}(\theta) = V_{jc}(\theta) - I. \tag{9.19}$$

The net present value of committing today by firm j to invest at a future time T as a follower (F) when demand first reaches θ_F ($\geq \theta$) is given by

$$NPV_{jc}(\theta_F; \theta) = E_\theta[e^{-rT}\{V_{jc}(\theta_F) - I\}], \tag{9.20}$$

where $E^\theta [\ ]$ is the risk-neutral expectation conditional on the current demand being θ; and T is the time demand first reaches θ_F, given that the current level of demand is θ:

$$T \equiv T(\theta_F; \theta) = \inf(t \geq 0 : \theta_t \geq \theta_F; \theta_0 = \theta). \tag{9.21}$$

From Dixit and Pindyck (1994, 315–16),

$$E_\theta[e^{-rt}] = \left(\frac{\theta}{\theta_F}\right)^{\beta_1}, \tag{9.22}$$

with $\beta_1 > 1$ as given in equation 9.17. Thus, the value to the follower (firm j) of committing now to undertake the investment when demand reaches θ_F can be simplified to

$$NPV_{jc}(\theta_F; \theta) = \left[\frac{(\theta_F - 2c_j + c_i)^2}{9\delta} - I\right]\left(\frac{\theta}{\theta_F}\right)^{\beta_1}. \tag{9.23}$$

If this value (from investing in the future time T) exceeds the NPV from immediate investment (even if it currently is positive), the firm should wait to invest (postponing the investment outlay). The higher the current demand, however, the greater is the opportunity cost of delaying investment from forgone profits. Maximizing the above future commitment value $NPV_{jC}(\theta_F; \theta)$ subject to $\theta_F \geq \theta$ can give the optimal entry demand level for firm j as the follower, θ_F^*.[20] The optimal entry demand level θ_F^* for firm j as a follower is higher (and investment should be postponed) the greater the required investment outlay I, the higher firm j's own unit operating cost c_j, and the lower the leader's unit cost c_i. The higher the required investment, the more cautious the firm should be in making the investment. The higher its unit operating cost, the less profitable its investment looks, and so it should wait for demand to increase further before it becomes attractive. Finally, the lower the incumbent's cost and the greater its comparative advantage and market power, the more cautious the challenger (late entrant) should be.

---

[20]The follower threshold is given by $\theta_F^* = 3\sqrt{q\delta I} + 2c_j - c_i$ where q corresponds to Tobin's q, market-to-book ratio or profitability index given by

$$q \equiv \frac{V^*}{I} = \frac{\beta_1}{\beta_1 - 1} (> 1 \text{ since } \beta_1 > 1).$$

The Leader's Decision to Enter First

Before the follower enters, the leader can temporarily earn excess monopoly profits. The follower will enter when demand reaches θ_F^*, thereby changing the market structure into a (Cournot-Nash) duopoly equilibrium. Firm i's value as a leader, V_{iL}, would be the sum of the value of its temporary monopoly profit flow up to time T plus the value of its future Cournot duopoly position.[21] By a similar argument as in the previous section, the value of firm i as a leader V_{iL} during the monopoly period must satisfy the following equation:

$$\tfrac{1}{2}\sigma^2\theta^2 V_{\theta\theta} + \hat{\alpha}\theta V_\theta - rV + V_t + \left[\frac{(\theta - c_i)^2}{4}\right] = 0, \tag{9.24}$$

where $V_\theta = \partial V/\partial\theta, V_{\theta\theta} = \partial^2 V/\partial\theta^2$. The first term is again the standard differential equation (given in appendix 9.1) capturing the option value of the leader's duopoly position. The last term now represents the value of the (temporary) profit flow for firm i as a monopolist (π_{iM} from equation 9.13). Since the value is again time-independent ($V_t = 0$), this results in the simplified solution[22]

$$V_{iL}(\theta) = A_i\theta^{\beta_1} + B_i\theta^{\beta_2} + \left[\frac{(\theta - c_i)^2}{4\delta}\right]. \tag{9.25}$$

The last term represents the current capitalized value of the monopoly profit flow if it were permanent (i.e., if firm i had no option to exit and firm j had no option to enter). The first two terms capture the value lost from potential competition, with A_i and B_i determined from the relevant boundary conditions. As demand θ drops, it becomes less likely that competition will enter (as θ approaches zero, the likelihood of competitive entry disappears) and so $B_i = 0$ (since $\beta_2 < 0$) and the leader's value reduces to

$$V_{iL}(\theta) = A_i\theta^{\beta_1} + \left[\frac{(\theta - c_i)^2}{4\delta}\right]. \tag{9.26}$$

As demand rises and the opportunity becomes more attractive, it is more likely competition will enter. When demand rises to θ_F^*, it will be optimal

---

[21]We use the subscript L in V_{iL} to indicate that firm i is the leader.

[22]Again, the more accurate expression is

$$V_{iL}(\theta) = A_i\theta^{\beta_1} + B_i\theta^{\beta_2} + \frac{1}{4}\left[\frac{\theta^2}{\delta'} - \frac{2\theta c_i}{\delta} + \frac{c_i^2}{r}\right]. \tag{9.25'}$$

for firm j to enter as a follower (F). At this time, the monopoly position (M) will disappear and the leader will become a Cournot-Nash duopolist (C). This justifies the following value-matching condition:

$$V_{iL}(\theta_F^*) = V_{ic}(\theta_F^*), \tag{9.27}$$

where (from equation 9.18)

$$V_{ic}(\theta_F^*) = \frac{(\theta_F^* - 2c_i + c_j)^2}{9\delta}. \tag{9.18'}$$

Substituting the expressions from equations 9.26 and 9.18′ into equation 9.27 uniquely specifies A_i.

Following a similar argument, the value of firm i's commitment today to invest in the project as the leader (during the monopoly stage) when demand reaches θ_L ($\geq \theta_M$ where θ_M is the monopoly demand threshold) is given by

$$NPV_{iL}(\theta_L; \theta) = \left[A_i \theta_L^{\beta_1} + \frac{(\theta_L - c_i)^2}{4\delta} - I \right] \left(\frac{\theta}{\theta_L} \right)^{\beta_1}. \tag{9.28}$$

The optimal entry demand level for firm i as a leader, θ_L^*, can be obtained by maximizing NPV_{iL} subject to $\theta_L > \theta$.[23] Assuming firm i will not be preempted by its competitor, its optimal entry demand threshold θ_L^* as a leader (during the monopoly period) is higher the greater the required investment outlay I, and the higher its own unit operating cost c_i. If the firm is not preempted by its competitor, it enters as a first investor at a higher demand level if it has a higher cost than if it had a lower cost. Unlike the symmetric cost case, both firms cannot be first entrants at different demand thresholds. The higher-cost firm will effectively be a second entrant (follower), entering later at θ_F^* ($\geq \theta_L^*$).

9.2.3. Equilibrium Entry and Critical Demand Thresholds

As noted earlier, there are two possible types of equilibrium in this duopoly competition: simultaneous entry and sequential entry. With simultaneous entry both firms in effect enter as second entrants, with neither enjoying temporary monopoly profits. Since the value payoff for a leader is higher than that for a follower, both firms would decide to invest simultaneously (resulting in a Cournot-Nash equilibrium) only if demand is sufficiently high (namely if $\theta \geq \theta_F^*$). Specifically, (simultaneous) entry would be optimal for both firms at the current demand level if it is greater

---

[23]For the leader threshold, one can first equalize the leader and follower values for the high-cost firm. This must be compared with the monopolistic threshold for the low-cost firm, choosing the lower threshold (see result 3 in Joaquin and Butler 2000).

than the optimal threshold entry levels for both firms as second entrants. Otherwise equilibrium will take the form of sequential entry.

The sequential entry game is characterized by a demand zone (θ_L^*, θ_F^*; θ), where θ_L^* is the threshold demand level at which the leader enters, θ_F^* the threshold demand level at which the follower enters (given earlier entry by the leader), and θ is the current demand level. It can be shown that if demand is not too high, there is a unique (subgame perfect) equilibrium where the lower-cost firm enters first as a leader (at θ_L^* and the higher-cost firm enters later as a follower (at θ_F^*) (see also Joaquin and Butler 2000). In the intermediate demand region, $\theta_L^* \leq \theta < \theta_F^*$, the higher-cost firm will be unprofitable ($NPV_j < 0$) and will therefore delay entry (until later when $\theta_T \geq \theta_F^*$), allowing the leader to (temporarily) enjoy Stackelberg leader (L) or monopoly profits (M). If demand is too low for either firm to operate profitably, namely if $\theta < \theta_L^*$, both firms will choose to wait until demand rises sufficiently.

The equilibrium entry, the values of the leader (L) and follower (F) and the critical demand entry thresholds (θ_L^*, θ_F^*) are depicted graphically in figure 9.1. The figure graphs the value of each firm V_i ($i = L$ or F) as a function of demand θ. As noted, the follower waits for $\theta < \theta_F^*$, and enters (invests) at (or above) θ_F^*, given that the leader has already entered. Thus, the follower's value $V_F(\theta)$ consists of two pieces: the convex call-option-like curve in the demand range from 0 to θ_F^* representing the option value of waiting; at θ_F^* this converges tangentially into the early exercise or immediate investment value $V - I$. Since in this demand zone ($\theta > \theta_F^*$ in region III) both firms invest (exercise the entry option) simultaneously, they receive Cournot-Nash equilibrium values as Cournot duopolists, $NPV_{jC}(\theta) = V_{jC}(\theta) - I$ as per equations 9.18–19. The probability that the leader or the follower would enter in this region are both 1 ($P_L = P_F = 1$).

Similarly, anticipating the follower's response, the leader waits for $\theta < \theta_L^*$, and enters (invests) at θ_L^* ($< \theta_F^*$). The leader's value $V_L(\theta)$ also consists of two parts: a concave part from 0 up to θ_F^* (incorporating temporary monopoly profits as well as an option value from waiting) and the part after θ_F^* representing immediate investment thereafter (similar to the follower). θ_L^* is exactly at the intersection of the value functions of the leader and the follower, that is, it is the demand threshold at which $V_L = V_F$. Below θ_L^*, the value of being a follower exceeds the value of being a leader as the leader must incur an upfront investment cost ($V_F > V_L$ in region I), so both firms would wait receiving the wait-and-see option value (and the game is repeated) until $\theta > \theta_L^*$. The probability that either the leader or the follower enters in this region is zero ($P_L = P_F = 0$).

In the intermediate demand region II, $\theta_L^* \leq \theta < \theta_F^*$, the value of being a leader exceeds that of being a follower ($V_L > V_F$), and the firm with the most comparative advantage will try to preempt the other. This will lead

FIGURE 9.1 VALUES OF LEADER (L) AND FOLLOWER (F) AND CRITICAL
DEMAND ENTRY THRESHOLDS IN DUOPOLY

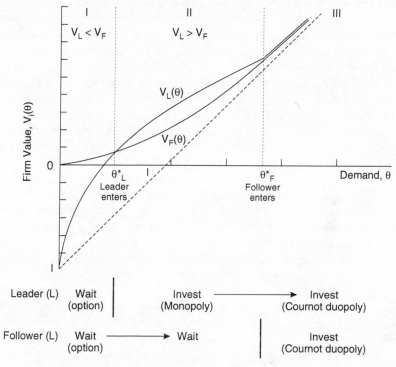

Region I.   Both wait (repeat game)
Region II. Leader: $P_L(1 - P_F)[V_{iL}(\theta) - I]$; Follower: $(1 - P_L)P_F V_{jF}(\theta)$
Region III. Both invest (simultaneously)

to sequential equilibrium entry, with the lower-cost firm entering first (becoming the leader) and earning temporary monopoly profits (and a positive NPV), while the follower must wait to enter until θ reaches θ_F^*. Thus
the differential costs or other asymmetries provide an intuitive and natural resolution as to which firm becomes the leader. In the special case that
the two firms are symmetric, which firm becomes the leader might be resolved by following a mixed strategy with a specified probability of entering first such that each firm is indifferent between investing and not
investing. In general, the leader's expected value from a mixed strategy
will be $P_L(1 - P_F)[V_{iL}(\theta) - I]$, and the follower's $(1 - P_L)P_F V_{jF}(\theta)$, where
P_L and P_F are the (independent) probabilities that the one or the other firm
will enter first. The values of the leader and follower, $V_{iL}(\theta)$ and $V_{jF}(\theta)$,
may be obtained from expressions similar to those in equations 9.26 and
9.23.

9.2.4. BENCHMARK CASES: SYMMETRIC COMPETITION AND MONOPOLY

Two well-known benchmark cases can result as special cases of this framework by varying the cost of the follower (c_F): (1) symmetric competition among identical firms whose unit costs are equal, as in the model of Dixit and Pindyck (1994, 309–16); and (2) an exclusive investment opportunity by an incumbent firm without fear of competitive preemption, as in the standard monopolistic option-pricing model of McDonald and Siegel (1986), here obtained by setting the unit cost of the higher-cost firm so high that it is never optimal for it to invest. The first benchmark case obtains when $c_F = c_L = c < \theta$. In this case, the above model reduces to one analogous to Dixit and Pindyck's (1994, 309–16), except that the firms have the additional flexibility to adjust their output level. In this equal-cost case with identical firms, several authors have suggested that one has to employ some random mechanism (e.g., flip of a coin) to decide which of the two identical firms will enter first in an equilibrium with sequential entry. This artificial decision setup is avoided in our more general model with asymmetric costs.[24]

The second benchmark case obtains when $c_F > \theta > c_L$. Here, the investment decision of the higher-cost firm becomes extreme: it will not invest at all, regardless of how favorable demand gets. Effectively, the low-cost firm obtains a permanent monopoly position being protected from competitive preemption. The entry demand threshold for the follower is effectively nonbinding (θ_F^* set at ∞). The first term of equation 9.26 disappears $(A_i = 0)$, reducing to the monopoly expression of McDonald and Siegel (1986) (see also equation 9.13).

9.3. Strategic Investment Timing under Uncertainty

This section discusses strategic investment timing issues. First, it discusses strategic interactions that may delay or speed up investment, and then it examines uncertainty over completion and time delays that may explain faster exit or delayed commercialization in innovative investments under uncertainty.

9.3.1. STRATEGIC INTERACTIONS AND THE TIMING OF INVESTMENT

In many industries firms often face competitors who may also exercise a shared option to invest that would significantly undermine the value of their own investment. As noted, when a rival firm has the ability to exercise a competing option, the fear of preemption comes in conflict with the

---

[24]See also footnote 3.

option value of delay. Accounting for competition between a small number of holders of interrelated or shared options necessitates use of game theory to analyze the strategic interactions between the parties, making real-options analysis considerably more involved. Strategic interactions can significantly affect investment threshold levels and the timing of investment in different ways.

Strategic Delay in Patent Races and First- versus Second-Mover Advantages

Weeds (2002) derives optimal investment strategies for two firms that compete for a patent. The research process for each individual firm involves both market and technological uncertainty, while investment is considered irreversible. The firms make separate investments, and their chances of making a breakthrough are uncorrelated. Due to the winner-takes-all nature of the patent system, success by one firm wipes out the value of the option held by the other, and the competition game ceases.

The analysis requires value functions to be derived for three situations: investing as the leader, investing as the follower, and continuing to hold the option to invest when the rival does so too. Preemption occurs when the value of becoming the leader exceeds that of continuing to hold the option. However, once it is clear that preemption will occur, the trigger point at which the leader invests is determined by the rent equalization principle of Fudenberg and Tirole (1985). This principle requires the values of the leader and follower to be equal at the point when the leader invests: if the leader's value were higher, a firm would preempt sooner, while if the follower's value were higher, both would wish to delay. The standard real-options "smooth-pasting" condition does not apply.

In a leader-follower equilibrium, one firm invests strictly earlier than its rival at the threshold determined by rent equalization, while the other can then exercise its option optimally (using standard "value-matching" and "smooth-pasting" conditions). The values of the firms, as viewed from the start of the game, are the same despite the different roles and investment timing. The leader gains the opportunity to win the patent before its rival even invests, but the value of the patent at this stage is lower. The follower has a lower probability of winning the patent, but if it does so, the value it gains is likely to be higher. Thus there is a trade-off between the two roles of the first or second mover.

In some cases, a second type of equilibrium may also be possible in which both firms invest at the same investment threshold. As long as the leader's value function never rises above the value of continuing to hold the option, there is no unilateral incentive for a firm to preempt its rival. Waiting until the threshold level at which it becomes optimal to invest,

knowing that the rival will also invest then, is a Pareto-dominant equilibrium in this situation. The investment threshold is the same as would
be chosen by two cooperating firms that agree upon an identical threshold and choose this level optimally (jointly). This simultaneous investment
outcome is very different from the leader-follower equilibrium: both firms
delay until a threshold level is reached that is higher than the single-firm
threshold. That is, strategic interactions between the firms induce an additional investment delay under uncertainty.

This result can be understood by considering the interactions between
the firms. There is a first-mover advantage, since the leader may innovate
before the follower invests. However, subsequent investment by the follower is harmful to the leader. In addition, the prospect of innovation by
the leader reduces the follower's option value of delay, speeding up its
competitive reaction to the leader's investment. Anticipating this reaction,
a firm may find it preferable to delay investment rather than to invest as
the leader. In effect, an investing firm chooses the time at which the patent
race begins, and each finds it preferable to delay this patent race. An analogy is the behavior of contestants in a long-distance race, who typically
remain in a pack proceeding at a moderate pace for most of the distance,
until near the end one breaks away and the sprint for the finish begins.

General Strategic Interactions with Externalities and Speedier Investment under Uncertainty

Mason and Weeds (2002) generalize the strategic interactions between
investing firms to combine an advantage of being the first-to-invest, with
externalities to investing (positive or negative) when another firm also
does so. As noted, a firm considering investing first may see the value of
its investment either be harmed by competition (shrinking the pie) or enhanced by spillover benefits from the other firm (enhancing the pie). For
example, when there are network benefits — as in telephony, where sub-
scribers care how many other people they may call — each firm gains from
investment by others since the total size of the market is expanded.

This broader framework raises the possibility that greater uncertainty
may hasten, rather than delay, investment. As above, there may be two
possible types of equilibrium: a leader-follower equilibrium and a simultaneous investment equilibrium. There are two ways in which investment
may be speeded up when uncertainty increases. First, in a leader-follower
equilibrium, greater uncertainty may lower the leader's investment threshold, entailing a speedier first investment. Second, the equilibrium may
switch between the leader-follower type and the simultaneous investment
pattern, such that the time taken for investment to occur is reduced. This
further emphasizes the point that interactions between firms may have

significant effects on option values and exercise strategies, demonstrating the importance of extending real-options analysis to incorporate such strategic interactions.

Real options must thus be analyzed in the context of a firm's competitive strategy. Competitive strategies affect real options through interactions such as those discussed above. In addition, real options can inform competitive strategy by guiding a firm's strategic alliances and acquisition strategies. When the options held by different firms interact, there may be advantages to managing them jointly to achieve optimal investment. This may be achieved by setting up a joint venture (e.g., in R & D) or through strategic acquisitions. This is becoming more important as markets converge and investment opportunities that were previously unrelated start to interact.

9.3.2. INNOVATION WITH UNCERTAINTY OVER COMPLETION AND TIME DELAYS

In many real-life situations, undertaking an investment project takes time: this is rarely an instantaneous process. There may be a considerable time, even several years, between the decision to invest and the time at which the project comes on stream and revenues are earned. Furthermore, there is often uncertainty over the exact time at which the project will be completed. One reason for completion uncertainty is innovation. When a firm undertakes research to create a new technology, it is generally unsure when — or even if — the breakthrough will be achieved. Such completion or technological uncertainty arises in a number of industries: biotechnology, computing, and oil exploration are just a few examples. Although innovation is perhaps an obvious context in which this issue arises, many physical investments also take time to build, and there is often uncertainty over exactly when the project will be completed. Building a factory, opening a mine, sinking telephone cables — all take time to complete, and the completion date is likely to be uncertain. Uncertainty over innovation completion in a single investment stage is examined in Weeds (2000a), while Weeds (2000b) extends the analysis to two investment stages to derive implications for sleeping patents.

Single Investment Stage: R & D Investment with Stochastic Innovation and Faster Exit

Consider an investment in innovation with completion or technological uncertainty in addition to the standard uncertainty over the value of the completed project. Specifically, suppose a firm holds the option to invest in research, where this investment is a sunk cost. The R & D process itself is stochastic: in any (short) time interval during which research is undertaken there is a probability that the breakthrough is achieved, with a given hazard rate for innovation. While the firm has not yet succeeded, it holds the option to abandon (and later restart) research. Once the innovation is made, the patent is obtained and the option expires. The value of the patent evolves according to a geometric Brownian motion.

The optimal investment strategy then takes the form of a pair of threshold patent values, describing the thresholds at which investment and abandonment should take place. The investment threshold exceeds the Marshallian zero-NPV investment level. However, the abandonment threshold may *exceed* the Marshallian exit point, giving rise to faster exit, or "reverse hysteresis." Thus, although the initial investment in research is delayed, the firm may abandon the project more rapidly as its profitability declines, ceasing research even while it would have a positive expected profit.

Two Investment Stages: Delayed Commercialization or Sleeping Patents

Suppose now the completed investment project involves two stages. First, the firm invests in research to create a patent. This process is stochastic, giving rise to completion uncertainty as described above. Second, once the patent is received, the firm makes a sunk capital investment in order to adopt the new technology, that is, to build a factory to produce the new product. Completion of this second stage is assumed certain and immediate. Thus the entire investment opportunity is a compound option, where the value of the (first-stage) research option is derived from the value of the (second-stage) commercial investment option, which is itself a standard call option.

Consider the threshold levels for the first- and second-stage investments. In the usual case without completion uncertainty or time to build, the trigger value for the first stage lies above that for the second. Thus, when investment takes place, both stages are undertaken at once with no delay between them. However, with uncertainty over completion or time to build, a delay may occur between the two stages. This delay results in the creation of a "sleeping patent" (or a similar unused asset in other contexts) that will be exploited only at a later date.

This pattern may arise for a number of reasons. At the time when research is commenced, profitability may be sufficiently high that if the patent were to be received at once, the new technology would also be adopted — and the second investment stage undertaken — immediately. However, when research takes time to produce results, conditions may deteriorate in the meantime and by the time the patent is obtained, profitability may no longer justify immediate adoption. Thus, a sleeping patent may arise due to potential deterioration of conditions during the research process.

It is also possible for research to be commenced at a time when prevailing conditions would *not* justify immediate adoption. In this case the investment trigger for the first stage lies below that for the second stage of investment. This pattern occurs particularly when the expected rate of innovation is low. When the first stage is likely to take some time to complete, research may be carried out prospectively, when current conditions are not so favorable, in order to ensure that the patent is available when profitability improves and it becomes desirable to undertake the second stage and commercialize the project. Meanwhile, a sleeping patent results that may be left dormant for some time.

When the first stage takes time to build, there is a trade-off between two potential costs facing the firm. If the first stage is completed before investing in the second stage becomes desirable, the cost of creating the patent could have been deferred for some period. The risk-free return on the invested funds over this interval is an opportunity cost incurred by early investment. On the other hand, if the first stage is not yet completed when the second-stage investment trigger is reached and the commercialized project becomes desirable, the second stage cannot be undertaken at once and an undesirable delay occurs. The opportunity cost of this delay is the revenues that are forgone because the completed project is unavailable at a time when it would have been desirable for it to be in place. Balancing these two costs may entail that research should be commenced even when current conditions would not justify proceeding with the second stage, and a sleeping patent may then arise.

This analysis has important policy implications for sleeping patents and compulsory licensing. Policymakers tend to regard sleeping patents as anticompetitive devices, employed by dominant firms to block entry into their market. Intellectual property laws in many jurisdictions, including a number of European countries (not the United States), contain compulsory licensing provisions so that a patent not utilized by its holder may be developed under license by another firm. In the absence of a coherent explanation as to why a firm would ever wish to create a new technology that it does not exploit, such measures appear readily justifiable.

However, as explained above, a sleeping patent (and similar dormant assets) may arise purely as a result of optimizing behavior when option values coexist with completion uncertainty. The mere existence of a sleeping patent cannot be taken as an indication of anticompetitive behavior. Therefore, compulsory licensing (or, for other assets, similar measures such as use-it-or-lose-it rules) may be unjustified. Furthermore, by restricting a firm's ability to delay after the patent is obtained but before the technology is adopted commercially, compulsory licensing may reduce option values and thereby weaken incentives to invest in research. If no delay at the intermediate stage may be allowed, the threshold for investing in research is raised. Thus, research will tend to be commenced later than when sleeping patents are permitted. This will have undesirable spillover effects on the rest of the economy.

9.4. Exercise Strategies under Incomplete Information with Applications

This section discusses entry or exit exercise strategies under incomplete information about the competitor, which may help explain delayed implementation of exercise decisions. Various applications are given explaining phenomena such as strategic sequential investments and sleeping patents, firm exit, product market competition and debt restructuring, as well as takeovers and restructuring activity.

9.4.1. ENTRY AND PREEMPTION UNDER INCOMPLETE INFORMATION

We have seen that first-mover advantages justify earlier investment that offsets a substantial part of the option value of waiting to invest. When there are many symmetric firms, the option value of waiting may be dissipated so that firms would again enter at (close to) the traditional Marshallian zero-NPV break-even threshold. In practice, however, we rarely observe this kind of extreme behavior. Firms most often do delay their entry beyond the break-even threshold, even when there are first-mover advantages. Lambrecht and Perraudin (2003) argue that this is partly because investors make their decisions under incomplete information. Incomplete information prevents investors from "marginally" preempting their competitors (as may usually be the case in complete information models), and consequently more option value of waiting is preserved. We first discuss the model of Lambrecht and Perraudin (1994), and next provide several applications from Lambrecht (2000, 2001, 2004).

Consider two firms, i and j, that can invest, respectively, amounts I_i and I_j in an indivisible technology that yields a flow of profits π_t, where π_t follows the geometric Brownian motion:

$$d\pi_t = \alpha \, \pi_t \, dt + \sigma \, \pi_t dz_t \qquad (\alpha < r, \sigma > 0). \tag{9.29}$$

Suppose that only the firm that invests first acquires the investment technology, whereas the preempted firm does not. Incomplete information about the competitor is introduced in two ways. First, each firm has imperfect knowledge (expressed via a probability distribution) of its competitor's investment (entry) threshold. Second, each firm faces a probability distribution of its competitor's investment cost, I. We next discuss the two competitors' investment thresholds that result in equilibrium.

Exogenous Competitor's Investment Threshold Distribution

To introduce incomplete information, assume that firm i conjectures that firm j invests when π_t first crosses some level $\overline{\pi}_j$, and that $\overline{\pi}_j$ is an independent draw from a distribution $F_j(\overline{\pi}_j)$, with positive support on an interval $[\overline{\pi}_L, \overline{\pi}_U]$. Lambrecht and Perraudin (1994, 2003) show that the value of firm i, which fears preemption by firm j, prior to investment by either firm is given by

$$V_i(\pi_t, \hat{\pi}_t \mid \overline{\pi}_{is}) = \left(\frac{\overline{\pi}_{is}}{\delta} - I_i\right)\left(\frac{\pi_t}{\overline{\pi}_{is}}\right)^{\beta_1} \frac{(1 - F_j(\overline{\pi}_{is}))}{(1 - F_j(\hat{\pi}_t))}, \tag{9.30}$$

where $\delta = r - \alpha$, and $\hat{\pi}_t$ is the highest level reached so far by π_t ($\hat{\pi}_\tau \equiv \sup\{\pi_\tau \mid 0 \le \tau \le t\}$). Firm i will invest when $\overline{\pi}_t$ first reaches the investment threshold $\overline{\pi}_{is}$, where $\overline{\pi}_{is}$ is given by

$$\overline{\pi}_{is} = \frac{(\beta_1 + h_j(\overline{\pi}_{is}))\delta I_i}{(\beta_1 - 1 + h_j(\overline{\pi}_{is}))}, \tag{9.31}$$

where $h_j(\pi)$ denotes the hazard rate $h_j(\pi) = \dfrac{\pi F'_j(\pi)}{1 - F_j(\pi)}$.

When there is no fear of preemption ($h_j(\pi) \cong 0$), the investment happens at the usual (nonstrategic) real-options threshold. As the competitive threat increases ($h_j(\pi) \to \infty$), the investment threshold converges to the Marshallian (zero-NPV) break-even threshold. This model can also incorporate learning: each time the state variable reaches a new high (and neither firm acts), firms update the conditional distribution of their opponent's trigger. This causes the value of their investment to go up as the opponent is perceived to be weaker than before.

Endogenous Competitor's Investment Threshold Distribution

Incomplete information is next introduced by assuming that the ith firm observes its own cost, I_i, but only knows that its competitor's cost I_j ($j \neq i$) is an independent draw from a distribution $G(I)$ with support $[I_L, I_U]$. We next determine the optimal investment strategy $\overline{\pi}_i(I)$ ($i = 1, 2$) for each firm. The inverse of this trigger mapping, $I_i(\pi)$, allows deriving the implied threshold distribution as: $F_i(\overline{\pi}) = G(I(\overline{\pi}))$, where $\overline{\pi}_L = \overline{\pi}_i(I_L)$ and $\overline{\pi}_H = \overline{\pi}_i(I_H)$. Lambrecht and Perraudin (1997) show that there is a unique symmetric equilibrium in which each firm's optimal investment threshold is the solution to the differential equation

$$I'(\overline{\pi}) = \left[\frac{1 - G(I)}{\overline{\pi}G'(I)}\right]\left[\frac{\overline{\pi} - \lambda(\overline{\pi} - \delta I)}{\overline{\pi} - \delta I}\right], \tag{9.32}$$

subject to the boundary condition that $I(\delta I_U) = I_U$.

9.4.2. APPLICATIONS

Strategic Sequential Investments and Sleeping Patents Revisited

Lambrecht (2000) applies the preceeding points to derive the optimal investment thresholds for two symmetric investors who hold an option to invest in a two-stage sequential investment and who have incomplete information on each other's profits. In the first stage, a patent of infinite duration can be acquired at known cost, C. Execution of this stage gives the investor the exclusive right to proceed to the second stage, the exploitation of the patent, which requires a further investment cost, I. Once the second stage is completed and the product is introduced on the market, profits start flowing in at a rate $a\pi_t$ (where a is a positive constant and π_t follows a geometric Brownian motion). It can be shown that if firm j's (first-stage) threshold distribution is given by $F_j(\overline{\pi}_{j1})$, then Firm i's investment thresholds for the first and second stage, $\overline{\pi}_{j1}$ and $\overline{\pi}_{i2}$, satisfy the following relationship:

$$\overline{\pi}_{i1} < \overline{\pi}_{i2} \Leftrightarrow \left[\frac{(\beta_1 + h_j(\overline{\pi}_{i1}))(\beta_1 - 1)}{h_j(\overline{\pi}_{i1})}\right] < \frac{1}{C}. \tag{9.33}$$

Since sleeping patents arise when $\overline{\pi}_{i1} < \overline{\pi}_{i2}$, the above relationship allows analyzing the determinants of sleeping patents. The first determinant is the size of the second-stage cost, I, relative to the patent fee, C. This makes intuitive sense. Think of the extreme case where the patent can be obtained costlessly. In this case, it is clearly optimal for firm i to grab the patent immediately and to let it sleep ($\overline{\pi}_{i1} < \overline{\pi}_{i2}$) until it is optimal to proceed with its exploitation. By doing this, the competitor is preempted at no cost. As the cost of patenting increases, it becomes more expensive to let the patent sleep. On the other hand, if the second-stage investment cost I is zero, there will be no reason for sleeping patents at all ($\overline{\pi}_{i1} \geq \overline{\pi}_{i2}$) because the patent holder would forgo free profits.

A second set of factors determining the occurrence of sleeping patents is the price volatility, σ, the interest rate, r, and the profit growth rate, α. As volatility increases, β_1 converges toward 1, causing the condition for sleeping patents to be satisfied. Similarly, sleeping patents are more likely to occur when interest rates are low and profit growth rates are high. Another crucial determinant of sleeping patents is competitive threat. As the competitive threat disappears ($h_j(.) \to 0$), the patent will not be taken out until the product is to be launched.

Exit, Product Market Competition, Debt Financing, and Restructuring

Lambrecht (2001) examines the impact of capital structure on the investment and foreclosure decisions of firms. He considers two firms, i and j, which have entered into a debt contract under which bondholders receive a perpetual flow of coupon payments, b_k ($k = i, j$), until the firm goes bankrupt. Each firm receives profits after interest payments of $a_k x_t - b_k$ ($k = i, j$), where x_t follows a geometric Brownian motion. Both firms are assumed to have complete information. If both firms have a single exit trigger strategy, the order in which firms leave is determined as follows:

Firm j leaves the market first

$$if \frac{b_i}{b_j} < \text{Max}\,[K_1, \text{Min}\,[K_2, K_3]\,]. \tag{9.34}$$

$$If \frac{b_i}{b_j} < K_1, \text{ then firm i strictly dominates, while}$$

$$if \frac{b_i}{b_j} > K_3, \text{ then firm j strictly dominates.}$$

$$If K_1 < \frac{b_i}{b_j} < K_3, \text{ then neither firm strictly dominates.}$$

This implies that the firm foreclosing last is the one with relatively high operating profits, lower debt repayments, and a larger incremental gain from becoming a monopolist, that is, survival of the "fittest, fattest, and greediest" firm. There is also a strong bias toward survival of the firm with the longest monopoly tenure (i.e., lowest monopoly exit threshold), which implies that it is more important to be "fat and greedy" than to be "fit." Interestingly, the extent to which higher operating profits can be substituted for lower debt repayments (and vice versa) depends on factors common to both firms, such as the interest rate, profit growth, and volatility. An important implication is that a change in these common economic factors may reverse the order in which firms are expected to foreclose.

Lambrecht (2001) extends this exit model by allowing financially distressed firms to reduce their debt repayments through a one-off "take it or leave it" debt exchange offer made by the equityholder. Bankruptcy occurs when both the equityholder and the bondholder refuse to support the firm any longer. Equityholders have an incentive to delay the exchange offer as long as possible, as bigger concessions can be obtained when the firm is more distressed. In addition, firms with higher bankruptcy costs, or with higher incremental monopoly benefits, can get bigger reductions on their debt repayments. Allowing for debt exchange offers can therefore reverse the order in which firms go bankrupt.

In terms of the impact of debt financing on market entry, in the presence of bankruptcy costs and in the absence of taxes, the need to borrow money will delay a firm's entry. Interestingly, the follower's entry timing also depends on the incumbent's capital structure if the follower is destined to outlive the incumbent. A higher coupon level set by the leader induces earlier entry by the follower, as the latter is keen to drive out the financially vulnerable opponent as soon as possible. Thus, a firm's product-market competition becomes "softer" when its leverage increases.

Takeovers and Restructuring Activity

Lambrecht (2004) presents a real-options model for the timing and terms of mergers and takeovers motivated by economies of scale, providing an explanation for the procyclicality of merger waves. He considers two firms whose production technology requires two inputs: a variable input (e.g., labor) and a fixed input (e.g., capital). Suppose the production technology displays economies of scale, in that both firms together can generate higher output than the sum of the outputs when they operate individually (without increasing production costs). The output increase can be a result of pure operational synergies (such as merging two complementary R & D teams, leading to increased research productivity), or it can be a consequence of the merged company being more competitive and attracting customers from its rivals (e.g., two telecom firms that by merging enhance the quality and size of their network coverage, making it superior to their rivals' network). The extra output can be sold at the market price, and hence the benefit of merging is an increasing function of the demand level, rising in economic booms and falling in economic downturns. Given that the industry demand is stochastic, the benefit of merging is stochastic also.

Mergers not only generate benefits, but also involve costs such as legal fees, fees to investment banks and other merger promoters, and costs of restructuring and integrating the two companies. These are typically one-off costs that, once incurred, are sunk. When merging, both companies have to trade off the stochastic benefit of merging against the cost of merging. Since both firms have the right, but not the obligation, to merge, each firm's payoff resembles an option, and the decision to merge resembles the exercise of an option. The higher profits that firms forgo by not merging act as an incentive to exercise this option, while the (at least partially) irreversible nature of the merger provides an incentive to delay. The optimal merger timing involves a balance between the two. Since the

gains from mergers motivated by economies of scale are positively correlated to product market demand, mergers happen in rising product markets. This creates merger activity at high output prices and merger
inactivity at low output prices. Cyclical product markets will therefore
generate a pattern of merger waves with mergers being procyclical.

Unlike financial options, the exercise of merger options is also influenced
by strategic considerations, since the payoff to each merged firm ultimately
depends on the postmerger ownership share it obtains in the new firm. The
restructuring mechanism (i.e., how the merger gains are divided up) can also
influence the timing of the restructuring. Thus friendly mergers and hostile
takeovers ceteris paribus should occur at different stages in a merger wave.

With friendly mergers it is in both parties' interest to first maximize
the total "pie" to be divided, and subsequently to argue about how to di-
vide the pie. In the absence of frictions it is in the interest of both parties
to adopt the globally efficient merger threshold. The second-round negotiation problem then boils down to identifying the merger terms that induce *both* firms to exercise their merger option at the globally efficient
merger threshold. Lambrecht (2004) shows that when firms are risk neutral there exists a unique Pareto optimal sharing rule that induces both
firms to execute the merger at the globally optimal time. By contrast, in
hostile takeovers negotiation about the surplus between the bidder and
the target is not possible. Consider the case where the target credibly pre-
commits to the terms it requires for relinquishing control, and the acquirer subsequently decides on the timing of the restructuring given those
terms. The target's increased bargaining power enables it to charge the
acquirer an extra bid premium. This bid premium is an additional cost to
the acquirer, raising the exercise price for the acquirer's takeover option
and causing hostile takeovers to take place later than mergers. The bid
premium is higher the higher the product market uncertainty and the
bidder-to-target-size ratio. Moreover, the higher the economies of scale
that motivate the takeover, the stronger will be the size effect.

9.5. General Equilibrium Investment Strategies under Imperfect Competition and Asymmetric Information

This section discusses general equilibrium investment exercise strategies,
first under imperfect competition and then under asymmetric information.

9.5.1. Equilibrium Investment Strategies under Imperfect Competition

Grenadier (2001) provides a general and tractable solution for deriving equilibrium investment policies in a continuous-time Cournot-Nash

framework. He argues that the impact of competition on exercise strategies is dramatic. In contrast to standard real-options models that emphasize that a valuable "option to wait" leads firms to invest only at large positive net present values, the impact of competition quickly erodes the value of the option to wait and leads to investment at near the zero-NPV threshold. The Nash equilibrium exercise strategies display the useful property that they are equivalent to those derived in an "artificial" perfectly competitive industry under a modified demand curve. This permits a simplified solution approach for including various realistic features into the analysis, such as time-to-build.

He considers an industry comprised of n identical firms producing a single, homogeneous good. Output is infinitely divisible. The price of a unit of output fluctuates stochastically over time so as to clear the market via a downward-sloping inverse demand curve. The demand for output is subject to continuous-time stochastic shocks. Each firm must choose its equilibrium investment strategy, subject to its beliefs about its competitors' investment strategies. A symmetric Nash equilibrium is obtained so that each firm's equilibrium exercise strategy is individually optimal conditional on its competitor's following the same equilibrium exercise strategy. The industry setting is quite general, that is, the underlying industry demand specification can be of a general form, as can the stochastic process underlying the demand shocks.

The search for an equilibrium can be simplified such that it becomes no more difficult than the standard real-options problem. Given that the Nash equilibrium can be determined via the solution of a particular myopic investor's problem, the entire solution approach becomes quite tractable. One can therefore apply this solution approach to analyze equilibrium investment strategies in a variety of settings. For a firm with monopolistic access to an investment opportunity, the option to "wait and see" can be quite valuable, leading to investment at triggers well above the standard zero-NPV threshold. However, the presence of competition quickly erodes the value of the option to wait. While for reasonable parameter values a monopolist may not invest until the net present value is about double the cost of investment, Grenadier finds that with competition the traditional net present value rule may become approximately correct even for industries with only a few competitors. The fact that the option to wait can be very valuable for a monopolist helps explain the large resources that firms expend in order to protect their position in various markets.

As the number of industry competitors increases, the likelihood of existing asset values falling below their investment cost increases. In many real-world asset markets, investments that initially appeared promising turned out poorly as the market quickly turned downward. In the traditional real-options framework, such ex post losses are not frequent. Since a monopolist would invest at a substantial option premium, the likelihood of large asset value reversals is remote. It would thus be difficult for the standard real-options framework that ignores such competitive effects to explain boom-and-bust markets such as real estate, where periodic bouts of overbuilding result in waves of high vacancy and foreclosure rates. However, given the much smaller option premiums in intensely competitive environments, such reversals become much more likely.

9.5.2. INVESTMENT STRATEGIES UNDER ASYMMETRIC INFORMATION

In many real-world situations, agents must formulate option exercise strategies under imperfect information. In such a setting, agents may infer the private signals of other agents through their observed exercise strategies. The construction of an office building, the drilling of an exploratory oil well, and the commitment of a pharmaceutical company toward the research of a new drug all convey private information to other market participants. Grenadier (1999) develops an equilibrium framework for option exercise games with asymmetric private information. This framework allows many interesting aspects of the patterns of equilibrium exercise to be analyzed. In particular, informational cascades, where agents ignore their private information and jump on the exercise bandwagon, may arise endogenously.

Consider the case of real estate investment as an example. As noted, the development of real estate is analogous to an American call option on a building, where the exercise price is equal to the construction cost. However, in real estate markets, there is a great deal of private information held by various market participants. Local developers may have particular knowledge of the suitability of particular locations, while large national developers may have greater expertise on market-wide factors and trends. The timing of construction will convey potentially valuable information about the value of a particular developer's private signal. Thus, the early entry of a local developer may convey positive information about the potential value of a particular location (just as the failure to enter would convey less positive information).

In Grenadier's (1999) model, private information is conveyed through the revealed exercise strategies of market participants. A set of n agents holds options contingent on a continuous-time stochastic price process, and each must determine the optimal time at which to exercise. Agents possess private information about a parameter that affects the option payoff. The private signals are informative but imperfect. Agents form exercise strategies that are contingent not only on their own signal but also on the revealed signals of other agents through their observed exercise policies. In equilibrium, as the potential payoff from exercise becomes greater, agents trade off the benefits of early exercise with the benefits of waiting for information to leak out through the actions of others. Equilibrium exercise is sequential, with the most informed agents allowing the least informed agents to free ride on the information conveyed by their exercise or failure to exercise.

While the observed exercise decisions of other agents may convey valuable private information, there are also times when no information can be inferred. This is the case when an informational cascade arises. As in information herding, an informational cascade occurs when agents ignore their own private information and instead emulate the behavior of those that preceded them. Specifically, an informational cascade can arise endogenously in which all agents, regardless of their private information, exercise immediately. Agents will find their private information overwhelmed by the information conveyed by others, and simply jump on the bandwagon.

Such option-exercise cascades may help explain the occurrence of "overbuilding" in real estate markets, that is, pronounced bursts of development in the face of declining rents and property values. Such overbuilding has not been limited to any region, property type, or even country. For example, when oil patch cities such as Denver and Houston experienced unprecedented waves of office construction during the early 1980s, local office vacancy rates were already above 27%. It seems unreasonable to assume that the developers (and their lenders) that had jumped on the bandwagon all had positive private signals about local market conditions. It is possible that a rational informational cascade was formed where agents found their private signals overwhelmed by the signals conveyed by previous developers. Grenadier's (1996) analysis of the timing of real estate development can help provide an explanation for why some markets experience building booms in the face of declining demand and property values. Developers, fearing preemption by a competitor's exercise, may proceed into a "panic" equilibrium in which development occurs during a market downturn.[25]

Unlike standard models of informational cascades where the ordering of actions is predetermined (exogenous), here timing is the essence of the

[25]Two building owners lease their existing properties in a local real estate market. Each holds the option to develop a new, superior building. Exercise of the development option by one building owner has repercussions on the value of both option holders. The first to build (the leader) will pay the construction cost earlier, but benefit by being able to lease the superior space without competition. The other developer (the follower) will see the value of its existing building rendered (relatively) obsolete by the presence of a new building. If the follower exercises his development option, he will gain the value from renting a new building. The leader will see his monopoly rentals discontinued, and must then compete in a duopoly.

game. Agents exercise strategically, and the revealed ordering of exercise is endogenous, that is, firms are free to choose the timing of their investment outlays. Thus one can analyze not simply "if" an informational cascade occurs, but also "when." Agents can not only use the actions of others to inform their behavior, but can also monitor the stochastic movement in some key underlying state variable (e.g., building rents) to guide their exercise policy.

This analysis reveals several interesting implications. With imperfect information, equilibrium exercise timing will almost always deviate from the full-information optimum. Those with the most informative signals will exercise the earliest, and will sometimes exercise earlier than optimal. Market observers may impute some form of "overbuilding," as is often implied in commercial real estate markets, using ex post information. In addition, the patterns of exercise across agents will differ across markets with varying structures. Markets with large information asymmetries will experience smooth exercise patterns over time, while markets with mild information asymmetries will experience quick bursts of exercise. The patterns of exercise will also vary according to the number of participants. Markets with large numbers of participants will be prone to longer lags between early exercisers, but more prone to bursts of exercise for later exercisers.

In many real-world situations, the exercise decision of an agent may not only impact the information set of other agents, but may also have a direct impact on the actual payoff from exercise. For example, certain technology markets exhibit network externalities in which the benefits from adoption are increasing in the total number of adopters. A classic example was the battle between VHS and Betamax in videocassette recorder technology. Such direct payoff externalities can have a powerful impact on the nature of the equilibrium. For example, if there are significant benefits from agglomeration, the likelihood of informational cascades increases substantially. Conversely, if negative externalities are associated with conformity, the likelihood of informational cascades can drop to zero.

9.6. Conclusions

In this chapter, we discussed the continuous-time analytic work of various authors, with some applications. Section 9.1 provided an overview of the relevant literature. Section 9.2 focused on a continuous-time version of the Smit-Trigeorgis approach discussed in earlier chapters. This represents a more general approach to strategic timing decisions by allowing duopolistic firms to have asymmetric costs and payoffs as well as flexibility in their choice of output levels. Variable output levels allow firms to optimally respond to entry by a competitor through a combination of output and timing decisions. This is an improvement over symmetric strategic models (which can be seen as a special case) in which some random mechanism must be used to decide which of two identical firms enters first. Section 9.3 revisited strategic interactions and their impact on investment thresholds and the timing of investment, and considered innovation with uncertainty over completion and time delays. This helped explain why there may be strategic delay in patent races, while in other situations (involving externalities) investment might be speeded up under uncertainty. It also helped explain phenomena like faster exit ("reverse hysteresis") and delayed commercialization (sleeping patents). Section 9.4 discussed entry and preemption under incomplete information concerning the competitor's entry threshold and investment outlay. It also discussed applications in sleeping patents, exit, product market competition, and debt restructuring, as well as takeovers and restructuring activity. The last section discussed general equilibrium investment (entry) strategies under imperfect competition and asymmetric information, explaining puzzling real estate development and other cascade phenomena.

Suggested Readings

Dixit, A., and R. Pindyck. *Investment under Uncertainty.* Princeton: Princeton University Press, 1994.

Grenadier, S. "Option Exercise Games: An Application to the Equilibrium Investment Strategies of Firms." *Review of Financial Studies* 15 (2001): 691–721.

Joaquin, D. C., and K. C. Butler. "Competitive Investment Decisions: A Synthesis." In *Project Flexibility, Agency, and Competition: New Developments in the Theory and Application of Real Options,* ed. M. J. Brennan and L. Trigeorgis. Oxford: Oxford University Press, 2000.

Lambrecht, B. M., and W. R. Perraudin. "Option Games." Working Paper 9414, University of Cambridge, 1994.

———. "Real Options and Preemption." *Journal of Economic Dynamics and Control* 27 (2003): 619–43.

McDonald, R., and D. Siegel. "The Value of Waiting to Invest." *Quarterly Journal of Economics* 101 (1986): 707–27.

Smit, H. T. J., and L. Trigeorgis. "Value Dynamics of R & D Strategies." Working Paper, Erasmus University, 1997.

Weeds, H. "Strategic Delay in a Real Options Model of R & D Competition." *Review of Economic Studies* 69 (2002): 729–47.

Appendix 9.1

Derivation of Differential Equation for Option Value of Waiting

This appendix obtains the standard differential equation for the option value of waiting for a single firm (first part of equations 9.15 and 9.24). Suppose the demand parameter θ_t follows the lognormal diffusion (or geometric Brownian motion) process:

$$d\theta = \alpha\theta dt + \sigma\theta \, dz, \qquad\qquad (9.A1.1)$$

where $d\theta$ is the change in demand θ over a small time interval dt, α is the constant growth rate (drift) of θ, σ is the constant instantaneous standard deviation in the drift rate, and dz is an increment of a standard Wiener process. Under risk-neutral (or no-arbitrage) valuation, α is replaced by the risk-neutral drift $\hat{\alpha} = \alpha - RP$ or $r - \delta$, where δ is the difference between the total required return and the actual growth rate or is a below-equilibrium return (analogous to a dividend yield).

The investment opportunity can then be seen as a contingent claim whose value, $V(\theta, t)$, depends on the current level of demand, θ_t, and time, t. To see how this value changes in a small time interval we can refer to Ito's Lemma, easier understood as a Taylor series expansion:

$$V(\theta + \Delta\theta, t + \Delta t) =$$

$$V(\theta, t) + \frac{\partial V}{\partial \theta} \Delta\theta + \frac{\partial V}{\partial t} \Delta t + 2\frac{\partial^2 V}{\partial \theta^2} (\Delta\theta)^2 + \dots, \text{ or}$$

$$\Delta V \equiv V(\theta + \Delta\theta, t + \Delta t) - V(\theta, t) =$$

$$\frac{\partial V}{\partial \theta} \Delta\theta + \frac{\partial V}{\partial t} \Delta t + 2\frac{\partial^2 V}{\partial \theta^2} (\Delta\theta)^2 + \dots$$

In the limit, as higher-order terms disappear,

$$dV = \frac{\partial V}{\partial \theta} d\theta + \frac{\partial V}{\partial t} dt + 2\frac{\partial^2 V}{\partial \theta^2} (d\theta)^2.$$

If θ follows the standard lognormal diffusion process in equation 9.A1.1, $(d\theta)^2$ behaves like $\sigma^2 \theta^2 dt$, and Ito's Lemma gives

$$dV = \frac{\partial V}{\partial \theta} d\theta + \frac{\partial V}{\partial t} dt + 2\frac{\partial^2 V}{\partial \theta^2} (\sigma^2 \theta^2 dt). \qquad (9.A1.2)$$

Since θ follows equation 9.A1.1, this can be written (as in equation 9.14)

$$dV = (\alpha\theta V_\theta + \tfrac{1}{2}\sigma^2\theta^2 V_{\theta\theta} + V_t)\, dt + \sigma\theta V_\theta\, dz, \qquad (9.A1.3)$$

where $V_\theta = \partial V/\partial \theta$, $V_{\theta\theta} = \partial^2 V/\partial\theta^2$, and $V_t = \partial V/\partial t$. Thus, the investment opportunity claim V follows a similar diffusion process involving the same dz (noise) term as the underlying demand θ, but with a different drift.

Using the standard risk-neutral valuation (no-arbitrage) argument as in Black and Scholes 1973 or Merton 1973, the (risk-neutral) expected return on the investment opportunity (growth option) must be the risk-free rate, that is,

$$\hat{E}(dV)/V = (\tfrac{1}{2}\sigma^2\theta^2 V_{\theta\theta} + \hat{\alpha}\theta V_\theta + V_t)/V = r.$$

Rearranging terms, this gives the standard equation for the option value of waiting to invest for a single firm:

$$\tfrac{1}{2}\sigma^2\theta^2 V_{\theta\theta} + \hat{\alpha}\theta V_\theta - rV + V_t = 0, \qquad (9.A1.4)$$

which is the first term in equations 9.15 and 9.24.

Appendix 9.2

Discounted Profit Flow and Value Function

As shown in earlier chapters, the profit flow for a firm i under Cournot-quantity competition is given by

$$\pi_i = \frac{(\theta - K_i)^2}{n} = \frac{1}{n}(\theta^2 - 2\theta K_i + K_i^2), \qquad (9.A2.1)$$

where $K_i = 2c_i - c_j$, n reflects the market structure (e.g., 4 for a monopolist, 9 for Cournot competition, 8 for Stackelberg leader, and 16 for Stackelberg follower), and θ is the market demand parameter. Assuming that θ follows a geometric Brownian motion, the present value of the profit flow, V, following risk-neutral valuation, is given by

$$V_i = E\left[\int_0^\infty e^{-rt}\pi_i(\theta_t)dt\right]; \qquad (9.A2.2)$$

$$V_i = \frac{1}{n}\int_0^\infty e^{-rt}(\theta^2 - 2\theta K_i + K_i^2)dt. \qquad (9.A2.2')$$

From Dixit and Pindyck 1994, 82, or Haanappel and Smit 2003, this yields

$$V_i = \frac{1}{n}\left[\frac{\theta^2}{\delta'} - \frac{2\theta K_i}{\delta} + \frac{K_i^2}{r}\right], \qquad (9.A2.3)$$

where $K_i = 2c_i - c_j$, $\delta = r - \hat{\alpha}$, $\delta' = r - 2\hat{\alpha} - \sigma^2$. Note that the discount rate depends on θ, with the quadratic θ term being discounted at δ', the linear term at δ, and the constant term at the riskless rate r. For expositional simplicity (and consistency with the discrete-time framework used in earlier chapters) we assume a constant discount rate δ and that the following value function holds: $V_i = \pi_i/\delta$.

Appendix 9.3

Sequential Stackelberg Leader–Follower Entry

If the two firms make their investments *sequentially* such that one firm observes the other's moves, then a Stackelberg leader-follower equilibrium can result. In case the low-cost firm i (the leader) invests first and the high-cost firm j defers investment until next period (I, D), the follower will set its quantity having first observed the leader's output (according to its reaction function, $R_j(Q_i)$, as in equation 9.6). Assuming the leader has already invested, Follower j's decision is to maximize its profit value (over its quantity Q_j) given the optimal output set by the leader. Anticipating this, the leader i will maximize its profit value $\pi_i(Q_i, R_j(Q_i))$ over Q_i, taking the follower's reaction function $R_j(Q_i)$ as given. Solving the above optimization problems simultaneously (since each firm's value and output decisions depend on the other's cost) results in the following equilibrium quantities and profit values for the Stackelberg leader (L):

$$Q_{iL} = \frac{(\theta - 2c_i + c_j)}{2} \quad \text{and} \quad V_{iL} = \frac{(\theta - 2c_i + c_j)^2}{8\delta}. \tag{9.A3.1}$$

The Stackelberg follower's (F) quantity and profit values are

$$Q_{jF} = \frac{(\theta - 2c_j + c_i)}{4} \quad \text{and} \quad V_{jF} = \frac{(\theta - 2c_j + c_i)^2}{16\delta}. \tag{9.A3.2}$$

As expected, the follower's equilibrium quantity and profit value are lower than the leader's ($Q_j < Q_i$, $V_j < V_i$) — except that the leader has to incur the investment outlay early on. If demand is not sufficiently high, the follower may be unable to cover its investment outlay I ($NPV_j < 0$) and may delay entry. The leader's profit value can then improve (temporarily) to the monopoly profit outcome. The above equilibrium output and profit value expressions are the same as those in chapters 6 and 7. In continuous time the value functions are simplifications assuming a constant discount rate. The exact expressions are given by equation 9.A2.3 in appendix 9.2, with $n = 8$ for the Stackelberg leader and 16 for the follower.

Chapter 10

Overview and Implications

A little knowledge is a dangerous thing.
So is a lot.
— Albert Einstein

10.1. Introduction

This closing chapter provides an overview and synthesis of some of the major ideas of the combined real-options and game theory framework developed in this book. Section 10.1 reviews the linkage between corporate finance and strategic planning via the expanded NPV framework. Section 10.2 discusses the main implications for strategic capital budgeting. Section 10.3 concludes with empirical implications for future work.

10.1.1. Linking Corporate Finance and Strategic Planning

The framework developed in this book is intended to align the design of an investment strategy with the market value of the firm. A new element presented here is to use real options and game theory not only to evaluate individual projects or acquisitions but to *shape* corporate strategy. One advantage of this approach is that it is consistent with and reinforces the intuitive strategic planning process. The options and games approach to corporate strategy is perhaps best viewed as an attempt to subject such intuition to the discipline of a more rigorous analytical process.

Figure 10.1 provides an overview of our framework, which connects strategic planning approaches and the underlying sources of value creation with the market value of the firm and its three value components. The starting point for the analysis are the various sources of economic value creation by the firm. A firm's growth opportunities and its strategic position in the industry are eventually reflected in stock market prices. As shown in the first column, the market value of a firm is not completely captured by the expected cash flows generated by the tangible assets that are currently in place (measured by its NPV) and the capabilities to utilize them efficiently. Stock market prices partly reflect a firm's strategic growth potential as well. Of course, different stocks generate different earnings streams and have a different growth potential. Growth stocks (e.g., in bio-tech, pharmaceuticals, or information technology) typically

FIGURE 10.1 IMPACT OF CORPORATE STRATEGIC PLANNING ON THE MARKET VALUE OF THE FIRM

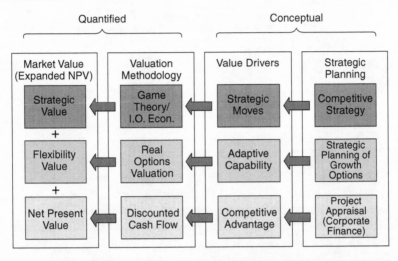

The broader strategy framework based on options and games recognizes three levels of planning that have an effect on the market value (expanded NPV) of investment opportunities. First (bottom row), project appraisal from corporate finance aims at determining the effect on the net present value of the projected cash flows resulting from establishing a competitive advantage. Second, strategic planning of growth opportunities aims at capturing the growth option value resulting from the firm's adaptive capabilities through real-options valuation. Third, competitive strategy aims at capturing the strategic value from establishing, enhancing, or deferring a strategic position vis-à-vis competitors based on game theory analysis and industrial organization economics.

have high price-earnings and market-to-book ratios. In fact, it is precisely the intangible and strategic value of their growth opportunities that determines most of the market value of high-tech firms in a dynamic environment. This growth option value derives from intangible assets, resources, and capabilities to adapt and generate options to undertake or capitalize on opportunities in the future under the right circumstances.

Because growth option value derives primarily from what the firm may invest in the future, rather than from investments it has undertaken in the past, it is particularly sensitive to future competitive moves. In fact, growth option value can be vulnerable not just to the actions of known incumbents, but also to the unanticipated entry of new rivals as new technologies can change drastically the competitive environment.

The flexibility and strategic value components of a business strategy are interwoven with that strategy's underlying logic and design. Quantitative tools like real options and game theory are intended to complement the strategic thinking process in an interactive way, not to replace it. The investor first has to reason why a particular business strategy leads to value creation. Combining these quantitative tools with qualitative insights from strategic management theory can provide a richer framework to help us understand better the investment and competitive behavior of firms and the substantial growth and strategic premiums embedded in certain stocks.

Strategic management and corporate finance are thus complementary for the design and valuation of an investment strategy. To properly link corporate strategy with the value creation of the firm one needs to identify the project's main value drivers. These value drivers help provide an interface between the quantitative project valuation methodology and the qualitative strategic planning process that focuses on competitive advantage and the sources of value creation. The two columns on the right-hand side of figure 10.1 indicate that to fully understand total strategic value creation, it is not sufficient to examine only the traditional value drivers that focus on *why* a particular project is more valuable for this company than for its competitors at the present time. One must consider also what are the important value drivers for capitalizing on or levering the firm's future growth opportunities in an uncertain environment, and *how* competitive strategic moves can help appropriate the benefits of those growth opportunities for the firm while limiting risk by cutting losses if unfavorable developments occur.

10.1.2. An Expanded Valuation Framework to Capture Flexibility and Strategic Value

An important step in bridging the gap between traditional corporate finance theory and strategic planning is the development of an expanded valuation framework that enables a complete analysis of all relevant value components. Besides the value of expected cash flows from already committed investments, valuation and capital appraisal methods should properly also capture the flexibility and strategic value components that may contribute significantly to an adaptive firm's market value in an uncertain competitive environment.

Our strategic framework proposes a dynamic strategy valuation that encompasses NPV analysis and incorporates the dynamic tree features of real options and game theory when they are relevant. NPV analysis can capture the value of management's expected scenario of cash flows, while real options provide an appropriate valuation procedure when future developments are likely to unfold differently than expected. Moreover, when competitors can affect each other's behavior, a broader strategic analysis (often relying on game theory principles) is called for.

The second column in figure 10.1 focuses on the new valuation approach based on the combined insights from real options and game theory, intended to capture the additional flexibility and strategic value beyond the narrow expected cash flow benefits of net present value. It views a firm's growth opportunities as a package of corporate real options that is actively managed by the firm, and which may be affected by competitive actions and the introduction of new technologies. If a firm's investment decisions are contingent upon and sensitive to competitors' moves, competitive strategies should be analyzed using a combination of option valuation and game-theoretic industrial organization principles, as the two may interact.

The strategic value of making an early investment commitment to influence competitive behavior in a way that is beneficial to the investing firm must be offset against the flexibility or option value of waiting, and may potentially justify early investment. In our proposed expanded or strategic NPV framework, investment can have two main effects on a firm's value compared to a wait-and-see strategy: (1) *A flexibility or option-value effect*, reflecting the value of management's ability to wait to invest in the business under uncertain conditions;[1] and (2) *A strategic commitment value effect*, since early investment may signal a credible commitment that can influence competitors' investment decisions.

In this broader context incorporating additional flexibility and strategic considerations of competitive interaction, besides the value of expected cash flows from passively committing to future plans, business strategy decisions must be based on an expanded NPV criterion reflecting total market value:

Expanded (strategic) NPV = (passive) NPV + flexibility (option) value + strategic (game-theoretic) value.

This expanded framework allows combining the three main value components presented in figure 10.1. Each is discussed in more detail below.

(Passive) NPV: Sustainable Competitive Advantage

To understand the sources of value creation behind a project's positive (expanded) NPV, one must first examine the various value drivers to understand *why* a particular project is more valuable for this particular company than for its competitors. How firms achieve and sustain com-

---

[1]Early investment would enhance the commitment value, but sacrifice flexibility value compared to a wait-and-see strategy.

petitive advantage that allows earning a return in excess of the opportunity cost of capital is a fundamental question in the field of strategic management. In competitive markets, excess profits attract new entrants or imitation by competitors. Such competitive forces would tend to drive a firm's rate of return down to its cost of capital. In rivalry, excess profits can only exist if the firm has a sustainable competitive advantage that can block pervasive forces of duplication by competitors.

Value creation due to competitive advantage can result from several broad generic strategies, for example, a cost advantage that allows the firm to produce at lower cost than its competitors or a differentiation advantage that allows the firm to charge a price premium. A cost leadership strategy exploits opportunities that are sources of cost advantage, provided they are not currently exploited by others. For instance, a firm can exploit economies of scale or learning by operating at large quantities while keeping its quality similar to its competitors. A cost leadership position is more likely to be adopted when demand sensitivity to price is highly elastic, more commodity-like, and customer services are hard to differentiate.

Differentiation can be an important competitive advantage when the firm can create distinctive capabilities and core competences that enable it to charge a price premium. This strategy can be relatively more attractive when price elasticity of demand is low, and when the differentiated nature of products or services allows enhancing its perceived value to customers.

Competitive advantage essentially reflects a firm's ability to perform superior relative to its competitors and eventually results in an excess return over industry profitability. When the advantage can persist over a long period and is resistant to current and potential competitor attempts to imitate, it will result in excess returns and positive (expanded) NPV. The internal resources and capabilities the firm has in its disposal to play the game in the market shape its strategic position in the industry. A superior strategic position will result in above-average profitability and attract efforts by potential rivals to duplicate the advantage. Sustainable competitive advantage depends on isolating mechanisms in the firm's resource position that can avoid imitation. Firms can make strategic moves such as obtaining first-mover advantages or patents to protect their value creation. But in dynamic market environments, excess profitability can only persist if the firm has gathered together a bundle of capabilities and options to adapt by reconfiguring and redeploying its resources more effectively than its competitors.

Real-Options Value: Adaptive Capabilities

Where does growth option value come from? To answer this question we must first understand that the internal resources and capabilities of a firm are explicitly linked to environmental opportunities. Firms who use their internal strengths in exploiting environmental opportunities, while moving in a prudent, staged fashion, are more likely to gain competitive advantage. An important question for value creation is, What opportunities exist for dynamically optimizing the use of a firm's resources? A firm's resources are more valuable if they lead to corporate growth options. Tangible resources, such as plant and machinery, may have simple options to expand. But the value of intangible resources, such as patents, critically depends on the generation of future growth options for the firm. Once management knows which of its resources and core capabilities are most important, it can leverage them to enhance competitive advantage.

The intangible value of investments that make up part of the firm's resources derives primarily from the set of options to invest in future growth. Strategic plans often encompass projects that, if measured by cash flows alone, appear to have a negative net present value, when in fact they may create a strategic position to invest in valuable follow-on opportunities. An early investment in research and development, for instance, may seem unattractive if its direct measurable cash flows are considered in isolation. Such a strategic R & D investment should not be seen as a one-time investment at the outset; proper analysis requires explicit consideration of its follow-on commercial and related spin-off applications. In practice firms use strategic investments to enhance their strategic position, and do appreciate the value of flexibility to react to a dynamic environment.

The real-options perspective suggests that, as information over the success of a multistage investment such as R & D is revealed, management has valuable flexibility to decide whether to proceed to the next stage, terminate, or otherwise alter its future investment plans. An R & D investment, a pilot project, or entry into a new geographical market has add-on strategic value precisely because it can create or exploit future investment opportunities. Like a call option, the value of the growth options of a firm is influenced by uncertainty, time to maturity, and interest rates.

Thinking of investment opportunities as real options can be facilitated via a classification scheme such as the one in figure 10.2. The first question managers must ask is, What are the value characteristics of the investment opportunity? Normal investment opportunities that realize their benefits primarily through operating cash inflows are similar to simple options. Compound or multistage options, on the other hand, have more strategic value. They should be seen as a first link in a sequence of investment opportunities over time. Strategic investments such as R & D, ex-

FIGURE 10.2 CLASSIFICATION FOR CORPORATE REAL (GROWTH) OPTIONS

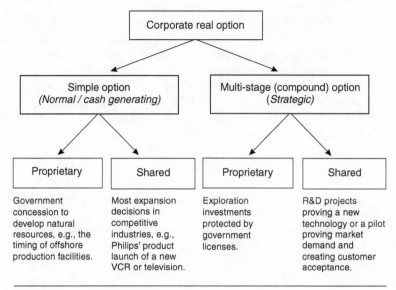

Source: Based on Trigeorgis 1988.

ploration drilling for oil, or a pilot project, create valuable follow-on investment opportunities.

Another major aspect affecting the value of a corporate real option concerns the corporation's ability to fully appropriate the resulting opportunities for itself. Proprietary options can result from license or patent protection. These options represent unique knowledge that cannot be duplicated by competitors, or that exist within a monopoly market structure. Shared options, on the other hand, are those held by more than one competitors in the industry. They include the opportunity to introduce a new product that is not protected from possible introduction of copies, or to penetrate a new geographic market without any barriers of entry by competitors.

Figure 10.2 reviews the option-based classification of corporate real options. Under this classification:

1. A production license that gives the right for a prespecified period to invest in production facilities to produce proven reserves is classified as a *simple proprietary* option.

2. An exploration license that allows an oil company to invest in exploration wells can be viewed as a *proprietary compound* option.

The investment in testing and appraisal wells creates an option to invest in production facilities.

3. Product launches, such as Philips' launch of 100 Hz television, CD, or high-density disk, which competed with similar products by Sony and others, are classified as *simple shared* options.

4. Investment in R & D with close substitutes can be classified as a *shared compound* option. Firms like Philips and Sony both competed and cooperated in the development of technologically innovative products, such as video and CD technology. The development of the CD technology resulted in various substitute product introductions.

A firm's business strategy involves developing and managing an optimal mix or portfolio of such simple (normal) and multistage (strategic) investment opportunities. Portfolio approaches that can optimize the bundle of simple and compound options can help managers to balance and manage their options portfolio. A portfolio approach should consider the balance between direct profitability from commercialization captured by NPV and the value of growth opportunities (PVGO). The mix of simple and compound options in the firm's options portfolio is closely related to the exploration-exploitation activity of the firm. Industries with a high level of innovation in dynamic environments have more compounded optional opportunities and higher PVGO-to-price ratios than firms with less R & D activities.

Growth firms (e.g., in information technology, pharmaceuticals, or consumer electronics) tend to have a higher growth option value component (PVGO) than income stocks, for two reasons. First, they operate in more volatile and rapidly evolving industries (characterized by more frequent technological innovations and a more intensely competitive environment), with the higher underlying volatility being translated into higher (simple) option value. Second, they tend to have a higher mix of compound (multistage or growth) options than simple (cash-generating) options, which further amplifies their strategic option value (being options on options). This higher (growth) option value, in turn, is translated into higher market valuations for high-tech or growth stocks that may appear excessive from the perspective of standard DCF valuation methods.

While technological opportunities may vary across industries, adaptive capabilities may be an important source of competitive advantage within industries. Adaptive capabilities reflecting the capacity of organizations to renew their competences and adapt flexibly can be an important source of competitive advantage in an environment characterized by rapid changes. The dynamic capabilities framework (Teece, Pisano, and Shuen 1997) emphasizes how organizations first develop firm-specific capabilities and how they renew their competences to respond to shifts in their business environment. Management must develop capabilities to appropriately adapt and reconfigure skills, resources, and competences to match the changing requirements of a dynamic environment. Learning and experimentation can help identify new production opportunities. This requires constant surveillance of markets and technologies for various types of opportunities that enable management to adapt more efficiently. The ability to effectuate necessary adjustments requires scanning the environment, evaluating markets and competitors, and quickly accomplishing reconfiguration and transformation ahead of competition.

From a real-options and dynamic capabilities perspective, where the firm is going in the future depends on the historical path it has traveled, the technological opportunities that lie ahead, and management's dynamic strategic plans. As soon as management starts down a path, it is faced with uncertainty about developments in the industry and competitive moves, and it needs to respond flexibly to these developments. As we begin to think in options terms, each project in a strategic investment program can be seen as a necessary link in generating follow-on options to invest, or as part of a bundle of corporate options and competences that extends over the long term. These options and competences may lose their value if they no longer matter in the marketplace or if they can be readily replicated by competitors.[2] Management should not treat the trajectory and pattern of related outlays along a strategic path as a static scenario, but instead dynamically adjust it depending on uncertain developments in the business environment. A firm engaged in R & D may find the path ahead closed off, though breakthroughs in related areas may be sufficiently attractive. Likewise, if the path ahead is extremely attractive, there may be no incentive for a firm to shift the allocation of resources away from its traditional pursuits.

Of course, a competence-building strategy is "history" dependent. The chosen path today does not only define which investment alternatives are open to the firm today, but also constrains choices in the future. Path dependencies arise when investment choices are costly to reverse and affect the value of future investment alternatives. Path dependencies limit options for switching along various available strategic paths.

Strategic (Game-Theoretic) Value: Strategic Moves and Positioning

Game theory, or strategic conflict in the strategic management literature, analyzes the nature of competitive interactions between firms. A game

---

[2]On the other hand, cooperation in R & D and coordination of a product standard among competitors may potentially increase the total economic pie for the industry.

describes a strategic context where the decisions of firms are interdependent. This can be a zero-sum game, involving the division of a given economic pie, as well as cooperation or mutual benefit decisions that can enhance total value. In the first case, the gain of one firm is the other firm's loss. For instance, in electronics or pharmaceuticals firms enter into patent races to improve their competitive position and their ability to appropriate the growth opportunities in the industry.

A strategic move is intended to influence a rival's behavior in a way that is advantageous to the pioneer firm, enhancing its value. Examples of strategic moves include an early irreversible investment, a threat of a price war or lawsuit, a promise to cooperate, or an announcement of a pathbreaking discovery. The move will have little effect or credibility if it can be costlessly undone. To be effective, such strategic moves must involve irreversible or costly commitments.

Similar to other mechanisms used to protect the profitability of an industry against potential entrants, like high entry or exit barriers, there are actions that can be taken by a firm to protect its competitive advantage against erosion or duplication from competitors. The company can use a deterrence strategy of signaling retaliation actions, or can adopt an early-mover strategy to exploit preempting advantages. Early-mover advantages in the competitive exercise of real options are important "isolating mechanisms" avoiding duplication by competitors. There are also potential interactions among the value components. The commitment effect of an early-mover advantage may help sustain a competitive advantage from assets in place (NPV) or help appropriate growth option value.

With first-mover advantages, precommitment can be used to influence competitive behavior to a firm's advantage, for example, by increasing the acquisition cost or reducing user revenues for competitors with a weaker position. Consider an early mover that invests aggressively in large-scale production facilities in a market with economies of scale. Investment in excess production capacity here can be viewed as a credible commitment. Later entrants would face less valuable expansion opportunities as they would expand with a reduced scale to avoid a market share battle. By making it more difficult for others to catch up, an early investment commitment can lead to higher profits for the early-moving firm. Similarly, first-mover advantages can be gained with proprietary technological leads, experience curve effects, customer loyalty with buyer switching costs, network externalities, reputation, and buyer choice under uncertainty.

Although an early investment commitment would kill the option value to wait-and-see and potentially invest later, it can make the firm better off from a strategic perspective. In addition, lack of flexibility to retreat from the market may alter a competitor's beliefs about the intensity of potential competition and the future profitability in the market. Inflexibility or "burning one's bridges" behind may signal commitment to pursue the chosen strategy to the very end. If a competitor is thereby forced to react in a desired way, this inflexibility has significant commitment value.

In some cases there may be early-mover disadvantages, which are in effect advantages of the late mover. For instance, in cases where the benefits of the strategic investment are shared, later movers may free ride on a pioneering firm's investment. This may be the case in R & D, some types of infrastructure investments, and buyer education. In addition to the ability to free ride on an early-mover investment, late movers may benefit from the resolution of technological and market uncertainty or from technological discontinuities that open up new technology options. The option value to wait is important when uncertainty is high and there is a benefit from waiting to exercise investments as uncertainty is resolved. Early movers may risk failure to establish a sustainable competitive advantage because they may bet on the wrong technology when there is substantial uncertainty about the future product standard. On the other hand, early entry might be attractive in cases where the firm can influence the way this uncertainty is resolved.

Game theory coupled with real-options valuation can yield powerful insights in these strategic situations. The combined framework provides a dynamic view of business strategy to assist practitioners in the building of long-run competitive advantage and strategic adaptability.

10.2. Implications of the Strategic Options and Games Framework

This book has taken a step in closing the gap between traditional corporate finance theory and strategic planning, combining the real-options approach with game theory principles. The proposed expanded NPV criterion can capture both the strategic commitment value of competitive initiatives or reactions and the flexibility value of altering planned investments in pursuing a business strategy under uncertainty. By contrast to the flexibility value implicit in a wait-and-see approach, early irreversible investment may entail commitment value if it informs competitors about the future profitability of their options in a given market. We develop several implications of our framework depending on the simple or compound nature of the firm's options, the type and competitive impact of the investment, and the strategic context of the market.

10.2.1. Timing Games for Simple Commercial Options

As noted, entry barriers and the number of competing firms determine the intensity of competition and market power in an industry. Competition can influence the value and timing of commercial projects. A deferrable project in a monopoly is seen as an exclusive investment opportunity that can benefit from a wait-and-see approach. On the other hand, postponement of a shared option in a fragmented competitive market implies a potential loss in the expected value of the project due to anticipated entry by competitors. In the absence of a structural competitive advantage, investing early to preclude this erosion of value may be justified.

An oligopoly situation lies between these extremes of monopoly and competition. Here, a few firms with individual market power are competing in the industry. Managers' investment decisions are made with the explicit recognition that they may invite competitive reaction, which in turn impacts the value of the investment opportunity. In a duopoly, a prisoners' dilemma can occur in which the competitive pressure of the other firm investing first and winning the innovation race induces both firms to invest prematurely. Instead, it would have been better for the two firms to defer investment in case of low project value and uncertain market demand. If the firms can (implicitly) coordinate their investment, they may find it preferable to postpone to jointly optimize against demand uncertainty.

If the competitors' market power differs, we can distinguish different investment timing strategies. When early-mover advantages are present, timing strategy is based on the firm's strength in relation to its competitors. A competitor with a stronger resource position would likely have more valuable options. Preemptive exercise of its options can affect the acquisition cost (exercise price) or the user revenues (underlying value) for weaker competitors. If the firm is able to use an early-mover advantage in its favor, it can create a situation where it becomes increasingly difficult for others to catch up. The value erosion for late movers will be greater if the market power of the leader is higher, because an early investment on its part will take away a large market share. A firm with substantial market power can sometimes preempt a competitor. Projects with low net present value from immediate exercise are more likely to be postponed. Low project value by weaker companies makes them vulnerable to preemption by a stronger competitor with high project value. As noted, early-mover advantages can be an important isolating mechanism for the resources of the firm, depending on such factors as economies of scale, experience effects, customer loyalty or network externalities.

Based on the strength of a firm in relation to its competitors (dominant or weak) and the value of the project in relation to the risk of preemption, one can develop simple option investment strategies as illustrated in figure 10.3.

1. Projects that have relatively small net present value from immediate investment and relatively larger flexibility value in uncertain markets are better candidates to be postponed. If a company has a dominant market position in its industry, there is little threat of complete preemption by a weaker competitor. This firm can safely postpone the project and decide to invest later if the market develops favorably or if the weaker competitor invests first, especially if it can prove the market without gaining a significant market share.

2. Projects with relatively high net present values in relation to the risk of preemption and relatively less flexibility value are less likely to be postponed. There may be a high opportunity cost from deferment in the form of lost operating cash flows during the deferment period, inducing a dominant company to invest early.

3. If the company has a weak position in the market, the project will not likely have a large net present value up front. Only later, if the market develops sufficiently, will it make sense to initiate the project.

4. If the company has a weak market position but its particular project nonetheless appears to have a positive net present value, it should invest immediately if it can preempt competitors or create a

FIGURE 10.3 TIMING STRATEGIES OF FOLLOW-ON INVESTMENTS UNDER COMPETITION

NPV FROM IMMEDIATE INVESTMENT

		Low	*High*	
MARKET POSITION	*Dominant*	Low commitment value and high flexibility value enhances postponement i No threat of preemption	High commitment value and ii low flexibility value enhances early investment No threat of preemption, dominant position increases the ability to expand market share	
	Weak	Low NPV value supports iii deferment until the market develops sufficiently for the firm to enter Threat of preemption	Early investment to capture iv high NPV and preclude erosion of value Risk of preemption in which case NPV might become negative	

cost advantage. However, because of its weak position, there is a risk that a stronger competitor can come in subsequently and erode its net present value, even turn it negative ex post.

In general, a company will tend to postpone commercial projects when net present value is low and market demand is uncertain. The degree of nonexclusiveness of the investment opportunity also influences the investment strategy. When there are many competitors, each with negligible market power, their entry can erode some of the value of the project and can be treated as exogeneous. When there are few competitors with great individual market power, however, competitive interaction must be considered and sometimes there can be a threat of complete preemption.

10.2.2. INVESTMENT GAMES INVOLVING STRATEGIC OPTIONS

In chapters 6 and 7 we considered a sequence of investment decisions by a pioneer firm in which a first-stage strategic (R & D) investment commitment influences its relative cost position vis-à-vis its competitor in the commercialization stage, and subsequent cash-generating investment decisions by either competitor. We illustrated the trade-off between flexibility and the strategic commitment value of the first-stage R & D investment that interacts with market structure by altering the competitor's equilibrium quantity or changing the market structure altogether.

We saw that an early strategic investment would necessarily reduce option or flexibility value, other things constant, but it can have a high or low (even negative) net commitment value, depending on the strategic effects. A key factor in determining the commitment value and an appropriate competitive strategy is whether an early strategic commitment makes the pioneer firm more "tough" (i.e., whether it can appropriate the resulting benefits and hurt its competitors), or "accommodating" (i.e., whether the resulting advantage can be shared with and benefit its rivals) in the commercialization phase. A second factor is whether competitive reactions are reciprocating or contrarian, that is, whether the competitors' reactions are similar (strategic substitutes), or whether they are opposite (strategic complements) (figure 10.4).

In some cases, an early investment commitment can be a strategic disadvantage if it reduces the firm's ability to respond toward aggressive competitors who can exploit shared benefits from the strategic investment, or if it provokes a retaliating competitive response and intense rivalry. Based on a combination of real-options valuation with basic game-theory principles from industrial organization, we have distinguished various competitive investment strategies, depending on whether competitive actions are reciprocating or contrarian, and whether the resulting benefits are proprietary (tough) or shared (accommodating):

FIGURE 10.4 SIGN OF THE STRATEGIC EFFECT AND COMPETITIVE
STRATEGIES FOLLOWING A TOUGH OR ACCOMMODATING POSITION
UNDER CONTRARIAN OR RECIPROCATING COMPETITION

COMPETITION

		Contrarian (down-sloping reaction/ substitutes) e.g., Quantity competition	*Reciprocating* (up-sloping reaction/ complements) e.g., Price competition
	Tough e.g., proprietary investment (hurt competition)	i **committing and offensive** Invest (+ strategic effect)	ii **flexible and inoffensive** Don't invest / wait (– strategic effect)
PIONEER	*Accommodating* e.g., shared investment (benefit competition)	iii **flexible and offensive** Don't invest / wait (–strategic effect)	iv **committing and inoffensive** Invest (+ strategic effect)

1. *When competitive actions are contrarian and the benefits of strategic investment can be appropriated by the pioneering firm at the expense of its competitors, the firm should commit to an offensive strategy and invest early.* Strategic commitment makes the firm tougher in the commercialization stage by creating a proprietary advantage when investing in follow-on projects. If competitive actions (e.g., quantities) are contrarian, competition will retreat in the commercial stage and the pioneering firm can become a leader as demand grows.

2. *When the benefits of strategic investment are shared and competition is contrarian, rivals would respond aggressively, and the firm should not invest immediately but rather follow a flexible but offensive strategy.* By delaying strategic investment, it prevents its competition from exploiting the resulting shared benefits to grow at its own expense.

3. *When the benefits of strategic investment can be appropriated by the firm at the expense of competitors and rivals may reciprocate with an aggressive response, the firm should follow a flexible and inoffensive strategy.* The firm should avoid committing to the strategic project to preserve its resources and flexibility and avoid intensified price competition in the later stage of the market.

4. *When the strategic investment benefits both the firm and its competitors, rivals would reciprocate with an accommodating position (e.g., maintaining high industry prices), the pioneer should follow a committing and inoffensive strategy.* It may invest in goodwill in an inoffensive way, avoiding intense price competition that would hurt the industry. Through maintaining higher prices, both firms may enjoy more profitable follow-on commercial options.

The preceding analysis of competitive strategies can be extended to incorporate the impact of additional factors, such as uncertainty in market demand and a stochastic outcome of the R & D effort, incomplete or asymmetric information, R & D competition versus cooperation in a joint research venture, and learning or experience cost effects. A number of implications result from this extended analysis regarding competitive R & D strategies.

5. *Uncertainty in the outcome of the R & D effort generally enhances flexibility value and reduces the strategic and commitment value of R & D compared to the situation of certain proprietary R & D.*

6. *Under incomplete information, the value of flexibility and strategic reaction becomes less important due to an "averaging out" in the competitor's response.* The value in case of R & D success declines compared to the situation of complete information. Competition would set a higher quantity based on its expectation and would intensify rivalry. By contrast, in case of R & D failure, competition would set a lower quantity. Naturally, if its R & D efforts are successful, the firm has an incentive to communicate this to competition to induce it to set a lower quantity and soften competition in the commercialization phase.

7. When the firms can cooperate in R & D via a joint research venture during the first stage, there are three influences on value compared to direct competition in R & D: (*a*) A joint research venture enables the cooperating firms to more fully appropriate the flexibility value from waiting. There is no sacrifice of flexibility value from the pressure to preempt the market as under direct R & D competition; (*b*) joint research has a beneficial impact on direct NPV and commitment value compared to R & D competition by achieving the same cost savings during commercialization with a lower (shared) first-stage R & D expenditure by each firm; (*c*) on the negative side, joint research results in potential sacrifice of strategic value because the firm cannot acquire a competitive advantage via an early R & D investment.

8. *Learning cost effects generally trigger earlier investment and erode flexibility value.* A learning cost experience by both firms has

the following influences on the value of a strategic R & D invest-ment: (a) It has a negative impact on the direct NPV of the pioneer firm because competition builds up production volume more quickly, i.e., the direct value of making an up-front strategic R & D invest-ment under learning declines. The strategic reaction value declines as well; (b) learning enhances the strategic pre-emption value of a strate-gic investment; (c) learning erodes flexibility value, since both firms have a cost-driven incentive to invest earlier rather than to wait.

The preceeding framework marrying real-options valuation with game-theoretic industrial organization principles enables simultaneous deter-mination of different market structure equilibrium games in the various states of demand within a binomial valuation decision tree. It also makes possible to properly account for interdependencies among the early strate-gic commitment and sequential follow-on decisions in a competitive in-teractive setting.

10.3. Empirical Implications

It is up to empirical testing to provide support for the validity of the in-sights derived from this analysis. The propositions developed herein are potentially testable since the growth option and commitment values are embedded in the firm's stock price. The implications of the above analy-sis can be tested against observed firm behavior using data on the competitors' relative market performance and their corresponding risk profiles. There is already sufficient evidence that valuable growth opportu-nities for innovative firms tend to be found in more volatile and rapidly evolving industries. Options thinking suggests that firms operating in in-dustries with more uncertain demand and technological innovation (such as biotechnology, information technology, and electronics) have higher embedded growth option value (PVGO/price). However, strategic pre-emption may cause additional value discontinuities and further enhance growth stock value asymmetry. The strategic reaction and preemption ef-fects of early commitment embedded in the firm's market value should be more significant when the firm has preferential or proprietary access to future opportunities (e.g., when patents in biotechnology or a dominant market position in information technology can ensure the R & D benefits are proprietary). However, technical uncertainty may interact with com-mitment value in that the preemption effect may manifest itself after the uncertainty of R & D success is resolved, but is smoothed out during the uncertain R & D phase. The value of firms operating in industries with high technical uncertainty, such as biotechnology and pharmaceuticals, should more fully reflect the strategic effect following the R & D phase when the product is launched. The effect of breakthrough inventions should also be reflected in the market value of competitors and be manifest in more asymmetric stock returns. Finally, cooperation in R & D would diminish the strategic preemption effect of R & D. We leave it for future research to empirically test the economic implications of the preceeding analysis in explaining actual firm behavior.

From a practical perspective, it is interesting to apply the above strategic framework to real-life cases in oligopolistic industries, such as consumer electronics (e.g., Philips, Matsushita, Sony), pharmaceuticals (Merck, Du Pont) and consumer products (Unilever, Procter and Gamble). It will be interesting to explain the historical business strategies of these firms incorporating strategic interactions, relative costs, outputs and profits. This framework may help shape new strategies and better understand the strategic value of investments such as R & D, cost-driven competitive advantage, and preemption of markets. From the increased attention already paid by corporations to such application and implementation issues, the practical use of real options and game theory analysis in the years ahead looks promising.

References

Abrams, M. 2002. "The Mathematics of Auctions." *Discover,* August.

Achstatter, G. A. 1996. "Let Game Theory Begin: Anticipating Your Rival." *Investor's Business Daily,* January 25.

Aggarwal, R. 1991. "Justifying Investments in Flexible Manufacturing Technology." *Managerial Finance,* 17, nos. 2–3:77–88.

Akerlof G. A. 1970. "The Market for 'Lemons,' Qualitative Uncertainty, and Market Mechanisms." *Quarterly Journal of Economics* 84:488–500.

Allen, J. R. 1996. "LBOs — The Evolution of Financial Structures and Strategies." *Journal of Applied Corporate Finance* 8, no. 4:18–29.

Amram, M., and N. Kulatilaka. 1999. *Real Options: Managing Strategic Investment in an Uncertain World.* Boston: Harvard Business School Press.

Anderson, S. P., and M. Engers. 1994. "Strategic Investment and Timing of Entry." *International Economic Review* 35:833–53.

Ang, J. S., and S. Dukas. 1991. "Capital Budgeting in a Competitive Environment." *Managerial Finance* 17, nos. 2–3:6–15.

Appelbaum, E., and C. Lim. 1985. "Contestable Markets under Uncertainty." *Rand Journal of Economics* 16:28–40.

Arthur Andersen & Co. 1988. "The Netherlands Offshore and Oil Guide." AA7000, item 77.

Axelrod, R. 1984. *The Evolution of Cooperation.* New York: Basic Books.

———. 1997. *The Complexity of Cooperation: Agent-Based Models of Competition and Collaboration.* Princeton: Princeton University Press.

Axelrod, R., and W. D. Hamilton. 1981. "The Evolution of Cooperation in Biological Systems." *Science* 211:1390–96.

Baldwin, C. 1982. "Optimal Sequential Investment When Capital Is Not Readily Reversible." *Journal of Finance* 37:763–82.

———. 1987a. "Preemption vs. Flexibility in New Product Introduction." Working paper, Harvard Business School.

———. 1987b. "Competing for Capital in a Global Environment." *Midland Corporate Finance Journal* 5, no. 1:43–64.

Baldwin, C., and K. Clark. 1992. "Capabilities and Capital Investment: New Perspectives on Capital Budgeting." *Journal of Applied Corporate Finance* 5, no. 2:67–87.

———. 1993. "Modularity and Real Options." Working Paper 93-026, Harvard Business School.

———. 2000. *Design Rules.* Vol. 1, *The Power of Modularity.* Cambridge: MIT Press.

Baldwin, C., and R. Ruback. 1986. "Inflation, Uncertainty, and Investment." *Journal of Finance* 41:657–69.

Baldwin, C., and L. Trigeorgis. 1993. "Toward Remedying the Underinvestment Problem: Competitiveness, Real Options, Capabilities, and TQM." Working Paper 93–025, Harvard Business School.

Barney, J. B. 1986. "Strategic Factor Markets: Expectations, Luck, and Business Strategy." *Management Science* 32:1231–41.

Baum, J. A. C., and H. J. Korn. 1996. "Competitive Dynamics of Interfirm Rivalry." *Academy of Management Journal* 39:255–91.

Bell, G. 1995. "Volatile Exchange Rates and the Multinational Firm: Entry, Exit, and Capacity Options." In *Real Options in Capital Investment: Models, Strategies, and Applications,* ed. L. Trigeorgis. Westport, Conn.: Praeger.

Berk, J. B., R. C. Green, and V. Naik. 1998. "The Valuation and Return Dynamics of New Ventures." NBER Working Paper No. W6745. Forthcoming in *Review of Financial Studies.*

Berkman, H. 1996. "The Value of Expected Cash Flows: Does the Market Value Real Options?" Working Paper, University of Auckland.

Bernardo, A., and B. Chowdhry. 2002. "Resources, Real Options, and Corporate Strategy." *Journal of Financial Economics* 63:211–34.

Besanko, D., D. Dranove, and M. Shanley. 2000. *Economics of Strategy.* 2d ed. New York: John Wiley.

Bettis, R., and M. Hitt. 1995. "The New Competitive Landscape." *Strategic Management Journal* 16:7–19.

Bierman, H. S., and L. Fernandez. 1998. *Game Theory with Economic Applications.* 2d ed. Reading, Mass.: Addison-Wesley.

Bjerksund, P., and S. Ekern. 1990. "Managing Investment Opportunities under Price Uncertainty: From 'Last Chance' to 'Wait-and-See' Strategies." *Financial Management* 19, no. 3:65–83.

———. 1995. "Contingent Claims Evaluation of Mean-Reverting Cash Flows in Shipping." In *Real Options in Capital Investment: Models, Strategies, and Applications,* ed. L. Trigeorgis. Westport, Conn.: Praeger.

Black, F., and M. Scholes. 1973. "The Pricing of Options and Corporate Liabilities." *Journal of Political Economy* 81:637– 54.

Blakeslee, S. 2000. "Paradox in Game Theory: Losing Strategy That Wins," *New York Times,* January 25.

Bowman, E. H., and D. Hurry. 1993. "Strategy through the Option Lens: An Integrated View of Resource Investments and the Incremental-Choice Process." *Academy of Management Journal* 18:760–82.

Boyer, M. 1997. "Capacity Commitment versus Flexibility." *Journal of Economics and Management Strategy* 6:347–76.

Brandenburger, A. M., and B. J. Nalebuff. 1995. "The Right Game: Use Game Theory to Shape Strategy." *Harvard Business Review* 73, no. 4:57–71.

———. 1996. *Co-opetition.* New York: Doubleday.

Brealey, R., and S. C. Myers. 2003. *Principles of Corporate Finance.* 7th ed. New York: McGraw-Hill.

Brennan, M., and E. Schwartz. 1985a. "Evaluating Natural Resource Investments." *Journal of Business,* 58, no. 2:135–57.

————. 1985b. "A New Approach to Evaluating Natural Resource Investments." *Midland Corporate Finance Journal* 3, no. 1:37–47.

Brennan, M., and L. Trigeorgis. 2000. *Project Flexibility, Agency, and Competition: New Developments in the Theory and Application of Real Options.* Oxford: Oxford University Press.

Camerer, C. F. 1991. "Does Strategy Research Need Game Theory?" *Strategic Management Journal* 12:137–52.

Capozza, D., and G. Sick. 1992. "Risk and Return in Land Markets." Working paper, University of British Columbia.

Carr, P. 1998. "The Valuation of Sequential Exchange Opportunities." *Journal of Finance* 43:1235–56.

Chandler, A. D., Jr. 1966. *Strategy and Structure.* New York: Anchor Books.

Chi, T. 2000. "Option to Acquire or Divest a Joint Venture." *Strategic Management Journal* 21:665–88.

Childs, P. D., and A. J. Triantis. 1999. "Dynamic R&D Investment Policies." *Management Science* 45:1359–77.

Chung, K., and C. Charoenwong. 1991. "Investment Options, Assets in Place, and the Risk of Stocks." *Financial Management* 20, no. 3:21–33.

Copeland, T., and V. Antikarov. 2001. *Real Options: A Practitioner's Guide.* New York: Texere.

Cortazar, G., E. Schwartz, and M. Salinas. 1994. "Evaluating Environmental Investments." Working paper, Pontificia Universidad Católica de Chile.

Cox, J., and S. A. Ross. 1976. "The Valuation of Options for Alternative Stochastic Processes." *Journal of Financial Economics* 3:145–66.

Cox, J. C., S. A. Ross, and M. Rubinstein. 1979. "Option Pricing: A Simplified Approach." *Journal of Financial Economics* 7:229–63.

Coy, P. 1999a. "Exploiting Uncertainty: The Real-Options Revolution in Decision-Making." *Business Week,* June 7.

————. 1999b. "Options, Options, Everywhere." *Business Week,* June 7.

————. 2000. "How 'Winner's Curse' Could Undermine This E-commerce Channel." *Business Week,* March 20.

————. 2002. "Game Theory's Hidden Holes." *Business Week,* March 18.

Dasgupta, P., and J. Stiglitz. 1980. "Uncertainty, Industrial Structure and the Speed of R&D." *Bell Journal of Economics* 11:1–28.

Daughety, A. F., and J. F. Reinganum. 1990. "Asymmetric Information Acquisition and Behavior in Roll Choice Models: An Endogenous Generated Signaling Game." Working paper, University of Iowa.

Dierickx, I., and K. Cool. 1989. "Asset Stock Accumulation and Sustainability of Competitive Advantage." *Management Science* 35:1504–11.

Dixit, A. 1979. "A Model of Duopoly Suggesting a Theory of Entry Barriers." *Bell Journal of Economics* 10, no. 1:20–32.

————. 1980. "The Role of Investment in Entry Deterrence." *Economic Journal* 90:95–106.

————. 1989. "Entry and Exit Decisions under Uncertainty." *Journal of Political Economy* 97:620–38.

Dixit, A., and B. J. Nalebuff. 1991. *Thinking Strategically: The Competitive Edge in Business, Politics, and Everyday Life.* New York: Norton Press.

Dixit, A., and R. Pindyck. 1994. *Investment under Uncertainty.* Princeton: Princeton University Press.

Dosi, G., D. J. Teece, and S. Winter. 1989. "Toward a Theory of Corporate Coherence: Preliminary Remarks." Center for Research in Management, University of California, Berkeley.

Edleson, M., and F. Reinhardt. 1995. "Investment in Pollution Compliance Options: The Case of Georgia Power." In *Real Options in Capital Investment: Models, Strategies, and Applications,* ed. L. Trigeorgis. Westport, Conn.: Praeger.

Eriv, I., and A. E. Roth. 1998. "Predicting How People Play Games: Reinforcement Learning in Experimental Games with Unique, Mixed Strategy Equilibria." *American Economic Review,* 88:848–81.

Fried, V. H., and R. Hisrich. 1994. "Toward a Model of Venture Capital Investment Decision Making." *Financial Management* 23:38–37.

Fudenberg, D., R. Gilbert, J. Stiglitz, and J. Tirole. 1983. "Preemption, Leapfrogging, and Competition in Patent Races." *European Economic Review* 22:3–31.

Fudenberg, D., and J. Tirole. 1984. "The Fat-Cat Effect, the Puppy-Dog Ploy, and the Lean and Hungry Look." *American Economic Review* 74:361–66.

————. 1985. "Preemption and Rent Equalization in the Adoption of New Technology." *Review of Economic Studies* 52:383–401.

————. *Game Theory.* 1991. Cambridge: MIT Press.

Garlappi, L. 2002. "Preemption Risk and the Valuation of R&D Ventures." Working paper, University of Texas, Austin.

Gertner, R., and M. Knez. 1999. "Mastering Strategy in the Real World." *Financial Times,* November 22.

Geske, R. 1979. "The Valuation of Compound Options." *Journal of Financial Economics* 7, no. 1:63–81.

Ghemawat, P. 1986. "Sustainable Advantage." *Harvard Business Review* 64, no. 5:53–58.

————. 1991. *Commitment: The Dynamics of Strategy.* New York: Free Press.

Ghemawat, P., and P. del Sol. 1998. "Commitment versus Flexibility?" *California Management Review* 40, no. 4:26–41.

Graham, J. R., and C. R. Harvey. 2001. "The Theory and Practice of Corporate Finance: Evidence from the Field." *Journal of Financial Economics* 60:187–243.

Grant, R. M. 1991. "The Resource-Based Theory of Competitive Advantage: Implications for Strategy Formulation." *California Management Review* 33:114–35.

————. 1995. *Contemporary Strategy Analysis.* Oxford: Blackwell Business.

Grenadier, S. R. 1996. "The Strategic Exercise of Options: Development Cascades and Overbuilding in Real Estate Markets." *Journal of Finance* 51:1653–79.

———. 1999. "Information Revelation through Option Exercise." *Review of Financial Studies* 12, no. 1:95–129.

———, ed. 2000. *Game Choices: The Intersection of Real Options and Game Theory.* London: Risk Books.

———. 2001. "Option Exercise Games: An Application to the Equilibrium Investment Strategies of Firms." *Review of Financial Studies* 15:691–721.

Grenadier, S. R. and A. M. Weiss. 1997. "Investment in Technological Innovations: An Option Pricing Approach." *Journal of Financial Economics* 44:397–416.

Grossman, G., and J. Shapiro. 1986. "Optimal Dynamic R&D Programs." *Rand Journal of Economics* 17:581–593.

———. 1987. "Optimal Dynamic R&D Competition." *Economic Journal* 97: 372–87.

Haanappel H. T., and H. T. J. Smit. 2003. "Returns Distributions of Strategic Options." Working paper, Erasmus University.

Hayes, R., and D. Garvin. 1982. "Managing as if Tomorrow Mattered." *Harvard Business Review* 60, no. 3:71–79.

Hayes, R., and S. Wheelwright. 1984. *Restoring Our Competitive Edge: Competing through Manufacturing.* New York: John Wiley.

Hendricks, D. 1991. "Optimal Policy Responses to an Uncertain Threat: The Case of Global Warming." Working paper, Kennedy School of Government, Harvard University.

Hendricks, K., and D. Kovenock. 1989. "Asymmetric Information, Information Externalities, and Efficiency: The Case of Oil Exploration." *Rand Journal of Economics* 20:164–82.

Hevert, K. T., R. M. McLaughlin, and R. A. Taggart. 1998. "Growth Options and Equity Duration." *Journal of Portfolio Management* 25:43–50.

Hodder, J., and H. Riggs. 1985. "Pitfalls in Evaluating Risky Projects." *Harvard Business Review* 63, no. 1:128–35.

Holden, S., and C. Riis. 1994. "Entry into a New Market: A Game of Timing." *International Journal of Industrial Organization* 12:549–568.

Huisman, K. J. M. 2001. *Technology Investment: A Game Theoretic Real Options Approach.* Dordrecht, The Netherlands: Kluwer Academic Publishers.

Huisman, K. J. M., and P. M. Kort. 1999. "Effects of Strategic Interactions on the Option Value of Waiting." CentER DP no. 9992, Tilburg University.

Hull, J.C. 1995. *Introduction to Futures and Options Markets.* 2d. Ed. Englewood Cliffs, N.J.: Prentice Hall.

———. 2000. *Options, Futures, and Other Derivatives.* Upper Saddle River, N.J.: Prentice Hall.

Ingersoll, J., and S. Ross. 1992. "Waiting to Invest: Investment and Uncertainty." *Journal of Business* 65, no. 1:1–29.

Joaquin D. C., and K. C. Butler. 2000. "Competitive Investment Decisions: A Synthesis." In *Project Flexibility, Agency, and Competition,* ed. M. J. Brennan and L. Trigeorgis. Oxford: Oxford University Press.

Kamrad, B., and R. Ernst. 1995. "Multiproduct Manufacturing with Stochastic Input Prices and Output Yield Uncertainty." In *Real Options in Capital*

Investment: Models, Strategies, and Applications. ed. L. Trigeorgis. Westport, Conn.: Praeger.

Kasanen, E. 1993. "Creating Value by Spawning Investment Opportunities." *Financial Management* 22, no. 3:251–58.

Katz, M. L., and C. Shapiro. 1985. "Network Externalities, Competition, and Compatibility." *American Economic Review* 75:424–40.

———. 1986. "Technology Adoption in the Presence of Network Externalities." *Journal of Political Economy* 94:822–41.

Kemna, A. G. Z. 1988. *"Options in Real and Financial Markets."* Ph.D. diss., Erasmus University.

Kemna, A. 1993. "Case Studies on Real Options." *Financial Management* 22, no. 3:259–70.

Kensinger, J. 1987. "Adding the Value of Active Management into the Capital Budgeting Equation." *Midland Corporate Finance Journal* 5, no. 1:31–42.

Kester, W. C. 1984. "Today's Options for Tomorrow's Growth." *Harvard Business Review* 62, no. 2:153–60.

———. 1993. "Turning Growth Options into Real Assets." In *Capital Budgeting under Uncertainty,* ed. R. Aggarwal. Englewood Cliffs, N.J.: Prentice-Hall.

Klemperer, P. 1987. "Markets with Consumer Switching Costs." *Quarterly Journal of Economics* 102:375–94.

Kogut, B. 1991. "Joint Ventures and the Option to Expand and Acquire." *Management Science* 37, no. 1:19–33.

Kogut, B., and N. Kulatilaka. 1994. "Operating Flexibility, Global Manufacturing, and the Option Value of a Multinational Network." *Management Science* 40, no. 1:123–39.

Kolbe, A. L., P. A. Morris. and E. O. Teisberg. 1991. "When Choosing R & D Projects, Go with Long Shots." *Research-Technology Management,* January–February: 35–40.

Kulatilaka, N. 1988. "Valuing the Flexibility of Flexible Manufacturing Systems." *IEEE Transactions in Engineering Management* 35, no. 4:250–57.

———. 1993. "The Value of Flexibility: The Case of a Dual-Fuel Industrial Steam Boiler." *Financial Management* 22, no. 3:271–79.

———. 1995a. "The Value of Flexibility: A General Model of Real Options." In *Real Options in Capital Investment: Models, Strategies, and Applications,* ed. L. Trigeorgis. Westport, Conn.: Praeger.

———. 1995b. "Operating Flexibilities in Capital Budgeting: Substitutability and Complementarity in Real Options." In *Real Options in Capital Investment: Models, Strategies, and Applications.* ed. L. Trigeorgis. Westport, Conn.: Praeger.

Kulatilaka, N., P. Balasubramanian, and J. Stork. 1996. "Managing Information Technology Investments: A Capability Based Real Options Approach." Working Paper 96-35, Boston University.

Kulatilaka, N., and A. Marcus. 1988. "A General Formulation of Corporate Operating Options." *Research in Finance* 7:183–200.

———. 1992. "Project Valuation under Uncertainty: When Does DCF Fail?" *Journal of Applied Corporate Finance* 5, no. 3:92–100.

Kulatilaka, N., and S. Marks. 1988. "The Strategic Value of Flexibility: Reducing the Ability to Compromise." *American Economic Review* 78:574–80.

Kulatilaka, N., and E. C. Perotti. 1998. "Strategic Growth Options." *Management Science* 44:1021–31.

Kulatilaka, N., and L. Trigeorgis. 1994. "The General Flexibility to Switch: Real Options Revisited." *International Journal of Finance* 6:778–98.

Lambrecht, B. M. 2000. "Strategic Sequential Investments and Sleeping Patents." In *Project Flexibility, Agency, and Product Market Competition: New Developments in the Theory and Application of Real Options Analysis*, ed. M. Brennan and L. Trigeorgis. Oxford: Oxford University Press.

———. 2001. "The Impact of Debt Financing on Entry and Exit in a Duopoly." *Review of Financial Studies* 14:765–804.

———. 2004. "The Timing and Terms of Mergers Motivated by Economies of Scale." Forthcoming in *Journal of Financial Economics*.

Lambrecht, B. M., and W. R. Perraudin. 1994. "Option Games." Working Paper 9414, University of Cambridge.

———. 2004. "Real Options and Preemption under Incomplete Information." *Journal of Economic Dynamics and Control* 27:619–43.

Laughton, D. G., and H. D. Jacoby. 1993. "Reversion, Timing Options, and Long-Term Decision-Making." *Financial Management* 22, no. 3:225–40.

Lerner, J. 1994. "The Syndication of Venture Capital Investments." *Financial Management* 23:16–27.

Lieberman M. B., and D. B. Montgomery. 1988. "First-Mover Advantages." *Strategic Management Journal* 9:41–58.

Lintner, J. 1965. "The Valuation of Risk Assets and the Selection of Risky Investments in Stock-Portfolios and Capital Budgets." *Review of Economics and Statistics* 7:13–37.

Luehrman, T. 1998. "Strategy as a Portfolio of Real Options." *Harvard Business Review* 76:89–99.

Majd, S., and R. Pindyck. 1987. "Time to Build, Option Value, and Investment Decisions." *Journal of Financial Economics* 18:7–27.

Margrabe, W. 1978. "The Value of an Option to Exchange One Asset for Another." *Journal of Finance* 33:177–86.

Mason, S. P., and C. Baldwin. 1998. "Evaluation of Government Subsidies to Large-Scale Energy Projects: A Contingent Claims Approach." *Advances in Futures and Options Research* 3:169–81.

Mason, S. P., and R. C. Merton. 1985. "The Role of Contingent Claims Analysis in Corporate Finance." In *Recent Advances in Corporate Finance*, ed. E. Altman and M. Subrahmanyam. Homewood, Ill.: R. D. Irwin.

Mason, R., and H. Weeds. 2002. "Can Greater Uncertainty Hasten Investment." Working paper, University of Southhampton, January.

Mauer, D., and A. Triantis. 1994. "Interactions of Corporate Financing and Investment Decisions: A Dynamic Framework." *Journal of Finance* 49:1253–77.

McDonald, R., and D. Siegel. 1985. "Investment and the Valuation of Firms When There Is an Option to Shut Down." *International Economic Review* 26:331–49.

———. 1986. "The Value of Waiting to Invest." *Quarterly Journal of Economics* 101:707–27.

McGahan, A. M. 1993a. "The Effect of Incomplete Information about Demand on Preemption." *International Journal of Industrial Organization* 11:327–46.

———. 1993b. "The Incentive Not to Invest: Capacity Commitments in Compact Disk Introduction." *Research and Technology Innovation, Management, and Policy* 5:177–97.

———. 1994. "The Incentive Not to Invest: Capacity Commitments in the Compact Disc Introduction." In *Research on Technical Innovation, Management, and Policy,* vol. 5, ed. R. A. Burgelman and R. S. Rosenbloom. Greenwich, Conn.: JAI Press.

McGrath, R. G. 1997. "A Real Options Logic for Initiating Technology Positioning Investments." *Academy of Management Review* 22:974–96.

———. 1999. "Falling Forward: Real Options Reasoning and Entrepreunerial Failure." *Academy of Management Review* 24:13–30.

McGrath, R. G. and I. C. MacMillan. 2000. "Assessing Technology Projects Using Real Options Reasoning." *Research-Technology Management* 43, no. 4:35–49.

McLaughlin, R., and R. A. Taggart. 1992. "The Opportunity Cost of Using Excess Capacity." *Financial Management* 21, no. 2:12–24.

Merton, R. C. 1973. "Theory of Rational Option Pricing." *Bell Journal of Economics and Management Science* 4:141–83.

Miltersen K. R., and E. S. Schwartz. 2003. "R&D Investments with Competitive Interactions." Working paper, Norwegian School of Economics and Business Administration.

Morck, R., E. Schwartz, and D. Stangeland. 1989. "The Valuation of Forestry Resources under Stochastic Prices and Inventories." *Journal of Financial and Quantitative Analysis* 24:473–87.

Morton, F. S. 1999. "Mastering Strategy 7: Strategic Complements and Substitutes." *Financial Times,* November 8.

Muoio, A. 1998. "Decisions, Decisions." *Fast Company,* October.

Myers, S. C. 1977. "Determinants of Corporate Borrowing." *Journal of Financial Economics* 5, no. 2:147–76.

———. 1987. "Finance Theory and Financial Strategy." *Midland Corporate Finance Journal* 5, no. 1:6–13.

Myers, S. C., and C. D. Howe. 1997. "A Life-Cycle Financial Model of Pharmaceutical R&D." Working paper, MIT.

Myers, S. C., and S. Majd. 1990. "Abandonment Value and Project Life." *Advances in Futures and Options Research* 4:1–21.

Naj, A. K. 1990. "In R & D, the Next Best Thing to a Gut Feeling." *Manager's Journal, Wall Street Journal,* May 21.

Nelson, R. 1996. "The Evolution of Competitive or Comparative Advantage: A Preliminary Report on a Study." Working Paper WP-96-21, International Institute for Applied Systems Analysis, Luxemberg, Austria.

Nelson, R., and S. Winter. 1982. *An Evolutionary Theory of Economic Change.* Cambridge: Harvard University Press.

Nichols, N. A. 1994. "Scientific Management at Merck: An Interview with CFO Judy Lewent." *Harvard Business Review* 72, no. 1:88–99.

Novy-Marx, R. 2003. "An Equilibirum Model of Investment under Uncertainty." Working paper, Haas School of Business, University of California, Berkeley.

NV Luchthaven Schiphol. 2001. Facts and Figures.

NV Luchthaven Schiphol Business Development and Planning. 1988. Masterplan 2003.

————. 1994. Masterplan 2015.

Ordover, J., and R. Willig. 1985. "Antitrust for High-Technology Industries: Assessing Research Joint Ventures and Mergers." *Journal of Law and Economics* 28:311–33.

Oster, S. M. 1999. *Modern Competitive Analysis*. 3d ed. Oxford: Oxford University Press.

Paddock, J., D. Siegel, and J. Smith. 1988. "Option Valuation of Claims on Physical Assets: The Case of Offshore Petroleum Leases." *Quarterly Journal of Economics* 103:479–508.

Page, E. S. 1998. "KanFax Kicks." *SportsJones,* July 21.

Parker, P. 1998. "Mastering Marketing 3: How Do Companies Collude?" *Financial Times,* September 28.

Pawlina, G., and P. M. Kort. 2001. "Real Options in an Asymmetric Duopoly: Who Benefits from Your Competitive Disadvantage?" Working Paper 2001-95, Department of Economics and CentER, Tilburg University.

Penrose, E. 1959. *The Theory of the Growth of the Firm.* Oxford: Basil Blackwell.

Perotti, E., and N. Kulatilaka. 1999. "Time-to-Market Capability as a Stackelberg Growth Option." Working paper, University of Amsterdam.

Perotti, E., and S. Rossetto. 2002. "Real Option Valuation of Strategic Platform Investments." Working paper, University of Amsterdam.

Pindyck, R. 1980. "Uncertainty and Exhaustible Resource Markets." *Journal of Political Economy* 86:1203–25.

————. 1988. "Irreversible Investment, Capacity Choice, and the Value of the Firm." *American Economic Review* 78:969–85.

————. 1991. "Irreversibility, Uncertainty, and Investment." *Journal of Economic Literature* 29:1110–48.

Porter, M. E. 1979. "How Competitive Forces Shape Strategy." *Harvard Business Review* 57, no. 2:137–45.

————. 1980. *Competitive Strategy.* London: Macmillan.

————. 1990. *The Competitive Advantage of Nations.* New York: Free Press.

Prahalad, C. K. 1999. "Mastering Strategy 2: Changes in the Competitive Battlefield." *Financial Times,* October 4.

Prahalad, C. K., and G. Hamel. 1990. "The Core Competence of the Corporation." *Harvard Business Review* 68, no. 3:79–91.

Quigg, L. 1993. "Empirical Testing of Real Option-Pricing Models." *Journal of Finance* 48:621–40.

————. 1995. "Optimal Land Development." In *Real Options in Capital Investment: Models, Strategies, and Applications,* ed. L. Trigeorgis. Westport, Conn.: Praeger.

Reinganum, J. 1983. "Uncertain Innovation and the Persistence of Monopoly." *American Economic Review* 73:741–48.

———. 1985. "Innovation and Industry Evolution." *Quarterly Journal of Economics* 100:81–100.

Roberts, K., and M. Weitzman. 1981. "Funding Criteria for Research, Development, and Exploration Projects." *Econometrica* 49:1261–88.

Roll, R. 1977. "A Critique of the Asset Pricing Theory's Tests, Part 1: On Past and Potential Testability of the Theory." *Journal of Financial Economics* 7:265–96.

Rosenberg, N. 1982. *Inside the Black Box: Technology and Economics.* Cambridge: Cambridge University Press.

Rubinstein, M. 1976. "The Valuation of Uncertain Income Streams and the Pricing of Options." *Bell Journal of Economics* 7:407–25.

Rumelt, R. P. 1984. "Towards a Strategic Theory of the Firm." In *Competitive Strategic Management,* ed. R. B. Lambrecht. Englewood Cliffs, N.J.: Prentice Hall.

Sadanand, A., and V. Sadanand. 1996. "Firm Scale and the Endogeneous Timing of Entry: A Choice between Commitment and Flexibility." *Journal of Economic Theory* 70:516–30.

Sahlman, W. 1988. "Aspects of Financial Contracting in Venture Capital." *Journal of Applied Corporate Finance* 1:23–36.

Schelling, T. 1980. *The Strategy of Conflict.* 2d ed. Cambridge: Harvard University Press.

Schmalensee, R. 1983. "Advertising and Entry Deterrence: An Exploratory Model." *Journal of Political Economy* 90:636–53.

Schumpeter, J. A. 1934. *Theory of Economic Development.* Cambridge: Harvard University Press.

———. 1942. *Capitalism, Socialism, and Democracy.* New York: Harper.

Schwartz, E. S. 2001. "Patents and R&D as Real Options." Working Paper no. 12-01, John E. Anderson Graduate School of Management, University of California, Los Angeles.

Schwartz, E. S., and M. Moon. 2000. "Evaluating Research and Development Investments in Innovation, Infrastructure, and Strategic Options." In *Project Flexibility, Agency, and Competition: New Developments in the Theory and Application of Real Options,* ed. M. J. Brennan and L. Trigeorgis, 85–106. Oxford: Oxford University Press.

Schwartz, E. S., and L. Trigeorgis, eds. 2001. *Real Options and Investment under Uncertainty: Classical Readings and Recent Contributions.* Cambridge: MIT Press.

Selten, R. 1965. "Spieltheorestische Behandlung eines Oligopolmodells mit Nachfragetragheit." *Zeitschrift für die gesamte Staatswissenschaft* 121:301–24.

Shapiro, A. C. 1985. "Corporate Strategy and the Capital Budgeting Decision." *Midland Corporate Finance Journal* 3, no. 1:22–36.

———. 1989. "The Theory of Business Strategy." *Rand Journal of Economics* 20, no. 1:125–37.

———. 1991. *Modern Corporate Finance.* London: Macmillan.

Sharpe, W. F. 1964. "Capital Asset Prices: A Theory of Market Equilibrium under Conditions of Risk." *Journal of Finance* 19:425–42.

Shell. 1988. *Op Zoek naar Olie en Gas.* Shell Rotterdam.

Sick, G. 1989. *Capital Budgeting with Real Options.* Salomon Brothers Center Monograph, New York University.

Siegel, D., J. Smith, and J. Paddock. 1987. "Valuing Offshore Oil Properties with Option Pricing Models." *Midland Corporate Finance Journal* 5, no. 1:22–30.

Smit, H. T. J. 1994. "The Flexibility Value of Strategic Investments under Competition." In *New Directions in Finance,* ed. D. K. Gosh and S. Khaksari. London: Routledge.

———. 1996. "The Valuation of Offshore Concessions in the Netherlands." *Financial Management* 26, no. 2:5–17.

———. 1999a. "The Options Characteristics of Growth Opportunities." Working paper, Erasmus University Rotterdam.

———. 1999b. "Option Characteristics of Stocks in High-Tech Industries." Working paper, Erasmus University, August.

———. 2001. "Acquisition Strategies as Option Games." *Journal of Applied Corporate Finance* 14, no. 2:79–89.

———. 2003. "Infrastructure Investment as a Real Options Game: The Case of European Airport Expansion." *Financial Management* 32, no. 4:27–57.

Smit, H. T. J., and L. A. Ankum. 1993. "A Real Options and Game-Theoretic Approach to Corporate Investment Strategy under Competition." *Financial Management* 22, no. 3:241–50.

Smit, H. T. J., and L. Trigeorgis. 1997. "Value Dynamics of R&D Strategies." Working paper, Erasmus University, August.

———. 1998. "Flexibility, Strategic Options, and Dynamic Competition in Technology Industries." Working paper, Erasmus University, September.

———. 2001. "Flexibility and Commitment in Strategic Investments." In *Real Options and Investment under Uncertainty: Classical Readings and Recent Contributions,* ed. E. S. Schwartz and L. Trigeorgis. Cambridge: MIT Press.

———. 2003. "Real Options: Examples and Principles of Valuation and Strategy." In *Venture Capital Contracting and the Valuation of High-Tech Firms,* ed. J. McCahery and L. Renneboog. Oxford: Oxford University Press.

Smith, K. W., and A. Triantis. 1994. "The Value of Options in Strategic Acquisitions." In *Real Options in Capital Investment: Models, Strategies, and Applications,* ed. L. Trigeorgis. Westport, Conn.: Praeger.

Smith, M. 1974. "The Theory of Games and the Evolution of Animal Conflicts." *Journal of Theoretical Biology* 47:209–21.

Spatt, C. S., and F. P. Sterbenz. 1985. "Learning, Preemption, and the Degree of Rivalry." *Rand Journal of Economics* 16, no. 1:84–92.

Spence, M. 1977. "Entry, Capacity, Investment, and Oligopolistic Pricing." *Bell Journal of Economics* 8:534–44.

———. 1979. "Investment Strategy and Growth in a New Market." *Bell Journal of Economics* 10:1–19.

Spencer, B. J., and J. A. Brander. 1992. "Pre-commitment and Flexibility Applications to Oligopoly Theory." *European Economic Review* 36:1601–26.

Stackelberg, H. von. 1934. *Marktform und Gleichgewicht*. Vienna: Springer-Verlag.

Stalk, G. 1988. "Time — the Next Source of Competitive Advantage." *Harvard Business Review* 66, no. 4:41–51.

Sutton, J. 1992. "Implementing Game Theoretical Models in Industrial Economies." In *Recent Developments in the Theory of Industrial Organization*, ed. A. Del Monte. Ann Arbor: University of Michigan Press.

Teece, D. J. 1980. "Economics of Scope and the Scope of the Enterprise." *Journal of Economic Behavior and Organisation* 1:223–47.

———. 1982. "Towards an Economic Theory of the Multiproduct Firm." *Journal of Economic Behavior and Organisation* 3:39–63.

———. 1984. "Economic Analysis and Strategic Management." *California Management Review* 26, no. 3:87–110.

———. 1986. "Profiting from Technological Innovation." *Research Policy* 15, no. 6:285–305.

———. 1988. "Technological Change and the Nature of the Firm." In *Technical Change and Economic Theory*, ed. G. Dosi, C. Freeman, R. Nelson, G. Silverberg and L. Soete. New York: Pinter.

Teece, D. J., G. Pisano, and A. Shuen. 1997. "Dynamic Capabilities and Strategic Management." *Strategic Management Journal* 18:509–34.

Teece, D. J., R. Rumelt, G. Dosi, and S. Winter. 1994. "Understanding Corporate Coherence: Theory and Evidence." *Journal of Economic Behavior and Organization* 23:1–30.

Teisberg, E. 1993. "An Option Valuation Analysis of Investment Choices by a Regulated Firm." *Management Science* 40:535–48.

———. 1995. "Methods for Evaluating Capital Investment Decisions under Uncertainty." In *Real Options in Capital Investment: Models, Strategies, and Applications*, ed. L. Trigeorgis. Westport, Conn.: Praeger.

Thakor, A. V. 1991. "Game Theory in Finance." *Financial Management* 22, no. 1:71–94.

Tirole, J. 1990. *The Theory of Industrial Organization*. Cambridge: MIT Press.

Titman, S. 1985. "Urban Land Prices under Uncertainty." *American Economic Review* 75:505–14.

Tourinho, O. 1979. "The Option Value of Reserves of Natural Resources." Working Paper 94, University of California, Berkeley.

Triantis, A., and J. Hodder. 1990. "Valuing Flexibility as a Complex Option." *Journal of Finance* 45:549–65.

Trigeorgis, L. 1986. "Valuing Real Investment Opportunities: An Options Approach to Strategic Capital Budgeting." Ph.D. diss., Harvard Business School.

———. 1988. "A Conceptual Options Framework for Capital Budgeting." *Advances in Futures and Options Research* 3:145–67.

———. 1990a. "A Real Options Application in Natural Resource Investments." *Advances in Futures and Options Research* 4:153–64.

———. 1990b. "Valuing the Impact of Uncertain Competitive Arrivals on Deferrable Real Investment Opportunities." Working paper, Boston University.

————. 1991a. "Anticipated Competitive Entry and Early Preemptive Investment in Deferrable Projects." *Journal of Economics and Business* 43, no. 2:143–56.

————. 1991b. "A Log-Transformed Binomial Numerical Analysis Method for Valuing Complex Multi-option Investments." *Journal of Financial and Quantitative Analysis* 26:309–26.

————. 1993a. "The Nature of Option Interactions and the Valuation of Investments with Multiple Real Options." *Journal of Financial and Quantitative Analysis* 28, no. 1:1–20.

————. 1993b. "Real Options and Interactions with Financial Flexibility." *Financial Management* 22, no. 3:202–24.

————. 1995. *Real Options in Capital Investment: Models, Strategies, and Applications.* Westport, Conn.: Praeger.

————. 1996a. *Real Options: Managerial Flexibility and Strategy in Resource Allocation.* Cambridge: MIT Press.

————. 1996b. "Evaluating Leases with Complex Operating Options." *European Journal of Operations Research* 91:315–29.

Trigeorgis, L., and E. Kasanen. 1991. "An Integrated Options-Based Strategic Planning and Control Model." *Managerial Finance* 17, nos. 2–3:16–28.

Trigeorgis, L., and S. P. Mason. 1987. "Valuing Managerial Flexibility." *Midland Corporate Finance Journal* 5, no. 1:14–21.

Trivers, R. L. 1971. "The Evolution of Reciprocal Altruism." *Quarterly Review of Biology* 46:35-57.

Vives, X. 1998. "Technological Competition, Uncertainty, and Oligopoly." *Journal of Economic Theory* 48:386–415.

Walker, P. 1995. "An Outline of the History of Game Theory." University of Canterbury, New Zealand.

Weeds, H. 2000a. "'Reverse Hysteresis': R&D Investment and Stochastic Innovation." Warwick Economics Research Paper 578.

————. 2000b. "Sleeping Patents and Compulsory Licensing: An Options Analysis." Warwick Economics Research Paper 579.

————. 2002. "Strategic Delay in a Real Options Model of R&D Competition." *Review of Economic Studies* 69:729–47.

Wernerfelt, B. 1984. "A Resource-Based View of the Firm." *Strategic Management Journal* 5, no. 2:171–80.

Williams, J. 1991. "Real Estate Development as an Option." *Journal of Real Estate Finance and Economics* 4, no. 2:191–208.

————. 1993. "Equilibrium and Options on Real Assets." *Review of Financial Studies* 6:825–50.

Williamson, O. E. 1975. *Markets and Hierarchies.* New York: Free Press.

————. 1985. *The Economic Institutions of Capitalism.* New York: Free Press.

Willner, R. 1995. "Valuing Start-up Venture Growth Options." In *Real Options in Capital Investment: Models, Strategies, and Applications,* ed. L. Trigeorgis. Westport, Conn.: Praeger.

Zhu, K. X. 1999. "Strategic Investment in Information Technologies: A Real Options and Game Theoretic Approach." Ph.D. diss., Stanford University.

Index